WILEY

Dual Reporting for Equity and Other Comprehensive Income

Dual Reporting for Equity and Other Comprehensive Income

Under IFRS and U.S. GAAP

By

Francesco Bellandi, CPA, CA, ACCADipIFR, MBA

A John Wiley & Sons, Ltd., Publication

To my sons
that they may follow
my parents' example
of intellectual honesty

Non est vir fortis et strenuus qui laborem fugit,
nisi crescit illi animus ipsa difficultate.

Non sum uni angulo natus,
patria mea totus hic mundus est.

Seneca, Ad Lucilium, Epistularum Libri I, VII.

CONTENTS

PREFACE

Dual Reporting for Equity and Other Comprehensive Income under IFRS and U.S. GAAP, examines and compares the reporting of stockholders' equity as required by U.S. GAAP, SEC rules and regulations, and International Financial Reporting Standards. Under all of those standards, most business enterprises and, in certain situations, not-for-profit organizations must provide certain information regarding equity items on the face of the statement of financial position, on the face of other specific statements, and/or in the notes to the financial statements.

Equity reporting explains the accumulated balances and the changes during the period in contributed capital, retained earnings, other comprehensive income, and their components. Subtopic 505-10 (APB Opinion No. 12, *Omnibus Opinion – 1967*), permits several alternatives for reporting changes in equity. Subtopic 220-10 (FASB Statement of Financial Accounting Standards No. 130, *Reporting Comprehensive Income*), allows alternative statements for reporting comprehensive income, recently amended by ASU 2011-05. SEC Regulation S-X requires a multi-step equity section of the balance sheet but allows an analysis of the changes in each caption of stockholders' equity in the form of a schedule or a note. International Accounting Standard No. 1, *Presentation of Financial Statements*, used to adopt two alternative forms of equity reporting as part of the basic financial statements but finally moved to a single format of the Statement of Changes in Equity. SEC Form 20-F is in some way similar to both the IFRS formats and SEC Regulation S-X.

This Book thoroughly analyzes and discusses in detail the concepts of capital and reserves, retained earnings, additional paid-in capital, other comprehensive income, and the relevant accounting literature. It explains the rules and alternatives, describes the mechanics of applying them, and illustrates the formatting of the related statements through samples of company's annual reports.

The pros and cons concerning the different approaches followed by the respective standards, their purpose and rationale and how to reconcile them are discussed. The Book also identifies gray areas and practical implementation issues, as well as the proposals currently under discussion to amend those standards. In addition it illustrates relevant joint efforts of the FASB and the IASB to converge domestic and international accounting standards. Finally, it deduces the major implications for companies and suggests planning points on how the pertinent standards inform the resolution of issues that practitioners are likely to encounter.

The Book also includes an analysis of the diverse relevance and implementation of the concept of defense of legal capital and appropriations of retained earnings in certain jurisdictions, the accounting for each caption of the equity section of the statement of financial position, the items directly affecting retained earnings, the concept and mechanics of recycling, also including, among other items, foreign currency translation adjustment, unrealized gains or losses on available-for-sale investments, effective portion of gains or losses on cash flow hedge and on hedge of a net investment in foreign operations, the impact of pension accounting, revaluation surplus, and taxes on items recognized in other comprehensive income or directly in equity.

The Book gives an inventory of the different accounting requirements, and their implications, for equity reserves, additional paid-in capital, retained earnings and other comprehensive income under current standards, proposed Exposure Drafts, and Discussion Papers. It then builds possible theoretical accounting models that explicitly or implicitly result from those requirements.

As the IASB Staff acknowledged, a conceptual basis for presentation of items in other comprehensive income is still missing, but this is a potential topic of the IASB Work plan.[1] This Book brings several suggestions together in a proposed overall approach to equity. This model gives a consistent response to the other comprehensive income dilemma, preserves the clean-surplus concept of income, develops from capital maintenance concepts, enhances the quality of earnings and the quality of equity, and at the same time does not violate jurisdictional corporate governance and defense of capital frameworks.

This Book treats the experience gathered first hand in an international context and becomes an indispensable tool for management decision making, as well as for academic study.

Additional material and worksheets can be found on the book's companion website at www.wiley.com/go/Bellandi_Equity.

Username: Bellandi_Reader
Password: equity

The username and password are both case sensitive.

---

[1] *Project Summary and Feedback Statement, June 2011. Presentation of Items of Other Comprehensive Income (Amendments to IAS 1), page 10.*

ABOUT THE AUTHOR

Francesco Bellandi holds a Degree in Economics (summa cum laude), LUISS University; M.B.A., SDA Bocconi School of Business, Bocconi University; Diploma in International Financial Reporting from the ACCA (The Association Of Chartered Certified Accountants, UK); and the Diploma in Private Equity from the A.I.F.I. (Italy's private equity association).

Francesco Bellandi, U.S. CPA (Certified Public Accountant) and Dottore Commercialista (Italian Chartered Accountant), is a practitioner in U.S. GAAP/IFRSs dual reporting. He is a member of the AICPA, the NYSSCPA (New York State Society of Certified Public Accountants), and the NYSSCPA's International Accounting & Auditing Committee.

He has served as a Board Director and Chief Financial Officer in Cobalt Waterline Group (2007–2008); Director Finance & Administration in Alitalia Maintenance Systems (Alitalia – Lufthansa Technik) (2003–2005); Chief Financial Officer in Alitalia North America & Mexico, New York (2001–2003); Director Business Planning & Finance Performance SEMEA Southern Europe, Middle East, and Africa in Société Internationale de Télécommunications Aéronautiques (1999–2001); Manager Finance & Administration/Shared Services, Reengineering & Restructuring in Ernst & Young (1997–1998); Financial Controller and Logistics Manager in Ericsson (1993–1997); Financial Analyst in IRI (Istituto per la Ricostruzione Industriale) (1988–1992).

Francesco Bellandi also holds executive seminars for CFOs on U.S. GAAP/IFRSs dual reporting. He can be reached at francesco_bellandi@yahoo.com or dualgaap.com, the website dedicated to U.S. GAAP/IFRSs Dual Reporting.

1 INTRODUCTION AND SCOPE OF BOOK

1.1 NATURE OF ACCOUNTING LITERATURE AND PERTINENT PRONOUNCEMENTS

Under both U.S. Generally Accepted Accounting Principles (GAAP) and International Financial Reporting Standards (IFRSs) there is no all inclusive general standard on stockholders' equity. Instead, authoritative literature on this subject consists of concepts from the FASB and the IASB frameworks and standards that apply to specific types of transactions or events or items in financial statements that affect stockholders' equity.

The principal accounting pronouncements, under U.S. GAAP, SEC guidance, and IFRSs respectively, are listed in Worksheet 80, grouped per specific category.

Starting from July 1, 2010, the International Accounting Standards Committee Foundation (IASCF) became the IFRS Foundation. The International Financial Reporting Interpretations Committee (IFRIC) had changed its name into the IFRS Interpretations Committee. The IASB had renamed its website as IFRS.org. The Accounting Standards Executive Committee (AcSEC) recently became the Financial Reporting Executive Committee (FinREC). This Book maintains the above original names for all references.

1.2 PERSPECTIVES AND MAJOR IMPLICATIONS OF THE CONCEPT OF EQUITY

Accounting for stockholders' equity refers to the recognition, measurement, presentation, and disclosure of equity on a company's financial statements. Along with such meaning, the Book particularly adopts the perspective of a comparative study, by means of criticism and contrast between the U.S. and the IFRSs' pronouncements and practice.

Comment: However, the topic of stockholders' equity is pervasive, well beyond accounting. In fact, according to circumstances, it may be relevant under a number of management, finance, legal, tax, and business viewpoints for several stakeholders, such as company managers, CPAs, financial analysts, and, in general, preparers and users of financial statements. Some of these angles are as follows:

- *Meaning, and rationale for, equity:* Firstly, equity is an element of the financial statements under the FASB and the IASB conceptual frameworks. Its location within an accounting framework may follow two different approaches: the asset liability (or balance sheet approach) or the revenue expense views. Derivation of income, under the former, is the result of certain changes in net assets during the accounting period, as opposed to the view, under the latter concept, of income producing activities of the enterprise as a major determinant of changes of equity.
- *Definition and classification of equity:* Finance theory makes a separation between financing activities and an entity's other activities. Within financing activities, accounting has

traditionally developed a dichotomy between financial liabilities and equity. The correspond
ing classification of interest versus dividends develops from the concept of income determi
nation (net of interest) as opposed to income distribution (to shareholders). The treatment of
compound financial instruments, instruments with both characteristics of equity and financial
liabilities, and share based payments moves traditional constraints.

- *Sources of capital, and assessment of "quality of equity"*: Disclosure of sources of equity
  firstly discriminates between capital that is contributed and equity that derives from earnings
  (i.e., retained earnings or other comprehensive income). The use of separate paid in capital
  accounts offers additional information for analysis of sources of capital and quality of equity.
  A specific point in this respect is whether or not a gain or loss that relates to distributions to, or
  contributions from, an entity's owners, should be recognized and, if yes, in which statement.
- *Rationale for capital and capital disclosures*: The presentation and disclosure of equity also
  includes the accounting for, and the classification of, specific captions and equity reserves.
  The definition and segregation of equity "reserves" serve the purpose of appropriation,
  distributability of earnings, or other forms of defense of capital, and in particular, the guarantee
  function of capital for an enterprise's creditors, to the extent of means that are statutorily or
  legally appropriated or restricted. Classification and disclosure of equity sources may also be
  required for taxation purposes under a specific jurisdiction.
- *Management of capital*: From a management viewpoint, an entity has to determine its capital
  structure optimization policy, the dividend policy, the objectives, policies and processes that
  it employs for the purpose of managing capital and, depending on the industry, how to cope
  with externally imposed capital requirements.
- *Owners' perspective*: Each one of the owners of a company is interested in understanding
  whether a certain jurisdiction provides for equality of shareholders' rights for each class of
  equity securities, which rights are associated with each class of equity securities, minority
  interest rights, and whether or not such rights are proportional to the equity interest. From an
  accounting perspective, this also translates into different presentations of minority interests
  in a partially owned subsidiary in consolidated financial statements, as a result of adopting
  the entity versus the parent company theory, and how gains or losses that are generated by
  capital transactions should be accounted for. Furthermore, financial reporting has produced
  indicators that serve information needs of the controlling interest (such as earnings per share
  that are attributable to ordinary equity holders of the parent entity) versus those of all owners
  (e.g., net income).
- *Definition of financial performance and performance metrics*: Shareholders are interested
  in understanding the return on their investment, as well as the performance of the company. A
  long standing debate exists on the definition of performance: financial versus economic versus
  nonfinancial performance; net income versus comprehensive income; capital maintenance
  concepts; short versus long term perspective; GAAP measures versus pro forma earnings.
  Financial reporting has responded by in computing earnings per share and diluted earnings per
  share. Financial analysis has developed ROE – Return on Equity, cost of equity, economic
  value added (EVA), and other models of shareholders' value and financial performance.
  Many financial ratios involve equity (such as debt to equity ratio), and specific accounting
  treatments may affect such ratios (such as recognition of a capital versus an operating lease).
  Furthermore, all this differs from market capitalization of a company, and value of equity
  from a stock exchange investor's viewpoint.
- *Business law and regulation*: Shareholders' contributions are a basic element of their obliga
  tions as part of the articles of incorporation. Depending on jurisdiction, types and categories
  of equity instruments differ, as do the related rules and regulations. A certain jurisdiction
  may require a minimum amount of capital stock for certain company forms, allow the is
  sue of shares with no par value, and sometimes mandate a minimum par, or stated value,
  or an integer amount only. Fundamental corporate changes involving capital must follow
  specific rules.

1.3 THE CONCEPT OF OTHER COMPREHENSIVE INCOME

The concepts of comprehensive income and other comprehensive income interact with the concept of equity. Comprehensive income, under a balance sheet approach, represents all the recognized changes in equity (net assets) of an entity from one reporting period date to the next that result from sources other than changes arising from investment by and distributions to owners. The balance sheet view is discussed in Section 2.1.4 later. Other comprehensive income is a part of comprehensive income. Other comprehensive income is a component of equity. Other comprehensive income is treated in Chapter 7, including its interactions with net income in representing financial performance.

1.4 THE FINANCIAL STATEMENT PRESENTATION PROJECT

The FASB and the IASB are jointly pursuing a comprehensive and consistent approach to financial statements presentation. Stockholders' equity also comprises presentation issues. Therefore, it is worth considering the development of this project to date and its connections to the topic of this Book.

1.4.1 Project History

The accounting and financial communities have long been discussing presentation models to enhance the relevance, quality, credibility, and usefulness of financial reporting, including whether its scope should extend to business issues, real time disclosures, financial metrics, and even nonfinancial information.[1]

In 1998 the FASB decided to undertake research on business reporting, also covering disclo sures that companies may decide to make even on a voluntary basis.[2]

The IASB and the FASB added independent projects on performance reporting, mainly fo cused on income statement presentation, to their agendas, in September and October 2001 respectively. Since April 2004 they have been conducting a joint project.

---

[1] *Among others: Association for Investment Management and Research (AIMR),* Financial Reporting in the 1990s and Beyond *(November 1993); AICPA Special Committee on Financial Reporting,* Improving Business Reporting – A Customer Focus *(December 1994); FASB Invitation to Comment,* Recommendations of the AICPA Special Committee on Financial Reporting and the Association for Investment Management and Research *(1996); L. Todd Johnson and Andrew Lennard, January 1998 Special Report, Reporting Financial Performance:* Current Developments and Future Directions, *published by the members of the former G4+1 standard setting organizations (January 1998); Kathryn Cearns, September 1999 Special Report,* Reporting Financial Performance: A Proposed Approach, *published by the members of the former G4+1 standard setting organizations (September 1999); UK's Accounting Standards Board (ASB) Financial Reporting Exposure Draft (FRED 22),* Reporting Financial Performance *(December 2000).*

[2] *Special Committee Report of the Business Reporting Research Project,* Improving Business Reporting: Insights into Enhancing Voluntary Disclosures *(January 2001); GAAP SEC Disclosure* Requirements *(March 2001);* Business and Financial Reporting: Challenges from the New Economy *(April 2001);* Update of Electronic Distribution of Business Reporting Information – Survey of Business Reporting Research Information on Companies' Internet Sites *(May 2002).*

During their joint meeting on March 18, 2006, the FASB and the IASB finally decided to rename the project previously entitled *Performance Reporting* as *Financial Statement Presen tation Project* to reflect its expanded scope to cover all financial statements.

The project now continues as part of the Memorandum of Understanding which sets out a Roadmap of Convergence between IFRSs and U.S. GAAP 2006–2008. The MoU called for issuance of one or more due process documents on the full range of topics in the Financial Statement Presentation project by 2008. The IASB and the FASB updated their Memorandum of Understanding. A timeline for convergence of IFRSs and U.S. GAAP by 2011 outlined in the Memorandum of Understanding was endorsed by the G20 Leaders on September 24–25, 2009 in Pittsburgh. In November 2009, the FASB and the IASB reaffirmed their commitment to their 2006 Memorandum of Understanding, as updated in 2008. They issued a joint statement indicating a pathway for completion of the major projects by 2011. In June 2010, they revised their convergence work plan to prioritize the major projects.

A Joint International Group (JIG), composed of experienced financial statements professionals, and a Financial Institutions Advisory Group (FIAG), for reporting issues regarding financial institutions, assist the Boards and their staff.

On March 16, 2006, the IASB issued its Phase A Exposure Draft, *Proposed Amendments to IAS 1 Presentation of Financial Statements: a Revised Presentation*. On September 2007, the IASB issued its revised version of IAS 1, *Presentation of Financial Statements*, which completed this first phase of the project. As to Phase B of the project, on October 16, 2008 the IASB and the FASB published for public comment a discussion paper. In July 2010, the staff of the IASB and the FASB published a Staff Draft. Progress on this project is not expected until later in 2011.[3]

1.4.2   Scope and Objectives of the Project

The *Financial Statement Presentation Project* limits its scope to presentation standards. Its objective is to improve the ability of financial statements users to assess the financial perfor mance of a business enterprise and the amounts, timing, and uncertainty of the enterprise's future cash flows. Through identification of decision relevant information, in a manner that is sufficient for financial analysis, with appropriate display and consistent classifications of data, users would be assisted in understanding an entity's past and present financial position and changes thereof, and the nature of the activities that caused those changes.

The project is divided into three segments, with the following scope:

- ***Phase A*** – Decision on which primary statements shall form a complete set of financial statements; the number of years and configuration of comparative information; and the use of a single statement of comprehensive income and its appropriate subtotals;
- ***Phase B*** – Definition of principles for disaggregating and totalizing financial in formation; whether to maintain the notion and mechanics of "recycling" of other

[3] *Discussion Paper,* Preliminary Views on Financial Statement Presentation *(October 2008); FASB and IASB,* Staff Draft of an Exposure Draft on Financial Statement Presentation *(July 2010);* FASB Technical Plan and Project Updates (last visited August 25, 2011) *www.fasb.org;* IASB Work Plan *as of July 26, 2011.*

comprehensive income items to net income; and whether the statement of cash flows should follow the direct or indirect method of presentation;

- **Phase C (FASB only)** – Decision on interim reporting, including which financial statements shall be involved; whether and how to use condensed formats; what periods are relevant for comparative information; and whether guidance should differentiate private versus public companies.

The project does not include recognition and measurement, presentation or disclosure of nonfinancial metrics, financial reporting other than financial statements (such as management discussion and analysis), and pro forma earnings.

Although discussed during the project, the Discussion Paper scoped out the accounting for other comprehensive income and its recycling to net income or reclassification to profit or loss.[4] To benefit from the shorter term improvements made through the *Financial Statement Presentation Project* and other projects, the Boards enucleated the aspects of presentation of other comprehensive income, resulting in June 2011 in Amendments to IAS 1 and in an Accounting Standards Update.[5]

1.4.3 Working Principles

The *Financial Statement Presentation Project* has been proceeding deductively from a num ber of working principles. Those working principles address the manner in which financial statements should present information. A short explanation of those principles follows. The Discussion Paper and then the Staff Paper revised them in number, definition, and priority.

1.4.3.1 Cohesiveness The first, and initially the governing, working principle states that financial statements should portray a cohesive financial picture of an entity. This principle initially included subprinciples on comparativeness and consistency. These subprinciples were subsequently removed, because they were already part of the overarching qualitative characteristics of financial reporting.[6] Qualitative characteristics make accounting or financial statements information helpful to users.[7] The *Financial Statement Presentation Project* instead translates general qualitative characteristics into working principles of financial statement presentation.[8] The Staff Draft gives a special relevance to cohesiveness as one of the core prin ciples. Cohesiveness structures financial statements similarly, by using sections, categories, and subcategories that make the interrelations of financial statements transparent. Depending

---

[4] *Discussion Paper,* Preliminary Views on Financial Statement Presentation, ¶ 1.22 (October 2008).

[5] *FASB Accounting Standards Update No. 2011 05,* Comprehensive Income (Topic 220) – Presentation of Comprehensive Income; *Amendments to IAS 1,* Presentation of Items of Other Comprehensive Income.

[6] *CON 8,* Conceptual Framework for Financial Reporting, Chapter 1, The Objective of General Purpose Financial Reporting, and Chapter 3, Qualitative Characteristics of Useful Financial Information, ¶¶ QC21, QC22; CON 2 (superseded), ¶¶ 111, 120; The Conceptual Framework for Financial Reporting 2010, ¶ QC21, QC22; IASB Framework, ¶ 39 (superseded).

[7] *CON 8,* ¶ QC1; CON 2 (superseded), ¶ 1; The Conceptual Framework for Financial Reporting 2010, ¶ QC1; IASB Framework, ¶ 24 (superseded).

[8] *IASB Meeting, September 19, 2006, Agenda Paper 9,* Application of Working Principles, ¶ 122 (September 2006).

on the granularity of the changes in assets or liabilities, financial statements may align at various levels, from category to line items.[9]

1.4.3.2 Categorization   The working principle of categorization requires that financial statements should separate an entity's financing activities from its business and other activities and further separate financing activities between transactions with owners in their capacity as owners and all other financing activities. The terminology used for the working principle has changed to specify *value creating activities* as *business and other activities* (e.g., business, investing, and others) and, symmetrically, to replace *financing activities* (i.e., financing of those business and other activities) to *capital activities*. Finally, the point on segregation between transactions with owners in their capacity as owners from all other financing activities, which was previously independent, was added to this working principle, to underline equity financing as one of the types of financing activities. This principle did not survive the Staff Draft and was embedded in other principles.

1.4.3.3 Liquidity   Under the working principle of liquidity, financial statements should present information in a manner that helps a user assess the liquidity of an entity's assets and liabilities (nearness to cash or time to conversion to cash). This working principle previously included an explanation of the importance of liquidity to predict future cash flows, and has subsequently incorporated a definition of liquidity as nearness to cash or time to maturity. Moreover, the Boards have been considering whether the notion of solvency should be included in this working principle. The Discussion Paper finally subsumed this working principle in that of "liquidity and financial flexibility."[10] The Staff Draft has eliminated the principle of liquidity and financial flexibility, as subsumed in the Conceptual Framework.[11]

1.4.3.4 Measurement   The working principle of measurement dictates that financial state ments help a user understand the following aspects concerning the measurement of assets and liabilities:

1. The basis on which assets and liabilities are measured (measurement basis);
2. The uncertainty in measurements of individual assets and liabilities (measurement uncertainty);
3. What causes a change in reported amounts of individual assets and liabilities (causes of asset and liability changes).

This is no longer a basic principle. Measurement is a dimension of the disaggregation principle.

1.4.3.5 Disaggregation   Financial statements should disaggregate line items, under the disaggregation working principle, if that disaggregation enhances the usefulness of the infor mation in predicting future cash flows. This working principle lost the previous component of the notion of totalization. Totalization is important as it consists in the aggregation on the face of the financial statements of line items into subtotals and totals that are considered

---

[9]   *FASB and IASB*, Staff Draft of an Exposure Draft on Financial Statement Presentation, ¶¶ *44–45, 57–58, 61 (July 2010).*

[10]   *Discussion Paper*, Preliminary Views on Financial Statement Presentation, ¶¶ *2.12–2.13 (October 2008).*

[11]   *FASB and IASB*, Staff Draft of an Exposure Draft on Financial Statement Presentation, ¶¶ *BC72–BC73 (July 2010).*

relevant. However, excessive totalization makes cluttered financial statements. Finally, the Discussion Paper proposes the presentation of meaningful subtotals for each section and cat egory within a section of the financial statements.[12] The Staff Draft gives a special relevance to disaggregation as one of the core principles. The keys of disaggregation are the functions, nature, and measurement basis of items. Disaggregation, by enucleating activities, cash flows, and relationships between assets or liabilities and the effects of their changes, makes financial statements clear and ready for financial analysis for appraisal of performance and prediction of future cash flows. The correct level of disaggregation depends on the interaction of materiality and understandability.[13]

1.4.3.6 Cash Flow Assessment This working principle was introduced in December 2006. It requires all financial statements, not just the statement of cash flows, to apply the objectives of the statement of cash flows under Subtopic 230 10 (FASB Statement No. 95, *Statement of Cash Flows*) and International Accounting Standard No. 7, *Cash Flow Statements*. Specifically, under this working principle, financial statements should be prepared in a manner that helps investors, creditors, and others to assess an entity's ability to generate future cash inflows, meet its obligations, and establish what transactions do not involve cash and their impact on an entity's financial position.[14]

The Discussion Paper finally subsumed this working principle within that of "liquidity and financial flexibility."[15]

1.4.3.7 Selection of Working Principles in the Financial Statement Presentation Project Among these working principles, the Discussion Paper of the *Financial Statement Presentation Project* selected cohesiveness, disaggregation, and liquidity and financial flexibility as the objectives of financial statement presentation and renamed them as objectives of financial statement presentation.[16] The objective of "liquidity and financial flexibility" included the former working principle of liquidity and that of cash flow assessment that were previously separate ones. Under the Staff Draft, disaggregation and cohesiveness remain the two core principles.[17]

1.4.4 Interrelationships and Conflicts among Working Principles

Some interrelationships (and conflicts) arguably arise from the working principles. Worksheet 1 illustrates those relationships.

---

[12] *Discussion Paper,* Preliminary Views on Financial Statement Presentation, *¶ 2.23 (October 2008).*

[13] *FASB and IASB,* Staff Draft of an Exposure Draft on Financial Statement Presentation, *¶¶ 44–46, 51, BC66, BC70–BC71 (July 2010).*

[14] *Financial Accounting Standards Advisory Council,* March 20, 2007 Agenda, *Attachment F – Exhibit 1, ¶ 3.*

[15] *Discussion Paper,* Preliminary Views on Financial Statement Presentation, *¶¶ 2.12–2.13 (October 2008).*

[16] *Discussion Paper,* Preliminary Views on Financial Statement Presentation, *¶ 2.4 (October 2008).*

[17] *FASB and IASB,* Staff Draft of an Exposure Draft on Financial Statement Presentation, *¶¶ 44, 45 (July 2010).*

1.4.5 Link to the Topic of This Book

The *Financial Statement Presentation Project* has raised some issues that have a connection to the topic of equity. The main aspects are illustrated in Worksheet 2 along with paragraph references in this Book.

1.5 MAIN INTERRELATIONSHIPS WITH OTHER PROJECTS

The FASB and the IASB are conducting several projects independently, or in conjunction as a result of the convergence effort. Some of these projects have points of contact with the topic of equity, as follows.

Within the context of deliberations on the elements of financial statements and on recognition as part of Phase B of the *Conceptual Framework Project*, the discussions compare alternative views on equity. Part of the debate regards an effort to define equity, as opposed to leaving it as a residual classification. Additionally, an approach to identifying a single element of *claims* is an alternative to a more traditional classification of equity versus liabilities. A Discussion Paper from the IASB and from the FASB on Phase B is not expected until after June 2011 and December 2011, respectively. Phase A was completed by publishing in September 2010 the Objectives and Qualitative Characteristics chapters.[18]

Debate on the adoption of the entity versus proprietary concepts is included as part of Phase D of the project, with a Discussion Paper issued on May 2008. Continuation of this Phase by the IASB and the FASB is not expected before June 2011 and December 2011, respectively.[19] This issue is treated extensively in Section 4.3.2 later.

The *Financial Instruments with Characteristics of Equity Project – former Financial Instruments: Liabilities and Equity Project –* (Phase 1 of which resulted in FASB Statement No. 150[20]), is intended to produce a comprehensive standard for all financial instruments, including those with characteristics of equity, liabilities, or both. As part of this project, three different approaches to equity – ownership, ownership settlement, and reassessed expected outcomes (REO) approaches – have been under discussion. Progress on this project is not expected until later in 2011.[21]

The *Financial Instruments Project* has the long term objective of adopting fair value measurement and simplification of accounting for financial instruments, including overcoming the current dichotomy between net income and other comprehensive income. In November 2009 the IASB issued IFRS 9, *Financial Instruments*, and in October 2010 revised it. In May 2010,

---

[18] The Conceptual Framework for Financial Reporting *2010; CON 8*, Conceptual Framework for Financial Reporting, *Chapter 1*, The Objective of General Purpose Financial Reporting, *and Chapter 3*, Qualitative Characteristics of Useful Financial Information; *FASB* Technical Plan and Project Updates *(last visited August 25, 2011) www.fasb.org;* IASB Work Plan *as of July 26, 2011.*

[19] *Discussion Paper,* Preliminary Views on an Improved Conceptual Framework for Financial Reporting: The Reporting Entity; *FASB Technical Plan and Project Updates (last visited August 25, 2011) www.fasb.org; IASB Work Plan as of July 26, 2011.*

[20] *FASB Statement No. 150,* Accounting for Certain Financial Instructions with Characteristics of Both Liabilities and Equity *(May 2003).*

[21] FASB Technical Plan and Project Updates *(last visited August 25, 2011) www.fasb.org;* IASB Work Plan *as of July 26, 2011.*

the FASB published a proposed Accounting Standards Update. A Final Document is planned by 2011.[22]

The *Business Combination Project* in its Phase II also included the accounting for, and reporting of, noncontrolling (minority) interests. Phase I of the project resulted in IFRS 3, and revised versions of International Accounting Standard No. 36[23] and International Accounting Standard No. 38.[24] Phase II resulted in IFRS 3 (Revised January 2008) and FASB Statement of Financial Accounting Standards No. 141 (Revised 2007),[25] as well as International Accounting Standards No. 27 (Revised January 2008)[26] and FASB Statement of Financial Accounting Standards No. 160, *Noncontrolling Interests in Consolidated Financial Statements*. The topic of noncontrolling (minority) interests is discussed in Section 4.3 later.

Both Phase 2 of the FASB's *Postretirement Benefit Obligations including Pensions Project* and Phase 1 of the IASB's *Post Employment Benefits (including Pensions) Project* aim at a comprehensive reconsideration of pension and postretirement benefit accounting. A first step was the issuance of FASB Statement No. 158 in September 2006. The implications on equity are analyzed in Section 7.18 later. In June 2011, the IASB issue a revision of IAS 19. However, this is not a comprehensive reconsideration of postemployment benefits. The FASB placed this project in a not active status.

The IASB's *Intangible Assets Project* was intended to address the accounting for intangible assets, resulting in the amendment of IAS 38. In December 2007, the IASB decided not to add this project to its active agenda. The effect of the revaluation model to equity is explained in Section 6.6 later and Section 7.16 later.

The *Income Tax Short Term Convergence Project* addresses selected differences between U.S. GAAP and IFRSs on income taxes, including those directly affecting other comprehensive income and equity. The IASB issued an Exposure Draft on March 2009. However, in October 2009, the IASB decided not to go forward with the Exposure Draft and to re introduce some of its proposals. It also resolved to address specific issues concerning income taxes in the short term and conduct a fundamental review with the FASB in a longer period.[27] Certain requirements proposed in the Exposure Draft are illustrated in Chapter 8 later.

1.6 SIGNIFICANCE OF EQUITY

Stockholders' equity has at all times been considered a significant item in financial statements for several reasons. Firstly, most transactions and events that involve assets and liabilities result, directly or indirectly, in changes in equity. Secondly, contributions from, and distributions to,

---

[22] *FASB, Proposed Accounting Standards Update,* Accounting for Financial Instruments and Revi sions to the Accounting for Derivative Instruments and Hedging Activities – Financial Instruments (Topic 825) and Derivatives and Hedging (Topic 815) *(May 2010).* FASB Technical Plan and Project Updates *(last visited August 25, 2011) www.fasb.org.*

[23] *International Accounting Standard No. 36,* Impairment of Assets.

[24] *International Accounting Standard No. 38,* Intangible Assets.

[25] *FASB Statement No. 141(R),* Business Combinations.

[26] *International Accounting Standards No. 27,* Consolidated and Separate Financial Statements.

[27] *Exposure Draft,* Income Tax *(March 2009); Amendments to IAS 12,* Deferred Tax: Recovery of Underlying Assets, ¶ BC3; IASB Update, November 2009; IASB Update, March 2010.

shareholders also affect equity. Additionally, transactions and events that determine income (or expenses), or gains (or losses), increase (decrease) stockholders' equity, through either net income (loss) or other comprehensive income (loss), although the percentage impact of income or expense (nature of flow) is alleviated by the cumulative nature of equity (nature of stock). Finally, changes in accounting principles and correction of errors generally impact equity, under FASB Statement No. 154 and IAS 8, mostly through retroactive restatement of retained earnings.

Some surveys on first time adoption of IFRSs illustrate the pervasive nature of accounting impacts on stockholders' equity. The percentage change in stockholders' equity due to 2005 first time adoption of IFRSs for 24 largest European banks was positive in France up to over 20% in one case, Belgium from over 5% up to 15%, generally decreasing in the United Kingdom up to less than –10% in one instance, and with mixed results in other countries with a range from +10% to less than –15%.[28] An analysis by Ernst & Young of the impact of 2005 first time adoption of IFRSs for six companies in the building materials sector (BPB, CRH, Hanson, Italcementi, Lafarge, and St Gobain)[29] showed a prevailing downward change, ranging from –4% to –10%, in total equity (only one player presenting a positive increase). An analysis of 35 listed companies that were part of the S&P/MIB index in Italy[30] showed that the first time adoption of IFRSs as of January 1, 2005 affected stockholders equity by 2.7% on average, and +15.8% for the insurance sector, +5.5% for industrial companies, +4.5% for media and telecom, –4.9% for energy and utilities, –3.5% for banking, and +51.9% for other trade and services. A survey on 2005 IFRSs' first time adoption by Italian listed companies showed that the change in stockholders' equity relative to previous local GAAP exceeded a +/–10% range for 29% out of 193 consolidated financial statements as of the beginning of 2004 (32% as of the end of 2004) and 35% out of 50 entity financial statements (25% as of the end of 2004).[31]

1.7 SCOPE OF BOOK

This Book analyzes the accounting for stockholders' equity and other comprehensive income from the point of view of an equity issuer, as well as the related accounting requirements, from the angle of a comparative study, by means of a critical appraisal of and comparison between the U.S. GAAP and the IFRSs pronouncements and practice.

This operational view is taken from a dual reporting approach. In fact, from a practical perspective, Chief Financial Officers, Financial Directors, and controllers of companies that plan to or are required to adopt IFRSs for the first time may need to implement dual reporting systems and processes. This would also apply to European companies that operate both in Europe and in the United States, or U.S. multinational companies that are present in countries where IFRSs are effective. Therefore, they must understand the similarities and differences

---

[28] *Ernst & Young,* The Impact or IFRS on European Banks – 2005 Reporting *(October 2006) (last visited October 2006) www.ey.com/ifrs.*

[29] *Ernst & Young, IFRS,* The Implications for the Building Materials Sector *(December 2005) (last visited December 2005) www.ey.com/ifrs.*

[30] *Protiviti,* Insight No. 6 2005 *(December 2005) www.protiviti.it (last visited January 2006)*

[31] *Osservatorio Bilanci Sezione di Ragioneria – Dipartimento di Economia Aziendale Universita degli Studi di Torino,* Summit 2005, Rapporto sui bilanci 2005 delle societa quotate, *Summa (October 16, 2006), (last visited August 5, 2007) www.m2a.unito.it.*

between U.S. GAAP and IFRSs. Furthermore, EC Regulation 1606/2002 permits EU Member States to defer the first time adoption of IFRSs to the financial year starting on or after January 2007 for companies, inter alia, that are listed in an EU non member State and report under U.S. GAAP.

As a result of those changes, the complexity for multinational companies has increased twofold. Firstly, migrating to IFRSs as the primary basis of accounting may be necessary in the relevant jurisdictions. Secondly, the accounting systems, processes, and corporate culture must initially change to allow reporting in (at least) two comprehensive bases of accounting, as opposed to just a one off exercise for reconciliation to U.S. GAAP, as some companies have been required to do.

This often involves transition costs and implementation difficulties, for which companies may seek external support. In this respect, the accounting industry also faces the challenge of digesting new accounting principles and confronting them with other sets of standards.

> **Planning Point:** Transition processes may result in expensive professional charges to clients, unless better time and result for money are achieved through a multidisciplinary and multi chartered ac counting environment that capitalizes on a dual reporting practice, as opposed to the traditional and costly approach of mobilizing staff from the U.S. and European practices of a professional firm.

Certain events reaffirm the need for an understanding of the similarities and differences between the two different sets of accounting principles.

Firstly, as is well known, the IASB and the FASB are committed to a joint work program as described in their Memorandum of Understanding. The Memorandum of Understanding establishes a Roadmap of Convergence between IFRSs and U.S. GAAP 2006–2008. The MoU called for issuance of one or more due process documents by 2008. In 2008, the FASB and the IASB updated the Memorandum of Understanding. On September 24–25, 2009 in Pittsburgh, the G20 Leaders endorsed a timeline for convergence of IFRSs and U.S. GAAP by 2011 outlined in the update of the Memorandum of Understanding. In November 2009, the FASB and the IASB reaffirmed their commitment to their Memorandum of Understanding. They issued a joint statement indicating a pathway for completion of the major projects by 2011. In June 2010, they revised their convergence Work plan to prioritize the major projects. As a consequence of this trend to convergence, economic players, such as academics, accountants, and financial analysts, received a notice to be ready for the changing requirements. Corporate executives must be even more on the alert, in order to plan for easier and more cost conscious migrations.

Secondly, to give preparers a relatively stable period to implement the IFRS platform, the IASB announced that it would not require the application of new standards before January 1, 2009,[32] although in the meantime it has developed new standards. In October 2010, the IASB and the FASB published a Discussion Paper soliciting feedback on the most effective

---

[32] *IASB Press Release, December 2006.* No new major standards to be effective before 2009. *[Online] IASB. Available at www.iasb.org (last visited February 2007).*

times and transition methods of standards that they are jointly developing.[33] In general, the effective date of major projects planned for completion by 2011 is the beginning of 2013.[34] Therefore, companies yet to adopt IFRSs still have an additional opportunity to get a better understanding of future directions and design their accounting systems according to multi standard compliance.

Thirdly, effective for financial years ending after November 15, 2007 and interim periods within those years contained in filings made after the effective date, the Securities and Exchange Commission recently eliminated the requirement for reconciliation of financial statements prepared in conformity with IFRSs as issued by the IASB to U.S. GAAP in Form 20 F, and allowed annual filings and registration statements without reconciliation to U.S. GAAP.[35]

The SEC also published a Concept Release on allowing U.S. issuers to file financial statements in accordance with IFRSs as issued by the IASB with the Commission.[36]

On August 27, 2008 the SEC also proposed a "roadmap" to IFRSs that would require all U.S. public companies to file their financial statements in IFRSs by 2016 and would also allow certain U.S. companies, based on certain criteria, to use IFRSs for their filings for fiscal years ending on or after December 15, 2009. In 2011 the SEC would evaluate the steps made in the roadmap and decide whether or not to require large accelerated filers (issuers with common equity of at least $700 million) to report under IFRSs starting from fiscal years ending on or after December 15, 2014, accelerated filers to report under IFRSs starting for fiscal years ending on or after December 15, 2015, and all other public companies from fiscal years ending on or after December 15, 2016.

However, on February 24, 2010, the SEC issued a statement calling for more study of IFRSs and setting 2015 as the earliest possible date for the required use of IFRSs by U.S. public companies. It confirmed year 2011 as the threshold for a decision on whether to move ahead. The SEC withdrew the proposed rules for limited early use of IFRS by certain U.S. issuers, although it did not exclude the possibility of early use or adoption. The statement does not rule out the possibility in the future that issuers may be permitted to choose between the use of IFRSs or U.S. GAAP. The Work plan addresses six specific areas of concern: 1) whether IFRSs are sufficiently developed and consistent in application for use in the U.S. reporting system; 2) the independence of standard setting; 3) investor understanding and education regarding the new standards and comparison with U.S. GAAP; 4) impact on U.S. laws or regulations;

---

[33] *FASB, October 2010. Discussion Paper,* Effective Dates and Transition Methods; *IASB, October 2010.* Request for Views on Effective Dates and Transition Methods.

[34] *IASB Update, December 2009.*

[35] *Security and Exchange Commission,* Acceptance from Foreign Private Issuers of Financial Statements Prepared in Accordance with International Financial Reporting Standards Without Reconciliation to U.S. GAAP *(March 4, 2008); Security and Exchange Commission, Proposed Rule (Release No. 33 8818),* Acceptance from Foreign Private Issuers of Financial Statements Prepared in Accordance with International Financial Reporting Standards Without Reconciliation to U.S. GAAP *(July 2, 2007). Hereinafter Proposed Rule.*

[36] *Securities and Exchange Commission, Release No. 33 8831,* Concept Release on Allowing U.S. Issuers to Prepare Financial Statements in Accordance With International Financial Reporting Standards *(August 2007), page 6. Hereinafter Concept Release.*

5) impact on both large and small companies; and 6) preparation of auditors. The successful completion of the FASB IASB convergence project is perceived as a critical milestone.

On May 26, 2011, the SEC published an update concerning its Work plan to IFRSs.[37] After analyzing the difference between enforcement and convergence, the SEC's paper addresses the so called "condorsement" approach. This approach intends to lead to IFRS compliance by U.S. issuers that are compliant with U.S. GAAP. At the end of a transitional period, U.S. GAAP would incorporate IFRSs. In this respect, it is similar to an enforcement approach. During a transitional period of five to seven years, differences between IFRS and U.S. GAAP would be addressed. In this respect, it is similar to a convergence approach. The transition period could permit a staged or phased implementation.

Finally, the FASB would also have a role in issuing supplementary or interpretative guidance, adding disclosure requirements, or setting requirements on issues not addressed by IFRSs. Finally, as of May 18, 2008 the IASB has been designated by the Council of the AICPA as the body to establish international financial reporting standards for both private and public entities pursuant to Rule 202 and Rule 203 of the AICPA Code of Professional Conduct. In three to five years, the Council will reassess this decision.[38]

Planning Point: This should be seen as an opportunity. Adopting high quality, understandable, transparent, and internationally accepted standards (such as IFRSs or U.S. GAAP) for financial reporting should be part of the corporate, marketing, and communication strategy to stakeholders and requires top management commitment.

It may be a unique opportunity to enhance decision usefulness for users of financial statements, aid the raising of foreign finance, and improve corporate image, competitiveness, financial transparency, and international visibility. In addition, it is an opportunity to shift business processes from report generation to streamlined and cost effective data gathering.

The adoption of modern financial reporting is not simply an accounting exercise, but it generates a pervasive change that involves virtually all the departments of a company.

Therefore, this may result in a new competitive tool for Chief Executive Officers, Directors, and Chief Financial Officers who know how to accept this challenge.

Most importantly, some major economies, e.g., Canada, which has announced IFRS conver gence by 2011, are migrating to IFRSs by 2010–2012 and beyond.

On July 24, 2007, the Council of the Institute of Chartered Accountants of India announced its IFRS convergence plan for listed entities, other public interest entities such as banks, insurance companies, and large sized entities from the accounting periods commencing on or after April 1, 2011.

---

[37] *SEC, 2011.* Work Plan for the Consideration of Incorporating International Financial Reporting Standards into the Financial Reporting System for U.S. Issuers. *[Online] Available at www.sec.gov (last visited May 29, 2011).*

[38] *Amendment to Code of Professional Conduct Appendix A* – Council Resolution Designating Bodies to Promulgate Professional Standards.

On January 28, 2010, the Brazilian Federal Council of Accounting and the Brazilian Accounting Pronouncements Committee signed a MoU with the IASB to converge fully to IFRS by end 2010.

On August 1, 2008, the Financial Reporting Foundation (FRF) and Malaysian Accounting Standards Board (MASB) announced their plan to bring Malaysia to full convergence with IFRSs by January 1, 2012. For the time being, private entities will continue to apply Private Entity Reporting Standards (PERS).

In November 2008, the National Banking and Securities Commission of Mexico together with the Mexican Board for Research and Development of Financial Reporting Standards communicated a plan to adopt IFRSs for listed entities starting for periods ending on December 31, 2012.

Public companies in Argentina will be required to adopt IFRSs starting in 2012, with an option to file financial statements in accordance with IFRSs starting in January 2011.

The South Korean government has approved mandatory adoption of IFRSs by 2011 for all listed companies and unlisted financial institutions in certain sectors. All companies except financial institutions could voluntarily adopt IFRSs from January 1, 2009.

On December 11, 2009, the Japan Financial Services Agency (FSA) announced regulatory changes to allow certain qualifying domestic listed companies to apply IFRSs in consolidated financial statements, starting from the fiscal year ending on or after March 31, 2010. A final decision on the mandatory requirement of IFRSs from 2015 or 2016 will be taken around 2012.

In such a context, this Book addresses the informational needs of policymakers, Chief Financial Officers, Financial Directors, controllers, financial analysts, CPAs, and academics to compare the U.S. GAAP and IFRS requirements for the presentation on the face of the balance sheet and on the alternative statements for reporting shareholders' equity. It also draws practical implications for IFRS/U.S. GAAP dual reporting.

This Book approaches the subject mainly from the angle of presentation standards for the statement of financial position[39] and other statements for equity reporting. Recognition, measurement, and disclosure are also addressed, although consequentially derived.

The Book also capitalizes on the study of Basis for Conclusions, proposed Exposure Drafts, Discussion Documents, and other convergence project works, in order to analyze the rationale and the practical implications of differences in accounting requirements.

Firstly, the scope of the applicable authoritative pronouncements and respective definitions is analyzed in depth. Importantly, the main difficulty that comparative studies usually encounter is in making an inventory of whether authoritative literature treats the same, similar, partially overlapping, or totally different issues. This is mostly due to the fact that different bodies of standards often move from different angles, scopes, or starting points.

---

[39] *In general, this Book uses the expression "statement of financial position" with reference to U.S. GAAP and IFRSs, consistently with IAS 1, unless used differently in a specific pronouncement. It uses the term "balance sheet" with reference to SEC rules and regulations.*

Then, the differences between the two sets of standards are identified as far as possible, based on a study of the literal wording of the texts involved.

This Book follows a pervasive, comprehensive, multidisciplinary and multistandard compar ison approach. Thus, the reader will discover how important the implications for managers may be. Presentation is viewed as a cross cutting feature, as opposed to the traditional way of looking at the presentation issue as a residual item. This Book does more than simply comment on IAS 1. Conversely, virtually all authoritative pronouncements may have direct or indirect effects on the display on the face of the financial statements. Additionally, determining the right presentation entails, as a prerequisite, a clear understanding of the scope of standards, the definitions, and the relative frameworks. Sometimes the issue is intrinsically commingled with recognition criteria. Furthermore, under certain circumstances, professional judgment and application of accounting policies by management may be required to decide whether to display or simply disclose a certain item in the notes. Even more importantly, in practice the topic of presentation is the first and most evident issue that a company faces, as the design of the chart of accounts and the formatting of the financial statements will depend on it.

Further, the Book uses an operating approach which is useful to companies, especially for the concept and precise techniques of dual reporting, guidelines for designing the chart of accounts, restating or reconciling financial statements for different GAAP, and first time adoption of IFRS.

This Book does not treat: 1) the aspects of share based compensation other than those related to its presentation in equity; 2) earnings per share; and 3) classification of equity versus financial liability.

2 VIEWS ON EQUITY AND IMPLICATIONS

2.1 TERMINOLOGY AND DEFINITIONS OF TERMS

Several terms are used to indicate equity and related concepts in authoritative accounting literature. The multitude of terminology is such that it may not be clear where overlapping or inconsistencies exist. While generally some of these expressions may appear synonymous,[1] each may be found to have specific meanings and implications, to the extent that any particular expression underlines a peculiar aspect of the notion of equity according to the context in which it is used.

Generally, two different points of view alternate in discussions on equity: the perspective of the enterprise (also called the entity perspective) and that of its owners, i.e., the proprietary perspective. Sometimes, however, such different meanings may not be interchangeable.

Comment: For instance, as this section illustrates, equity may exist with no ownership interest (e.g., not-for-profit organization).

A residual-type interest may exist without equity (e.g., certain economic interests, or variable interests).

Criteria to distinguish equity from a liability may sometimes differ from those to define an interest in net assets.

One may argue that common dividends declared and not yet paid accrue to the shareholders and thus dividends payable are equity, not liabilities. This would be similar to the notion that retained earnings accrue to shareholders and that noncontrolling interests are part of equity. IFRS 17 acknowledges that using the proprietary versus the entity perspective ends up with different conclusions.[2] Under the view that an enterprise is a separate entity from its owners, the declaration of dividends separates the period in which retained earnings are an indistinct component of equity from the moment that the entity assumes an obligation to its owners considered as a party distinct from the company itself.

Finally, Section 5.2.10 later illustrates that the adoption of the entity versus the proprietary perspective may affect the choice of grant date versus exercise date measurement of stock options.

---

[1] For example, FASB Statement No. 150, ¶ 5 uses, for the purpose of this standard, the term "shares" to include different forms of ownership, although in Footnote 4 it acknowledges the use of several specialized names.
[2] IFRIC 17, ¶ BC41, BC42.

This section develops an analysis of conceptual views on equity through a framework of four layers, with reference to the following four categories related to the notion of equity:

1. Equity;
2. Equity owners;
3. Equity instruments;
4. Equity interest.

In fact, at least four angles are ordinarily embedded in the notion of equity: 1) equity as synonymous with an entity's capital; 2) shareholders, owners, or equity participants; 3) the financial instruments or securities through which equity materializes; and 4) the set of rights and privileges that attach to its beneficiaries.

Comment: Each of these layers refers to a different perspective, emphasis, and issues. However, as will become clear in the following paragraphs, when some overlaps and inconsistencies in definitions and uses of terms exist, it is not uncommon that a term relating to one of these layers is defined or used with reference to another of those contexts. This fact further complicates the debate on the classification of equity versus liabilities. Sometimes a term may cut across more than one of the different layers mentioned above. For example, security refers to the instrument layer, while equity instrument is sometime used at equity classification level. Similarly, residual interest sometimes mixes a definition of total equity with the concept of holdings at owner level.

Most importantly, this section illustrates how different conceptual views draw practical implications for financial statements preparers and users.

2.1.1 Equity

In both the IASB Framework and the U.S. Concepts, equity is an element of the financial statements. Different terminology for equity exists. Each term originates from different conceptual views and may have diverse implications. Expressions such as *shareholders' equity*, *stockholders' equity*, *net assets*, and *capital* are analyzed in Section 4.1 later.

In particular, designating equity as net assets is more than a semantic distinction. Net assets identify equity as a residual concept (see Section 2.1.4.1 following). Furthermore, under U.S. GAAP, not-for-profit organizations[3] use the term *net assets*, although this is not explicitly indicated as mandatory.[4] Finally, the term *net assets* is normally considered a substitute for *equity*.[5] However, the IASB Framework specifies that the use of *capital* as a substitute for *equity* or *net assets* holds under a financial concept of capital maintenance only.[6] Capital maintenance concepts are analyzed in Section 7.6 later.

---

[3] *CON 6, ¶ 50.*
[4] *CON 6, Footnote 26.*
[5] *CON 6, Footnote 26.*
[6] The Conceptual Framework for Financial Reporting 2010, *¶ 4.57; IASB Framework, ¶ 102.*

2.1.2   Equity Owners

As shown below, in authoritative accounting literature several terms may indicate *equity owners*.

Comment: Although no explicit or intentional pattern of use exists, some generalization may be drawn, as in the analysis below.

2.1.2.1   Shareholders   The definition of *shareholder* as a residual interest holder is found in U.S. GAAP.[7]

One pattern of utilization of such a term is to subcategorize holders of stock. Firstly, shareholders may be found as part of stakeholders.[8] Secondly, shareholders are identified as a subset, or a particular type, of investors that, in turn, are users of financial statements. The new common framework does not use the term *shareholders* but simply refers to investors.[9] Then, the term may be found to differentiate common or ordinary shareholders,[10] or to denote a specific class, type, or technical category of shareholders.[11] Furthermore, such a name may distinguish controlling, or parent, from noncontrolling shareholders.[12] Finally, it sometimes identifies the position of an individual versus a class of owners.[13]

Additionally, the term *shareholder* applies to corporate entities only. It is generally employed to characterize a relation, corporate governance issue, or transaction between a corporation and its shareholders, i.e., contributions of funds,[14] or with reference to a company's legal obligation to make a distribution,[15] or with reference to changes in the tax status of an entity or of its shareholders,[16] or regarding a requirement for shareholders approval.[17]

---

[7]   *EITF Issue 88-16, Issue.*

[8]   *IAS 1, ¶ IG10.*

[9]   The Conceptual Framework for Financial Reporting 2010, *¶ OB2; IASB Framework, ¶ 9 (superseded).*

[10]   *For example FASB Statement No. 128, ¶ 115, and IAS 33, ¶¶ 10, 31 for* ordinary *and* common shareholders *for purpose of computing earnings per share.*

[11]   *For example, principal shareholder in FASB Statement No. 123(R), ¶ B107; common shareholders in ARB 51, Ch. 7B, ¶ 2; nominee shareholder in EITF Issue No. 97-2,* Application of FASB Statement No. 94 and APB Opinion No. 16 to Physician Practice Management Entities and Certain Other Entities with Contractual Management Arrangements, *Footnote 1.*

[12]   *FASB ASC 255-10-55-12 (FASB Statement No. 89, ¶ 107); FASB ASC 740-30-25 (FASB Statement No. 109, ¶ 33); FASB Statement No. 142, ¶ B154; FASB ASC 810-10 (EITF Issue No. 96-16,* Investor's Accounting for an Investee When the Investor Has a Majority of the Voting Interest but the Minority Shareholder or Shareholders Have Certain Approval or Veto Rights, *Issue); IAS 27 (2010), ¶¶ 22, BC9. SEC Form 20-F, Item 7 uses the term major shareholders, for beneficial owners of 5% or more of each class voting securities.*

[13]   *FASB ASC 505-30-25-3 (FTB 85-6, ¶ 14); IAS 1, ¶ BC51.*

[14]   The Conceptual Framework for Financial Reporting 2010, *¶ 4.20; IASB Framework, ¶ 65.*

[15]   *IAS 32, ¶ AG13.*

[16]   *SIC-25.*

[17]   *FASB ASC 815-40-25-19 (EITF Issue 00-19, ¶ 19).*

2.1.2.2   Owners   U.S. GAAP and IFRSs offered no general definition of *owner*.[18] The 2007 Revision of IAS 1 provided a definition of owners in relation to instruments being classified as equity and instead uses this term "equity holders" to converge with Subtopic 220-10 (FASB Statement No. 130).[19] A definition exists in the specialized meaning of a *principal owner* (which is when interest of such a person amounts to more than 10% of the entity's voting interest).[20] Arguably, the inclusion of both an owner of record and a beneficial owner can be derived from this.

SEC Form 20-F identifies a beneficial ownership of securities in situations where the direct or indirect (through trustees, brokers, agents, legal representatives, other intermediaries, or controlled companies) possession or sharing of the underlying benefits of ownership exists, including when a beneficial owner has the right to acquire the securities within 60 days by option or other agreement. The power to direct the voting or the disposition of the securities and the direct or indirect power to direct the management and policies of the entity may be part of these benefits.[21]

In general, ownership relates to propriety.[22] Ownership is often used with reference to legal ownership, although in accounting terms this is only a type of ownership, as ownership may be substantiated even without the existence of a right to it, to the extent that an entity controls the benefits which are associated with ownership.

The pattern of use of the term *ownership* and its derivations is to designate the existence of an interest in an entity,[23] the relative weight of such interest and who effectively has it,[24] the level of influence, or control exercised through it,[25] whether it was obtained directly

---

[18] *As part of the Financial Statement Presentation Project, Agenda Paper 14*, Exposure Draft of Proposed Amendments to IAS 1 Presentation of Financial Statements – Comment Letter Analysis *(December 14, 2006), ¶ 45, the IASB staff notes that the fact that criteria for ownership are jurisdiction related and that some accounting literature does not focus on the concept of control may explain the lack of a definition of ownership.*

[19] *IAS 1, ¶¶ 7, BC38.*

[20] *FASB of Financial Accounting Standards No. 57,* Related Party Disclosures, *¶ 24; SEC Regulation S-X, ¶ 210.1-02(r). However, FASB Statement No. 123,* Accounting for Stock-Based Compensation, *¶ 395 (superseded by FASB of Financial Accounting Standards No. 123(R)) identified a* principal stockholder *as owning at least 10% of common stock or having direct or indirect power of control or significantly influence.*

[21] *SEC Form 20-F, General Instructions, F.*

[22] *As examples of such implicit use of the term: FASB ASC 323-10-35 (AICPA Accounting Interpretations AIN-APB 18,* The Equity Method of Accounting for Investments in Common Stock: Accounting Interpretations of APB Opinion No. 18, *¶ #1), and CON 6, Footnote 30, which explains ownership as proprietary interest.*

[23] *For example: EITF Issue 90-5,* Exchanges of Ownership Interests between Entities under Common Control, *Issue; IAS 27 (2010), ¶ IG6; IFRIC 2, ¶ 3;* The Conceptual Framework for Financial Reporting 2010, *¶ 4.20; IASB Framework, ¶ 65.*

[24] *For example: FASB ASC 323-10-05-5 and 323-10-15 (FASB of Financial Accounting Standards No. 94, ¶ 10; APB 18, ¶¶ 12, 17); FASB ASC 810-10-15 (ARB 51, ¶ 2); EITF Issue 85-21, Issue; IAS 27 (2010), ¶¶ IN6, 21, BC8.*

[25] *For example: FASB Statement of Financial Accounting Standards No. 13,* Accounting for Leases, *¶ 5; APB 18, ¶ 3; IAS 27 (2010), ¶ 13; IAS 28 (2010), ¶ 2; International Accounting Standard No. 31,* Interests in Joint Ventures, *¶ 3.*

or indirectly through subsidiaries,[26] or whether the exercise of such influence is actual or potential.[27]

Furthermore, ownership is often associated to the distinction between transactions with owners and with nonowners.[28]

SEC Form 20-F also uses the term *share ownership*.[29]

2.1.2.3 Equity Holders   Some accounting standards use the expressions, although undefined, of *equity holders* or *holder of equity investments*. Unlike the 2007 Revision of IAS 1, the Exposure Draft to IAS 1 extensively used *equity holder*.[30]

In general, the term *holder* is used, depending on the circumstances, with reference to a holder of a share or equity[31] in the same sense as it may be used relating to the holder of a contract, security,[32] option,[33] or right, or other financial instrument,[34] as the person or entity that owns it, materially holds it, or benefits from its respective rights.

2.1.2.4 Beneficiaries   Occasionally, the term beneficiary is used with specialized meanings, such as unitholders of noncorporate entities,[35] and primary beneficiary of a variable interest entity. Obviously, the concept of primary beneficiary of a variable interest entity is wider than that of owner, as the notion of variable interest is broader than ownership.[36]

2.1.2.5 Equity Investors   The term *equity investor* is used in certain circumstances.[37]

Investor generally refers to the person or entity that invests (employs money), irrespectively of whether this investment is in the form of debt or equity, and of which rights attach to this investment.

---

[26]   *For example: FASB ASC 810-10-15-10 (ARB 51, ¶ 3); IAS 27 (2010), ¶ 40.*

[27]   *For example: IAS 27 (2010), ¶¶ 23, IG 3.*

[28]   *For example: FASB ASC 220-10-55-3 (FASB Statement No. 130, ¶ 8); FASB ASC 845-10-05-4 (APB 29, ¶ 5); CON 6, ¶ 70; The Conceptual Framework for Financial Reporting 2010, ¶ OB21, 4.10, 4.23, 4.59; IASB Framework, ¶¶ 15 (superseded), 55, 68, 104.*

[29]   *SEC Form-20F, Item 6.E. FASB Statement No. 123 (R) and IFRS 2, ¶¶ BC10, BC13 use this term with reference to share ownership plans.*

[30]   *Agenda Paper 14,* Exposure Draft of Proposed Amendments to IAS 1 Presentation of Financial Statements – Comment Letter Analysis *(December 14, 2006), ¶ 46: the IASB staff notes that, inconsistently, the Basis for Conclusions and the Invitation to Comment refer to the terms* owner *and* equity holders.

[31]   *For example: FASB Statement No. 13, ¶ 61; SEC Form 20-F, Item 12.A; FASB ASC 810-10-15-14 (FASB Interpretation No. 46(R), ¶ 5); IAS 32, ¶¶ IN14, 17, 35; IAS 33, ¶ 5.*

[32]   *For example: FASB ASC 260-10-45-21 (FASB Statement No. 128, ¶ 12).*

[33]   *For example: IAS 32, ¶ 18; IFRS 2, ¶ B38.*

[34]   *For example: FASB Statement of Financial Accounting Standards No. 155,* Accounting for Certain Hybrid Financial Instruments an Amendment of FASB Statements No. 133 and 140, *¶ A22; IAS 32, ¶¶ IN10, AG30.*

[35]   The Conceptual Framework for Financial Reporting 2010, *¶ 4.23; IASB Framework, ¶ 68.*

[36]   *FASB Interpretation No. 46(R), Summary.*

[37]   *FASB ASC 944-235-S99-3 (SEC Regulation S-X, 210.12-18). Under FASB ASC 810-10-15-14 (FASB Interpretation No. 46(R), ¶ Footnote 6) equity investments in an entity are those interests that must be classified as equity in that entity's financial statements.*

A first inference is in the meaning of present and potential investors, including providers of risk capital, as users of financial statements.[38] Thus, the term is also used with reference to the logic of investment and its consequences, such as return on investment.[39] Consequently, investor-owned, or all-investor entities, distinguish themselves from mutual entities.[40] The Discussion Paper on the conceptual framework used the term investor as a present or potential investor in equity, whether equity was represented by securities or partnership or other interests, and included advisors of an investor in the definition of an investor. The conceptual framework mentions investors, lenders, and other creditors but does not rigidly define such terminology.[41]

A specialized use of the term under IFRSs distinguishes an investor in an associate or in a joint venture, for the purposes of the cost and equity method of accounting, as opposed to a parent for the purposes of consolidation accounting.[42] By contrast, under APB 18 an investor is any business entity that holds a voting stock interest in another company. Such a standard then uses the term investor for the cost and the equity method of accounting.[43] IFRS 10 also uses the term investor for a parent.

2.1.2.6   Equity Participants   Finally, IFRSs also refer to *equity participants* in contrasting transactions with owners to transactions with non-owners.[44] Referring to owners as participants is also typical of mutual organizations.[45]

2.1.2.7   Interchangeability, Inconsistency, and Dissimilarity   It may be argued that the abovementioned names are interchangeable.[46] Some assertions also exist that *owners* is the most comprehensive term of all.[47] Sometimes, from a different angle, some are considered as general terms (e.g., investors), others as specialized names (e.g., shareholders, partners, and proprietors).[48]

---

[38]   *CON 8, ¶ OB3; CON 1 (superseded), Highlights;* The Conceptual Framework for Financial Reporting 2010, *¶ OB3; IASB Framework, ¶¶ 9, 10 (superseded).*

[39]   *CON 8, ¶ BC3.14; CON 1 (superseded), ¶ 38;* The Conceptual Framework for Financial Reporting 2010, *¶ BC3.14; IASB Framework, ¶ 9 (superseded)*

[40]   *CON 1 (superseded), ¶ 12; IFRS 3, Appendix A.*

[41]   FASB, *Preliminary Views,* Conceptual Framework for Financial Reporting: Objective of Financial Reporting and Qualitative Characteristics of Decision-Useful Financial Reporting Information *(July 2006), ¶ OB7.*

[42]   *IAS 27 (2010), ¶ 4; IAS 28 (2010), ¶ 2; IAS 31, ¶ 3.*

[43]   *APB 18, ¶ 3.*

[44]   The Conceptual Framework for Financial Reporting 2010, *¶ 4.25; IASB Framework, ¶ 70; International Accounting Standard No. 18,* Revenue, *¶ 7. In accounting for leveraged leases, FASB Statement No. 13, ¶ 42 offers a specialized meaning of* equity participants *that is unrelated to the topic of this Book.*

[45]   *CON 6, Footnote 30.*

[46]   *In this sense, Agenda Paper 14,* Exposure Draft of Proposed Amendments to IAS 1 Presentation of Financial Statements – Comment Letter Analysis (December 14, 2006), *¶¶ 48, 51. The IASB staff believes that* owner *is equivalent to* equity holder, *because the latter is a holder of an ownership interest in an entity.*

[47]   *In this sense, FASB Statement No. 150, Footnote 4, and CON 6, Footnote 30.*

[48]   *FASB Statement No. 150, Footnote 4.*

Comment: From the above research, however, it can be concluded that the adoption of different terminology, although often undefined and not systematic, generally emphasizes a peculiar aspect of the notion of equity according to the context in which it is used. Furthermore, as shown above, even *investor* may have both a general and specialized meaning under IFRSs.

Under certain circumstances the terms are not synonymous with each other.

For example, mutual entities are not investor-owned entities. Therefore, while the notion of net assets holds for mutual entities, the concept of investor's share of net assets or equity investor would not be applicable. Similarly, they do not have stockholders (and, arguably, owners), but participants.[49]

Moreover, the notion of equity may be dissociated from that of interest in net assets and from ownership. In fact, equity classification is an accounting matter, which may result in net assets being classified as financial liabilities, e.g., for an entity having mandatorily redeemable shares only (see Section 4.8 later).

Furthermore, depending on the specific jurisdiction, different ownership rights (or even none) may result from holding an interest in an entity's net assets, based on the number of shares or on the type of shares. This point is dealt with Section 2.1.4.4 following.

Finally, some duplications and inconsistencies emerge both within IFRSs and between U.S. GAAP and IFRSs. Particularly, both *owner* and *equity holder* are used to discriminate between transactions with owners versus with nonowners, to indicate the boundaries of comprehensive income, and to identify the statement of changes in equity.[50]

2.1.3 Equity Instruments

The SEC Securities Act of 1933 and Exchange Act of 1934 provide the fundamental definition of *security*.[51] These definitions are very broad. In practice, they are interpreted to include any occurrence of investment in a common enterprise with a reasonable expectation of profits, which result solely from the efforts of a promoter or third party and not from the investors (although this latter requirement is not always deemed essential).

More succinctly instead, the definition of security given by SEC Regulation S-X comprises any stock or similar security and any convertible, warrant, or right relating to a security.[52]

---

[49] *Similarly, in this sense, CON 6, Footnote 30.*

[50] The Conceptual Framework for Financial Reporting 2010, *IASB Framework, and CON 6 ¶ 70, use the term* owners, *while IAS 1, ¶¶ 8, 98 use the term* equity holders. *Interestingly, SEC Form 20-F, Item 8.A which essentially incorporates paragraph 8 of IAS 1 (Revised 2005) changes the term* equity holders *to* owners.

[51] *Security Act of 1933, Section 2(a)(1) and Security Exchange Act of 1934, Section 3(a)(10) define* security. *Security Exchange Act of 1934, Section 3(a)(11) defines* equity security. *There is no definition of the term* equity security *in the Securities Act of 1933.*

[52] *Regulation S-X, ¶ 210.1-02.*

Subtopic 320-10 (FASB Statement No. 115)[53] acknowledges that it defines *security* by reference to the definition in the Uniform Commercial Code[54] instead of that of the Exchange Act of 1934. Subtopic 320-10 (FASB Statement No. 115) intentionally offers a narrower definition of security[55] for the purpose of accounting under this standard.[56]

Subtopic 320-10 (FASB Statement No. 115)[57] includes in the definition of an equity security any security, be it an ownership interest in itself, such as common, preferred, or other capital stock or a right to acquire (as the case may be for warrants, rights, and call options) or dispose of (for example, put options) an ownership interest in an enterprise at fixed or determinable prices.[58]

It excludes a convertible debt, a mandatorily redeemable preferred stock, a written equity option (because it is an obligation of the writer), a cash-settled option on equity securities or option on equity-based indexes (because they are not considered to be ownership interests).[59]

The scope of Subtopic 320-10 (FASB Statement No. 115), for the purpose of accounting for investments, applies to a still narrower set of this definition.[60]

Comment: While U.S. GAAP use the terms *security* and *equity security*, IFRSs do not employ such terms, unless with reference to specific securities, but subsume them within the broader concept of *financial instrument*, and *equity instrument* in particular. IAS 39 avoids the term *security* because IFRSs speak to too many different legal jurisdictions.[61]

---

[53] *FASB Statement No. 115, ¶¶ 46, 47.*

[54] *The Uniform Commercial Code, Section 8-102(a)(15) includes in the term security obligation of an issuer or a share, participation, or other interest in it or its property or enterprise. It may be in bearer or registered form or, one of a class or series or by its terms divisible into a class or series of shares, participations, interests, or obligations. It can be dealt in or traded on securities exchanges or securities markets or a medium for investment and by its terms expressly provides that it is a security governed by the UCC. The Uniform Commercial Code does not define or use the term* equity security, *although Section 8-103(a) explicitly considers a share or similar equity interest a security.*

[55] *FASB Statement No. 115, ¶ 137 defines a security from the perspective of an issuer as a share, its participation, other interest in property or in an enterprise, or obligation. It may be in bearer or registered form or as a record in books kept by a registrar. It may be dealt in on securities exchanges or markets or an instrument commonly recognized as a medium for investment. It may be one of a class or series or by its terms divisible into a class or series.*

[56] *The definition of equity security in this standard is finalized to the measurement of investments and, as a consequence, it excludes equity securities with no readily determinable fair values from its scope.*

[57] *FASB Statement No. 115, ¶ 137.*

[58] *Under the Uniform Commercial Code, Section 8-103(e) an option issued by a security corporation to its participants is not a security but a financial asset.*

[59] *FASB ASC 320-10-55-5, 958-320-55-4 (FASB Staff Implementations Guides – Q&A 115, A Guide to Implementation of Statement 115 on Accounting for Certain Investments in Debt and Equity Securities: Questions and Answers, #3).*

[60] *The accounting for investments falls outside of the scope of this Book.*

[61] *IASB,* Request for Views on Proposed FASB Amendments on Fair Value Measurement and Proposed FASB Amendments to Impairment Requirements for Certain Investments in Debt and Equity Securities, *¶ 27 (March 2009).*

IAS 32 offers two definitions of *equity instrument*. A first definition refers to the concept of *interest* in an entity's net assets,[62] as is similarly employed under U.S. GAAP.[63]

Additionally, under both U.S. GAAP and IFRSs, an equity security (or equity instrument under IFRSs) – as seen from an investor's viewpoint – is a financial instrument, and in particular a financial asset.[64] In fact, the definitions of financial instrument and financial asset also comprise an equity instrument of another entity[65] (or the evidence of an ownership interest in an entity[66]). Similarly, to a certain extent, the Uniform Commercial Code includes a security in the definition of financial asset.[67]

Comment: These are two main similarities between *equity instrument* under IFRSs and *security* under U.S. GAAP.

IAS 32 gives a second definition of *equity instrument*, which operates instead for the purpose of equity versus financial liability classification.[68]

Comment: There is a fundamental difference between U.S. GAAP and IFRSs in the context in which the definition is located. The way IAS 32 treats *equity instrument* places it within the framework of the classification of financial instruments as equity versus financial liabilities. This Book classifies such an approach as level no. 1 in the working model at the start of this Section (Section 2.1 previously). The term *security*, under U.S. GAAP, is in the setting of financial markets instruments (classified in this Book as level no. 3 in the working model at the start of this Section). By contrast, U.S. GAAP provides no definition of *equity instrument* at a level related to the notion of equity, although it also uses such a term in other circumstances, mainly with reference to stock-based compensation and earnings per share.

Planning Point: Lastly, the U.S. GAAP terminology shows some internal inconsistency. On the one hand, the expressions *financial instrument* and *financial asset* are extensively used: for the purposes of fair value disclosure under Subtopic 825-10 (FASB Statement No. 107), accounting for

---

[62] *Under IAS 32, ¶ 11 an equity interest is any contract that provides with a residual interest in the net assets of an entity.*

[63] *As cited, FASB Statement No. 115, ¶ 137 refers to ownership interest. Similarly, under FASB Statement No. 128, ¶ 171 a security comprises substantiation of debt or ownership or related rights.*

[64] *Under both U.S. GAAP and IFRSs the notion of financial instrument is at a higher level than financial asset, including both financial assets and financial liabilities, as substantiated by comparing FASB Statement No. 133, ¶ 540 to IAS 32, ¶ 11.*

[65] *IAS 32, ¶ 11.*

[66] *FASB Statement No. 107, ¶ 3; FASB Statement No. 133, ¶ 540; FASB Statement No. 140, ¶ 364; FASB Statement No. 150, D1; FASB Statement No. 156, ¶ 3.*

[67] *The Uniform Commercial Code, Section 8-102(a)(9) states that a financial asset, except as otherwise provided in Section 8-103, is a security, an obligation of a person or a share, participation, or other interest in a person or property or enterprise, dealt in or traded on financial markets or as a medium for investment, or any property that is held by a securities for another person in a securities and treated as a financial asset under the UCC. The term* security *may refer to the interest itself or the means of evidence of the claim, such as a certificated or uncertificated security, a security certificate, or a security.*

[68] *IAS 32, ¶ 16.*

derivatives and hedges under Topic 815 (FASB Statement No. 133), transfer of financial assets under Topic 860 (FASB Statement No. 140), liability versus equity classification under Subtopic 480-10 (FASB Statement No. 150), hybrid financial instruments under Subtopic 815-15 (FASB Statement No. 155).[69] Those standards however do not elaborate on the definition of security. On the other hand, the term *security* is used in accounting for an investment under Subtopic 320-10 (FASB Statement No. 115) which does not define or discuss financial assets. A link between those two approaches appears to be missing.[70]

2.1.4 Equity Interest

2.1.4.1 Residual Interest

(1) Definition of Residual Interest Both the U.S. Concepts and the IASB Framework define equity as residual interest in an entity's assets minus liabilities.[71] Equity is considered residual as a whole,[72] even though for regulatory, corporate governance, appropriations, tax, legal, or other reasons it may be further subdivided.

Sometimes, the residual interest of an entity is also put in relation to the residual interest of a specific shareholder[73] or of an equity instrument.[74]

(2) Implications of the Residual Interest Model The idea of residual interest has some important implications.

Firstly, if equity is residual, its determination is a derivative function of transactions, events, and circumstances that affect assets and liabilities, and recognition and measurement of assets and liabilities. Under this view, equity cannot be determined otherwise.[75]

Comment: This further implies that, unless a pure fair value measurement model is adopted for all assets and liabilities, equity as expressed through financial statements by definition does not reflect its fair value.[76] This parallels some inconsistencies in the debate about the purpose of financial reporting,

---

[69] *On the contrary, SEC Securities Act of 1933, Exchange Act of 1934, and Regulation S-X do not use the term* financial asset.

[70] *In addition, FASB Statement No. 123(R), ¶ E1 and FASB Statement No. 150, ¶ 5 use the term* shares *to signify various forms of ownership, including securities, irrespectively of the classification as liabilities or equity on the financial statements, and* equity shares *when classified as equity.*

[71] *CON 6, ¶ 49;* The Conceptual Framework for Financial Reporting 2010, *¶ 4.4(c); IASB Framework, ¶ 49(c).*

[72] *Similarly, CON 6, Footnote 29.*

[73] *EITF Issue No. 88-16,* Basis in Leveraged Buyout Transactions, *Issue equates shareholder to residual interest holders.*

[74] *Under IAS 32, ¶ 11 an equity instrument is any contract that embodies a residual interest in an entity's net assets.*

[75] *CON 6, ¶¶ 50, 54, 63, 213, 222;* The Conceptual Framework for Financial Reporting 2010, *¶ 4.22; IASB Framework, ¶ 67.*

[76] *As this may be implicitly derived from IASB Framework, ¶ 67.*

according to which on the one hand financial reporting is not directed to company valuation, although it ordinarily is a starting point for it, and on the other hand it is suggested as being of most benefit to its users including for company valuation.[77]

As a further consequence, equity instruments are not subsequently remeasured.[78]

> **Comment:** The acceptance of this principle has practical repercussions, for example, for share-based compensation, or for bifurcation of embedded derivatives. The residual theory of equity is one of the reasons why IFRS 2 adopts grant-date measurement for share-based payment transactions and rejects both exercise-date and vesting-date measurements.[79] IAS 39 explains that not only the embedded derivative but also the residual interest characteristics of a host contract shall be taken into consideration to determine whether their economic characteristics and risks are closely related.[80] Finally, U.S. GAAP prohibits remeasurement of equity-classified obligations for contingent payments after the acquisition date.[81]

> **Comment:** As part of the *Liabilities and Equity Project*, the FASB proposed that basic ownership instruments and components with redemption requirements would be remeasured at each balance sheet date at the current redemption value and changes in the redemption value be reported as a separate equity account.[82]

Also, under this theory, transactions which do not determine changes in net assets, such as conversion of one type of equity interest into another, should not result in changes in total equity. In this sense, a similar conclusion applies for appropriations of retained earnings.[83]

Additionally, if equity is a residual, changes in net assets translate into changes in equity. This concept has various consequences. Firstly, a specific implication of equity as *residual* is that it is a claim on changes in a company's value, which arise from increases and decreases in the value of assets or liabilities. From a different angle, a claim on changes in a company's value implies an association with the risks and rewards of ownership.

Furthermore, as a residual, equity is subordinated to other sources of capital (e.g., debt), and thus is named *capital at risk* or *risk capital*, in the sense that the ranking in priority of equity, as a claim on assets, comes after liabilities.[84]

> **Comment:** However, as the following paragraphs will illustrate, an equity interest, conceptually, is a subset of residual interests as intended here, which may also arise from certain economic interests and variable interests.

---

[77] *CON 8, ¶¶ OB2, OB7; CON 1 (superseded), ¶¶ 34, 41;* The Conceptual Framework for Financial Reporting 2010, *¶¶ OB2, OB7.*
[78] *IFRS 2, ¶ BC64.*
[79] *IFRS 2, ¶¶ BC98, BC103, BC105.*
[80] *IFRS 9, ¶ B4.3.2; IAS 39, ¶ AG27.*
[81] *FASB Statement No. 141(R), ¶ B353.*
[82] *Financial Accounting Standards Board, Preliminary Views,* Financial Instruments with Characteristics of Equity, *¶ 32 (November 30, 2007).*
[83] *FASB ASC 505-10-25-2 (IFRS 2, ¶ BC101; APB 9, ¶ 28).*
[84] *CON 6, ¶ 60.*

Additionally, the residual interest model may be put in relation to the so-called alternative accounting equation, that is, assets minus liabilities equals equity.[85] As a residual, equity indistinctly counterbalances net assets, although relationships with some components of equity may be established for tax, legal, defense of capital, or other purposes depending on jurisdictions.

Another implication of the concept of residual interest is its translation in the so-called *equity format* of the balance sheet layout.[86] This is explained in Section 4.1.4 later.

Finally, *net assets* become synonymous with equity.[87] This does not hold if equity is not a residual, as under a physical capital maintenance concept.[88]

> **Comment:** IFRSs classify certain puttable instruments as equity, except when certain characteristics of those instruments make them representative of the ultimate residual interest of the entity. These requirements are detailed prescriptions that are intended to ensure the existence of the characteristics of a residual interest, i.e., subordination, that the class of instruments as a whole is the residual class, and that there should be no financial instrument or contract with a return that is more residual. Prior to these amendments to IAS 32 made in March 2008,[89] a puttable instrument was classified as liability, irrespectively of whether or not it was residual.[90]

> **Comment:** One aspect of Phase B of the FASB and IASB joint *Conceptual Framework Project* concerns whether equity should be defined or whether it should it be a residual classification.

Worksheet 3 illustrates the residual interest model.

(3)   The Balance Sheet Approach   Residual interest is also an alternative expression for the balance sheet approach (also called asset and liability view of earnings).

Both the FASB and the IASB are formally committed to a balance sheet approach to setting financial standards, although with different emphasis. Under the IASB Framework[91] the elements of equity, income, and expenses, and under CON 6[92] the elements of equity, revenues, expenses, gains, losses, and comprehensive income are derived from the elements of assets and liabilities (and, depending on which element, equity itself).

---

[85] *In this sense, IFRS 2, ¶ BC63.*

[86] *See Francesco Bellandi, Dual Reporting Under U.S. GAAP and IFRS – Layout of the Statement of Financial Position for Commercial and Industrial Entities,* The CPA Journal *(December 2007).*

[87] *CON 6, ¶ 60.*

[88] *CON 6, ¶ 213 always equates equity to net assets. Conversely,* The Conceptual Framework for Financial Reporting 2010, *¶ 4.57 (IASB Framework, ¶ 102) relates this equation to a financial concept of capital maintenance.*

[89] *Amendments to IAS 32 Financial Instruments: Presentation and IAS 1 Presentation of Financial Statements,* Puttable Financial Instruments and Obligations Arising on Liquidation.

[90] *In this sense, IAS 32 (2005 revision) ¶ BC7, which gives the example of the case of a puttable instrument.*

[91] The Conceptual Framework for Financial Reporting 2010, *¶¶ 4.4, 4.25; IASB Framework, ¶¶ 49, 70.*

[92] *CON 6, ¶¶ 25, 32, 49, 66, 67, 70, 78, 80, 82, 83, 212.*

The balance sheet approach:

- Focuses on transactions and events depicted as flows to assets and liabilities;
- Places a primary focus on the definition and recognition of assets and liabilities;
- Views revenues, income, expenses, gains, losses, and earnings as secondary and derivative from assets and liabilities, as determined by those flows (changes) in the net economic resources of the enterprise during a period, other than as a result of investments by or distributions to owners.

On the other hand, the revenue-expense approach:

- Views earnings as directly arising from transactions and events, seen as an autonomous measure of an enterprise's effectiveness in using its inputs to obtain and sell outputs;
- Places primary emphasis on the income statement;
- Derives assets and liabilities from transactions and events that determine revenues and expenses.

Comment: The accounting theory has seen waves of acceptance of the two concepts: a balance sheet driven financial reporting in the nineteenth century, a focus on the income statement in the twentieth century, followed by a certain convergence on the balance sheet approach.

Comment: Adopting a balance sheet or income statement orientation may have very practical implications, as explained below. In fact, the use of the balance sheet or other approaches may result in recognition differences of assets and liabilities, or different measurement, or different presentation. Worksheet 4 illustrates those examples.

Example: An example of different treatment for recognition, measurement, and presentation is the accounting for income taxes.

Under U.S. GAAP, the debate over measurement strategy has moved from the accent on the income statement, and therefore on the deferred method of accounting for taxes under APB Opinion No. 11, *Accounting for Income Taxes*, in the 1960s–70s to the balance sheet, and therefore to the liability method of interperiod tax allocation in the late 1970s.

Both U.S. GAAP and IFRSs follow the balance sheet liability method of income tax accounting, which determines the amount of future tax benefits or obligations as of each reporting period date and calculates income tax as an adjustment necessary to bring the deferred taxes to the correct balance.

Differently from the income statement liability method that focused on timing differences, the balance sheet liability method emphasizes temporary differences, which may arise even if the income statement is unaffected.

Under the net-of-tax method deferred tax credits were valuation accounts of individual assets related to the effects of taxability.

Under the deferred method, the annual income tax position consisting of current and deferred portions was calculated based on the expected relationship to pretax accounting income. Any defect/excess was a balance sheet position that was considered definitive and not changed in case of a subsequent change in tax rules. Under this method, deferred taxes were not liabilities and asset valuation account, but residual deferred debits or credits.

Example: A case of presentation difference arising from the choice of the balance sheet approach versus other approaches is exemplified by deferred gross profit on instalment sales. CON 6[93] explains that deferred gross profit is an asset valuation (that is a reduction of asset) used to measure the accounts receivable at unrecovered cost. Under alternative approaches it would be considered as unearned revenue classified as a current liability; or as a deferred credit classified among liabilities and equity. International Accounting Standard No. 18, *Revenue*,[94] instead seems to follow another approach, because revenue is recorded at the date of sale at present value, while interest is recognized at the effective interest method when earned. Therefore there is no recognition at point of sale of an asset for the interest portion and no need for a valuation account.

Example: Both U.S. GAAP and IFRSs follow a balance sheet approach for receivable or payable discounts or premiums, as they are assets or liabilities valuation accounts, respectively, that is to say they are a reduction or increase of the face amount of the related asset or liability, and do not meet the definition of liabilities and assets by themselves.

Example: Debt issue costs under CON 6[95] are either expenses or liability valuation account. However, under U.S. GAAP practice, differently from IFRSs, they are treated as deferred charges.

Example: Under U.S. GAAP, an estimated loss on noncancellable commitment to purchase specific quantities of goods at fixed prices in the future is recognized in case of a decline in market value below the contract price at the reporting period date. This reflects the fact that the future economic benefit of the right to receive that asset has decreased. Although this results in recognizing a loss on an unrecorded asset (as purchase commitments generally are executory in nature and therefore not recognized – but this is a recognition issue and not an issue related on the definition of asset or liability), estimated loss on commitment is an asset valuation account. The related asset is missing and the estimated loss is shown among the liabilities.[96] Executory contracts are contracts under which neither party has performed any of its obligations or both parties have partially performed their obligations to an equal extent.

Under the IASB Framework, a future commitment may be a present obligation only to the extent it is an irrevocable agreement that, by its terms, the entity cannot avoid.[97] Under IAS 37, an estimated loss on noncancellable commitment may qualify as an onerous contract[98] but only if it meets the definition requirements. The standard requires the use of more restrictive recognition and measurement criteria, which may likely lead to non-recognition, as contract unavoidable costs must exceed its expected

---

[93] *CON 6, ¶ 234.*

[94] *International Accounting Standard No. 18*, Revenue, *¶ 8.*

[95] *CON 6, ¶ 237.*

[96] *CON 6, ¶¶ 251–253.*

[97] The Conceptual Framework for Financial Reporting 2010, *¶ 4.16; IASB Framework, ¶ 61.*

[98] *International Accounting Standard No. 37*, Provisions, Contingent Liabilities and Contingent Assets, *¶¶ 66–69.*

economic benefits. If recognized (to the extent this may be permitted under IAS 37), it would be a provision, not an asset valuation as there is no recognized asset.

Example: Through a balance sheet approach, in both U.S. GAAP and IFRSs, a property under capital leases for a lessee is recognized as an asset, as the agreement unbundles the future economic benefits giving the lessee a right to possess and use the property and the lessor a right to receive rents and residual value.

Example: Under CON 6,[99] noncontrolling (minority) interest is not a present obligation that meets the definition of liability. However, different practices displayed it as either a separate item among consolidated liabilities and equity, or as a separate item among liabilities, or as a separate item among equity, or as part of an item such as "other liabilities." From these different points of view, noncontrolling interest did not follow a balance sheet approach but was mainly seen as a deduction in the income statement (sometimes among items of other expenses and sometimes as a separate item), in order to arrive at net income. Section 4.3.3 later illustrates the recent changes to these practices.

Example: Revenue recognition under both IFRSs and U.S. GAAP is very much income statement driven. This, in theory, may lead to situations of debit balances that are not necessarily assets and credit balances that are not necessarily liabilities.

The revenue recognition joint project conducted by the FASB and the IASB was intended to shift from the risks and rewards approach and the principle of earnings and realization process to a recognition of revenue based on changes in assets and liabilities, and is expected to produce a new general standard on revenue recognition, replacing IAS 18, International Accounting Standard No. 11, *Construction Contracts*, and also amending the IASB Framework.

Example: Finally, the concept of performance, intended as *comprehensive* income (see Section 7.5.6 later), also including items debited or credited in other comprehensive income or directly to equity (or outside profit or loss), as opposed to net income, is deducted from the balance sheet rather than from the income statement approach.

Example: The capital maintenance concept (see Section 7.6 later) is balance-sheet oriented, as under the financial concept of capital maintenance capital is net assets or equity.

There are many other examples that do not strictly follow a balance sheet approach under U.S. GAAP as opposed to IFRSs. One of these is the classification of refinance agreements and of obligations where a covenant has been breached.

2.1.4.2 Ownership Interest   The concept of equity as ownership interest emphasizes the property of its owners, and their relationship, in their role as owners, with the enterprise.[100]

---

[99]   *CON 6, ¶ 254.*
[100]   *CON 6, ¶ 60.*

(1)   Ownership Versus Residual Interest   Worksheet 5 shows the relationships between changes in equity, changes in residual interest, and changes in ownership interest.

The notion of ownership interest presents the following implications.

Firstly, ownership interest is a feature distinguishing business enterprises from not-for-profit organizations that do not have owners, and from non-investor organizations, such as mutual entities, whose equity technically is not ownership interest, although still a residual interest.[101]

> **Comment:** Therefore, the concept of residual interest exists irrespective of whether or not ownership interest exists, as in the case of not-for-profit organizations.

Secondly, changes in ownership interest result from contributions from owners (increase in ownership interest), and distributions to owners (decrease in ownership interest).

> **Comment:** Thus, while residual interest focuses on the entity's assets and liabilities and determines changes in equity as a result, ownership interest focuses directly on changes in equity, and may indirectly affect residual interest. In fact, distributions to owners also determine a decrease in residual interest, but only indirectly because either cash decreases or other assets have been transferred, services rendered, or liabilities incurred. When a dividend is declared, and therefore an entity's liability arises, owners become creditors with respect to the dividend. This also causes a decrease in net assets due to such liability. Similarly, investments by owners also increase residual interest, but again only indirectly because of either increases in cash or other assets, or receipt of services, or conversion of the entity's liabilities.[102]

Thirdly, contributions from, and distributions to, owners translate into changes in equity only to the extent that they arise from transactions with the enterprise. A transfer among owners without involving the enterprise is a change in each owner's ownership interest that does not result in a change in residual interest.[103] A stock dividend, i.e., a change within equity that does not affect assets or liabilities, does not result in any change in residual interest, while it may determine a change in ownership interest if the stock dividend of the entity is not proportional among owners.

> **Comment:** Therefore a change in ownership interest does not necessarily mean a change in residual interest.
>
> However, comprehensive income that accrues to owners also determines a change in net assets: it affects residual interest, and also total ownership interest in absolute terms, but not as the pro rata interest of any of the owners.

---

[101]   *CON 6, ¶¶ 60, 90.*
[102]   *CON 6, ¶ 66–69.*
[103]   *CON 6, ¶ 68.*

(2) The Invested and Earned Equity Model The ownership interest model can also be related to an alternative definition of the equity of business enterprises, that is, the *invested and earned equity* model.[104] In this perspective, equity is the result of cumulative contributions from and distributions to owners plus accumulated comprehensive income. This approach emphasizes the sources and uses of equity. CON 6 also calls investments by owners *invested* or *contributed capital* and comprehensive income *earned capital* or *capital from operations*. Comprehensive income is discussed in Chapter 7 later.

> **Comment:** As discussed in Section 4.1.4 later, the concept of invested and earned risk capital and debt (non-risk capital) as sources of the finance of the entity's assets, is employed under the balanced format of the statement of financial position.

Worksheet 3 illustrates the interrelationships between the residual interest model and the invested and earned equity model and locates these links in the framework of the elements of financial statements.

> **Comment:** It is to be noted that while both the U.S. Concepts and the IASB Framework adopt the residual interest approach, the latter also discusses the invested and earned equity model. The U.S. Concepts define obtaining or increasing ownership interest as the purpose of contributions from owners.[105] This is an evidence of the relationship between the invested and earned equity and the ownership interest approaches. Conversely, according to the IASB Framework, contributions from and distributions to owners are not among the elements of the financial statements, although the definitions of the elements of revenue and expenses in the IASB Framework mention them.[106]
>
> Finally, as mentioned in Section 2.1.3 previously regarding equity instruments, both U.S. GAAP and IFRSs offer a definition of *equity instrument* that refers to the concept of ownership *interest* in an entity's net assets.[107] This definition is similarly employed under U.S. GAAP.[108]

> **Comment:** As was noted in a meeting of the *Financial Statement Presentation Project*, the current statement of changes in equity does not provide information about changes between ownership interests (which would require a detailed display of equity instruments).[109]

2.1.4.3 Economic Interest The definition of an *economic interest* in an entity given by Subtopic 718-10 (FASB Statement No. 123(R)) is quite wide, as it includes any pecuniary interest or arrangement, irrespective of type or form, that an entity could issue or be party to.

---

[104] *CON 6, ¶¶ 63, 212, 214.*

[105] *CON 6, ¶ 66.*

[106] The Conceptual Framework for Financial Reporting 2010, *¶ 4.25; IASB Framework, ¶ 70.*

[107] *Under IAS 32, ¶ 11 an equity interest is any contract that embodies a residual interest in the net assets of an entity.*

[108] *As cited, FASB Statement No. 115, ¶ 137 refers to* ownership interest. *Similarly, under FASB Statement No. 128, ¶ 171 a security comprises substantiation of debt or ownership or related rights.*

[109] *IASB Meeting, January 25, 2007, Agenda paper 13D:* Financial Statement Presentation – Statement of Changes in Equity, *¶ 33 (January 2007).*

This pronouncement gives examples of equity securities, financial instruments with characteristics of equity, liabilities, or both, debt-financing, leases, and management contracts, service contracts, or intellectual property licenses.[110]

Under Subtopic 718-10 (FASB Statement No. 123(R)), a transaction, where a holder of an economic interest in an entity awards share-based payment to an employee of that enterprise, equates and shall be accounted for as a capital contribution to the entity plus a share-based payment to that employee in exchange for services rendered, if the entity benefits from the transfer and unless this is clearly the purpose of the transaction.[111]

Under Subtopic 718-10 (FASB Statement No. 123(R)), contrary to IFRS 2, such a holder of an economic interest need not necessarily be a shareholder.[112]

The FASB acknowledged that in theory this principle should also apply to compensation arrangements that are outside the scope of FASB Statement No. 123(R). However, the FASB did not proceed in that sense as it would have required reconsidering accounting for related party transactions.[113]

The SEC Staff extended this accounting treatment to other transactions where a principal stockholder (for example, a parent company) pays an expense for the company (or the company's debt[114]), unless the payment is completely unrelated to his position as a stockholder or when such action clearly does not benefit the company.[115]

Comment: The common characteristics of all these situations are that the entity is part of the transaction because it benefits from it (as in the case of services rendered by employees to the entity[116]), and the holder of an economic interest also benefits from the transaction (as in the case of a shareholder that in this way increases or maintains previous investment value).

Topic 958 (FASB Statement No. 136) also discusses a similar concept of *economic interest*, for not-for-profit organizations. A recipient organization shall recognize, as a contribution, cash or other financial assets contributed by a donor with the agreement to use them on behalf of, or to transfer them, or their return on investment, to a beneficiary, if the donor explicitly grants the recipient variance power or if recipient and beneficiary are financially interrelated organizations. The beneficiary shall recognize an interest in the net assets of the recipient organization. An ongoing economic interest in net assets is one of the two conditions in which two or more not-for-profit organizations are considered to be financially interrelated. The other condition is that one of the organizations shall have the ability to influence the operating and financial decisions of the other. Thus, if the economic interest is ongoing and residual, the

---

[110] *FASB Statement No. 123(R), ¶ E1.*

[111] *FASB ASC 718-10-15-4 (FASB Statement No. 123(R), ¶ 11).*

[112] *Also see FASB Statement No. 123(R), ¶ B109; IFRS 2, ¶ 3.*

[113] *FASB Statement No. 123(R), ¶ B111.*

[114] *AICPA Technical Practice Aids § 4160.*

[115] *FASB ASC 225-10-S99-4 (SAB 5-T).*

[116] *IFRS 2, ¶ BC35.*

beneficiary's interest is assimilated to a parent's or equity-method investor's residual interest, and considered as residual rights.[117]

Comment: The above discussion illustrates that, conceptually, it may be inferred that economic interest may result in a type of residual interest, and also that ownership interest might be intended as a subset of economic interest.

2.1.4.4 Voting Interest Voting rights are but one of the rights deriving from an ownership interest. Other rights are the right to receive dividends or repayment of contributed capital, and additional rights that may differ according to jurisdiction.

From its particular perspective, Subtopic 810-10 (FASB Interpretation No. 46(R)) confirms that, in a traditional voting interest, holders of equity investment at risk have, as a group, direct or indirect decision ability regarding the entity's activities through voting or similar rights.[118] If both the equity group and outside parties have this ability, then the extent of this ability is assessed with special reference to decisions that have a significant impact on the success of the entity.[119]

Comment: Thus, generally voting interest may be conceived as a consequence of ownership interest, because this attributes ownership rights. However, a voting interest may be different from an economic interest, which – as we saw – is a wider concept. In addition, control may derive from forms of residual interest in the fair value of net assets other than ownership interest, such as a variable interest.

Depending on the type of entity, voting interest may have a different relationship to the notions of an equity instrument and of ownership interest.

Comment: For corporate entities, some of those rights generally equally attach to each share within an equity class. Therefore, each share carries some rights autonomously. A shareholder may enhance cumulatively its position by holding more shares. In such a way shares attribute a plurality of positions, and a shareholder can exercise the rights attached to each share individually (e.g., selling some shares and receiving dividends on the remaining ones), and sometimes differently for each share, according to which rights and whether or not this is permitted in the specific jurisdiction.

By contrast, for unincorporated entities, those rights generally attach to the interest itself, so that an interest holder has a unitary position related to its pro rata interest in the entity.

Although voting interest generally derives from ownership interest, it need not equal ownership interest.

---

[117] *FASB ASC 958-20-15-2 (FASB Statement No. 136, Summary, ¶¶ 13, 102).*
[118] *FASB ASC 810-10-15-14 (FASB Interpretation No. 46(R), ¶ 5(b)(1)).*
[119] *FASB ASC 810-10-55-5 (FASB Staff Position FASB Interpretation No. 46(R)-3,* Evaluating Whether as a Group the Holders of the Equity Investment at Risk Lack the Direct or Indirect Ability to Make Decisions about an Entity's Activities through Voting Rights or Similar Rights under FASB Interpretation No. 46(R), *¶ 2).*

> **Comment:** Depending on the different classes of equity, parties with ownership interests in an entity may have differing rights, in relation to voting power, receipt of dividends, or the repayment of contributed equity, or other rights.[120] This is even truer in an international context, depending on jurisdiction.
>
> Some minority rights – voting or otherwise – may attach to even one share or to a qualified interest, individual or in the aggregate. Section 810-10-25 (EITF Issue No. 96-16)[121] considers minority rights from the perspective of consolidation of corporations or analogous entities. It identifies protective rights which do not overcome presumptions of consolidation by a majority voting interest investor and substantive participating rights which defeat such presumptions. EITF Issue No. 04-5 extends such a concept to include limited partnerships and similar entities.
>
> According to jurisdiction, minority rights granted by law or contract may also include calling on shareholders' meetings, requesting intervention of statutory auditors, initiating actions against directors, etc.

The existence of ownership rights, or some voting rights, however, does not necessarily imply equity classification.

> **Comment:** As an example, under IFRSs, financial instruments, including members' shares which carry ownership rights such as voting and dividend rights but include or are subject to limits on whether the instruments will be redeemed, are not equity if the issuer does not have an unconditional right to refuse redemption.[122] Similarly, in some jurisdictions financial instruments may attribute some ownership rights, but not or only limited voting rights, so that they are not considered equity at least from a legal perspective.[123]
>
> Additionally, some debt instruments may have voting rights attached, as in the case of debt covenants.

Operationally, some guidance exists about practical computation of voting interest.

Under IFRSs, the existence and effect of potential voting rights shall be considered in assessing control or significant influence and in applying consolidation and the equity method of accounting, under IFRS 10 when these rights are substantive and under IAS 27 currently exercisable or convertible and when, in substance, they give access at present to the economic benefits associated with an ownership interest, irrespective of the intention of management and the financial ability to exercise or convert.[124] However, potential voting rights are not

---

[120] *CON 6, ¶ 62;* The Conceptual Framework for Financial Reporting 2010, *¶ 4.20; IASB Framework,* *¶ 65.*

[121] *FASB ASC 810-10-25 (EITF Issue No. 96-16,* Investor's Accounting for an Investee When the Investor Has a Majority of the Voting Interest but the Minority Shareholder or Shareholders Have Certain Approval or Veto Rights).

[122] *IFRIC 2, ¶¶ 4, 7.*

[123] *For example, Italy's civil code, Section 2346, ¶ 6 establishes a category of financial instruments that are akin to shares but that are not considered equity. They may provide several rights, including limited voting rights or the appointment of an independent director, but no general voting rights in shareholders' meeting.*

[124] *IAS 27 (2010), ¶¶, 14, 15, IG5.*

considered for the purpose of allocating profit or loss and changes in equity to the parent and minority interests.[125]

Under Section 232-10-15 (APB 18), potential voting privileges should not be considered in assessing significant influence.[126]

However, a specialized definition in the context of leveraged buyouts computes a shareholder's interest as an investor's fully diluted post-liquidation and post-redemption percentage of equity.[127]

2.1.4.5 Controlling Financial Interest One of the most important applications of voting interest is in determining control for consolidation purposes, or significance influence for equity-method accounting. In fact, a direct or indirect majority voting interest, when the entity also has control of an investee, is a typical situation of a controlling financial interest.[128]

The relative, not absolute, ownership and voting rights are relevant for the determination of control and significant influence.[129]

Comment: Nevertheless, a controlling financial interest may arise from sources other than a voting interest. In fact, IFRSs consider situations of control by means other than a majority voting interest. These situations may arise out of contractual, statutory, or de facto criteria.[130] In particular, under IFRSs, in-substance control of a Special Purpose Entity (SPE) may exist even with no ownership interest, based on four additional criteria: 1) conducting activities on behalf of the entity so that it benefits from the SPE's operation; 2) decision-making powers to obtain the majority of the benefits of the activities of the SPE; 3) rights to obtain the majority of the benefits of the SPE; and 4) retainage of the majority of the residual or ownership risks.[131]

Conceptual and practical difficulties in defining control had prevented U.S. GAAP from replacing ownership with control for a long time.[132]

Topic 460 (FASB Interpretation of Financial Accounting Standard No. 45)[133] acknowledges that, under certain circumstances where guarantees benefit related parties, controlling financial interest cannot be assessed through the analysis of voting interests, and requires additional disclosures.

Subtopic 810-10 (FASB Interpretation of Financial Accounting Standard No. 46(R)) defines three criteria that the group of holders of equity investment at risk shall collectively have in order to qualify

---

[125] *IAS 27 (2010), ¶ 23.*

[126] *FASB ASC 323-10-15-9 (APB 18, ¶ 18).*

[127] *EITF Issue 88-16, Issue.*

[128] *FASB ASC 810-10-15-8 (ARB 51, ¶ 2); IAS 27 (2010), ¶ 13.*

[129] *IAS 27 (2010), ¶ 13; IAS 28 (2010), ¶¶ 6, 7.*

[130] *IAS 27 (2010), ¶ 13. This topic falls outside of the scope of this Book. We mention it here within the context of the meaning and implications of the notion of voting interest.*

[131] *SIC Interpretation No.12, Consolidation – Special Purpose Entities, ¶¶ 2, 9, 10.*

[132] *FASB Statement of Financial Accounting Standards No. 94, Consolidation of All Majority-Owned Subsidiaries, ¶ 10 and FASB Statement of Financial Accounting Standards No. 141, Business Combinations, ¶ 9 acknowledge but do not address such an issue.*

[133] *FASB Interpretation of Financial Accounting Standard No. 45, Guarantor's Accounting and Disclosure Requirements for Guarantees, Including Indirect Guarantees of Indebtedness of Others, ¶ A62.*

a financial interest as controlling: 1) voting or similar rights to make decisions, directly or indirectly, about the entity's activities that significantly affect the entity's success; 2) obligation to absorb the entity's expected losses; and 3) right to receive the entity's expected residual returns. In the absence of any one of those characteristics, the at-risk equity investors collectively lack a controlling financial interest. In those circumstances, or when the equity investment at risk is not sufficient to finance the entity's activities without additional subordinated financial support, a controlling financial interest cannot be identified based on voting interests.[134] In that situation, the entity is a variable interest entity (VIE),[135] as defined by the interpretation.

Another case applies to limited partnerships or similar entities that are not variable interest entities under Interpretation 46(R). Control by a general partner is presumed, independently of its ownership interest, unless the limited partners have substantive kick-out rights or substantive participating rights.[136]

Finally, under Section 810-10-15 (EITF Issue No. 97-2),[137] a physician practice management entity can establish a controlling financial interest in a physician's practice through a contractual management arrangement if certain requirements are met.

Phase D of the *Conceptual Framework Project* also includes deliberations on the concept and models of control.[138]

2.1.4.6 Variable Interest   As mentioned in the previous paragraph, a variable interest may arise, if the other requirements of Interpretation 46(R) are met, when total equity investment at risk does not provide the holders with the characteristics of a controlling financial interest, or when there would be a controlling financial interest but total at-risk equity investment is not sufficient to finance the entity's activities.

Contractual, ownership, or other pecuniary interests become variable interests in a VIE when they change with changes in the fair value of an entity's net assets excluding the variable interests themselves.[139]

Situations that result in potentially variable interests may include, but are not limited to, the following:[140]

- At-risk equity investments in a VIE;
- Investments in subordinated debt instruments issued by a VIE;
- Investments in subordinated beneficial interests issued by a VIE;

---

[134] *FASB ASC 810-10-15-14 (FASB Interpretation No. 46(R), ¶¶ 5(b), D2).*
[135] *Hereinafter VIE.*
[136] *FASB ASC 810-20-25-3 (EITF Issue No. 04-5, Determining Whether a General Partner, or the General Partners as a Group, Controls a Limited Partnership or Similar Entity When the Limited Partners Have Certain Rights, ¶ 6).*
[137] *FASB ASC 810-10-15-21 (EITF Issue No. 97-2, Application of FASB Statement No. 94 and APB Opinion No. 16 to Physician Practice Management Entities and Certain Entities with Contractual Management Arrangements, Discussion).*
[138] *Discussion Paper, Preliminary Views on an Improved Conceptual Framework for Financial Reporting, The Reporting Entity (May 2008).*
[139] *FASB Interpretation No. 46(R), ¶ 2(c).*
[140] *FASB ASC 810-10-55-23, 810-10-55-24, 810-10-55-25, 810-10-55-28, 810-10-55-29, 810-10-55-30, 810-10-55-33, 810-10-55-37, 810-10-55-38, 810-10-55-39, 810-10-55-40, 810-10-55-41 (FASB Interpretation No. 46(R), ¶¶ B8, B9, B10, B13, B14, B15, B18, B22, B23, B24, B25, B26).*

- Guarantees of the value of a VIE's assets or liabilities;
- Written put options on the assets of a VIE or similar obligations that protect senior interests from suffering losses;
- Forward contracts to sell assets owned by the entity at a fixed price;
- Stand-alone or embedded derivative instruments including total return swaps and similar arrangements;
- Contracts or agreements for fees to be paid to a decision maker, unless under an employee-employer or a "hired service provider" relationship;
- Other service contracts with non-decision makers;
- Operating leases that include residual value guarantees and/or lessee option to purchase the leased property at a specified price;
- Variable interests of a VIE in another VIE;
- Interests retained by a transferor of financial assets to a VIE.

Comment: In the context of our discussion on equity interest, variable interest illustrates another occurrence of the disassociation between the concept of ownership interest and residual interest. In fact, in one VIE situation, a sponsor or a holder of interests other than voting equity interests may reach effects similar to a controlling interest without having ownership or voting interest, or having a voting interest in a measure that is not sufficient to substantiate a controlling financial interest.[141] In such a situation, equity investors do not bear the residual economic risks.[142] From a different angle, an equity interest may be part of the concept of variable interest, if the entity is a VIE and total at-risk equity investment is not sufficient to finance the entity's activities.[143]

The model of control of IFRS 10 now includes the consideration of variable returns arising from the performance of an investee. Consistently, IFRS 12 defines an interest in another entity in terms of such variability, irrespective of whether it results from a contractual or other arrangement.[144]

2.2 BASIC CHARACTERISTICS OF EQUITY

Accounting literature identifies some main characteristics of equity. It employs those features in order to arrive at both a definition of equity as well as a distinction between equity and financial liabilities.

The previous paragraphs analyzed the terminology and definitions of terms relating to equity. Although the equity/liability distinction falls outside the scope of this Book, as well as its determination from a legal or tax viewpoint,[145] the following paragraphs elaborate on points already discussed and on the main characteristics of equity as a base for a definition of equity itself, according to the following:

- Ownership rights;
- Dependency on an entity's dynamics;

---

[141] *FASB Interpretation No. 46(R), ¶ E29.*
[142] *FASB Interpretation No. 46(R), Summary.*
[143] *FASB Interpretation No. 46(R), ¶ 2(c).*
[144] *IFRS 12,* Disclosure of Interests in Other Entities, *¶ Appendix A.*
[145] *Among many relevant sources, see Peter C. Barton and Clayton R. Sager, "Sixth Circuit Court of Appeals Reverses Debt-Versus-Equity Issue,"* The CPA Journal *(April 2007).*

- Risks and rewards of ownership;
- Subordination; and
- Discretion of distributions to owners.

2.2.1   Ownership Rights

Shareholders' interest conveys certain ownership rights, e.g., voting, participation, and other rights. Section 2.1.4 previously discusses the relationships between ownership interest, voting interests, and owners' rights.

Also, the equity of business enterprises is the source of distributions to owners. Section 2.1.4.2 previously analyzes such an assertion, its implications, and its relation to the notion of ownership interest.

Comment: The basic ownership approach proposed by the FASB as part of the *Financial Instruments with Characteristics of Equity Project* focuses on the concept of residual interest in order to classify the most residual claim as equity. A claim that reduces the residual net assets available for distribution to the holders of basic ownership instruments would be classified as liability.[146]

2.2.2   Dependency on an Entity's Dynamics

Section 2.1.4.1 previously shows that, as an implication of the notion of residual interest, the dynamics of equity, and of attached economic rights, are a function of the entity's operations and other events and circumstances that reflect in its profitability.

Example: As mentioned, the amendments to IAS 32 made in February 2008 introduce a limited scope exclusion from financial liability classification for certain financial instruments that meet the definition of a financial liability but represent the residual interest in the net assets of the entity. This is because they represent the ultimate residual interest of the entity. Among other characteristics, one of the features of these instruments is that their total expected cash flows over the life of the instrument are based substantially on profit or loss, or the change in net assets, or the change in their fair value (i.e., the entity's dynamics). One of the points for this exception was that classifying an instrument as a liability when its redemption value depends on the profit or loss would increase the liability when the entity has a profit and vice versa, which is counter-intuitive accounting.[147]

Comment: For the purpose of classifying certain obligations to issue a variable number of shares as liabilities, Subtopic 480-10 (FASB Statement No. 150) analyzes the initial sole or predominant variability and direction of the relationship between the monetary value of an instrument (i.e., its fair

---

[146] *FASB, Preliminary Views,* Financial Instruments with Characteristics of Equity, *¶¶ 16(a), D10 (November 2007).*

[147] *Amendments to IAS 32* Financial Instruments: Presentation and IAS 1 Presentation of Financial Statements, Puttable Financial Instruments and Obligations Arising on Liquidation, *¶ BC50(b).*

value at settlement date under specified market conditions) and the fair value changes of stock. The lack of a direct relationship determines liability status and precludes equity classification.[148]

The reassessed expected outcome (REO) approach (i.e., a model to distinguish between liability instruments and equity instruments that the FASB presented but rejected during the *Financial Instruments with Characteristics of Equity Project*) would classify an instrument as equity or contra-equity based on its type of ownership return, i.e., a contractual link that makes changes in its fair value to move in the same direction or the opposite direction as changes in the fair value of a basic ownership instrument.[149]

Under the ownership-settlement approach (also rejected by the FASB), indirect ownership instruments settled by issuing related basic ownership instruments would be classified as equity when, among other requirements, their fair value changes in the same direction as the fair value of the basic ownership instrument.[150]

2.2.3 Risks and Rewards of Ownership

As seen in Section 2.1.4.1 previously, the association of equity to risks and rewards of ownership is inherent in its definition as residual interest. Risks and rewards of ownership also derive from the fact that changes in equity are a function of entity dynamics.

Accounting literature has developed such association under different angles.

Firstly, risk and return on investment is intrinsic to investing risk capital.[151] However, an entity may have several classes of equity with different levels of risks and rewards.[152]

Secondly, one of the pervasive concepts under Subtopic 480-10 (FASB Statement No. 150) is that obligations that establish the type of relationship that exists between an entity and its owners are not liabilities.[153]

Under Subtopic 480-10 (FASB Statement No. 150), an obligation establishes a liability when it creates either a debtor-creditor relationship, or a relationship that is akin to a leveraged treasury stock purchase, or the conversion of shares to be delivered into a mandatorily convertible instrument (e.g., the case of a forward purchase contract), or a relationship that is different from an ownership relationship.

For obligations to issue a variable number of shares, Subtopic 480-10 (FASB Statement No. 150) uses the criterion of the variability and type of direction at inception of the sole or predominant relationship between the monetary value (defined as fair value at settlement date

---

[148] *FASB Statement No. 150, ¶¶ 4, 12.*
[149] *FASB, Preliminary Views,* Financial Instruments with Characteristics of Equity, *¶ B2 (November 2007).*
[150] *FASB, Preliminary Views,* Financial Instruments with Characteristics of Equity, *¶ A4 (November 2007).*
[151] *CON 1 (superseded), ¶ 13; CON 6, ¶ 51; IASB Framework, ¶ 9a (superseded).*
[152] *CON 6, ¶ 62;* The Conceptual Framework for Financial Reporting 2010, *¶ 4.20; IASB Framework, ¶ 65.*
[153] *See for example FASB Statement No. 150, ¶ B36.*

under specified market conditions) of the instrument embodying the obligation and the changes in fair value of the issuer's own shares.

Comment: Ownership relationship is a concept derived from the traditional notion of residual interest, and thus basically reflects the conventional definition of equity, whereby an instrument, in order to be considered equity, must expose its holder to the risks and benefits or returns similar to those of common stock. In fact, the principle that is implicit in the monetary value model is that an obligation that does not establish a direct relationship is not an ownership relationship and therefore not equity.

A different perspective is implicit in the variability criterion in IAS 32.[154]

Comment: By contrast, under IAS 32, the definition of residual interest (equity) is incompatible with an obligation for a total amount that is fixed. Stated in other terms, if the unit amount of the economic rights attached to one equity instrument is not variable it cannot be an equity instrument. From the angle of the impact on ownership interest, in order to be classified as equity, a contract shall be of a specific equity interest, which instead would not be fixed if the number of equity instruments were variable or were not determinable before settlement because they depend on an underlying variable.[155]

Thirdly, under Section 815-40-25 (EITF Issue 00-19) a guaranteed return or a collateral back-up precludes equity classification.[156] Under Subtopic 810-10 (FASB Interpretation No. 46(R)) a guaranteed return prevents the group of holders of equity investment at risk from sharing the obligation to absorb expected losses of the entity, and thus to qualify as a controlling financial interest.[157] Under IAS 32 the guarantee of a receipt for at least a cash-settled amount also calls for liability status.[158]

In parallel, several pronouncements underline some linkages between equity and risks and rewards implications.

Under Section 323-10-15 (EITF Issue 02-14), in-substance common stock investments include non-equity investments in an entity that have risks and rewards of ownership (e.g., participation in earnings, and capital appreciation and depreciation, in addition to subordination and no obligation to transfer value) that are substantially similar to an investment in the entity's common stock.[159]

Other characteristics of these instruments are mentioned in Section 2.2.4 and Section 2.2.5 following.

---

[154] *IAS 32, ¶ 16.*
[155] *As mentioned, the analysis and comparison of these two models, which are subject of a yet-to publish work by the author, is outside of the scope of this Book.*
[156] *FASB ASC 815-40-25-35 (EITF Issue No. 00-19, Footnote 1, ¶ 32).*
[157] *FASB ASC 810-10-15-14 (FASB Interpretation No. 46(R), ¶ 5(b)(2)).*
[158] *IAS 32, ¶ 20.*
[159] *FASB ASC 323-10-15-13 (EITF Issue 02-14, ¶ 6(b)).*

The Amendments to IAS 32 made in February 2008 identify certain instruments that entitle the holder to a pro rata share of the entity's net assets in the event of the entity's liquidation as largely equivalent to ordinary shares to be classified as equity.[160]

Under Subtopic 810-10 (FASB Interpretation No. 46(R)), significant participation in profits and losses is a defining element of total at-risk equity investment.[161] When the right to receive the expected residual returns and the obligation to absorb the expected losses of the entity reside with other interests,[162] total at-risk equity investment is in fact deprived of its otherwise controlling ownership nature, for the purpose of consolidation accounting.

Some SAB guidance refers to when a disposal of a subsidiary or business shall not be recognized as a divestiture for accounting purposes. By reading it in reverse, the principal consideration on derecognizing or recognizing a residual interest in an entity's net assets again depends on whether the risks and other incidents of ownership have been transferred to the buyer with sufficient certainty. This guidance also provides some indicators for such an assessment.[163]

Finally, a recent development that elaborates on a risk perspective is the loss absorption approach, under which equity is considered as a buffer or shield for other sources of capital, and therefore the distinction between equity and debt should be based on the ability or inability of capital to absorb losses incurred by an entity.[164] The FASB Preliminary Views and the IASB Discussion Paper on financial instruments with characteristics of equity acknowledge the loss absorption approach but do not develop such a method and leave it to a possible analysis at a later stage.[165]

2.2.4 Subordination

As a derivation of the residual interest concept (see Section 2.1.4.1 previously), equity is subordinated to liabilities in priorities of claims.[166]

---

[160] *Amendments to IAS 32* Financial *Instruments: Presentation and IAS 1* Presentation of Financial Statements, Puttable Financial Instruments and Obligations Arising on Liquidation, *¶¶ 16A(a), 16C(a), BC70.*

[161] *FASB ASC 810-10-15-14 (FASB Interpretation No. 46(R), ¶ 5a).*

[162] *FASB ASC 810-10-15-14 (FASB Interpretation No. 46(R), ¶ 5b).*

[163] *FASB ASC 605-40-S99-1 (SEC Staff Accounting Bulletin, Topic 5-E; SEC Staff Accounting Bulletin, Topic 5-U), removed by SAB 112, ¶ 2.d as deemed no longer necessary, and superseded by FASB Accounting Standards Update No. 2010-22,* Accounting for Various Topics – Technical Corrections to SEC Paragraphs, An Announcement made by the Staff of the U.S. Securities and Exchange Commission, *¶ 4.*

[164] Distinguishing Between Liabilities and Equity – Preliminary Views on the Classification of Liabilities and Equity and Under International Financial Reporting Standards, *¶ ES.5, A discussion paper prepared by staff of the Accounting Standards Committee of Germany on behalf of the European Financial Reporting Advisory Group and the German Accounting Standards Board under the Pro-active Accounting Activities in Europe Initiative of the European Financial Reporting Advisory Group and the European National Standard Setters (Brussels/Berlin, 2007).*

[165] *FASB, Preliminary Views,* Financial Instruments with Characteristics of Equity, *¶ E11 (November 2007); IASB, Discussion Paper,* Financial Instruments with Characteristics of Equity, *¶ 42, Invitation to Comment, Para. 6 (February 2008).*

[166] *CON 6, ¶¶ 54, 60, 213, 222.*

Comment: This has practical significance in several different contexts.

For example, a prerequisite for equity classification of a contract under Section 815-40-25 (EITF Issue 00-19) is that in the event of bankruptcy the counterparty's rights shall not rank higher than those of a shareholder of the stock underlying the contract.[167]

Under Section 323-10-15 (EITF Issue 02-14), an investment that has a substantive liquidation preference over common stock is not in-substance common stock. In this context, the liquidation preference is not substantive if it is not significant in relation to the purchase price of the investment or if the investee has little or no subordinated equity, such as common stock, from a fair value perspective.[168]

Finally, the subordination to all other classes of instruments and the fact that all financial instruments in the subordinated class have identical features are two of the requisites for classifying certain instruments in the scope of the February 2008 Amendments to IAS 32 as equity. A preferential right on liquidation negates those characteristics.[169]

Comment: The concept of liquidation plays mixed roles in accounting pronouncements. On one hand, as mentioned above, priority in liquidation of certain instruments may prevent their classification as equity. On the other hand, under certain circumstances settlement features in case of normal liquidation or liquidation preferences do not influence equity versus liability classification of an instrument, as they are considered outside the going concern assumption. For example, under IAS 32 the presence of a contingent settlement provision for settlement by transfer of cash or other financial asset only in the event of liquidation does not trigger the classification of the instrument as a liability.[170] Therefore, such situation may result in an instrument with liquidation preferences being classified as equity. Under EITF Issue No. 00-19, cash payment that is required only in the event of final liquidation of an entity need not be considered for the purpose of equity versus liability classification.[171] Similarly, under Section 480-10-S99 (EITF Topic No. D-98), ordinary liquidation or redemption events of all equity securities do not trigger temporary equity classification.[172]

However, different priorities may also exist even among different classes of stock.[173] For example, junior stock is subordinated to regular common stock for voting, liquidation, and dividend rights, but is convertible into regular common stock on the occurrence of certain future events.[174]

---

[167] *FASB ASC 815-40-25-31, 815-40-25-32, 815-40-25-33 (EITF Issue 00-19, ¶¶ 29–31).*

[168] *FASB ASC 323-10-15-13 (EITF Issue 02-14, ¶ 6a).*

[169] *Amendments to IAS 32* Financial Instruments: Presentation and IAS 1 Presentation of Financial Statements, Puttable Financial Instruments and Obligations Arising on Liquidation, *¶¶ 16A(b), 16A(c), AG14C, BC59.*

[170] *IAS 32, ¶¶ 25(b), BC18.*

[171] *EITF Issue No. 00-19, ¶ 12.*

[172] *FASB ASC 480-10-S99-3A (EITF Topic No. D-98, ¶¶ 5-6, as amended by Accounting Standards Update No. 2009-04,* Accounting for Redeemable Equity Instruments*).*

[173] *CON 6, ¶ 62.*

[174] *FASB Interpretation of Financial Accounting Standard No. 38,* Determining the Measurement Date for Stock Option, Purchase, and Award Plans Involving Junior Stock, *superseded by FASB Statement No. 123(R), ¶ D7(c).*

> **Comment:** Subtopic 810-10 (FASB Interpretation No. 46(R)) enlarges the concept of subordination, as the degree to which an interest in an entity absorbs all or part of the entity's expected losses (as the term *subordination* term is used in Interpretation 46(R)), therefore it comes after senior interests. Equity becomes a specific type of subordinated interest, the most subordinated for a voting interest entity. However, for a variable interest entity, a subordinated interest may consist in a non-equity interest.[175] The existence of subordinated financial support in excess of 50% of total equity triggers the need for evaluation as to whether the entity is a variable interest entity.[176] Subordination also takes a larger meaning, as "priority on claims to the entity's cash flows." The weight of the subordinated interest in relation to the overall expected losses and residual returns is considered in determining whether subordination is substantive. A subordinated interest that is capital-at-risk under Subtopic 810-10 (FASB Interpretation No. 46(R)) is substantive and therefore will be consider as determining variability.[177]

Subordination is the key feature of the basic ownership approach described in the FASB's Preliminary Views on financial instruments with characteristics of equity, whereas only the most residual claim would be classified as equity, although there may be different levels of residual interests in an entity.[178]

Publicly held companies in the U.S. must not present subordinated debt within stockholders' equity or commingled with any of such captions.[179]

Somehow, IAS 1 considers it possible that an entity regards subordinated debt as part of "adjusted capital," for the purpose of disclosure on capital only.[180]

2.2.5 Discretion on Distributions to Owners

Another characterization of equity is that distributions to owners, whether as dividends or any other transfer of value, are discretionary.[181]

Under the so-called *present obligation approach*, owners bear no unconditional right, and the entity has no contractual obligation to them in this respect, except in the event of the enterprise's liquidation or by formal act. In other words, the entity has an unconditional right to avoid a monetary transfer, except in liquidation.[182] Also, the lack of an entity's unconditional right to refuse share redemption in a non-liquidation situation characterizes such instruments as liabilities.[183] The triggering of cash (or other financial asset) settlement under the contractual terms of an instrument by the occurrence of an uncertain future event that is outside of the control of both the issuer and the holder implies that its issuer does not have the unconditional

---

[175] *FASB ASC 810-10-55-23 (FASB Interpretation No. 46(R), ¶ B8).*

[176] *FASB Interpretation No. 46(R), ¶ 8.*

[177] *FASB ASC 810-10-25-32 (FASB Staff Position FIN 46(R)-6, Determining the Variability to Be Considered in Applying FASB Interpretation No. 46(R), ¶ 11).*

[178] *FASB, Preliminary Views, Financial Instruments with Characteristics of Equity, ¶¶ 16(a), 18, 53 (November 2007).*

[179] *FASB ASC 470-10-S99-2 (SEC SAB Topic 4-A).*

[180] *IAS 1, ¶ 135.*

[181] *CON 6, ¶¶ 54, 61.*

[182] *FASB Statement No. 150, ¶ B23; CON 6, ¶ 62; IAS 32, ¶¶ 17, 19, 25(b), AG13, BC18.*

[183] *FASB ASC 480-10-25-4 (FASB Statement No. 150, ¶ 9); IAS 32, ¶ AG25; IFRIC 2, ¶ 7, A3.*

right to avoid the settlement. This calls for financial liability under IAS 32, unless this applies only in the event of liquidation of the issuer.[184] However, IAS 32 overrides financial liability classification in the above situations for certain instruments that entitle the holder to a pro rata share of the entity's net assets in the event of the entity's liquidation. However, again, the contractual obligation to deliver cash or another financial asset must be limited to a situation of liquidation.[185]

> **Comment:** An analogy may be drawn between this presentation and the requirement in Subtopic 480-10 (FASB Statement No. 150) not to present a subsidiary's mandatorily redeemable financial instruments whose redemption is required to occur only upon the liquidation or termination of such subsidiary as liability in the subsidiary's statement of financial position. However, here the rationale is that otherwise the going concern assumption of the subsidiary would be violated.[186]

Similarly, under Subtopic 815-40 (EITF Issue 00-19), any contract provision that could require net cash settlement for an instrument based on the occurrence of an event which is beyond the issuer's control precludes equity classification, unless the holders of the underlying shares would also receive cash, or if such payment is only required in the event of final liquidation of the entity.[187]

Section 323-10-15 (EITF Issue 02-14), by taking the perspective of the holder of investments other than common stock, defines risk and reward characteristics of common stock. Investments other than common stock are deemed to be in-substance common stock if their features are substantially similar to the entity's common stock. Among other criteria, Section 323-10-15 (EITF Issue 02-14) considers an investment not to be substantially similar to common stock if the investee is expected to transfer value that is substantive to the investor, and that is not similarly available to common shareholders.[188] However, contrary to the traditional conception of equity, this notion does not require a lack of obligation to transfer value per se.

> **Comment:** Therefore, equity classification is incompatible with the existence of an obligation, which instead characterizes the definition of a liability under the IASB Framework and the U.S. Concepts. Somewhat differently, under the basic ownership approach proposed by the FASB as part of the *Financial Instruments with Characteristics of Equity Project*, the existence of an obligation is not a necessary prerequisite of a liability, as in the case of a perpetual preferred stock which under that approach would be classified as liability even when it bears no dividend requirement.[189]

---

[184] *IAS 32,* ¶ *25.*

[185] *Amendments to IAS 32* Financial Instruments: Presentation and IAS 1 Presentation of Financial Statements, Puttable Financial Instruments and Obligations Arising on Liquidation, ¶¶ *16A(d), BC67.*

[186] *FASB ASC 480-10-25-4 (FASB Statement No. 150, ¶ 9).*

[187] *FASB ASC 815-40-25-4, 815-40-25-7, 815-40-25-10 (EITF Issue No. 00-19, ¶¶ 8, 12, 13).*

[188] *FASB ASC 323-10-15-13 (EITF Issue 02-14, ¶ 6c).*

[189] *Financial Accounting Standards Board, Preliminary Views,* Financial Instruments with Characteristics of Equity, ¶ *D11 (November 30, 2007).*

2.3 MAJOR IMPLICATIONS FOR COMPANIES

This Book analyzes accounting for equity and other comprehensive income from the standpoint of the comparison between U.S. GAAP and SEC requirements and IFRSs.

The implications that arise from such a perspective are at different levels. Firstly, the previous paragraphs highlighted some consequences of different conceptual views on equity. Secondly, other Sections of the Book will illustrate specific technical implications of issues relating to equity and other comprehensive income. In so doing, it is useful to include, when appropriate, some considerations made by SEC staff as well as by foreign regulators with regard to companies that adopted IFRSs for the first time. Although this is a much wider topic that falls outside the scope of this Book, given the pervasive nature of equity, the next paragraphs will enucleate the main lessons learned from the first migrations to IFRSs, mainly with reference to both consequences for stockholders' equity and the dual reporting perspective.

> **Comment:** It is evident that the experience gained in several countries from the first transition to IFRSs offers a tremendous opportunity to learn insights on how to manage the impact of both the enlarging of the IFRS base and the dual reporting wave. The SEC also acknowledges that the U.S. public capital market has never experienced the magnitude of an event that requires either a massive change in the comprehensive basis of accounting, or the use of different basis of accounting for purposes of preparing primary financial statements.[190]

Massive first-time adoption of IFRSs happened in 2005 and 2006. This involved many countries outside the United States, and in particular the European Union in connection with EC Regulation 1606/2002.[191] Such a move by the EU has been estimated to have affected approximately 8000 companies from January 2005 to the beginning of 2007.[192] In 2005, IFRS adopters with securities admitted to trading on a regulated market in the EU numbered 7365.[193]

In the United States, foreign registrants have also been permitted to file IFRS financial statements with the SEC with reconciliation to U.S. GAAP, with some accommodations for first-time adoption of IFRSs. In 2006 approximately 110 foreign private issuers filed IASB-compliant IFRSs financial statements with the SEC, and approximately 70 IFRSs with a jurisdictional variation of IFRSs. In 2006, IFRS filings with the Commission were principally

---

[190] *Concept Release, page 40.*

[191] *Regulation (EC) No 1606/2002 of The European Parliament and of The Council of 19 July 2002 on the application of international accounting standards. Hereinafter EC Regulation 1606/2002.*

[192] *Committee of European Securities Regulators, Press Statement, CESR/07-121b (April 2007).*

[193] *Committee of European Securities Regulators, CESR, Press Statement, CESR/07-121b, April 2007; Committee of European Securities Regulators, CESR, November 2007. 07-352, CESR's Review of the Implementation and Enforcement of IFRS in the EU, ¶ Appendix 1. [Online] CESR, France. Available at www.cesr.eu (last visited May 25, 2009); Commission of The European Communities, Report from the Commission to The Council and The European Parliament on The Operation of Regulation (EC) No 1606/2002 of 19 July 2002 on The Application of International Accounting Standards (April 24, 2008), ¶ 2.3.*

from European and Australian issuers.[194] The Commission expects Canada's announced move to IFRSs to boost the IFRS trend even further.[195]

It should also be taken into consideration that EC Regulation 1606/2002 permitted EU Member States to defer the first-time adoption of IFRSs to a financial year starting on or after January 2007 for companies, inter alia, that are listed in a non-member State and report under U.S. GAAP.[196] Thus, some companies had to adopt IFRSs in 2007 or still are in the process of adopting IFRSs.

In 2006 the SEC staff reviewed the annual reports of more than 100 foreign private issuers.[197]

Additional trends are emerging. Firstly, as a next step, the SEC amended Form 20-F and Regulation S-X, and other regulations, forms, and rules under the Securities Act of 1933 and the Exchange Act of 1934, to accept IFRS financial statements without reconciliation to U.S. GAAP from foreign private issuers, but this is limited to English language financial statements prepared under the IASB (International Accounting Standards Board) version of IFRSs.[198] Regulation S-X continues to apply to filings from such foreign private issuers with the exception of their financial statement form and content.

Additionally, the SEC considered allowing U.S. issuers, including investment companies subject to the Investment Company Act of 1940, to prepare financial statements in accordance with International Financial Reporting Standards as published by the IASB for purposes of complying with the rules and regulations of the Commission.[199] On August 27, 2008 the SEC also proposed a "roadmap" to IFRSs that would require all U.S. public companies to file their financial statements in IFRSs by 2016 and would also allow certain U.S. companies, based on certain criteria, to use IFRSs for their filings for fiscal years ending on or after December 15, 2009. In 2011 the SEC would evaluate the steps made in the roadmap and decide whether or not to require large accelerated filers (issuers with common equity of at least $700 million) to report under IFRSs starting from fiscal years ending on or after December 15, 2014, accelerated filers to report under IFRSs starting from fiscal years ending on or after December 15, 2015, and all other public companies from fiscal years ending on or after December 15, 2016.

However, on February 24, 2010, the SEC issued a statement calling for more study of IFRSs and setting 2015 as the earliest possible date for the required use of IFRSs by U.S. public companies. It confirmed the year 2011 as the threshold for a decision on whether to move ahead. The SEC withdrew the proposed rules for limited early use of IFRS by certain U.S. issuers, although it did not exclude the possibility of early use or adoption. The statement does not rule out the possibility in the future that issuers may be permitted to choose between the use of IFRS or U.S. GAAP. The Work plan addresses six specific areas of concern: 1) whether

---

[194] *Proposed Rule, page 29.*
[195] *Concept Release, page 6.*
[196] *EC Regulation 1606/2002, article 9(b).*
[197] Observations in the Review of IFRS Financial Statements, *July 2, 2007 (last visited July 6, 2007)* *http://www.sec.gov/divisions/corpfin/ifrs_staffobservations.htm*
[198] *Rule, Summary.*
[199] *Concept Release, Summary.*

IFRS is sufficiently developed and consistent in application for use in the U.S. reporting system; 2) the independence of standard setting; 3) investor understanding and education regarding the new standards and comparison with U.S. GAAP; 4) impact on U.S. laws or regulations; 5) impact on both large and small companies; and 6) preparation of auditors. The successful completion of the FASB-IASB convergence project is perceived as a critical milestone.

On May 26, 2011, the SEC published an update concerning the Work plan to IFRSs.[200] After analyzing the difference between enforcement and convergence, the SEC's paper addresses the so-called "condorsement" approach. This approach intends to lead to IFRS compliance by U.S. issuers that are compliant with U.S. GAAP. At the end of a transitional period, U.S. GAAP would incorporate IFRSs. In this respect, this is similar to an enforcement approach. During a transitional period of five to seven years, differences between IFRS and U.S. GAAP would be addressed. In this respect, it is similar to a convergence approach. The transition period could permit a staged or phased implementation. Finally, the FASB would also have a role to issue supplement or interpretative guidance, adding disclosure requirements, or setting requirements on issues not addressed by IFRSs.

As of May 18, 2008, the Council of the AICPA designated the IASB as the body to establish international financial reporting standards for both private and public entities pursuant to Rule 202 and Rule 203 of the AICPA Code of Professional Conduct. In three to five years, the Council will reassess this decision.[201] In particular, the AICPA's recognition of the IASB as a designated standard setter has opened the route for the use of IFRSs by nonpublic entities in the U.S., especially IFRSs for small and medium-sized entities.

All over the world, several patterns of adoptions, or combinations of approaches, have arisen depending on the country involved. Some countries have required the use of IFRSs for consolidated financial statements of listed companies. Others have required or permitted this to listed companies, or extended to unlisted companies with an option to use local accounting principles. Certain jurisdictions, for example Ukraine, have permitted IFRSs for all companies with no reconciliation to local GAAP; others (e.g., Bangladesh) have required them for all companies; still others have prohibited IFRSs to any extent (for example, Iran). The U.S. traditional approach was a limited permission with reconciliation to local GAAP. The EU has chosen a clearance process resulting in a jurisdictional version of IFRSs. Amendment of local GAAP to conform partly or entirely to IFRSs is another pattern (for example, Australia). Other countries – the U.S., Canada, Japan, India – have plans in progress to adopt IFRSs.

Most importantly, some major economies, e.g., Canada, which has announced IFRS convergence by 2011, are migrating to IFRSs by 2010–2012 and beyond.

In 2006, China promulgated a new set of accounting standards substantially in line with IFRSs.

---

[200] *SEC, 2011*. Work Plan for the Consideration of Incorporating International Financial Reporting Standards into the Financial Reporting System for U.S. Issuers. *[Online] Available at www.sec.gov (last visited May 29, 2011)*.

[201] *AICPA. Amendment to Code of Professional Conduct, Appendix A* – Council Resolution Designating Bodies to Promulgate Professional Standards.

On July 24, 2007, the Council of the Institute of Chartered Accountants of India announced its IFRS convergence plan for listed entities, other public interest entities such as banks, insurance companies, and large-sized entities from the accounting periods commencing on or after April 1, 2011.

On January 28, 2010, the Brazilian Federal Council of Accounting and the Brazilian Accounting Pronouncements Committee signed a MOU with the IASB to converge fully to IFRS by end 2010.

On August 1, 2008, the Financial Reporting Foundation (FRF) and Malaysian Accounting Standards Board (MASB) announced their plan to bring Malaysia to full convergence with IFRSs by January 1, 2012. For the time being, private entities will continue to apply Private Entity Reporting Standards (PERS).

In November 2008, the National Banking and Securities Commission of Mexico together with the Mexican Board for Research and Development of Financial Reporting Standards communicated a plan to adopt IFRS for listed entities starting for periods ending on December 31, 2012.

Public companies in Argentina will be required to adopt IFRSs starting in 2012, with an option to file financial statements in accordance with IFRS starting in January 2011.

The South Korean government has approved mandatory adoption of IFRSs by 2011 for all listed companies and unlisted financial institutions in certain sectors. All companies except financial institutions could voluntarily adopt IFRSs from January 1, 2009.

On December 11, 2009, the Japan Financial Services Agency (FSA) announced regulatory changes to allow certain qualifying domestic listed companies to apply IFRSs in consolidated financial statements, starting from the fiscal year ending on or after March 31, 2010. A final decision on the mandatory requirement for IFRSs from 2015 or 2016 will be taken around 2012.

Planning Point: Therefore, some companies find themselves in the position of reporting under both bodies of standards as the primary basis of accounting. In other words, they may need to embed this situation in their systems, an approach that we call dual reporting in this Book (see Section 1.7 previously).[202]

The abovementioned U.S. companies are likely to be large multinationals that are also present in IFRSs jurisdictions, that may share some of the reasons for adopting IFRSs with other non-U.S. enterprises, to the extent such standards may provide them some of the general benefits that are normally associated with the concept of a single set of high quality globally accepted accounting standards.

---

[202] *The Concept Release, page 7 acknowledges this phenomenon for certain U.S. issuers because it allows them to compete for capital globally, or because of their broad subsidiaries base in IFRSs jurisdictions, or because required to file under IFRSs by regulatory or statutory purposes.*

Comment: The main advantages at entity level are, but are not limited to: raising foreign finance, including non-U.S.-based finance, reducing costs of global investment and of restating financial statements,[203] improving corporate image, competitiveness, financial transparency and international visibility with customers, investors and financial markets, and providing a common accounting language to enhance internal management.

Similarly, the financial community as a whole (both global capital markets and investors) is presumed to gain from comparability and reduced costs and time in comparing financial information and investment opportunities across borders,[204] and from the reliable basis for corporate analysis that contribute to the strength of capital markets, investor protection, and promoting the free flow of capital between nations.

2.3.1 Financial Impact

2.3.1.1 Financial Statement Performance   Among the many other implications the experience of a change in the comprehensive basis of accounting to IFRSs has shown some main features on financial statements performance and equity. As mentioned, the Book will illustrate in detail most of these and other specific technical issues. Although these examples, which are not intended to be comprehensive, have generally arisen in jurisdictions where local accounting standards were less restrictive than IFRSs, some may also be valid to a certain extent for migration from U.S. GAAP to IFRSs or instances of dual reporting, due to the difference between the two bodies of standards. However, the potential for impact is more limited when moving from U.S. GAAP, due to wider similarities to IFRSs than when moving from national local GAAP in many other jurisdictions.

Further, some differences are diminishing, following some current changes in respective standards, such as those for accounting for a change in accounting principle after the issuance of FASB Statement No. 154.

The main aspects potentially impacting stockholders' equity and other comprehensive income are the following:

- Possible different and more volatile earnings and equity to the extent that an entity is required to use fair value measurement more extensively, in particular depending on different measurement criteria for financial assets and financial liabilities,[205] or for other specific items such as the fair value model for investment property;
- The expensing of all share-based payment transactions, including to subjects other than employees, in line with IFRS 2;

---

[203] *Similarly, the Concept Release, page 13 regarding the lowering of costs in preparing consolidated financial statements as a possible driving force in a situation where a U.S. issuer has a large number of subsidiaries reporting under IFRSs, as long as an increase in cost of capital does not offset such benefit.*

[204] *The Concept Release, page 12 also takes into consideration the possible pressure for comparability from investors in industries with a critical mass of companies reporting under IFRSs.*

[205] *A readiness survey of over 300 European companies by PriceWaterhouseCoopers,* International Financial Reporting Standards, Ready to Take the Plunge? *(May 2004), pages 23, 24 rated financial instruments, employee benefits, and deferred tax accounting as high or medium priority topics for the majority of the sample.*

- The different treatment of employee benefits, including pension and postemployment benefits. In particular the lack of additional pension liability under IFRSs, and on the other hand, the more comprehensive reporting in other comprehensive income required recently under Subtopic 715-20 (FASB Statement No. 158);
- The elimination of mezzanine or any other intermediate classification of certain instruments with characteristics of both equity and liabilities, or their different classification as either equity or liabilities, or the split into their respective components under IAS 32;
- The presentation within equity of minority interests, recently also adopted under Subtopic 810-10 (FASB Statement No. 160);
- The possible different scope of consolidation. In particular whether an entity may be consolidated as a variable interest entity under U.S. GAAP or a special purpose entity under IAS 32 and SIC 12. A related issue is whether the same transfer transaction may result in a sale and consequently the derecognition of financial assets under one of the two sets of accounting principles or a guaranteed loan under the other;
- The impact of choosing a group reporting currency that is different from the parent's functional currency for multinationals with many foreign entities, as consolidated financial statements may be prepared with any presentation currency under IAS 21;
- The revaluation model for property, plant, and equipment, or for some intangible assets;
- The impact on distributable reserves and taxation from adopting IFRSs, when permitted, for local statutory reporting.

Additionally, under IFRS 1 the retroactive application of most changes has made it necessary to restate the opening IFRS statement of financial position as of the date of transition to IFRSs, that is, the beginning of the first IFRS full comparative period in an entity's first IFRS financial statements,[206] including recomputing opening retained earnings balance (see Section 6.4.4 later).

2.3.1.2   Taxation   Traditionally, the purpose and rules of tax reporting are recognized to be different from those of financial reporting. Further, the relationship between tax and financial reporting is different according to the tax legislation in each jurisdiction.

This subject falls outside the scope of this Book. However, it is evident that to the extent to which the move to IFRSs involves an entity's financial statements and not only consolidated statements, depending on each specific EU Member State use of EC Regulation 1606/2002 options (see Section 2.3.2.1 following), the adoption of IFRSs could substantially impact corporate tax, and legal or regulatory regimes. IFRS consolidated financial statements may also have tax effects in jurisdictions that allow consolidated tax return.

In any event the tax legislation of each IFRS jurisdiction has been facing the need for updating in order to adjust for IFRS impact. Further, companies have been facing changes in their tax computations and tax accounting systems in order to comply with newly-enacted rules.

2.3.1.3   Financial Analysis   Some financial analysis implications of the first adoption of IFRSs are as follows:

- Financial ratios are impacted as long as financial statements performance is affected, as seen in the previous paragraph;

---

[206]   *IFRS 1, Appendix A.*

- The extent and quality of disclosures further enable financial modeling, analysis, and assessment of business and financial risks, and thus may influence rating;
- Consequently, restrictive covenants in existing financing agreements or lease contracts may be affected by the changes in financial ratios;
- The degree of freedom in setting dividend policy may also be altered.

Example: As an example, the use of split accounting for compound financial instruments under IAS 32 determines a lower initial liability (because it refers to the liability component only). Instead, interest expense are generally computed with a higher market rate than that resulting implicitly from considering the equity upside potential of the instrument.[207]

Valuation of company shares may also be affected. A survey by KPMG reported that 77% of analysts expected share valuation impact from the introduction of IFRSs, especially in relation to increased volatility. Further, analysts have rated the consistency of application and interpretation and comparability between financial statements of companies in different countries as essential.[208]

Another study by Ernst & Young argues that while in theory accounting does not impact cash flows, apart from tax effects, these indeed are affected, as long as credit ratings are altered, employee benefits practices change, reported profits impact share prices, and migration involves implementation costs.[209]

Comment: Avoiding consolidation, including SPEs, is one of the main reasons for certain companies not to adopt IFRSs even when this is permitted by local laws. This may have a very significant impact on financial performance. Similarly, the impact of accounting for business consolidation needs to be considered. Some jurisdictions have minimized or delayed impacts by not permitting or not requesting IFRSs for entity's unconsolidated financial statements.

In such a context, financial analysts and CPAs also need to understand how to read, or prepare, IFRS financial statements.

2.3.2 Strategic Impact

2.3.2.1 International Expansion As mentioned, IFRS is in force, either mandatorily for listed companies in certain jurisdictions such as the EU Member States or on an optional basis, in more than 100 countries. Worksheet 6 illustrates the use by EU Member States of the options allowed under EC Regulation 1606/2002. Worksheet 7 shows the use of IFRSs by domestic companies in non-EU countries. Worksheet 8 lists EC Directives and Regulations that endorse IFRSs. An analysis on IFRSs in 175 jurisdictions found out that for domestic listed companies 30 countries do not permit IFRSs, 24 permit them, six require IFRSs for some

---

[207] *Similarly, Ernst & Young,* Converting to IFRS – An Analysis of Implementation Issues *(November 2005), page 67 (last visited December 2005) www.ey.com/ifrs.*

[208] *KPMG,* On the Threshold of IFRS, Analyst Research Survey *(November 2005) (last visited January 2006) kpmgifrg.com pages 7, 10.*

[209] *Ernst & Young, IFRS,* The Implications for the Building Materials Sector *(December 2005), page 3 (last visited December 2005) www.ey.com/ifrs.*

companies, 94 require IFRSs or full IFRS equivalent or substantially-converged standards for all companies, and 21 have no stock exchange. Of 136 jurisdictions for which information concerning unlisted companies is available, 37 jurisdictions do not permit IFRSs, 44 permit IFRSs for all or some companies, 30 require them for some companies, and 25 for general-purpose financial statements of all companies.[210]

> **Comment:** All over the world, several patterns of adoptions, or combinations of approaches, have arisen depending on the country involved. Some countries have required the use of IFRSs for consolidated financial statements of listed companies. Others have required or permitted this to listed companies, or extended to unlisted companies with an option to use local accounting principles. Certain jurisdictions, for example Ukraine, have permitted IFRSs for all companies with no reconciliation to local GAAP, others (e.g., Bangladesh) have required them for all companies, still others have prohibited IFRSs to any extent (for example, Iran). The U.S. traditional approach was a limited permission with reconciliation to local GAAP. The EU has chosen a clearance process resulting in a jurisdictional version of IFRSs. Amendment of local GAAP to conform partly or entirely to IFRSs is another pattern (for example, Australia). Other countries, such as the U.S., Canada, Japan, and India, have plans in progress to adopt IFRSs.

Therefore, an entity may be required to migrate to IFRSs for primary financial statements for the purpose of reporting in certain countries. Depending on the magnitude of an entity's presence in such foreign markets it may consider changing financial reporting practices globally. Of course, some companies with limited geographical presence will have little or no incentive for such transition. Certain academic research found that the perception of benefits of IFRSs is greater for larger companies that use equity financing to a greater extent.[211]

> **Comment:** There are barriers and benefits related to this move. Migration implies initial costs and complexity. This may generate resistance to change by companies themselves. Furthermore, some may fear losing a competitive advantage because of enhanced disclosure, as stated above, especially on consolidation. Others may want to avoid disclosing information that they believe confidential or competitive.
>
> The national accounting bodies may perceive loss of power, and resist IFRSs. Particularly before the development of the 2005 stable platform, IFRSs have been accused, especially in the United States, of lacking proper rigor and detail and permitting too many options. Additionally, notwithstanding the recent issuance of some specialized industry standards,[212] IFRSs still do not deal extensively with

[210] *Adapted from: Deloitte,* Use of IFRSs for Reporting by Jurisdiction *(last visited August 25, 2011)* www.iasplus.com/country/useias.htm.

[211] *The Institute of Chartered Accountants in England and Wales (ICAEW), 2007.* EU Implementation of IFRS and the Fair Value Directive, a Report for the European Commission, ¶ 6.3. [Online] London: ICAEW. Available at www.icaew.com/ecifrsstudy (last visited July 31, 2010).

[212] *Such as International Accounting Standard No. 41,* Agriculture, *International Financial Reporting Standards No. 4,* Insurance Contracts, *International Financial Reporting Standards No. 6,* Exploration for and Evaluation of Mineral Resources, *IFRIC Interpretation No. 2,* Members' Shares in Co-operative Entities and Similar Instruments; *IFRIC Interpretation No. 12,* Service Concession Arrangements, *IFRIC Interpretation No. 15,* Agreements for the Construction of Real Estate *which add to the pre-existing International Accounting Standard No. 26,* Accounting and Reporting by Retirement Benefit Plans, *and International Accounting Standard No. 30,* Disclosures in the Financial Statements of Banks and Similar Financial Institutions, *now superseded by IFRS 7.*

specialized industries and its perceived principles-based approach may be seen as difficult to apply in situations where specific standards or interpretations are missing.

As to the normative environment, some countries with a legal or tax-driven approach to financial reporting may oppose global accounting standards. National tax authorities generally do not accept GAAP, including IFRSs, for taxation purposes. Possible conflict with local corporate governance or legal framework may arise.

However, a unique or dual accounting platform and related routines may even be a deliberate optimizing choice by a company.

Planning Point: Firstly, this step may be functional to expanding internationally for business opportunities or finance raising. A prerequisite of this move is an analysis of which local entities are allowed to use IFRSs for local reporting, and its impact on financial performance. Worksheet 9 summarizes the options that U.S. listed companies have in connection with EC Regulation 1606/2002. Worksheet 10 instead illustrates options, according to U.S. requirements, for a U.S. entity that reports under IFRSs. Worksheet 11 shows options that are available to non-U.S. entities that report in the U.S. either under IFRSs or under U.S. GAAP.

Additionally, if such changes are faced systematically by structured accounting routines, the company is likely to benefit in the future from reduced need to reconcile and use an ad hoc approach each time.

Finally, the application in different jurisdictions of IFRSs, even in their IASB version, may result in more transparent and robust, although not necessarily uniform, disclosures to financial statements users, particularly in cases where local securities regulators require provision of a greater amount of information to investors.

In this regard, however, the previously mentioned SEC Concept Release describes some interesting issues that would arise if the Commission decided to accept financial statements from U.S. issuers that are prepared in accordance with IFRSs as published by the IASB.[213] In particular, the specificity of Regulation S-X on format or content of financial statements is greater than that under IFRSs, particularly IAS 1.[214] Additionally, investment company financial statements have unique disclosure requirements under Regulation S-X. Finally, Regulation S-K refers to specific U.S. GAAP pronouncements for the purpose of disclosures for the nonfinancial statement portion of filings with the SEC.

Planning Point: Even if no jurisdictional version of IFRSs is required by a certain country, IFRSs as a "neutral" blanket (i.e., IASB-IFRSs) would likely be required to be complemented, besides financial statements themselves, by additional disclosures as set by securities regulators in each jurisdiction, or for nonlisted companies by other disclosures depending on sector regulations, or specific corporate laws. As an example, under the rule to permit IFRS filing without reconciliation

---

[213] *Concept Release, pages 37–39.*

[214] *For a comparison between Regulation S-X and IFRSs on the format of the statement of financial position, see Francesco Bellandi, "Dual Reporting Under U.S. GAAP and IFRS – Layout of the Statement of Financial Position for Commercial and Industrial Entities,"* The CPA Journal *(December 2007).*

to U.S. GAAP, foreign private issuers reporting under IFRSs in the U.S. would need to provide additional disclosures as required by Regulation S-X.

Nevertheless, in any event multinational companies would need to deal with more securities regulators in markets where they are present. With a unique platform, however, regulators' comments would relate to IFRS financial statements only. In any case this fact reduces the complexity of managing multiple local GAAP bases. It must also be remembered that the efforts by securities regulators exist to facilitate the sharing of experience with IFRSs and avoiding conflicting conclusions.[215] Thus, this may even result in a cross-fertilizing experience to find useful interpretations for the application of IFRSs in situations where an IFRS standard or interpretation that specifically applies to a transaction or event does not exist.

2.3.2.2   Board Decisions   A change in the comprehensive basis of accounting or dual reporting is a strategic event that requires top priority from a company's Board of Directors, which has the ultimate responsibility for such a move.

The following are some key considerations that should involve the Board of Directors, that should take the lead and communicate its decisions to the IFRS migration project team for further cascading to the entire organization:

• Decide on options that IFRSs permit, including first-time adoption exemptions under IFRS 1;
• Identify, review, and select accounting policies;
• Assess the high-level impact of migration on financial statements performance and associated risks;
• Identify critical changes in business processes (see Section 2.3.3 following);
• Ensure that corporate governance applicable in the jurisdiction is not violated;
• Understand how stakeholders perceive, and should be directed to perceive, all such changes.

Comment: Worksheet 12 illustrates IFRS accounting options that involve stockholders' equity. These decisions are also of utmost importance for the users of financial statements. In fact, the CESR[216] has identified the use of options as a specific situation that warrants transparent disclosure. Other

[215] *IOSCO developed a database to share such experience: see IOSCO Press Release,* Regulators to Share Information on International Financial Reporting Standards *(last visited August 28, 2007) http://www.iosco.org/news/pdf/IOSCONEWS92.pdf. Additionally, efforts in this sense have been made by the European Commission, the SEC, and the CESR: see SEC Press Release No. 2006-17,* Accounting Standards: SEC Chairman Cox and EU Commissioner McCreevy Affirm Commitment to Elimination of the Need for Reconciliation Requirements *(February 8, 2006) (SEC Press Release No. 2006-17) (last visited August 28, 2007) http://www.sec.gov/news/press/2006-17.htm;* SEC and CESR Launch Work Plan Focused on Financial Reporting, *SEC Press Release 2006-130 (August 2, 2006) (last visited August 28, 2007) http://www.sec.gov/news/press/2006/2006-130.htm;* CESR Publishes Key Information from Its Database of Enforcement Decisions Taken by EU National Enforcers of Financial Information (IFRS) *CESR/07-163 (April 2007) (last visited August 28, 2007) http://www.cesr-eu.org/index.php?page=groups&mac=0&id=13.*
[216] *Committee of European Securities Regulators, Public Statement,* CESR Reminds Issuers and Investors about the Importance of Clear and Transparent Disclosure on the Use of Any Options Made Available by Applicable Financial Reporting Standards, *CESR/05-758 (January 12, 2006).*

particular circumstances comprise issues where IFRSs provide no guidance, accounting in areas where the EU has not, or has not yet, fully endorsed a standard or interpretation, or the decision for the early adoption of an accounting standard. This also includes a situation where a company uses the EU permission to adopt a standard that becomes effective after the reporting date but before the financial statements are signed. Certain disclosures of early adoptions are in any case required by IAS 8.

2.3.2.3 Top Management Role The adoption of modern financial reporting may result in a new competitive tool for CEOs, Directors, and CFOs who know how to face this challenge.

Comment: Adopting high quality, understandable, transparent, and internationally accepted standards (such as IFRSs or U.S. GAAP) for financial reporting should be part of the corporate, marketing, and communication strategy to stakeholders. This requires top management commitment. It may be a unique opportunity to enhance the decision usefulness for users of financial statements, the raising of foreign finance, corporate image, competitiveness, financial transparency, and international visibility. In addition, it is a tremendous opportunity to shift the business processes from report production to streamlined and cost-effective data capture and generation.

The adoption of modern financial reporting is not simply an accounting exercise, but it generates a pervasive change that involves virtually all the departments of a company.

Comment: Management shall ensure that a project management migration strategy is in place, its importance is cascaded down the hierarchy levels, action plans are developed and followed up, the project team is appropriately staffed and trained, and project migration steps, including communication strategy, are implemented as scheduled (see Section 2.3.4.1 following).

2.3.3 Business Processes Impact

Business processes and systems are largely affected by the adoption of a new primary basis of accounting or by the adoption of dual reporting.

Example: Firstly, the internal management in each process or function may change in some respect. As an example, banking and financing agreements may require renegotiation, when the counterparty uses IFRSs to monitor compliance with financial ratios or covenants. SPE arrangements may need to be re-discussed or terminated. Lease contracts will need to be reviewed.

Definition and measurement of revenue may require amending in commercial or vendor contracts. The computation of the results of business units, lines, or product/services may be affected. In regulated industries, tariffs and several obligations might be impacted.

Treasury should analyze the consistency of risk management and hedging policies with hedge accounting requirements, and review contracts if required. Documentation, hedge effectiveness, and disclosures as required by IAS 39 shall be assured. It should analyze whether embedded derivatives emerge that should be bifurcated. Adopting fair value option, when permitted, should be evaluated as opposed to hedging strategies.

Secondly, some interactions between processes or functions become mandatory.

Example: The legal department shall become aware of what discriminants to communicate to the accounting department for it to be able to classify a financing contract as financial liability or equity.

The accounting department shall distribute check lists to virtually all other functions to be satisfied that relevant information for disclosures is completely and promptly collected.

Thirdly, this is a tremendous opportunity for business process re-engineering, to better enable financial reporting, to build comprehensive data warehousing which comprises data for financial reporting as well, and to make sure that internal controls are expanded to the issue of the new standards.

Other implications for accounting and business processes, such as human resources, management reporting, investor relationship, information systems, as well as internal control and auditing are discussed in the following paragraphs.

2.3.4   Implementation Considerations

2.3.4.1   Migration Project Management   The impact of change management requires a knowledgeable transition management. Each company that has been involved in such change must have developed a migration strategy, although surveys have generally evidenced some implementation delay.[217] In a group of companies, generally the parent leads action. Although for many companies this process has taken place, many others are still in a learning process. From a professional perspective, several accounting firms have developed different approaches. Worksheet 13 shows a general framework check list for GAAP transition management.

Comment: Accounting standards change, companies expand internationally, and thus sooner or later may face additional GAAP to report on. The key is an approach of integrating IFRS into the company systems, which in its more extreme application is what this Book denotes as *dual reporting*. Avoiding developing short-term solutions will save cost and time.

2.3.4.2   Accounting Procedures   Worksheet 14 reports a check list of accounting implications for transition to IFRSs.

Comment: In particular, with specific reference to stockholders' equity, under IFRS 1 most of the first-time adoption changes generate adjustments to the opening balance of retained earnings. IFRS 1 also requires specific reconciliation of equity as compared with previous GAAP (see Section 6.4.4 following).

---

[217]   *For example, the survey by PriceWaterhouseCoopers,* International Financial Reporting Standard – Ready to Take-off? *(December 2004) (last visited February 2, 2007) of 323 companies in 20 countries in the third quarter of 2004 described the pace of integrating IFRS in core systems, processes, and controls as slow. Only 44% of companies surveyed had identified data needs and 79% had collected no or little data. European companies registered with the SEC (16% of the survey) were a little advanced in putting IFRSs into operation.*

2.3.4.3 Management Reporting Systems The implications of GAAP migration in management reporting require a review of the internal reporting systems and the upgrade of internal manuals and procedures. According to a 2007 survey of European publicly listed and unlisted companies, 69% of preparers used IFRSs for internal reporting; 48% of them found them beneficial while 21% were not sure of this.[218]

> **Comment:** A long-term solution to IFRS migration is to ensure compatibility with internal management, budgeting, and reporting systems. This also helps prevent a company that is not accustomed to those standards from carrying out forecasting, for internal reporting purposes, on the basis of outdated models with unrealistic targeted results. This requires collaboration between accounting departments and planning, control and management reporting. Additionally, disconnection between financial reporting and management reporting would cause reworks and waste of effort.

2.3.4.4 Information Systems Worksheet 15 illustrates a check list for assessment of the impact of IFRS migration on information systems or information technology.

> **Comment:** A practical and pervasive issue is that under IFRS 1 an entity's estimates at the date of transition to IFRSs shall be consistent with estimates under previous GAAP. Keeping track or having systems to trace this may in practice be very difficult, if not appropriately addressed.

2.3.4.5 Internal Control Audit Committees and management shall review what additional internal controls are required by the adoption of a new comprehensive basis of accounting or by the use of dual reporting.

> **Comment:** This is relevant from several angles. Firstly, relevance and robustness of new data collected shall be assured. Secondly, management shall envisage what arbitrage opportunities exist under the new standards and identify ways to prevent them. To the extent a body of standards differs from that already adopted by a company, internal control check lists shall be amended. This also comprises consistency and efficiency of financial reporting.
>
> Additionally, SEC registrants based in Europe have to coordinate IFRS implementations with the U.S. Sarbanes-Oxley requirements. The existence of appropriate control over financial reporting under IFRSs should be demonstrated. Also, changes in internal controls from the IFRS migration project should be compliant with Sarbanes-Oxley. Importantly, to the extent a company is able to leverage on interdependencies between those two projects, their total costs would decrease.
>
> Further, to the extent business processes are affected, line and staff controls on efficiency and effectiveness of operations may necessitate amendment.
>
> Finally, audit committee members must assure the timeliness and quality of IFRS migration, through appropriate project management and regular feedback. They will be required to approve IFRS accounting policies and financial information.

---

[218] *The Institute of Chartered Accountants in England and Wales (ICAEW), 2007.* EU Implementation of IFRS and the Fair Value Directive, a Report for the European Commission, ¶ *Figure 4.22. [Online] London: ICAEW. Available at www.icaew.com/ecifrsstudy (last visited July 31, 2010).*

2.3.4.6 Auditing As to audit firms, the SEC highlighted[219] some effects, with reference to auditing and to reporting on the effectiveness of internal controls over financial reporting, that would arise if the use of IFRS were extended to U.S. issuers. In fact, auditing quality control systems would likely need amendment. Also, audit firms should decide whether the benefits of hiring new personnel and assigning to engagements, building competence, training and developing staff, and adequate supervision outweigh the investment. A firm's procedures should be updated accordingly. The lower level of experience that U.S. auditors have with IFRSs than with U.S. GAAP would initially likely require a greater effort. Certainly this is a challenge to the accounting industry. However, further new business may derive from being members of global audit networks, thanks to foreign affiliates of U.S. issuers or U.S. subsidiaries of foreign companies.

> **Planning Point:** In this context, the development of a practice of dual reporting may prevent those efforts from resulting in expensive professional charges to clients, who are always increasingly cost conscious. In fact, better time and result for money is achieved through a multidisciplinary and multi-chartered accounting environment that capitalizes on multiple-GAAP practices, as opposed to the traditional and costly approach of involving staff from the U.S. and European practices of a professional firm.

2.3.4.7 Human Resources The human resources impacts of IFRS migration are among the most important, as personnel is the base for the proper working of an enterprise. Worksheet 16 shows a check list of human resources implications of GAAP transition.

> **Comment:** Implications are twofold: Firstly, human resources department shall pursue some specific action plans. Secondly, interaction between staff across departments of a company is going to increase, because financial statements figures and disclosures should be sourced, captured, and verified based on structured and systematic inputs from operating departments.

Further human resources managers shall be satisfied that subsidiaries received proper communication, guidelines, and appropriate training programs.

On the other hand, as the SEC explains,[220] investors, CPAs, auditors, financial analysts, rating agencies, actuaries, valuation experts, professional associations, industry groups, and professors would also need training to understand and use IFRSs.

2.3.4.8 Communication and Investor Relationship Communication is of strategic importance to make all stakeholders understand the implications of IFRS migration and to manage their expectations and perceptions.

Investor relationship plays a fundamental role. In fact, CESR indicated a transition process made of four milestones, consisting of 2003 annual financial statements, 2004 annual or

---

[219] *Concept Release, pages 32–33.*
[220] *SEC Concept Release, pages 28–29. The Concept Release goes on to state that to date in the United States a comprehensive curriculum does not include IFRSs, and that eventually it may be appropriate to include it in the Uniform CPA Examination.*

interim financial statements, 2005 interim financial statements, and 2005 annual financial statements. CESR had already encouraged listed companies to include in 2003 financial statements narrative disclosure of migration plans, their status, and major differences with prior GAAP that they knew with sufficient certainty.[221]

Comment: Communication need not be limited to external and professional communication, as it also includes a warning to all the organization about the right weight to attribute to this stage of a company's life. Sometimes, communication will also be bottom up, leading from the CFO to top management and Boards of Directors, as the challenges of this step may be overlooked.

In more detail, a communication strategy involves:

- Drawing a communication plan to top management regarding needs, benefits, and costs of IFRSs, and the need to develop a clear transition strategy;
- Increasing awareness of key stakeholders within the company of how staff may be affected – particularly in respect to training;
- Communicating the financial effects of change to shareholders, financial analysts, employees, lenders, and other stakeholders.

Section 2.3.1.3 previously indicates some financial analysis implications on which companies should assure capital markets that the process is under control and that no surprises will arise. Unfortunately, as some surveys report,[222] communication to financial markets has not always been addressed to the appropriate level.

---

[221] *Committee of European Securities Regulators,* European Regulation on the Application of IFRS in 2005 – Recommendation for Additional Guidance Regarding the Transition to IFRS, *CESR/03-323e (December 2003), ¶¶ 11, 17, 18.*

[222] *For example, the survey Citigate Dewe Rogerson Fallonstewart,* The Adoption of International Financial Reporting Standards, Who should lead the way? *(March 2005) (last visited July 2006) www.non-execs.com, of the top 12 investment banks in London and their analysts, for combined market value accounting for over 70% of total market capitalization of the FTSE 100 indicated on page 1 a lack of companies' communication about IFRSs to almost a third of the sample and that only 18% of the sample were satisfied with the communication received. This survey also reports some recommendations to avoid misunderstandings and enhance the building of forecasting models on the company by financial analysts, such as early presentation of IFRS impact, even ahead of the mandatory deadlines, and in a manner that is customized to financial analysts, specific quantitative reconciliations, preparation of Questions & Answers sections, regular and pro-active communications, details on balance sheet and distributable reserves.*

3 RESERVES

3.1 TERMINOLOGY AND DEFINITIONS OF TERMS

3.1.1 U.S. GAAP Terminology and Practice

In U.S. accounting the word *reserves* should be used only for appropriations of retained earnings for general or specific purposes.[1] Appropriations of retained earnings must be displayed as part of stockholders' equity.[2] General purpose contingency reserves displayed as part of equity are examples.[3] However, somewhat inconsistently, the term *accounting reserve*, in its general meaning, sometimes refers to accruing or provisioning expenses for certain purposes to deduct from reported earnings.[4] In accounting practice, *reserve* is often used as a synonym for an accrual for estimated liabilities, or valuation allowance, or a specific asset valuation account, as *depreciation reserve*, *LIFO reserve*, or *bad debts reserve*.[5] Forensic accounting language expands from that (e.g., *cookie jar reserves*[6]), to mean unrealistically estimated liabilities to stabilize earnings across years. A different utilization of this word exists in the sense of deferred credit.[7] The use of the term *reserve* can also be found in the sense of contingent liability or provision in the balance sheet or in the income statement,[8] sometimes with special meaning. This is the case of *reserve for bad debts* and *general reserves* as used in the Internal Revenue Code,[9] *catastrophe reserve accounting*,[10] or *general reserves* of stock savings and loan associations[11] or with reference to insurance.[12] According to the *AICPA Accounting Trends & Techniques* the term *reserve* appeared in 2009 and 2005 for 68% and 73% of companies surveyed, respectively (66% in 2002), to describe accruals (10% and 19% for estimated expenses relating to property abandonment or discontinued operations, 11% and 14% for environmental costs, 8% and 13% for warranty, 11% in both years for insurance, 10% and 9% for litigation, and 4% and 7% for employee benefits and others) and for 32% and 27%, respectively (44% in 2002), to describe deductions from assets (9% for LIFO allowance, 8% and 9% for inventory obsolescence, 10% and 4% for doubtful accounts, and 5% for others).[13]

---

[1] *The Committee on Terminology of the AICPA, Accounting Terminology Bulletin No. 1, Review and Resume, ¶¶ 59.3, 60.*

[2] *FASB ASC 505-10-45-3 (FASB Statement No. 5, ¶ 15).*

[3] *ARB 43, Appendix B, ¶ 8.*

[4] *In this sense, FASB ASC 450-20-05-9 (FASB Statement No. 5, ¶ 65).*

[5] *In this sense, Accounting Terminology Bulletin No. 1, ¶ 59.1.*

[6] *A. Levitt,* The Numbers Game, *Remarks to New York University Center for Law and Business, page 4 (September 29, 1998).*

[7] *CON 6, ¶ 97.*

[8] *Accounting Terminology Bulletin No. 1, ¶¶ 59.2, 59.4.*

[9] *FASB ASC 942-740-05-2 (APB Opinion No. 23, Accounting for Income Taxes – Special Areas, Footnote 8).*

[10] *FASB Statement No. 5, ¶ 92.*

[11] *APB Opinion No. 23, ¶ 1.*

[12] *Accounting Terminology Bulletin No. 1, ¶ 59.2.*

[13] *Calderisi, M. C., Bowman, D., and Cohen, D., eds, 2010. Accounting Trends & Techniques. 64th edn. New York: AICPA, ¶ Table 2-32 (hereinafter AICPA ATT 2010); Lofe, Y. and Calderisi, M. C., eds., 2006. Accounting Trends & Techniques. 60th edn. New York: AICPA, ¶ Table 2-32 (hereinafter AICPA ATT 2006).*

3.1.2   IFRS Terminology

Unlike certain U.S. GAAP pronouncements, IFRSs do not associate the term *reserve* with accruals, provisions, or contingent liabilities.

Comment: In fact, the word *reserve* is not even mentioned in IAS 37. The only occurrences in this sense can be found incidentally in IFRS 4 and IAS 39, when treating impairment or bad debt losses on financial assets.[14]

The IASB Framework characterizes reserves as logical subclassifications within equity,[15] somewhat similar to the notion that ATB 1 proposed.[16] Some IFRS standards make this point absolutely clear. In fact, IFRS 4 prohibits insurance catastrophe or equalization provisions for claims that are not in existence at the reporting date and considers those reserves as appropriations of retained earnings, and therefore a component of equity, not liabilities. Similarly, IAS 30, now superseded, prohibited provisions for amounts set aside for general banking risks and required disclosure as appropriations of retained earnings.[17]

Comment: Components of equity are notional subclassifications. In fact, under the residual theory of equity (Section 2.1.4.1 previously), adopted by the IASB Framework and the U.S. Concepts, equity is a single amount. On a practical basis, however, a company manages equity based on its subcomponents.

In its implementation of this concept, IAS 1 mentions *issued capital and reserves* as one of the minimum line items for display on the face of the statement of financial position.[18] A "reserves" subclassification within equity may be displayed separately or disclosed in the notes, including details of nature and purposes.[19] As for each of the other components of equity, the statement of changes in equity must separately show period changes to reconcile beginning and ending balances.[20]

Comment: IFRSs generally do not often use the term *reserve*. For example, expressions like *revaluation surplus* are preferred to *revaluation reserve* (however, this term is used). Additionally, the example of statement of financial position in the Implementation Guidance IG6 of IAS 1 (revised 2007) amended the previously used term *other reserves* to *other components of equity*.

---

[14]   *IAS 39, ¶ Implementation Guidance, E.4.6 (deleted by IFRS 9). However, IASB Update December 2002 and IASB Update July 2003 also use the term* reserve account *for allowance account.*

[15]   The Conceptual Framework for Financial Reporting 2010, ¶ 4.20; IASB Framework, ¶ 65.

[16]   *Accounting Terminology Bulletin No. 1, ¶¶ 69.4, 69.5.*

[17]   *International Financial Reporting Standards No. 4,* Insurance Contracts, *¶¶ 14, IG58, BC89; IAS 30, ¶ 30.*

[18]   *IAS 1, ¶ 54.*

[19]   *IAS 1, ¶ 78–79.*

[20]   *IAS 1, ¶ 106.*

> **Comment:** The term *reserve* as component of equity is used by the EU and is current practice in some European jurisdictions. For example, in the United Kingdom, companies use a tabular disclosure of movements on reserves.

3.2   RECONCILIATION

3.2.1   Reserves Versus Provisions

As mentioned, sometimes the U.S. practice gives to the term *reserve* a connotation of contingent liability while IFRSs treats it as a component of equity.

Mixed meanings have been adopted in some continental European countries, to assimilate expressions like accrued warranty, valuation allowance, at lower of cost or market valuation, negative goodwill, inventory obsolescence, sales returns, and accruals for fiscal and legal claims to "reserves." The term *fund* is often used as a substitute for *reserve* (e.g., severance fund). Pre-IAS 37 practices in some countries have seen profit-smoothing abuses consisting of provisioning for future losses and expenses, for generic risks, general reserves, or classifying in extraordinary items in order to minimize the adverse impact of events, or accruing based on management intentions. IAS 37 prevented these practices through making present obligation a prerequisite for a provision. Although the first-time adoption of IFRSs has caused the restating of such reserves, sometimes local terminology for *reserve* is still in effect for both components of equity and contingent liabilities.

3.2.2   Reserves Versus Other Components of Equity

The term *reserve* under IFRSs is undefined, although extensively used.

> **Comment:** The IASB Framework does not define what *reserves* do include or exclude, as opposed to other elements of equity. It simply mentions funds contributed by shareholders, retained earnings, and reserves, part of which may consist of appropriations of retained earnings.[21] By contrast, IAS 1 seems to apply the term extensively to all equity other than issued capital.[22] Arguably, along this line, 1) components of equity arising from capital surplus, such as share premium; and 2) components of other comprehensive income would be denoted as "reserves." This seems to be confirmed by the fact that the sample statement of financial position in IAS 1 illustrates shareholders' equity as made of share capital, retained earnings, and other components of equity, while the previous version of IAS 1 mentioned share capital, other reserves, and retained earnings as components of equity: components of equity other than share capital and retained earnings would then also be characterized as reserves.

3.2.3   Reserves Versus Additional Paid-In Capital

Reserves other than retained earnings under IFRSs would correspond to different items under U.S. GAAP. One of these is additional paid-in capital under U.S. GAAP.

---

[21]   The Conceptual Framework for Financial Reporting 2010, ¶ 4.20; IASB Framework, ¶ 65.

[22]   IAS 1, ¶ 54.

> **Comment:** Share premium is a reserve under IFRSs (as opposed to issued capital), while it is part of contributed capital under U.S. GAAP. This conclusion seems to be confirmed by the illustration of the statement of changes in equity in the Implementation Guidance of the December 2005 revision of IAS 1 that shows in a column format share capital, *other reserves* (or each separately, if material), translation reserve, and retained earnings. Thus, other reserves include all components of equity where not otherwise indicated.

3.2.4 Reserves Versus Other Comprehensive Income

Reserves under IFRSs may also correspond to a second component under U.S. GAAP: other comprehensive income.

> **Comment:** To illustrate, in amending the statement of changes in equity, the Implementation Guidance of the September 2007 revision of IAS 1 shows separate columns for individual components of accumulated other comprehensive income (such as columns for translation of foreign operations, available-for-sale financial assets, cash flow hedges, revaluation surplus) in place of the former term *reserves*. The Implementation Guidance of IAS 39 also referred to *available-for-sale reserve.*[23]

It is also to be noted that under certain circumstances the EC Directives use reserves for certain items that U.S. GAAP would classify as other comprehensive income.

> **Example:** EC Directive 2001/65 amends EC Directive 78/660 to require a fair value reserve within equity for a cash flow hedge through financial instruments that are measured at fair value or for a net investment in a foreign operation. It leaves EU Member States free to use such fair value reserve for nonderivative available-for-sale financial instruments.[24]

Finally, IAS 16 permits a direct transfer from revaluation surplus to retained earnings (see Section 6.6.1 later) for the difference between depreciation at revalued carrying amount and at historical cost of the corresponding item of property, plant, and equipment.[25]

> **Comment:** The standard does not comment this treatment. A traditional defense of capital theory would justify it as a revaluation surplus (unrealized) that becomes retained earnings (realized). Alternatively, this concept could be seen as an appropriated amount that becomes unappropriated (and therefore distributable). The latter interpretation brings to mind the U.S. GAAP approach that does not permit the revaluation model for long-lived assets (Section 7.16 later), but permits an appropriation for replacement of fixed assets in case current values largely differ from historical cost.[26]

---

[23] *IAS 39, ¶ Implementation Guidance E.4.10 (deleted by IFRS 9).*

[24] *EC Directive 2001/65 (September 27, 2001), Art. 1, which also introduces the Art. 42-quater into EC Directive 78/660.*

[25] *IAS 16, ¶ 41.*

[26] *ARB 43,* Restatement and Revision of Accounting Research Bulletins, *Ch.9A, ¶ 6.*

3.2.5 Reserves Versus Retained Earnings

Under IFRSs, retained earnings would also be part of reserves.

> **Comment:** IAS 1 (December 2005) referred to "other reserves" (reserves other than retained earnings).

> **Comment:** As said, the IASB Framework includes appropriations of retained earnings in the notion of reserves. Subtopic 450-20 (FASB Statement No. 5) also includes appropriations of retained earnings in equity, although (unlike ATB 1[27]) it does not name them as *reserves*.

> **Comment:** According to certain local GAAP (for example in certain European countries), retained earnings are naturally classified as a reserve created from profit.

3.3   TYPES OF RESERVES

The IASB Framework generally classifies reserves as either appropriations of retained earnings or capital maintenance adjustments.[28]

By means of examples,[29] it subclassifies appropriations of retained earnings as:

- Reserves required by corporate legal requirements;
- Statutory reserves, that is, determined by statute or other law (or, depending on jurisdictions, by the articles of incorporation or bylaws);
- Tax reserves, required for the company to get tax reductions or exemptions generally in connection with their distribution, deficit reorganization, or other different applications of those reserves.

As to capital maintenance adjustments (Section 7.6.3 later), the IASB Framework[30] states revaluation reserve, also called revaluation surplus, as an example. In its implementation of the IASB Framework, IFRSs also expand the term *reserve* to other income and expenses that are recognized in other comprehensive income.[31]

Many EU Member States, as well as some other countries, have a long history in reserve accounting. In practice, although classification of reserves depends on each jurisdiction, generally certain common logical categories exist.

A first classification distinguishes reserves according to the authority that has jurisdiction. Legal reserves are those required by the law under which the company is incorporated.

---

[27] *Accounting Terminology Bulletin No. 1,* ¶¶ *59.3, 69.4.*
[28] The Conceptual Framework for Financial Reporting 2010, ¶ *4.20; IASB Framework,* ¶ *65.*
[29] The Conceptual Framework for Financial Reporting 2010, ¶ *4.21; IASB Framework,* ¶ *66.*
[30] The Conceptual Framework for Financial Reporting 2010, ¶ *4.36; IASB Framework,* ¶ *81; IAS 1,* ¶¶ *IG10.*
[31] *In this sense, IAS 39,* ¶ *Implementation Guidance E.4.10 (deleted by IFRS 9) referred to* available-for-sale reserve. *IFRS 1,* ¶ *IG Example 11 (before amendments by IFRS 9) and IFRIC 1,* ¶ *BC29 also use the term* revaluation reserve.

Statutory reserves may exist insofar as corporate statutes, articles of incorporation, or bylaws permit them. Finally, contingency and general reserves may be determined by the shareholders' meeting once the mandatory reserves of the other two sources have been appropriated.

> **Comment:** Statutory reverses should not be confused with legal reserves: in countries where law dictates some accounting, legal reserves are mandated by the operation of law, while "statutory" reserves generally originate from the provisions of bylaws. By contrast, in countries where the state determines accounting by statute, the two kinds of reserves are likely to be used as synonymous with each other. For contingency reserves, again terminology changes from country to country, as sometimes contingency reserves are also based on the provisions of corporate bylaws.

> **Example:** The appropriation of a reserve of 10% of net income annually until this reserve amounts to 50% of the company's equity is common in some Middle Eastern jurisdictions.

> **Example:** In Japan, a legal reserve must be formed from at least 10% out of earnings until it amounts to 25% of capital stock.

> **Example:** In the Netherlands, shareholders' equity is composed of issued capital, share premium, revaluation reserves, reserves defined by the articles of associations, and undistributed profit.

A second categorization sees reserves divided, according to their sources, into capital reserves and income reserves (also called revenue reserves, or reserves created from profit). The former category results from contributed capital, i.e., shareholders' contributions. Typically, in certain jurisdictions these reserves include share premium (called additional paid-in capital in the U.S.), which corresponds to the amount contributed in excess of the shares' par or stated value, and other sorts of paid-in capital accounts (see Chapter 5 later). They may comprise legal reserve, in countries where law ties its annual changes to a certain percentage of share capital, and certain revaluation reserve required by special laws. Income reserves generally arise from appropriations of retained earnings or from items that were accounted for in the determination of net income or comprehensive income. Examples are legal reserve when it is created annually based on the amount of net income, and reserves appropriated from net income or retained earnings on a discretionary basis for specific purposes (e.g., to pay bonuses to employees or management, or to appropriate an amount in excess of the accumulated depreciation required by GAAP in consideration of replacing or enhancing certain fixed assets).

> **Comment:** Although U.S. GAAP does not use the term *reserve* as components of equity, a similar segregation by sources of equity may be found in the U.S. Concepts. In fact, the invested and earned equity model (see Section 2.1.4.2 previously) distinguishes equity in the two sources of contributed capital and earned capital.[32] ATB 1 supported a display by source of equity, namely legal capital, additional paid-in capital, and retained earnings.[33]

---

[32] *CON 6, ¶ 212.*
[33] *Accounting Terminology Bulletin No. 1*, Review and Resume, ¶¶ 65–66, 68, 69.2.

A third taxonomy discriminates reserves according to their use. They may be restricted, that is not available for distribution except as provided by law or until they reach a certain threshold. Other reserves may be free and distributable. Generally, legal reserves are also restricted. Reserves may also have different treatment depending on whether or not they can be capitalized (transferred to capital accounts), or used for deficit reorganization.

> **Example:** Accounting in Norway has a twofold classification of equity: as arising from paid-in capital or retained earnings, and as free or restricted capital.

Finally, reserves may have special nomenclature based on their tax treatment (see Section 3.5.4 following).

3.4 TRACKING OF EQUITY

The use of reserve accounting makes tracking of changes in equity operationally complex. Sometimes, unless sophisticated accounting is used, tracing the creation and use of income versus capital reserves may become impossible, and in any case arbitrary. CON 6 acknowledges this point, as sources of equity of invested versus earned capital may become intricately mixed in the case of transactions or events such as stock dividends or treasury stock transactions.[34]

> **Example:** Worksheet 17 illustrates the classification of equity reserves for financial statement purposes in Italy. As may be seen from the Worksheet, the main purpose of reserve accounting in that country is the preservation of principles of distributability of profit for the period, income reserves, capital and capital reserves, and their interaction with deficit reorganization and the capitalization of reserves. The intricacy of the subject may be seen from the number of meanings the term *reserves* may have, depending on whether it is used in respect of defense of capital, tax, conservatism, or other purposes.

3.5 FUNCTION OF RESERVES

The sources that require the creation of certain reserves may vary, depending on specific jurisdictions, as well as the functions that such reserves would serve. Generally, the function of legal reserves, and under certain circumstances of statutory reserves, may be twofold: 1) for the purpose of disclosing sources from which the capital was derived; and 2) for the purpose of defense of capital (either through reserves or appropriations of retained earnings). This Section also analyzes additional rationales.

3.5.1 Sources of Equity

Disclosure of sources of capital is an objective of stockholders' equity accounting that is served under both U.S. GAAP and IFRSs through display on the face of the financial statements or note disclosure of capital accounts.[35] Presentation by sources of equity was reaffirmed by

---

[34] *CON 6, ¶ 212.*
[35] *FASB ASC 505-10-50-3 (FASB Statement No. 129, ¶ 4); IAS 1, ¶ 79.*

ATB 1.[36] Furthermore, the IASB Framework acknowledges that the use of equity subclassifications may be a way to discriminate dividend or liquidating rights of different classes of ownership interests.[37]

3.5.2 Defense of Legal Capital

3.5.2.1 The Concept of Defense of Legal Capital   The notion of defense of legal capital refers to all means that may assure the preservation of legal capital under the business corporation laws in the specific jurisdiction where a company is incorporated. From the viewpoint of a defense of legal capital, legal capital is the portion of equity that remains available for the satisfaction of creditor's claims. The remainder of such capital only may be returned to shareholders. Therefore, equity is seen as a cushion to absorb real and potential losses: the higher the level of this cushion, the better the position of creditors. Although protection of creditors is the main focus, shareholders are also protected against actions by the directors that might reduce their interest.

> **Comment:** Based on the notion of defense of capital, the segregation of components of equity intends to give creditors and other stakeholders a sort of protection against losses. A reserve, or an appropriation of retained earnings, under this category generally signals restrictions on distributable income sources.[38] Protection would derive from enhanced disclosure and from avoidance of distribution of funds corresponding to the appropriated amount (Section 3.7 later expands this topic). Although this is usually a legal or corporate governance issue, it may affect accounting, especially where financial reporting derives from a legal framework in the context of the relevant laws of the state where the company is chartered. In fact, defense of legal capital is one of the main rationales for legal and statutory reserves.

3.5.2.2 Implications of Defense of Legal Capital   This Section is not a comprehensive illustration of the basic notion of defense of legal capital, but it offers a highlight of some of its accounting implications.

First of all, a minimum level of capital stock may be required depending on the jurisdiction.

> **Example:** Directive 77/91/EEC on the formation of public limited-liability companies and the maintenance and alteration of their capital requires a minimum subscribed capital of 25,000 ECUs, to be revised every five years by the European Council.[39]

In addition, stock may be required to have a par value. Par value is a basic concept in defense of legal capital, which is at the origin of a capital reserve such as additional paid-in capital.

> **Example:** In the U.S., defense of legal capital requirements are specified at state law level. In states where a share must have a par value, the excess amount at which stock is issued is credited to

---

[36] *Accounting Terminology Bulletin No. 1,* Review and Resume, ¶ *68.*
[37] The Conceptual Framework for Financial Reporting 2010, ¶ *4.20; IASB Framework, ¶ 65.*
[38] *IFRIC 2, ¶ A13 uses the term* reserve *with this meaning (i.e.,* distributable reserves*).*
[39] *Directive 77/91/EEC, Art 6.*

additional paid-in capital. Although the articles of incorporation may state a par value for shares, the Model Business Corporation Act has removed the distinction between par value and the excess that goes to additional paid-in capital. In states that have adopted those provisions, directors may decide to issue no-par value stock. When no-par value stock is issued, stated capital is credited with the entire proceeds of the issue unless directors allocate an amount to capital surplus. If a stated value is determined by the Board of Directors, such value is accounted for in the same way as for par value. The Board of Directors must resolve that the consideration exchanged for the issuance of shares is adequate. Directors' valuation of stated value is conclusive unless fraud is proved.[40]

Whether or not shares may be issued at a discount also falls under defense of capital rules. The main meaning of requiring consideration not to be lower than par value is to avoid watered stock, which is when stock exceeds the consideration exchanged for its issuance. If the corporation becomes insolvent, original shareholders remain liable for this difference in amount.

Example: The Directive 77/91/EEC on the formation of public limited-liability companies and the maintenance and alteration of their capital requires that shares are not issued for less than their nominal or par value.[41]

Example: Under the Companies Amendment Act 37 of 1999 in South Africa, a discount issue is permitted provided that terms are established by a special resolution, for already-issued classes of shares, with court approval, and subject to some timing constraints.

Example: The 2004 corporate law reform in Italy has permitted the previously-prohibited issuance of stock at face value below par, provided the overall consideration exceeds nominal value of stock.

Example: In the U.S. an original discount issue (stock sold below par) would be accounted for by debiting a "discount on issue" account. This makes users of financial statements aware of the contingent liability of shareholders.

Distributability of retained earnings and of income reserves must also follow certain restrictive criteria. Distributability of profit might be restricted to amounts that are earned, realized, existing as of the balance sheet date, resulting from issued and approved or audited financial statements. The foundation of such a tenet is that only earned income can be distributed through dividends. Otherwise, the true wealth of a corporation would be reduced and creditors would be potentially damaged in their claims.

Comment: In the U.S. in a context of defense of legal capital (but not under the Model Business Corporation Act that has eliminated the difference between stated capital and surplus) or of aged accounting terminology, the term *surplus* generally indicates the excess of net assets over stated capital.

---

[40] *American Bar Foundation,* Model Business Corporation Act, *Subchapter B,* § *6.21 (c) (2003).*
[41] *Directive 77/91/EEC, Art 8.*

Earned surplus is usually used for retained earnings, and *capital surplus* for surplus minus earned surplus, generally to correspond to additional paid-in capital.[42] For criticism on such terminology, see Section 5.1 and Section 6.1.1 later.

Example: Distribution of dividends to shareholders in excess of earned surplus (retained earnings) is prohibited in some U.S. states. Others permit a liquidating dividend (distribution out of capital surplus), provided it is allowed by bylaws and approved by shareholders. A corporation would not be able to declare dividends if this impeded paying its debts as they become due in the usual course of business. In addition, in states adopting the Model Business Corporation Act, net assets, after deduction of the rights that preferential shareholders would have upon dissolution, must be positive after the dividend distribution. However, the Board of Directors would be able to distribute dividends out of unrealized appreciation if it determined and disclosed that the fair value of net assets remained positive after such distribution.[43]

Example: Tests similar to the two mentioned above (liquidity test and solvency test) are also required for payment of dividends under the Companies Amendment Act 37 of 1999 in South Africa.

Example: In the United Kingdom, under common law, a distribution out of capital is unlawful. Under FRS 18, *Accounting Policies*, a profit is realized when converted to cash or other assets of reasonably certain cash realization. TECH 3/07, *Guidance on The Determination of Realised Profits and Losses in the Context of Distributions Under The Companies Act 1985*, by The Institute of Chartered Accountants in England and Wales and by The Institute of Chartered Accountants of Scotland, provides the basic guidance on principles of realization.

Example: Under Directive 77/91/EEC, no distribution to shareholders can result in a decrease of subscribed capital and undistributable reserves, and it cannot exceed approved profits and reserves available for distribution.[44]

Comment: IAS 29 requires an entity that operates in an economy that has become hyperinflationary to restate the components of equity, except retained earnings and revaluation surplus, by applying a general price index from the date.[45] In case these revaluations are not permitted under a specific jurisdiction they would be considered undistributable. The entity would provide appropriate disclosures.

Depending on jurisdictions, acquisition of treasury shares may fall under defense of capital provisions. These may also include prohibition or constraints to the company giving direct or indirect financial assistance for the purchase or subscription of such shares, as this

---

[42] *The terms* earned surplus *and* capital surplus *are also used in some authoritative literature, such as ARB 43, Ch. 1A, ¶ 3; ARB 43, Ch. 1B, ¶ 5.*
[43] *American Bar Foundation,* Model Business Corporation Act, *Subchapter D, § 6.40 (c) (2003).*
[44] *Directive 77/91/EEC, Art 15.*
[45] *IAS 29, ¶¶ 24–25.*

would result in the company being creditor of money that had been used to purchase its own shares.

Example: The accounting for treasury stock under U.S. GAAP is treated in Section 4.14 later. Nevertheless, some U.S. states require debiting retained earnings for total purchased amount of treasury stock or accounting for the excess purchase cost over the amount of common stock as a distribution to shareholders similar to dividends.

Comment: In some states, a requirement for appropriation of retained earnings in case of acquisition of treasury stock may be based on the fact that such purchase reduces the availability of retained earnings for declaration of dividends.

Example: Under the Companies Amendment Act 37 of 1999 in South Africa the acquisition of treasury shares, provided it is authorized by the articles of incorporation and adopted through a special resolution, is permitted provided the liquidity test and the solvency test, similarly to the case of payment of dividends, are reasonably met.

Example: In Italy purchase of treasury shares is permitted, provided some rules are followed. In particular, the amount purchased shall not exceed distributable profits and free and available reserves based on the latest approved financial statements; a special report by the Board of Directors is required; the Board of Directors must stay within the main terms and limits of purchase that are decided by the shareholders' meeting; fully paid shares only may be purchased; the par value amount purchased must not exceed 10% of capital stock; the number and par value of shares purchased, held, and sold must be disclosed; and an undistributable reserve must be appropriated for the corresponding amount.[46]

Example: In the United Kingdom, before the Companies Act 2006 became law, financial assistance to buy a private company's own shares was prohibited, unless a "whitewash" procedure was followed.

Priority may be established in order for reserves to be used to offset a loss of the period or a deficit in retained earnings. In addition, depending on jurisdiction, the return of capital and of capital reserves may be prohibited for a company not in liquidation, or special criteria may be set out.

Example: The interaction of principles of distributability and procedures for deficit reorganization may be very complex. Worksheet 17 illustrates how intricate the implementation of legal capital concepts may be in jurisdictions, like Italy, where accounting has a legal derivation or translates into requirements that are sanctioned from a legal standpoint.

Example: From October 2009, in the United Kingdom, the Companies Act of 2006 will permit reduction of share capital by special resolution supported by a solvency statement by directors.

---

[46] *Italian Civil Code, Art. 2357, 2357-ter.*

> **Example:** In response to the SEC Staff with reference to its Form 20-F for the fiscal year ended December 31, 2005 containing financial statements prepared for the first time on the basis of IFRSs, a British foreign private issuer explained that in the United Kingdom share premium account and capital redemption reserve may be offset against a retained earnings deficit, with the excess credited to a nondistributable special reserve. This requires the approval of the High Court of England and Wales and certain undertakings by the company for the sake of protection of existing creditors.[47]

Depending on jurisdiction, capitalization of earnings (transfer of retained earnings or income reserves to capital accounts) may be allowed under certain circumstances. This point has twofold relevance for defense of capital: firstly, stricter rules generally apply to distribution of capital as opposed to distribution of retained earnings; in addition, particular procedures may then be envisioned to prevent schemes to distribute formerly-appropriated earnings subsequently pretending to be return of capital.

> **Example:** Worksheet 17 also illustrates the ranking of reserve sources that may be capitalized in Italy.

> **Example:** Under U.S. GAAP, in case of small stock dividends (when the issuance of shares does not reduce the per-unit price by more than 20–25% of the outstanding shares before declaration), retained earnings are capitalized on the grounds that the market perceives it as a distribution of dividend. Capitalization is here considered a mechanism in defense of the public interest in avoiding possible future distributions of such retained earnings.[48] Furthermore, states that require maintenance of stated capital generally make capitalization of retained earnings in case of stock dividends mandatory.

Certain disclosures of capital adequacy are illustrated in Section 4.6 later.

3.5.2.3 Defense of Legal Capital Versus Capital Maintenance The notion of defense of capital must not be confused with capital maintenance, although the two are related. The confusion may arise from the fact that the former is sometimes referred to as "maintenance of stated capital." As an example, the Simplification of Capital Maintenance EC Directive (2206/68/EC) uses such an expression with the meaning of defense of capital. Capital maintenance refers to whether an increase or decrease of capital maintains the original wealth and the relationship with the profit or loss for the period. This follows one accounting view and is discussed in Section 7.6 later. Defense of capital relates to the way corporate business law may prevent capital from being illegally reduced or not maintained. This is a corporate governance and business law view.

3.5.2.4 Defense of Legal Capital and Other Comprehensive Income Section 7.5.7 later illustrates the fundamental impact that recognition in other comprehensive income may have on profit distributability or quasi-reorganization procedures in jurisdictions when defense of capital is heavily enforced in the legal environment.

---

[47] *Letter by the SEC, File No. 1-15206, Note 25 (December 12, 2006). Reply by the company (January 20, 2007) www.sec.gov/divisions/corpfin/ifrs_reviews (last visited January 7, 2008).*

[48] *FASB ASC 505-20-30-3, 505-20-05-2 (ARB 43, Ch. 7B, ¶ 10).*

3.5.3 Appropriations of Retained Earnings

Appropriations are segregations of retained earnings. Their main purpose is to disclose that a portion of retained earnings is restricted or nondistributable.

3.5.3.1 Accounting for Appropriations An appropriation must not be confused with any setting aside of assets. It simply results in an accounting entry. Under U.S. GAAP it is permitted as long as it is clearly identified as an appropriation of retained earnings within the stockholders' equity section.[49] ATB 1 already supported the presentation of transfers to restricted capital by resolution of the Board of Directors, amounts restricted as to withdrawal and other sorts of appropriations in the equity section of the balance sheet and the illustration of such reductions in the retained earnings caption.[50] An appropriation must then eventually be reversed to retained earnings. The nature of, and reasons for, restriction and the amount of appropriation and changes thereof must be disclosed.

An appropriation is never debited/credited to net income or results of operations.[51] The actual amount of the expense incurred or gains/losses resulting from transactions and events in reference to which the appropriation was made is irrelevant to the amount to be reversed, which must always equal the amount that had been appropriated (debit: appropriated retained earnings; credit: retained earnings or unappropriated retained earnings).

Under U.S. GAAP, banks and similar financial institutions must show any general purpose contingency reserve under stockholders' equity.[52]

Section 210-10-S99 (Regulation S-X)[53] requires separate display of appropriated and unappropriated retained earnings. It also requires disclosure on the face of the appropriate statement or in notes of the most significant restrictions, other than those referring to preferred shares, on the payment of dividends by the registrant, indicating their sources, their pertinent provisions, the amount of retained earnings or net income restricted or free of restrictions, and the amount of consolidated retained earnings which represents undistributed earnings of 50% or less owned persons accounted for by the equity method.[54]

3.5.3.2 Minimum Dividends The AICPA International Practices Task Force interpreted that retained earnings required to be distributed should be considered temporary equity, as in the case of certain jurisdictions. For example, Chilean companies are required to distribute 30% of their net income to shareholders unless a majority of shareholders approves the retention of the profits. Consistently with the new developments concerning equity versus financial liability classification after the issuance of FASB Statement No. 150, the SEC Staff clarified its preference for presentation of minimum dividends as a liability.[55]

---

[49] *FASB ASC 505-10-45-3 (FASB Statement No. 5, ¶ 15).*
[50] *Accounting Terminology Bulletin No. 1,* Review and Resume, *¶¶ 68, 69.4, 69.5.*
[51] *FASB ASC 505-10-45-4 (FASB Statement No. 5, ¶ 15); FASB ASC 505-10-25-2 (APB Opinion No. 9, Reporting the Results of Operations, ¶ 28).*
[52] *ARB 43, Appendix B, ¶ 8.*
[53] *FASB ASC 210-10-S99-1 (Regulation S-X, ¶ 210.5-02).*
[54] *FASB ASC 235-10-S99-1 (Regulation S-X, ¶ 210.4-08(e)).*
[55] *AICPA International Practices Task Force, August 15, 1996, ¶ VIII; AICPA International Practices Task Force, November 22, 2005, ¶ 8; AICPA International Practices Task Force, March 7, 2006, ¶ 2; AICPA International Practices Task Force, November 21, 2006, Discussion Document F; U.S.*

> **Comment:** Local GAAP of certain European countries account for minimum dividends as appropriations of retained earnings. The rationale for temporary equity treatment is that such a distribution is beyond the control of the company, while appropriations of retained earnings generally assume (but not necessarily) a voluntary company resolution. Unlike both these treatments, liability classification reduces net income and total equity.

3.5.3.3 Sources of Appropriations The sources for appropriations may arise from legal requirements, contractual requirements (such as compliance with the terms of a bond indenture), or determination by the Board of Directors (such as for internally financed expansion, or anticipation of losses, or general purpose contingency reserve).

> **Comment:** Generally, appropriating retained earnings for dividends in arrears, which are not considered a liability, is considered not to be correct. The same applies to cash restricted for retirement of bonds, unless segregation is required by law or by the Board of Directors. In some states, an appropriation is required at purchase of treasury stock, to be released upon reissuance. This is based on the fact that such purchase reduces availability of retained earnings for declaration of dividends. However, the amount of appropriation may also depend on the accounting method used. In fact, if the cost method is used (see Section 4.14.5 later) and a beginning balance of the paid-in capital – treasury stock account already exists, no appropriation would be required in some states. Such appropriation would be needed under the par-value method, as in this case the account paid-in capital – common stock, would be used. An allocation corresponding to accumulated depreciation is considered acceptable for common interest realty associations that are cooperatives. Common interest realty associations that use non-fund reporting show fund for major repairs and replacements presented as appropriation of retained earnings.[56]

3.5.3.4 Are Income Taxes a Form of Appropriation? As part of the *Financial Statement Presentation Project*, the IASB Staff considered income taxes as a form of appropriation of income to tax authorities, before the remainder is retained within the entity.[57]

> **Comment:** This analysis is placed in the context of methods of presentation of income taxes in the financial statements, and the term "appropriation" is here used with reference to income and not to retained earnings. In the traditional context, however, income taxes are not appropriations. In fact, they enter into the determination of income and are not a segregation of retained earnings. They are transactions with non-owners, unlike retained earnings that are ultimately distributed to shareholders. Finally, from a different angle, tax payments are mandatory, while dividends are discretionary.

3.5.3.5 Appropriations Versus Defense of Capital An appropriation of retained earnings is of a disclosing nature. In other words, it is a technical tool for defense of capital.

    Securities and Exchange Commission, International Reporting and Disclosure Issues in the Division of Corporate Finance, *Appendix A,* Country Specific Issues *(November 1, 2004) www.sec.gov (last visited April 26, 2006).*

[56] *FASB ASC 972-205-45-5, 972-205-50-1 (AICPA Accounting and Audit Guide,* Common Interest Realty Associations, *¶¶ 4.02, 9.12).*

[57] *IASB Meeting, September 19, 2006, Agenda Paper 9,* Application of Working Principles, *¶¶ 52, 58 (September 2006).*

3.5.4   Influence of Taxation

The degree of freedom or, vice versa, constraints exerted by tax laws on accounting principles varies with jurisdictions. For example, Germany and Italy have a tradition of a close relationship between tax and financial reporting, while United Kingdom provides several discrepancies. Depending on such relationships, taxation rules may require special treatment in accounts, and especially the creation of specific reserves.

Certain jurisdictions have special classification of reserves for tax purposes.[58]

> **Example:** In Scandinavia there is a way of openly showing hidden reserves intended to reduce taxation, such as excess depreciation or undervaluation of assets, in a special caption of "untaxed reserves" that is classified between equity and liabilities or alternatively presented partly in equity and partly in deferred taxes. Changes in such reserves are transferred to the income statement and affect the determination of taxable income.

In certain jurisdictions expenses must be accounted in financial statements in order to be deductible for tax purposes. The use of tax criteria for financial reporting purposes and the need for accounting on the books in order to minimize tax often determine the creation of hidden reserves by applying tax accelerated depreciation rates or prudent valuation of assets.

Finally, one tax objective is generally to recapture tax on hidden reserves or on distributions of profits. This results in certain tax laws mandating special classifications of reserves in the balance sheet. For this purpose, sometimes reserves may be considered appropriated or "frozen" for tax purposes, unless tax is computed and paid on them, in which case they become free and add up to income reserves. Section 8.2.17.4 later expands this topic.

> **Example:** In response to the SEC's review of Form 20-F of an Italian foreign private issuer for the year ended December 31, 2005 containing financial statements prepared for the first time on the basis of IFRSs, the company explained that certain reserves were recorded separately in shareholders' equity as taxable upon distribution.[59]

3.5.5   The IFRS Approach

Under the IASB Framework, subcassifications of equity – whether legal, statutory, regulatory, agreement-based, tax-imposed, standard-based (e.g., revaluation surplus) or voluntary – may have varied informative reasons, such as to indicate undistributability of profits, different owners' rights to dividends and capital distributions, appropriations of accumulated profit, logical segregation of funds, capital maintenance adjustments, or similar purposes. However, although IFRSs require some reserves (see Section 3.6.1 following), it mandates no defense of legal capital or appropriations of retained earnings.

---

[58] *Classification of reserves for tax purposes falls beyond the scope of this Book.*

[59] *Letter by the SEC, File No. 333-12334, Note 13 (September 26, 2006). Reply by the company (October 20, 2006) www.sec.gov/divisions/corpfin/ifrs_reviews (last visited January 7, 2008).*

Comment: The decision on whether or not reserves should exist is considered not to be a matter for GAAP, but of national legislation, taxation, corporate governance, or business decision. However, once a need for reserves is established, the IASB Framework permits, or better welcomes, their disclosure as it deems them relevant in assisting informational needs of users of financial statements.[60]

Planning Point: However, IAS 1 does require some disclosures, irrespective of legal requirements, which are not intended to replace regulatory disclosures, on the level of an entity's capital and how it manages capital. One rationale is to assist users in assessing an entity's risk profile and its flexibility in the event of unexpected adverse events, including its ability to pay dividends:[61] this has, in effect, something in common with the concept of defense of capital.

Comment: IAS 16 requires the disclosure of restriction on the distribution of the balance of revaluation surplus.[62]

Comment: On the first adoption of IAS 29, as mentioned in Section 3.5.2.2 previously, the procedures of IAS 29 may result in the restatement of components of equity other than retained earnings and revaluation surplus. As explained in Section 6.6.5 and Section 6.6.1 later, this may translate into an implicit transfer of a pre-existing accumulated other comprehensive income to retained earnings. This might not be permitted under a specific jurisdiction or might affect the amount of earnings that are legally distributable.

Comment: As explained is Section 7.5.7 later, jurisdictions where equity cannot be negative or go below a certain floor cannot account for a component of equity without considering restrictions mandated by local corporate governance and business law frameworks. In theory IFRSs intend to be neutral with regard to implications on defense of capital, but they are not. What may be valid in a common law country is not necessarily so in Roman or civil law jurisdictions. Accounting standards that ignore this fundamental difference may have unintended effects on financial markets through their effect on business financial reporting.

3.6   IFRS IMPLEMENTATION IN SOME JURISDICTIONS

3.6.1   Do IFRSs Require Specific Reserves?

Some reserves are required by IFRSs. Reserves, such as foreign currency translation adjustment, revaluation surplus, reserve for available-for-sale investments, cash flow hedge reserve, reserve for net investment hedge in foreign operations, or option to convert a compound instrument, have sometimes been introduced in jurisdictions that previously did not contemplate those accounts. Section 3.6.7 following analyzes presentation requirements of reserves.

---

[60]   The Conceptual Framework for Financial Reporting 2010, ¶¶ 4.20, 4.21; IASB Framework, ¶¶ 65-66; IAS 19 (2007), ¶ BC48Y.

[61]   IAS 1, ¶¶ BC86–BC87.

[62]   IAS 16, ¶ 77(f).

3.6.2 Does the IFRS First-Time Adoption Affect the Use of Previously-Existing Reserves?

In the United Kingdom, revaluation reserves existing under previous GAAP should not be presented as a revaluation surplus.[63] In Italy, revaluation reserves that existed before transition to IFRSs have been either reclassified to revaluation surplus or reversed to retained earnings where they had been determined on different bases. Reserves for own shares (Section 4.14.3 later) have been reversed to retained earnings. Reserves that had been used to account for government grants in equity following a capital approach have been reversed to retained earnings. The capital approach[64] is inconsistent with the income approach adopted by International Accounting Standard No. 20, *Accounting for Government Grants and Disclosure of Government Assistance*. Several reserves that were previously used to segment profit or loss of prior years, interim dividends paid, or losses offset before the close of the reporting period (see Section 6.1.2 later) have been reversed to retained earnings or re-classified as subledgers of retained earnings. Other reserves have been maintained, to the extent they were not inconsistent with IFRSs, and presented in the statement of changes in equity or in the statement of recognized income and expense (before the 2007 Revision of IAS 1).

3.6.3 Merger Relief

In the local GAAP or laws of certain jurisdictions, the acquirer company may account in its separate financial statements for the cost of the investment, through a share-for-share exchange, in a subsidiary, associate, or jointly-owned entity at the nominal value of the shares given, as opposed to the fair value of the consideration given. In the United Kingdom, this is called "merger relief" (Section 612 of the Companies Act of 2006), whereby the company may take advantage of journalizing the investment by debiting cost of investment and crediting share capital only for the nominal value of the shares issued, or "group reconstruction relief" (Section 611 of the Companies Act of 2006), whereby the company may set share premium value at a minimum. Then, on consolidated financial statements, a merger reserve arises for the excess value over par value of shares issued as consideration for the acquisition of the investee. An example of group reconstruction may be the sale at under value of an already-existing subsidiary by the parent company to another subsidiary against an issue of shares by the new parent with a nominal value below the prior parent's carrying cost of the investment. In such a case, the new parent would account for a share premium only to make up the amount of the original cost to the original parent, and not the higher fair value.

The issue arises of how a merger relief shall be accounted under U.S. GAAP and IFRS and its first adoption in separate financial statements and in consolidated financial statements.

As far as separate financial statements are concerned, under IAS 27[65] a parent, investor, or joint venturer must record an investment either at cost (that is, the fair value of the consideration paid less any impairment loss) or at fair value. On transition to IFRSs, in order to apply IAS 27 in separate financial statements when merger relief or group reconstruction relief had been used for local GAAP or laws purposes, IAS 27, IAS 28, and IAS 32 would ordinarily require

---

[63] *The Institute of Chartered Accountants in England and Wales and The Institute of Chartered Accountants of Scotland, TECH 21/05,* Distributable Profits: Implication of IFRS, *page 35.*

[64] *IAS 20,* Accounting for Government Grants and Disclosure of Government Assistance, *¶¶ 13–14.*

[65] *IAS 27 (2010), ¶ 38.*

retrospective application to the investment starting from the fair value of the consideration given, as IFRS 1 had no exemption in this respect. This resulted in a restatement of share premium or capital reserves.

Given the possible difficulty of such a restatement, the Amendments to IFRS 1 and to IAS 27 add an exemption in IFRS 1, whereby a first-time adopter that measures the investment at cost in its separate financial statements may elect to use a deemed cost represented by either the fair value or the previous GAAP carrying amount of the investment at the entity's date of transition to IFRSs in its separate opening IFRS statement of financial position. In addition, in a group reconstruction (provided there is no change in the absolute and relative ownership interests of the owner of the original parent or entity and in the assets and liabilities of the group), in its separate financial statements a new parent that is formed to obtain control of a previously-existing subsidiary of the same group through shares exchange would measure the cost of its investment in such previously-existing subsidiary of the original parent at the carrying amount of its share of the equity items shown in the separate financial statements of the original parent for the existing subsidiary at the date of formation of the new parent.[66]

Comment: U.S. GAAP has no explicit treatment of first-time adoption of U.S. GAAP, and therefore retroactive restatement applies as a general rule.[67] Furthermore, U.S. GAAP contemplates only consolidated financial statements as general-purpose financial statements of a parent company with consolidated subsidiaries, even if it does not prohibit the use of parent-only financial statements for other uses.[68] However, in most instances a parent company would use the equity method to account for its subsidiary in parent-only financial statements. As under U.S. GAAP, the equity method must make retained earnings equal to consolidated retained earnings; retrospective restatement would also apply under U.S. GAAP in parent- or investor-only financial statements to restate a merger relief that was used to account for the cost of a subsidiary under prior local GAAP, to the extent that the business combination would also be measured at the fair value exchanged for consolidation purposes.

Comment: As far as consolidated financial statements are concerned, a merger reserve that in consolidation had been used under UK GAAP would eliminate the effect of merger relief, to the extent that such reserve had been computed to gross up the cost of investment to the fair value as of the date of acquisition. IFRSs do not treat merger relief for consolidation purposes. However, on first adoption of IFRSs a company may elect, under the IFRS 1 exemption, not to restate past business combinations retroactively under IFRS 3. Past business combinations are those that occurred before transition date to IFRSs. If the election is taken, the carrying amount under previous GAAP of assets acquired and liabilities assumed in past business combination, apart from some recognition adjustments, are considered at their deemed cost under IFRSs at that date.[69]

---

[66] *Amendments to IFRS 1,* First-time Adoption of International Financial Reporting Standards *and IAS 27,* Consolidated and Separate Financial Statements, Cost of an Investment in a Subsidiary, Jointly Controlled Entity or Associate, *¶¶ 23B, 38B–38C (May 2008).*

[67] *FASB ASC 250-10-45-3 (FASB Statement No. 154, ¶ 6).*

[68] *FASB Statement No. 94,* Consolidation of All Majority-Owned Subsidiaries, *¶ 15; APB 18, ¶ 14; FASB ASC 810-10-45-11 (ARB 51, ¶ 24, as amended by FASB Statement No. 160); AICPA TPA 1400.32,* Parent-Only Financial Statements and Relationship to GAAP.

[69] *IFRS 1, ¶ C4 (e).*

Example: The SEC Staff, in its review of Form 20-F of a British foreign private issuer for the fiscal year ended December 31, 2005 containing financial statements prepared for the first time on the basis of IFRSs, requested repetition of disclosure explaining a merger reserve resulting from merger relief in an acquisition made in 2001 that was "grandfathered" under the IFRS 1 exemption.[70]

Under U.S. GAAP, a group reconstruction may fall under a transfer of assets or exchange of shares between entities under common control, to be recorded at the same carrying values (i.e., using the carry over basis) at the date of transfer. If a parent transfers its ownership interest in a subsidiary to another subsidiary in exchange for additional shares of the new parent, the consolidated financial statements of the new parent shall reflect the net assets of the acquiree at their historical cost in the consolidated financial statement of the previous parent.[71]

Example: The SEC Staff, in its review of Form 20-F of a British foreign private issuer for the fiscal year ended March 31, 2006 containing financial statements prepared for the first time on the basis of IFRSs, challenged in consolidated U.S. GAAP financial information a separate classification in equity as "other reserves" of a merger reserve arising from a group reconstruction which involved the creation of a new parent company, and that was as a transaction between entities under common control for purposes of U.S. GAAP.[72]

Comment: Business combinations between entities under common control are also scoped out of IFRS 3, as out of Subtopic 805-10 (FASB Statement No. 141(R))[73] and therefore from their accounting at acquisition method for consolidation purposes. However, IFRS 3 makes it clear that, to be scoped out, control of all of the combining entities must remain with the same entity both before and after the business combination and it must be not transitory.[74] This is intended to avoid the acquisition method being circumvented by common control assumed for a brief period immediately before the combination.[75] Furthermore, IFRS 3 requires the existence of a contractual arrangement and of ultimate nontransitory collective control power for more than one individual to be considered as controlling entity. Those characteristics absent, a group reconstruction where the shareholders are a group of individuals would not be considered a transaction under common control.[76] In addition, based on the definition of a business combination in IFRS 3, the standard generally does not apply when one company creates another nonpre-existing entity (such as in certain group reconstructions) or when such a company was not a business (such as a newly-created or nonoperating company to receive assets divested or spun-off), as such entity did not constitute a business.[77]

---

[70] *Letters by the SEC, File No. 001-14602, Note 25 (September 25, 2006 and October 19, 2006). Reply by the company (October 6, 2006) www.sec.gov/divisions/corpfin/ifrs_reviews (last visited January 7, 2008).*

[71] *FASB ASC 805-50-30-5 (FASB Statement No. 141(R) ¶ D9).*

[72] *Letters by the SEC, File No. 1-14958, Note 38.18 (October 31, 2006 and January 9, 2007). Replies by the company (December 7, 2006 and February 2, 2007) www.sec.gov/divisions/corpfin/ifrs_reviews (last visited January 7, 2008).*

[73] *FASB ASC 805-10-15-4 (FASB Statement No. 141(R), ¶ 2); IFRS 3, ¶ 2(c).*

[74] *IFRS 3, ¶ B1.*

[75] *IFRS 3 (Revised 2005), ¶ BC28.*

[76] *IFRS 3, ¶ B2; IFRIC 17, ¶ BC13.*

[77] *IFRS 3, ¶¶ IN6, 2(b).*

3.6.4 Merger Reserve Arising from Pooling of Interests

In certain jurisdictions, merger relief is often used as a factor of merger accounting. However, merger relief must not be confused with merger accounting, which is a method of accounting for business combinations and consolidation as opposed to the acquisition method. Merger accounting was called uniting of interests and accounted for as pooling of interests method under International Accounting Standard No. 22, *Business Combinations* and under U.S. GAAP. A "merger reserve" also arose under merger accounting. This reserve was a cancellation adjustment to equal the difference between the parent's carrying cost of investment in a previously-existing subsidiary (or the par/stated value of newly-issued acquirer's common stock) and the parent share of the subsidiary's (or acquiree's) share capital. Under IAS 22, if this difference was negative, it was accounted for as capital reserve in the consolidated balance sheet. If positive, it first reduced the subsidiary's pre-existing share premium, then other reserves, then retained earnings. Under U.S. GAAP this difference was debited to additional paid-in capital and any remaining amount to retained earnings.

In the U.S. uniting of interests was banned beginning July 1, 2001 for all business combinations, except those involving not-for-profit organizations and combinations of entities under common control. This method was also prohibited under Australian and Canadian GAAPs. Similarly, IFRS 3, *Business Combinations*, superseded IAS 22 and no longer permitted pooling of interests. Both U.S. GAAP and IFRSs now require measuring the consideration transferred in a business combination at the fair value exchanged.[78]

On transition to IFRSs, a company that elects the exemption under IFRS 1 on business combinations does not reclassify a past business combination that had been accounted as pooling of interests as an acquisition[79] and does not restate any previously unrecognized goodwill.[80]

A foreign private issuer that used to consistently account for all business combinations under IAS 22, *Business Combinations*, then superseded by IFRS 3, could benefit from a special accommodation in Form 20-F to maintain the method of accounting used under IFRSs (i.e., the acquisition method or the pooling of interests) in filing with the SEC even though the transaction would have resulted in a different method of accounting under U.S. GAAP. This accommodation was not permitted for mergers of entities under common control. However, once the method of accounting was determined, reconciling to the purchase method of accounting under U.S. GAAP was required.[81]

3.6.5 Goodwill Displayed as a Reserve

The EC Seventh Directive allows Member States to permit deduction of goodwill from equity reserves.[82] Both IFRSs and U.S. GAAP prohibit this treatment.[83] On transition to IFRSs, a

---

[78] *FASB ASC 805-30-30-7 (FASB Statement of Financial Accounting Standards No. 141(R), ¶ 39); IFRS 3, ¶ 37.*

[79] *IFRS 1, ¶ C4(a).*

[80] *IFRS 1, ¶ C4(b) (ii).*

[81] *Form 20-F, Part III, Item 17, Instructions, 6 (then amended).*

[82] *Seventh Council Directive 83/349/EEC (June 13, 1983), Art. 30.2.*

[83] *FASB Statement No. 141(R), ¶ B 312; IFRS 3, ¶ BC312.*

company that adopted such accounting must not recognize goodwill in its opening IFRS statement of financial position as well as its subsequent impacts on profit or loss on derecognition or impairment of the investment. Furthermore, in this case, resolution of a contingency involving the purchase consideration affects retained earnings and not goodwill.[84]

3.6.6 What Disclosure of Reserves is Required under IFRSs?

As mentioned, the IASB Framework welcomes disclosure of reserves. IAS 1 requires appropriate subclassifications of classes of equity capital and reserves either in the statement of financial position or in the notes,[85] and a description of the nature and purpose of each reserve within equity either in the statement of financial position or the statement of changes in equity, or in the notes.[86] The standard states a disaggregation of paid-in capital, share premium, and reserves as examples of equity disclosures. Details of those other reserves are shown in the statement of changes of equity or in the notes, as there is no requirement to accumulate them separately on the face of the statement of financial position.[87] The display of reserves in other statements under IFRSs is analyzed in Section 6.8 later, Section 5.3 later, and Section 7.9 later.

Comment: Under U.S. GAAP appropriations of retained earnings must be clearly identified within the stockholders' equity section.[88] Specific standards may require separate display or disclosure, such as in the case of a one-time reclassification of available-for-sale securities to trading securities to entities that, based on the same standard, have elected subsequent fair value measurement of separately recognized servicing assets and liabilities (see Section 6.4.12 later).

Example: The SEC Staff, in its review of Form 20-F of a French foreign private issuer for the year ended March 31, 2006 containing financial statements prepared for the first time on the basis of IFRSs, required disclosure of nondistributable reserves, and the nature and computation of the statutory reserve balance. The company explained that statutory reserve included appropriations made by annual shareholders' meetings, and disclosed that nondistributable reserves comprised cash flow hedge reserve, available-for-sale securities reserve, and undistributed earnings of consolidated subsidiaries.[89]

Example: The SEC Staff, in its review of Form 20-F of a Spanish foreign private issuer for the year ended December 31, 2005 containing financial statements prepared for the first time on the basis of IFRSs, required separate disclosure of retained earnings, legal reserve, and revaluation reserve that were combined under the heading "Other reserves."[90]

---

[84] *IFRS 1, ¶ C4 (i).*

[85] *IAS 1, ¶ 78.*

[86] *IAS 1, ¶ 79.*

[87] *IAS 1, ¶¶ 106(d)–108; IAS 19 (2007), ¶ BC48Z; IASB Update October 2005.*

[88] *FASB ASC 505-10-45-3 (FASB Statement No. 5, ¶ 15).*

[89] *Letter by the SEC, File No. 001-32139, Note 26.4 (December 1, 2006). Reply by the company (January 12, 2007) www.sec.gov/divisions/corpfin/ifrs_reviews (last visited July 6, 2007).*

[90] *Letter by the SEC, File No. 1-15158, Note 14 (September 20, 2006). Replies by the company (October 18, 2006 and February 2, 2007) www.sec.gov/divisions/corpfin/ifrs_reviews (last visited January 7, 2008).*

> **Comment:** In the United Kingdom, the "movements on reserves" is a tabular form in addition to the "reconciliation of movements in shareholders' funds" required by FRS 3, *Reporting Financial Performance*, a statement that reports the changes in components of equity. The two statements are somehow equivalent to the statement of changes in equity under IFRSs. Reserves typically include accounts such as share premium, revaluation reserve, and retained earnings.

Depending on jurisdiction, additional disclosures of reserves from other perspectives, such as defense of capital, may be required.

> **Example:** The Italian Civil Code and Italian accounting principles require the disclosure of the sources of reserves, their actual use in the last three annual periods, and their future availability and distributability.[91]

3.6.7   Have Specific Display Requirements Been Introduced for the Reserves Required by IFRSs?

Each country may have introduced specific display or disclosure requirements for reserves required by IFRSs.

> **Example:** In Italy, the operating guidelines by OIC[92] required that changes in opening balance of retained earnings under IFRS 1 for IFRSs first-time adoption be displayed as separate subreserves, with appropriate disclosures, based on the nature of items that determined such changes (such as prior period profit or loss, translation adjustments, fair value measurement), and that fair value reserve be separately presented based on the type of instruments or transactions from which it arose (such as available-for-sale financial assets, etc.).

> **Example:** In the United Kingdom, FRS 3, *Reporting Financial Performance* requires some statements on shareholders' equity, such as a statement of total recognized gains and losses and a reconciliation of movements in shareholders' funds. The reporting of reserves on these statements overlaps with the statement of comprehensive income (or the statement of recognized income and expense under the previous revision of IAS 1) and the statement of changes in equity.

3.6.8   Did New Reserves Arise from The Implementation of IFRSs?

Some jurisdictions have mandated the use of additional reserves in conjunction with the first-time adoption of IFRSs, or have made some of the reserves required by IFRSs not distributable. This is because IFRSs make use, to a certain extent, of fair value and recognize some items of income and expense in other comprehensive income or directly in equity, something that was

---

[91]   *Italian Civil Code, Art. 2427.7-bis; Italian OIC – Organismo Italiano di Contabilità, Principio Contabile No. 28, Il Patrimonio Netto, ¶ IV.*

[92]   *OIC – Organismo Italiano di Contabilità, Guida Operativa per la Transizione ai Principi Contabili Internazionali (IAS/IFRS) (October 2005), pages 102–103.*

not permitted under certain prior local standards. Insofar as those items are considered to be unearned, their distributability is sanctioned under the principle of defense of capital.

Example: In Italy some new reserves have been mandated in conjunction with the first-time adoption of IFRSs:[93] 1) an undistributable reserve for gains recognized in the income statement, net of tax impact, that results from the use of the fair value option or equity method, other than arising from financial instruments held for trading or hedging, or foreign exchange transactions; 2) an undistributable reserve for valuation of financial instruments at fair value directly in equity under IFRSs and for revaluation surplus on PP&E and intangible assets; 3) an undistributable reserve for the IFRS 1 election to use fair value or revaluation as deemed cost at first-time adoption of IFRSs; and 4) an undistributable reserve for the first-time adoption of IFRSs, arising from items different from those above and other than gains/losses on financial instruments held for trading, hedging, foreign exchange transactions, and derecognition of capitalizations and provisions made under prior GAAP.

Example: In the United Kingdom, the Companies Act of 2006 establishes the rules for distributable profits. A gain or loss on hedging instruments is considered unrealized, and therefore not distributable, when the corresponding gain or loss on the hedged item is deemed so.[94] In substance, those principles have not been changed after the adoption of IFRSs, although they are better detailed in the context of IFRSs.[95]

3.6.9 Can Newly-Established Reserves be Used for Deficit Reorganization?

The issue is whether or not the newly-created reserves may be used for deficit reorganization (see Section 5.2.3 later and Section 6.5.3 later) and under what circumstances.

Example: In Italy, the undistributable jurisdictional reserve for gains recognized in the income statement, net of tax impact, that results from the use of fair value option or equity method, other than those arising from financial instruments held for trading or hedging, or foreign exchange transaction, and the reserve for the election to use fair value or revaluation as deemed cost at first-time adoption of IFRSs can be used for deficit reorganization. However, they must be brought back to their original amount, or reduced by the same amount by an extraordinary shareholders' meeting, before any distribution of dividends.[96]

3.6.10 Can Newly-Established Reserves be Used to Offset a Deficit Arising from the First-Time Adoption of IFRS?

The issue is whether or not offsetting a deficit in retained earnings created by the first-time adoption of IFRSs may follow the same procedures as those for deficit reorganization. Of course, the answer depends on the specific jurisdiction.

---

[93] *Decreto legislativo 28 febbraio 2005, n. 38.*
[94] *The Institute of Chartered Accountants in England and Wales and The Institute of Chartered Accountants of Scotland, TECH 7-03*, Guidance on the Determination of Realised Profits and Losses in the Context of Distributions under the Companies Act of 1985.
[95] *The Institute of Chartered Accountants in England and Wales and The Institute of Chartered Accountants of Scotland, TECH 21-05*, Distributable Profits: Implications of IFRS.
[96] *Decreto legislativo 28 febbraio 2005, n. 38, art. 7.6.*

Example: In Italy, the reserve for the election to make use of fair value or revaluation as deemed cost at first-time adoption of IFRSs may also be used to offset a deficit in retained earnings determined by the first-time adoption of IFRS.[97]

3.6.11   Does a Deficit in Retained Earnings that Has Originated from the First-Time Adoption of IFRSs Call for Deficit Reorganization?

The issue is whether or not a deficit in retained earnings that was determined by derecognizing previously capitalized assets that are not capitalizable under IFRSs, as mandated by the first-time adoption of IFRSs, calls for deficit reorganization procedures. Of course, the answer depends on the specific jurisdiction.

Example: In Italy, such a case in not defined by the law relating to the first-time adoption of IFRSs.[98] In 2006, the Consob (Italy's securities regulator) required no formal deficit reorganization procedure for some listed companies that were in such a situation,[99] but asked for print releases on such estimates and related effects. Furthermore, the ABI (Italy's banking association) excluded formal deficit reorganization procedures in such circumstances for banks incorporated as cooperative entities.[100]

3.6.12   Distributability of Preacquisition Profits

In theory, as the use of a different set of GAAP affects the computation of profit or loss, so also is the determination of profit available for distribution to shareholders. A particular situation arises in the case of preacquisition dividends.

Under IFRSs a parent company may account for its investment in subsidiaries at the cost method in its separate financial statements.[101] Only dividends that originated from accumulated profits of the investee after the date of acquisition had to be accounted for as dividend income. Preacquisition earnings had to be treated as a reduction of the cost of the investment, as they represented distribution of the assets at acquisition (realization of part of the investment).[102] If, as part of a group reorganization, the subsidiary was sold from the parent to another company of the group, any dividends that had been or would be distributed to the new parent but had arisen out of previously-accumulated profit would be preacquisition dividends with respect to the new parent and would not be part of its income (and therefore its distributable profit). Hence, preacquisition retained earnings of the subsidiary purchased would also not become

---

[97]   *ABI – Associazione Bancaria Italiana, Soluzioni IAS ABI No. 13 (February 28, 2006).*

[98]   *Decreto legislativo 28 febbraio 2005, n. 38.*

[99]   *CONSOB,* Indagine conoscitiva sulle recenti vicende relative al calcio professionistico con partico- lare riferimento al sistema delle regole e dei controlli – *Audizione di Massimo Ferrari (Responsabile della divisione emittenti) presso la Camera dei Deputati, VII Commissione permanente (Cultura, scienza e istruzione) (October 11, 2006).*

[100] *ABI – Associazione Bancaria Italiana,* Soluzioni IAS ABI No. 24 *(November 9, 2006).*

[101] *IAS 27 (2010), ¶ 38.*

[102] *IAS 18, ¶ 32 and IAS 27, ¶ 4, before Amendments to IFRS 1,* First-time Adoption of International Financial Reporting Standards *and IAS 27,* Consolidated and Separate Financial Statements, Cost of an Investment in a Subsidiary, Jointly Controlled Entity or Associate, *(May 2008).*

distributable to its new parent and indirectly to the former parent (the seller).[103] As IFRS 1 had no exemption for preacquisition dividends, a parent company was required to retroactively restate, at the date of transition to IFRSs, its subsidiaries' preacquisition accumulated earnings, preacquisition dividends, and thus the cost of investment and retained earnings, as if IAS 27 had always been applied. As part of the IASB's Project on *Cost of an Investment in a Subsidiary, Jointly Controlled Entity or Associate*, discussions had initially been directed to either allowing all accumulated profits of the subsidiary at the parent's transition date to be considered as deemed preacquisition profits, or considering the preacquisition accumulated profits of the subsidiary under the previous national GAAP as deemed preacquisition profits.[104] The final amendments did not add an exemption to IFRS 1. Instead, the IASB decided that dividends from a subsidiary, associate, or jointly controlled entity (similarly to UK GAAP) must be recognized as income in a parent's separate financial statements, subject to assessment for impairment in the value of the investment. These amendments apply for annual periods beginning on or after January 1, 2009.[105]

Comment: U.S. GAAP also considers preacquisition dividends as reduction of cost of investment, although it addresses this issue simply with reference to consolidated statements.[106] In fact, U.S. GAAP contemplates only consolidated financial statements as general-purpose financial statements of a parent company with consolidated subsidiaries, although it does not prohibit the use of parent-only financial statements for other uses.[107] In addition, in its parent-only financial statements, a company would account for its subsidiaries at equity method and not at cost. Furthermore, in the U.S. as well as in several other jurisdictions, dividends that are paid in intrayear acquisition are computed either as paid out from post acquisition profits first and from preacquisition profits for the excess, or as arising evenly throughout the year, unless they are directly declared out of preacquisition profits.

3.6.13   Implications of Reserves Appropriated for Tax Reasons

As mentioned, taxation may be one reason for the creation of reserves. In some jurisdictions, tax laws may require that certain profits, or part of retained earnings that are exempted from taxation, be appropriated, and be taxed (at lower or higher rates) when they are subsequently distributed as dividends. One associated issue is in what period deferred tax assets and liabilities, referring to the additional benefits or taxes that will be assessed in relation to those dividends, must be recognized. A similar issue arises in case of an income tax refund or payment triggered by dividend declaration and distribution in a subsequent period (at a lower or higher tax rate on distributed profit as opposed to undistributed earnings). Section 8.2.17.4 later develops this topic.

---

[103]   *The impact of this situation in the UK is analyzed in Ernst & Young,* IFRS in Individual Company Accounts *(2005). The paper concluded that in the UK the adoption of IFRS in the parent's separate financial statements might be unachievable.*

[104]   *IASB Update, September 2006, page 9.*

[105]   *Amendments to IFRS 1,* First-time Adoption of International Financial Reporting Standards and IAS 27, Consolidated and Separate Financial Statements, Cost of an Investment in a Subsidiary, Jointly Controlled Entity or Associate, *(May 2008).*

[106]   *APB 18, ¶ 6; FASB ASC 810-10-45-4 (ARB 51, ¶ 11).*

[107]   *FASB Statement No. 94,* Consolidation of All Majority-Owned Subsidiaries, *¶ 15; APB 18, ¶ 14; FASB ASC 810-10-45-11 (ARB 51, ¶ 24, as amended by FASB Statement No. 160); AICPA TPA 1400.32,* Parent-Only Financial Statements and Relationship to GAAP.

3.7 CONSERVATISM, TRUE-AND-FAIR VIEW, AND INVESTORS' PROTECTION

This paragraph describes certain links between the notion of *reserves* and investors' protection, conservatism or prudence, faithful representation and true-and-fair view, and the context of equity.

> **Comment:** This discussion is relevant for the topic of reserves as components of equity. In fact, there is a link between a reserve in the meaning of a provision and a reserve as an appropriation of equity. Firstly, depending on jurisdictions, when undervaluation of assets or overvaluation of liabilities are permitted or required for tax purposes, tax laws may also require appropriations of retained earnings on the financial statements in order to identify those amounts and track taxation on their distribution for the corresponding amounts. Secondly, corporate laws may also provide for similar appropriations with the purpose of defending capital from distribution of profits that in effect have not been realized.

Reserve accounting in its meaning of provisioning general expenses (see Section 3.1.1 previously) is sometimes warranted on the ground of protection of investors, depositors, or other external stakeholders. In this respect, the FASB expressed the view that reserves, in their meaning as accrual accounting, do not per se provide financial protection against losses and, unlike insurance, do not reduce or eliminate risk, as no real fund is set aside, but cost is simply allocated across accounting periods.[108]

> **Comment:** Requirements for creating such reserves may come from the operation of laws or regulatory authorities. Examples are catastrophe accounting,[109] generally justified for the sake of protection of policyholders, and general reserves of banks, mutual savings, and loan associations.[110]

The notion of *reserves* (as loss contingencies or provisions) is often argued on the basis of conservatism or prudence.

> **Comment:** In its extreme form, this concept may lead to hidden reserves. This term is used to mean an understatement of assets or an overstatement of liabilities that is made, often intentionally, to decrease net income. Such reserves are sometimes employed to minimize tax or stabilize and smooth fluctuations in earnings.

The response of both the FASB and the IASB is clear on this matter. Although both the FASB's and IASB's conceptual frameworks have introduced conservatism and prudence, respectively, as a consequence of estimates under conditions of uncertainty in financial reporting, this may determine some bias in financial reporting, as conservatism may conflict with other qualitative characteristics. Therefore, under both the frameworks, reserves (whether hidden or not) that result, whether intentionally or not, from an excess use of prudence are not permitted.[111] Loss

---

[108] *FASB ASC 450-20-05-8, 450-20-05-9 (FASB Statement No. 5, ¶¶ 61–65).*

[109] *IFRS 4,* Insurance Contracts, *¶ IG58.*

[110] *FASB ASC 942-740-05-2 (APB Opinion No. 23,* Accounting for Income Taxes – Special Areas, *¶ 19); IAS 30 (superseded), ¶ 51.*

[111] *CON 8, ¶ BC3.27; CON 2 (superseded), ¶¶ 91–94, 97; IASB Framework, ¶ 37 (superseded);* The Conceptual Framework for Financial Reporting 2010, *¶ BC3.27.*

contingencies and provisions, in order to be recognized, must meet the criteria of Subtopic 450-20 (FASB Statement No. 5) and of IAS 37. The probability that an asset has been impaired or that a liability has been incurred and reasonable estimability of the resulting loss are two prerequisites for provisioning: in their absence disclosure, not accruing, may be warranted. These conditions are not considered to be in conflict with the convention of conservatism,[112] but conservatism per se is not a valid reason for provisioning. Furthermore, under both U.S. GAAP and IFRSs general business risk cannot be provisioned.[113] Also, reserves for contingency are not considered acceptable under U.S. GAAP.[114]

Comment: The borderline between measurement of assets and liabilities and creation of hidden reserves rests with the trade-off between conservatism (the term generally used under U.S. GAAP) or prudence (the term employed under IFRSs) and reliability and representational faithfulness (under the new common framework, faithful representation). Different levels of this balance are reached depending on jurisdiction. In EU jurisdictions this trade-off is named with respect to "true-and-fair view," an expression which is used by the EC Accounting Directives.[115] U.S. GAAP and IFRSs do not use such a term, but this concept roughly corresponds to the application of the principal qualitative characteristics of financial information and in particular faithful representation.[116] The notion of the "true-and-fair view" is often incorporated in a country's legal system. The use of the term also connects to the perspective of investors' protection discussed above.[117] The IASB Framework included neutrality and prudence as part of reliability, which is one of the qualitative characteristics of financial information. CON 2 placed neutrality under reliability, although as a secondary and interactive quality, but not conservatism, as an ingredient of qualitative characteristics. The new conceptual framework leaves neutrality as part of faithful representation but does not repropose prudence or conservatism as they would undermine neutrality. The common framework replaces the term "reliability" with "faithful representation."[118] IAS 1 does not include a discussion on prudence in overall considerations on financial statements.[119] By contrast, the EC Fourth Directive attaches greater importance to prudence.[120] Under GAAP in most European countries prudence is even more a general principle that deeply informs the preparation of financial statements. This is the case of some EU Member States, such as Austria, Germany, and Luxembourg, as opposed to the

---

[112] *FASB ASC 450-20-25-3 (FASB Statement No. 5, ¶ 84).*

[113] *FASB ASC 450-20-25-8 (FASB Statement No. 5, ¶ 14); IAS 37, ¶ 18.*

[114] *FASB ASC 450-20-05-8, 450-20-05-9 (FASB Statement No. 5, ¶ 61); EITF Topic No. D-35, FASB Staff Views on Issue No. 93-6, "Accounting for Multiple-Year Retrospectively Rated Contracts by Ceding and Assuming Enterprises," Q&A # 28.*

[115] *Fourth Council Directive 78/660/EEC (25 July 1978), Art. 2.3; Seventh Council Directive 83/349/EEC (June 13, 1983), Art. 16.3.*

[116] The Conceptual Framework for Financial Reporting 2010, *¶ BC3.44; IASB Framework, ¶ 46 (superseded).*

[117] *For example, Committee of European Securities Regulators, Consultation Paper, Draft Technical Advice on Equivalence of Certain Third Country GAAP and On Description of Certain Third Countries Mechanisms of Enforcement of Financial Information, CESR/05-230 (April 2005), page 14 instructs its respondents that assuring the protection of investors must be the primary focus in assessing whether financial statements prepared under third country GAAP provide a true and fair view of the issuer's financial position and performance.*

[118] *CON 2 (superseded), ¶¶ 62, 96; CON 8, ¶¶ QC12, BC3.19, BC3.27; IASB Framework, ¶¶ 36–37 (superseded);* The Conceptual Framework for Financial Reporting 2010, *¶¶ QC12, BC3.19, BC3.27.*

[119] *A similar conclusion is found in EC, DG Mercato Interno,* Informazione finanziaria e diritto della società, Esame della compatibilità tra gli IAS da 1 e 41 e le direttive contabili europee *(April 2001), page 8.*

[120] *Fourth Council Directive 78/660/EEC (July 25, 1978), Art. 31.1.*

Anglo-Saxon countries, where this concept is reinforced by their strict interpretation of the EC Fourth Directive.[121] Depending on jurisdiction, the weight given to conservatism may originate from the importance of the legal, tax, or banking connotation that it attaches to financial statements.[122] In this context, although it is generally acknowledged that conservatism should not reach an extreme form, in certain jurisdictions hidden reserves are silently set aside or explicitly permitted, sometimes with the additional requirement to disclose the fact through appropriation of retained earnings.

3.8   PERSPECTIVES AND ALTERNATIVE MODELS

3.8.1   Defense of Capital Versus Financial Performance

The dichotomy between recognized profit and distributable profit partly resembles the debate on what metrics must represent the financial performance of a company, and whether or not different performance indicators should address different meanings of "performance" to users of financial statements.

Comment: While the dispute on financial performance (treated in Section 7.5 later) proceeds from net income to the larger picture of comprehensive income to look for a measure of global performance, the search for distributable income moves from net income to the smaller set of realized and available profit. This also includes the issue of whether or not principles of profit distributability should be based on accounting data based on GAAP or on tests on other grounds.

3.8.2   Appropriations as an Alternative to Recycling

Depending on jurisdictions, appropriations of retained earnings and recycling (treated in Section 7.8 later) may be used as tools to pursue some common purposes within different accounting frameworks.

Planning Point: Under both U.S. GAAP and IFRSs income and expenses that are recognized in other comprehensive income are generally recycled (reclassified, under IFRSs) into profit or loss or, in limited circumstances under IFRSs, are transferred directly to retained earnings. Net income or loss is then accumulated in retained earnings. To the extent that items of income and expenses recognized in other comprehensive income are unrealized and that recycling arises from the use or derecognition of related assets and liabilities, other comprehensive income becomes net income. Then net income becomes distributable profit, when ultimately realized, based on jurisdictional legal requirements.[123]

---

[121] *FEE Study,* Comparison of the EC Accounting Directives and IASs: A Contribution to International Accounting Developments *(April 1999), pages 20–21.*

[122] *Similarly, CON 2 (superseded), ¶ 93 acknowledged that in the U.S. the great importance attributed to conservatism derived from the primary purpose of financial statements being their use by bankers and lenders.*

[123] *From a different angle,* Distinguishing Between Liabilities and Equity – Preliminary Views on the Classification of Liabilities and Equity and Under International Financial Reporting Standards, *A discussion paper prepared by staff of the Accounting Standards Committee of Germany on behalf of the European Financial Reporting Advisory Group and the German Accounting Standards Board under the Pro-active Accounting Activities in Europe Initiative of the European Financial Reporting Advisory Group and the European National Standard Setters (Brussels/Berlin, 2007), ¶ 3.21 con-cludes that, as recognizing income directly in equity is an accounting convention, measurements of reserves are ultimately available for loss absorption as retained earnings.*

Alternatively, some jurisdictions do not have items of income and expenses that are recognized in other comprehensive income. Appropriations of retained earnings and reserves are in fact used as a warning sign (all within the same equity section of the statement of financial position without the need for recycling to profit or loss) that net income or accumulated profits or losses are unrealized, undistributable, or otherwise restricted. Consequently, transfer among reserves and capitalization of reserves becomes an important accounting subject. Such different approaches will be read in the light of different interpretations of the clean-surplus concept in Section 7.3 later and will be wrapped up into a general model of equity reporting and comprehensive income (Section 7.21 later).

4 EQUITY SECTION OF THE STATEMENT OF FINANCIAL POSITION

4.1 TERMINOLOGY AND DEFINITION OF TERMS

4.1.1 Shareholders' Versus Stockholders' Versus Owners' Equity

.U.S. GAAP and SEC Form 20-F utilize both *stockholders'* and, less frequently, *shareholders'* and *owners' equity*. SEC Regulation S-X uses *stockholders' equity* and occasionally *shareholders' equity*. Subtopic 480-10 (FASB Statement No. 150) clarifies that several names for equity of business enterprises, such as *stockholders' equity* or *owners' equity*, are commonly used interchangeably under U.S. GAAP.[1] The term *shareholders' equity* prevails under IFRSs.

> **Comment:** Some terminology differences come from the use of British English versus American English. Nevertheless, the terms appear synonymous under IFRSs and U.S. rules.

4.1.2 Net Assets Versus Equity

The term *net assets* can be found in both U.S. GAAP and IFRSs. Under the FASB's Concepts, the term *net assets* refers to assets minus liabilities,[2] although it is undefined under IFRSs.

Designating equity as net assets is more than a semantic distinction. Firstly, net assets identify equity as a residual concept (see Section 2.1.4.1 previously). The Discussion Paper of the *Common Conceptual Project* highlights that presenting equity as a separate section (as opposed to a separate category within the financing section) shows that equity equals net assets.[3]

Secondly, the term *net assets* is normally considered a substitute for *equity*.[4] However, the IASB Framework specifies that such an equivalence applies only to the financial concept of capital maintenance.[5] Capital maintenance refers to whether an increase or decrease of capital maintains the original wealth and to the relationship with the profit or loss for the period. This notion, and its implications, is analyzed in Section 7.6 later.

---

[1] *FASB Statement No. 150, Footnote 4.*

[2] *CON 6, ¶ 50.*

[3] *Discussion Paper,* Preliminary Views on an Improved Conceptual Framework for Financial Reporting, The Reporting Entity *(May 2008), ¶ 2.55.*

[4] *CON 6, Footnote 26.*

[5] The Conceptual Framework for Financial Reporting 2010, *¶ 4.57; IASB Framework, ¶ 102.*

Thirdly, net assets and equity are generally equated for business enterprises.[6] However, under U.S. GAAP the term *net assets* applies to not-for-profit organizations,[7] although it is not explicitly indicated as mandatory.[8] Diverse expressions, such as "fund balance," may apply to specific purposes relevant only to not-for-profit entities, such as reporting by fund groups.[9] In contrast, under IFRSs, general-purpose financial statements explicitly address for-profit entities only, including public sector business entities, although not-for-profit private or governmental organizations and cooperative entities are not prohibited from seeking to apply IFRSs, provided some descriptions in the financial statements are appropriately amended or customized.[10]

Finally, in its literal meaning, the term *net assets* may denote the net of only certain assets minus certain liabilities, a figure that does not equal equity. For example, the Discussion Paper mentions the net assets in business or financing activities.[11]

4.1.3 Capital Versus Equity

The proper GAAP discussion on the notion of *capital* remains in the context of the debate on the concepts of capital maintenance. As mentioned, from a terminological angle, the use of *capital* as a substitute for *equity* holds under a financial concept of capital maintenance only. Capital maintenance concepts are analyzed in Section 7.6 later.

This section explains the use of the term *capital* in accounting pronouncements and compares IFRSs to U.S. GAAP on the concept of management of capital.

As acknowledged by the U.S. Concepts,[12] the use of the term *capital* in accounting literature is diverse and not clearly defined. This is true for IFRSs as well.

Sometimes, *capital* is a general surrogate for financing, as implicit in expressions such as *raising capital*,[13] *capital needs*,[14] and *suppliers of capital*.[15]

---

[6] *Example of such use can be found in FASB Statement No. 89,* Financial Reporting on Changing Prices, *¶ 27; CON 6, ¶ 49; The Conceptual Framework for Financial Reporting 2010, ¶ 4.57; IASB Framework, ¶ 102.*

[7] *CON 6, ¶ 50.*

[8] *CON 6, Footnote 26.*

[9] *FASB ASC 958-205-05-07 (FASB Statement No. 117, Footnote 5); FASB Implementation Guide No. 116/117,* Not-for-Profit Organizations: Guidance on Applying FASB Statements 116 and 117, *¶ 11.*

[10] *IAS 1, ¶ 5.*

[11] *Discussion Paper,* Preliminary Views on an Improved Conceptual Framework for Financial Reporting, The Reporting Entity *(May 2008), ¶ 2.51.*

[12] *CON 6, ¶ 212.*

[13] *FASB ASC 915-10-05-2 (FASB Statement No. 7, ¶ 9); FASB Statement of Financial Accounting Standards No. 19,* Financial Accounting and Reporting by Oil and Gas Producing Companies, *¶ 157; FASB Concepts Statement No. 1,* Objectives of Financial Reporting by Business Enterprises, *¶ 13.*

[14] *FASB Concepts Statement No. 4,* Objectives of Financial Reporting by Nonbusiness Organizations, *¶ 8.*

[15] *FASB Statement No. 7, ¶ 48.*

In certain instances, the embedding of both components of debt and equity financing is explicit, or is inherent in the technical meanings used, such as *company's weighted average cost of capital,*[16] *capital at risk,*[17] or *capital structure.*[18]

In other circumstances, capital is instead synonymous with equity, as for example *equity transactions,*[19] *equity capital,*[20] or *investee's capital.*[21] SEC Regulation S-X uses the term *capital shares* (not *equity shares*, the term usually used in U.S. GAAP).

Going further into the use of terminology, the adjective *capital* then may label contributions from, and distributions to, owners: for example, *capital accounts*[22] and *capital transactions.*[23] It also underlines derived concepts of *contributed capital* versus *earned capital,*[24] *capitalization of stock dividends,*[25] or *paid-in*[26] or *contributed capital,*[27] to include *legal capital*[28] or *capital stock,*[29] *additional paid-in capital* – also referred to as *capital surplus*[30] (see Section 5.1 later), and *donated capital*, as opposed to retained earnings and other comprehensive income.

In this set of uses of the term *capital*, there may be a legal connotation, as *statutory capital,*[31] or *regulatory capital requirements* or *regulatory capital.*[32]

More narrowly, capital occasionally implies the perspective of the individual investor: *capital investment,*[33] *capital gains or losses,*[34] or *cost of capital.*[35]

More extensively, the term *capital* is also associated with the notion of its utilization (that is, investing) in selected assets or certain assets net of liabilities, as *capital employed,*[36] or *working capital* or *net working capital.*[37]

---

[16] *FASB Statement No. 19, ¶ 122.*

[17] *EITF Issue No. 88-16,* Basis in Leveraged Buyout Transactions, *Footnote 4.*

[18] *FASB ASC 718-10-55-37 (FASB Statement No. 123(R), ¶ A32); FASB ASC 260-10-45-2 (FASB Statement No. 128, ¶ 36); FASB Statement No. 129, ¶ 14; IFRS 2, ¶¶ B38–B41.*

[19] *EITF Issue No. 88-16,* Basis in Leveraged Buyout Transactions, *Footnote 4; CON 5, ¶ 11.*

[20] *FASB Statement No. 150, Footnote 4; APB Opinion No. 26,* Early Extinguishment of Debt, *¶ 13; IAS 1, ¶ 75(e).*

[21] *APB 18, ¶ 6.*

[22] *ARB 43, Ch. 7.*

[23] *FASB Concepts Statement No. 2,* Qualitative Characteristics of Accounting Information, *¶ 22.*

[24] *CON 6, ¶ 214.*

[25] *FASB ASC 505-30-30-8 (ARB 43, Ch. 1B, ¶ 7).*

[26] *IAS 1, ¶ 75(e).*

[27] *CON 6, ¶ 214.*

[28] *CON 6, Footnote 29.*

[29] *ARB 43, Ch. 1A, ¶ 6.*

[30] *ARB 43, Ch. 1B, ¶ 5.*

[31] *FASB Statement of Financial Accounting Standards No. 60,* Accounting and Reporting by Insurance Enterprises, *¶ 60.*

[32] *FASB ASC 320-10-25-6 (FASB Statement No. 115, ¶ 8); IAS 39, Appendix A, AG22(e) (deleted by IFRS 9).*

[33] *FASB Interpretation No. 46(R), ¶ F1.*

[34] *FASB ASC 740-10-30-9 (FASB Statement No. 109, ¶ 18).*

[35] *FASB Statement No. 2, ¶ 36.*

[36] *ARB 43, Ch. 3A, ¶ 3.*

[37] *ARB 43, Ch. 3A; IAS 1, ¶ 53.*

Under certain conditions, *capital* suggests the long-term or financial nature of certain assets or liabilities that may result from its use: *capital assets* for property, plant & equipment and similar assets,[38] *capital investment*,[39] *capital expenditures*,[40] *capital intensiveness*,[41] *capital leases* and *obligations under capital leases*,[42] *capitalization* or *capital treatment* as opposed to expensing in net income of the period,[43] *capital cash flows*.[44] In this sense it may even be applied to unrecognized resources, e.g., *intellectual capital*.[45]

Section 4.6 following expands the concept of management of capital.

4.1.4   Liabilities and Stockholders' Equity Versus Equity

IFRSs also display and make use of the expression *total equity and liabilities* (not *liabilities and shareholders' equity*). On the other hand, SEC Regulation S-X utilizes the term *total liabilities and stockholders' equity*. Interestingly, though, in U.S. GAAP, only a few standards display or employ the terminology *liabilities and stockholders' equity* or *liabilities and equity*.[46] Other U.S. GAAP pronouncements generally use equity and liabilities separately.

> **Comment:** Importantly, referring to just *net assets* or *equity* may denote the use of the equity format of the statement of financial position (i.e., the balance sheet). On the other hand, typical of some jurisdictions, the counterbalancing of liabilities and shareholders' equity (or total equity and liabilities) to total assets identifies the so-called "balanced format" of the balance sheet. Such a difference is explained below.

As part of the *Financial Statement Presentation Project* the FASB and the IASB tentatively decided on a format of the statement of financial position where equity financing is separate from debt financing.

---

[38] *FASB Statement of Financial Accounting Standards No. 15*, Accounting by Debtors and Creditors for Troubled Debt Restructuring, ¶ 122.

[39] *FASB Statement No. 19*, ¶ 117.

[40] *FASB Statement No. 19*, ¶ 199.

[41] *FASB Statement No. 52*, ¶ 104.

[42] *FASB Statement of Financial Accounting Standards No. 13*, Accounting for Leases, ¶¶ 6, 122.

[43] *FASB Statement No. 2*, ¶ 53; *IAS 23*, ¶ 11.

[44] *FASB Statement of Financial Accounting Standards No. 117*, Financial Statements of Not-for-Profit Organizations, ¶ 141.

[45] *FASB Statement No. 130*, ¶ 71.

[46] *FASB Statement No. 66*, Accounting for Sales of Real Estate, *Appendix D*, ¶ 95; *FASB Statement No. 89*, Financial Reporting and Changing Prices, *Appendix A*, ¶ 73; *FASB Statement No. 95*, Statement of Cash Flows, *Appendix C*, ¶ 133; *FASB Statement No. 102*, Statement of Cash Flows – Net Reporting of Certain Enterprises and Classification of Cash Flows from Certain Securities Acquired for Resale; *FASB Statement No. 113*, Accounting and Reporting for Reinsurance of Short-Duration and Long-Duration Contracts, *Appendix B*, ¶ 120; *FASB Statement No. 130*, Reporting Comprehensive Income, *Appendix B*, ¶ 131; *FASB Statement No. 133*, Accounting for Derivative Instruments and Hedging Activities, *Appendix C*, ¶ 225; *FASB Statement No. 154*, Accounting Changes and Error Corrections – a replacement of APB Opinion No. 20 and FASB Statement No. 3.

> **Comment:** The main rationale here is to enhance transparency and cohesiveness among the financial statements.[47] However, a clear distinction of equity from debt financing is an implicit confirmation of the concept of equity as residual interest (as discussed in Section 2.1.4.1 previously).

Worksheet 18 illustrates the basic formats and basic forms of the statement of financial position.

> **Comment:** Accounting practice in different countries has been developing around the two basic formats – the balanced and the equity formats – with varied column or page arrangements.
>
> The balanced format, which is the graphic representation of the so-called "fundamental accounting (or balance sheet) equation," whereby assets equal the sum of liabilities and equity, emphasizes sources of finance (liabilities and equity) and how they are used or invested (assets) as of the reporting date. Under this view, equity is the source of contributed and earned risk capital which together with debt (non-risk capital) finances the entity's assets. Alternatively, both equity and liabilities embody rights, although different, on an entity's assets.
>
> It is typically employed in the Franco-Italian-German tradition. Incidentally, these countries denominate each side of the balance sheet with specific terms, while in the English language there is a split in the sources side of the balance sheet between the terms equity and liabilities.
>
> The equity format (also known as net asset or United Kingdom GAAP format) represents the so-called "alternative accounting equation," whereby assets minus liabilities equal net assets (or equity or capital in a larger sense). It is typically used by British companies, and by a minority of U.S. companies. It emphasizes equity as a residual element. Also, the concept of capital invested or employed is in line with this approach.

For each format there may be two basic forms:

The account (or horizontal) form: assets on the left-hand side or column, and liabilities and equity on the right-hand side or column;

The report (or vertical) form: top-to-bottom or running presentation (assets then liabilities then equity).

> **Comment:** In conjunction with a classified balance sheet in report form, the equity format brings out net working capital (as opposed to working capital when a classified balance is associated with the balanced format), and the elaboration of permanent financing. This type of variation is sometimes called the financial position format. Therefore, this is the type of format that is generally used for the financial re-classification of the balance sheet and for the calculation of ROI in its several variants based on a strict financial orientation. It is commonly used internationally, although not so much in the United States. In 2009 and in 2005, 87% and 84% of survey U.S. GAAP companies used a report form of the statement of financial position, respectively, while the remaining companies used the account form.[48]

---

[47] *FASB Meeting, January 31, 2007, FASB Memoranda No. 46A-C, ¶ 49 (January 31, 2007); IASB Meeting, January 25, 2007, Agenda Paper 13d*, Application of Working Principles, *¶¶ 21, 28 (January 25, 2007)*.

[48] *AICPA ATT 2010, ¶ Table 2-2; AICPA ATT 2006, ¶ Table 2-2*.

> **Comment:** Both formats are compatible with U.S. GAAP and IFRSs, based on nonpromulgated GAAP, although the equity format – equity as a residual – is typically employed under both the IASB and the FASB conceptual frameworks. It should be noted, however, that IAS 1 Implementation Guidance (which accompanies but is not part of the standard) shows an example of a balance sheet under balanced format and report form.

> **Planning Point:** The way financial statements are divided across categories and sections may favor different notions and uses of equity, thus suggesting different ways of reading them by financial analysts and other users. The FASB and IASB joint *Financial Statement Presentation Project* addresses different display formats. However, the Boards' discussion on the categorization working principle would seem not to have really related their consideration on presentation layouts to the long-standing debate on the equity format versus the balanced format. The different uses behind these two formats serve users' needs in several ways. Practices in many jurisdictions of reclassifying financial statement along the lines of the equity format demonstrate such purposes.

> **Comment:** Actually, both financial analysis and accounting practices of reclassification in management commentary have for a long time brought about a solution, in certain jurisdictions, to the debate on what primary categories should be presented on the face of the financial statements, by having both a traditional (financial reporting according to GAAP) presentation and a reclassification based on financial markets practices. This is supposed to have reached cohesiveness (or to be more cohesive), as well as to separate different angles of analysis, such as financing versus operating or other categories, internal versus external financing, working capital versus permanent financing, liquidity information, or balance sheet classification, for capital structure analysis.

4.2   SINGLE- VERSUS MULTI-STEP EQUITY SECTION

The equity section of the statement of financial position may be either in the form of a stand-alone section or as part of a total liabilities and equity section.

> **Comment:** This often depends on whether the "equity format" or the "balance sheet format" of the statement of financial position is employed (see Section 4.1.4 previously).

Section 210-10-S99 (Regulation S-X) adopts a multi-step display of the equity section of the statement of financial position, whereby in lieu of a total equity heading separate captions apply to nonredeemable preferred stocks, common stocks, and other stockholders' equity.[49] SEC registrants must report certain items as "temporary equity" which is presented under line items separately from "permanent equity" and long-term debt. Therefore, this classification is commonly referred to as "mezzanine." These line items must not be reported under stockholders' equity or combined in a total with items of stockholders' equity.[50] Section 4.3 following analyzes noncontrolling interest and their mezzanine classification for publicly-held companies. Section 4.4 later discusses the other situations of temporary equity.

---

[49]   *FASB ASC 210-10-S99-1 (Regulation S-X, ¶ 210.5-02).*
[50]   *FASB ASC 210-10-S99-1 (Regulation S-X, ¶ 210.5-02.28(d)).*

> **Comment:** When a single-step display is used, a financial instrument must be classified either as equity or as a financial liability/asset. Conversely, Regulation S-X distinguishes "permanent" from "temporary" equity (e.g., redeemable preferred stocks and minority interests). Therefore, a multi-step format firstly permits this segregation, and secondly avoids the totalizing of equity.

Temporary equity classification requirements are set out for publicly-held companies in Accounting Series Release No. 268 – Section 210-10-S99 (Rule 210.5-02.28 of Regulation S-X) and Section 480-10-S99 (EITF Topic No. D-98). Accounting Series Release No. 268 was intended to be an interim solution until the conceptual boundaries between equity and liability classification had been revised.[51]

> **Comment:** The FASB recently rejected the "mezzanine approach" to avoid adding a separate residual caption in which to place difficult classification issues. Furthermore, this approach is inconsistent with the definition of a liability in CON 6, based on which mandatorily redeemable equity instruments are liabilities.[52]

4.3   NONCONTROLLING INTEREST

4.3.1   Terminology

Both U.S. GAAP and IFRSs are moving from the term *minority interest* to *noncontrolling interest*.

> **Comment:** The expression *minority interest* derives from the traditional "ownership" model of consolidation, whereby legal ownership determines the status of an entity as subsidiary within a group. U.S. GAAP was the first to start using *noncontrolling interest*,[53] although Subtopic 810-10 (FASB Statement No. 160) still retains both the terms *noncontrolling* and *minority interest*.[54] The term *noncontrolling interest* is now adopted by both U.S. GAAP and IFRSs. This is because the characteristic of control, and not the attribute of being a majority, is ultimately the determinant for consolidation purposes.[55] In the particular situation of a business combination achieved by contract alone, a party may end up having the whole equity interests in a subsidiary and nonetheless retain the status of being the noncontrolling interest.[56]

4.3.2   Noncontrolling Interest and Consolidation Theories

Two traditional main alternative presentation and measurement bases may be found with reference to noncontrolling interest. They somehow relate to whether the "entity theory"

---

[51]   *FASB ASC 480-10-S99-3 (EITF Topic No. D-98, ¶ 13), superseded by Accounting Standards Update No. 2009-04,* Accounting for Redeemable Equity Instruments *(August 2009).*

[52]   *Financial Accounting Standards Board, Preliminary Views,* Financial Instruments with Characteristics of Equity, *¶¶ D6, E10 (November 30, 2007).*

[53]   *The term* noncontrolling interest *was used in the FASB Exposure Draft,* Consolidations *(1995) and in the FASB Exposure Draft,* Consolidated Financial Statements *(1999).*

[54]   *FASB ASC 810-10-45-15 (ARB 51 ¶ 25, as amended by FASB Statement No. 160,* Noncontrolling Interests in Consolidated Financial Statements – an amendment of ARB No. 51*).*

[55]   *FASB Statement No. 160, ¶ B28; IAS 27 (2010), ¶ BC28.*

[56]   *IFRS 3, ¶ 44.*

or the "parent company theory "(also called "parent entity" concept) of consolidation is used. However, this is not a necessary relationship.[57] Under the parent company theory, noncontrolling interests are not considered equity (but quasi-liabilities) and are generally measured at an amount equal to the minority's share of the carrying amount of the subsidiary's identifiable net assets. Noncontrolling interests do not include the minority's share of the fair value adjustments and goodwill.

Comment: The "parent company theory" focuses on what the parent company owns and owes and treats minority stockholders as outsiders – not a party in the business combination transaction, leaving them unaffected by the transaction of the majority shareholder. The assets and liabilities of the subsidiary are included on a "mixed" basis in the consolidated statement of financial position, i.e., at fair value to the extent of the parent's share and at preacquisition carrying cost for the minority's share. The rationale is that the cost of acquisition only relates to the percentage of the identifiable assets and liabilities purchased by the acquirer, while the minority's proportion has not been part of the exchange transaction to effect the acquisition. As a result, the consolidated statement of financial position is essentially a variant of the parent's statement of financial position with the assets and liabilities of all subsidiaries substituted for the parent's investment in those subsidiaries. The extreme of the parent company concept is the "proprietary" concept, which emphasizes the central role of owners as opposed to the entity itself.[58] An accounting translation of the proprietary concept is the proportionate consolidation method (which IFRSs, prior to IFRS 11, adopt for jointly controlled entities), whereby only the parent's share of the acquiree's assets and liabilities is consolidated and minority interest is completely ignored.

Comment: Conceptually, the selection of one of these approaches to consolidated financial statements must affect the scope of comprehensive income. As comprehensive income is defined as a period change in an entity's net assets arising other than from transactions with owners in their capacity as owners (see Section 7.2.1 later), whether or not noncontrolling interests are considered owners would determine whether gains and losses arising from a transaction with them shall be accounted for in equity or in a statement of income. Section 4.14.2 later illustrates this issue with reference to treasury stock.

Under the entity theory, however, noncontrolling interest is computed as the minority's share of the net assets' fair value, with several calculation alternatives. Under a variant of the entity theory, known as the "parent entity extension" concept or "economic-unit/purchased goodwill" method, noncontrolling interest is stated at minority's share of the net assets' fair value, with no goodwill attributed to minority interest. The "economic unit" concept refers to the treatment of two or more legal entities as a single reporting entity.[59] By contrast, the pure entity theory

---

[57] *IAS 27 (2010), ¶ BC43 explains that the IASB has not yet comprehensively considered the entity and proprietary concepts. Furthermore, IASB Update March 2009, page 1 reports that, as part of the* Conceptual Framework *Project, the IASB tentatively decided to avoid referring to the entity or proprietary perspectives as those do not convey the views of the IASB and the FASB.*

[58] *Discussion Paper,* Preliminary Views on an Improved Conceptual Framework for Financial Reporting, The Reporting Entity *(May 2008), ¶ 108.*

[59] *Discussion Paper,* Preliminary Views on an Improved Conceptual Framework for Financial Reporting, The Reporting Entity *(May 2008), ¶ 116.*

(also referred to as "economic-unit/full goodwill" method or "economic-control" approach[60]) determines the goodwill that would be applied as if the subsidiary were wholly owned, and the computation of noncontrolling interests comprises both the minority's share of the net fair value of subsidiary's assets and liabilities and the part of goodwill that is attributable to noncontrolling interest.

> **Comment:** According to the entity theory the whole assets and liabilities of a subsidiary are measured at their fair value at the date of acquisition. This concept emphasizes control by the acquirer as opposed to ownership. It also focuses on the single management of the consolidated group.

Both theories have been represented in U.S. practice, although the prevailing accounting in the U.S. to date has been along the parent-company concept.

> **Comment:** The fact that the noncontrolling interest refers to subsidiaries as opposed to the parent has been a resistance factor for not considering it as part of the equity of the consolidated group. In fact, even considering minority interests as shareholders, such status, as referred to the consolidated group, mathematically results from their interest in only a part (the subsidiaries) of the consolidated entity. Noncontrolling shareholders have a residual claim on the net assets of the subsidiaries, not the consolidated group. Therefore their risks and benefit are different from those of controlling interest.[61] From a consolidated financial analysis perspective, noncontrolling interest may be somehow akin to preferred stock, as both creditors and controlling shareholders of the parent company may benefit, indirectly through channels of control and rights and limitations set out by corporate law frameworks, from net assets of the subsidiaries only after satisfying the claims of its minority shareholders. The IASB acknowledged such a particular situation, but decided to maintain the accounting for noncontrolling interest consistent with the IASB Framework,[62] as explained next. Conversely, from the perspective of the subsidiary, both the parent and noncontrolling interest have no further obligation to contribute assets to it.[63]

Despite accounting practice, both the U.S. Concepts and IASB Framework support the entity theory.

> **Comment:** Minority interest lacks the present obligation characteristics that define a liability in both the IASB Framework and U.S. Concepts.[64] At the same time, it meets the definition of equity as residual interest in the net assets of subsidiaries that are not held, directly or indirectly, by the parent.[65] The presentation of minority interest outside equity is in contrast with the U.S. Concepts which consider noncontrolling interest as equity. However, CON 6 does not discuss specific display formats, and does not rule out a separate presentation from majority interest or giving prominence

---

[60] *A conceptual codification of the economic-control approach is in Seventh Council Directive 83/349/EEC (June 13, 1983).*

[61] *Similarly, IAS 27 (2010), ¶ DO6.*

[62] *IASB, Business Combinations Phase II, Project Summary and Feedback Statement, page 16 (January 2008).*

[63] *IAS 27 (2010), ¶ BC38.*

[64] *CON 6, ¶ 35; The Conceptual Framework for Financial Reporting 2010, ¶ 4.15; IASB Framework, ¶ 60.*

[65] *FASB Statement No. 141(R), ¶ B34; IAS 27 (2010), ¶¶ BC31–BC32.*

to majority interest in consolidated financial statements.[66] Furthermore, the FASB has recently taken the position that the U.S. Concepts do not define noncontrolling interest as an element of the financial statements and therefore mezzanine classification would not be justified.[67] ARB 51,[68] before being amended by FASB Statement No. 160, in sustaining that consolidation represented a single business enterprise, also seemed to be consistent with the entity theory. However, earlier practice, even before the issuance of the superseded APB Opinion No. 16, *Business Combinations*, was to compute minority interest by using preacquisition carrying amounts. APB Opinion No. 16 did not provide guidance for accounting for less-than-wholly owned subsidiaries strong enough to change such accounting. Recently, the *Joint Conceptual Framework Project* also supports the entity perspective view.[69]

4.3.3 Presentation of Noncontrolling Interest

From a presentation standpoint, minority interest has long been shown separately in the balance sheet, but generally not as part of stockholders' equity, either under noncurrent liabilities, or other liabilities, or as "mezzanine," that is a caption between total liabilities and shareholders' equity. In the income statement, minority interest has been shown as a deduction, that is, an expense, to arrive at net income. The *AICPA Accounting Trends & Techniques* records 173 occurrences in 2005 of display of minority interest in other noncurrent liabilities, and 110 cases of charges in income statement after income from continuing operations. Entities included it in losses in 57 instances.[70]

Comment: Before the *Business Combination Project* (added to the FASB agenda in 1996) the FASB had deliberated noncontrolling interest issues as part of the *Consolidations Project* (added to the FASB agenda in 1982), the Discussion Memorandum, *Consolidation Policy and Procedures* (1991), and the *Financial Instruments Project* (added to the FASB agenda in 1986). One of the objectives of the *Financial Instruments with Characteristics of Equity Project* – former *Financial Instruments: Liabilities and Equity Project* was also to eliminate the classification of minority interest as mezzanine.

An SEC registrant must present "net income attributable to the noncontrolling interest" in the income statement after net income or loss.[71] SEC registrants must report an item for noncontrolling interests in the statement of financial position. Although the rule is not specific about the location of this item, entities have generally placed it between the long-term debt section and the equity section and before redeemable preferred stock. Alternatively, presentation within debt, with an appropriate description in the notes, has been considered acceptable.

Recently, Regulation S-X changed its position to a line after other stockholders' equity. In fact, the SEC Staff took the view that registrants must now abide by the presentation requirements

---

[66] *CON 6, ¶ 254.*
[67] *FASB Statement No. 160, ¶ B32.*
[68] *FASB ASC 810-10-45-6 (ARB 51, ¶ 14).*
[69] *Discussion Paper,* Preliminary Views on an Improved Conceptual Framework for Financial Reporting, The Reporting Entity, *¶ S8 (May 2008).*
[70] *AICPA ATT 2006, ¶¶ Tables 2-31, 3.7, 3.17.*
[71] *FASB ASC 225-10-S99-2 (Regulation S-X, ¶ 210.5-03(b).19).*

of Subtopic 810-10 (FASB Statement No. 160).[72] Furthermore, the SEC announced that classification as liability is no longer acceptable.[73] The minority interest related to preferred stock and the applicable dividend requirements, if the preferred stock is material in relation to the consolidated stockholders' equity, presumes separate indication in a note.[74]

As part of the *Business Combination Project*, Subtopic 810-10 (ARB 51, as amended by FASB Statement No. 160) now requires that noncontrolling interests be clearly and separately presented within consolidated equity, but separate from the parent's equity, and that net income or loss and comprehensive income or loss that are attributed to the parent and to the noncontrolling interest be separately displayed.[75]

Comment: It is to be noted, however, that in the way Subtopic 810-10 (FASB Statement No. 160) illustrates, this new consolidated income statement[76] is similar to current practice, as net income attributable to the noncontrolling interests is still deducted from net income to arrive at net income attributable to the parent.

IAS 22 permitted the entity concept as an allowed alternative to the benchmark treatment, which used to be in line with the parent-company concept. The 1997 version of IAS 1 and the 2000 version of IAS 27 used a sort of "mezzanine" presentation of minority interest on the balance sheet, between liabilities and consolidated equity. IFRS 3 superseded IAS 22 and determined noncontrolling interest to be the minority's share times the fair value of the acquiree's identifiable net assets. The 2003 and 2005 versions of IAS 1 and IAS 27 treated it in the statement of financial position as part of equity, separately from controlling interests, and in income statement as allocation of profit or loss (as opposed to a deduction as an expense).[77] IFRSs, as a result of the *Business Combination Project*, maintain noncontrolling interest as a separate caption in equity in the statement of financial position and now also need to determine the portions of profit or loss and total comprehensive income that are attributable to noncontrolling interests and to present total comprehensive income for the period separately in the newly-established single statement of comprehensive income or in the income statement and in the statement of comprehensive income (when the two-statement approach is elected).[78] U.S. GAAP also requires the display of amounts of net income and comprehensive income that are attributable to noncontrolling interests on the face of the income statement or

---

[72] *SEC Regulations Committee, April 9, 2008 – Joint Meeting with SEC Staff, Discussion Document A, ¶ 4,* Presentation of Minority Interest in Consolidated Financial Statements under Article 5 of Regulation S-X Upon Adoption of FAS 160 *www.sec.gov (last visited July 20, 2010).*

[73] *Revised SEC Staff Announcement, EITF Abstract, Topic No. D-98,* Classification and Measurement of Redeemable Securities, *¶ 38*

[74] *FASB ASC 210-10-S99-1 (Regulation S-X, ¶¶ 210.5-02.31); FASB ASC 944-210-S99-1 (Regulation S-X, ¶ 210.7-03.24); FASB ASC 942-210-S99-1 (Regulation S-X, ¶ 201.9-03.22).*

[75] *FASB ASC 810-10-45-16 (ARB 51, ¶ 26, as amended by FASB Statement No. 160 and FASB Statement No.141(R), ¶¶ 26); FASB ASC 810-10-45-20 (ARB 51, ¶ 30); FASB ASC 810-10-50-1A (ARB 51, ¶ 38).*

[76] *FASB ASC 805-10-55-4 (FASB Statement No. 141(R), ¶ A4); FASB ASC 810-10-55-4J, 810-10-55-4K (ARB 51, ¶¶ A4, A5, as amended by FASB Statement No. 160). In fact, FASB Statement No. 141(R), ¶ B36 reports that the new requirement is believed not to change current practice.*

[77] *IAS 1 (revised 2005), ¶¶ 82, BC19.*

[78] *IFRS 10, ¶ 22; IAS 1, ¶¶ 54, 82, 83; IAS 27 (2010), ¶¶ 27–28.*

the statement of comprehensive income.[79] Subtopic 810-10 (FASB Statement No. 160) also amends Subtopic 220-1 (FASB Statement No. 130) to require the display of comprehensive income attributed to controlling and noncontrolling interests on the face of the statement where comprehensive income is presented.[80] Furthermore, under Subtopic 810-10 (FASB Statement No. 160), the statement of changes in equity must segregate the amounts of net income, total comprehensive income for the period, and each component of other comprehensive income that are attributable to noncontrolling interests from that of the owners of the parent. Effective for fiscal years ending after December 15, 2012 and subsequent annual and interim periods, with early adoption permitted, and for fiscal years (and related interim periods) beginning after December 15, 2011 for public entities, ASU 2011-05 shows the attribution of only the total of other comprehensive income to noncontrolling interests on the face of the statement of changes in equity.[81] IAS 1 also requires balances reconciliation as part of the statement of changes in equity, but does not state the attribution to controlling and noncontrolling interests. However, this is shown in the Implementation Guidance.[82]

Comment: There are subtle differences for the latter requirement. Firstly, unlike IAS 1, Subtopic 810-10 (FASB Statement No. 160) allows note disclosure as an option. This is because nonregistered companies are not obliged to present the statement of changes in equity.[83] Secondly, the wording of IAS 1 literally calls for the change in equity balances arising from profit or loss, each item of other comprehensive income, and transactions with owners. Instead, the wording of Subtopic 810-10 (FASB Statement No. 160) requires the showing of net income, each component of other comprehensive income, and transactions with owners. Implementation Guidance shows these differences.

Example: In its review of Form 20-F for the year ended December 31, 2005 of a foreign private issuer from The Netherlands, the SEC Staff challenged the mezzanine presentation of minority interest.[84]

Example: In its Form 20-F for the year ended December 31, 2005 containing financial statements prepared for the first time on the basis of IFRSs, a British foreign private issuer presented a reconciliation between profit for the year under U.K. GAAP (that under IFRSs includes noncontrolling interest) and the profit for the year attributable to the controlling shareholders.[85]

---

[79] *FASB ASC 810-10-50-1A, 810-10-55-4J, 810-10-55-4K (ARB 51, ¶¶ 38(a), A4, A5, as amended by FASB Statement No. 160).*

[80] *FASB Statement No. 130, ¶ 14, as amended by FASB Statement No. 160, ¶ C9.*

[81] *FASB ASC 220-10-45-8 superseded, 220-10-55-11, 220-10-55-12, 810-10-55-4L as amended by ASU 2011-05.*

[82] *FASB ASC 810-10-50-1A, 810-10-55-AL (ARB 51, ¶¶ 38(c), A6, as amended by FASB Statement No. 160); IAS 1, ¶ 106(d) as amended by IAS 27 (Revised 2008); IAS 27 (2010), ¶ 28.*

[83] *FASB Statement No. 160, ¶ B66.*

[84] *Letter by the SEC, File No. 0-17444, Note 1 (October 3, 2006) www.sec.gov/divisions/corpfin/ifrs_reviews (last visited January 7, 2008).*

[85] *Letter by the SEC, File No. 000-25670, Note 54 (September 28, 2006). Reply by the company (October 30, 2006) www.sec.gov/divisions/corpfin/ifrs_reviews (last visited January 7, 2008).*

Under both U.S. GAAP and IFRSs, the part of income from continuing operations, discontinued operations, and extraordinary items (U.S. GAAP only) that is attributed to the parent must be disclosed either on the face of the income statement (U.S. GAAP) or the statement of comprehensive income (IFRSs) or in the notes.[86]

IAS 27 (R) and Subtopic 810-10 (FASB Statement No. 160) are effective, respectively, for fiscal years beginning on or after July 1, 2009, and for fiscal years and interim periods within those fiscal years beginning on or after December 15, 2008. Earlier application of Subtopic 810-10 (FASB Statement No. 160) is prohibited while it is permitted for IAS 27 (R), provided IFRS 3 (R) is also applied. Prospective application is required as of the beginning of the year of first application. Retrospective reclassification of noncontrolling interest is required by Subtopic 810-10 (FASB Statement No. 160), but IAS 27 (R) does not permit restating the attribution of total comprehensive income to the owners of the parent and to the noncontrolling interests. A first-time adopter cannot restate, unless it applies IFRS 3 retrospectively to past business combinations. Subtopic 805-10 (FASB Statement No. 141(R)) and IFRS 3(R) must be applied prospectively to business combinations for which the acquisition date is on or after the beginning of the first annual reporting period beginning on or after December 15, 2008 or July 1, 2009, respectively. Under both the standards, assets and liabilities of previous business combinations shall not be retroactively adjusted. Earlier application of Subtopic 805-10 (FASB Statement No. 141 (R)) is prohibited. Earlier application of IFRS 3 is permitted only for an annual reporting period that begins on or after June 30, 2007.[87]

The SEC Staff considers appropriate the separate presentation of income or loss applicable to common stock on the face of the consolidated income statement in case of a material difference (or more than 10%) with reported net income or loss or when it is indicative of significant trends or other qualitative considerations. Its presentation is mandatory when the entity adopts a single statement of income and comprehensive income. The reconciliation between net income and income available to common stock may be presented below comprehensive income.[88]

Comment: As a related issue, Subtopic 810-10 (FASB Statement No. 160)[89] has confirmed (and the revisions of IFRS 3 and IAS 27 have not amended) the way income for continuing operations available to common shareholders and net income have been computed under current practice (i.e., after adjusting for minority interest)[90] for the purpose of calculating earnings per share based on the consolidated financial statements.

The computational note in the definition of "significant subsidiary" in Regulation S-X[91] also refers to income from continuing operations, which is net of minority interest.[92]

---

[86] *FASB ASC 810-10-50-1A (ARB 51, as amended, ¶ 38(b)); IFRS 5, as amended by IAS 27 (2008), ¶ 33(d).*

[87] *FASB ASC 805-10-65-1 (FASB Statement No. 141(R), ¶¶ 74–75); IFRS 3 R, ¶¶ 64–65; IAS 27 (2010), ¶¶ 44–45, A2.*

[88] *SEC Staff Accounting Bulletin, Topic 6-B, Accounting Series Release 280 – General Revision of Regulation S-X: Income or Loss Applicable To Common Stock.*

[89] *FASB Statement No. 160, ¶ C8.*

[90] *FASB Statement No. 128,* Earnings per Share, *¶¶ 140–141; IAS 33, ¶ A1.*

[91] *Regulation S-X, ¶ 210.1-02(w)(3).*

[92] *FASB ASC 225-10-S99-2 (Regulation S-X, ¶ 210.5-03(b)).*

> **Comment:** A possible revision of such guidance may affect which equity-method investees or unconsolidated subsidiaries are deemed "significant," therefore triggering disclosure of summarized financial information.

4.3.4 Different Classifications of Noncontrolling Interests in Subsidiary's and Consolidated Financial Statements

Subtopic 810-10 (FASB Statement No. 160) and Subtopic 805-10 (FASB Statement No.141(R)) have not affected the classification of a financial instrument under Subtopic 480-10 (FASB Statement No. 150 and FASB Staff Position FAS 150-3, *Effective Date, Disclosures, and Transition for Mandatorily Redeemable Financial Instruments of Certain Nonpublic Entities and Certain Mandatorily Redeemable Noncontrolling Interests under FASB Statement No. 150*), and SEC Accounting Series Release 268, *Presentation in Financial Statements of "Redeemable Preferred Stocks."* Subtopic 810-10 (FASB Statement No. 160) also acknowledged the inconsistency between the standard and EITF Issue No. 00-6, now superseded by EITF Issue No. 08-8, that does not consider the stock of a subsidiary as equity of the parent company.[93]

Section 810-10-45 (ARB 51) requires that a financial instrument, issued by the parent or a subsidiary, and classified in the subsidiary's financial statements as a liability by other standards cannot be considered a noncontrolling interest in consolidated financial statements.[94]

> **Comment:** Conversely, under IFRSs, a different treatment of noncontrolling interest in consolidated versus subsidiary's financial statements may exist, when additional terms and conditions agreed directly between a parent company and the minority holders of equity instruments result in an obligation or settlement provision that forces a liability classification of those instruments in consolidated financial statements.[95]

4.3.4.1 Put Options on Noncontrolling Interests In particular, put options on noncontrolling interests are a case of possible different treatment between IFRSs and U.S. GAAP. Under IFRSs, written put options for cash or other financial assets on an entity's own equity instruments granted to noncontrolling shareholders are financial liabilities, not noncontrolling interests, whose changes affect profit or loss. They are measured at the present value of their redemption amount.[96] The IFRS Interpretations Committee is considering whether to introduce a scope exclusion from IAS 32 that would result in derivative treatment.[97]

> **Example:** The Corporate Reporting Standing Committee (EECS), a forum of the EU National Enforcers of Financial Information, accepted an issuer's treatment of a written puttable instrument of

---

[93] *FASB Statement No. 160, ¶ B35.*
[94] *FASB ASC 810-10-45-16A, 810-10-45-17 (ARB 51, ¶ 27, as amended by FASB Statement No. 160).*
[95] *IAS 32, ¶ AG29.*
[96] *IFRS 9, ¶¶ 5.7.2–5.7.4; IAS 32, ¶¶ 23, AG29; IAS 39, ¶¶ 55, 56.*
[97] *IFRIC Update, March 2011; IFRIC Update January 2011; IFRIC Update November 2010; IFRIC Update, September 2010; IFRIC Update, July 2010; IFRIC Update, May 2010.*

noncontrolling interest as financial liability with the derecognition of the minority interest previously accounted in equity.[98] In another case, the EECS rejected the treatment of minority puts as contingent liabilities.[99]

Comment: Therefore, if the put option is agreed upon only by the parent, those financial instruments will be equity in the financial statements of the subsidiary and financial liabilities in the consolidated financial statement.

Under FASB Statement No. 150, freestanding written put options on the issuer's shares that must be physically or net cash settled are also financial liabilities. Conversely, before EITF Issue No. 08-8, put options embedded in nonderivative host contracts were accounted for as embedded derivative liabilities, if the other conditions for considering them embedded derivatives were met, and were measured at fair value.[100] EITF Issue No. 08-8, effective for fiscal years beginning on or after December 15, 2008 and related interim periods, deals with the accounting for a freestanding financial instrument that is not within the scope of FASB Statement No. 150 (or a separately recorded embedded feature) for which the payoff of the counterparty fully or partially depends on the stock of a consolidated subsidiary. When the subsidiary is considered to be a substantive entity and both under EITF Issue No. 07-5[101] such an instrument is determined to be indexed to the entity's own stock and under EITF Issue No. 00-19 it is classified as equity, the instrument qualifies for the scope exception in Subtopic 815-10 (FASB Statement No. 133) for instruments both indexed to their own stock and classified in equity. Therefore is not considered to be a derivative. Conversely, this instrument must be presented as a noncontrolling interest in the consolidated financial statements, irrespective of whether it was entered into by the parent or the subsidiary. If it expires unexercised, an equity-classified instrument that was entered into by the parent must be reclassified to the controlling interest.[102]

Example: Two French foreign private issuers explained to the SEC Staff the differences in accounting for put options on noncontrolling interests as financial liabilities under IFRSs and under derivatives U.S. GAAP.[103]

---

[98] *Committee of European Securities Regulators (CESR), 2007. CESR/07-120,* Extract from EECS's Database of Enforcement Decisions, *Paris: CESR, ¶ Decision ref. EECS/0407-16. [Online] CESR. Available at www.cesr.eu (last visited July 20, 2010).*

[99] *Committee of European Securities Regulators (CESR), 2009. CESR/09-252, 5th* Extract from EECS's Database of Enforcement Decisions, *Paris: CESR, ¶ Decision ref. EECS/0209-06. [Online] CESR. Available at www.cesr.eu (last visited July 20, 2010).*

[100] *FASB ASC 815-20-25-20 (FASB Statement No. 133, ¶ 61(e)); FASB Statement No. 150, ¶ 11; EITF Issue No. 00-6, ¶ 21; IAS 32, ¶ 23.*

[101] *EITF Issue No. 07-5,* Determining Whether an Instrument (or an Embedded Feature) is Indexed to an Entity's Own Stock.

[102] *FASB ASC 815-40-45-5C (EITF Issue No. 08-8,* Accounting for an Instrument (or an Embedded Feature) with a Settlement Amount That is Based on the Stock of an Entity's Consolidated Subsidiary, *¶¶ 5, 7, 9); EITH Issue No. 08-8, ¶¶ 3, 10.*

[103] *Reply by the company to the SEC, File No. 001-14734, Note 3 (December 28, 2006). Reply by the company to the SEC, File 1-15248, Note 23 (September 25, 2006) www.sec.gov/divisions/ corpfin/ifrs_reviews (last visited January 7, 2008).*

4.3.4.2 Mandatorily Redeemable Noncontrolling Interests   As a second situation, under IFRSs, mandatorily redeemable noncontrolling interests are financial liabilities, again also considering terms agreed upon by the parent and irrespective of the classification given by the subsidiary. Under Subtopic 480-10 (FASB Statement No. 150), an entity also classifies a mandatorily redeemable noncontrolling interest as a financial liability. However, Section 810-10-45 (ARB 51, as amended by FASB Statement No. 160) scopes out equity classification of financial instruments issued by a subsidiary that are not classified as equity in the subsidiary's financial statements.[104] SEC registrants classify mandatorily redeemable noncontrolling interests in temporary equity, unless they fall within the scope of FASB Statement No. 150 or the redemption feature is a freestanding option within the scope of FASB Statement No. 150. FASB Statement No. 150 requires their classification as liabilities. FASB ASC 480-10-65-1 (FASB Staff Position FAS 150-3) deferred indefinitely the measurement – not the classification provisions of FASB Statement No. 150 for mandatorily redeemable noncontrolling interests, other than those redeemable only upon the liquidation or termination of the subsidiary. However, SEC registrants must apply both the classification and measurement guidance of EITF Issue D-98, if these instruments had been issued by the subsidiary before November 5, 2003 both in consolidated financial statements and in subsidiary's financial statements. Whether the subsidiary classifies these instruments as liabilities or temporary equity, Section 810-10-45 (ARB 51, as amended by FASB Statement No. 160), prohibits equity classification as noncontrolling interests in consolidated financial statements. Therefore, the SEC has instructed that adjustments to those instruments do not affect net income but result in direct debit or credit to the equity of the parent. The same effect occurs for the portion of the gain or loss that arises from the derecognition of the carrying amount of noncontrolling interest when the parent deconsolidates the former subsidiary because of disposal or loss of control. The adjustment to noncontrolling interests resulting from a change in a parent's ownership interest with no loss of control is accounted for as an equity transaction as for all other companies, although it may affect retained earnings instead of additional paid-in capital. Upon the retrospective application of these provisions, an entity must disclose the redemption amount of those securities on the face of the statement of financial position and provide note disclosure of their features.[105]

Finally, an SEC registrant that is also a finance subsidiary must not present outstanding mandatorily redeemable securities as noncontrolling interest, particularly when guaranteed by the parent and matched by the cash flows of the debt to its parent, without appropriate disclosure of the effective capitalization and leverage.[106]

4.3.4.3 Certain Instruments Associated to the Event of Liquidation   Under IFRSs, if certain subordinated puttable financial instruments that entitle the holder to a pro rata share of the entity's net assets in the event of the entity's liquidation, and certain instruments or components of instruments that impose on the entity an obligation to deliver to another party

---

[104] *FASB Staterment No. 150, ¶¶ 30, A30; FASB 810-10-45-17 ARB 51, ¶ 27(c), as amended by FASB Statement No. 160); IAS 32, ¶¶ 23, AG29.*

[105] *FASB Statement No. 150, ¶¶ 30, A30; FASB ASC 810-10-45-16A, 810-10-45-17 (ARB 51, ¶ 27(c)), as amended by FASB Statement No. 160; FASB Statement No. 160, ¶ B35; FASB ASC 480-10-S99-3A (EITF Topic No. D-98, ¶¶ 2, 17B, 19A, 25, as amended by Accounting Standards Update No. 2009-04,* Accounting for Redeemable Equity Instruments*); EITF Topic No. D-98, ¶¶ 21A, 40, 41; FASB ASC 480-10-65-1 (FASB Staff Position FAS 150-3, ¶ 7b).*

[106] *Securities and Exchange Commission, Division of Corporate Finance,* Current Issues and Rulemaking Projects, *page 81 (November 14, 2000).*

a pro rata share of the net assets of the entity only on liquidation,[107] refer to noncontrolling interest, they are equity in the separate or individual financial statements of the issuer but financial liabilities in the consolidated financial statements. This is because they are not residual interest in the consolidated financial statements as they are not in the most subordinated class of instruments from the perspective of the group.[108] Therefore, in the consolidated financial statements such instruments will be classified as equity to the extent of the controlling interest and financial liabilities for the noncontrolling interest.

Conversely, if a subsidiary issues mandatorily redeemable financial instruments whose redemption is required to occur only upon the liquidation or termination of such subsidiary, FASB Statement No. 150, as issued,[109] required that they were not classified as liability in the subsidiary's statement of financial position (otherwise the going concern assumption of the subsidiaries would be violated) while those mandatorily redeemable noncontrolling interests had to be displayed as such in the consolidated financial statement (because the possible liquidation or termination of such subsidiary did not violate the going concern assumption of the parent). This provision was deferred indefinitely for both public and nonpublic entities.[110]

4.3.5 Computation of Noncontrolling Interest

The computation of full goodwill under a pure entity theory may follow different mechanics. One way is to determine the "implied" amount that a purchaser of a 100% interest would pay as goodwill, based on a proportional calculation applied to the percentage of ownership acquired. An alternative is to determine the full goodwill as the difference between a direct measure of the fair value of the business as a whole and the sum of the fair values of the assets acquired and the liabilities assumed. The difference between the direct and implied methods potentially includes a control premium or minority discount. IFRS 3 (Revised 2008) and Subtopic 805-20 (FASB Statement No. 141 (Revised 2007)) instead innovate by defining a measurement attribute for noncontrolling interests and measuring them using a direct valuation (e.g., through the use of market prices or valuation techniques) as opposed to a residual measurement of the acquisition-date fair value. Valuation technique(s) and significant inputs to measure fair value must be disclosed.[111]

Comment: IFRS 3 (Revised 2008) does not proceed with the full goodwill method, which assesses the value of the business as a whole and determines noncontrolling interest residually after attributing a hypothetical portion of goodwill to it. Instead, it shifts in focus to assessing the values of the components of business (such as the consideration transferred, assets, liabilities and equity instruments of the acquiree) including a stand-alone determination of noncontrolling interest.[112]

---

[107] *Amendments to IAS 32* Financial Instruments: Presentation *and IAS 1* Presentation of Financial Statements, Puttable Financial Instruments and Obligations Arising on Liquidation, ¶¶ *16A–16D.*

[108] *Amendments to IAS 32* Financial Instruments: Presentation *and IAS 1* Presentation of Financial Statements, Puttable Financial Instruments and Obligations Arising on Liquidation, ¶¶ *AG29A, BC68.*

[109] *FASB ASC 480-10-25-4 (FASB Statement No. 150, ¶¶ 9); FASB Statement No. 150, ¶ B21.*

[110] *FASB ASC 480-10-65-1 (FASB Staff Position FAS 150-3,* Effective Date, Disclosures, and Transition for Mandatorily Redeemable Financial Instruments of Certain Nonpublic Entities and Certain Mandatorily Redeemable Noncontrolling Interests under FASB Statement No. 150, *¶ 7a).*

[111] *FASB ASC 805-20-50-1 (FASB Statement No. 141(R), ¶ 68(p)); IFRS 3, ¶ B64(o).*

[112] *IASB, Business Combinations Phase II,* Project Summary and Feedback Statement, *page 13 (January 2008).*

Worksheet 19 illustrates the computation of some of these different methods.

Under the 2008 version of IFRS 3, the acquirer in a business combination has the option, on a transaction-by-transaction basis, to measure noncontrolling interest either at acquisition-date fair value method or at the proportionate share of the acquiree's identifiable net assets[113] (the latter is sometimes referred to as "modified parent company theory"). This diverges from Topic 805 (FASB Statement No. 141(R)), which permits the acquisition-date fair value method only. The IASB recently limited this option to noncontrolling interests that are present ownership instruments (e.g., not an equity component of a compound instrument, or an equity-classified share-based transaction) and that entitle their holders to a pro rata share of net assets in the event of liquidation. In those cases, the proportionate share is that arising from the present ownership. These amendments are prospectively effective for annual periods beginning on or after July 1, 2010, with earlier application permitted.[114] Generally, the fair value method gives a higher noncontrolling interest and goodwill as opposed to the other method, a higher subsequent possible impairment of goodwill attributable to the noncontrolling interest, and a higher equity attributable to the controlling interest in case the parent subsequently increases its share. This is because under IAS 27(R) the difference between the consideration paid and the noncontrolling interests acquired for a change in a parent's ownership interest in a subsidiary accrues to the equity attributable to the parent. If noncontrolling interest is measured at its proportionate share of the acquiree's identifiable net assets, that difference corresponds to any unrecognized fair value changes that have arisen from the acquisition date, including goodwill, and that are instead paid to the noncontrolling interest.[115]

4.4   OTHER CLASSIFICATIONS IN TEMPORARY EQUITY

In addition to the no longer valid mezzanine classification of noncontrolling interests, there are several situations where SEC registrants must report some instruments in temporary equity, as explained in this paragraph. By contrast, IFRSs have no such temporary equity classification. Section 3.5.3.2 previously explains the particular case of minimum dividends.

Comment: These requirements are set out for publicly-held companies in Accounting Series Release No. 268 – Section 210-10-S99 (Rule 210.5-02.28 of Regulation S-X) and Section 480-10-S99 (EITF Topic No. D-98). These pronouncements no longer apply to instruments within the scope of Subtopic 480-10 (FASB Statement No. 150) after the effective date of this standard, but still apply under certain circumstances, including certain instruments under EITF Issue No. 00-19.[116]

4.4.1   Mandatorily Redeemable Preferred Shares

A mandatorily redeemable preferred share falls within the scope of Subtopic 480-10 (FASB Statement No. 150) if it imposes on the issuer an unconditional obligation to redeem it by

---

[113]   *IFRS 3, ¶ 19.*

[114]   Improvements to IFRSs, Amendments to IFRS 3 Business; *IFRIC Update, January 2010.*

[115]   *IAS 27 (2010), ¶ 31; IFRS 3, BC217–BC218.*

[116]   *FASB ASC 480-10-S99-3A (Accounting Standards Update No. 2009-04, Accounting for Redeemable Equity Instruments, 3); EITF Topic No. D-98 (superseded), ¶ 3.*

transferring its assets at specified or determinable date(s) or upon an event certain to occur.[117] In this case, it is classified as a liability. However, public companies must report such instruments in temporary equity, it they do not fall within the scope of Subtopic 480-10 (FASB Statement No. 150). This may be the case of a contingently or optionally redeemable instrument, which is outside the scope of FASB Statement No. 150 because there is no unconditional obligation to redeem the shares by transferring assets at a specified or determinable date or upon an event certain to occur. Liability reclassification applies when the uncertainty is resolved once the event has occurred, the condition has been resolved, or the event has become certain to occur.[118] The FASB indefinitely delayed the classification, measurement, and disclosure provisions of Subtopic 480-10 (FASB Statement No. 150) for mandatorily redeemable financial instruments of nonpublic, non-SEC registrant entities. For these companies, liability classification holds only for those financial instruments that are mandatorily redeemable on fixed dates for amounts that are either fixed or determinable through an external index.[119]

Under those circumstances, an SEC registrant must report in mezzanine a preferred stock when its redemption is outside the issuer's control. The specific line is called "preferred stocks subject to mandatory redemption requirements or whose redemption is outside the control of the issuer." "Outside issuer's control" means that the instrument is redeemable for cash or other assets at a fixed or determinable price on fixed or determinable dates, or that it is redeemable at the option of the holder, or when the conditions or events that trigger redemption are not solely within the control of the issuer.[120] Some "deemed" liquidation events, other than normal liquidation of the company, may also warrant temporary equity classification of related securities. These deemed liquidation events may include, according to relevant facts and circumstances, a redemption provision that requires approval by the board of directors, a provision that makes such securities become redeemable in case of a change in control, or other redemption clauses that are not solely within the issuer's control, such as a violation of a conversion provision or of another covenant, a delisting from a stock exchange, a failure to have an IPO declared effective by a particular date, a failure to achieve specific earnings targets, a reduction of the holder's credit rating, or similar events.[121] The SEC Staff clarifies that the same classification applies even if these events were not described as "deemed liquidation" events in the "liquidation" section of the preferred stock indentures to avoid ASR 268 treatment.[122]

> **Comment:** As a prerequisite for this classification, the instrument must be an equity, not debt, host instrument with certain features that preclude permanent equity classification.[123]

---

[117] *FASB ASC 480-10-05-3, 480-10-25-4, 480-10-55-5 (FASB Statement No. 150, ¶¶ 3, 9, A3); FASB Statement No. 150, ¶ B20.*

[118] *FASB ASC 480-10-55-39, 480-10-55-40 (FASB Statement No. 150, ¶ A28); FASB ASC 480-10-S99-3 (EITF Topic No. D-98, ¶ 26).*

[119] *FASB ASC 480-10-65-1 (FASB Staff Position FAS 150-3, ¶ 3).*

[120] *FASB ASC 210-10-S99-1 (Regulation S-X, ¶ 210.5-02.28, adopted in Accounting Series Release No. 268,* Presentation in Financial Statements of "Redeemable Preferred Stocks").

[121] *FASB ASC 480-10-S99-3A, (Accounting Standards Update No. 2009-04); EITF Topic No. D-98 (superseded), ¶¶ 7–9.*

[122] *Securities and Exchange Commission, Division of Corporate Finance,* Frequently Requested Accounting and Financial Reporting Interpretations and Guidance, *¶ I.A (March 31, 2001).*

[123] *See letter by the SEC to Alcatel, Note 5 (July 31, 2006) www.sec.gov/divisions/corpfin/ifrs_reviews (last visited January 7, 2008).*

Under Section 480-10-S99 (EITF Topic No. D-98), those instruments must be initially measured at fair value at date of issue and, if then currently redeemable or if redemption is probable, subsequently adjusted (against retained earnings or, in the absence of retained earnings, by charges against paid-in capital) to their maximum redemption amount at each reporting period date, also including undeclared or unpaid dividends but which will be payable under the mandatory redemption features, or for which the ultimate payment is not solely within the control of the issuer. If redeemable at a future determinable date and it is probable that the equity instrument will become redeemable, the security should be accreted in each period to the ultimate contractual redemption amount using an appropriate methodology, usually the interest method.[124]

Comment: Subtopic 825-10 (FASB Statement No. 159) excludes measurement under the fair value option of financial instruments that are, in whole or in part, classified as permanent or temporary equity, because changes in fair value would affect earnings while equity is not remeasured under current standards.[125] As part of the *Financial Instruments with Characteristics of Equity Project* – former *Financial Instruments: Liabilities and Equity Project* – the FASB proposed that such instruments be classified as liabilities. However, basic ownership instruments and components (i.e., common shares, not preferred shares) with redemption requirements would be remeasured at each balance sheet date at the current redemption value and changes in the redemption value be reported as a separate equity account.[126]

When mandatorily redeemable securities issued by an SEC registrant that is a financial subsidiary are guaranteed by the parent and matched by the cash flows of the debt to its parent, the consolidated balance sheet must separately present them in a line item captioned "company-obligated mandatorily redeemable security of subsidiary holding solely parent debentures," "guaranteed preferred beneficial interests in company's debentures," or similar description, with appropriate note disclosure.[127]

SEC registrants classify mandatorily redeemable noncontrolling interests in temporary equity, unless they fall within the scope of FASB Statement No. 150 or the redemption feature is a freestanding option within the scope of FASB Statement No. 150. Section 4.3.4 previously explains the accounting treatment in consolidated financial statements.

By contrast, under IAS 32, a mandatorily redeemable preferred share contains (eventually through split accounting if only a component of the instrument is mandatorily redeemable) a financial liability when the substance of the transaction is an obligation to transfer financial

---

[124] *FASB ASC 480-10-S99-3A (Accounting Standard Update No. 2009-04); EITF Topic No. D-98 (superseded), ¶ 15; FASB ASC 480-10-S99-2 (SEC Staff Accounting Bulletin, Topic 3-C,* Redeemable Preferred Stock*); Securities and Exchange Commission, Division of Corporate Finance,* Frequently Requested Accounting and Financial Reporting Interpretations and Guidance, *¶ I.A (March 31, 2001).*

[125] *FASB ASC 825-10-15-5 (FASB Statement No. 159,* The Fair Value Option for Financial Assets and Financial Liabilities, *¶ 8(f)); FASB Statement No. 159, ¶ A8(e).*

[126] *Financial Accounting Standards Board, Preliminary Views,* Financial Instruments with Characteristics of Equity, *¶ 32 (November 30, 2007).*

[127] *Securities and Exchange Commission, Division of Corporate Finance,* Current Issues and Rulemaking Projects, *page 81 (November 14, 2000).*

assets to the holder. This happens if the redemption amount is fixed or determinable and at a fixed or determinable future date. The liability is valued at the present value of its redemption amount.[128]

4.4.2 Contingently or Optionally Redeemable Instruments

Generally, for nonpublic companies, instruments that are outside the scope of Subtopic 480-10 (FASB Statement No. 150), such as contingently or optionally redeemable instruments, should be evaluated under Topic 815 (FASB Statement No. 133 and EITF Issue No. 00-19). Subtopic 815-40 (EITF Issue No. 00-19) has certain criteria to classify a contract that is indexed to, and potentially settled in, the issuer's own stock as equity. As an additional requirement, settlement in shares must be within the control of the company (it must not ultimately result in cash settlement), otherwise it would be a liability (or asset), except in certain circumstances in which the holder also receives cash.[129]

IAS 32 requires the same accounting for conditionally redeemable instruments as for mandatorily redeemable instruments. A preferred share that is redeemable at the option of the holder at or after a particular date for a fixed or determinable amount is also a financial liability, because the obligation to transfer cash or another financial asset for the redemption amount is beyond the control of the entity.[130]

Example: The Corporate Reporting Standing Committee (EECS), a forum of the EU National Enforcers of Financial Information, assessed that mandatorily redeemable participating preferred shares were financial liabilities.[131]

For public companies in the U.S., under similar circumstances where redemption is not fully under the issuer's control, temporary equity treatment (subject to amendments made by other pronouncements) may extend to equity securities other than preferred stock, such as stock subject to rescission rights, or to certain financial instruments indexed to, and potentially settled in, a publicly-held company's own stock that are classified as equity under EITF Issue No. 00-19 and that do not fall within the scope of Subtopic 480-10 (FASB Statement No. 150).[132]

In particular, a public company must reclassify into temporary equity an amount corresponding to the common shares that have been issued with an embedded written put option that requires physical settlement.[133]

---

[128] *IAS 32, ¶¶ 18, AG25, AG27(a), AG37.*

[129] *FASB ASC 815-40-25-7 (EITF Issue No. 00-19, ¶ 12).*

[130] *IAS 32, ¶¶ 18, AG25, BC12*

[131] *Committee of European Securities Regulators (CESR), 2009. CESR/09-720, 6th Extract from EECS's Database of Enforcement Decisions, Paris: CESR, ¶ Decision ref. EECS/0809-08. [Online] CESR. Available at www.cesr.eu (last visited July 20, 2010).*

[132] *FASB ASC 480-10-S99-3A (Accounting Standards Update No. 2009-04); EITF Topic No. D-98 (superseded), ¶ 2; Securities and Exchange Commission, Division of Corporate Finance, Frequently Requested Accounting and Financial Reporting Interpretations and Guidance, ¶ I.A (March 31, 2001).*

[133] *FASB ASC 815-15-55-82 (Statement 133 Implementation Issues, Issue No. C2, Application of the Exception to Contracts Classified in Temporary Equity).*

Additionally, as Subtopic 480-10 (FASB Statement No. 150) deferred the decision on the classification of puttable and contingently redeemable stock to a subsequent phase,[134] nonpublic companies would analyze it under EITF Issue No. 00-19.

However, under IAS 32 financial instruments that are puttable for cash or other financial assets at the option of the holder are liabilities.[135] Whether or not the obligation is conditional on the counterparty's exercise of a redemption right is irrelevant under IAS 32, as the existence of holder's option for a cash settlement by the issuer is beyond the issuer's control, thus confirming a contractual obligation, such as in the case of a written put option. As an exception, effective from annual periods beginning on or after January 1, 2009, certain subordinated puttable financial instruments are classified as equity, if they entitle the holder to a pro rata share of the entity's net assets in the event of the entity's liquidation and if they meet certain additional requirements. The same classification also holds for certain instruments, or components of instruments, that impose on the entity an obligation to deliver to another party a pro rata share of the net assets of the entity only on liquidation.[136]

4.4.3 Convertible Mandatorily Redeemable Preferred Stock

A convertible preferred stock with a mandatory redemption date would generally not be within the scope of Subtopic 480-10 (FASB Statement No. 150) and therefore would not be classified as a liability, because it is generally redeemed if the holder does not exercise its option to convert into a fixed number of shares, and not a variable number of shares which would make them fall within the scope of Subtopic 480-10 (FASB Statement No. 150).[137] Once the conversion option expires, a mandatorily redeemable share would be classified as a liability under FASB Statement No. 150.[138] As long as it is outside the scope of Subtopic 480-10 (FASB Statement No. 150), a financial instrument would be valued under the relevant GAAP, including Subtopic 815-40 (EITF Issue No. 00-19) if indexed to, and potentially settled in, the issuer's own stock.[139] EITF Issue No. 05-2 confirmed that convertible preferred stock with debt-like features, such as preferred stock with a mandatory redemption date, may qualify as a "conventional convertible debt" for the purposes of applying EITF Issue No. 00-19 when its economic characteristics indicate that it is more akin to debt than equity, that is, the equity conversion feature is not clearly and closely related to the host instrument. A convertible debt instrument is conventional under EITF Issue No. 00-19 when the holder may only realize the value of the conversion option by exercising the option and receiving the entire proceeds either in a fixed number of shares or equivalent amount of cash at the issuer's option and discretion.[140] Section 815-40-25 (EITF Issue No. 00-19) exempts a conventional convertible debt instrument from being evaluated for additional conditions necessary for equity classification under the Issue and therefore whether or not an embedded derivative that is indexed to the company's own stock would require, if freestanding, bifurcation under Topic 815 (FASB Statement

---

[134] *FASB Statement No. 150,* ¶ 6.
[135] *IAS 32,* ¶¶ *18(b), BC12.*
[136] *Amendments to IAS 32* Financial Instruments: Presentation and IAS 1 Presentation of Financial Statements, Puttable Financial Instruments and Obligations Arising on Liquidation, ¶¶ *16A–16D.*
[137] *EITF Issue No. 05-2,* The Meaning of "Conventional Convertible Debt Instrument" in Issue No. 00-19, ¶ 5.
[138] *FASB ASC 480-10-55-11 (FASB Statement No. 150,* ¶ *A9).*
[139] *EITF Issue No. 00-19,* ¶ 72.
[140] *EITF Issue No. 05-2,* ¶ 9.

No. 133).[141] The embedded conversion feature would qualify for equity classification EITF Issue No. 00-19, and a public company must classify it as temporary equity under Accounting Series Release No. 268 and EITF Topic D-98, if the convertible preferred stock has redemption features that are not under issuer's control and outside of the scope of FASB Statement No. 150.[142]

On the other hand, a convertible preferred stock is classified as equity under IAS 32 unless the substance is of debt, such as a mandatorily redeemable feature, or, in case redemption is not mandatory, when distributions are not at the discretion of the issuer, apart for certain exceptions. In such a case, it would be a compound financial instrument, where the liability component is measured at the present value of the redemption amount.[143]

> **Example:** The Corporate Reporting Standing Committee (EECS), a forum of the EU National Enforcers of Financial Information, assessed that nonredeemable preferred shares that guaranteed fixed net cash dividends plus a participating dividend were compound financial instruments. The fixed net cash dividend was to be classified as a finance cost.[144]

4.4.4 Nonconventional Convertible Debt

For contracts other than conventional convertible debt, Subtopic 815-40 (EITF Issue No. 00-19) also applies to analyze whether an embedded derivative that is indexed to the issuer's own stock would be classified as liability or equity instrument for the purpose of applying Topic 815 (FASB Statement No. 133), if it were a freestanding derivative.[145] If classified as equity under Subtopic 815-40 (EITF Issue No. 00-19), it would not be considered a derivative under Topic 815 (Statement No. 133), as this case would fall under the FASB Statement No. 133 scope exclusion of a contract that is both indexed into the issuer's own stock and classified as equity.[146] If the contract does not meet the definition of a derivative under Topic 815 (FASB Statement No. 133), then EITF Issue No. 00-19 applies.[147] Therefore, SEC registrants need to evaluate whether the terms of such instruments required temporary equity classification under Accounting Series Release No. 268 and Subtopic 480-10 (EITF Topic No. D-98).

4.4.5 Preferred Shares with Beneficial Conversion Features

An SEC registrant that issues convertible preferred shares with nondetachable beneficial conversion options (that is, that are in-the-money – i.e., the market value is greater than the conversion price – at the purchase commitment date or that become such upon the occurrence

---

[141] *FASB ASC 815-40-25-39 (EITF Issue No. 00-19,* Accounting for Derivative Financial Instruments Indexed to, and Potentially Settled in, a Company's Own Stock, *¶ 4).*

[142] *EITF Issue No. 05-2, ¶ 5.*

[143] *IAS 32, ¶¶ 18, AG25, AG26, AG37.*

[144] *Committee of European Securities Regulators (CESR), 2009. CESR/09-252, 5th* Extract from EECS's Database of Enforcement Decisions, *Paris: CESR, ¶ Decision ref. EECS/0209-10. [Online] CESR. Available at www.cesr.eu (last visited July 20, 2010).*

[145] *FASB ASC 815-40-25-39 (EITF Issue No. 00-19, ¶ 4).*

[146] *FASB ASC 815-10-15-74 (FASB Statement No. 133,* Accounting for Derivative Instruments and Hedging Activities, *¶ 11(a)).*

[147] *EITF Issue No. 00-19, ¶ 65.*

of a future event) must classify them as mezzanine (because cash settlement is presumed) if it does not control (based on criteria established by EITF Issue No. 00-19) the actions or events necessary to issue the number of required shares in case the holder exercises the conversion option. The same accounting applies to the discount on perpetual preferred stock that has no stated redemption date but that is redeemable upon occurrence of a future event beyond the control of the issuer.[148]

4.4.6   Redeemable Instruments Granted in Conjunction with Share-Based Payment Arrangements

A financial instrument given to an employee in a share-based payment transaction whose redemption is outside the control of the issuer (in the meaning used by Accounting Series Release No. 268) gives rise to further considerations. When it does not qualify for liability classification under Statement 123(R), SEC registrants must evaluate whether the terms of such an instrument result in the need to classify it as temporary equity under Accounting Series Release No. 268 and EITF Topic No. D-98. Also, when a freestanding financial instrument ceases to be subject to Subtopic 718-10 (FASB Statement No. 123(R)), i.e., when its rights no longer depend on the holder's status as employee, the application of Subtopic 480-10 (FASB Statement No. 150), or other suitable GAAP, including Accounting Series Release No. 268 must be reconsidered to determine its classification as equity or liability.[149] Firstly, Subtopic 718-10 (FASB Statement No. 123(R)) refers to evaluation under Subtopic 480-10 (FASB Statement No. 150) to classify a freestanding financial instrument given to an employee in a share-based payment transaction, and therefore instruments within its scope will be classified as liabilities. Furthermore, Subtopic 718-10 (FASB Statement No. 123(R)) itself requires liability classification in certain cases, that is, for an option or similar instrument on underlying shares that are classified as liabilities, or when the entity would be required under all circumstances to settle an option or similar instrument by transferring cash or other assets, or when the occurrence of a contingent event outside of the issuer's control that triggers cash settlement becomes probable. Instead, outstanding shares awarded to an employee in conjunction with share-based payment arrangements that embody a conditional obligation to transfer cash or other assets, as in the case of puttable shares or put rights, are outside of the scope of Subtopic 480-10 (FASB Statement No. 150). They are equity under Subtopic 718-10 (FASB Statement No. 123(R)) if the employee bears the risks and rewards normally associated with share ownership for a reasonable period of time (at least six months) from the date the share is issued.[150] Temporary equity classification will not be warranted if the instrument does not, by its terms, require redemption for cash or other assets, even when the contract permits the company to net share or physically settle by delivering registered shares, notwithstanding that these circumstances are considered by Subtopic 815-40 (EITF Issue No. 00-19) to be

---

[148]   *EITF Issue No. 00-27, Application of Issue No. 98-5 to Certain Convertible Instruments, ¶¶ 20, 60.*

[149]   *FASB ASC 718-10-35-12, 718-10-35-13, 718-10-35-14 (FASB Statement No. 123(R), ¶¶ A230–A232); FASB ASC 718-10-S99-1 (SEC Staff Accounting Bulletin, Topic 14-E).*

[150]   *FASB ASC 718-10-25-7 to FASB ASC 718-10-25-12 (FASB Statement No. 123(R), Share-Based Payments, ¶¶ 29–32); FASB ASC 480-10-55-10, 480-10-55-38, 480-10-55-39, 480-10-55-40 (FASB Statement No. 150, ¶¶ A8, A28); FASB Statement No. 150, ¶ B25; FASB ASC 480-10-S99-3A (EITF Topic No. D-98, ¶ 28); FASB ASC 718-10-S99-1 (SEC Staff Accounting Bulletin, Topic 14-E,* Statement 123R and Certain Redeemable Financial Instruments).

beyond the control of the issuer and the Issue would therefore assume net cash settlement.[151] When temporary equity presentation is warranted, it must reflect the redemption amount of the instrument and be increased over time as services are rendered during the requisite service period. At each reporting period date it would correspond to the percentage of the value of the shares or share options that are vested. Similar guidance generally applies to non-employee awards.[152]

IFRS 2 provides no guidance on share-based transactions in which under the arrangement the choice or the terms of settlement are beyond the control of the issuer.[153]

4.4.7 Settlement Methods and Choices

Another situation within the scope of Subtopic 480-10 (FASB Statement No. 150) is that of a freestanding financial instrument that provides for a gross settlement where the issuer is or can be required to deliver cash to the counterparty in exchange for the company's shares. The instrument is then classified as a liability (or an asset in some circumstances) and measured at fair value or at the present value of the redemption amount. Prior to Subtopic 480-10 (FASB Statement No. 150), a publicly-held company that issued such an instrument that qualified as equity under Subtopic 815-40 (EITF Issue No. 00-19), had to transfer the maximum redemption amount of cash required to be delivered from permanent equity to temporary equity, with no assessment of the likelihood of such redemption.[154] Nonpublic entities instead had to classify those instruments as assets or liabilities under Subtopic 815-40 (EITF Issue No. 00-19). A similar situation arose for public companies when the issuer had the option to choose a settlement method either at physical settlement that required a cash payment or at net cash settlement, or the holder had the option of a net share settlement versus a physical settlement by means of a cash payment by the issuer. However, nonpublic companies classified those instruments, under Subtopic 815-40 (EITF Issue No. 00-19), as equity if the option between gross or net settlement and net cash, or between net cash and net share settlement with a cash delivery was left to the issuer (because gross physical or net share settlement was assumed) and as assets or liabilities if the option was left to the holder (because net cash settlement was assumed).[155] However, if in these and other situations, the amount were contingently or optionally redeemable, the instrument would be outside of the scope of Subtopic 480-10 (FASB Statement No. 150)[156] and thus a public company would classify it in temporary equity.

Under IAS 32, an instrument is classified as equity if it provides for gross settlement in shares or a purchase of a fixed number of shares for a fixed amount of cash or another financial asset. However, the issuer classifies as a liability the present value of the redemption amount which it is obligated to deliver in cash or in another financial asset to the counterparty at a fixed or determinable date or on demand in exchange for the company's shares, unless such

---

[151] *FASB Statement No. 123(R), Footnote 152; EITF Topic No. D-98 (superseded), ¶ 29; FASB ASC 718-10-S99-1 (SEC Staff Accounting Bulletin, Topic 14-E).*

[152] *FASB ASC 718-10-S99-1 (SEC Staff Accounting Bulletin, Topic 14-E).*

[153] *IFRIC Update, January 2010.*

[154] *EITF Issue No. 00-19, ¶¶ 9, 12, 74*

[155] *EITF Issue No. 00-19, ¶ 9.*

[156] *FASB Statement No. 150, ¶ B28.*

obligation is classified as equity because it is a puttable instrument or an instrument with certain characteristics, or a component of it, that imposes on the entity an obligation to deliver to another party a pro rata share of the net assets of the entity only on liquidation.[157] Under IAS 32, a contract that is settled in net cash or net share is generally classified as a financial liability, even if indexed on the entity's own equity price.[158]

4.4.8 Employee Stock Ownership Plans

Under U.S. GAAP, the sponsor of an Employee Stock Ownership Plan must report in mezzanine, for the maximum cash obligation, equity securities held by the ESOP where the holders have, by the terms of the securities, a put option to the sponsor for cash in exchange for such securities when its obligation is outside of the scope of Topic 815 (FASB Statement No. 133) and Subtopic 460-10 (FASB Interpretation No. 45). In this situation, a similar classification applies to a proportional amount of the contra-equity items ("loan to ESOP" or "deferred compensation") in the sponsor's equity section of the balance sheet.[159]

4.5 LAYOUT OF THE EQUITY SECTION OF THE STATEMENT OF FINANCIAL POSITION

4.5.1 Minimum Line-Item Display Requirements

Under U.S. GAAP, the typical stockholders' equity section of the statement of financial position includes at least contributed (or paid-in) capital, retained earnings, and accumulated other comprehensive income.[160] ATB 1 supported a display by source of equity, namely legal capital, additional paid-in capital, and retained earnings.[161]

IAS 1 lists "issued capital and reserves" attributable to the controlling interest as one of the minimum line items for display on the face of the statement of financial position.[162]

Comment: In summary, those minimum line-items reconcile as follows:

U.S. GAAP	*IFRSs*
Contributed capital	Issued capital and reserves
Retained earnings	
Accumulated other comprehensive income	

---

[157] *IAS 32, ¶¶ AG13, AG27(a).*
[158] *IAS 32, ¶ AG27(c).*
[159] *FASB ASC 480-10-S99-4 (EITF Issue No. 89-11, Sponsor's Balance Sheet Classification of Capital Stock with a Put Option Held by an Employee Stock Ownership Plan, Discussion).*
[160] *FASB ASC 220-10-45-14 (FASB Statement No. 130, ¶¶ 26); FASB Statement No. 130, ¶ 95.*
[161] *Accounting Terminology Bulletin No. 1, Review and Resume, ¶¶ 65–66, 68, 69.2.*
[162] *IAS 1, ¶ 54.*

or, in more detail:

U.S. GAAP	**IFRSs**
Contributed capital	Issued capital
Retained earnings	Retained earnings
Accumulated other comprehensive income	Other reserves or components of equity

In addition, IFRS 5 requires separate presentation of accumulated other comprehensive income related to noncurrent assets held for sale in the statement of financial position.[163]

SEC registrants shall present certain separate items on the face of the balance sheet, as follows:[164]

> Non-Redeemable Preferred Stocks
> Common Stocks
> Other Stockholders' Equity
> > Additional paid-in capital
> > Other additional capital
> > Retained earnings
> > > Appropriated
> > > Unappropriated
> > > Deficit eliminated in a quasi-reorganization for at least three years
> > Noncontrolling interests
> Total Liabilities and Equity

Subsection 480-10-S99-1 (CFRR 211) prohibits SEC registrants that have redeemable preferred stock to use a stockholders' equity heading inclusive of redeemable preferred stock.[165]

Worksheet 20 compares minimum display requirements under IFRSs, U.S. GAAP, and SEC guidance.

Comment: Typically, U.S. practice has a more detailed display of individual classes of equity on the face of the statement of financial position. It is also interesting to note that IAS 1 does not require the display of share premium and retained earnings on the face of the statement of financial position. Furthermore, the IFRS for small and medium-sized entities considers the manner of presentation of shares and equity instruments on the face of the statement of financial position, such as whether or not par value and share premium shall be presented separately, to be a matter of corporate law.[166]

---

[163] *IFRS 5, ¶ 38.*

[164] *FASB ASC 210-10-S99-1 (Regulation S-X, ¶ 210.5-02).*

[165] *FASB ASC 480-10-S99-1 (Codification of Financial Reporting Release, CFRR 211,* Redeemable Preferred Stock, *¶¶ 1, 3).*

[166] *IASB,* International Financial Reporting Standards for Small and Medium-sized Entities, *¶ 22.10 (2009).*

Under U.S. GAAP, investment companies show only two components of capital: shareholder capital and distributable earnings.[167] Investment companies show net assets reflecting all investments at fair value, adjustment from fair value to contract value for fully benefit-responsive investment contracts, and a total for net assets. Benefit plans do the same with reference to net assets available for benefits.[168] Subsection 958-210-45-1 (FASB Statement No. 117) requires separate presentation of total net assets of not-for-profit entities.[169]

The equity section of the balance sheet of agricultural cooperatives differentiates investments by members and nonmembers and patronage allocations. They may allocate retained earnings arising from nonpatronage earnings.[170]

4.5.2 Contributed Capital

U.S. GAAP refers to equity contributed by owners in exchange for stock as *contributed*[171] or *paid-in capital*. This is composed of *legal capital*,[172] or *capital stock*,[173] *additional paid-in capital* (or *capital surplus*), and *donated capital*, if any. Legal capital may comprise par- or no-par-value common and preferred capital stock.

Comment: IFRSs generically refer to components of equity, and do not use the term *contributed capital* and rarely *contributed equity*[174] and *legal capital*.[175] This is made up of *share*[176], or *issued*[177] or *equity*[178] *capital*, share premium, and generically other components of equity.

---

[167] *FASB ASC 946-20-50-11 (AICPA Audit and Accounting Guide, INV, ¶ 12.36).*

[168] *FASB ASC 960-205-55-1 (FASB Statement No. 35, ¶ Exhibit D-1); FASB ASC 965-20-45-1, 965-205-55-4 (AICPA Statement of Position No. 92-6, ¶¶ 64, Exhibit A); FASB ASC 962-325-55-16 (AICPA Statement of Position No. 99-3*, Accounting for and Reporting of Certain Defined Contribution Plan Investments and Other Disclosure Matters, *¶ 33); FASB ASC 962-205-45-2 (AICPA Statement of Position No. 94-4*, Reporting of Investment Contracts Held by Health and Welfare Benefit Plans and Defined-Contribution Pension Plans, *¶ 15); FASB ASC 960-205-55-2, 956-205-55-8 (AICPA Statement of Position No. 99-2*, Accounting for and Reporting of Postretirement Medical Benefit (401(h)) Features of Defined Benefit Pension Plans, *¶¶ Appendix B Example 1, Appendix C Example 1); FASB ASC 946-210-45-9, 946-210-45-15, 946-210-45-16, 946-210-50-14, 946-210-55-2 (FASB Staff Position Nos. AAG INV-1 and SOP 94-4-1*, Reporting of Fully Benefit-Responsive Investment Contracts Held by Certain Investment Companies Subject to the AICPA Investment Company Guide and Defined-Contribution Health and Welfare and Pension Plans, *¶¶ 1, 8, 9, 11, A1).*

[169] *FASB ASC 958-210-45-1 (FASB Statement No. 117, ¶ 10).*

[170] *FASB ASC 905-505-45-2 (AICPA Audit and Accounting Guide, ¶* Accounting by Agricultural Producers and Agricultural Cooperatives, *11.24)*

[171] *FASB Statement No. 16*, Prior Period Adjustments, *¶ 32; FASB ASC 740-20-45-11, 852-740-45-3 (FASB Statement No. 109, ¶¶ 36, 39); EITF Issue No. 00-19, ¶ 9; CON 6, ¶ 214.*

[172] *CON 6, Footnote 29.*

[173] *ARB 43, Ch. 1A, ¶ 6.*

[174] The Conceptual Framework for Financial Reporting 2010, *¶ 4.20; IASB Framework, ¶ 65; IAS 1, ¶ 108; IAS 7*, Cash Flow Statements, *¶ 6; IAS 32, ¶ 18.*

[175] *IFRS 3, ¶ B21. The example in IAS 14*, Segment Reporting, *Appendix B also used the term "capital stock."*

[176] *IAS 1, ¶¶ 6, 79, 80, IG6; IAS 8*, Implementation Guidance; *IAS 12*, Income Taxes, *Appendix B; IAS 21*, The Effects of Changes in Foreign Exchange Rates *¶ 49; IAS 27 (2010), ¶ 49; IAS 32, ¶¶ IN10, IE35.*

[177] *IAS 1, ¶ 54.*

[178] *IAS 1, ¶ 78(e); IFRS 4*, Insurance Contracts, *¶ IG 48(g).*

The term *paid-in capital* may be found in U.S. practice as a substitute for contributed capital, although several pronouncements use it as a synonym for additional paid-in capital.[179] Contrary to U.S. GAAP, the term *paid-in capital*[180] is found in IFRSs with reference to capital stock, and not to total contributed capital.

4.5.3 Classification of Equity Instruments by Manner of Issuance

Equity instruments may be categorized by manner of issuance. Equity instruments may be issued either 1) on a stand-alone basis; or 2) as part of a share-based payment transaction; or 3) as consideration in a business combination; or 4) may result from an equity component of a compound financial instrument (as a result of split accounting).

Comment: Split accounting exists only under IFRSs.[181] Under U.S. GAAP instead, a freestanding contract that is indexed to, and potentially settled in, the issuer's own stock would be classified as either asset/liability or equity, based on relevant GAAP, such as Subtopic 480-10 (FASB Statement No. 150) and Subtopic 815-40 (EITF Issue No. 00-19). However, as part of the *Liabilities and Equity Project*, the FASB proposed that the separation of an instrument with a basic ownership component and a liability or asset component be reported as if it were two separate freestanding instruments.[182]

4.5.4 Sequence of Display

Neither set of standards provides a mandatory sequence of display of items on the face of the statement of financial position in general.

Comment: However, under U.S. GAAP, the typical sequence of display on the face of the statement of financial position is: preferred stock, common stock, additional paid-in capital, retained earnings, and cumulative other comprehensive income. IFRSs typically display, as a minimum, issued capital, retained earnings, and other components of equity.[183]

Depending on its pre-IAS accounting practice, a specific jurisdiction might have maintained specific presentation requirements of equity on the balance sheet, provided it proved to be consistent with IFRSs.

---

[179] *FASB ASC 718-10-35-2 (FASB Statement No. 123(R), ¶ 39); FASB Statement No. 130, ¶ 113; APB Opinion No. 14,* Accounting for Convertible Debt and Debt Issued with Stock Purchase Warrants, *¶ 1; APB Opinion No. 26,* Early Extinguishment of Debt, *¶ 13.*

[180] *IAS 1, ¶ 78(e); IFRIC 2, ¶ 9.*

[181] *Compound financial instruments, as well as the classification of financial instruments as equity versus financial liability fall outside the scope of the book.*

[182] *Financial Accounting Standards Board, Preliminary Views,* Financial Instruments with Characteristics of Equity, *¶ 25 (November 30, 2007).*

[183] *IAS 1, ¶¶ 54, Guidance on Implementation.*

Comment: For example, the Italian civil code requires that certain equity items be shown, and according to a specific sequence, that is, common stock, additional paid-in capital, revaluation reserves, legal reserve, statutory reserves, treasury stock reserve, other reserves, prior period retained earnings, profit or loss of the period, total shareholders' equity.[184]

4.5.5 Sorting Order

As a matter of accounting practice, U.S. GAAP and IFRSs have opposite ways of sorting components of equity on the face of the statement of financial position, e.g., according to a descending or ascending order of priority in liquidation, respectively. Worksheet 21 compares samples of sorting orders under U.S. GAAP and IFRSs.

An SEC registrant may choose various sorting orders, provided this is consistent throughout the filing.[185]

Comment: The sorting order of items on the statement of financial position should not be confused with whether or not a classified statement of financial position (with a current/noncurrent distinction) or presentation in order of decreasing/increasing liquidity is adopted (under IAS 1 this is permitted only in certain circumstances[186]).

IFRS Accounting Trends & Techniques illustrates that 82% of survey IFRS companies using a classified statement of financial position use a sorting from least current to most current and 18% use the reverse order. 64% of companies using a liquidity criterion use a sorting from most current to least current.[187]

4.5.6 Parenthetical Explanation

Under U.S. GAAP, the relationship between the aggregate preference in involuntary liquidations of preferred shares and par or stated value of stock must be disclosed in parenthetical format in the respective line items, when such preference rights are in excess of par or stated value.[188] Section 235-10-S99 (Regulation S-X) requires a similar disclosure either on the face of the financial statements or in the notes, including any restrictions on retained earnings.[189]

Under Section 210-10-S99 (Regulation S-X),[190] for each issue of common, redeemable, or nonredeemable preferred stocks, the following must be displayed on the balance sheet (details may be disclosed in notes if more than one issue exists):

---

[184] *Italian Civil Code, Art. 2424.*
[185] *FASB ASC 205-10-S99-9 (SEC Staff Accounting Bulletin, Topic 11-E,* Chronological Ordering of Data).
[186] *IAS 1, ¶ 60.*
[187] *Doran Walters, P., Bowman, D., 2010.* IFRS Accounting Trends & Techniques – 2009. *New York: AICPA, ¶ Table 2-1 (hereinafter AICPA IFRS ATT 2009).*
[188] *FASB ASC 505-10-50-4 (FASB Statement No. 129, ¶ 6).*
[189] *FASB ASC 235-10-S99-1 (Regulation S-X, ¶ 210.4-08(d)).*
[190] *FASB ASC 210-10-S99-1 (Regulation S-X, ¶ 210.5-02).*

- Title;
- Carrying amount;
- Redemption amount;
- Number of shares authorized, issued, or outstanding;[191]
- Amount of shares subscribed but unissued;[192]
- Subscriptions receivable;
- Discount on shares;
- The basis of conversion of convertible stock (either on the face of the balance sheet or in the notes).

Comment: IFRSs do not specifically treat parenthetical information as a disclosure technique.

4.5.7 Subclassifications on the Face of the Statement of Financial Position and Disclosures in the Notes

Subtopic 505-10 (FASB Statement No. 129) requires certain disclosures of equity within the financial statements, therefore either on the face of the statement of financial position or in the notes.

IFRSs do not require further display of subclassifications, although those may be warranted on the face of the statement of financial position or in the notes based on size, nature, and function of capital and reserves.[193] Additionally, other information may be needed if relevant to an understanding of the financial statements.[194] Unlike full IFRSs, IFRS for SMEs also mentions the separate presentation in the statement of financial position or the disclosure in the notes of items of other comprehensive income.[195]

Form 20-F requires the disclosure of issued capital and other information.[196]

Worksheet 22 compares U.S. GAAP, SEC rules and regulations, and IFRS requirements on disclosures relating to equity stock that are required on the face of the statement of financial position, statement of changes in equity or in the notes, or simply in the notes.

---

[191] *FASB ASC 210-10-S99-1 (Regulation S-X, ¶ 210.5-02) requires, for each class of common shares, the disclosure on the face of the balance sheet of the number of shares issued or outstanding, while it prescribes, for each issue of both nonredeemable and mandatorily redeemable preferred shares, the disclosure either on the face of the balance sheet or in the notes of the number of shares authorized, issued, or outstanding.*

[192] *FASB ASC 210-10-S99-1 (Regulation S-X, ¶ 210.5-02) requires the disclosure of the amount subscribed but unissued either in the balance sheet or in the notes for each class of common shares, while it prescribes display in the balance sheet, for each issue of both nonredeemable and mandatorily redeemable preferred shares.*

[193] *IAS 1, ¶ 78.*

[194] *IAS 1, ¶ 112(c).*

[195] *IASB, International Financial Reporting Standards for Small and Medium-sized Entities, ¶ 4.11(f) (2009).*

[196] *Form 20-F, Item 10.A.1.*

> **Example:** In certain jurisdictions the shareholders' meeting may authorize the Board of Directors to issue a certain number or shares or shares up to a maximum amount subject to certain conditions (see Section 3.5.2.2). The SEC Staff, in its review of Form 20-F of a French foreign private issuer for the fiscal year ended December 31, 2006 containing financial statements prepared for the first time on the basis of IFRSs, requested the company to disclose the number of shares authorized according to IAS 1. The company explained in a note that the shareholders had delegated the Board of Directors to issue shares up to a certain maximum number.[197]

4.6 CAPITAL DISCLOSURES

IAS 1 (Revised 2005) prescribed certain disclosures, for annual periods beginning on or after January 1, 2007, of an entity's management of capital. Subtopic 505-10 (FASB Statement No. 129) also requires certain disclosures on capital structure.

> **Comment:** IAS 1 capital disclosure requirements, although initially exposed to comment as part of ED 7 *Financial Instruments: Disclosures*, were finalized as of general bearing to all entities, irrespective of whether or not they have issued financial instruments. However, although neither Subtopic 505-10 (FASB Statement No. 129) nor IAS 1 scope out any particular type of entity, public or private, the rationale for those disclosures in Subtopic 505-10 (FASB Statement No. 129) exists insofar as an entity has certain types of securities with features described in the standard.

The notion of *management of capital* in IAS 1 has peculiar and new characteristics.

Firstly, it pertains to strategy, that is, to objectives, policies, and processes for managing capital.[198]

> **Comment:** While capital structure under Subtopic 505-10 (FASB Statement No. 129) appears to be a mechanical and quantitative derivation of the existence of certain securities, under IAS 1 management of capital results from an entity-specific strategic policy, which is largely independent of whether or not certain financial instruments are issued.

Secondly, such disclosures are based on information provided to the entity's key management personnel.[199]

> **Comment:** Assessing a policy on capital follows a management approach that is internal to the entity. By referring to *management of capital*, IAS 1 takes an open-ended approach on how capital is subjectively intended or managed at a specific entity level.

---

[197] *Letter by the SEC, File No. 001-32139, Note 26 (December 1, 2006). Reply by the company (January 12, 2007) www.sec.gov/divisions/corpfin/ifrs_reviews (last visited January 7, 2008).*
[198] *IAS 1, ¶ BC90.*
[199] *IAS 1, ¶ 135.*

Thirdly, an entity must describe what it manages as capital.[200]

> **Comment:** Capital need not equate with equity (see Section 4.1.3 previously), and this is a ground for disclosure, both quantitatively and qualitatively, of what constitutes capital and how an entity monitors it. Therefore, at the entity-specific level and as far as the managerial aspects of capital are concerned, the traditional dichotomy between equity and financial liabilities is subjectively resolved. In fact, the standard states as an example that an entity might decide to define an "adjusted capital" that includes some type of subordinated debt in the notion of capital, or conversely excludes some components such as cumulative gain or loss arising from cash flow hedges that had been recognized directly in equity.[201]

Finally, the main focus of managing capital under IAS 1 is capital adequacy, which can be inferred as maintaining appropriate cushion equity levels, providing returns to shareholders, including dividends, assuring safety margins to preserve the going concern assumption and flexibility to face adverse events. It may embed a risk-based determination of capital in relation to assets and liabilities. It may also include the impact of entity-specific (not industry-wide) capital requirements on the adequacy of its capital resources.[202]

> **Comment:** This brings to mind part of the discussion on the objectives of financial reporting under both the FASB and the IASB conceptual frameworks. Although differently phrased, both the U.S. Concepts and the IASB Framework elaborate on the assessment of financial structure, liquidity, solvency and their impact on borrowing needs, future interest and dividend distributions,[203] or liquidity, solvency, financial flexibility, and funds flows.[204] The IASB Framework[205] defines solvency (undefined under U.S. GAAP) based on a concept of longer-term cash availability proportionate to financial commitments falling due. CON 5[206] defines financial flexibility based on a concept of ability to effectively and proactively manage cash flows and their timing to face unexpected needs and opportunities. This term is undefined under IFRSs.
>
> Incidentally, the *Financial Statement Presentation Project* has discussed the possible inclusion of capital adequacy, with similar meaning, into the liquidity principle.[207]
>
> Further, it is to be noted that such a concept of managing capital may resemble some of the typical disclosures that, according to the entity's jurisdiction, may be signaled through segregated items that are appropriations of retained earnings for defense of capital purposes (examined at Section 3.5.3 previously).

---

[200] *IAS 1, ¶ 135.*

[201] *IAS 1, ¶¶ BC91, IG10.*

[202] *IAS 1, ¶¶ BC94, IG10.*

[203] *IASB Framework, ¶ 16 (superseded).*

[204] *FASB Concepts Statement No. 1*, Objectives of Financial Reporting by Business Enterprises, *¶¶ 41, 49; CON 5, ¶ 24a.*

[205] *IASB Framework, ¶ 16 (superseded).*

[206] *CON 5, Footnote 13.*

[207] *IASB Meeting, May 17, 2007, Agenda Paper 6A*, Presentation of Liquidity Information, *¶¶ 8, 30 (May 2007). Also see: FASB Meeting, February 26, 2002*, Summary of User Interviews, Reporting Financial Performance by Business Enterprises, *Par. Content of Note Disclosures (a) (February 2002). Additionally, a possible statement of wealth creation and capital allocation was examined as part of this project: IASB Meeting, January 25, 2007, Agenda Paper 13D*, Statement of Changes in Equity and Other Equity-Related Issues, *¶¶ 29–32 (January 2007).*

In contrast, Subtopic 505-10 (FASB Statement No. 129) focuses on capital structure, starting from its title. Its disclosures are restricted to securities (in terms of number of actual and potential shares and their rights and privileges), liquidation preference of preferred stock, and redeemable stock. Thus, the standard focuses on most critical features that may substantiate capital structure and determine changes thereof.

Comment: Although the two pronouncements have different approaches, in practice, however, IAS 1 also states as an example debt-to-equity ratio, i.e., capital structure.

IAS 1 differentiates between disclosure about capital, which is deemed to be useful to users of general-purpose financial statements,[208] and disclosure required by regulators, which is not a matter of financial reporting. Accordingly, it also applies to nonregulated entities. Disclosure extends to information on noncompliance about externally imposed capital requirements, but not to such requirements per se.[209] Conversely, U.S. GAAP requires certain regulatory capital disclosures for depository and lending institutions.

Planning Point: Incidentally, the location of disclosures on managing capital may seem somewhat inconsistent within IAS 1.[211] In fact, IAS 1 also connotes some information of a similar nature, such as an entity's financial performance policies, funding and target capital structure, or dividend policy,[212] as information that is generally located in Management Discussion and Analysis, as being outside financial statements,[213] as the IFRS Practice Statement permits.[214]

The IASB Framework has considered disclosure in the notes to be appropriate for additional information that is relevant to the needs of users, when items are recognized in the financial statements.[215] Similarly, as a general criterion, the U.S. Concepts[216] leave to the notes, or parenthetical presentation on the face of the financial statements, the sort of information that is essential in understanding, complementing, or amplifying elements recognized in the financial statements and that is an integral part of them, as opposed to other supplementary information and other means of financial reporting that contain information that is additional to the financial statements or notes.

---

[208] *Similarly, the IASB Framework, ¶ 16 (superseded) emphasized the importance of information about the financial structure of an entity.*

[209] *IAS 1, ¶ BC87.*

[210] *FASB ASC 942-505-50 (AICPA Audit and Accounting Guide,* Depository and Lending Institutions, *¶¶ 17.15–17.18.*

[211] *However, IAS 1, ¶¶ 134–136 do not indicate that disclosures should be provided in the notes to the financial statements, although under IFRSs the term disclosure ordinarily may include either display on the face of the financial statements or information in the notes (IAS 1, ¶ 48). On the contrary, in the same standard, when location in the notes is required for other disclosures, this fact is indicated (IAS 11, ¶¶ 125, 137).*

[212] *IAS 1, ¶ 13.*

[213] *International Organization of Securities Commissions,* International Disclosure Standards for Cross-Border Offerings and Initial Listings for Foreign Issuers, *¶ 4 (1998) also requires in Management Discussion and Analysis the disclosure of factors materially affecting capital resources.*

[214] *IFRS Practice Statement,* Management Commentary. A Framework for Presentation, *¶ 30.*

[215] *IASB Framework, ¶ 21 (superseded).*

[216] *CON 5, ¶ 7; CON 6, ¶ 5.*

Also, under IFRSs, information that if omitted would make the financial statements incomplete and potentially misleading should be given in the financial statements or incorporated by cross-reference to some other document that is simultaneously available, as shown for example by IFRS 7 requirement of disclosure of risks arising from financial instruments.[217]

Therefore, it could be argued that this option might seem applicable to capital disclosures, under circumstances in which separate report information is provided elsewhere for regulatory purposes.[218]

4.7 EQUITY OF PARTNERSHIPS AND SIMILAR ENTITIES

Both under IFRSs and U.S. GAAP partners' capital and proprietorship are not precluded from consideration as a form of equity.[219] In fact, these are business entities. Under the SEC's Regulation S-X, the term *person* also includes an individual, a partnership, an association, a joint-stock company, a business trust, or an unincorporated organization.[220]

Although relevant GAAP ordinarily applies, U.S. GAAP has an established practice of accounting for partnerships. Under IFRSs, general standards also apply to noncorporate entities, such as partnerships or trusts, with appropriate amendment of terminology.[221]

In their joint project on conceptual framework, the IASB and the FASB tentatively decided that organizational structures other than legal entities, such as sole proprietorships, should be included in the concept of financial reporting entities.[222]

Under U.S. GAAP, the term "members' equity" or "partners' capital" generally apply to the net worth section of Limited Liability Companies and Partnerships.

In the U.S., partnership equity is recorded in capital accounts, to include invested capital and accumulated earnings. Partnerships generally maintain capital accounts by individual partner or class of partners, general or limited (a single capital account is usually used for sole partnerships). Drawing accounts are optional nominal accounts, to record withdrawals of capital by partners, that are closed to partnership capital at the end of each period. LLCs and LLPs usually do not disaggregate members' equity by individual membership.

The statement of financial position of publicly held partnerships should separately display general partners' and limited partners' equity, with the respective number of equity units

---

[217] *IFRS 7, ¶ B6.*

[218] *Similarly: IFRS 7, ¶ BC46.*

[219] *FASB ASC 480-10-05-6 (FASB Statement No. 150, ¶¶ 5, Footnote 4), and IAS 32, ¶ 14 make it clear that they apply to such types of entities.* The Conceptual Framework for Financial Reporting 2010, *¶ 4.23 (IASB Framework, ¶ 68) specifies that the definition of equity also applies to noncorporate entities.*

[220] *SEC Regulation S-X, ¶ 210.1-02.q.*

[221] *IAS 1, ¶ 80.*

[222] *Discussion Paper,* Preliminary Views on an Improved Conceptual Framework for Financial Reporting, The Reporting Entity *(May 2008), ¶ 21(e); FASB Minutes of Meeting, September 27, 2006, Conceptual Framework Project – Elements 7: Asset Definition (VI); Reporting Entity (September 2006), page 2; IASB Minutes of Meeting, September 21, 2006, Conceptual Framework Project – Agenda Paper 5A, Reporting Entity, ¶ 17.*

authorized and outstanding (generally explained parenthetically). A separate statement of changes in partnership equity must relate to each ownership class. Similarly, the income statements must present separate line items for the aggregate amount of net income (loss) attributable to the general partners and to the limited partners.[223] Nonregistered investment partnerships that report capital by investor class must include cumulative unrealized gains and losses into the ending balances of each class of shareholders' or partners' interest in that entity at the balance sheet date, as if net assets were realized and distributed based on the partnership's governing documents. They must also show a deduction from the general partner's capital account for clawback obligations.[224]

Investment partnerships and other pass-through entities aggregate all elements of equity into partners' capital.[225]

Subsection 272-10-45-3 (PB 14) requires the title of members' equity for Limited Liability Companies. LLCs must show or disclose any separate account for components of members' equity (such as undistributed earnings, earnings available for withdrawal, or unallocated capital). LLCs may present equity attributable to each class of members on the face of the statement of financial position or in the notes.[226]

Comment: Under IFRSs, noncorporate entities, such as partnerships or trusts, must adapt appropriately the terminology, presentation, and equity disclosures required of corporations.[227] As such disclosures also include the number of equity units authorized, issued, fully and not fully paid, and rights, preferences, and restrictions attaching to each ownership class, and period changes of each category of equity, its main difference from the SEC guidance is that such disclosure under IFRSs may be either on the face of the statement of financial position or in the notes.

Additionally, under IFRSs, a requirement to disclose the legal form of the entity[228] and to give prominent identification on the financial statements of the name of the reporting entity or other means of identification[229] exists to further improve transparency. There is a similar provision under PB 14 and SEC Form 20-F.[230]

4.8   NET ASSETS OF ENTITIES WITH NO CONTRIBUTED EQUITY OR WITH OWNERS' INTEREST THAT HAS CHARACTERISTICS OF EQUITY AND LIABILITIES

IAS 32 gives special consideration to: 1) entities that do not have equity as defined in IAS 32; and 2) entities whose share capital is not equity. It identifies the former situation as when all financial instruments representative of unitholders' interest are puttable, and the latter as

---

[223] *FASB ASC 505-10-S99-5 (SAB 4-F).*
[224] *AICPA, TIS Section 6910,* Investment Companies, *¶ 29.*
[225] *FASB ASC 946-20-50-14 (AICPA Audit and Accounting Guide, INV, ¶ 7.38).*
[226] *FASB ASC 272-10-45-3 (AICPA, Practice Bulletin No. 14,* Accounting and Reporting by Limited Liability Companies and Limited Liability Partnerships, *¶¶ 10, 12).*
[227] *IAS 1, ¶ 80.*
[228] *IAS 1, ¶ 138.*
[229] *IAS 1, ¶ 51(a).*
[230] *AICPA, Practice Bulletin No. 14, ¶ 9; Form 20-F, Part I, Item 4A.1.*

when the entity has an obligation to repay some share capital on demand (which would prevent equity classification under IAS 32).

In the former situation, expressions such as net asset value attributable to unitholders and changes in net asset value attributable to unitholders (for profit or loss) are not prohibited.[231]

As a result, from a presentation viewpoint, the entity would have no contributed equity in the meaning used by the standard. Conversely, *net assets*, although they may still be named so, are classified among liabilities (see Section 4.1.2 previously for a conceptual discussion on the topic). However, alternative names, such as *members'* or *unitholders' interests* may be warranted as appropriate.[232]

Comment: Under certain circumstances, IFRSs permit the use of the term *net assets* but disassociate it in its literal meaning (e.g., assets minus liabilities) from its connotation as equity.[233] This happens because, under IAS 32, the substance of a part of or all such instruments calls for their classification as financial liabilities instead of equity, although residual interest in net assets formally rests on the holders of those financial instruments. This standard clarifies that generally this may involve open-ended mutual funds, unit trusts, partnerships, and some cooperative entities.[234] A specific application is when members' shares in cooperative entities meet the requirements of IFRIC 2[235] for classification as liabilities.[236]

Comment: However, the IASB recently amended IAS 32 to introduce an exception to the basic definition of a financial liability, pending the conclusion of its long-term project on liabilities and equity. Under certain circumstances, certain puttable and other financial instruments that meet the definition of a financial liability because they embody a contractual obligation to transfer cash or other financial assets but represent the residual interest in the net assets of the entity are classified as equity. Therefore, contrary to the situation explained above, when all financial instruments representative of unitholders' interest are of those types, the issuer maintains their classification as equity. One of the arguments for this presentation is avoiding the entire market capitalization and all the financial instruments of the entity being recognized as financial liabilities.[237] This, however, contrasts with the presentation that Subtopic 480-10 (FASB Statement No. 150) requires for mandatorily redeemable shares that are the entity's only outstanding financial instruments, as explained below.

Under Subtopic 480-10 (FASB Statement No. 150), mandatorily redeemable shares that are the entity's only outstanding financial instruments shall be displayed among liabilities in the balance sheet as *shares subject to mandatory redemption*. Companies must also separately

---

[231] *IAS 32, ¶ 18(b).*

[232] *IAS 1,¶ 6.*

[233] *On the contrary, CON 6, ¶ 213 confirms that equity always equals net assets.*

[234] *IAS 32, ¶ 18(b).*

[235] *IFRIC 2, ¶ B20.*

[236] *Being among entities other than investor-owned entities is one of the characteristics of the definition of a mutual entity, including a mutual cooperative, given by IFRS 3, Appendix A. The U.S. Concepts consider both all investor-owned enterprises and mutual organizations to be outside of not-for-profit organizations: see FASB Concept Statement No. 4, ¶ 7.*

[237] *Amendments to IAS 32 Financial Instruments: Presentation and IAS 1 Presentation of Financial Statements, Puttable Financial Instruments and Obligations Arising on Liquidation, ¶¶ BC50, BC55.*

present interests in income statement and related payments in the statement of cash flows.[238] The same treatment applies to shares that are required to be redeemed upon the death of the holder and those instruments that represent the only shares or units of the entity.

Subsection 210-10-S99-1 (SEC Regulation S-X) by default requires a balance sheet item named "Preferred stocks subject to mandatory redemption requirements or whose redemption is outside the control of the issuer," within the limitation discussed in Section 4.4 previously.[239]

Comment: Therefore, contrary to IAS 32, Subtopic 480-10 (FASB Statement No. 150) does not use the term *net assets* (or discusses whether or not such use is permitted) in circumstances where all shares are classified as liabilities.

In the case of an entity that has an obligation to repay the share capital on demand, IAS 32 does not require or prohibit additional disclosure of the composition of total members' interest, which is composed of items that show up in equity and items that are displayed among liabilities.[240] Additionally, those items that are classified in liabilities would be presented as separate line items and disclosed.[241]

Subtopic 480-10 (FASB Statement No. 150), contrary to IAS 32, requires, among other information, separate disclosure of the components of the liability that would otherwise be related to shareholders' interest.[242]

Worksheet 23 illustrates related reporting formats under IAS 32. Worksheet 24 illustrates related reporting formats under Subtopic 480-10 (FASB Statement No. 150).

---

[238] *FASB ASC 480-10-45-2 (FASB Statement No. 150, ¶ 19).*
[239] *FASB ASC 210-10-S99-1 (SEC Regulation S-X, ¶ 210.5-02).*
[240] *IAS 32, ¶ 18(b).*
[241] *IAS 1, ¶ 59 requires separate line items for classes of assets that have different measurement bases. An extensive interpretation of IAS 1 would then apply this requirement to classes of liabilities as well.*

Furthermore, IAS 1, ¶¶ 117–118 require disclosure in the summary of significant accounting policies of measurement bases used in the financial statements. U.S. GAAP has no such general guidance, although it may be inferred from APB Opinion No. 22, Disclosure of Accounting Policies, *¶ 12a and CON 5, ¶ 7a. Other pronouncements have similar provisions for specific items.*

As part of the Financial Statement Presentation Project, the IASB and the FASB tentatively decided to require disclosure of measurement bases as part of the summary of significant accounting policies and that different measurement bases should not be mixed in the same line item of the statement of financial position. See Minutes of IASB and FASB Meeting, October 2006, (last visited June 25, 2007), www.iasb.org. This position has been confirmed in the Discussion Paper, Preliminary Views on Financial Statement Presentation, *¶ 3.19 (October 2008).*

FASB ASC 820-10-50-2, 820-10-50-2A then superseded, 820-10-50-2B (FASB Statement No. 157, as amended by Accounting Standards Update No. 2010-06, Fair Value Measurements and Disclosures (Topic 820), Improving Disclosures about Fair Value Measurements *and by Accounting Standards Update No. 2011-4,* Fair Value Measurement (Topic 820) – Amendments to Achieve Common Fair Value Measurement and Disclosure Requirements in U.S. GAAP and IFRSs) *asks for a greater level of disaggregation within line items of assets and liabilities in order to determine, using appropriate judgment, the classes for which to provide fair value measurements.*

[242] *FASB ASC 480-10-55-64 (FASB Statement No. 150, ¶ A6).*

> **Comment:** Disclosure requirements are not equivalent.

Unlike IAS 32, Subtopic 480-10 (FASB Statement No. 150) scopes out both obligations that are embedded in other instruments and conditional instruments, such as contingent obligations embodied in shares, and embedded written stock put options. Subtopic 480-10 (FASB Statement No. 150) classifies a share purchase by asset transfer (such as a forward purchase contract or a written put option) as a liability to the extent that it is freestanding and the relationship is akin to leveraged treasury stock purchase. It classifies conditionally mandatorily redeemable instruments as liabilities only once they become unconditional.

Similarly, an obligation to repay the share capital on demand, if it is in the form of outstanding shares, is outside of the scope of Subtopic 480-10 (FASB Statement No. 150). Otherwise, a financial instrument that, at inception, embodies an obligation to repurchase the issuer's own equity shares by transferring assets is a financial liability.

In cases where Subtopic 480-10 (FASB Statement No. 150) is scoped out, the classification is determined by applying Topic 815 (EITF Issue No. 00-19) and FASB Statement No. 133. This topic of classification of equity versus liability is outside of the scope of this Book. For reference purposes however, Worksheet 25 depicts a general decision workflow under U.S. GAAP.

> **Comment:** Therefore, some differences in scope between the two standards are relevant to the topic of this paragraph. Entities that face such situations should be aware that differences in scope may require them to revise loan agreements for debt covenants.

4.9   DISCOUNT ON ISSUANCE

Original issue discount (discount on shares, or discount on capital stock) refers to issuing stock below par.[243]

> **Comment:** This is generally avoided by setting low par values. The issue does not arise in case of no-par value stock. Section 3.5.2.2 previously discusses discount on issuance from the perspective of defense of legal capital.

In the U.S. an original discount issue would be accounted for by debiting a "discount on issue" account for the difference between the par value and the amount actually received. This makes users of financial statements aware of the contingent liability of shareholders if, in the event of liquidation, creditors sustain a loss. This contingent liability from the shareholders' perspective arises only upon original issue of the stock and does not occur for a purchaser of a treasury stock resold below par. Alternatively, a charge to additional paid-in capital is possible to the extent this account is available from the same class of stock.

---

[243] *This Section does not treat share purchase plans that provide employees with an opportunity to buy shares at a discount.*

Section 510-10-S99 (Regulation S-X)[244] clarifies that discount on shares, or any unamortized balance thereof, must be separately deducted from the appropriate account(s).

IFRSs have no explicit guidance on the subject.

> **Comment:** IFRSs typically do not address corporate or business matters, as of competence of regulators. However, under both sets of standards, disclosure would be required as part of the information on par value of shares, issued and paid amounts (see Section 4.5.7 previously).

4.10   INCREASING RATE PREFERRED STOCK

Increasing rate preferred shares are nonredeemable (or their redemption is not outside the control of the issuer) preferred shares (whether cumulative or not) that are issued at a discount (or at a premium in the reverse situation) to counterbalance either a low, below-market, or zero dividend in earlier years or a gradually increasing dividend.

The discount at time of issuance is the present value of the difference between the dividends during the initial periods less the dividends that would be available from similar instruments with no increasing-rate dividend feature, discounted at the market rate for dividend yield on comparable preferred stocks.

Under both IFRSs and SEC rules and regulations, as the original discount represents a prepaid unstated dividend cost, it is amortized at the effective interest method over the period(s) preceding the inception of normal dividend, through a debit to retained earnings against a credit to dividends, and then an increase of the carrying amount of preferred stock against a debit of dividends.[245]

Therefore, the amortization for the total period and any stated dividend for the period results in a constant rate (that is, the market rate that was used to determine the discount at initial issuance) on the carrying amount of the preferred stock. SAB Topic 5-Q adds that if stated dividends rates are variable (e.g., linked to a market index), changes of the index subsequent to date of issuance must not affect the amounts of initial discount and subsequent amortization.

Subtopic 480-10 (FASB Statement No. 150) did not take a position on whether increasing rate preferred shares are liabilities or equity instruments when no enforceable obligation to redeem the shares and pay dividends exists.[246] Similarly, under IFRSs a form of economic compulsion, as opposed to a contractual obligation, does not make an instrument a financial liability.

The accounting for increasing-rate preferred stock is under FASB's revision as part of the *Financial Instruments with Characteristics of Equity Project* – former *Financial Instruments: Liabilities and Equity Project.*

---

[244] *FASB ASC 510-10-S99-2 (Regulation S-X, ¶ 210.4-07).*
[245] *FASB ASC 505-10-S99-7 (SEC Staff Accounting Bulletin, Topic 5-Q,* Increasing Rate Preferred Stock; *International Accounting Standard No. 33,* Earnings per Share, *¶¶ 15, IE).*
[246] *FASB Statement No. 150, ¶ B24.*

4.11 EQUITY ISSUANCE COSTS

Under IFRSs, equity issuance costs are referred to as part of "transaction costs."

Comment: "Transaction costs" is a general term. Such costs are accounted for differently depending on whether they refer to the issuance of debt or equity, or to the acquisition, transfer, or disposal of an asset or a liability, and to the extent they refer to the issuer or the holder. Specific terms apply in both sets of standards depending on the type of transaction (e.g., "costs to sell" of a long-lived asset classified as held for disposal under Subtopic 360-10 (FASB Statement No. 144) and IFRS 5,[247] "point-of-sale costs" for biological assets under IAS 41, then replaced by "costs to sell"[248]). Now, Subtopic 820-10 (FASB Statement No. 157) also uses this term.[249] In particular, transaction costs in issuing equity are a greater set than issue costs because they may also include the cost of services from external professionals, such as lawyers, investment bankers, or accountants.

Issuing costs may be direct or indirect. In general, transaction costs are direct and incremental, directly attributable to the transaction they refer to, and those that would otherwise have been avoided had the transaction not taken place.[250]

Examples of direct transaction costs incurred in issuing or acquiring an entity's own equity may include registration, regulatory, legal, accounting, and underwriting and other advisors' fees, stamp duties and printing costs.[251] Records maintenance and ownership transfers (e.g., registrar's fees) are examples of indirect transaction costs of equity issue.

Under U.S. practice, costs of registering and issuing equity are deducted from the proceeds of issue.[252] Similar accounting applies to equity redemption costs. SEC guidance confirms that specific external incremental costs directly attributable to an offering may be deferred and deducted from the proceeds of the offering.[253] EITF Issue No. 09-1 and Accounting Standard Update No. 2009-15, effective for fiscal years beginning on or after December 15, 2009 and related interim periods for arrangements outstanding as of the beginnings of those years, treat an own share-lending arrangement that a company executes (including when in a separate

---

[247] *FASB ASC 360-10-35-38 (FASB Statement No. 144*, Accounting for the Impairment or Disposal of Long-Lived Assets, ¶ 35); FASB Statement No. 144, ¶ B81; IFRS 5, Non-current Assets Held for Sale and Discontinued Operations, Appendix A.*

[248] *IAS 41*, Agriculture, *¶ 14*. Improvements to IFRSs, *Part II, Amendment to IAS 41 (May 2008) deleted the term "point-of-sale costs" in IAS 41 and added the definition of "costs to sell" in paragraph 5 of IAS 41.*

[249] *FASB ASC 820-10-35-7 moved to 820-10-35-9B (FASB Statement No. 157, ¶ 9, as amended by Accounting Standards Update No. 2011-04*, Fair Value Measurement (Topic 820) – Amendments to Achieve Common Fair Value Measurement and Disclosure Requirements in U.S. GAAP and IFRSs*).*

[250] *FASB ASC 820-10-35-7 amended and moved to 820-10-35-9B (FASB Statement No. 157, Footnote 6, as amended by ASU No. 2011-04); FASB ASC 360-10-35-38 (FASB Statement No. 144, ¶ 35); IAS 32, ¶ 37; IAS 39, ¶¶ 9, AG13;* Improvements to IFRSs, *Part II, Amendment to Appendix of IAS 18 (May 2008).*

[251] *IAS 32, ¶ 37.*

[252] *FASB ASC 470-60-35-12 (FASB Statement No. 15*, Accounting by Debtors and Creditors for Troubled Debt Restructuring, *¶ 24); FASB Statement No. 15, ¶ 100.*

[253] *FASB ASC 340-10-S99-1 (SEC Staff Accounting Bulletin, Topic 5-A*, Expenses of Offering*).*

transaction) in connection or in contemplation of the issuance of convertible debt or other financing. The entity loans shares to an investment bank or a third-party investor, to be returned upon maturity or conversion for no additional expenditure. The loaned shares are legally outstanding. The loan processing fees generally correspond to the par value of the newly-issued shares, which is considerably lower than their fair value. Other GAAP, such as FASB Statement No. 133 or Subtopic 815-40 (EITF Issue No. 00-19), determine whether liability or equity classification applies. At issuance date the company records an adjustment to additional paid-in capital for issuance cost, i.e., own-share lending arrangement issuance costs.[254]

Comment: However, as part of the *Financial Instruments with Characteristics of Equity Project* – former *Financial Instruments: Liabilities and Equity Project*, the FASB proposed that equity transaction costs be charged to income immediately.[255]

Under IFRSs, direct costs of an equity transaction, if incremental, external, and directly attributable to the equity transaction, and which would otherwise have been avoided had the transaction not taken place (and therefore, necessary to complete the transaction), are also netted from the proceeds of issue, while indirect costs of issuance are expensed.[256] IAS 32 sees this as a way to allow the representation in equity of the total cost of the transaction.[257] Typically under U.S. GAAP direct costs are debited in additional paid-in capital.[258] Under both IFRSs and SEC guidance, costs of an aborted offering (i.e., under SAB Topic 5-A, if postponed for more than 90 days) must be charged to profit or loss.[259]

Under IAS 32, a rational allocation, consistently with similar transactions, must be used for costs related to more than one transaction. In case of a compound instrument, this treatment is simply pro-rated based on the proceeds allocated to the equity component of the transaction. An early redemption or repurchase of a convertible instrument before maturity triggers a reallocation of the consideration paid and the related transaction costs.[260]

In a business combination, IAS 22, then superseded, considered transaction costs as part of the cost of acquisition (therefore they were measured as part of goodwill). When pooling of interest was permitted, in such a business combination all registration and issuance costs were expensed. Then IFRS 3 and FASB Statement No. 141 used to treat direct external costs (as defined above) incurred in issuing equity instruments as a reduction of the proceeds of

---

[254] *FASB ASC 471-20-05-12A, 12B, 470-20-25-20A, 470-20-65-3 (Accounting Standards Update No. 2009-15,* Accounting for Own-Share Landing Arrangements in Contemplation of Convertible Debt Issuance or Other Financing, *amending Accounting Standards Codification as the result of EITF Issue No. 09-1,* Accounting for Own-Share Landing Arrangements in Contemplation of Convertible Debt Issuance, ¶¶ 2, 3, 6, 7, 11).

[255] *Financial Accounting Standards Board, Preliminary Views,* Financial Instruments with Characteristics of Equity, *¶ 30 (November 30, 2007).*

[256] *IAS 1, ¶ 109; IAS 32, ¶¶ IN15, 35, 37.*

[257] *IAS 32, ¶ BC33.*

[258] *IFRSs do not specify the component of equity from which issuance costs are to be deducted.*

[259] *FASB ASC 340-10-S99-1 (SEC Staff Accounting Bulletin, Topic 5-A,* Expenses of Offering*); IAS 32, ¶¶ 37–38.*

[260] *IAS 32, ¶ AG33.*

the equity instruments issued, while indirect and internal costs were expensed. However, the cost of a business combination still included any direct cost.[261] IFRS 3 (Revised 2008) and Subtopic 815-10 (FASB Statement No. 141 (Revised 2007)) require a consistent accounting for all acquisition-related costs, i.e., to be treated separately from both the fair value of the consideration transferred and the fair value of net assets acquired and to be expensed as incurred (rather than included in goodwill), apart from the costs to issue debt or equity securities that are treated according relevant standards (thus, equity issue costs deducted from equity under IAS 32). Acquisition-related costs are not assets, and therefore their inclusion in goodwill as part of the allocation of the cost of an acquisition is not justified. Furthermore, the new requirement is consistent with Subtopic 820-10 (FASB Statement No. 157) which views those costs as not being part of the fair value exchange between the buyer and seller in a business combination, and therefore not to be recognized in the cost of acquisition or in its allocation to the acquiree's identifiable assets and liabilities.[262] Transaction costs directly related to the acquisition or disposal of noncontrolling interests with no loss of control are recognized in equity as the underlying transaction. Although the wording is not specific, related guidance in abovementioned standards is applicable.[263]

> **Example:** The Corporate Reporting Standing Committee (EECS), a forum of the EU National Enforcers of Financial Information, assessed that an issuer did not comply with IFRS 3 because it did not deduct the costs related to the issue of equity instruments in a business combination from equity.[264]

> **Comment:** Fair value less costs to sell is the measurement principle under IFRS 5. When applied to a subsidiary acquired exclusively with a view to its subsequent disposal, costs to sell are costs to dispose of that subsidiary. On initial recognition, subtracting those costs from the fair value of the subsidiary's assets in practice results in deducting disposal (not acquisition) costs from the acquired goodwill related to that subsidiary. The IASB acknowledged that conceptually, they should be expensed.[265]

An SEC registrant must make an allocation of fees that are charged by an investment banker that, in connection with a business combination or asset acquisition, also provides interim financing or underwriting services, based on relative fair value of services provided and the guidance in Topic 805 (FASB Statement No. 141(R)) on acquisition-related costs.[266]

---

[261] *FASB Statement No. 141, ¶¶ 24, A9; IFRS 3 (Revised 2004), ¶¶ 24, 31, BC71–BC72.*

[262] *FASB Statement No. 141(R), ¶¶ B251, B365–BC70; IFRS 3, ¶¶ 53, BC251, BC365–BC370*

[263] *IAS 1, ¶¶ 106(d)(iii), 109; IFRIC Update, May 2009.*

[264] *Committee of European Securities Regulators (CESR), 2007. CESR/07-120,* Extract from EECS's Database of Enforcement Decisions, *Paris: CESR, ¶ Decision ref. EECS/0407-13. [Online] CESR. Available at www.cesr.eu (last visited July 20, 2010).*

[265] *IFRS 5, ¶¶ BC42, BC44–BC45.*

[266] *FASB ASC 340-10-S99-2 (SEC Staff Accounting Bulletin, Topic 2-A.6* Purchase Method, Debt Issue Costs*).*

Under IFRSs, a company must disclose acquisition-related costs by transaction and separately disclose the amount expensed and the respective line items in which they are recognized.[267]

Comment: The IASB acknowledged that it would need to consider whether to amend other standards, such as IAS 16, IAS 39, and IFRS 5, to have a consistent treatment of transaction costs,[268] irrespective of whether they are related to equity, debt, or assets. Similarly, in the *Financial Instruments with Characteristics of Equity Project* the FASB considered charging equity transaction costs to income immediately.[269]

4.12   SUBSCRIPTIONS RECEIVABLE

Subscription receivable must be presented as a deduction from equity. This also applies to limited liability companies.[270] An SEC registrant must separately present subscriptions receivable on the face of the balance sheet, as a deduction from equity (referred to common stock or preferred stock as applicable). If related to mandatorily redeemable preferred stock or preferred stock whose redemption is solely at the option of the issuer, subscriptions receivable must be shown as a deduction from this item.[271]

Comment: Under IFRSs, however, the display as a separate line item in equity is not mandatory. In fact, IAS 1 requires disclosure either in the statement of financial position or the statement of changes in equity or in the notes of shares that have been issued but not fully paid,[272] which in any case are reported within equity.

Under U.S. practice,[273] the accounting entries would be as follows:

	Debit:	*Credit:*
At initial subscription:	Cash	
	Stock subscription receivable	
		Preferred stock subscribed (at par or stated value)
		Common stock subscribed (at par or stated value)
		Additional paid-in – preferred stock
		Additional paid-in – common stock

---

[267] *IFRS 3, ¶ B64(m).*

[268] *IASB, Business Combinations Phase II,* Project Summary and Feedback Statement, *page 19 (January 2008).*

[269] *Financial Accounting Standards Board, Preliminary Views,* Financial Instruments with Characteristics of Equity, *¶ 30 (November 30, 2007).*

[270] *AICPA, Practice Bulletin No. 14, ¶ 13.*

[271] *FASB ASC 210-10-S99-1 (Regulation S-X, ¶¶ 210.5-02.28-30).*

[272] *IAS 1, ¶ 79.*

[273] *Also see EITF Issue No. 88-16,* Basis in Leveraged Buyout Transactions, *¶ Section 3.b.*

At full payment and share issuance:	Cash	Stock subscription receivable
	Preferred stock subscribed	Preferred stock
	Common stock subscribed	Common stock

The pre-IAS treatment in many European jurisdictions was to recognize subscriptions receivable as an asset.

> **Comment:** This treatment traditionally arose from different corporate law frameworks. In the U.S., shares must be generally fully paid for actual issuance of the shares. Subscribed shares generally do not carry the rights and liabilities of actual outstanding stock, and consequently must be deducted from equity. Depending on the specific foreign jurisdiction, issuance of partially paid stock might be possible. Where partially-paid shares are considered issued shares, subscriptions receivable is reported as an asset. The rights of those shareholders are generally limited.

As part of the first-time adoption of IFRSs, in countries where subscriptions receivables are accounted for as assets, a company has to reverse such amounts against equity.

> **Example:** The Implementation Guidance by OIC in Italy for first-time adoption of IFRSs suggested separate display of capital stock, subscriptions receivable, and stock already paid at the reporting date.[274]

4.13 SHARES ISSUED IN EXCHANGE FOR A NOTE RECEIVABLE

In general, the accounting treatment of shares issued in exchange for a note receivable, where this is permitted by state statute or laws, is assimilated to the accounting for subscription receivables (see Section 4.12 above).

> **Comment:** In particular, the SEC guidance considers such circumstances comparable to subscriptions receivable, which are also accounted for as reduction of equity.[275] Although IFRSs provide no explicit guidance on the subject, this may be associated to the treatment of subscriptions receivable.

---

[274] *OIC – Organismo Italiano di Contabilità,* Guida Operativa per la Transizione ai Principi Contabili Internazionali (IAS/IFRS) *(October 2005), page 100, Footnote 86.*

[275] *FASB ASC 310-10-S99-2 (SEC Staff Accounting Bulletin, Topic 4-E,* Receivables From Sale Of Stock*); FASB ASC 310-10-S99-3 (SEC Staff Accounting Bulletin, Topic 4-G,* Notes And Other Receivables From Affiliates).

A note receivable that is exchanged for issuance or sale of stock (or an issuance of stock before its cash collection) must be reported as a deduction in equity.[276] As mentioned, IFRS does not impose a separate line presentation.

> **Comment:** From a defense of capital perspective, reporting unpaid accounts receivable as assets may end up with raising equity through an increase in gross assets that might result in being uncollectible.

Under U.S. GAAP however, in rare cases, a company may report a note receivable as an asset, when the note is collected in cash before the issue of the financial statements, the payment date is disclosed in the notes, and the payment is not subsequently refunded. In addition, a nonpublic company might recognize the note as an asset if there is substantial evidence of both the ability and intent to pay it in a reasonably short period of time. Other situations where this may be presented as an asset arise if the note that has a short stated maturity is collateralized (e.g., by an irrevocable letter of credit) or is discountable at a bank.[277]

> **Comment:** This is not permitted under IFRSs.

The SEC guidance requires that the note receivable, whether presented as an asset or as a contra-equity account, must be separately displayed if received from a related party (e.g., a general partner) also including from employees when the receivables arise other than in the ordinary course of business.[278]

> **Comment:** IAS 24 requires disclosure either on the statement of financial position or in the notes of amounts receivable from related parties as distinguished in the standard (also including key management personnel of the entity or its parent).[279] Contrary to Subtopic 850-10 (FASB Statement No. 57) and SEC guidance, IAS 24 does not exempt from disclosure certain related party transactions (e.g., with employees) in the normal course of business.

The SEC Staff clarifies that the characteristic of control in the relationship between the parties (e.g., a parent or another affiliate contributes the note receivable) qualifies the note for contra-equity account treatment.[280]

---

[276] *FASB ASC 310-10-S99-2 (SEC Staff Accounting Bulletin, Topic 4-E); FASB ASC 505-10-45-2 (EITF Issue No. 85-1,* Classifying Notes Received for Capital Stock*).*

[277] *FASB ASC 310-10-S99-2 (SEC Staff Accounting Bulletin, Topic 4-E); FASB ASC 505-10-45-2 (EITF Issue No. 85-1).*

[278] *FASB ASC 310-10-S99-3 (SEC Staff Accounting Bulletin, Topic 4-G). According to FASB ASC 210-10-S99-1 (Regulation S-X, ¶ 210.5-02.3) such separate display is also a general requirement for accounts and notes receivable from related parties.*

[279] *IAS 24,* Related Party Disclosures, *¶ 19.*

[280] *FASB ASC 310-10-S99-3 (SEC Staff Accounting Bulletin, Topic 4-G).*

> **Comment:** Similarly, in a leveraged buyout transaction, a loan from the Old Co., or other form of proceeds not independent of the Old Co., that had permitted the controlling shareholders of the New Co. to obtain such controlling interest, must reduce the reported equity of the New Co.[281]

Whether or not the contributed capital is then actually paid does not change the accounting. SAB Topic 4-G explains that this does not change the substance of the transaction.

> **Comment:** From the perspective of the investor, a situation of an unpaid subscription receivable might by analogy be treated as a long-term interest that is in substance a net investment in the investee accounted for at equity method, for which settlement is neither planned nor likely to occur in the foreseeable future.[282]

4.14   TREASURY STOCK

4.14.1   Terminology

Different terminology may be found for treasury stock.

> **Comment:** U.S. GAAP generally uses the term *treasury stock* or *own stock* for stock that a corporation issued and then repurchased and that is not yet reissued or cancelled, and rarely the expression *treasury shares*.[283] The expression often used by U.S. business law and regulation is *own stock*. The Model Business Corporation Act calls such shares *own shares*[284] and describes them as shares that are *reacquired, redeemed, converted, or cancelled*. Such shares have the status of authorized but unissued shares.[285] Section 3.5.2.2 previously highlights how acquisition of treasury shares may fall under defense of capital. IFRSs generally refer to equity instruments reacquired and held by the issuer or its subsidiaries[286] as *treasury shares* or *own shares* (i.e., shares held in treasury or own shares held[287]). The EC Accounting Directives use the term *own shares*.[288] Furthermore, as described in Section 4.14.5 following, under U.S. GAAP different account names may be used depending on the accounting method used.

---

[281]   *EITF Issue No. 86-16*, Basis in Leveraged Buyout Transactions, *Discussion, Section 3.*

[282]   *FASB ASC 323-10-35-19 (EITF Topic D-68:* Accounting by an Equity Method Investor for Investee Losses When the Investor Has Loans to and Investments in Other Securities of an Investee*); IAS 28 (2010), ¶ 29.*

[283]   *FASB ASC 718-10-50-2 (FASB Statement No. 123(R), ¶ A240); FASB Statement No. 128, ¶ 100; FASB ASC 220-10-55-3 (FASB Statement No. 130, ¶ 110); FASB ASC 505-30-30-2 (FASB Technical Bulletins No. 85-6,* Accounting for a Purchase of Treasury Shares and Costs Incurred in Defending against a Takeover Attempt*); EITF Issue No. 85-2,* Classification of Costs Incurred in a Takeover Defense*; EITF Issue No. 99-7,* Accounting for an Accelerated Share Repurchase Program, *¶ 6;*

[284]   *American Bar Foundation,* Model Business Corporation Act, *Subchapter A, § 6.31 (a) (2003).*

[285]   *American Bar Foundation,* Model Business Corporation Act, *Subchapter A, § 6.03 (a) (2003).*

[286]   *IAS 33, ¶ IE, Example 2, note a).*

[287]   *IFRS 2, ¶ Footnote to BC2.*

[288]   *Fourth Council Directive 78/660/EEC (July 25, 1978), Art. 9.*

4.14.2   Gains or Losses on Treasury Stock Transactions

Under U.S. GAAP[289] and IAS 32, gains and losses on treasury stock transactions (purchase, sale, issuance, or cancellation), and dividends on treasury shares,[290] shall affect directly equity and not the income statement. Treasury stock is recognized as a deduction from equity, and proceeds from resale are credited directly in equity, unless an agency relationship exists (that is, when an entity holds its own equity on behalf of others).[291]

> **Comment:** This may be seen as an application of the "entity" approach to consolidated financial statements (see Section 4.3.2 previously). Conceptually, gains or losses arising from transactions between a parent company and noncontrolling interests are recognized in equity and not in profit or loss to the extent noncontrolling interests are considered owners.[292] Conversely, the proprietary perspective (Section 2.1 previously) would see a loss to pre-existing shareholders resulting from a resale of treasury stock above cost as a dirty-surplus loss.

> **Comment:** The treasury stock principle may be pictured from another perspective. Assume that a company liquidates and its shareholders obtain the net assets. Total equity is brought to zero and any gain or loss included in net assets is now a gain or loss realized by the shareholders. They would obtain the same results if the company sold all of its shares and distributed the proceeds to its shareholders.

4.14.3   Applications of the Treasury Stock Principle

Several applications of this principle may be found in accounting pronouncements, as discussed below.

A treatment similar to treasury share accounting applies to a forward purchase contract that requires a fixed number of outstanding shares of the issuer to be repurchased in exchange for cash. In fact, equity must be initially reduced by the fair value of the shares.[293] Equity treatment (gain/loss recognized in equity) applies for any difference between the initial reduction of minority interest and its carrying amount that arises under such a contract.[294]

Under U.S. GAAP, the acquisition phase of an accelerated share repurchase program must be recorded as a purchase of treasury stock. In a share repurchase program a company purchases a certain number of own shares immediately, but the price is based on a volume-weighted average market price over a fixed period of time through a forward contract with an investment banker, whereby the entity will receive cash when the contract is in a gain position but pay

---

[289]   *APB Opinion No. 6,* Status of Accounting Research Bulletins, *¶ 12; FASB ASC 505-10-25-2 (APB Opinion No. 9,* Reporting the Results of Operations, *¶ 28).*

[290]   *Current Text, General Standards ¶ C23.101.*

[291]   *IAS 32, ¶¶ 33, AG36.*

[292]   *Discussion Paper,* Preliminary Views on an Improved Conceptual Framework for Financial Reporting, The Reporting Entity *(May 2008), ¶ 114.*

[293]   *FASB ASC 480-10-30-3, 480-10-30-5 (FASB Statement No. 150, ¶ 21).*

[294]   *FASB Statement No. 160, ¶ D7.a, amending EITF Issue No. 00-6,* Accounting for Freestanding Derivative Financial Instruments Indexed to, and Potentially Settled in, the Stock of a Consolidated Subsidiary, *¶ 20.*

cash or stock in the reverse situation. This second phase must be accounted for as a forward contract indexed to the issuer's own common stock.[295]

> **Comment:** IFRSs provide no exception to such accounting for treasury stock. The IFRIC also confirmed that even if own shares are held for trading they must not be measured at fair value with changes in value reported in profit or loss.[296] By contrast, certain limited exceptions to treasury stock treatment existed, and some are still in force, under U.S. GAAP, as explained below.

Under APB 25, now superseded, cash paid to an employee to settle an earlier award of stock or a grant of option (i.e., a repurchase), if shortly after issuance, was part of compensation cost.[297]

Furthermore, if treasury shares are acquired at a price significantly above open market price that reflects stated or unstated rights or privileges or additional agreements, such excess must be attributed to these other elements, accounted for according to their substance and disclosed accordingly. The cost of treasury stock must instead reflect the fair value of shares (at quoted market price[298]) at the date of agreement of the main terms of purchase. Generally this situation arises when the seller is a specific (group of) shareholder(s) or when the identity of the seller is relevant. Examples of additional agreements may be an accord where the selling shareholder agrees to dump certain acquisition plans or transactions, or to settle litigation or employment contracts. A "standstill" agreement not to purchase additional shares for a period or a "greenmail" to avert a takeover attempt must be expensed. However, if no additional stated or unstated rights, privileges, or agreements can be identified, as the excess price is intrinsic in the type of treasury stock transaction (e.g., a tender offer, a purchase of a block of shares over current market price) treasury shares are measured at the entire purchase price.[299]

> **Comment:** This case is not explicitly treated under IFRSs. The accounting is controversial. On one hand, the general principle of treasury stock would result in no income or expense recognition. However, IAS 32 does not explain what happens in case own shares are repurchased or resold at an amount other than their fair value. On the other hand, a different interpretation arises by analogy from the application of IFRS 2. In fact, under IFRS 2, the difference between the settlement in cash or other asset of a share-settled award and its fair value is recognized in profit or loss.

Further exceptions, consisting in treating treasury stock as an asset, are discussed in the next paragraph.

Although it may be argued that an extinguishment of convertible debt may be seen as equivalent to a treasury stock purchase, under U.S. GAAP the accounting for such an extinguishment is independent of the source from which the required cash is obtained. Consequently treasury

---

[295] *FASB ASC 505-30-25-5, 505-30-25-6 (EITF Issue No. 99-7*, Accounting for an Accelerated Share Repurchase Program*)*.

[296] *IFRIC Update, August 2002*.

[297] *APB Opinion No. 25, ¶ 11(g)*.

[298] *EITF Issue No. 85-2*, Classification of Costs Incurred in a Takeover Defense, *¶ Status*.

[299] *FASB ASC 505-30-30-2 (FASB Technical Bulletins No. 85-6)*.

stock accounting does not apply and any difference between the acquisition price (which, under certain circumstances, may equal the fair value of the shares into which the debt is convertible) and the net carrying amount of debt affects current income in the period of extinguishment.[300]

As to measurement, Subtopic 845-10 (APB 29) classifies a treasury stock purchase as a non-reciprocal transfer with owners.[301] A nonmonetary asset transferred in exchange for treasury stock is measured at fair value of the asset transferred. The standard indicates that the fair value of the treasury stock may be a more clearly evident measure of the fair value of the asset if the transaction is to eliminate a disproportionate part of owners' interest.[302]

4.14.4 Whether or not Treasury Stock is an Asset

As a consequence of its equity treatment mentioned above, treasury stock is not an asset, as it lacks the ability to provide future economic benefits.[303]

FASB Statement No. 135 eliminated prior limited exceptions to classify treasury stock as assets.[304] In one of these situations SEC guidance permitted shares, which were expected to be reissued under existing stock plans within one year of repurchase, to be presented as an asset. In connection with the issue of EITF Issue No. 97-14, the SEC repealed such requirement.[305]

IFRSs do not permit asset presentation of treasury shares on the ground that this would be inconsistent with the definition of asset in the IASB Framework.

> **Comment:** An interest in the entity's net assets is not an asset. As a proof, receiving dividends from itself would result in no change in net assets and therefore in no future economic benefits (i.e., a required characteristic for asset definition). Furthermore, as the result of reselling treasury shares at a higher amount may be replicated through issuing new shares at a higher price, accounting as an asset would also result in treating an entity's shares as assets.[306]

As part of the *Conceptual Framework Project*, the FASB and the IASB reconsidered whether an entity's unissued shares, own shares, or treasury shares are assets of the issuing entity or not and confirmed that they are not assets. In fact, the existence of an economic resource resulting in cash inflows, which is one of the three essential characteristics of the definition of an asset, is not present here. Unlike an asset that can be sold against cash or other assets, unissued shares or treasury shares cannot be transferred (that is, issued or reissued) to a third party for a cash inflow without giving something in exchange, i.e., an ownership interest, at the same time. To originate an asset, an economic resource must have a net positive economic value. Here, the net value is nil. In other terms, before issuance or after reacquisition they are a promise with no external counterparty; they are simply evidence of one-sided promissory

---

[300] *FASB ASC 470-50-40-4 (APB Opinion No. 26*, Early Extinguishment of Debt, ¶ 21).

[301] *FASB ASC 845-10-05-4 (APB Opinion No. 29*, Accounting for Nonmonetary Transactions, ¶ 3(d)); APB 29, ¶ 5.

[302] *FASB ASC 845-10-30-1 (APB 29*, ¶ 18).

[303] *IAS 32, ¶ AG36.*

[304] *FASB Statement No. 135*, Rescission of FASB Statement No. 75 and Technical Corrections, ¶¶ 4(a), 4(b), 20(a).

[305] *FASB Statement No. 135, ¶ 20(a); EITF Issue No. 97-14*, Accounting for Deferred Compensation Arrangements Where Amounts Earned Are Held in a Rabbi Trust and Invested, ¶ *Discussion*.

[306] *IFRS 2, ¶¶ BC73, BC331.*

capacity. Furthermore, once issued, shares are a claim on one's cash flows; this fact cannot create an asset of the issuing entity. Instead, issued shares are an economic burden.[307]

The Fédération des Experts Comptables Européens (FEE)[308] argued from a different standpoint against recognizing treasury stock as an asset. In particular, this would result in capitalizing an issuer's internally generated goodwill, as this value is included in the stock price of a company. In addition, if treasury stock transactions that are not intended for stock retirement result in a change of minority interest, this fact should ordinarily not trigger a remeasurement of assets (see Section 4.14.10 following for an update on recent U.S. and international standards on this point).

Comment: The pre-IAS accounting in certain European jurisdictions required the presentation of treasury stock as a current or noncurrent asset. To a certain extent this was under the umbrella of the EC Fourth Directive, which classifies treasury shares as an asset to the extent this is permitted by national laws.

The EC Fourth Directive prescribes a separate line for own shares and/or shares in affiliates, and a reserve for own shares to the extent that this is required by national laws.[309] The EC Second Directive requires such a reserve in case the laws of a Member State are in favor of the presentation of treasury shares as an asset.[310]

Example: In Italy, a company that does not report under IFRSs must still present treasury shares as assets. In addition, a purchase of own shares requires a transfer from reserves to an undistributable "treasury stock" reserve within equity. Once treasury shares are resold or retired, such a reserve becomes free to the extent of the excess of purchase value over par value per share, and is reversed to the equity reserves from which it was originally sourced.[311] On first-time adoption of IFRSs, such companies have to reclassify treasury stock from asset to equity and to reverse the treasury stock reserve to the equity reserves from which it was originally sourced or to the beginning balance of retained earnings in the opening IFRS statement of financial position.[312]

---

[307] *FASB, Minutes of Meeting, June 20, 2006, Conceptual Framework Project*, Element 5: Asset Definition (IV) and Liability Definition (III), ¶¶ *10–12 (June 27, 2006) (last visited June 21, 2007) www.fasb.org; FASB/IASB, Conceptual Framework Project, Agenda Paper 7, Elements 5:* Asset Definition (IV) & Liability Definition (III): Application of the Working Definitions to Certain Contracts—a Forward Contract and an Entity's Own Shares, ¶¶ *4, 40, 42, 46 (June 2006) (last visited June 21, 2007) www.fasb.org; IASB, Conceptual Framework Project, Agenda Paper 3,* Phase B: Elements: Definition of an Asset, ¶¶ *A4, A8 (November 16, 2006) (last visited June 21, 2007) www.iasb.org; IASB, SAC Meeting, February 2007, Conceptual Framework Project, Agenda Paper 4A,* Phase B: Elements: Definition of an Asset, ¶¶ *A22, A23 (last visited December 23, 2009) www.iasb.org.*

[308] *Fédération des Experts Comptables Européens, FEE Study,* Comparison of the EC Accounting Directives and IASs. A Contribution to International Accounting Developments *(April 1999).*

[309] *Fourth Council Directive 78/660/EEC (July 25, 1978), Articles 9, 10, 13.*

[310] *Second Council Directive 77/91/EEC, Art. 22(1)(b).*

[311] *OIC – Organismo Italiano di Contabilità, Principio Contabile No. 28,* Il Patrimonio Netto, *page 25.*

[312] *OIC – Organismo Italiano di Contabilità,* Guida Operativa per la Transizione ai Principi Contabili Internazionali (IAS/IFRS) *(October 2005), page 102.*

> **Comment:** Thus, the amount of such treasury stock reserve that is ultimately used would correspond, under U.S. GAAP, to the sum of the debit of additional paid-in capital and retained earnings at formal retirement under cost method.

4.14.5   Relationship between Treasury Stock and Share-Based Payment Transactions

Several cross-references exist between treasury stock accounting and share-based payment transactions.

Firstly, a direct relation arises when the issuer's treasury shares are used in share schemes for the benefit of all or certain employees.

Under IFRSs, treasury share accounting (i.e., recognition within equity) also applies to shares purchased, sold, issued, or cancelled in connection with share-based payment transactions,[313] although IFRSs do not provide specific guidelines for presentation of treasury shares acquired in connection with equity compensation plans.

> **Comment:** IFRS 2 extends treasury equity accounting to issuer's shares purchased, sold, issued, or cancelled in connection with share-based payment transactions. The standard justifies this in the light of avoiding a double hit in the statement of comprehensive income. This would come, on one hand, from the expense of the goods or services received in exchange for the issue of equity instruments and, on the other hand, from the write down of treasury shares, if they were recognized as an asset (Section 4.14.3 previously), that corresponds to the defect of exercise price versus purchase price.[314]

A special case is when a principal shareholder provides the entity's shares needed for compensating the employees or suppliers under a share plan. The arrangement is an equity-settled share-based payment, independently of whether the entity itself or a third party (such as the principal shareholder) granted the employee's rights to the shares or whether the entity itself or a third party settled the transaction.[315]

> **Example:** In its reply to the SEC's review of Form 20-F for the year ended March 31, 2006, a French foreign private issuer classified own shares that were granted to its employee by the French State, the Company's principal stockholder, as held in treasury.[316]

Shares reacquired as a consequence of a clawback feature in a share-based payment transaction, such as where an employee must return to the company for no consideration shares granted and earned in the share-based payment transaction or their cash equivalent upon the occurrence

---

[313] *IAS 32, ¶ 4(f)(ii).*

[314] *IFRS 2, ¶¶ BC332–BC333.*

[315] *FASB ASC 718-10-15-4 (FASB Statement No. 123(R), ¶ 11); IFRS 2, ¶ 3; IFRIC 11, ¶ 7 (then incorporated into IFRS 2).*

[316] *Letter by the SEC, File No. 001-32139, Note 1 (January 22, 2007). Reply by the company (February 23, 2007) www.sec.gov/divisions/corpfin/ifrs_reviews (last visited January 7, 2008).*

of a certain event defined by the award (e.g., termination and subsequent employment by a competitor), are also accounted for as treasury shares.[317]

Under U.S. GAAP, a rabbi trust is a grantor trust, used to fund deferred compensation of a selected group of management or executives through placing amounts earned by them in the trust and investing in the employer's stock and then often diversifying in other securities. The assets must be available to satisfy the claims of general creditors in the event of the employer's bankruptcy. Under EITF Issue No. 97-14, employer stock held in a rabbi trust must be accounted for in equity similarly to treasury stock in such employer's financial statements. If the plan allows for diversification and the employee has actually diversified, the accounting must follow GAAP applicable to the specific type of financial assets. Subsequent changes in the fair value of the employer's stock are not recognized.[318]

Secondly, an indirect link results from consolidation of a special-purpose entity that holds the issuer's shares for the purpose of share-based awards to the sponsor's employees.

Under IFRSs, following the amendment of SIC-12 (effective from annual periods beginning on or after January 1, 2005, unless an entity applies IFRS 2 from an earlier date), equity compensation plans held within a special purpose entity, such as an employee benefit trust, are included within the scope of SIC-12 and should be consolidated when, in substance, they are controlled by the entity. Shares held by the trust are then treated as treasury shares under IAS 32 and deducted from equity for the reporting entity.[319] IFRS 10 replaces IAS 27 and SIC-12. It is effective for annual periods beginning on or after January 1, 2013, with earlier application permitted. It introduces a single model of consolidation based on control for all types of entities.[320]

> **Example:** Prudential Plc in its Form 20-F for the fiscal year ended December 31, 2005 reported own shares held by trusts established to facilitate the delivery of shares under employee incentive and saving plans as treasury shares. Those trusts did not continue to hold the shares once they were issued to employees.[321]

Similar treatment generally applies under U.S. GAAP for share trusts other than employee stock ownership plans (ESOPs).[322] In an ESOP employees receive shares of the sponsoring entity as additional compensation as part of a defined contribution employee benefit plan. The plan may obtain the sponsor's shares in alternative ways, directly from the sponsor through either installments or a block purchase, or through a purchase from an existing shareholder. Under U.S. GAAP, a contra-equity line item "unearned ESOP shares" accounts for shares issued from an employer to the ESOP or treasury shares transferred from an employer to the

---

[317] *FASB ASC 718-20-35-2, 718-10-55-8, 718-10-55-47, 718-20-55-85, 718-20-55-86 (FASB Statement No. 123(R), ¶¶ 27, A5, A42, A190–A191).*

[318] *EITF Issue No. 97-14,* Accounting for Deferred Compensation Arrangements Where Amounts Earned are Held in a Rabbi Trust and Invested.

[319] *IFRIC Amendment to SIC-12,* Scope of SIC-12 Consolidation – Special Purpose Entities, *¶ 15C.*

[320] *IFRS 10, ¶¶ IN2, C9.*

[321] *Reply by Prudential Plc to the SEC (October 31, 2006) www.sec.gov/divisions/corpfin/ifrs_reviews (last visited January 7, 2008).*

[322] *FASB ASC 810-10-S99-2 (Regulation S-X, ¶¶ 210.1-02(g), 210-3A-02(a)).*

ESOP or when the ESOP buys employer's stock on the open market.[323] This is because such shares are not legally released but committed to release in the future, and the sponsor has a commitment to make future contributions to the plan and thus has no claim to resources. Once they are released because they are allocated to participants' accounts for services provided or the ESOP services the debt (either through contributions made by the sponsor or dividends received on sponsor shares held by the plan) the sponsor reduces the contra-equity account on its balance sheet.

> **Comment:** IFRSs do not treat accounting for ESOP (see Section 8.2.17.5 later). However, if the ESOP were determined to hold shares on behalf of others (i.e., the employer) those shares would not be treated as property of the ESOP but as employer's treasury shares under IAS 32.[324]

> **Comment:** The IFRIC analyzed whether treasury stock accounting should also apply to the separate financial statements of an entity sponsoring an employee benefit trust, that is, whether the employee benefit trust should be considered an extension of the sponsoring entity or whether the investment in the employee benefit trust should be recorded as an asset (a separate legal entity view). The IFRIC decided not to take the issue onto its agenda. The topic was related to the notion of "entity" being analyzed in the *Conceptual Framework Project* and to whether or not to account for the net investment in the trust, an issue that was related to the revision of IAS 27.[325]

4.14.6 Accounting Methods

Under U.S. GAAP treasury stock may be accounted for at cost method (as the simplest method), at par-value method, or formal or constructive retirement methods according to circumstances. Generally, cost method is used where stock will not be retired or when such a decision has not yet been taken. Constructive retirement method usually applies when management does not intend to reissue the shares within a reasonable time period, or when state laws define reacquired shares as retired. However, the use of formal or constructive retirement of stock, as an alternative to cost or par-value method, is allowed to account for treasury shares purchased for purposes other than retirement or pending a decision on disposition of stock.[326]

> **Comment:** The cost method is based on the "one-transaction concept," whereby a treasury stock transaction is simply considered a transfer among shareholders, even if mediated by the corporation. Therefore the transaction is not expected to affect total equity, and gains and losses should not be recognized in equity until they materialize through a subsequent decision to formally retire the shares acquired. At that point, in fact, the transaction becomes a "distribution to shareholders" and is no longer a transaction among them. Conversely, the par value and the constructive retirement methods are consistent with the "two-transaction concept," whereby the capital structure must end up being

---

[323] *FASB Statement No. 130,* ¶ *110; AICPA Statement of Position No. 93-6,* Employer's Accounting for Employee Stock Ownership Plans, ¶ *13.*

[324] *IAS 32,* ¶ *AG36.*

[325] *IFRIC Update, May 2006; IFRIC Update, November 2006.*

[326] *Accounting Research Bulletin No. 43,* Restatement and Revisions of Accounting Research Bulletins, *Ch.1.B,* ¶ *7(b).*

affected by both the acquisition of own stock as a retirement (a quasi-retirement, in case of par-value method) and a reissuance as an issuance of new shares (a quasi-issuance, in case of par-value method). Therefore, under this theory, excess and deficiency of purchase or resale price over par or stated value is recognized immediately at the date of the transaction. As a result, treasury stock transactions are considered distributions to, and contributions from, owners. The par value method is somehow in the middle as a "quasi-retirement": hence it uses a "treasury stock" and not a "common stock" account. The par-value method therefore uses an "additional paid-in capital – treasury (or retired) stock" account, as opposed to "additional paid-in capital – common stock" account, to the extent that an increase in additional paid-in capital does not correspond to a reversal of a previous decrease in additional paid-in capital – common stock. The cost method also uses "treasury stock" and "additional paid-in capital – treasury (or retired) stock" accounts.

Worksheet 26 illustrates the accounting entries for treasury stock transactions under U.S. GAAP.

U.S. state laws, if different, prevail; for example, some states treat reacquired shares as retired or excess cost over reacquired shares as equivalent to dividend distribution. In such circumstances, a company must disclose any limitation on distributability of retained earnings or similar restrictions.[327]

Comment: The accounting for treasury stock implicitly makes reference to two traditional accounting principles. Firstly, retained earnings may decrease but never increase as a result of transactions directly affecting equity without passing through the income statement. This point is analyzed in Section 6.2 later. Secondly, treasury stock transactions must not affect the income statement as a result of their being investments by, or distributions to, shareholders: this fact excludes their inclusion in comprehensive income. This aspect is analyzed in Section 7.2.1 later.

Contrary to U.S. GAAP, IFRSs do not prescribe specific accounting methods.

Comment: ARB 43, Ch.1.B explicitly states that the purchase and resale of treasury stock is equivalent to the purchase and retirement of an entity's own stock and issue of new stock (i.e., the two-transaction concept), a fact which would not affect the income statement.[328] By contrast, IAS 32 reasoning is twofold. On the one hand, it seems to resemble the "one-transaction concept" by considering treasury stock as transactions among shareholders.[329] On the other hand, it acknowledges the equivalence, typical of the "two-transaction concept," between share repurchase and retirement and between share resale and new issuance. Furthermore, IFRS 2 equates distribution of cash to buy back shares to a return of capital to shareholders.[330] IASB Update argues that the purchase consideration in excess of the carrying amount of preferred shares classified as equity is in effect a dividend to the preference shareholders.[331]

---

[327]   *APB 6, ¶ 13.*
[328]   *ARB 43, Ch.1.B, ¶ 7.*
[329]   *IAS 32, ¶¶ IN14, BC32.*
[330]   *IFRS 2, ¶¶ BC73, BC331.*
[331]   *IASB Update, November 2001.*

4.14.7   Presentation of Treasury Stock

As mentioned, under both U.S. GAAP and IFRS treasury stock is accounted for as a contra-equity account.

From a presentation standpoint under U.S. GAAP, when treasury stock is acquired for formal or constructive retirement or if the decision on its ultimate use has not yet been taken (and therefore either constructive retirement method or par-value method is adopted), treasury stock is deducted from the issued capital stock of the same class. When the par-value method is used, the par value is deducted from capital stock and excess/deficiencies from other paid-in capital or retained earnings consistently with their accounting under that method. Otherwise, when the cost method is employed, it is usually separately shown as an unallocated amount and deducted from the total of capital stock, additional paid-in capital, and retained earnings.[332] In practice, under the cost method it is found as a deduction from total equity, or alternatively from total stockholders' equity and liabilities, as follows:

> . . . Equity items
> Less: common stock in treasury, [number of] shares at cost
> Total stockholders' equity

Or, alternatively:

> . . . Total stockholders' equity
> Less: common stock in treasury, [number of] shares at cost
> Total stockholders' equity and liabilities

The *AICPA Accounting Trends & Techniques* illustrates that in 2009 68% of the survey U.S. GAAP companies disclosed treasury stock (65% in 2005 and 66% in 2002). Approximately 93%, 94%, and 92% of them, respectively, displayed it at cost method as a deduction from shareholders' equity.[333] However, if a U.S. state law views excess purchase cost as equivalent to dividends, it must be displayed with dividends in the retained earnings section.

Comment: The presentation of treasury stock under U.S. GAAP depends on the purpose for purchasing, and therefore on the accounting method used, with some variants in practice. Conversely, under IAS 32, separate presentation as deduction from equity on the face of the statement of financial position does not depend on the purpose of acquisition.[334] Furthermore, separate note disclosure is an available option, as an alternative to displaying the amount of treasury stock on the statement of financial position.[335]

Comment: Contrary to U.S. GAAP, IFRSs do not state under what caption within equity an entity must or may report treasury shares. The superseded SIC-16 stated as an example that treasury shares might be presented either as a one-line adjustment of equity or as a deduction from par value and a

---

[332]   *APB 6, ¶ 12(b).*
[333]   *AICPA ATT 2010 and AICPA ATT 2006, ¶ Table 2-41.*
[334]   *IAS 32, ¶ AG36.*
[335]   *IAS 32, ¶ 34.*

separate deduction of premium/discounts from other components of equity or as different adjustments to several categories of equity.[336] Depending on IFRS jurisdiction, specific guidance exists by the local accounting bodies.

Example: The Italian accounting body (OIC) suggested the separate display of treasury shares at par value as a deduction from issued capital. The difference between purchase price and par value has to adjust the other component of equity to which it relates. The details may be provided in the notes.[337]

Example: In contrast, an Irish foreign private issuer in its reply to the SEC's review or its Form 20-F for the fiscal year ended March 31, 2006 explained that the total issued share capital represents the legally issued share capital and therefore cannot change regardless of the existence of treasury shares.[338]

4.14.8 Disclosure of Treasury Stock

Worksheet 27 contrasts treasury stock disclosures under U.S. GAAP and IFRSs.

Comment: The main purpose for disclosure concerning treasury stock is to make their existence clear to users of financial statements, inform on whether or not such transactions involved related parties, and on their expected use, such as utilization in employee share schemes, resale, or cancellation.

When national laws permit a company to acquire own shares, the EC Second Directive requires disclosure in the annual report of the reasons for treasury share purchase, the number and nominal value of shares purchased and disposed of, both in the period and in total, the corresponding proportion of subscribed capital, and the consideration received or paid.[339]

4.14.9 Shares of the Parent Held by a Subsidiary

Under U.S. GAAP, a subsidiary's investment in the parent's shares is not treated as outstanding stock in the consolidated statement of financial position: in consolidation the subsidiary's "investment in parent" account is reclassified as treasury stock and deducted from consolidated equity.[340]

---

[336] *Standing Interpretations Committee, Interpretation SIC-16,* Share Capital – Reacquired Own Equity Instruments (Treasury Shares), ¶ 10.

[337] *OIC – Organismo Italiano di Contabilità,* Guida Operativa per la Transizione ai Principi Contabili Internazionali (IAS/IFRS) *(October 2005), page 100.*

[338] *Letter by the SEC, File No. 001-14452, Note 3 (January 25, 2007). Reply by the company (February 16, 2007) www.sec.gov/divisions/corpfin/ifrs_reviews (last visited January 7, 2008).*

[339] *Second Council Directive 77/91/EEC, Art. 22(2); Fourth Council Directive 78/660/EEC (July 25, 1978), Art. 46(d).*

[340] *FASB ASC 810-10-45-5 (ARB 51, ¶ 13).*

> **Comment:** Depending on jurisdiction, defense of capital laws may prohibit or limit the amount or percentage of mutual holdings.

> **Comment:** This is one case of a situation of mutual holdings (also known as bilateral or reciprocal holdings), which include both parent–subsidiary relationships (where the subsidiary owns some shares of the parent) and connecting affiliates (where subsidiaries own some of each other's shares). Under U.S. GAAP, in a situation of connecting affiliates, treasury stock interpretation is not applicable as none of the parent's shares are held by the subsidiaries.

Under IAS 32, shares of the entity that are acquired or held by other members of the consolidated group are also considered as treasury shares in consolidated financial statements.[341] The parent must disclose, for each class of share capital, the number of shares held by its subsidiaries or associates either on the face of the statement of financial position or in the statement of changes in equity or in the notes for both consolidated and separate financial statements.[342]

> **Comment:** As an analogy, from a consolidated perspective, transfers of equity instruments of an entity's parent or shareholders to employees or other providers in exchange for their goods or services are treated as share-based payment transactions.[343]

In U.S. practice, in case of a partially-owned subsidiary, two alternative approaches of consolidation exist: the treasury stock method and the traditional allocation method.

> **Comment:** Under the former, the subsidiary's investment in the parent account is reclassified as treasury stock. Under the latter, the subsidiary's investment in the parent account is eliminated against the equity of the parent. In this case, in line with the constructive retirement method for accounting for treasury stock, any implicit purchase premium is debited in additional paid-in capital and retained earnings. These two methods lead to different consolidated net income, retained earnings and additional paid-in capital.[344]
>
> Arguably, under IFRSs, the traditional allocation method is not an available option or in any case does not give rise to the issue of the implicit purchase premium, because the parent and an investor use cost (or fair value) method and not equity method in their separate financial statements.

Under U.S. GAAP, an investment in the parent should probably be reported as treasury stock in the subsidiary's financial statements, especially if the investment in the subsidiary is the only significant asset for the parent. The policy for accounting for investment in the parent must be disclosed in the accounting policy note. An EITF tentative conclusion, since then withdrawn, was that in its financial statements a joint venture should account for an investment in a joint

---

[341] *IAS 32, ¶ 33.*
[342] *IAS 1, ¶ 79(a)(vi); IAS 32, ¶ 34.*
[343] *IFRS 2, ¶ 3.*
[344] *See Ronald J. Huefner, James A. Largay III, and Susan S. Hamlen,* Advanced Financial Accounting, *DAME Thomson Learning, ¶ 7-41 (2002).*

venture partner that has substantive operations apart from the joint venture, as an equity-method investment with an elimination of the reciprocal ownership investments.[345]

IFRSs do not treat this case explicitly.

> **Comment:** IFRIC 11 gives an answer to this point indirectly: at purchase, a subsidiary accounts for holding shares of its parent as an investment in the parent (asset).[346]

4.14.10 Shares of an Investor Held by Its Associate

The treatment of shares of an investor held by its associate depends on whether or not the investor in an associate (with the meaning of "associate" under IAS 28[347]) is also a parent that issues consolidated financial statements. In addition different treatment arises for consolidated and parent's or investor's separate financial statements.

> **Comment:** The accounting of an associate's investment in an investor that is also a parent is a controversial issue. A view is that it would not be treated as treasury stock in consolidated financial statements. Firstly, intercompany balances with an associate are not eliminated in consolidation. Furthermore, IAS 32 does not specify the meaning of a member of the consolidated group for the purpose of treasury stock accounting.[348] Under IFRSs, a group is made up of a parent and all its subsidiaries.[349] Therefore, in theory it would exclude associates, although consolidated financial statements include them with specific rules. However, IAS 28 has some inconsistent guidance. The aggregate of the holdings in an associate by the parent and its subsidiaries is considered to determine significant influence and apply equity method. IAS 28 explicitly states that the holding of the group's other associates or joint ventures is ignored. On the other hand, the associate's financial statements, including its interest in other associates or joint ventures, must be considered for the purpose of equity method.[350] Furthermore, the 2009 revision of IAS 24 considers an associate's subsidiary as a party related to the investor in that associate.[351] By contrast, the concept of group is not defined by ARB 51 and FASB Statement No. 94. In addition, U.S. GAAP makes a distinction between consolidated and nonconsolidated group. Under Regulation S-X, a group is made of two or more persons who act together for the purposes of acquiring, holding, voting, or disposing of securities of a registrant.[352] Under Form 20-F it is composed of the parent and all its subsidiaries.[353]
>
> Another view is that treating an investment in a parent held by an associate as treasury stock is consistent with the substance of the guidance of IAS 32 on subsidiaries. Furthermore, IAS 28 specified that many consolidation procedures related to subsidiaries also apply to associates.[354]

---

[345] *EITF Issue No. 98-2*, Accounting by a Subsidiary or Joint Venture for an Investment in the Stock of Its Parent Company or Joint Venture Partner.

[346] *IFRIC Interpretation No. 11, IFRS 2 - Group and Treasury Share Transactions, ¶ BC14 (then incorporated into IFRS 2).*

[347] *IAS 28 (2010), ¶ 2.*

[348] *IAS 32, ¶ 33.*

[349] *IFRS 10, Appendix A; IAS 27 (2010), ¶ 4.*

[350] *IAS 28 (2011), ¶ 27; IAS 28 (2010), ¶ 21.*

[351] *IAS 24,* Related Party Disclosures, *¶ 12.*

[352] *Regulation S-X, ¶ 210.2-01.f(12).*

[353] *Form 20-F, General Instructions, F.*

[354] *IAS 28 (2010), ¶ 20.*

The case of an investor in an associate that is not a parent is similar to the accounting analyzed in the previous paragraph. A related issue of how to calculate equity method income accrual arises under U.S. GAAP for both consolidated and parent's financial statements. This is further complicated in the case of parent's dividends received by the associate.

Comment: As explained in the previous paragraph, under U.S. GAAP the accounting depends on whether the parent uses the treasury stock method or the traditional allocation method. Under the former, the parent computes the equity method income accrual in consolidated or in its separate financial statements either as a) parent's share of subsidiary's net income excluding parent's dividends, less minority's share of parent's dividends received by the subsidiary; or as b) parent's share of subsidiary's reported net income including parent's dividends, less all intercompany dividends received by the subsidiary. Under the traditional allocation method the calculation would be circular.

Comment: The problem of how to determine equity method income accrual, in the parent or in an investor's separate financial statements, does not arise under IFRSs, as such investment is accounted for at cost method (or at fair value method in certain circumstances).[355] In theory, it may arise for an investor that does not issue consolidated financial statements, as under IAS 28 it would use equity method. However, the traditional allocation method could not apply because the associate would not account for its reciprocal investment at equity method.

4.14.11   Purchase or Sale of Treasury Shares by a Subsidiary

The accounting for a purchase or sale of treasury shares by a subsidiary may be compared to the accounting of change in a parent's ownership interest in that subsidiary.

Comment: A purchase or sale of treasury shares by a subsidiary from/to outsiders achieves the same result in consolidated financial statements as, respectively, a sale or purchase by the parent of a noncontrolling interest in the subsidiary. In fact, the parent can reduce its controlling interest by selling some of the subsidiary's shares to outsiders or by instructing the subsidiary to sell treasury shares to outsiders. The impact of a sale of treasury shares by the subsidiary may also be replicated through an issue of additional shares to outsiders by the subsidiary. FASB Statement No. 160 contains a similar conclusion.[356] Both EITF Issue No. 08-6 and the IFRIC drew a similar conclusion with reference to the context of an investor and an associate.[357]

Under FASB Statement No. 160 and IAS 27 (Revised 2008) a change in a parent's ownership interest in a subsidiary, after control is obtained and with no loss of control, must result in adjusting the carrying amount of the controlling and noncontrolling interests in consolidated financial statements to reflect the change in their respective shares in the subsidiary's net assets. This is considered an equity transaction, because noncontrolling interests are a separate component of equity.

---

[355]   *IAS 28 (2010), ¶ 35.*
[356]   *FASB ASC 810-10-45-22 (ARB 51, ¶ 32, as amended by FASB Statement No. 160).*
[357]   *EITF Issue No. 08-6, Equity Method Investment Accounting Considerations, ¶ 9; IFRIC Update, May 2009.*

> **Comment:** This would be consistent with the entity theory of consolidation (see Section 4.3.2 previously).

As an equity transaction, no adjustment arises in the carrying amounts of the subsidiary's assets, including goodwill and liabilities, and any gain or loss arising from the difference between the fair value of the consideration paid or received for the additional stock and its book value is recognized directly in equity. Such gain or loss is attributed to the controlling interest. No additional goodwill is recognized on acquisition of noncontrolling interests of a controlled subsidiary, because obtaining control in a business combination, and not the percentage of ownership that provides that control, is deemed the significant economic event that determines the fair value measurement of the subsidiary's identifiable net assets. The entity of the ownership interest instead determines the pro rata share of the subsidiary's net income and liquidation preferences that accrues to the parent. Under this approach, any possible additional synergies that might be obtained through a higher ownership interest and any changes in the fair value of the subsidiary's net assets from the date when control was obtained would be unrecognized and subsumed within equity. The standards require the disclosure of a separate schedule of the effects on the equity attributable to owners of the parent.[358]

> **Comment:** Investment account, subsidiary's equity account, and noncontrolling interest account change depending on whether price is higher/lower than book value. For example, if the subsidiary purchases treasury stock below book value, the end-of-year controlling interest will increase, parent's investment account in the subsidiary will increase by the change in parent's share of subsidiary's equity, subsidiary's equity will decrease by the cost of the treasury shares, and noncontrolling interest will increase to equal the minority's share of the subsidiary's equity.

Before its latest revision, FASB Statement No. 141 required that the acquisition of noncontrolling interest in a subsidiary by the parent, or the subsidiary, or another affiliate, be accounted for in consolidated financial statements by using the purchase method on business combinations.[359] FASB Statement No. 160 also nullifies Issue 2 of EITF Issue No. 90-5[360] that required the purchase method to record the acquisition by one subsidiary of another subsidiary's minority interest when both entities were under common control. Under the new standard, such a transaction would be recorded as an equity transaction, because control had already been obtained and there is no loss of control.[361]

Similarly, FASB Statement No. 160[362] nullifies Issue 2 of EITF Issue No. 90-13[363] that considered a transaction where a parent purchased a controlling interest in a company and, at

---

[358]   *FASB ASC 810-10-45-23 (ARB 51, ¶ 33, as amended by FASB Statement No. 160); FASB Statement No. 160, ¶¶ B44, B47: IAS 27 (2010), ¶¶ 30–31, BC41–BC51, DO4–DO5.*

[359]   *FASB Statement No. 141, ¶¶ 14, A5, A6, D13.*

[360]   EITF Issue No. 90-5, Exchanges of Ownership Interests between Entities under Common Control; FASB Technical Bulletins No. 85-5, Issues Relating to Accounting for Business Combinations, Including Stock Transactions between Companies under Common Control.

[361]   *FASB Statement No. 160, ¶ D3.*

[362]   *FASB Statement No. 160, ¶ D3.*

[363]   EITF Issue No. 90-13, Accounting for Simultaneous Common Control Mergers.

the same time, in exchange for an extra percentage ownership, sold a noncontrolling interest in one of its subsidiaries to that company, as a partial acquisition of the company and a partial sale of the subsidiary to the minority shareholders of the acquired company. The parent recognized a gain or loss in consolidated financial statements on the partial sale of the subsidiary. Again, a sale of noncontrolling interests in subsidiaries without a loss of control is now an equity transaction.

FASB Statement No. 160[364] objected to the continuation of the SEC's interim guidance that permitted, in certain circumstances where realization of the gain was reasonably assured, the recognition of gains or losses in the consolidated financial statements on a subsidiary's direct sale of its unissued shares in a public offering, or in other issues as long as the value of the proceeds could be objectively determined. SAB 112 removed SAB 5-H and ASU 2010-22 superseded it.[365] This treatment was acceptable for SEC registrants provided such sale was not a part of a broader corporate reorganization contemplated or planned by the registrant, no share repurchase plan existed at the time of issuance (and no repurchase was effected within one year of issuance), and no other subsequent capital transactions were contemplated that would undermine the likelihood of gain realization. Gain recognition was not appropriate for a newly-formed, nonoperating subsidiary, a research and development or start-up or development stage company, or an entity whose going concern assumption was in question, and like circumstances. In case of subsequent repurchase of shares by the subsidiary, its parent, or any affiliate, no gain would be recognized on additional issues until all repurchased shares had been reissued. An SEC registrant had to show such gains or losses separately within nonoperating items in the consolidated income statement. This income statement treatment in consolidation for issuances of stock by a subsidiary was considered an accounting policy that, if chosen, had to be applied consistently to all qualifying stock transactions and disclosed in the accounting policy note. For all the issuances of subsidiary stock that had occurred during all periods presented, note disclosure was required about the description of the transaction, the subsidiary and nature of its operations, the number of shares issued, the price per share and the total dollar amount, the nature of consideration received, the percentage ownership of the parent both before and after the transaction, and any related provision of deferred income taxes. Information on the impact of transactions and likelihood of future similar transactions was to be provided in Management Discussion and Analysis.[366]

Finally, if a company purchases its own shares to the extent that an existing investor in such company obtains control in it, the transaction is considered a business combination without a transfer of consideration, and is accounted for at the acquisition method.[367]

---

[364] *FASB Statement No. 160, ¶¶ B50–B51.*

[365] *FASB Accounting Standards Update No. 2010-22,* Accounting for Various Topics – Technical Corrections to SEC Paragraphs, An Announcement made by the Staff of the U.S. Securities and Exchange Commission, *¶ 3; SEC, Staff Accounting Bulletin No. 112 (June 4, 2009), ¶ 2.b.*

[366] *FASB ASC 505-10-S99-6 (SEC Staff Accounting Bulletin, Topic 5-H,* Accounting for Sales of Stock by a Subsidiary*).*

[367] *FASB ASC 805-10-25-11 (FASB Statement No. 141(R), ¶ 49); IFRS 3, ¶ 43.*

5 ADDITIONAL PAID-IN CAPITAL

5.1 TERMINOLOGY

The term *additional paid-in capital* under U.S. GAAP corresponds to *share premium* under IFRSs. An aged U.S. terminology for additional paid-in capital is *capital surplus* or *paid-in surplus*,[1] expressions already criticized by ATB 1, which supported its discontinuance because the notion of redundancy was generally considered not appropriate with reference to capital or used with different meanings in economics or legal contexts.[2]

> **Comment:** Several U.S. pronouncements use the term *paid-in capital* as a synonym for additional paid-in capital,[3] although in general this is also a substitute for contributed capital.

The *AICPA Accounting Trends & Techniques* shows that approximately 63% and 61% of the survey companies that in 2009 and 2005, respectively, presented an additional paid-in capital account used the term *additional paid-in capital* on the face of the balance sheet, 11% and 10% the term *paid-in capital*, 3% *capital surplus*, approximately 17% and 20% the expression *capital in excess of par or stated value*, and the other companies used other terms. No one used *paid-in surplus*.[4]

5.2 ADDITIONAL PAID-IN CAPITAL VERSUS OTHER PAID-IN CAPITAL ACCOUNTS

In an issuance of stock (common or preferred), additional paid-in capital results from the difference between the proceeds for contributed capital and the par value of shares. Section 4.1 previously mentions certain transactions and events that affect additional paid-in capital as well as disclosures of additional paid-in capital.

Under U.S. GAAP several paid-in capital accounts, other than additional paid-in capital, may arise in the course of certain transactions. Companies describe such accounts when material, although they do not necessarily segregate additional paid-in capital from those paid-in capital accounts on the face of the statement of financial position. This Section analyzes those transactions and compares their treatment under U.S. GAAP with IFRSs.

5.2.1 Paid-In Capital – Treasury Stock

Section 4.14.5 previously illustrates the mechanics of the "additional paid-in capital – treasury stock," "additional paid-in capital – retired stock," "additional paid-in capital – common stock" accounts in treasury stock transactions, and retirement of stock.

---

[1] *ARB 43, Ch. 1B, ¶ 5.*
[2] *Accounting Terminology Bulletin No. 1*, Review and Resume, *¶¶ 67, 69.1, 70.*
[3] *FASB ASC 718-10-35-2 (FASB Statement No. 123(R), ¶ 39); FASB Statement No. 130, ¶ 113; APB Opinion No. 14*, Accounting for Convertible Debt and Debt Issued with Stock Purchase Warrants, *¶ 1; APB Opinion No. 26*, Early Extinguishment of Debt, *¶ 13.*
[4] *AICPA ATT 2010 and AICPA ATT 2006, ¶ Table 2-37.*

5.2.2 Paid-In Capital – Forfeiture of Stock Subscription

In the U.S., a forfeiture of stock subscription determines a credit to additional paid-in capital and a debit to stock subscribed for the amount defaulted. This depends on the rules of the specific state.

Comment: As explained in Section 4.12 previously, in certain jurisdictions the treatment of sub-scriptions receivable as an asset traditionally arose from different corporate law framework. This difference in approach also translates into a different accounting of default in fully paying stock. In the U.S., depending on state laws, failure to fully pay shares may result in forfeiture of the entire amount (the company recognizes this amount as "additional paid-in capital – forfeiture of stock subscription"), or in issuing to the subscriber a proportionate number of shares corresponding to the amount already paid, sometimes reduced by the cost of selling the defaulted shares to other stockholders. In jurisdictions where partially-paid shares are issued (although limited) shares, failure to pay may ultimately result in losing shareholder status, and in reduction of contributed capital if shares are not sold to other shareholders.

An analogy may be made to a different situation. In case of probable default of the counterparty to an own share-lending arrangement in contemplation of the issuance of convertible debt or other financing, the issuer expenses the fair value of the unreturned shares that will probably not be recovered against additional paid-in capital.[5]

5.2.3 Paid-In Capital – Quasi-Reorganization

An "additional paid-in capital – quasi-reorganization" or similar account arises in case of quasi-reorganization. Deficit reorganization is analyzed in Section 6.5.3 later. The deficit in retained earnings is eliminated by first debiting pre-existing additional paid-in capital and then capital stock, through reducing par value and creating this new additional paid-in capital account for the difference. This new account must date from the effective date of readjustment.[6]

Comment: IFRSs have no specific guidance for quasi-reorganization. Quasi-reorganization proce-dures depend on the specific jurisdiction in which a company is incorporated. Such requirements are not considered to be a matter for GAAP, but of national legislation or corporate governance. However, the IASB Framework permits, or better, welcomes their disclosure as it deems it relevant in assisting informational needs of users of financial statements.[7] In addition to compliance with specific financial reporting that may be mandated by law, disclosure of quasi-reorganization might also be seen as required by IAS 1 as part of capital disclosures, to inform on externally-imposed capital requirements, their nature, and how the entity has complied with them (see Section 4.6 previously).[8]

---

[5] *FASB ASC 470-20-35-11A (Accounting Standards Update No. 2009-15*, Accounting for Own-Share Landing Arrangements in Contemplation of Convertible Debt Issuance or Other Financing, *amending Accounting Standards Codification as the result of EITF Issue No. 09-1*, Accounting for Own-Share Landing Arrangements in Contemplation of Convertible Debt Issuance*)*.

[6] *ARB 43, Appendix B, ¶ 9.*

[7] The Conceptual Framework for Financial Reporting 2010, *¶¶ 4.20, 4.21; IASB Framework, ¶¶ 65–66.*

[8] *IAS 1, ¶ 135.*

5.2.4 Paid-In Capital – Stock Dividend

An "additional paid-in capital – common stock for stock dividend declared" or similar account arises in case of declaration of stock dividends that are accounted for as a real dividend. This, in addition to when mandated by legal requirements of the state of incorporation of the entity, may generally take place for public companies when the stock dividends issuance is deemed to be of relatively "insignificant" amount (this threshold depends on individual company and market conditions, but is generally assumed to be below 20–25% of the number of shares outstanding before declaration). In such a case, retained earnings are capitalized, in excess of legal requirements, for the fair value of the additional shares issued. ATB 1 supported the indication of such a reduction in retained earnings on the face of the balance sheet.[9] Therefore, capital stock account is credited for the par value and additional paid-in capital for the amount of fair value in excess of par value. Above this threshold, stock dividends are recorded at par value and thus no capitalization to an additional paid-in capital account arises.[10]

Comment: IFRSs provide no specific guidelines for stock dividends from the standpoint of accounting for equity, but simply with reference to earnings per share. IAS 33 refers to stock dividends as a capitalization or bonus issue.[11] IAS 33 arguably acknowledges capitalization of retained earnings by indirectly referring to stock dividends as changes in number of shares outstanding without a corresponding change in entity's resources.[12]

Comment: A difference with U.S. GAAP may arise because capitalization from retained earnings or other free reserves to share capital for stock dividends is in general for the nominal value of the shares.

Comment: A declaration of a stock dividend after the reporting period date but before authorization to issue the financial statements requires retrospective adjustment for the purpose of earning per share calculation,[13] although in theory it would be a nonadjusting event under IAS 10.[14] It is an adjusting event in the U.S. GAAP and AU Section 560.

Under U.S. GAAP, the fact that a subsidiary has proceeded to a stock dividend does not require capitalization of retained earnings in consolidated financial statements as it is the capitalization by the parent company that matters for the consolidated group.[15]

Comment: A related issue may instead arise, on migration to IFRSs, for companies that, under United Kingdom GAAP, revalued investments in subsidiaries and then capitalized some amount of the resulting revaluation surplus or reserve through a stock dividend. TECH 21/05 indicates that when such a company, on first adoption of IFRSs for the purpose of its individual company's financial

---

[9] *Accounting Terminology Bulletin No. 1*, Review and Resume, ¶ 69.5.
[10] *FASB ASC 505-20-25-3, 505-20-25-6 (ARB 43, Ch. 7B, ¶¶ 10–14).*
[11] *IAS 33, ¶ 27.*
[12] *IAS 33, ¶ 26.*
[13] *IAS 33, ¶ 64.*
[14] *IAS 10, ¶ 22(f).*
[15] *FASB ASC 810-10-45-9 (ARB 51, ¶ 18 as amended by FASB Statement No. 160).*

statements, has to restate its investments in subsidiaries to historical cost as required by IAS 27, a debit entry to reverse such revaluation surplus may be treated as an unrealized loss, provided the recoverable amount of the investment is equal to or greater than its revalued value. Such loss will be considered realized in the event of a subsequent disposal of the investment.[16]

Comment: Arguably, considerations similar to what was discussed in Section 3.6.3 previously with reference to the accommodation made by the amendments to IFRS 1 and IAS 27[17] for the treatment of cost of an investment in a subsidiary on first adoption of IFRSs may apply.

5.2.5   Paid-In Capital – Conversion of Convertible Debt

A convertible debt that is "conventional" or a nonconventional convertible debt that is classified as equity under Subtopic 815-40 (EITF Issue No. 00-19) or that does not meet the bifurcation criteria in Subtopic 815-10 (FASB Statement No. 133) (see Worksheet 28), is accounted for under Subtopic 470-20 (APB 14)[18] entirely as a nonconvertible debt (therefore the conversion option is an unrecognized equity feature), if the conversion right is in essence nondetachable (that is when the debt must be tendered to exercise the conversion right), on the basis that such element is inseparable and thus to do so would be difficult in practice.

Under U.S. GAAP, however, a substantial premium on issuance of convertible debt is presumed to be paid-in capital, unless the substance of the transaction is different, so as not to overstate the convertible debt and thereby recognize an abnormal interest expense.[19]

Comment: IAS 32, by moving from the assumption that transactions with like economic effect should have like accounting treatment, does not consider relevant, contrary to Subtopic 470-20 (APB 14), whether or not the option is detachable. It considers split accounting to be more representationally faithful, as the presentation of a convertible debt must be the same as the presentation of debt with an early settlement provision and warrant on common shares, assuming their substantial equivalence.[20]

A convertible debt instrument is conventional under Subtopic 815-40 (EITF Issue No 00-19) and EITF Issue No 05-2[21] when it is convertible entirely into a fixed number of shares or equivalent amount of cash at the discretion of the issuer and the exercisability of the option is based on the passage of time or a contingent event, even if it contains a standard antidilution provision (based on which the conversion ratio is adjusted in case of an equity restructuring transaction, such as a stock split, spinoff, rights offering, recapitalization through a large nonrecurring cash dividend). Convertible preferred stock with debt-like features, such as a

---

[16]   *The Institute of Chartered Accountants in England and Wales and The Institute of Chartered Accountants of Scotland, TECH 21/05,* Distributable Profits: Implication of IFRS, ¶¶ *6.41–6.42.*

[17]   *Amendments to IFRS 1, First-*time Adoption of International Financial Reporting Standards *and IAS 27,* Consolidated and Separate Financial Statements, Cost of an Investment in a Subsidiary, Jointly Controlled Entity or Associate, *(May 2008).*

[18]   *FASB ASC 470-20-25-12 (APB 14, ¶ 12).*

[19]   *FASB ASC 470-20-25-13 (APB 14, ¶ 18).*

[20]   *IAS 32, ¶ 29.*

[21]   *EITF Issue No. 00-19, ¶ 4; EITF Issue 05-2, ¶ 8.*

mandatory redemption date, also qualifies as conventional when the equity conversion feature is clearly and closely related to the host instrument.

> **Comment:** Under IFRSs there is no such distinction between conventional or nonconventional convertible debt.

Under IAS 32, from the issuer's perspective, a nonderivative debt instrument that is convertible by the holder for a specified period of time into a fixed number of ordinary shares of the issuer is initially accounted for as a compound financial instrument. Therefore, the proceeds are allocated to the debt and equity components and separately presented on the statement of financial position (so-called "split accounting"). The embedded call option is classified as equity, to an item such as "option to convert."[22]

> **Comment:** This contrasts with the classification of the entire convertible debt as liability under Subtopic 470-20 (APB 14). Such classification of the conversion option as equity is in line with the requirement of a fixed number of shares in exchange for a fixed amount of cash or another financial asset, when read in conjunction with the IAS 32 definition of equity. Under such definition, in fact, in order to be considered equity a nonderivative should have no contractual obligation for the issuer to deliver a variable number of its own equity instruments.[23]

Under U.S. GAAP, the conversion of a convertible debt results in a credit to additional paid-in capital for the difference between the net carrying amount of the debt and the par value of the newly-issued stock, when the market value approach of conversion is used (as opposed to the book value approach). Under this method, the new stock is recorded at market price or at market price of the bonds converted, whichever is more easily determinable, and additional paid-in capital records the difference between market price and the par value of the stock.

> **Comment:** The difference between the market value of the shares issued in the conversion and the book value of the security converted is unrecognized under the book value method. Under the proprietary perspective (Section 2.1 previously), this would be a hidden dirty-surplus loss. However, under the entity perspective, equity refers to all shareholders, not only pre-existing common shareholders. Therefore, such a loss is offset by a gain to the new shareholders and does not affect total equity.

Furthermore, a debt issuer must debit an interest expense against a credit to additional paid-in capital for unpaid interest that accrues at the date of conversion when such interest, under the terms of a convertible debt instrument, must be forfeited at conversion of the instrument. Such amount is considered to be part of the cost of stock issued.[24]

Under IAS 32, upon conversion the liability component is derecognized against equity on conversion with no creation of gains or losses and the original equity component may be

---

[22] *IAS 32, ¶¶ 32, AG31.*

[23] *IAS 32, ¶ 16(b)(i).*

[24] *FASB ASC 470-20-40-11 (EITF Issue No. 85-17, Accrued Interest upon Conversion of Convertible Debt).*

transferred from one line item within equity to another. In the case of extinguishment before maturity with no change in terms, equity may change as the result of allocation of the consideration paid. Again, an entity has freedom as to the classification of such an equity component.[25]

Worksheet 29 illustrates the impact of the various methods of accounting for a convertible debt.

5.2.6 Paid-In Capital – Warrants

Under U.S. GAAP, a freestanding warrant is classified as equity or liability under Subtopic 815-40 (EITF Issue No. 00-19) according to related rules, depending on settlement methods and on the issuer's or the holder's possible settlement choices. Generally, traditional detachable warrants, where settlement is in shares, are classified as equity, in which case Subtopic 470-20 (APB 14) applies. Under Subtopic 470-20 (APB 14), if a debt security (such as a bond) is issued with detachable stock purchase warrants, the proceeds received for the purchase price are allocated to the bond and the warrants based on the relative market values of the debt security without the warrants and of the warrants at the time of issuance. If one component cannot be determined, it is quantified by difference between the total price and the other component. An "additional paid-in capital – warrants," "warrant outstanding," or equivalent account arises for the portion of the proceeds allocated to the warrants. This equals the difference between the total proceeds received and the discount on bond payable minus the face value of the bond. The discount on bond payable amounts to the purchase price allocated to the bonds minus its face value.[26] At warrant exercise, additional paid-in capital amounts to the reversal of additional paid-in capital – warrants account plus any difference between the proceeds from the exercise price of the warrant and the stock par value.

However, as per Subtopic 815-40 (EITF Issue No. 00-19), some additional conditions are prerequisites for equity classification. A typical situation, for a public company, where warrants may be classified as liabilities is when cash settlement may ultimately result upon the occurrence of certain events, such as a delisting, or ineffectiveness of the registration statement of the underlying shares. No consideration is given to the probability of the event occurring. Similarly, under Subtopic 815-40 (EITF Issue No. 00-19) warrants are liabilities if significant liquidated damages that are payable to the holder in the event of some failure in compliance to the registration statement are intended as a penalty, unless this indemnifies for the difference in fair value between registered and unregistered shares. Similarly, the likelihood of those penalties or their significance is not a determinant, as the maximum penalty that could occur must be considered.[27]

By contrast, under IAS 32 detachable warrants are classified as equity at issuance.

---

[25] *IAS 32, ¶¶ AG32–AG34, IE46.*

[26] *FASB ASC 470-20-25-2, 470-20-25-3 (APB Opinion No. 14,* Accounting for Convertible Debt and Debt Issued with Stock Purchase Warrants, *¶¶ 15–16).*

[27] *FASB ASC 815-40-25-8 (EITF Issue No. 00-19, ¶ 16); Accounting Staff Members in the Division of Corporation Finance U.S. Securities and Exchange Commission, Washington, D.C.,* Current Accounting and Disclosure Issues in the Division of Corporation Finance, *¶ II.B.1 (November 30, 2006) www.sec.gov (last visited January 8, 2007).*

> **Comment:** However, the prerequisites are different. Detachability is not a prerequisite. IAS 32 instead requires that, in order to meet the equity definition, the number of equity instruments must be fixed and that the exchange must be for a fixed amount of cash or another financial asset (such as a fixed price or a fixed stated principal amount of a bond), and both must be unaffected by changes in the fair value of the contract that arise from variations in market interest rates.[28]

Under U.S. GAAP, an entity that issues warrants or similar instruments to third parties, as part of a research and development arrangement, must report a portion of the related proceeds as paid-in capital, based on the fair value of the instruments at the date of the arrangement.[29]

Under U.S. GAAP, if the warrants expire unexercised, the "additional paid-in capital – warrants" account is reversed to "additional paid-in capital – expired warrants" or similar account.[30]

> **Comment:** Under IFRSs, similarly to U.S. GAAP, when a warrant is recognized in equity, the fact that it lapses unexercised does not determine a recognition of gain in the income statement because equity is not remeasured and there is no change in the entity's net assets.[31]

> **Comment:** Under the proprietary perspective (Section 2.1 previously), equity would include a hidden dirty-surplus loss, as there is no recognition of a loss to the pre-existing common shareholders for the difference between the exercise price and the market price of the stock at exercise date. However, under the entity perspective, equity refers to all shareholders, not only pre-existing common shareholders. Therefore, such a loss is offset by a gain to the new shareholders and does not affect total equity.

Worksheet 30 compares the classification of detachable warrants under U.S. GAAP and IFRSs.

5.2.7 Paid-In Capital – Unexercised Premium Put

A convertible bond issued with a premium put is an instrument with mutually exclusive choices where the holder may either redeem the instrument for cash at a multiple of the bond's par value at a certain date before maturity or convert the debt to equity at maturity. The issuer accounts for such features as embedded derivatives to be separated under Subtopic 815-10 (FASB Statement No. 133) and provides disclosures required by Subtopic 460-10 (FASB Interpretation No. 45) for market value guarantees.[32] However, if the issuer elected either January 1, 1998 or January 1, 1999 as a transition date for accounting for embedded derivatives under Subtopic 815-10 (FASB Statement No. 133),[33] a convertible bond issued with a premium put that had been issued, acquired, or substantively modified before that date

---

[28] *IAS 32, ¶ 22.*
[29] *FASB ASC 730-20-25-12 (FASB Statement No. 68, Research and Development Arrangements, ¶ 13).*
[30] *FASB Statement No. 123(R), ¶ B160.*
[31] *IFRS 2, ¶ BC220.*
[32] *FASB ASC 460-10-25-1 (FASB Interpretation No. 45, Guarantor's Accounting and Disclosure Requirements, Including Indirect Guarantees of Indebtedness of Others, ¶ 7(a)).*
[33] *FASB Statement No. 133, ¶ 50.*

would be subject to EITF Issue No. 85-29. In such a case, the premium is considered a liability, to be accrued over the period from the date of issuance to the initial put date. If the put expires unexercised, such accrued liability is reversed to additional paid-in capital if the market value of common stock under conversion exceeds the put price. In the reverse situation, the put premium is amortized as a yield adjustment over the remaining term of the debt.[34]

Under IFRSs, the instrument considered here is an example of a financial instrument with interdependent multiple embedded derivatives that have equity and non-equity derivative features.

Comment: By simply looking at the put option, the embedded derivative would be separated from the host instrument, like U.S. GAAP. IAS 39 requires the issuer to assess whether an instrument shall be bifurcated before the application of split accounting. Under IAS 39, if the host instrument is debt or an insurance contract, an embedded call or put or prepayment option is not closely related to the host contract, unless its exercise price is approximately equal on each exercise date to the amortized cost of the host debt instrument or the carrying amount of the host insurance contract.[35] A similar conclusion results from looking at the instrument with both the embedded features from the perspective of IAS 39. In fact, IAS 39 requires that multiple derivatives that are embedded in a single hybrid contract be accounted for separately when some are classified differently from the others, as equity, assets, or liabilities; or some relate to different risk exposures from the others; or they are readily separable and independent of each other; or they are interdependent but have equity and non-equity derivative features.[36] Thus, as the option to convert is classified as equity and an embedded put option is classified as a financial liability under IAS 32,[37] although these features are interdependent, they would be separated.

However, contrary to U.S. GAAP, under IAS 32 the issuer applies split accounting to a convertible debt. In addition, when a compound instrument with multiple embedded derivatives has a non-equity derivative feature (as in this case the put option), its value is included in the liability component. The difference between the total consideration received and such liability component is then recognized in equity (i.e., the equity conversion option).[38] However, while IAS 32 requires separate presentation of liability and equity components of a compound financial instrument, it does not address whether or not multiple embedded derivatives with the same characteristics of liability or equity should be separately presented on the face of the statement of financial position.

Comment: When embedded derivatives are interdependent, a separate determination of their value plus the equity component would not equal the value of the whole compound instrument. Therefore, the joint value attributable to the interdependence is arbitrarily included in the liability component, based on the IASB Framework definition of equity as residual. This is why IFRS 7 requires the disclosure of the effect of multiple embedded derivatives that are interdependent.[39]

---

[34] *EITF Issue No. 85-29,* Convertible Bonds with a "Premium Put."
[35] *IFRS 9, ¶ B4.3.5(e); IAS 39, ¶ AG30(g).*
[36] *IFRS 9, ¶ B4.3.4; IAS 39, ¶ AG29.*
[37] *IAS 32, ¶ 18(b).*
[38] *IAS 32, ¶¶ 31–32.*
[39] *IFRS 7, ¶¶ 17, BC28–BC31.*

5.2.8 Paid-In Capital – Beneficial Conversion

An issuer of a convertible security with a nondetachable embedded beneficial conversion feature ("beneficial" means that it is in-the-money at the purchase commitment date or that becomes such upon the occurrence of a future event – i.e., the market value is greater than the conversion price) first assesses whether such instrument falls under Subtopic 480-10 (FASB Statement No. 150) and thus must be classified as a liability. This is the case if the security is issued in the form of shares and is unconditionally convertible into a variable number of shares under one of the three conditions of Subtopic 480-10 (FASB Statement No. 150)[40] and is required to be redeemed by transfer of assets in the event of nonconversion.[41]

> **Comment:** IFRSs do not explicitly treat convertible instruments with beneficial conversion features, apart from contingently issuable convertible shares for earnings per share computation purposes. Arguably, some unconditionally convertible preferred stock that would be a liability under Subtopic 480-10 (FASB Statement No. 150) would likely be a compound instrument under IAS 32. However, their accounting, and therefore whether they should be split into equity and liability components, would vary depending on whether the host instrument is classified as equity or liability. This would depend on the rights attached and the substance of the instrument, including whether dividends are discretionary or not. Thus, preferred stock that is mandatorily convertible into a variable number of shares designed to get a fixed amount or an amount based on changes in an underlying variable, such as a commodity, and where dividends are discretionary, would likely be host equity, with a liability component being the present value of the dividend amounts. Instead, nondiscretionary dividends would make the entire instrument a liability.[42]

> **Comment:** Similarly, but in a context of bifurcation of an hybrid financial instrument issued in the form of a share, the SEC Staff highlights that the determination of whether a host contract is an equity or debt instrument rests with the judgment of the economic characteristics and risks of the host contract itself, considering all stated or implied substantive terms and features of the hybrid financial instrument.[43]

If the instrument is out of scope of Subtopic 480-10 (FASB Statement No. 150), the issuer assesses whether the host contract and embedded derivative must be bifurcated under FASB Statement No. 133.

> **Comment:** Instead, a convertible debt host instrument that is bifurcated under FASB Statement No. 133 would likely require split accounting under IAS 32.

---

[40] *Under FASB ASC 480-10-25-14 (FASB Statement No. 150, ¶ 12), when at inception the monetary value of the obligation is based solely or predominantly on a fixed monetary amount known at inception, or variations in something other than the fair value of the issuer's shares, or variations inversely related to changes in the fair value of the issuer's shares.*

[41] *FASB ASC 470-20-35-8, 470-20-35-9 (EITF Issue No. 00-27, ¶¶ 63); EITF Issue No. 00-27, ¶ 64.*

[42] *IAS 32, ¶¶ AG25, AG37.*

[43] *FASB ASC 815-10-S99-3 (EITF Topic D-109, Determining the Nature of a Host Contract Related to a Hybrid Financial Instrument Issued in the Form of a Share under FASB Statement No. 133, as amended by Accounting Standards Update No. 2010-04, Accounting for Various Topics, Technical Corrections to SEC Paragraphs, ¶ 15).*

If Subtopic 815-10 (FASB Statement No. 133) does not apply (e.g., a convertible preferred security that would likely meet the scope exclusion from Subtopic 815-10 (FASB Statement No. 133) because both indexed only to the issuer's stock and classified as equity,[44] or an equity-classified freestanding warrant that allows the holder to acquire nonredeemable convertible preferred shares and that contains a beneficial conversion feature), Subtopic 470-20 (EITF Issue No. 98-5) applies and the issuer separately measures at issuance such features at their intrinsic value. The issuer allocates a portion of the proceeds to such features and debits a discount against a credit to an "additional paid-in capital – beneficial conversion amount" account.[45]

Comment: Conceptually, this is somehow similar to increasing-rate preferred stock (see Section 4.10 previously). Under U.S. GAAP in fact, in case of convertible preferred securities, the beneficial conversion amount is considered analogous to a dividend, to be amortized at effective interest method over the period to the earliest conversion date or the most beneficial conversion date in case of conversion at multiple steps. Arguably, from the perspective of IFRSs, the two situations cannot be analogous. Firstly, in increasing-rate preferred stock, dividends are set out in the dividend payment terms of the instrument. Here, instead dividends refer to the stock into which the preferred securities may be converted. Furthermore, even if converted, the dividend payment terms are those of ordinary shares. Secondly, even if likely, such conversion is not assured. Under IAS 32, the likelihood of conversion or changes thereof is irrelevant in classifying as equity or liability the components of a compound instrument.[46] Therefore, it is not the fact of being in the money or not that makes an embedded conversion feature equity or liability.

5.2.9   Paid-In Capital – Modified Conversion Terms

Although Subtopic 470-20 (APB 14) does not permit separate initial recognition of an embedded conversion option of a convertible instrument, under EITF Issue No. 05-7 when an exchange of debt instruments or a modification of the terms of an existing debt instrument shall not be accounted for as a debt extinguishment under EITF Issue 96-19 (that is, when the new or amended terms of the debt instrument are not "substantially" different from the original terms), the value exchanged by the holder for the difference in fair value of an embedded conversion option immediately before and after the modification must be recognized as a premium/discount (to be amortized during the remaining term of the instrument) counterbalanced by additional paid-in capital.[47] The same treatment applies when the modification adds or deletes an embedded conversion option provided that it is not required to be bifurcated under Subtopic 815-10 (FASB Statement No. 133).[48] EITF Issue No. 05-7 applies to modifications beginning in the first interim or annual reporting period beginning after December 15, 2005.

As under U.S. GAAP, under IAS 39 the accounting for an exchange of debt instruments or a modification of the terms of an existing financial liability also depends on whether the amended

---

[44]   *FASB ASC 815-10-15-74 (FASB Statement No. 133, ¶ 11(a)).*

[45]   *FASB ASC 470-20-25-5 (EITF Issue No. 98-5,* Accounting for Convertible Securities with Beneficial Conversion Features or Contingently Adjustable Conversion Ratios, *¶ 5).*

[46]   *IAS 32, ¶ 30.*

[47]   *EITF Issue No. 05-7,* Accounting for Modifications to Conversion Options Embedded in Debt Instruments and Related Issues, *¶ 6.*

[48]   *EITF Issue No. 05-7, ¶ 10.*

terms of a debt instrument are substantially different or not from the original terms. In the first situation, the transaction is accounted for as an extinguishment of the original financial liability and the recognition of a new debt instrument with consequent gain or loss recognition; in the latter, it is accounted for as a modified financial liability.[49]

Comment: Under IAS 32 however, the option to convert a convertible debt is classified as equity from inception. A change in the likelihood of conversion (and therefore even when such change is determined by modification of terms) does not trigger a change in classification or remeasurement of the equity component of the compound instrument.[50]

5.2.10   Paid-In Capital – Stock Options Outstanding

Under U.S. GAAP, the compensation cost for share-based payment transactions classified as equity is credited to equity, generally under additional paid-in capital.[51] In the case of stock options, at their exercise additional paid-in capital is reversed to capital accounts to record the issuance of common stock.[52]

APB 25 required separate deduction from equity of compensation expense that was unearned (deferred compensation expense account) because of stock issued before employees had performed their services (when the issuance of stock for future services is permitted by state laws), and to reverse deferred compensation expense to compensation expense in the income statement to the extent services had been provided.[53] Thus, the paid-in section of equity in the balance sheet separately displays stock options outstanding and a deduction for deferred compensation expense. Section 6.4.20 later expands this topic.

Alternatively, this account may be found within stockholders' equity accounts other than capital stock, additional paid-in capital, retained earnings, and accumulated other comprehensive income. The *AICPA Accounting Trends & Techniques* show that approximately 76% of the survey companies that in 2005 presented other stockholders' equity accounts (excluding noncontrolling interests) included unearned compensation in that caption.[54]

Comment: IFRS 2 recognizes the compensation cost against increase in equity over the service period.[55] Therefore, no deferred compensation expense account is necessary. However, IFRS 2 provides no specific guidance on how to display the increase in equity for goods or services received in relation to equity-settled share-based payment transactions in the equity section of the statement of financial position. Display in a separate equity reserve helps to isolate that component of equity and highlights amounts for future issuance of shares. This may be seen as a way of complying with IAS 1 disclosure requirement of shares reserved for issue under options and contracts for the sale of shares.[56] This approach also maintains the fundamental principle that retained earnings

---

[49] *IFRS) 9, ¶¶ 3.3.2, B3.3.6; IAS 39, ¶¶ 40, AG62.*

[50] *IAS 32, ¶ 30.*

[51] *FASB ASC 718-10-35-2 (FASB Statement No. 123(R), ¶ 39).*

[52] *FASB ASC 718-20-25-18, 718-20-25-19 (FASB Statement No. 123(R), ¶ A93).*

[53] *APB Opinion No. 25 (superseded), Accounting for Stock Issued to Employees, ¶ 14.*

[54] *AICPA ATT 2006, ¶ Table 2-42.*

[55] *IFRS 2, ¶¶ 7, 14, 15.*

[56] *IAS 1, ¶ 79.*

may be decreased but not increased from company's operations unless passing through the income statement. Conversely, a credit to retained earnings would be substantiated by the fact that retained earnings is not yet defined as the cumulative total of undistributed profit or loss, as the IASB acknowledges.[57] Other forms of presentation have developed in practice, including a capital reserve, or other equity reserves. A study by the ICAEW of EU implementation of IFRSs in 2005 showed that out of 20 companies presenting share-based payments in equity 30% used retained earnings, 20% a capital reserve, 15% a specific reserve, and the remainder other reserves or did not make it visible.[58]

Both U.S. GAAP and IFRSs use grant-date accounting. A company does not recognize any additional expense as the market price of the stock moves into the money, as well as when options are exercised. A forfeiture of share-based payment after the vesting period would not result, under IFRS 2, contrary to Topic 718 (FASB Statement No. 123(R)), in a reversal of the accrued compensation cost and of the corresponding increase in equity, although a transfer from one component of equity to another would possibly occur.[59]

Comment: When adopting a proprietary perspective (Section 2.1 previously), pre-existing common shareholders lose when the market price of the stock goes into the money, because the new shareholders obtain stock at a lower price than market price at grant date. Similarly, if no expense is reversed upon forfeiture, an expense is recognized for something that has not occurred, hence an unrealized loss. Under this view, equity would include a hidden dirty-surplus expense. However, under the entity perspective, equity refers to all shareholders, not only pre-existing common shareholders. Similarly, employees have provided services or non-employees delivered goods. Therefore, IFRS 2 permits a transfer within equity to reflect such a dilution, but not a change in total net assets.[60]

Section 6.4.20 later also illustrates the impact on additional paid-in capital and retained earnings of the transitional provisions of Topic 718 (FASB Statement No. 123(R)).

5.2.11   Paid-In Capital – Clawback in a Share-Based Payment Transaction

Under U.S. GAAP, a noncompete clause that is part of a share-based payment transaction is recognized upon the occurrence of the related contingent event. This is a clawback feature where an employee must return to the company shares granted and earned or their cash equivalent upon the occurrence of termination and subsequent employment by a competitor, as defined by the award, for consideration that is less than the fair value of the equity instruments at the date of grant. If the noncompete provision is not met during the vesting period, the difference between the market value of shares received (debited as treasury stock) or the corresponding cash amount received and any other income is credited to additional paid-in capital. Other income is recorded in the income statement for the lesser of the recognized

[57] *IAS 19 (2007), ¶ BC48W; IAS 19 (2011), ¶ BC100.*
[58] *The Institute of Chartered Accountants in England and Wales,* EU Implementation of IFRS and the Fair Value Directive, A Report for the European Commission, *Table 23.4 (October 2007).*
[59] *IFRS 2, ¶ 23.*
[60] *IFRS 2, ¶ BC219.*

compensation cost of the share-based payment arrangement that contained such contingent feature or the fair value of the consideration received. Such recognition in income comes from the fact that the party is acting in its quality as employee or former employee and not as an equity owner.[61]

Comment: Under U.S. GAAP, a noncompete agreement included in a share-based payment transaction is an example of a contingent feature, under which an employee might end up by returning to the entity either equity instruments earned or realized gains from the sale of those instruments.[62] Under IFRSs there is no such contingent feature category. A noncompete agreement is a type of nonvesting condition.[63] Contrary to Topic 718 (FASB Statement No. 123(R)), under IFRSs the probability of a nonvesting condition being met is included in the estimate of grant-date fair value of the equity instruments granted.[64] For agreements that are classified as equity-settled arrangements, if the noncompete provision is subsequently not met during the vesting period, the event is deemed to be a cancellation because the counterparty could choose whether or not that nonvesting condition be met. Consequently, on one hand the entity immediately debits an expense against equity for the full amount of services under the plan over the remainder of the vesting period (an acceleration of vesting) and, on the other hand, it records a decrease in equity for any refund payment to the employee to the extent of the fair value of the equity instruments granted and as an expense for any excess.[65] This case is similar to the treatment under U.S. GAAP.[66] Instead, if the noncompete provision is not met after the vesting period, contrary to U.S. GAAP where the compensation cost previously recognized is adjusted when such contingent event occurs, under IFRSs no adjustment is made to the compensation expense recognized and to total equity after vesting date, other than possibly a transfer from one component of equity to another.[67] However, in case of repurchase of vested equity instruments with lower consideration than their fair value at grant date (including no consideration), IFRS 2 is not specific on the credit side of the accounting entry.[68]

5.2.12 Paid-In Capital – Undistributed Earnings of an S Corporation

Under SAB 4-B, the undistributed earnings of an S corporation on the date of termination of its S election are reported as additional paid-in capital, as if it had distributed them constructively to the owners and then those had contributed capital to the newly-established C corporation.[69]

Comment: IFRSs provide no explicit guidance for flow-through entities, apart from applicability of general standards.

---

[61] *FASB ASC 718-20-35-2, 718-10-55-8, 718-10-55-47, 718-20-55-85, 718-20-55-86 (FASB Statement No. 123(R), ¶¶ 27, A5, A42, A190–A191).*

[62] *FASB ASC 718-10-55-8 (FASB Statement No. 123(R), ¶ A5).*

[63] *Amendment to International Financial Reporting Standards,* IFRS 2 Share-based Payment – Vesting Conditions and Cancellations, *¶ BC171B (January 2008).*

[64] *FASB ASC 718-10-55-8 (FASB Statement No. 123(R), ¶ A5); IASB,* Amendment to IFRS 2, *¶ 21A (January 2008).*

[65] *IASB,* Amendment to IFRS 2, *¶¶ 28A, IG15A (January 2008); IFRS 2, ¶ 28.*

[66] *FASB ASC 718-20-35-7 (FASB Statement No. 123(R), ¶ 55).*

[67] *IFRS 2, ¶ 23.*

[68] *IFRS 2, ¶ 29.*

[69] *FASB ASC 505-10-S99-3 (SEC SAB Topic 4-B, S Corporations).*

5.2.13   Paid-In Capital – In-Substance Capital Contributions

Under Subsection 225-10-S99-4 (SAB 5-T),[70] when a principal stockholder (or a holder of an "economic interest" in an entity, as defined by Topic 718 (FASB Statement No 123(R))[71]), pays an expense on behalf of the company that would otherwise have resulted in a direct expense by the company (e.g., he/she transfers a portion of his/her shares to a third party to settle a litigation of the company with a third party; or similarly, under SAB 1-B,[72] any expenses incurred by the parent on a subsidiary's behalf), the company must record an expense against an increase in paid-in capital. This is because the transaction is in substance a payment of an expense of the company through a capital contribution by the shareholder. A prerequisite for such accounting is that the stockholder act in his quality of stockholder and this clearly does benefit both the company and the shareholder by protecting its investment. The concept of economic interest is analyzed in Section 2.1.4.3 previously.

5.2.14   Paid-In Capital – Transaction Costs

Section 4.11 previously analyzes the treatment of equity issuing costs as a deduction from paid-in capital and the evolution of the accounting for such topic.

5.2.15   Paid-In Capital – Certain Preferred Stock

Section 4.4 previously analyzes the treatment of preferred shares when redemption is outside the issuer's control. Under Subtopic 480-10 (EITF Topic No. D-98), the subsequent adjustment to their redemption amount at each reporting period date may be charged against retained earnings or, in the absence of retained earnings, against paid-in capital.[73]

5.2.16   Paid-In Capital – Changes in a Parent's Ownership Interest in a Controlled Subsidiary

Section 7.17.2 later illustrates the accounting for a change in a parent's interest in a controlled subsidiary. In particular, a purchase of an additional interest in a controlled subsidiary at a consideration paid in excess of book value determines a loss recognized in equity attributable to the controlling interest. Subtopic 810-10 (FASB Statement No. 160) explains that additional paid-in capital is reduced by the excess amount paid. The reverse situation arises in case of a purchase at less than book value. In addition, the reallocation of other comprehensive income is accounted for as an increase in the controlling interest's proportionate share of other comprehensive income counterbalanced by a decrease in additional paid-in capital.[74] For SEC registrants that classify mandatorily redeemable noncontrolling interests in temporary equity,

---

[70] *FASB ASC 225-10-S99-4 (SEC SAB Topic 5-T,* Accounting for Expenses or Liabilities Paid by Principal Stockholder(s)).

[71] *FASB Statement No. 123(R), ¶ E1.*

[72] *FASB ASC 225-10-S99-3 (SEC SAB Topic 1-B,* Allocation Of Expenses And Related Disclosure In Financial Statements Of Subsidiaries, Divisions Or Lesser Business Components Of Another Entity).

[73] *FASB ASC 480-10-S99-3A (EITF Topic No. D-98, ¶ 15, as amended by Accounting Standards Update No. 2009-04,* Accounting for Redeemable Equity Instruments); *FASB ASC 480-10-S99-2 (SEC Staff Accounting Bulletin, Topic 3-C,* Redeemable Preferred Stock); *Securities and Exchange Commission, Division of Corporate Finance,* Frequently Requested Accounting and Financial Reporting Interpretations and Guidance, *¶ I.A (March 31, 2001).*

[74] *FASB ASC 810-10-45-23, 810-10-45-24 (ARB 51, ¶¶ 33, 34, as amended by FASB Statement No. 160).*

the adjustment to noncontrolling interests resulting from a change in a parent's ownership interest with no loss of control may affect retained earnings instead of additional paid-in capital.[75]

Comment: The same treatment in equity applies under the 2008 Revision of IAS 27, but that standard is not specific on the presentation within equity.

5.2.17 Paid-In Capital – Income Tax Impact

Specific accounting applies to matters relating to income taxes on items recorded as additional paid-in capital.

As an example, an enterprise reorganized under the Bankruptcy Code that realizes tax benefits from the carryforward of net operating losses incurred before reorganization, arising from transactions that were recorded in equity upon reorganization, charges tax expenses at full tax rate in the income statement against a credit to additional paid-in capital, to the extent of those tax benefits that exceed reorganization values that are not allocatable to identifiable assets and other intangibles.[76] Section 8.2.11 later expands on this topic.

An important issue is how income tax on share-based compensation affects additional paid-in capital. Another subject relates to the impact of deferred tax on additional paid-in capital for convertible debt with beneficial conversion features.

These and other tax issues are analyzed in Chapter 8 later.

5.3 PRESENTATION OF ADDITIONAL PAID-IN CAPITAL

Two different formats of presentation of additional paid-in capital accounts may be found under U.S. practice in the statement of financial position: either all together in a separate section, or separately under the section of each related source of contributed capital. Worksheet 31 illustrates those alternative display arrangements.

However, *The AICPA Accounting Trends & Techniques* illustrates that in 2009 and 2005, respectively, out of the U.S. GAAP companies that reported additional paid-in capital, almost all used the statement of stockholders' equity, with a schedule in the notes ranking as the second most popular method.[77]

Under IFRSs, share premium need not be shown separately on the statement of financial position (although this is allowed as a subclassification) but in the statement of changes in equity.[78]

---

[75] *FASB ASC 480-10-S99-3A (EITF Topic No. D-98, ¶ 19A, as amended by Accounting Standards Update No. 2009-04, Accounting for Redeemable Equity Instruments).*

[76] *FASB ASC 220-10-55-3 (FASB Statement No. 130, ¶¶ 113-115); FASB ASC 852-10-15-1 (AICPA Statement of Position No. 90-7, Financial Reporting by Entities in Reorganization Under the Bankruptcy Code).*

[77] *AICPA ATT 2010 and AICPA ATT 2006, ¶ Table 5-5.*

[78] *IAS 1, ¶¶ 54, 78, 106.*

> **Comment:** As part of the *Financial Statement Presentation Project*, the IASB and the FASB discussed whether to locate proceeds from all the capital components of each capital transaction (such as additional paid-in capital) under the same heading of the respective instrument, and whether this would result in loss of information or not. Furthermore, the Staff suggested modifications to the format of the statement of changes in equity for items that are reported in additional-paid-in capital under U.S. GAAP and were recognized directly in equity under IFRS.[79] The 2007 revision of IAS 1 requires a separate presentation on the statement of changes in equity of contributions by, and distributions to, owners (as opposed to the requirement of the previous revision of the standard to separately disclose distributions to owners, either on that statement or in the notes).[80] The 2008 Revision of IAS 27, effective for annual periods beginning on or after July 1, 2009, amended that statement in IAS 1 to require a reconciliation of beginning and ending balances with separate indication of changes in transactions with owners in their capacity as owners, including contributions, distributions, and changes in ownership interests in subsidiaries that do not result in a loss of control.[81]

An entity that has no equity instruments outstanding and, under Subtopic 480-10 (FASB Statement No. 150), presents all shares as subject to mandatory redemption in the liability section of the statement of financial position must disclose separately, contrary to IAS 32, the components of such instruments that would be par value, additional paid-in capital, retained earnings, accumulated other comprehensive income had the instrument not been classified as a liability.[82] This topic is discussed in more detail in Section 4.8 previously.

5.4   THE CAPITAL SURPLUS MODEL

Under U.S. GAAP, as a general principle, additional paid-in capital should not be directly reduced by entity's operations other than transactions with owners, except in a quasi-reorganization (Section 6.5.3 later) or correction of prior period errors (Section 6.4.2 later) that affected additional paid-in capital. This derives from the traditional dichotomy between earned surplus and capital surplus (Section 5.1 previously and Section 6.1.1 later). Income and expenses measure the accounting impact of business transactions and events directly in the income statement or in the statement of comprehensive income.[83] The concept of "clean surplus" is discussed in Section 7.3 later.

> **Comment:** From an entity perspective (see Section 2.1 previously), equity does not measure only the rights of common shareholders. Additional paid-in capital takes care of some gains or losses that affect common shareholders versus other shareholders, or common shareholders pre-existing the transaction as opposed to new shareholders. Conversely, the proprietary perspective would require that those gains and losses pass through profit or loss, because it sees equity as accruing to common shareholders only.

---

[79] *IASB Meeting, January 25, 2007, Agenda Paper 13D,* Statement of Changes in Equity and Other Equity-Related Issues, ¶¶ *10–16 (January 2007); FASB Meeting, January 31, 2007, Financial Statement Presentation*—Discontinued Operations, Hybrid Entities, and Equity-Related Issues, ¶¶ *50, 60 (January 2007).*

[80] *IAS 1, ¶ 106(c); IAS 1 (Revised 2005), ¶ 97(a).*

[81] *IAS 27 (2010), ¶ A4.*

[82] *FASB Statement No. 130, ¶¶ 28, B60.*

[83] *FASB ASC 505-10-25-1 (ARB 43, Ch.1A, ¶ 2); FASB ASC 852-20-25-2, 825-20-30-2, 825-20-30-3, 825-20-30-4, 852-20-35-2, 825-20-15-2, 825-20-15-3 (ARB 43, Ch.7A, ¶¶ 1, 4–5, 12).*

Planning point: However, from the above list of the types of transactions that may affect additional paid-in capital, it is evident the additional paid-in capital may result from both contributions from owners (as in case of issuance of shares of stock above par) and from capital surplus that accrues to stockholders in certain capital transactions. In addition, sometimes this caption is used as a residual category, when no other recognition in the net income, retained earnings, or other comprehensive income is found to be appropriate. Additional paid-in capital is sometimes used as a substitute for equity reserve, a concept that is largely missing in U.S. accounting pronouncements (see Section 3.2 previously). The logical classification of share premium under equity reserves is explained in Section 3.2.3 previously. Subtopic 220-10 (FASB Statement No. 130) maintains outside of its scope certain transactions that directly affect additional paid-in capital or other equity accounts and may have characteristics similar to items of other comprehensive income. At the time, the FASB reserved reconsidering this issue in a broader project on comprehensive income.[84]

Therefore, it may be argued that the current model is somehow hybrid, including in the same item both elements of a capital nature and of economic return, in its broader meaning from the shareholders' viewpoint. Section 7.21 later highlights this inconsistency and discusses suggestions for alternative models.

[84] *FASB Statement No. 130, ¶ 119.*

6 RETAINED EARNINGS

6.1 TERMINOLOGY AND DEFINITIONS OF TERMS

6.1.1 Terminology

Both U.S. GAAP and IFRSs use the term *retained earnings*.

> **Comment:** The 2007 revision of IAS 1 substituted the term *retained earnings* for the expressions "accumulated profits" or "accumulated profit or loss" that were previously used.[1]

An alternative terminology used in U.S. GAAP is *earned surplus*,[2] as opposed to *capital surplus* (additional paid-in capital, that is, surplus minus earned surplus). The term *surplus* generally indicates the excess of net assets over stated capital.

> **Comment:** The importance of the concept of surplus from a defense of legal capital perspective is discussed in Section 3.5.2.2 previously. Earned surplus, or better earned capital, also has a relation with the "invested and earned equity" model, as opposed to the residual interest model. This is discussed in Section 2.1.4.2 (2) previously.

> **Comment:** The expression *earned surplus* was criticized by ATB 1, which acknowledged the use of alternative expressions, such as cumulative balance of profit and loss (or income), undivided profits, retained income, retained earnings, or accumulated earnings, suggested its discontinuance, and recommended terminology that indicated source, such as retained earnings, retained income, accumulated earnings, or earnings retained for use in the business.[3]

> **Comment:** The term *surplus* survives in IFRSs with reference to revaluation surplus, to distributable surplus for insurers' contracts with discretionary participation features,[4] and to fund accounting.[5]

The *AICPA Accounting Trends & Techniques* show that in 2002–2009, approximately 82–84% of the survey companies used expressions that contained the words *retained earnings* on the face of the statement of financial position, approximately 11–13% the term *accumulated deficit*, and approximately 5–6% expressions that did not contain the word *retained*.[6]

---

[1] *IAS 1, ¶¶ A20, BCA2, IGA14.*

[2] *ARB 43, Ch. 1, ¶¶ 3, 5. However, the term* earned surplus *is still used in certain recent authoritative pronouncements, for example FASB ASC 810-10-45-9 (ARB 51, ¶ 18, as amended by FASB Statement No. 160).*

[3] *Accounting Terminology Bulletin No. 1, ¶¶ 32, 34, 65, 67, 69.*

[4] *IFRS 4, Insurance Contracts, ¶ BC115.*

[5] *IAS 19 (2011), ¶ 148; IAS 19 (2007), ¶ 30; IFRIC Interpretation No. 5, Rights to Interests Arising from Decommissioning, Restoration and Environmental Rehabilitation Funds, ¶ 3.*

[6] *AICPA ATT 2010 and AICPA ATT 2006, ¶ Table 2-38.*

6.1.2 Definitions

The obvious and traditional definition of retained earnings is that retained earnings are earnings that are retained (i.e., not distributed), that is, the undistributed earnings of the firm.

Under U.S. practice, as a general formula, retained earnings amount to:

> Accumulated amount of earnings from the date of inception or of reorganization;
> Plus/Minus: prior period adjustments;
> Minus: the cumulative amount of distributions made to shareholders (e.g., dividends);
> Minus: other charges to retained earnings (e.g., impact of treasury stock);
> Minus/Plus: Appropriations/returns of appropriations.

Comment: U.S. GAAP do not contain a current definition of *retained earnings*. ATB 1 did refer to a definition by a special committee,[7] in the sense of retained earnings as the cumulative balance of profit and expenses, gains and losses from the inception of a company (or from the date of a quasi-reorganization – see Section 6.5.3 following), minus amounts distributed to owners and transfers to other components of equity. The meaning of retained earnings is also undefined in IFRSs, as the IASB acknowledges.[8] The 2003 revision of IAS 1 did not contain a formal definition of retained earnings, but simply stated them as accumulated profit or loss.[9] Although undefined and without an explicit meaning of accumulated profits under IFRSs, the previous version of IAS 1 also used the two expressions as equivalent. Now, as mentioned, the expression *accumulated profit or loss* is not used any longer. In addition, the connotation of retained earnings as cumulative income is not explicitly acknowledged by the IASB. As a result, accounting for retained earnings, as demonstrated by the remainder of this Section, has been largely dictated by practical considerations.[10] Section 6.10 later expands on this issue, after illustration of the diverse ways of treating retained earnings.

Comment: Interestingly, several EU jurisdictions have no retained earnings concept. In fact, net income remains displayed as such in the balance sheet and it is not automatically reclassified into a retained earnings account. Net income for prior years goes into a sort of accumulated profit/loss reserve which, however, does not include the profit or loss for the period and therefore is not equal to retained earnings. Profit or loss for the period is displayed separately. Often, in order to make this transfer or to effect deficit reorganization (see Section 5.2.3 previously and Section 6.5.3 later) and thus change the balance of this accumulated profit/loss reserve a decision by shareholders' meeting is required.

Example: In response to the SEC Staff, a foreign private issuer from The Netherlands explained that, in its Form 20-F for the fiscal year ended January 1, 2006 containing financial statements prepared for the first time on the basis of IFRSs, Dutch law requires a separate line on the face of the balance sheet for net income before appropriation of current year result, to indicate net income before shareholders' declaration of dividends and approval of the amount to plow back to retained earnings.[11]

---

[7] *Accounting Terminology Bulletin No. 1, ¶¶ 33–34.*
[8] *IAS 19 (2011), ¶ BC100.*
[9] *IAS 1 (Revised 2003), ¶ 97(b).*
[10] *IAS 19 (2007), ¶¶ BC48W–BC48X.*
[11] *Letter by the SEC, File No. 1-2510, Note 1 (December 29, 2006). Reply by the company (January 11, 2007) www.sec.gov/divisions/corpfin/ifrs_reviews (last visited January 7, 2008).*

> **Example:** The SEC Staff, in its review of Form 20-F of a French foreign private issuer for the fiscal year ended December 1, 2005 containing financial statements prepared for the first time on the basis of IFRSs, requested explanation of reclassification from "Appropriation of Earnings/(Loss)" to additional paid-in capital. Under French Law, an offset of prior periods accumulated losses against additional paid-in capital was done based on a shareholders' meeting decision.[12]

6.1.3 Relationship to Earnings

Earnings are a part of retained earnings.

> **Comment:** The previous Section explains that under certain local GAAP there is no such concept as single retained earnings; instead a line "accumulated profit or loss" is shown on the statement of financial position as opposed to "profit or loss for the period."

The term earnings also presents mixed meanings.

> **Comment:** The definition and recognition of earnings are mainly related to measuring performance and to the recognition criteria of revenues, gains, expenses, and losses.[13] ATB 1 mentioned the use of *earnings* with reference to service operations as opposed to *profits* for manufacturing and mercantile industries.[14] CON 5 defines "earnings" as net income for the period minus the cumulative effects of a change in accounting principle (see Section 6.4.3 later) that are recognized in the current period.[15] Under CON 3, now superseded, *earnings* was an undefined term that was reserved for possible subcomponents of comprehensive income,[16] while the term "comprehensive income" (see Section 7.1.3 later) in CON 3 had the same meaning of measure of performance as *earnings* in CON 1.[17] CON 5 expected that the notion of earnings would be subject to future evolution, also as a consequence of the debate on the concept of clean-surplus (see Section 7.3 later). However, in practice, different terminology, such as net income, profit, or loss, is used in practice as synonymous with earnings.[18]
>
> In contrast to U.S. GAAP, IFRSs do not generally use the term *earnings*, apart from technical terminology, such as earnings per share, and have no such intermediate component of performance.

6.1.4 Relationship to Equity Reserves

Section 3.2.5 previously analyzes the position of retained earnings among "equity reserves" in IFRSs, and the change that occurred compared to the prior revision of IAS 1.

---

[12] *Letter by the SEC, File No. 1-14838, Note 5 (September 26, 2006). Reply by the company (October 10, 2006) www.sec.gov/divisions/corpfin/ifrs_reviews (last visited January 7, 2008).*

[13] *CON 1 (superseded), ¶ 43; CON 5, ¶¶ 33–34, 36.*

[14] *Accounting Terminology Bulletin No. 1, Review and Resume, ¶ 30.*

[15] *CON 5, ¶¶ 34, 42.*

[16] *CON 3, Elements of Financial Statements of Business Enterprises, ¶58.*

[17] *CON 1 (superseded), ¶¶ 42, Footnote 1, 43; CON 5, Footnote 7; CON 6, Footnote 1 and ¶ 2.*

[18] *FASB Statement No. 130, ¶ 81; CON 5, ¶ 35; Accounting Terminology Bulletin No. 2, Proceeds, Revenue, Income, Profit, and Earnings, ¶ 11.*

6.2   BASIC PRINCIPLE OF RETAINED EARNINGS

The traditional principle underlying retained earnings is that they can be reduced but never increased by transactions directly affecting equity without passing through net income. Conversely, a capital excess is generally credited to paid-in capital, as in case of transactions in own stocks. The U.S. accounting literature confirms this principle with reference to specific transactions, such as treasury stock purchase and resale (see Section 4.14.2 previously), quasi-reorganization[19] (see Section 6.5.3 following), or capitalization of earnings due to a small stock dividend (see Section 5.2.4 previously).[20]

> **Comment:** As illustrated in Section 5.4 previously, a similar principle exists under U.S. GAAP for capital surplus (additional paid-in capital) that in theory should not be reduced by losses except in case of quasi-reorganization.[21] However, again, as demonstrated in that Section, this pure model is not fully implemented in the U.S. pronouncements.

This basic principle is neither stated nor implemented under IFRSs.

> **Comment:** There are in fact some outstanding exceptions, as analyzed in Section 6.6 later. For example, under IAS 16 and IAS 38 revaluation surplus may be transferred directly to retained earnings (it is not reclassified into profit or loss), even though in connection to the use or realization of the asset that takes place through depreciation/amortization or disposal of the asset.

> **Comment:** Affecting retained earnings without passing through net income is a violation of the "clean-surplus" or "all-inclusive" concept of income, that is, all items of profit or loss recognized during a period must be included in net income.[22] The concept of "clean-surplus" is discussed in Section 6.4.1 following and Section 7.3 later.

6.3   CATEGORIZATION OF ITEMS THAT MAY AFFECT RETAINED EARNINGS

Worksheet 32 categorizes transactions and events involving retained earnings on the basis of the moment in which they are affected. The following paragraphs treat the specific items of each category under U.S. GAAP and IFRSs.

> **Comment:** Net income ordinarily determines the accumulation of retained earnings, and dividends reduce its ending balance. However, depending on the specific GAAP, some items may have an effect on retained earnings by directly affecting its opening balance. Other entries may directly change the ending balance of retained earnings without passing through the income statement. Finally, a direct transfer to retained earnings from other comprehensive income is possible under IFRSs. Under no circumstances this can happen under U.S. GAAP. This case is further discussed in under Section 6.6 following.

---

[19] *FASB ASC 505-30-25-8 (ARB 43*, Restatement and Revision of Accounting Research Bulletins, *Ch.1.B, ¶ 10; FASB ASC 852-20-25-4 (ARB 43, Ch.7A, ¶ 6).*

[20] *FASB ASC 505-20-30-3 (ARB 43, Ch.7B, ¶ 10).*

[21] *FASB ASC 505-10-25-1 (ARB 43, Ch.1A, ¶ 2).*

[22] *FASB ASC 250-10-45-22 (FASB Statement No. 16, ¶ 10).*

6.4   ITEMS THAT MAY DIRECTLY AFFECT THE BEGINNING BALANCE OF RETAINED EARNINGS

The following paragraphs illustrate the items that, under U.S. GAAP and IFRSs, may directly affect the opening balance of retained earnings without passing through net income.[23]

6.4.1   Retrospective Approach: General Considerations

Both Subtopic 250-10 (FASB Statement No. 16) and IAS 1 acknowledge the accounting for prior period adjustments and changes in accounting principles directly in retained earnings as an exception to including all profits and losses in net income.[24] Subtopic 250-10 (FASB Statement No. 154) carries forward the accounting for prior period adjustments contained in APB 20.

Comment: This is one of the exceptions to the "all-inclusive" or "clean-surplus" concept of income (another exception is, for example, other comprehensive income – see Section 7.3 later). The debate on whether or not the opening balance of retained earnings should be adjusted is linked to the topic of the clean-surplus concept of income (Section 7.3 later). Subtopic 250-10 (FASB Statement No. 154) and IAS 8 justify retroactive treatment on the grounds of consistency of financial information between periods and of comparability, especially of cross-border financial reporting. IAS 8 explains that faithful presentation of profit or loss is more important than avoiding bypassing the income statement in some period though direct credit or debit to retained earnings. Furthermore, retroactive treatment avoids repeating errors in comparative information.[25] The longer the period of time a certain transaction exerts its effects, the greater is the need for such inter-period comparability.[26] Although the predecessor APB 20 also acknowledged this point, it gave more weight to avoiding impaired public confidence in financial reporting as a result of restatement of financial statements.[27]

Objectives of transitional provisions on first application of a standard also include minimizing costs, issues, and disruption arising from its implementation.[28] When major effects derive from the adoption of a new standard, impact of financial markets, including factors such as variability in financial reporting, must also be considered. Therefore a practical approach is often followed, resulting in the adoption of mixed transition methods.

Another purpose of the clean-surplus concept is to limit or avoid abuses consisting in not charging all income and expenses to the net income of the current period.[29] With appropriate disclosure, judgment of financial statements users may be more effective and independent than that of management.[30] The issuance of APB 9 also pursued this objective. Avoiding use of hindsight when a standard relies on intent of management and reducing transition costs have been rationales against a retroactive approach.[31]

---

[23] *Correction of errors and changes in accounting principles fall outside of the scope of this Book: they are treated here insofar as they may affect retained earnings.*

[24] *FASB ASC 250-10-45-22 (FASB Statement No. 16, ¶ 10); IAS 1, ¶ 89.*

[25] *FASB Statement No. 154, Summary; IAS 8, ¶¶ BC7, BC8, BC11.*

[26] *IFRIC 4, ¶ Determining Whether an Arrangement Contains a Lease, ¶ BC49.*

[27] *APB 20, ¶ 18.*

[28] *FASB Statement No. 106, Employers' Accounting for Postretirement Benefits Other Than Pensions, Appendix A ¶ 250.*

[29] *APB 9, ¶ 14; CON 5, ¶ 35.*

[30] *ARB 4, Ch.8 (superseded), ¶ 7.*

[31] *FASB Statement No. 150, ¶ B73.*

Furthermore, financial statements under an all-inclusive concept are easier to prepare and understand.

The consideration that those adjustments were unrelated to operations of the current period was also one rationale in FASB Statement No. 16 behind the proposal of the retroactive treatment as prior period adjustment.[32]

From a different angle, related to the debate on financial performance, getting rid of nonrecurring or other items that, depending on management's experience, are sometimes not representative of a base to forecast future performance and cash flows has been considered a motivation for moving out of the traditional all-inclusive concept of income.[33] Part of the issue is, in fact, whether a retroactive application of a change in accounting principle and a correction of error must be considered as non-owner changes in equity (i.e., comprehensive income, either as items of profit or loss, or of other comprehensive income), or as other changes in equity (i.e., as owner changes in equity). In reply to some comment letters to the Exposure Draft of the amendments to IAS 1,[34] the 2007 Revision of IAS 1 specifies that such items are not period changes in equity, as they do not arise from changes in net assets during the period, but are simply reconciling opening items. For the first time, a distinction is made between other comprehensive income and other items that are credited or charged directly to equity.[35] IAS 1 requires their separate presentation as part of the statement of changes in equity. Section 505-10-S99 (Regulation S-X) also requires disclosure of retroactive adjustments to retained earnings in a separate statement of changes in stockholders' equity but permits note disclosure.[36] The previous version of IAS 1 included both those items in the statement of changes in equity and in the statement of recognized income and expenses.[37] They are neither transactions with owners acting in their capacity as owners, or components of profit or loss, or components of other comprehensive income. However, the IASB did not consider it necessary to remove the inconsistency in the definition of "total comprehensive income" that does not explicitly exclude such adjustments.[38] Conversely, FASB Statement No. 130 considers prior period adjustments as part of comprehensive income for prior periods, not for the current period.[39] Instead, CON 5 and FASB Statement No. 130 consider cumulative accounting adjustments that U.S. GAAP used to report under current-method (see later in this Section) as part of comprehensive income (reported in net income, not other comprehensive income) as they are recognized in the current period as changes in equity and therefore meet the definition of comprehensive income under the U.S. Concepts.[40] CON 5 classifies a change in accounting principle as being part of net income but not of earnings, while prior period adjustments, such as corrections of errors, are outside both.[41] Arguably, here a different way of accounting (by retroactive approach or by catch-up method) for the same transactions or events determines a different scope of an element of the financial statements, by the simple fact that focus shifts from the period of occurrence of the original transaction to the period of reporting of the adjustment. The "clean-surplus" concept of income is further discussed in Section 7.3 later.

---

[32] *FASB Statement No. 16, ¶¶ 26, 41, 49; CON 5, Footnote 21.*
[33] *APB 9, ¶¶ 11, 12; CON 5, ¶ 35.*
[34] *IASB Meeting, December 14, 2006, Agenda Paper 14:* Exposure Draft of Proposed Amendments to IAS 1 Presentation of Financial Statements – Comment Letter Analysis, *¶ 53 (December 14, 2006).*
[35] *IAS 1, ¶¶ 106, 109-110, BC74, Implementation Guidance.*
[36] *FASB ASC 505-10-S99-1 (Regulation S-X, ¶ 210.3-04).*
[37] *IAS 1 (Revised 2005), ¶ 96.*
[38] *IAS 1, ¶ 7; IASB Meeting, December 14, 2006, Agenda Paper 14:* Exposure Draft of Proposed Amendments to IAS 1 Presentation of Financial Statements – Comment Letter Analysis, *¶ 55 (December 14, 2006).*
[39] *FASB Statement No. 130, ¶ 106.*
[40] *FASB Statement No. 130, ¶ 79; CON 5, ¶ 39.*
[41] *CON 5, ¶¶ 34, 42.*

> **Example:** In its response to the SEC's review of Form 20-F for the fiscal year ended December 31, 2005, a French foreign private issuer explained its first adoption of IAS 32 and IAS 39. The retroactive application of those standards also affected other comprehensive income. However, based on analogy with FASB Statement No. 130, the company did not include such an effect in comprehensive income but treated it as an adjustment in the statement of changes in equity.[42]

Retroactive application of equity items has been traditionally prohibited in certain jurisdictions, mainly where accounting standards have a legal derivation, e.g., Italy or Germany.

> **Comment:** Italian accounting standards (for companies that do not report under IFRSs) interpret the EU Fourth Directive[43] to reject such a treatment on the grounds that opening balances of a balance sheet must correspond to the closing balances of the prior period's balance sheet.[44] This position has also been adopted by countries such as Belgium, France, Luxembourg, Spain, Finland, Norway, Sweden, and Switzerland, with certain exceptions. Furthermore, the Consob (Italy's securities regulator) instructed that the benchmark treatment under the previous version of IAS 8 could not be used for listed companies in Italy and required the use of only the alternative treatment permitted. As this later method reduces comparability, the Commission required note disclosure of the cumulative and current effect of changes of accounting policies and correction of errors, and of the effect on equity, net income (before and after tax), and each real account. In addition, it prescribed pro forma disclosures as if retroactive restatement were applied.[45] Other countries, such as Denmark, Ireland, and the United Kingdom, have been interpreting the EU Fourth Directive less narrowly, by allowing retroactive accounting, subject to appropriate disclosure. The Fédération des Experts Comptables Européens (FEE) acknowledged both these interpretations, but did not deny the compliance of retroactive restatement with the EU Fourth Directive when interpreted widely.[46]

> **Comment:** IAS 1 explains the behavior to adopt in the extremely rare circumstances in which maintaining the objective of financial statements as set out in the IASB Framework would require a "true-and-fair-view override" of IFRSs,[47] but local laws prohibit departure from their requirements. However, it does not treat the reverse situation, when national laws require a certain treatment that is not permitted under IFRSs, as it would be in the situation where a national law prohibited a retroactive approach. In a similar case concerning a conflict between the particular requirements of UK GAAP and the UK Companies Act of 2006, the SEC Staff admitted true-and-fair-view overrides, provided disclosure requirements were fully complied with, plus an explanation of the reason for such a departure, the key assumptions or estimates used, and the quantification of the effects on the financial statements.[48]

---

[42] *Letter by the SEC, File No. 1-15234, Note 37 (September 7, 2006). Reply by the company (November 24, 2006) www.sec.gov/divisions/corpfin/ifrs_reviews (last visited January 7, 2008).*

[43] *Fourth Council Directive 78/660/EEC (25 July 1978), Art 31.1(f).*

[44] *OIC – Organismo Italiano di Contabilità, Principio Contabile No. 29, Cambiamenti di principi contabili, cambiamenti di stime contabili, correzione di errori, eventi ed operazioni straordinari, fatti intervenuti dopo la data di chiusura dell'esercizio, ¶ A.III.b.2.*

[45] *Consob, Comunicazione No. DAC/99016997 (March 11, 1999), Comunicazione No. DAC/99059009 (July 30, 1999).*

[46] *Fédération des Experts Comptables Européens, FEE Study, Comparison of the EC Accounting Directives and IASs. A Contribution to International Accounting Developments (April 1999).*

[47] *IAS 1, ¶ 23.*

[48] *U.S. Securities and Exchange Commission, International Reporting and Disclosure Issues in the Division of Corporate Finance, ¶ V(I) (November 1, 2004) (last visited April 26, 2006).*

Planning Point: For the sake of formal legal compliance, in case a retroactive adjustment is required, some companies open the annual accounts at the amounts of prior period closing and, immediately after (in the new accounting year), make an adjustment to the beginning balance.

The term "restatement" may have a variety of technical connotations. However, the meaning of this term is not exactly the same under U.S. GAAP and IFRSs, depending on the legal environment.

Comment: Before FASB Statement No. 154, the term "restatement" was undefined in authoritative literature, although largely used in practice with a variety of meanings. FASB Statement No. 154[49] reserves the term "restatement" to retroactive corrections of errors, as opposed to "retrospective application" of a change in accounting principle or of a change in reporting entity. IAS 8 uses "retrospective application" and, occasionally, "retrospective adjustments" for a change in accounting policy while "retrospective restatement" is used for a correction of error.[50] IAS 8 intends "restatement" to be a correction as if the error had never occurred.[51] IAS 8 and IAS 34 use a restatement of prior period financial data, even with reference to a retrospective application of a change in accounting policy, as the action taken to remeasure, re-present, and re-disclose comparative data.[52] It is clear from IAS 8 that a restatement is made to the current financial statements on comparative period data, and does not require, per se, a republication of previously issued financial statements. Such a restatement is presented on the face of the financial statements.[53] Elsewhere, depending on the country, republication is generally a matter of corporate law, in addition to auditing standards. In fact, the alternative treatment by which the 1993 version of IAS 8 allowed the report of a correction of errors in net profit or loss had been contemplated for those jurisdictions that prohibited the restatement of previously-issued financial statements. That version of IAS 8 also clarified that a restatement did not necessarily give rise to a republication of financial statements, unless required by national laws.[54]

A mixed implication arises from the 2007 amendments to IAS 1. In order to better serve the interests of financial analysts, the 2007 version of IAS 1 added a statement of financial position as of the beginning of the earliest comparative period presented to a complete set of financial statements, but only in case of retroactive applications of an accounting policy, a correction of error, or a reclassification of items.[55] Under such circumstances, it may be argued that this is partial republication of those financial statements.

Conversely, FASB Statement No. 154 defines a "restatement" in terms of a revision of previously issued financial statements.[56] The term "restatement" suggests that previously-issued financial statements, not simply some lines, are revised. On the other hand, also in the U.S., restatement does not necessarily mean republication. Firstly, whether or not prior period financial statements must be reissued for the current period or for comparative purposes is a matter of auditing standards. Secondly, the example in Subtopic 250-10 (FASB Statement No. 154) illustrates amended comparative figures

---

[49] *FASB Statement No. 154, ¶ B8.*

[50] *IAS 8, ¶¶ 4–5.*

[51] *IAS 8, ¶ 5.*

[52] *IAS 34, ¶ 44.*

[53] *IAS 8, ¶¶ 42, Implementation Guidance Example 1.*

[54] *IAS 8 (1993), ¶¶ 36, 51.*

[55] *IAS 1, ¶ 10; Exposure Draft of* Proposed Amendments to IAS 1 Presentation of Financial Statements, *¶ BC6 (March 2006).*

[56] *FASB Statement No. 154, ¶ 2j.*

in current, not republished, financial statements and in the respective notes.[57] Finally, in the context of subsequent events guidance, Subtopic 855-10 (ASU 2010-09) clarifies that revised financial statements, in contrast to reissued financial statements, include revisions as a result of corrections of errors or retrospective changes in accounting policies. Again, however, the term "reissuance" appears to be misleading, to the extent that the amendment classifies restated financial statements as part of reissued financial statements.[58]

Conversely, an SEC registrant must first announce restatements for correction of errors in a press release, filed on Form 8-K, if the company's Board of Directors, officers, or outside auditor concludes that any previously issued financial statements should not be relied upon.[59] However, if the company, four days prior to such a conclusion, issues a quarterly or an annual report that includes the restated information, Form 8-K is not required. The company must file an amended quarterly or annual report (Form 10-K/A or Form 10-Q/A), but many companies simply restate prior periods in their next quarterly or annual filings.[60] Furthermore, a company should cite the fact that the restatement is the reason for a late quarterly or annual report in a Form 12b-25 "NT" filing. In case of a change in accounting principle that requires a material retroactive restatement of financial statements, an SEC registrant that files subsequent interim period financial statements that reflect such change must include fully restated financial statements, or incorporate by reference, when filing a registration statement or proxy/information statement. However, prior filing of annual report on Form 20-F that is incorporated by reference need not be amended, although restated financial statements should be filed in the registration statement or under cover of a Form 6-K that is incorporated by reference.[61] Finally, under SEC rules and regulations, the topic of pre-event financial statements also focuses on whether and when an entity must reissue them. This concerns certain subsequent events (i.e., a discontinued operation, a change in reportable segments, or a change in accounting principle) to be retrospectively applied that occur after the end of a financial year whose financial statements are reissued after the subsequent financial statements have already been filed.[62]

IAS 8 is effective for annual periods beginning on or after January 1, 2005. Earlier application is permitted.[63] The 1993 release of IAS 8 prescribed a retroactive approach to changes in accounting policies and corrections of errors as the "benchmark treatment" but allowed a prospective approach as the "alternative method." Subtopic 250-10 (FASB Statement No. 154) is effective for accounting changes and corrections of errors made in fiscal years beginning after December 15, 2005. Earlier application is permitted.[64] This standard also adopts a retroactive approach. Prior to FASB Statement No. 154, APB 20 required retroactive treatment only in certain situations, while the so-called "current-method" (also known as "cumulative-effect" or "catch-up" method) was the general rule.[65] A change in accounting principle affected

---

[57] *FASB ASC 250-10-55-2 (FASB Statement No. 154, ¶ Appendix A); FASB ASC 250-10-50-8, 250-10-50-9 (APB 9, ¶ 26).*

[58] *FASB ASC 855-10-50-5 (Accounting Standards Update No. 2010-09, Subsequent Events (Topic 855), Amendments to Certain Recognition and Disclosure Requirements, ¶ 5 (February 2010)); ASU No. 2010-09, ¶ BC5.*

[59] *Form 8-K, Item 4.02.*

[60] *See Lynn E. Turner and Thomas R. Weirich, "A Closer Look at Financial Statement Restatements,"* The CPA Journal *(December 2006).*

[61] *AICPA International Practices Task Force, March 22, 2005 meeting, 6(c).*

[62] *SEC, Financial Reporting Manual, ¶ 13100.*

[63] *IAS 8, ¶ 54.*

[64] *FASB ASC 250-10-15-4 (FASB Statement No. 154, ¶ 27).*

[65] *CON 5, Footnote 20.*

the income statement, which placed an aggregate for income before cumulative effects of a change in accounting principle after extraordinary items and before net income. Regulation S-X also requires a caption for cumulative effects of changes in accounting principles, but not an income or loss subtotal.[66] Pro forma information of income before extraordinary items and net income was required on the face of the income statement for all periods presented. Few circumstances required a retroactive approach, that is, a change from LIFO to another inventory method, a change in method of accounting for long-term contracts, a change to or from the full cost method for exploration costs in the extractive industries, a change from retirement-replacement-betterment accounting to depreciation accounting, any change by a closely-held company first issuing financial statements for the purpose of obtaining additional equity capital, effecting a business combination, or registering securities, and a change that was required by an authoritative pronouncement which had no transitional provisions.[67] The latter was not explicitly stated in APB 20 but was the general practice.

> **Comment:** The "current-method" was similar to the then superseded alternative treatment allowed by IAS 8, which presented cumulative effect of a change in accounting policy as of the beginning of the period in the income statement. However, this was different from the allowed alternative treatment for correction of errors because the latter did not use a single line. Pro forma information was required to be shown, if practicable. According to the "current-method" under APB 20, actual and pro forma amounts for the current period differed because pro forma calculation did not include the cumulative-type effect of the change.

> **Comment:** Therefore in general, unless otherwise required by a specific pronouncement and except specific situations where retroactive method was required under U.S. GAAP, changes in accounting principles and corrections of errors made in 2005 are likely to be on a retroactive basis under IFRSs and on a catch-up basis under U.S. GAAP. Thereafter, they are both likely to be on a retroactive method. It would be more common to find a catch-up approach used under both U.S. GAAP and IASs for accounting changes made before 2005.

In the case of a retrospective accounting or a reclassification, IAS 1 requires the presentation of an additional statement of financial position as of the beginning of the earliest period presented.[68]

6.4.2   Corrections of Errors

A *correction of an error* occurs when the error relates to a prior period and is corrected after the issue of the financial statements that contained such error.[69] In order to qualify for a restatement, an error must be discovered and corrected after prior financial statements were issued. IAS 8 refers to them as *prior period errors.*[70]

---

[66] *FASB ASC 225-10-S99-2, 944-225-S99-1, 942-225-S99-1 (Regulation S-X, ¶¶ 210.5-03.18, 210.7-04.16, 210.9-04.19).*

[67] *APB 20, ¶¶ 27, 29; FASB Statement No. 73,* Reporting a Change in Accounting for Railroad Track Structures, *¶ 2.*

[68] *IAS 1, ¶ 10(f).*

[69] *FASB ASC 250-10-45-23 (FASB Statement No. 154, ¶ 25).*

[70] *IAS 8, ¶ 5.*

> **Comment:** Under U.S. GAAP, the correction of an error is a type of *prior period adjustments*. For this category, APB 9 used to set certain restrictive conditions, that is, such adjustments had to be material, identified with or directly related to business activities of a prior period, resulting from economic events reported in prior financial statements. Their determination had to be independent of management, and they had to be subject to reasonable estimation.[71] FASB Statement No. 16 maintained retroactive restatement accounting for corrections of errors, but eliminated such treatment for many other types of prior-period adjustments.

> **Comment:** The 1993 revision of IAS 8 used to distinguish between *errors* (that were normally corrected in the net profit or loss for the current period) and *fundamental errors* (that were corrected through the benchmark treatment and restatement of comparative information, or alternatively in the net profit or loss for the current period plus presentation of additional pro forma information). Therefore, the expression *correction of fundamental errors* used to apply. An error was deemed to be fundamental when it was so significant as to undermine the reliability of prior period financial statements.[72] IAS 8 subsequently eliminated the concept of fundamental errors, and simply referred to prior period errors.[73] However, in defining material omissions or misstatements,[74] it introduced the concept of *material errors* and immaterial errors that are made intentionally, which both disturbed the compliance of financial statements with IFRSs. Such errors now require retroactive restatement. This treatment used to apply to fundamental errors only, on the grounds that all these kinds of errors make financial statements unreliable.[75] U.S. GAAP simply defines errors. However, for interim reporting only, an adjustment related to prior interim periods of the current fiscal year (which is a technical expression to include certain types of adjustments or settlements only, i.e., related to litigation or similar claims, income taxes, renegotiation proceedings, or utility revenue under rate-making processes) must be material and have certain other characteristics to be accounted for retrospectively.[76]

> **Comment:** On a practical basis, the revision of IAS 8 translated into an increased number of occurrences that require retroactive correction of prior period errors in IFRS jurisdictions. Conversely, fundamental errors were expected to be reported very rarely. The 1993 revision of IAS 8 opened to different interpretations as to whether or not the error was simply material or fundamental. In practice, reporting fundamental errors was seen as a negative incident to be avoided as far as possible, due to potential harmful consequences on the auditing of financial statements and on the impact on regulatory conditions and corporate governance.

Under both U.S. GAAP and IFRSs, errors include mathematical mistakes, mistakes in applying accounting principles, use of unacceptable or incorrect principles, fraud, and failure to use, as well as oversight or misinterpretation in the use of reliable information that was known, available, or reasonably expected to become available with due effort.[77]

---

[71] *APB 9, ¶ 23.*

[72] *IAS 8 (Revised 1993), Net Profit or Loss for the Period, Fundamental Errors and Changes in Accounting Policies, ¶¶ 31–32.*

[73] *IAS 8 (Revised 2005), Accounting Policies, Changes in Accounting Estimates and Errors, ¶ IN12.*

[74] *IAS 8 (Revised 2005), ¶¶ IN3(d), IN7(b)–(c), 5.*

[75] *IAS 8 (Revised 2005), ¶¶ 8, 41–42, BC12.*

[76] *FASB ASC 270-10-15-17 (FASB Statement No. 16, ¶ 13).*

[77] *FASB Statement No. 154, ¶ 2.h; IAS 8, ¶¶ 5, 41.*

Comment: Under U.S. GAAP the threshold for availability of information was the date of issuance of the financial statements, while under IFRSs it is the date of authorization for issue. This different interpretation of the relevant date is consistent with the date used under the two sets of standards for purposes of defining subsequent events.[78] However, now Subtopic 855-10 (FASB Statement No. 165, as amended by ASU 2010-9), for the purpose of evaluating subsequent events, requires the use of the issuance date for an SEC filer and a conduit bond obligor for conduit debt securities that are traded in a public market, and the date financial statements are available to be issued for all other entities. The standard requires the disclosure of whether subsequent events have been evaluated at the date of issuance of financial statements or at the date the financial statements are available to be issued and what this date is.[79] ASU 2010-9 eliminates such a disclosure for an entity that is an SEC filer, thus removing conflicts with SEC guidance.[80] Under FASB Statement No. 165, effective prospectively for interim and annual periods ending after June 15, 2009, the issuance date is to be intended as the date of wide distribution of GAAP-compliant financial statements to all shareholders for general use and reliance. The date of availability for issue is when financial statements are completed in form and format that is compliant with GAAP and all relevant authorizations, including shareholders' meeting when required, have been obtained.[81] For SEC registrants, the issuance date is the earlier of the date above (adding that annual financial statements must have been audited) or the date of filing with the SEC.[82] Conversely, under IAS 10, the date of authorization for issue is the date on which the Board of Directors authorizes the issuance of the financial statements to the shareholders' meeting for their approval. However, in case management issues financial statements to a supervisory board made up only of non-executive directors for its approval (apart from representatives of other external parties), it is the date on which management authorizes their issuance to that supervisory board. All this is irrespective of any public announcement of profit or loss or other selected financial information.[83]

Under both U.S. GAAP and IFRSs, errors differ from changes in accounting estimate insofar as a change in accounting estimate arises from new or additional information, new developments in information, more experience, changes in circumstances, or information that was not available or susceptible to reasonable estimation by management (or not expected to be available) at the threshold date. Estimation is made by management while a prior period adjustment is determinable by persons other than management. A change in accounting estimate need not relate to prior periods. It results from changes in judgments due to changes in events or circumstances that determine a change in information available.[84]

Comment: This concept has a specific important application for the first-time adoption of IFRSs. IFRS 1 requires, as of the transition date, that no change is made in the estimates that had been made under previous GAAP. New information received after the date of transition or the end of a comparative period must be accounted for prospectively in the current and future periods, as

---

[78] *IAS 10, ¶ 18.*

[79] *FASB Statement No. 165, Subsequent Events, ¶¶ 6, 12.*

[80] *FASB ASC 855-10-25-1A, 855-10-50-1, 855-10-50-4 (FASB Accounting Standards Update No. 2010-9, Subsequent Events (Topic 855): Amendments to Certain Recognition and Disclosure Requirements, ¶¶ 4–6, 8).*

[81] *FASB Statement No. 165, ¶¶ 5–6, A13.*

[82] *FASB ASC 855-10-S99-2 (EITF Topic No. D-86, Issuance of Financial Statements, as amended by Accounting Standards Update No. 2010-04, Accounting for Various Topics, Technical Corrections to SEC Paragraphs, ¶ 6).*

[83] *IAS 10, ¶¶ 5–7.*

[84] *APB 9, ¶ 23; APB 20, ¶ 13 (now superseded); IAS 8, ¶¶ 5, 34.*

appropriate, as changes in estimates. The only adjustments that are required are those to reflect any difference in accounting policies and on correction of errors. It may be the case that prior GAAP did not require certain estimates to record a transaction at the date of transition, while IFRSs do. In such a situation, consistently with the definition of adjusting events in IAS 10, a company must formulate such estimates only by considering the conditions (market prices, interest rates, foreign exchange rates, etc.) that existed at that date.[85]

Comment: IAS 8 states that hindsight should not be used to correct an error. The impossibility of isolating information that reflects the circumstance that existed when the transaction occurred is a case of the impracticability exemption from retroactive application under IAS 8.[86] FASB Statement No. 154 presents similar conclusions, although limited to a change in accounting principle (this pronouncement calls it impracticability exception).[87] The 1993 version of IAS 8 also limited the impracticability exception from a change in accounting policy.[88]

Comment: Subsequent events fall outside of the scope of this Book. However, it is to be noted that IFRSs, contrary to U.S. GAAP, show a very consistent application across standards of the principle of adjusting versus nonadjusting events, as for example for the case of long-term obligations that contain call provisions or the case of refinancing agreements on a long-term basis.[89]

Under both U.S. GAAP and IFRSs, prior period adjustments are accounted for retroactively, by restating the opening balance of retained earnings of the current period by the cumulative effect of error net of tax, if the error occurred in the prior period. If the error occurred in a period before the prior period, the opening balance of retained earnings presented for that prior period is also adjusted by the amount corresponding to the cumulative effects of error (net of tax) as of the beginning of the prior period. The same treatment applies to any additional prior periods that may have been presented. For comparative information purposes, the ending balance of retained earnings of a prior period in which the error occurred is also restated. Any adjustments to the profit or loss that affect current operations are reported as appropriate in the income statement (or, under IFRSs, in the single statement of comprehensive income) of the current period, in the line items required by the accounting of the specific transaction. For comparative information purposes, the line items of the income statement or statement of comprehensive income are restated as appropriate. The ending balances of assets and liabilities, if affected, are adjusted in the prior period in which the error occurred. The opening balances of assets and liabilities, if affected, are also adjusted for the earliest prior period presented, if the error occurred before that period.[90]

---

[85] *IFRS 1, ¶¶ 14–17.*

[86] *IAS 8, ¶¶ 52–53.*

[87] *FASB Statement No. 154, ¶¶ B15–B16.*

[88] *IAS 8 (1993), ¶ 52; IAS 8, ¶ BC28.*

[89] *See IAS 1, ¶¶ 72–74 versus FASB Statement No. 6,* Classification of Short-Term Obligations Expected to Be Refinanced; *FASB ASC 470-10-45-12 (FASB Statement No. 78,* Classification of Obligations That Are Callable by the Creditor*); FASB ASC 470-10-55-34 (FASB Interpretation No. 8,* Classification of Short-Term Obligations Repaid Prior to Being Replaced by a Long-Term Security*); FASB ASC 470-10-45-1 (EITF Issue No. 86-30,* Classification of Obligations When a Violation Is Waived by the Creditor*).*

[90] *FASB ASC 250-10-45-23 (FASB Statement No. 154, ¶ 25); FASB ASC 250-10-45-24 (APB 9, ¶ 18); IAS 8, ¶ 42.*

Comment: One reason for retroactive applications is that prior period financial statements would have been different, had the error not occurred. FASB Statement No. 16 highlights this characteristic as a distinguishing feature of a correction of error from other situations that were previously considered as prior period adjustments under APB 9. FASB Statement No. 16 excludes the retroactive approach in circumstances where management was not in a position to correctly determine the required accounting in the originally-issued financial statements.[91]

Worksheet 33 illustrates retroactive restatement for correction of errors under U.S. GAAP and IFRSs. The tax treatment related to adjustments of retained earnings is analyzed in Section 8.2.9 later.

Comment: When treating changes in accounting policies, IAS 8 specifies that a retrospective application may be made in an equity item other than retained earnings, if required by a standard or interpretation.[92] Although IAS 8 does not repeat this with reference to corrections of errors, the treatment is arguably the same, as the standard generically refers to adjustment to equity without mentioning retained earnings.[93] For a correction of error, Subtopic 250-10 (FASB Statement No. 154) states that the opening balance of a component of equity other than retained earnings may be affected, as appropriate.[94]

IAS 8 contains an impracticability exception to retroactive restatement, in case either the cumulative effect or the period-specific effects cannot be determined.[95]

Comment: In such a case, an entity must disclose related circumstances and how and from when the error has been corrected.[96] The simple fact that information is not readily available cannot be an excuse.

Comment: U.S. GAAP has an impracticability exception for a change in accounting principle, and not for a correction of error.[97]

The 1995 revision of IAS 8 referred to the retroactive restatement as the benchmark treatment and allowed an alternative treatment consisting in adjusting current net profit or loss.

Comment: However, U.S. GAAP did not allow current-method for prior period adjustments.

[91] *FASB Statement No. 16, ¶ 41.*
[92] *IAS 8, ¶ 26.*
[93] *IAS 8, ¶ 42.*
[94] *FASB ASC 250-10-45-23 (FASB Statement No. 154, ¶ 25.b).*
[95] *IAS 8, ¶¶ 43–48.*
[96] *IAS 8, ¶ 49(d).*
[97] *FASB Statement No. 154, ¶ B32.*

U.S. GAAP and IFRSs require certain disclosures for correction of errors. They include the nature of errors, the amount of corrections (IFRSs), the amount of the effects on net income of prior periods, on beginning retained earnings for each period presented and on each financial statements line item (U.S. GAAP), the line items affected (IFRSs), the impact on basic and diluted earnings per share (if applicable), and the cumulative effect in equity as of the beginning of the earliest period presented, and whether the impracticability exception was used and how correction was pursued (IFRSs only).[98] Section 505-10-S99 (Regulation S-X) requires separate information of prior period adjustments affecting the opening balances of the earliest period presented, as note disclosure or as a specific statement of changes in other stockholders' equity.[99]

6.4.3   Changes in Accounting Principles

Both U.S. GAAP and IFRSs account for changes in accounting principles retroactively.

> **Comment:** "Accounting policies" under IFRSs correspond to "accounting principles" under U.S. GAAP.

FASB Statement No. 154 largely converged with the retroactive application provisions of IAS 8.

> **Comment:** Technically, under U.S. GAAP, a change in accounting principle is not a prior period adjustment,[100] although it is now accounted for retroactively under FASB Statement No. 154, and sometimes referred to as such by certain pronouncements.[101]

Such a retrospective approach requires showing the cumulative effect of the change in the opening balance of retained earnings and (under IFRSs) or (under U.S. GAAP) other components of equity as appropriate, as of the earliest period presented. Current and future periods apply the newly adopted accounting principle. The opening balance of assets and liabilities as of the earliest period presented must also be affected as appropriate. The illustrations given by both standards also show the restatement of the income statement of comparative periods.[102]

Section 250-10-45 (FASB Statement No. 154) now clarifies that under no circumstances must the cumulative effect of a voluntary change in accounting principle affect the income statement.[103]

---

[98]   *FASB ASC 250-10-50-7 (FASB Statement No. 154, ¶ 26); FASB ASC 210-10-50-8, 210-10-50-9 (APB 9, ¶ 26); IAS 8, ¶ 49.*

[99]   *FASB ASC 505-10-S99-1 (Regulation S-X, ¶ 210.3-04).*

[100]   *FASB Statement No. 16, ¶ 11.*

[101]   *FASB Interpretation No. 7, Applying FASB Statement No. 7 in Financial Statements of Established Operation Enterprises, ¶ 5.*

[102]   *FASB ASC 250-10-45-5, 250-10-55-11 (FASB Statement No. 154, ¶¶ 7, A7; IAS 8, ¶¶ 22, IG Example 2.*

[103]   *FASB ASC 250-10-45-6, 250-10-45-7 (FASB Statement No. 154, ¶¶ 8, 9); FASB Statement No. 154, ¶¶ B12, C19; IAS 8, ¶¶ 24, 25.*

> **Comment:** This does not exclude transitional provisions of a specific pronouncement imposing an accounting similar to the current-method. Furthermore, Subsection 250-10-S99-3 (SAB 5-F) does not allow an adjustment of beginning retained earnings without restating prior periods' financial statements. An entity that does not restate because the cumulative effect is immaterial must include the impact in current period net income, but not in a specific line.[104] IAS 8 also requires adjustment of other comparative amounts disclosed for each period presented, including historical summaries of financial data. Section 250-10-45 (APB 9) recommends restatement of historical summaries of financial data.[105]

> **Comment:** It is interesting to note subtle differences between the examples provided by IAS 8 and Subtopic 250-10 (FASB Statement No. 154) and some inconsistencies between IAS 1 and IAS 8. Firstly, as illustrated in Worksheet 34, Example No. 1 (for a correction of errors) and the former Example No. 2 for a change in accounting policy (then deleted) of the Implementation Guidance of IAS 8 report the original opening balance and the restatement of retained earnings at the beginning of the first period presented in rows, but do not do so for ending retained earnings of the first period presented and of the current period even when the beginning balance is also restated. Conversely, they show this as part of the restated profit or loss for a period presented. On the other hand, IAS 1 explains that the effects of retrospective application or retrospective restatement must be shown in the statement of changes in equity in accordance with IAS 8.[106] However, the statement of changes in equity has no line for profit or loss or its restatement. Instead, it simply reports a line for changes in accounting policy and a line for total comprehensive income of the year, as illustrated by the Implementation Guidance of the standard. Finally, IAS 8 illustrates the presentation of a change in accounting policy with retrospective application in a statement of changes in equity as part of the basic financial statements. By contrast, Illustration No. 1 of FASB Statement No. 154 shows a statement of financial position, an income statement, and a statement of cash flows (but not the statement of changes in equity), with columns for unrestated, restated amounts, and effect of changes, for both the current and the prior period. Therefore, all lines are detailed as to beginning and ending balances and respective adjustments. However, it does so as part of the notes. In effect, both standards require "adjustment" of accounts and certain note disclosures but do not clearly mandate specific presentation formats on the face of the financial statements.

Under both U.S. GAAP and IFRSs, the adjustment to the beginning balance of retained earnings shows parenthetically gross and net of income tax effect[107] (see Section 8.2.9 later).

> **Comment:** In case of IFRS first-time adoption, recasting of historical summaries of financial data is not required, provided prior GAAP data are prominently labeled and the nature of adjustments that would be required to comply with IFRSs is disclosed.[108]

---

[104] *FASB ASC 250-10-S99-3 (SEC Staff Accounting Bulletin, Topic 5-F, Accounting Changes Not Retroactively Applied Due to Immateriality).*

[105] *FASB ASC 250-10-45-28 (APB 9, ¶ 27).*

[106] *IAS 1, ¶ 106(b).*

[107] *FASB ASC 250-10-45-8 (FASB Statement No. 154, ¶¶ 2g, 10); FASB ASC 250-10-50-8, 250-10-50-9 (APB 9, ¶ 26); IAS 8, Implementation Guidance, Example 2; IAS 12, ¶ 62(b). However, the examples in FASB Statement No. 154 do not show such gross and net display.*

[108] *IFRS 1, ¶ 22.*

Under Subtopic 250-10 (FASB Statement No. 154), retrospective application of a change in accounting principle is measured at the direct effects of the change, including related tax implications and any impairment adjustments. Any indirect effects are recognized in the period of the accounting change. In such a period, both the amount recognized and the portion that is attributable to each prior period presented must be disclosed in aggregate and per-share amounts. When the current-method was used under APB 20, pro forma income before extraordinary items and net income also included indirect effects.[109]

> **Comment:** In contrast to U.S. GAAP, IAS 8 does not make a distinction between the direct and indirect effects of a change in accounting policy.

As a consequence of FASB Statement No. 154, the accounting treatments for a change in accounting principle and for a correction of error are similar, apart from disclosures. U.S. GAAP and IFRSs require certain disclosures for a change in accounting principle, including the nature and reason for the change, description of the retroactive adjustments, the effects on aggregate and per-share income from continuing operations (U.S. GAAP), net income, equity and financial statements line items, the cumulative effect on retained earnings or other equity component, the fact that and reason why retrospective application is impracticable and alternative methods used.[110] For interim financial statements, Section 270-10-S99 (Regulation S-X) adds the disclosure of the date of the change and a letter from the registrant's independent accountants, as an exhibit in the first Form 10-Q subsequently filed, confirming the preferability of a material change in accounting principle that is voluntary.[111] Furthermore, SEC registrants must determine other appropriate disclosures as required by SAB 11-M for accounting standards that have been issued but do not require adoption until some future date.[112] IAS 8 also has some disclosures when a new standard has been issued but is not yet effective.[113]

Both Subtopic 250-10 (FASB Statement No. 154) and IAS 8 now have an impracticability exception to the retrospective accounting for a change in accounting principle. When it is impracticable to determine the cumulative effect at the beginning of the current period, they apply the new accounting principle prospectively from the earliest date practicable. If it is impracticable to determine the period-specific effects, the cumulative-type adjustment affects the beginning balance of retained earnings of the first feasible period. Previously, under U.S. GAAP, if the cumulative effect could not be determined or reasonably estimated in the cases in which APB 20 required retroactive application, an entity had to show the effect of changes on the current income statement and reasons given in the notes. Instead, FASB Statement No. 154

---

[109] *FASB ASC 250-10-50-1 (FASB Statement No. 154, ¶¶ 2g, 2i, 17); FASB Statement No. 154, ¶¶ B33; APB 20, Footnote 6 to ¶ 19.*
[110] *FASB ASC 250-10-50-1 (FASB Statement No. 154, ¶ 17); IAS 8, ¶ 49.*
[111] *FASB ASC 270-10-S99-1 (Regulation S-X, ¶ 10-01(b)(6)).*
[112] *FASB ASC 250-10-S99-5 (SEC Staff Accounting Bulletin, Topic 11-M, Disclosure Of The Impact That Recently Issued Accounting Standards Will Have On The Financial Statements Of The Registrant When Adopted In A Future Period).*
[113] *IAS 8, ¶¶ 30, 31.*

now clarifies that under no circumstances will the period-specific effects of a voluntary change in accounting principle affect the income statement.[114]

> **Comment:** This does not prevent an accounting pronouncement from requiring transitional provisions similar to the current-method. Furthermore, SAB 5-F does not allow an adjustment of beginning retained earnings without restating prior periods' financial statements. An entity that does not restate because the cumulative effect is immaterial must include it in current period net income, but not in a specific line.[115]

> **Comment:** The impracticability exception is not necessarily equivalent to prospective application. In fact, the impracticability of determining the period-specific effects on comparative information for one or more prior periods presented is a limited retrospective application.[116] Instead, prospective application pertains to when even the cumulative effect as of the beginning of the current period is undeterminable, as in that case no form of retrospective application is possible. Therefore, prospective application under the previous version of IAS 8 would only have corresponded to this particular case of the current impracticability exception. However, in this case, it is evident that although the income statement does not report a line for cumulative effects, some of them may be present in profit or loss. For example, if the beginning balance of inventories is at FIFO and the ending balance follows another method, the part of the change included in cost of sales may include amounts related to prior periods.

Subtopic 250-10 (FASB Statement No. 154) and IAS 34 now have an approach on accounting for policy changes for interim reporting purposes that is consistent with that used for annual reporting, that is retrospective application. IAS 34 requires restating, if practicable, the financial statements of prior interim periods of the current financial year and of comparable interim periods of prior financial years that will be restated for annual reporting purposes.[117]

> **Comment:** Subtopic 250-50 (FASB Statement No. 154), limits the impracticability exception to prior financial year only. In case of impracticability in prechange interim periods of the current annual period, the change will be postponed to the beginning of the subsequent year. Similarly under IAS 34, if retrospective application of any change in accounting policy is impracticable, prospective application must be applied from no later than the beginning of the current year. Accounting policies must be consistent throughout a financial year. In any other event, the next financial year will reflect the changes.[118]

Changes of accounting principles as compared with prechange interim periods, interim periods of prior year, and prior annual report must be disclosed.[119] Previously, under FASB Statement No. 3, the income statement of the first quarter of the reporting annual period (or any

---

[114]   *FASB Statement No. 154, ¶¶ 8, 9, B12; IAS 8, ¶¶ 24, 25.*
[115]   *SEC Staff Accounting Bulletin, Topic 5-F,* Accounting Changes Not Retroactively Applied Due to Immateriality.
[116]   *FASB Statement No. 154, ¶ B11.*
[117]   *IAS 34,* Interim Financial Reporting, *¶ 43.*
[118]   *FASB ASC 250-50-45-14 (FASB Statement No. 154, ¶ 15); IAS 34, ¶¶ 28, 43, 44.*
[119]   *FASB ASC 270-10-45-12 (APB 28,* Interim Financial Reporting, *¶ 23).*

year-to-date or other financial statements that included the first quarter) had to show the cumulative effect of the change in a single line item. The comparative prior periods were not restated, while previous interim periods of the year were retroactively restated. Absolute and per-share pro forma income from continuing operations and net income were disclosed, as if the new principle had been applied retroactively.

Comment: Actual and pro forma amounts were equal only for quarters subsequent to the first quarter of the current annual period because pro forma calculation did not include the cumulative-type effect of the change.[120]

6.4.4 Changes Arising from First-Time Adoption of a Comprehensive Basis of Accounting

Before discussing the first-time adoption of a comprehensive basis of accounting, this Section introduces the distinction between voluntary and involuntary changes in accounting principle. Both U.S. GAAP and IFRSs distinguish between voluntary and involuntary changes in accounting principle. As mentioned, as a general rule, a change that is mandated by authoritative pronouncements is accounted for retrospectively, except for certain FASB Staff Positions and generally EITF Abstracts, unless different requirements are imposed by the transitional provisions of a specific pronouncement.[121] IAS 8 requires retrospective application, subject to an impracticability exception, of an involuntary change in accounting policy for which a standard or an interpretation does not provide any transitional provision. However, contrary to the previous version of the standard, the IAS 8 impracticability exception also holds when the retrospective application required in a transitional provision is not practicable (not only when that standard or interpretation has no transitional provision and therefore retrospective application under IAS 8 would apply, but results to be impracticable).[122]

Comment: Transitional provisions of certain standards are compared in the following Section when the accounting is different under U.S. GAAP and IFRSs. If periods over which certain transactions or events exert their effects overlap, at least in part, a comparability issue may arise.

A pooling of interests was a case for adjustment to retained earnings before 2002. Such method was banned for business combinations initiated after June 30, 2001.

A particular case of transition is the first-time adoption of a comprehensive basis of accounting. IFRS 1 treats this with reference to IFRSs. At the date of transition to IFRSs, the adjustments in the opening IFRS statement of financial position arising from applying IFRSs instead of previous GAAP to events and transactions before the date of transition to IFRSs must be recognized directly in retained earnings (or, if appropriate, in another category of equity, such as in the case of revaluation surplus for certain property, plant and equipment or certain

---

[120] *FASB Statement No. 3 (superseded),* Reporting Accounting Changes in Interim Financial Statements, ¶¶ *9-11.*

[121] *FASB ASC 250-10-45-3 (FASB Statement No. 154, ¶ 6); EITF Topic D-1; IAS 8, ¶ 19.*

[122] *IAS 8, ¶¶ 22, BC29.*

intangible assets, gain or loss of available-for-sale financial assets, or derivatives qualified as cash flow hedges).[123] As the transition date is the beginning of the earliest period for which an entity presents full comparative information under IFRSs in its first IFRSs financial statements, those adjustments affect the beginning balance of retained earnings.

Comment: U.S. GAAP has no similar guidance. However, as stated, retrospective application is the general rule. Furthermore, an entity that describes its financial statements as prepared "in conformity with generally accepted accounting principles" must apply all relevant authoritative accounting pronouncements.[124] The same concept is valid under IFRSs: the notes must contain an explicit and unreserved statement of compliance with IFRSs only if financial statements comply with all applicable standards and interpretations.[125] IFRS 1 applies to entities whose financial statements previously did not make such a representation.[126] Had IFRS 1 not been issued, a new entrant would have been forced to a one-off full retrospective application. IFRS 1 replaced SIC-8, *First-time Application of IASs as the Primary Basis of Accounting*. This interpretation required a strict full retrospective application, unless impracticable, and did not allow the exemptions and the exceptions of IFRS 1. In addition, some of its provisions (e.g., as to which version of standards to use, the use of hindsight in estimates, interaction with standard-specific transitional provisions) were not so clearly stated. This caused doubts and debate. Therefore, IFRS 1 moved in the direction of making transition to IFRSs more appealing to the IFRSs' large potential audience, through reducing possible undue costs of managing the change. It looked to achieve comparability among companies over time, initially among first-time adopters, and between those and companies that already applied IFRSs as a next step.[127]

Planning Point: Section 3.6.6 previously explains that, depending on jurisdiction, the changes in the opening balance of retained earnings may be awarded specific line-item display. On top of this, special tracing for tax treatment may be needed. Therefore, even if not required by IFRSs or in jurisdictions that do not impose additional prescriptions on the subject, it would be appropriate to separately identify an account within retained earnings for first-time adoption adjustment and possibly subclassifications by type of adjustments.

Comment: Failure to adjust retained earnings for a first-time adoption item results in a correction of error when this is adjusted in the subsequent period. Therefore, even though such correction again affects retained earnings, it should be accounted for in a separate retained earnings sub account other than that used for the purpose of IFRS first-time adoption.

IFRS 1 provides first-time adopters with certain exceptions to the retroactive application of IFRSs. Under such circumstances, Form 20-F requires a foreign registrant to describe the exception elected, the items to which it applies, the accounting principle and its application, and its impact, in the financial and operating review and prospects.[128]

---

[123] *IFRS 1, ¶ 11.*

[124] *FASB Interpretation No. 40,* Applicability of Generally Accepted Accounting Principles to Mutual Life Insurance and Other Enterprises, *¶¶ Summary, 2, 16.*

[125] *IAS 1, ¶ 16.*

[126] *IFRS 1, ¶ 4.*

[127] *IFRS 1 (Revised 2005), ¶¶ IN1, IN7, BC10.*

[128] *Form 20-F, Item 5, Instruction No. 4; AICPA International Practices Task Force, May 17, 2005 meeting, Questions 11 and 12.*

6.4.5 Changes in Reporting Entity

Changes in reporting entity are those that, in effect, make the resulting entity into a different entity. Under U.S. GAAP, changes in reporting entity consist of presenting consolidated or combined financial statements in place of entity's financial statements, or a change in the group of subsidiaries for which consolidated statements are prepared, or a change in companies included in combined statements. A change in reporting entity requires a retroactive application to the financial statements of all periods presented. The nature and reason for change have to be disclosed, as well as the aggregate and per share effects on income before extraordinary items and net income, and the effects on other comprehensive income and other appropriate equity caption for all periods presented.[129] A transfer of a parent's interest in subsidiaries to other wholly owned subsidiaries is a change in legal entity but not a change in reporting entity.[130]

Comment: IFRSs, in contrast to U.S. GAAP, do not provide guidance for changes in the reporting entity. While under U.S. GAAP consolidated financial statements of a company that has subsidiaries are its general-purpose financial statements, under IFRSs, the fact that consolidated financial statements are presented does not negate or interfere with the parent's separate financial statements. Consolidated or combined financial statements cannot be presented in place of entity's financial statements, and the two types of statements have separate lives. Hence, under such circumstances, no need arises for creating a change in reporting entity category for a change from entity's financial statements to consolidated or combined financial statements. In December 2007 the IASB added the common control project to its agenda. This project will also consider the accounting for demergers.[131]

Under U.S. GAAP, another situation arises when an unconsolidated investee that was accounted for at the equity method is subsequently line-by-line consolidated, resulting in a change in reporting entity.

Example: In its review of Form 20-F for the year ended December 31, 2005 of a French foreign private issuer, the SEC requested additional disclosures related to the consolidation of entities that were previously accounted for by the equity method as well as an explanation of the reason why the new policy had not been retroactively applied.[132]

Comment: Under IFRSs, the issue is irrelevant for the purpose of an investor's separate financial statements. In fact an investor that also presents consolidated financial statements would, in its separate financial statements, account for both an associate and a subsidiary at cost method or fair value. It would use the equity method only in case it presented individual financial statements only, a situation that would arise if it had no subsidiary or joint venture and thus presented no consolidated financial statements. In any case, it would carry on presenting its individual or separate financial statements.

---

[129] *FASB ASC 250-10-45-21, 250-10-50-6 (FASB Statement No. 154, ¶¶ 2f, 23–24).*
[130] *FASB Statement No. 141, ¶ D8.*
[131] *IFRIC Update, November 2009; IFRIC Update, January 2010.*
[132] *Letter by the SEC, File No. 1-14410, ¶ 14 (September 25, 2006). Reply by the company on October 31, 2006 www.sec.gov/divisions/corpfin/ifrs_reviews (last visited January 7, 2008).*

However, if the equity-method investment included capitalized interest according to Subtopic 835-20 (FASB Statement No. 58, *Capitalization of Interest Cost in Financial Statements That Include Investments Accounted for by the Equity Method*), as the investee was using funds to acquire assets qualifying for capitalization of interest costs for its principal operations which have not yet begun, such interest capitalized in prior periods must not be restated as part of the change in reporting entity.[133]

> **Comment:** Under IAS 23, an investee accounted for at equity method does not qualify for capitalization of borrowing costs.[134]

Under U.S. GAAP, an entity must retroactively restate the investment account, results of operations, and retained earnings for all periods presented, when an investee that was not accounted for at equity method subsequently qualifies for the equity method because ownership rises to over 20%. However, again, any capitalized interest costs are not restated.[135] Worksheet 35 illustrates the computations and the accounting.

> **Comment:** Arguably, IFRSs do not permit retroactive adjustments of financial statements for return to the equity method. In fact, the equity method applies from the date at which the investment qualifies as an associate or a jointly controlled entity (prior to IFRS 11).[136] By permitting a restatement, the investor would recognize a portion of the associate's results for the prior period during which it did not exert significant influence over the investee.

> **Comment:** Apart from whether or not a retroactive adjustment for a change in reporting entity exists under the respective sets of standards, both U.S. GAAP and IFRSs require disclosure of certain circumstances that give rise to a change in the group of subsidiaries for which consolidated statements are prepared.

In fact, both U.S. GAAP and IFRSs require certain disclosures of material business combinations affected during the period, and aggregate disclosures of individually immaterial business combinations that are material in aggregate, including information on major classes of assets and liabilities of the acquiree.[137] Furthermore, both Subtopic 805-10 (FASB Statement No. 141(R)) and IFRS 3 (revised 2007) require the disclosure of the parts of the post-combination consolidated revenue and profit or loss (IFRSs) or earnings (U.S. GAAP) that are attributable to a company acquired in the period, if practicable. However, Subtopic 805-10 (FASB Statement No. 141(R)) limits this "post-combination versus the organic growth approach" disclosure to public business enterprises.[138] In addition, U.S. GAAP continues its

---

[133] *FASB ASC 250-10-45-21 (FASB Statement No. 154, ¶ 23).*

[134] *IAS 23, Borrowing Costs, ¶ BC22.*

[135] *FASB ASC 323-10-35-33 (APB 18, ¶ 19(m), as amended by Accounting Standards Update No. 2010-08, Technical Corrections to Various Topics, ¶ 11).*

[136] *IAS 28 (2010), ¶ 23.*

[137] *FASB ASC 805-20-50-1, 805-10-50-3 (FASB Statement No. 141(R), ¶¶ 68(i), 69; IFRS 3, ¶¶ B64(i), B65.*

[138] *FASB ASC 805-10-50-2 (FASB Statement No. 141(R), ¶ 68(r)(1)).*

"comparative" approach requirement for public business enterprises that present comparative financial statements (but only if practicable) of supplemental pro forma information of the revenue and earnings on a combined basis for the preceding fiscal year as if the acquisition had occurred as of the beginning of prior year.[139] IFRSs do not require such information, on the basis that it is supposed to be too costly and unfeasible in an international environment.[140] Finally, in case of an intrayear acquisition, under both U.S. GAAP and IFRSs the pro forma revenue and profit or loss as if business combination had occurred as of the beginning of the annual reporting period must be disclosed, if practicable.[141]

> **Comment:** Certain particular situations, as explained below, may arise in dual-reporting circumstances, if there are differences in the area of consolidation between U.S. GAAP and IFRSs. This gives rise to a sort of "cross-border" change in the group of subsidiaries for which consolidated statements are prepared.

For a foreign private issuer in particular, the SEC Staff requires, at a minimum, summarized financial information of an equity investee that is "significant," as for the meaning of this term according to Regulation S-X,[142] when it is consolidated under IFRSs but would be accounted at equity method under U.S. GAAP. The registrant must also include a sufficiently detailed reconciliation to allow an investor to reconstruct financial statements prepared in accordance with U.S. GAAP and Regulation S-X.[143] Summarized financial information consists of note disclosure of assets, liabilities, results of operations, current assets, noncurrent assets, current liabilities, noncurrent liabilities, redeemable preferred stocks, and minority interests, other income statement items, and major components of assets and liabilities for specialized industries in which classified balance sheets are normally not presented.[144] Form 20-F has an accommodation in case a jointly owned entity is proportionately consolidated under IFRSs but would be accounted for at equity method under U.S. GAAP. Classification as, or display reconciliation to, the equity method may be omitted when proportionate consolidation is accepted under the issuer's home country GAAP, the joint venture would not be consolidated under U.S. GAAP, and that would be an operating entity whose significant financial operating policies are jointly controlled by contractual arrangements by all parties having an equity interest in the entity. Summarized footnote disclosure of the amounts proportionately consolidated is required.[145] IFRS 12 recently added specific disclosure requirements of summarized financial information of subsidiaries, associates, and joint ventures.[146]

6.4.6 Prior Period Adjustments of an Associate

Under U.S. GAAP, an investor's share of an equity-method investee's prior period adjustments is presented as prior period adjustments in the investor's financial statements.[147]

---

[139] *FASB ASC 805-10-50-2 (FASB Statement No. 141(R), ¶ 68(r)(3)).*

[140] *IFRS 3, ¶¶ BC423–BC428.*

[141] *FASB ASC 805-10-50-2 (FASB Statement No. 141(R), ¶ 68(r)(2)); IFRS 3, ¶ B64(q).*

[142] *Regulation S-X, ¶ 210.1-02(w).*

[143] *U.S. Securities and Exchange Commission,* International Reporting and Disclosure Issues in the Division of Corporate Finance, *¶ VI(c) (November 1, 2004) (last visited April 26, 2006).*

[144] *Regulation S-X, ¶ 210.1-02(bb).*

[145] *Form 20F, Part III, Item 17(c)(2)(vii).*

[146] *IFRS 12, Disclosure of Interests in Other Entities, ¶¶ 12(g), 21(b)(ii).*

[147] *APB 18, ¶ 19d.*

IAS 1 and IAS 28 are specific with reference to other comprehensive income, but not to retrospective adjustments.[148] An investor in an associate or in a joint venture accounted for at equity method adjusts its carrying amount of the investment and displays in its consolidated statement of comprehensive income its share (after tax and minority interest) of the changes in the investee's other comprehensive income. Prior to the 2007 amendments of IAS 1, it adjusted its equity in the statement of changes in equity for its share in income and expense that the investor had recognized directly in equity.[149] IAS 28 states revaluation surplus and foreign exchange translation differences as examples. The statement of comprehensive income in the Implementation Guidance of IAS 1 shows a line for share of other comprehensive income of associates. This subject is further discussed in Section 7.17.6 later.

Comment: IAS 8 does not specifically mention situations that require the retroactive approach, such as changes in accounting policies and corrections of errors, in relation to associates. However, an associate's retrospective adjustment would be reflected in the investor's financial statements based on general principles in IAS 8, i.e., retrospectively. The issue is whether or not separate presentation of the adjustment is warranted. IAS 28 prior to the amendments made by IAS 1 used to refer to changes in the investee's equity that had been recognized directly in the investee's equity, and not only to other comprehensive income. It used to require separate presentation of those adjustments in the statement of changes in equity. Therefore, it could be argued that separate presentation also applied to changes in accounting policies and corrections of errors.

Comment: Subtopic 323-10 (FASB Statement No. 130) also requires display in equity for the investor's share of an investee's equity adjustments of other comprehensive income, but it does not clarify how it should be displayed. It permits the combining with the investor's other comprehensive income items.[150]

6.4.7 Prior Period Adjustments of a Development Stage Subsidiary or Associate

Under Topic 915 (FASB Interpretation No. 7), an established operating parent company accounts in the consolidated financial statements for a development stage subsidiary's change in accounting principle arising from adopting Topic 915 (FASB Statement No. 7) as a prior period adjustment. The same treatment applies in case of a development stage enterprise that is an equity-method investee.[151] Reporting by development stage enterprises is treated in Section 6.8.5 following.

Comment: As IFRSs have no specific guidance for the development stage enterprise, arguably the same accounting applies whether or not the subsidiaries or the associate are development stage or established operating enterprises (like under FASB Statement No. 7). Therefore, in general, a change in the accounting policy of a subsidiary will be accounted for under IAS 8 in consolidated financial statements. A change in the accounting policy of an associate will be accounted for under IAS 28 in consolidated financial statements as mentioned in the previous paragraph.

---

[148] *IAS 1, ¶ 82(g) and (h); IAS 28 (2010), ¶¶ 11, 39.*
[149] *IAS 28 (2005), ¶¶ 11, 39.*
[150] *FASB ASC 323-10-45-3 (FASB Statement No. 130 ¶¶ 121–122).*
[151] *Topic 915 (FASB Interpretation No. 7, Accounting and Reporting by Development Stage Enterprises).*

6.4.8 Prior Period Adjustments of an Investment that is Classified as Held for Sale

IFRS 5 requires that cumulative income or expenses that relate to a noncurrent asset (or disposal group) classified as held for sale and that are recognized in other comprehensive income must be separately presented. The same requirement applies to a subsidiary that is acquired and held exclusively with a view to resale that meets the criteria to be classified as held for sale.[152]

Comment: Again, the standard refers to other comprehensive income. IFRS 5 prior to the amendments made by IAS 1 used to refer to cumulative income or expense recognized directly in equity, and not only to other comprehensive income. Therefore, it could be argued that separate presentation also applied to changes in accounting policies and corrections of errors.

Comment: FASB Statement No. 144 has no such guidance. Furthermore, it deleted a provision of ARB 51 that required separate presentation in consolidated financial statements of the parent's interest in the predisposal earnings of a deconsolidated subsidiary that had been disposed of during the year.[153]

To better explain the context of this topic, both U.S. GAAP and IFRSs now consolidate subsidiaries held on a temporary basis, such as subsidiaries acquired and held exclusively with a view to resale.[154] Under IFRS 5, if a subsidiary that is acquired and held exclusively with a view to resale meets the criteria to be classified as held for sale, it is consolidated but with the special rules of IFRS 5. It is presented on the face of the statement of financial position in at least two amounts – one for the assets under the caption "non-current assets classified as held for sale" and one for the liabilities under the caption "liabilities directly associated with noncurrent assets classified as held for sale," and it is measured at the lower of carrying amount and fair value less costs to sell. Display or note disclosure of the major classes of assets and liabilities is permitted but not required.[155]

Comment: Contrary to IFRS 5, FASB Statement No. 144 does not explicitly treat a subsidiary that is acquired and held exclusively with a view to resale. A similar classification would result to the extent that a temporarily controlled subsidiary (not necessarily a subsidiary that is acquired and held exclusively with a view to resale as in IFRS 5) is determined to meet the criteria for being a "component" of an entity that is classified as held for sale, in which case the requirements of FASB Statement No. 144 would apply. The major classes of assets and liabilities, measured at the lower of carrying amount or fair value less cost to sell, would be either separately presented or disclosed in the notes.[156]

FASB Statement No. 144 is effective as of the beginning of fiscal years beginning after December 15, 2001 and interim periods during those years, for disposal activities initiated by

---

[152] *IFRS 5, ¶ 38.*
[153] *FASB Statement No. 144, ¶ C2; ARB 51, ¶ 12 (deleted).*
[154] *FASB Statement No. 144, ¶¶ B119, C2; IFRS 5, ¶ BC53.*
[155] *IFRS 5, ¶¶ 32, 38, 39, BC54, BC79; IFRS 3, ¶ 31; IAS 27 (2010), ¶ BC19.*
[156] *FASB Statement No. 144, ¶¶ 41, B119, B133.*

an entity's commitment to a plan after the effective date or initial application of the standard.[157] IFRS 5 is effective for annual periods beginning on or after January 1, 2005.[158]

> **Comment:** Transition provisions of the two standards differ. IFRS 5 applies prospectively.[159] However, an IFRS first-time adopter with a date of transition to IFRSs on or after January 1, 2005 applies IFRS 5 retrospectively.[160] Under FASB Statement No. 144, comparative statement of financial position must be restated for reporting disposal groups classified as held for sale.[161] IFRS 5 requires no restatement of prior periods.[162]

For the purpose of the parent's separate financial statements, an investment in a subsidiary accounted for at cost method that is classified as held for sale or included in a disposal group is measured under IFRS 5 at the lower of carrying amount and fair value less costs to sell and presented as a net one line figure under the caption "non-current assets classified as held for sale." Conversely, if measurement under IAS 39 applies to the investment then it is accounted for at fair value under IAS 39, but the classification and presentation provisions of IFRS 5 still hold. This is because IFRS 5 scopes out of its measurement provisions financial assets in the scope of IAS 39 or IFRS 9 that are carried at fair value with changes in fair value recognized in profit or loss.[163]

> **Comment:** Subtopic 360-10 (FASB Statement No. 144) does not apply to financial instruments, as an investment in a subsidiary would be for the purpose of parent-only financial statements.[164]

IFRS 5 does not specifically clarify whether the separate classification in equity mentioned above applies to an investment in an associate or in another investee that is classified as held for sale.

> **Comment:** On one hand, under IFRS 5 an investment in an associate or in a jointly controlled entity that meets the criteria to be classified as held for sale is also presented as a net one-line figure under the caption "non-current assets classified as held for sale" in both consolidated and investor's separate financial statements.[165] On the other hand, the IAS 8 revision prior to the IAS 1 amendments required that an investor in an associate separately reflected income or expenses that had directly affected the equity of the associate (see Section 6.4.6 previously).

If an investment in an associate or in a jointly controlled entity (after IFRS 11, a subsidiary, an associate, a joint operation, a joint venture, or a portion of an interest in a joint venture or in an

---

[157] *FASB Statement No. 144, ¶¶ 49–50.*

[158] *IFRS 5, ¶ 44.*

[159] *IFRS 5, ¶ 43.*

[160] *IFRS 1 (Revised 2005), ¶ 34B.*

[161] *FASB Statement No. 144, ¶¶ 49, BC133.*

[162] *IFRS 5, ¶¶ 40.*

[163] *IFRS 5, ¶ 5; IAS 27 (2010), ¶¶ 38, BC66A, BC66B, BC66C.*

[164] *FASB ASC 360-10-15-5 (FASB Statement No. 144, ¶ 5).*

[165] *IAS 27 (2010), ¶ 38; IAS 28 (2010), Footnote to ¶ IN9, ¶ 14; IFRS 5, ¶ 2.*

associate) ceases to qualify as held for sale, it is reclassified to equity-method investment (or, prior to IFRS 11, proportionate consolidation or equity-method, in case of a jointly controlled entity) as from the date of previous classification as held for sale, including comparative information.[166]

Comment: Subtopic 360-10 (FASB Statement No. 144) does not apply to financial instruments, including investments in equity securities accounted by the cost or equity method.[167]

As part of the *Reporting Discontinued Operations Project* (whose scope has been removed from the *Financial Statement Presentation Project*) the FASB is considering including in the definition of discontinued operations a newly acquired subsidiary that meets the criteria to be classified as held for sale on acquisition.

6.4.9 Consolidation Adjustments of Beginning Retained Earnings

As a matter of practice, both under U.S. GAAP and IFRSs, worksheet entries are used in consolidation. These are not accounting entries and therefore are not reflected in the general ledger. Therefore, in consolidation in years subsequent to the first one, a consolidation entry that rectifies the unearned profits of a prior period must adjust the beginning balance of retained earnings, as net income of the prior period was not affected in the ledger accounts.

Example: In consolidation in years subsequent to the first, the prior years' depreciation or amortization of some fair value adjustments is accounted for by affecting the "retained earning" account, because consolidation in the prior years did not use book entries.

6.4.10 Reclassification of Investment Property

IAS 40 allows the use of either the "cost model" or the "fair value model" for investment property. Note that the fair value model differs from the revaluation model that is used instead for property, plant, and equipment or certain intangible assets. One of the differences is that the former recognizes all changes in fair value in profit or loss and not in other comprehensive income as the revaluation model does. When an entity that had applied the revaluation model under IAS 16 to investment property first adopts IAS 40, it has to reclassify any amount that it had previously credited to revaluation surplus in relation to investment property to the opening balance of retained earnings. However, for an entity that chooses to adopt the fair value model under IAS 40, restatement of prior periods, that otherwise would have been mandated by IAS 8, is prohibited, in order to avoid any possible manipulation in allocating fair values across periods. Disclosure of the fact that prior periods have not been restated is required.[168] The 2005 revision of IAS 40 is effective for annual periods beginning on or after January 1, 2005.

---

[166] *IFRS 5, ¶ 28, as amended by IFRS 11; IAS 28 (2011), ¶ 21; IAS 28 (2010), ¶ 15; IAS 31, ¶ 43.*
[167] *FASB ASC 360-10-15-5 (FASB Statement No. 144, ¶ 5).*
[168] *IAS 40, ¶¶ 80–83, B67(h).*

> **Comment:** Before the issuance of IAS 40 this case might apply either to an entity that used the revaluation model for investment property (no longer permitted after the issuance of IAS 40), or to an entity already applying IAS 40 that elects for the first time to treat some or all eligible property interests held under operating leases as investment property, as permitted by the 2003 amendments to IAS 40. In the latter case, restatement of prior period is permitted only for an entity that had already publicly disclosed fair values for prior periods.[169]

6.4.11   Measurement of Servicing Assets and Liabilities at Fair Value

FASB Statement No. 156, effective for the fiscal year that begins after September 15, 2006, requires initial fair value measurement, if practicable, of separately recognized servicing assets and servicing liabilities that arise from a contract to serve financial assets. For the purpose of subsequent measurement, an entity may irrevocably elect fair value, individually for each class of separately recognized servicing assets and servicing liabilities, in which case this must be separately or parenthetically presented on the statement of financial position. Such election, that may be taken either as of the beginning of the year of adoption of the standard or as of the beginning of subsequent years, requires prospective application to all new and existing separately recognized servicing assets and liabilities within each class. The cumulative-type difference between the fair value and the net carrying amount of existing separately recognized servicing assets and liabilities is adjusted to the beginning retained earnings and separately disclosed.[170]

> **Comment:** Similarly to U.S. GAAP, under IFRSs a separately recognized servicing liability is measured at fair value. Contrary to U.S. GAAP, a separately recognized servicing asset is measured at an amount that results from allocating the carrying amount of the transferred larger financial asset, based on such servicing asset's relative fair value at the date of transfer in relation to other parts of this larger financial asset that are derecognized and those parts that continue to be recognized by the transferor.[171] This treatment is similar to that required by FASB Statement No. 140 before its amendments by FASB Statement No. 156.[172] Now, under FASB Statement No. 156, a servicing asset is no longer considered as part of the interests that continue to be held by the transferor of the larger financial asset, because fair value was considered the most relevant measurement basis for financial instruments.[173] Contrary to FASB Statement No. 156, IAS 39 requires retroactive application and restatement of prior periods.[174]

6.4.12   Available-for-Sale Securities Designated as Offset of Changes in Fair Value of Servicing Assets or Liabilities

FASB Statement No. 156, as of the beginning of the fiscal year of its initial adoption, permits a one-time reclassification of available-for-sale securities to trading securities for entities that,

---

[169] *IAS 40, ¶ 3.*

[170] *FASB ASC 860-50-50-5, 860-50-35-3 (FASB Statement No. 156,* Accounting for Servicing of Financial Assets, *¶¶ 4(f), 7–9, 11).*

[171] *IFRS 9, ¶¶ 3.2.10, 3.2.13; IAS 39, ¶¶ 24, 27.*

[172] *FASB ASC 860-10-35-3 (FASB Statement No. 140,* Accounting for Transfers and Servicing of Financial Assets and Extinguishments of Liabilities, *¶ 10).*

[173] *FASB Statement No. 156, ¶ A10.*

[174] *IAS 39, ¶ 104.*

based on the same standard, have elected subsequent fair value measurement of separately recognized servicing assets and liabilities (see Section 6.4.11 previously). A precondition is that such securities must be designated as offsetting changes in fair value of those servicing assets or liabilities. The gains or losses on such available-for-sale securities that had been recorded as unrealized in other comprehensive income must be recorded as a separately-disclosed cumulative adjustment to the beginning balance of retained earnings.[175] On the other hand, under Topic 825 (FASB Statement No. 159, effective for the fiscal year that begins after November 15, 2007), an entity may elect to use the fair value option for eligible items, including available-for-sale securities. Cumulative unrealized gains or losses on those securities at the effective date must be reclassified from other comprehensive income to the beginning balance of retained earnings as a cumulative-effect adjustment to be separately disclosed.[176] On both cases, this treatment is different from the ordinary one prescribed by Subtopic 320-10 (FASB Statement No. 115), based on which a reclassification from available-for-sale securities to trading securities determines the recognition of a gain or loss in current earnings, including the amount that had been recognized in other comprehensive income.[177]

Comment: IFRSs have no such election in relation to servicing rights. However, an analogy might be drawn with the circumstances of irrevocable designation of certain financial instruments as at fair value through profit or loss under IAS 39. One of the situations in which an entity may designate a financial asset or financial liability as at fair value through profit or loss on initial recognition is when this eliminates the accounting mismatch resulting from adopting mixed bases of measurement or when such assets or liabilities (after IFRS 9, a group of financial liabilities or of financial assets and financial liabilities only) are managed as part of a group of financial instruments on a fair value basis. This should be substantiated by a documented risk or investment strategy that is internally monitored by the company's key management. Such circumstances are special cases of the revised fair value option under IAS 39. They are not contemplated by the fair value election under FASB Statement No. 155.[178] However, such circumstances are similar to the concept of designating certain instruments as offsetting changes in fair value mentioned by Subtopic 860-50 (FASB Statement No. 156). Although the fair value option under Subtopic 825-10 (FASB Statement No. 159) does not have the stringent qualifying criteria of IAS 39, such circumstances may also be an implicit motivation for such an option.[179] In such cases, contrary to Subtopic 860-50 (FASB Statement No. 156), IAS 39 requires retroactive application and restatement of prior periods, although with certain limitations as explained in Section 6.4.13 below.[180] It is to be noted that the 2000 revision of IAS 39 allowed an option to recognize unrealized gains or losses of an available-for-sale financial asset either directly in equity (as other comprehensive income) or in profit or loss. The already mentioned fair value option made this accommodation no longer necessary.[181] The transitional provisions relating to the elimination of this option are analyzed in Section 6.4.14 later.

6.4.13 Fair Value Measurements

Both Topic 820 (FASB Statement No. 157) and IAS 39 define fair value measurement criteria.

---

[175] *FASB Statement No. 156, Accounting for Servicing of Financial Assets, ¶¶ 10, A19.*
[176] *FASB Statement No. 159, The Fair Value Option for Financial Assets and Financial Liabilities, ¶ 28.*
[177] *FASB ASC 320-10-35-10 (FASB Statement No. 115, ¶ 15); FASB Statement No. 159, ¶ 29.*
[178] *FASB Statement No. 155, Accounting for Certain Hybrid Financial Instruments.*
[179] *FASB Statement No. 159, ¶ A3.*
[180] *IFRS 9 (October 2010), ¶ 4.1.5; IFRS 9, ¶ 4.5 (November 2009); IAS 39, ¶¶ 9(b)(i), 9(b)(ii) (as amended by IFRS 9), 105D.*
[181] *IFRS 9, ¶ BCZ4.59; IAS 39, ¶ BC74A.*

> **Comment:** The fair value measurements criteria of Topic 820 (FASB Statement No. 157) apply to most pronouncements that adopt the fair value attribute, as IFRS 13 effective from annual periods beginning on or after January 1, 2013, with earlier application permitted. Conversely, the pre-IFRS 13 fair value measurements of IAS 39 apply to financial assets and financial liabilities only, while other standards apply to fair value measurement in other contexts.[182]

FASB Statement No. 157 is effective for fiscal years beginning after November 15, 2007. It applies prospectively as of the beginning of the fiscal year of first application, given the difficulty in separating a change in fair value measurement from a change in the method of measuring fair value (a change in accounting principle). As an exception, however, certain situations are accounted for retrospectively limited to the beginning of the year of adoption of the standard with no restatement of prior periods. In this case, a cumulative-effect adjustment to the beginning balance of retained earnings or other component of equity must be separately displayed for the difference between carrying amounts and fair values of related instruments.[183] One of those situations is a derivative or other financial instrument that, prior to the initial application of Topic 820 (FASB Statement No. 157), was measured at fair value at initial recognition under Topic 815 (FASB Statement No. 133) using the transaction price and for which unrealized gain or loss between transaction price and fair value was not recognized in earnings under EITF Issue No. 02-3 as the fair value was determined using significant unobservable inputs.[184] Now fair value, as measured under Topic 820 (FASB Statement No 157), applies to those instruments and if a difference between a model-based estimate of fair value and the transaction price exists this is recognized in earnings at initial recognition (so-called day-one gain or loss).

IAS 39 must be applied retrospectively by adjusting the opening balance of retained earnings, with certain exceptions.[185] One of these exceptions concerns the initial gain or loss recognition on financial instruments. When an entity measures a financial instrument for which there is no quoted price in an active market, and the transaction price is different from the fair value computed otherwise, the entity may recognize gain or loss on inception given by the difference between fair value and the transaction price only if fair value is evidenced by comparison with other observable current market transactions in the same instrument without modification or repackaging or is based on a valuation technique that incorporates observable market data only. Under such circumstances, the entity may choose to recognize gains or losses on initial recognition of financial instruments either retrospectively, or prospectively to transactions entered into after October 25, 2002, or prospectively to transactions entered into after January 1, 2004.[186] IFRS 1 with no earlier adoption extends this accommodation to IFRS first-time adopters that do not apply IFRS 9 early.[187] IFRS 13, for annual periods beginning on or after January 1, 2013 with earlier application permitted, refers to fair value as evidenced by a Level 1 input in the fair value hierarchy, i.e., a quoted price in an active market for an identical asset

---

[182]   *FASB ASC 820-10-15-1 (FASB Statement No. 157, Fair Value Measurements, ¶ 2, as amended by ASU No. 2011-04); IFRS 9, ¶ 5.4.1; IAS 39, ¶ 48; IFRS 13, Fair Value Measurement, ¶¶ 5, C1.*

[183]   *FASB ASC 820-10-65-1 (FASB Statement No. 157, ¶¶ 36, superseded after the end of the transition period stated in FASB Staff Position FAS 157-2); FASB Statement No. 157, ¶ 37.*

[184]   *FASB Statement No. 157, ¶¶ 37, C10–C11, C108.*

[185]   *IAS 39, ¶ 104.*

[186]   *IFRS 9, ¶¶ B5.4.8, B5.4.9; IAS 39, ¶¶ 107A, AG76, AG76A, BC222.*

[187]   *IFRS 1, ¶¶ D20, BC83A; IFRS 1 (Revised 2005), ¶¶ 25G, BC83A.*

or liability.[188] Subsequent recognition of a previously unrecognized day-one gain or loss is limited to the extent that it arises from a change in factors, including the time variable, that market participants regard as relevant for price setting.[189]

> **Comment:** The date of October 25, 2002 was to converge with EITF Issue No. 02-3, now nullified by FASB Statement No. 157 on this point.[190] The effects of that Issue were reported by the cumulative-effect method, now changed to limited retrospective application under Topic 820 (FASB Statement No. 157).

IFRS 9 does not re-propose these transitional provisions, and therefore the day-one gain or loss rules apply retrospectively to ongoing IFRS entities.

> **Planning Point:** IFRS 9 (November 2009) did not amend IFRS 1. Therefore, an entity migrating to IFRSs that adopts IFRS 9 early still uses this exemption with reference to IAS 39. Conversely, IFRS 9 (October 2010) amended IFRS 1 to re-propose the accommodation with the same date but with reference to IFRS 9. In practice there is no impact, because IFRS 9 reproduces the provisions of IAS 39 on day-one gain or loss.[191]

A cumulative-effect adjustment to the beginning balance of retained earnings or other components of equity also arises on the first remeasurement to fair value of eligible items that existed at the date of election of the fair value option under Topic 825 (FASB Statement No. 159). This adjustment refers to the fiscal year of adoption of the standard and not to the beginning of the earliest comparative period presented, because comparative information is not restated. The pre-tax portion of such an adjustment must be illustrated as part of a note disclosure in the form of a schedule.[192]

Pre-IFRS 9 IAS 39 has a fair value option (previously already revised in IAS 39) to design a financial asset or financial liability at fair value through profit or loss.[193] In general, IAS 39 requires retrospective application, with adjustment of the beginning balance of retained earnings of the earliest prior period presented and all comparative periods, with certain exceptions.[194] On the first adoption of IAS 39, an entity must de-designate financial assets or financial liabilities that it had previously designated as such but which do not meet the new requirements[195] (IFRS 9 has a similar requirements for a financial asset[196]). An entity that first applied the IAS 39 revised fair value option in its annual period beginning on or after

---

[188] *IFRS 9, ¶¶ B5.1.2A, B5.2.2A as added by IFRS 3, Fair Value Measurement; IFRS 3, ¶ C1.*

[189] *IFRS 9, ¶¶ B5.4.8, B5.4.9; IAS 39, ¶¶ AG76, AG76A, BC104, BC221(e).*

[190] *FASB Statement No. 157, Footnote 17; EITF Issue No. 02-3, Issues Involved in Accounting for Derivative Contracts Held for Trading Purposes and Contracts Involved in Energy Trading and Risk Management Activities, ¶ 22.*

[191] *IFRS 9 (October 2010), ¶ C3.*

[192] *FASB Statement No. 159, ¶¶ 25, 27(a), A46.*

[193] *IAS 39, ¶¶ 9(b)(i), 9(b)(ii) (as amended by IFRS 9), 11A (as amended by IFRS 9), 12, 13, AG4B–AG4K (as amended by IFRS 9), AG33A–AG33B.*

[194] *IAS 39, ¶ 104.*

[195] *IAS 39, ¶¶ 105B(c), 105C(a).*

[196] *IFRS 9, ¶ 8.2.8(a).*

January 1, 2006 (the date of fair value option amendments) could not designate any previously recognized financial assets or financial liabilities as at fair value through profit or loss (in case of adoption of the standard in annual period beginning before January 1, 2006 and after September 1, 2005, an entity was permitted to make such designation provided the new criteria were met). For an entity whose annual period began before September 1, 2005, such designations did not need to be completed until such date and might also include financial assets and financial liabilities recognized between the beginning of that period and September 1, 2005. Comparative information had to be restated only if those instruments would have met the fair value option criteria as of the earlier of the beginning of comparative period and the date of initial recognition of the financial assets or liabilities, if acquired later.[197]

At first adoption of IFRSs, an entity is permitted to designate a financial asset (under criteria in IFRS 9, if after the effective date of this standard) and a financial liability as at fair value through profit or loss, provided the pre-IFRS 9 IAS 39 revised fair value option criteria are met at the date of transition to IFRSs[198] (or at the start of its first IFRS reporting period, if the entity presented its first IFRS financial statements for an annual period beginning before January 1, 2006). When the transition date was before September 1, 2005 (to be read as the beginning of the first IFRS reporting period, if the entity presented its first IFRS financial statements for an annual period beginning before January 1, 2006), such designations did not need to be completed until such date and might also include financial assets and financial liabilities recognized between the transition date (to be read as the beginning of that period in the latter case) and September 1, 2005. Restatement of comparative information was required if restatement had been made for the purpose of IAS 39 and if the revised fair value option criteria were met as of the earlier of the transition date to IFRSs and the date of initial recognition. Restatement was required for the financial assets, financial liabilities, or groups of financial assets, financial liabilities, or both that were classified as at fair value through profit or loss at the start of the first IFRS reporting period. Groups of financial assets, financial liabilities, or both managed and evaluated on a fair value basis had to be restated even if individually derecognized during the comparative period.[199]

Another situation of the abovementioned limited retrospective application method that may arise under Topic 820 (FASB Statement No. 157) is for a hybrid financial instrument that, prior to the initial application of that standard, was measured at fair value at initial recognition using the transaction price as a result of the fair value election under FASB Statement No. 155.[200] Such a transitional provision is consistent with that of FASB Statement No. 155. FASB Statement No. 155 is effective for all financial instruments acquired, issued, or subject to remeasurement after the beginning of an entity's first fiscal year that begins after September 15, 2006. Its fair value option may be applied to pre-existing hybrid financial instruments that had been bifurcated under Topic 815 (FASB Statement No. 133). FASB Statement No. 155 requires an adjustment to the beginning balance of retained earnings for the cumulative effect corresponding to the difference between the sum of carrying amount of the previously bifurcated components of a hybrid financial instrument and the fair value of the combined instrument as of the adoption of such standard, with no requirement to restate prior periods.[201]

---

[197]   *IAS 39, ¶¶ 104, 105A–105D.*
[198]   *IFRS 1, ¶ D19.*
[199]   *IFRS 1 (Revised 2005), ¶¶ 25A (then amended by IFRS 9), IG56(d)(iv).*
[200]   *FASB Statement No. 157, ¶¶ 37; FASB Statement No. 155, ¶¶ A39–A40.*
[201]   *FASB Statement No. 155, ¶¶ 6–7.*

The fair value option under IAS 39 also includes the designation of an entire hybrid contract as a financial asset or financial liability at fair value through profit or loss under certain circumstances.

> **Comment:** The IAS 39 fair value option is similar but not equivalent to the fair value election under FASB Statement No. 155.

Under IFRS 9, an entity may also designate a financial asset as at fair value though profit or loss on its initial recognition, provided the more limited criteria for fair value option in IFRS 9 are met. This fair value option is also permitted at the date of initial application of IFRS 9, based on facts and circumstances existing at that date. IFRS 9 is effective for annual periods beginning on or after January 1, 2013, with earlier application permitted. Retrospective application, with certain exceptions, applies. An entity that adopts IFRS 9 for reporting periods beginning before January 1, 2012 is exempted from applying IFRS 9 to comparative periods. In this case, any difference between amounts as of the beginning of the annual period of initial application of IFRS 9 and those relating to prior GAAP affects the beginning balance of retained earnings or other equity component, as applicable.[202]

In particular, at initial application of IFRS 9, the comparative period value of a hybrid contract measured at fair value (when not available because not determined at those reporting periods) is deemed to be the sum of the fair values of the nonderivative host and the embedded derivative at the end of those periods. Any difference with the fair value of the entire hybrid contract affects the beginning balance of retained earnings of the period of initial application of IFRS 9, or profit or loss if the entity applies IFRS 9 in an interim period (which is permitted if the entity applies IFRS 9 before January 1, 2011).[203] In addition, an adjustment to the beginning balance of retained earnings of the reporting period that includes the date of initial application of IFRS 9 must reflect any difference between the fair value at the date of initial application of IFRS 9 of an investment in an unquoted equity instrument (or a linked or a related to-be-physically-settled derivative) and its previous carrying amount at cost under IAS 39.[204]

An IFRS first-time adopter has a fair value option similar to that under IFRS 9 explained above, based on facts and circumstances existing at the date of transition to IFRSs. In its first IFRS financial statements, an entity that adopts IFRSs including IFRS 9 for annual periods beginning before January 1, 2012 is exempted from applying IFRS 9 disclosures and IFRS 7 disclosures related to assets within the scope of IFRS 9 to comparative periods. In this case, reference to transition date must be intended as the beginning of the first IFRS reporting period. Previous GAAP applies to comparative information in lieu of IAS 39 and IFRS 9. Any difference between amounts as of the beginning of the first IFRS reporting period and those relating to the prior GAAP comparative period is accounted for as a change in accounting principles and the entity must give most of the disclosures required by IAS 8 for earlier application of a standard.[205]

---

[202] *IFRS 9 (October 2010), ¶¶ 4.1.5, 7.1.1, 7.2.7, 7.2.14, BC7.21; IFRS 9 (November 2009), ¶¶ 4.5, 8.1.1, 8.2.7, 8.2.12, BC107.*

[203] *IFRS 9 (October 2010), ¶¶ 4.1.5, 7.2.2, 7.2.5, 7.2.6; IFRS 9 (November 2009), ¶¶ 4.5, 8.2.2, 8.2.5, 8.2.6.*

[204] *IFRS 9 (October 2010), ¶ 7.2.11; IFRS 9 (November 2009), ¶ 8.2.11.*

[205] *IFRS 1 (2008, as amended by IFRS 9), ¶¶ B8, D19A, E1, E2; IFRS 1 (2003, as amended by IFRS 9), ¶¶ 25AA, 34E, 36D, 36E.*

Finally, an entity that under prior GAAP used to recognize unrealized gains on investment measured at fair value directly in equity, must retroactively adjust the beginning balance of retained earnings at the date of first-time transition to IFRSs, if it classifies such instruments as at fair value through profit and loss on initial application of IAS 39 and IFRS 9.[206]

6.4.14 First-Time Classification as Available-for-Sale Investments

With the introduction of the fair value option, IAS 39 eliminated the option to recognize gains and losses on available-for-sale financial assets contained in the 2000 release of the standard either in profit or loss or directly in equity. Available-for-sale investments had then to be reclassified with retrospective application.[207]

Furthermore, prior to the effective date of IFRS 9, on first application of IAS 39 or on first-time adoption of IFRSs, an entity can redesignate a previously recognized financial asset as available for sale. In this case, it has to restate comparative information based on the new classification of the financial assets and reclassify all cumulative changes in fair value in a separate component of equity.[208]

Contrary to IFRSs, the transitional provisions of Topic 320 (FASB Statement No. 115) prohibited retrospective application to prior periods and requested the use of the cumulative-effect method under APB 20 and the adjustment of the balance of the separate component of equity for the unrealized gain or loss net of tax effect.[209]

6.4.15 Other-Than-Temporary Impairment of Certain Debt Securities

Section 7.14.4 later illustrates the recognition of other-than-temporary impairments of debt available-for-sale and held-to-maturity securities and presentation of those securities and of equity available-for-sale securities under FSP FAS 115-2 and FAS 124-2. The FSP is effective for interim and annual periods ending after June 15, 2009. It applies to existing and new investments held as of the beginning of the interim period in which it is adopted.

This FSP has a special transitional provision for previously other-than-temporary impaired debt securities that an entity holds at the beginning of the interim period of its adoption and that it does not intend to sell and that it is not more likely than not that it will be required to sell before recovery of their amortized cost basis. An adjustment to the opening balance of retained earnings, including related tax effects and with a corresponding adjustment to accumulated other comprehensive income, must reflect the cumulative effect of initially applying this FSP, as the difference between the present value of the cash flows expected to be collected and the beginning amortized cost basis of the debt security. The difference between the amortized cost basis of the securities adjusted for this cumulative effect gross of tax and the cash flows expected to be collected shall be accreted in accordance with existing guidance as interest income. In the period of adoption, the disclosures required by Subtopic 250-10 (FASB Statement No. 154) for a change in accounting principles apply.[210]

---

[206] *IFRS 1, ¶¶ IG58A (amended by IFRS 9), IG59 (amended by IFRS 9).*

[207] *IAS 32, ¶ 97; IAS 39, ¶ 104.*

[208] *IAS 39, ¶ 105; IFRS 1, ¶¶ D19(a) (deleted by IFRS 9), IG59 (partially deleted by IFRS 9).*

[209] *FASB Statement No. 115, ¶ 25.*

[210] *FASB ASC 320-10-65-1 (FSP FAS 115-2 and FAS 124-2, Recognition and Presentation of Other-Than-Temporary Impairments, ¶¶ 44–47).*

6.4.16 Changes in Decommissioning, Restoration, and Similar Liabilities

Under both U.S. GAAP and IFRSs, a decommissioning, restoration, or similar obligation is capitalized to the depreciable cost of the related asset against an offsetting liability (named asset retirement obligation – ARO – under Subtopic 410-20 (FASB Statement No. 143)[211]) and depreciated within the long-lived asset prospectively over the remaining useful life of the asset. Under IAS 16 this happens to the extent that such obligation is recognized as a liability under IAS 37.[212] Subtopic 410-20 (FASB Statement No. 143) is effective for financial statements issued for fiscal years beginning after June 15, 2002. IFRIC 1 is effective for fiscal years beginning on or after September 1, 2004. This paragraph highlights the differences in retained earnings between U.S. GAAP and IFRSs arising from the changes in value of such liabilities.

IFRIC 1 establishes that, when an asset is carried at the revaluation model, a change in the estimates of amount or timing determinants of the estimated cash outflows of a related existing decommissioning, restoration, or similar liability, or a change in the current market-based discount rate affects such liability and follows IAS 16 revaluation rules. Such revaluation rules are here read in the reverse order as compared with IAS 16, as they refer to changes in value of a liability and not of an asset. A decrease in the liability increases revaluation surplus, unless it is recognized in income to the extent it reverses a revaluation deficit that had previously been expensed. In case the liability decreases in excess of the carrying amount of the related asset that would result if the cost model were adopted, the asset is reduced to nil against the revaluation surplus and any excess is recognized in profit or loss. An increase in the liability first reduces revaluation surplus of that asset, then it is expensed to the extent of the excess. All changes in the liability subsequent to when the related asset has reached the end of its useful life must be recognized in profit or loss as they occur.[213]

> **Comment:** As the revaluation model is not allowed under U.S. GAAP, Subtopic 410-20 (FASB Statement No. 143) may be compared to IFRIC 1 only with reference to the cost model. Under both standards, if the entity uses this model, a change in estimate of the liability is capitalized to the cost of the related asset against an offsetting change in liability. However under Subtopic 410-20 (FASB Statement No. 143), if the expected present value of the liability increases, separate ARO liabilities arise per period of revision to record incremental obligations, unless this is not practical, in which case a weighted-average credit-adjusted risk-free rate can be used. The incremental ARO is depreciated prospectively. If the revision increase impacts one period only, the incremental ARO is fully depreciated in that period.[214] If the expected present value decreases, IFRIC 1 recognizes a gain only to the extent of the excess of the decrease over the asset's carrying amount.[215] Subtopic 410-20 (FASB Statement No. 143) uses the current credit-adjusted free-risk rate for decreases and an historical credit-adjusted free-risk rate for increases, while IFRIC 1 includes all changes in current market-based discount rate in the calculation of both the present value and the unwinding of discount.[216] Furthermore, contrary to Subtopic 410-20 (FASB Statement No. 143), IFRIC 1 does not

---

[211] *FASB Statement No. 143, Accounting for Asset Retirement Obligations, Footnote 1.*

[212] *IAS 16, ¶¶ 16(c), 18; IAS 37, Provisions, Contingent Liabilities and Contingent Assets, Appendix C, Example 3.*

[213] *IFRIC Interpretation No. 1, Changes in Existing Decommissioning, Restoration and Similar Liabilities, ¶¶ 6–8, B25(d).*

[214] *FASB ASC 410-20-35-8, 410-20-55-19, 410-20-55-20 (FASB Statement No. 143, ¶¶ 15, A26–A27.*

[215] *IFRIC 1, ¶ 5.*

[216] *FASB ASC 410-20-35-8 (FASB Statement No. 143, ¶ 15); FASB Statement No. 143, ¶ B54; IFRIC 1, ¶¶ IE5, BC3, BC19.*

address changes in decommissioning, restoration, and similar liabilities resulting from new legal or contractual requirements.[217] Under both standards (and with both the revaluation and cost models, under IFRSs), accretion cost for the periodic unwinding of the discount due to passage of time is charged in the income statement as it occurs, and is counterbalanced by an increase in the liability.[218] However, Subtopic 410-20 (FASB Statement No. 143) accounts for the unwinding of the discount before determining the impact of a change in estimate.[219]

Entities already reporting under IFRSs must retrospectively apply IFRIC 1, if practicable, while this is an option for IFRS first-time adopters.

Comment: A change of the decommissioning liability is retrospectively capitalized and depreciated from the date of the revised estimate. The impact on the beginning balance of retained earnings amounts to the cumulative unwinding of the discount related to the change in estimate plus (in case of the cost model) the accumulated depreciation on the change in estimate that would have been capitalized on the asset. If the entity adopts the revaluation model, retrospective application also affects revaluation surplus for the changes in value of the liability and revaluation of the asset. The policy followed by the entity to account for the accumulated depreciation at revaluation date also influences accumulated depreciation.

Comment: Some constituents found retrospective application inconsistent with the IAS 8 prospective accounting for changes in accounting estimates, for example for changes in the estimate of an asset's residual value or useful life.[220] Furthermore, retrospective application seems somewhat inconsistent with the transitional provision for adopting the fair value model of IAS 40 for the first time (see Section 6.4.10 previously) that seeks to avoid any possible manipulation in allocating fair values across periods.

Comment: On its first application, Subtopic 410-20 (FASB Statement No. 143) requires the recognition of AROs adjusted by cumulative accretion, of asset retirement costs capitalized on assets, and of accumulated depreciation. The cumulative-effect adjustment is recognized in the income statement as per the current-method under APB 20, including pro forma information as if Subtopic 410-20 (FASB Statement No. 143) had been applied from the date of the obligation.[221] However, the transitional provisions of Subtopic 410-20 (FASB Statement No. 143) require the use of assumptions and information current as of the date of adoption, as opposed to the full retrospective approach of IFRIC 1 (although IFRIC 1 contains an impracticability exception).[222]

Alternatively, as an accommodation for changes that occurred before the date of transition to IFRSs, an IFRS first-time adopter may opt to measure the liability at transition date at its revised estimate under IAS 37, discount it to the date it was first incurred at the historical risk-adjusted discount rates applicable in that period, and compute the accretion costs of

---

[217] *FASB ASC 410-20-55-19 (FASB Statement No. 143, ¶ A26); IFRIC 1, ¶ BC23.*
[218] *FASB ASC 410-20-55-18 (FASB Statement No. 143, ¶ A25); IFRIC 1, ¶ 8.*
[219] *FASB ASC 410-20-35-3 (FASB Statement No. 143, ¶ 13).*
[220] *IFRIC 1, ¶¶ BC14–BC18.*
[221] *FASB Statement No. 143, ¶¶ 24–27.*
[222] *FASB Statement No. 143, ¶¶ 25, B82–B84, B90.*

prior periods as unwinding of the discount. It then capitalizes the change in valuation into the cost of the asset and depreciates it to the transition date using the current estimate of the useful life of the asset. This accommodation avoids modifying the depreciable basis by considering all the historical record of changes in estimates that occurred before the transition date. However, this exemption does not neutralize the effect in opening retained earnings of any difference between the carrying amount of the liability and the amount of the decommissioning obligation included in the asset value that is due to its depreciation and any asset impairment loss.[223]

Comment: The impact of such IFRS 1 exemption on the opening balance of retained earnings at the transition date, as opposed to the retroactive application, amounts to the change in estimate that would have been capitalized on the asset and the related accumulated depreciation. The liability at transition date and the cumulative unwinding of discount are equal under the two methods.

Effectively for annual periods beginning on or after January 1, 2010 (with earlier application permitted), IFRS 1 requires a treatment different from either retroactive application of IFRIC 1 or from the alternative accounting under IFRS 1 to an IFRS first-time adopter that used the full cost method under prior GAAP to account for oil and gas properties in the development or production phases. Of course, the prerequisite is that such an entity elects the full cost method under prior GAAP as deemed cost at transition date (a further IFRS 1 exemption). In this case, the difference between the decommissioning, restoration, or similar liability measured at the transition date under IAS 37 and the carrying amount at the same date under prior GAAP affects the opening balance of retained earnings.[224]

6.4.17   Defined Pension and Other Postretirement Plans

Topic 715 (FASB Statement No. 158) requires recognition of the overfunded or underfunded status of defined benefit pension or other postretirement plans in the statement of financial position and of period changes in comprehensive income. Gains or losses and prior service costs or credits that are not recognized as components of net periodic costs are reported net of tax in other comprehensive income. This is better analyzed in Section 7.18.1 later. This paragraph focuses on the impact on retained earnings. Application of the standard is prospective and retrospective application is not permitted. The impact of first adoption on other comprehensive income affects year-end balances and the effect of change of measurement date on net periodic cost affects the beginning balance of retained earnings. In fact, in the year of first adoption of the standard, an entity that used to have a measurement date other than fiscal year end must remeasure plan assets and the defined benefit obligation as of the beginning of the fiscal year of adoption of the standard. The company must adjust the opening balance of retained earnings, through a separate line item, by the net periodic cost net of tax (exclusive of any curtailment or settlement gain or loss) that would have been recognized on a delayed basis under Topic 715 (FASB Statement No. 87) in the first interim period fiscal year of adoption of the standard. Alternatively, such entity must prorate, based on passage of time, net periodic cost (exclusive of any curtailment or settlement gain or loss) of the period from the earlier measurement date

---

[223]   *IFRS 1, ¶¶ D21, IG13, BC63C; IFRIC 1, ¶¶ 10, BC33.*
[224]   *IFRS 1, ¶¶ D21A, BC63CA.*

to the end of the fiscal year of adoption of the standard between an adjustment to the opening balance of retained earnings and current earnings.[225] Entities must separately disclose the effects of the initial application of the measurement provisions of FASB Statement No. 158 on retained earnings either in the statement of changes in equity or in the notes.[226]

6.4.18 Leases

EITF Issue 01-8 and IFRIC 4 provide guidance to distinguish leases from service contracts and from take-or-pay and similar contracts. IFRIC 4 applies for annual periods beginning on or after January 1, 2006. It permits either retrospective or prospective application for arrangements existing as of the beginning of the earliest comparative period presented to be assessed on the basis of facts and circumstances existing at that date.[227] By analogy with entities that already apply IFRSs, an IFRS first-time adopter may apply IFRIC 4 prospectively, as an accommodation, from the date of transition to IFRSs, based on facts and circumstances existing at that date, as opposed to retrospectively applying the interpretation and subsequently reassessing the arrangements.[228] Effectively for annual periods beginning on or after January 1, 2010 (with earlier application permitted), reassessment of whether an arrangement contains a lease is not required of an IFRS first-time adopter that under prior GAAP reached the same (not similar) conclusion as IFRIC 4 but at a different date.[229]

EITF Issue 01-8 applies to arrangements agreed to (or committed to, if earlier), modified, or acquired in a business combination after the beginning of an entity's next reporting period beginning after May 28, 2003.[230]

IAS 17 might be applied either retrospectively to each lease from the inception of the arrangement, or prospectively, in which case the balance of any finance lease existing before annual periods beginning on or after January 1, 2005 was deemed to have been properly determined by the lessor. If the entity had applied the 1997 revision of IAS 17 retroactively, subsequent amendments concerning leases of land and buildings must have been applied retroactively; otherwise prospectively from the inception of each arrangement subsequent to the first adoption of the standard.[231] An IFRS first-time adopter must apply IAS 17 retroactively. This may create some differences between new adopters and companies that already applied IFRSs because, contrary to the method that a first-time adopter must follow, the net cash investment method for recognizing the finance income of lessors was prospectively eliminated by the 1997 revision of IAS 17 and the accounting for incentives under SIC 15 did not require retrospective application either.[232]

---

[225] *FASB ASC 715-20-65-1, 958-715-65-1 (FASB Statement No. 158,* Employers' Accounting for Defined Benefit Pension and Other Postretirement Plans, ¶¶ *15–19, 21); FASB Statement No. 158,* ¶¶ *B68, B90.*

[226] *FASB ASC 715-20-65-1 (FASB Statement No. 158, ¶ 21); FASB Statement No. 158, ¶ B60.*

[227] *IFRIC 4,* Determining Whether an Arrangement Contains a Lease, ¶¶ *16–17.*

[228] *IFRS 1,* ¶¶ *D9, BC63D, IG205.*

[229] *Amendments to IFRS 1,* Additional Exemptions for First/time Adopters, ¶¶ *D9A, BC63DA, BC63DB (July 2009).*

[230] *EITF Issue No. 01-8, ¶ 16.*

[231] *IAS 17,* Leases, ¶¶ *66–68*

[232] *IFRS 1,* ¶¶ *IG15–IG16.*

FASB Statement No. 13 permitted either retroactive or prospective application for transactions entered into on or after January 1, 1977 and requested retroactive application, including restatement of prior periods, for years beginning after December 31, 1980. The cumulative effect on retained earnings as of the beginning of the earliest period restated was accounted for by a variant of the current-method under APB 20 where only the income statement of the first period restated, even if prior to the first period presented, showed the cumulative-effect adjustment.[233]

6.4.19 Compound Financial Instruments

Under IFRSs, contrary to U.S. GAAP, split accounting applies to the equity and liability components of a compound financial instrument. An IFRS first-time adopter must retroactively apply spit accounting to a compound financial instrument outstanding at the transition date, thus adjusting the opening balance of retained earnings by the cumulative interest accreted to the liability component of the compound financial instrument and reporting the original equity component separately as another component in equity. However, if at the date of transition to IFRSs the liability component is no longer outstanding it is exempted from this separation. Upon the application of the February 2008 amendments to IAS 32, the same exemption applies, under the same circumstances, to a compound instrument that includes an obligation to deliver a pro rata share of net assets only on liquidation.[234]

6.4.20 Share-Based Payments

IFRS 2 is effective for annual periods beginning on or after January 1, 2005. IFRS 2 encourages but does not mandate a full retroactive approach. The restatement of prior periods and the adjustment of the beginning balance of retained earnings for the earliest period presented is limited to equity instruments granted after November 7, 2002 and not yet vested at the effective date of the standard (for an IFRS first-time adopter such equity instruments must not have vested at the later of the date of transition to IFRSs and January 1, 2005). The same retroactive approach is required for liabilities arising from share-based payment transactions that are still in place at the effective date of the standard, but only to the extent of information that dates back to later than November 7, 2002. Certain disclosures are required for instruments that were granted before that date.[235]

As mentioned in Section 5.2.10 previously, IFRS 2 provides no specific guidance on how to display the increase in equity for goods or services received in relation to equity-settled share-based payment transactions in the equity section of the statement of financial position. As explained, display in retained earnings is one of the approaches found in practice.

FASB Statement No. 123(R) applies to awards granted, modified, repurchased, or cancelled after December 15, 2005, or June 15, 2005 for public entities that do not file as small business issuers. A full retrospective transition was rejected on the grounds of impracticability of certain estimation aspects. For entities that already used the fair value-based recognition or disclosure under Subtopic 718-740 (FASB Statement No. 123), the revised standard requires

---

[233] *FASB Statement No. 13*, Accounting for Leases, ¶¶ *48–51; FASB Technical Bulletin No. 79-17*, Reporting Cumulative Effect Adjustment from Retroactive Application of FASB Statement No. 13.

[234] *IFRS 1*, ¶¶ *D18, BC56–BC58; IAS 32*, ¶¶ *97, 97C.*

[235] *IFRS 2*, ¶¶ *53, 55, 56, 58–60, IG8; IFRS 1*, ¶¶ *D2, D3; IFRS 1 (Revised 2005)*, ¶¶ *25B–25C.*

a modified prospective application under which compensation cost is recorded at the effective date only for the portion of outstanding awards for which the requisite service has not yet been rendered, based on their grant-date fair value calculated under FASB Statement No. 123, *Accounting for Stock-Based Compensation*. Changes to the grant-date fair value are accounted for prospectively. Any contra-equity accounts for unearned or deferred compensation related to those earlier awards must be eliminated within equity. A modified retrospective application based on pro forma calculation under FASB Statement No. 123 is optional for periods before the effective date of FASB Statement No. 123(R), either for prior interim periods in the year of adoption of FASB Statement No. 123(R) or for all periods in which FASB Statement No. 123 was effective. In the latter case, which is mandatory for a nonpublic company that applied FASB Statement No. 123 after its effective date, the beginning balances of retained earnings, paid-in capital, and deferred taxes for the earliest period presented are adjusted and disclosed in the year of adoption of the standard. For both modified prospective and modified retrospective applications, the initial adjustment to measure a freestanding financial instrument at fair value (or a portion of it if the requisite service has not been rendered) that is classified as liability under the standard and under Subtopic 480-10 (FASB Statement No. 150) is accounted for as a cumulative effect of a change in accounting principle. If such instrument was previously classified as equity, firstly it is generally reversed from paid-in capital and any difference is then accounted for as mentioned above. A prospective method applies to nonpublic entities that used the minimum value method of measuring equity share options and similar instruments for recognition or pro forma disclosure under FASB Statement No. 123.[236]

Previously, with regard to the recognition (not disclosure) of stock-based employee compensation, an entity could apply FASB Statement No. 123 in a fiscal year beginning before December 16, 2003 by adopting either a prospective, or a modified prospective, or a retroactive restatement method. The modified prospective method consisted of applying the fair value-based accounting method of FASB Statement No. 123, as of the beginning of the year of adoption of such recognition provisions of the standard, to all employee awards granted, modified, or settled in fiscal years beginning after December 15, 1994. The retroactive restatement method reflected the application of the recognition provisions of the standards to those awards by restating prior periods but only for the periods presented. An adjustment to the beginning balance of retained earnings and of additional paid-in capital accounted for the cumulative effects on those accounts of the restatement of periods before the earliest period presented. An entity that applied the recognition provisions of FASB Statement No 123 in a fiscal year beginning after December 15, 2003 could use the two latter methods only.[237]

6.4.21 Past Business Combinations

IFRS 1 gives an IFRS first-time adopter the option to apply IFRS 3 retroactively to past business combinations (that is, those that occurred before transition date to IFRSs), or apply it retrospectively from a chosen prior date (in such a case all later combinations must also be restated and the related revisions of IAS 36 and IAS 38 must be applied from the same date of adoption of IFRS 3), or be exempted from applying IFRS 3 retrospectively.[238] In the latter

---

[236] *FASB Statement No. 123(R)*, Share-Based Payment, ¶¶ 69–72, 74, 76, 77, 79, 83, B251, B256.

[237] *FASB ASC 718-10-S99-1 (FASB Statement No. 153*, Accounting for Stock-Based Compensation, ¶¶ 52–53; *SEC Staff Accounting Bulletin, Topic 14-H*, First Time Adoption of Statement 123R in an Interim Period).

[238] *IFRS 1, ¶ C1; IFRS 1 (Revised 2005), ¶ B1.*

case, certain procedures, as illustrated in Worksheet 36, apply. As shown, retained earnings are affected, and such impact must be considered when reconciling to U.S. GAAP.

6.4.22 Cumulative Translation Adjustment

Cumulative foreign currency translation adjustment is analyzed in Section 7.10 later. An IFRS first-time adopter may use an exemption under IFRS 1 from retroactively accounting for all qualifying foreign operations since they were acquired or created. In such a case, at the date of transition to IFRSs it must reset any translation reserve that existed in equity against retained earnings.[239]

6.4.23 Hyperinflation

The initial application of IAS 29, *Financial Reporting in Hyperinflationary Economies*, requires the restatement of the opening statement of financial position as of the beginning of the earliest period presented. Equity, except retained earnings and revaluation surplus (that is eliminated), is also restated by applying a general price index from the date of contribution or otherwise origination of each component of equity. The restatement of retained earnings then results as the balancing figure of the restated statement of financial position. At the end of the first period of application of IAS 29 and in subsequent periods, all equity components must be restated in terms of the measuring unit current at the reporting period date by applying a general price index from the beginning of the current year or the date of contribution, if later. The gain or loss on the net monetary position is included in profit or loss, which is then added to the restated opening balance of retained earnings to determine the closing balance of retained earnings.[240]

Contrary to IAS 29, Subtopic 830-10 (FASB Statement No. 52) does not permit the presentation of inflation-adjusted primary financial statements for a company that uses the U.S. dollar as its reporting currency, but requires the remeasurement method as if the functional currency were the reporting currency.[241] However, Subtopic 255-10 (FASB Statement No. 89) encourages, but does not require, a business enterprise that prepares its financial statements in U.S. dollars and in accordance with U.S. GAAP to disclose supplementary information on the effects of changing prices based on current cost/constant purchasing power accounting.[242] Subtopic 255-10 (FASB Statement No. 89) permits a restate-translate method (see Section 7.12 later), to a certain extent similarly to that used under IAS 29 and IAS 21. A parity adjustment measures the effect of the difference between local and U.S. inflation for the year on net assets measured in nominal dollars. As explained in Section 7.12 later, the parity adjustment may be combined with the translation adjustment and displayed as a component of equity.[243]

---

[239] *IFRS 1, ¶ D13.*

[240] *IAS 29, ¶¶ 8, 24, 28, 34; IFRIC Interpretation No. 7, Applying the Restatement Approach Under IAS 29 Financial Reporting in Hyperinflationary Economies, ¶ 3.*

[241] *FASB ASC 830-10-45-11 (FASB Statement No. 52, Foreign Currency Translation, ¶ 11); FASB Statement No. 52, ¶ Appendix C, 105.*

[242] *FASB Statement No. 89, Financial Reporting and Changing Prices, ¶ 1.*

[243] *FASB ASC 255-10-50-49, 255-10-55-85, 255-10-55-86, 255-10-55-87, 255-10-55-88, 255-10-55-89 (FASB Statement No. 89, ¶¶ 39, 44, 95).*

A foreign private issuer based in countries with highly inflationary economies:[244]

- Can present U.S. GAAP financial statements in U.S. dollars at remeasurement method under Subtopic 830-10 (FASB Statement No. 52);
- Can present its primary financial statements in the highly-inflationary currency with a convenience translation to USD, subject to the limitations applicable to convenience translations;
- Can present its primary financial statements with supplemental information under the historical cost/constant currency or current cost approach, such as Subtopic 255-10 (FASB Statement No. 89) information, or disclose quantification of the effects of changing prices;
- If it reports under U.S. GAAP, can apply the guidance of APB Statement No. 3 rescinded by SOP 93-3 (FASB ASC 255-10-45) to present, to a certain extent similarly to IAS 29, primary price-level-adjusted financial statements (retroactively restated in equivalent purchasing power units of the reporting currency), where required or permitted by home-country GAAP and to the extent that that presentation is not inconsistent with the guidance in FASB Statement No. 89, with no reconciliation with historical cost financial statements, if the financial statements are intended for readers in the U.S.; or
- Can apply historical-cost-based primary financial statements for restatement under the historical cost/constant currency or current cost approach under home-country GAAP, with no reconciliation with U.S. GAAP on the effects of price level changes, provided the basis of presentation of the price-level adjustments and that such effects are excluded from the reconciliation to U.S. GAAP are disclosed. In particular, the use of IAS 29 falls into this accommodation;
- If a parent, may provide consolidated financial statements where the subsidiary's statements are first restated under IAS 29 and then translated under IAS 21, without reconciling the difference in methods with U.S. GAAP. However, a U.S. entity with a subsidiary or equity investee in hyperinflationary economies must use the remeasurement method under Subtopic 830-10 (FASB Statement No. 52).

6.4.24 Negative Goodwill

Under the 2004 revision of IFRS 3, negative goodwill (then referred to as "excess of the acquirer's interest," now under IFRS 3 R and Subtopic 805-10 (FASB Statement No. 141(R)) simply "excess"), that had been recognized on a business combination for which the agreement date was before March 31, 2004 or that had originated before March 31, 2004 as part of an equity-method investment or of an interest in a jointly controlled entity accounted for at proportionate consolidation, had to be derecognized at the beginning of the period starting on or after March 31, 2004, with a corresponding adjustment to the opening balance of retained earnings.[245]

---

[244] *FASB ASC 255-10-45 (AICPA Statement of Position No. 93-3*, Rescission of Accounting Principles Board Statements, ¶ 08); *Regulation S-X, ¶ 210.3-20; Form 20-F, Item 17(c)(2)(IV); U.S. Securities and Exchange Commission*, International Reporting and Disclosure Issues in the Division of Corporate Finance, ¶ XI, Reporting in Highly Inflationary Economies, *(November 1, 2004); SEC*, Financial Reporting Manual, ¶¶ 6540.2, 6700.

[245] *IFRS 3 (Revised 2004), ¶¶ 81, 84.*

> **Comment:** Under IAS 22 (superseded), negative goodwill was presented as a deduction from the assets in the same balance sheet classification as goodwill. Under certain local GAAP it was recorded as a component of shareholders' equity in a "consolidation reserve."

The original FASB Statement No. 141 was effective for all business combinations initiated on or after July 1, 2001. FASB Statement No. 142 is effective for fiscal years beginning after December 15, 2001. Unamortized negative goodwill that referred to business combination or equity-method investments acquired before July 1, 2001 and that was remaining at the earlier of the start of fiscal years beginning after December 15, 2001 or the date of adoption of Statement No. 142 in its entirety, had to be written off and be reported as cumulative change in accounting principle in the income statement, after reclassifying intangible assets that did or did not warrant individual recognition under those standards.[246]

6.4.25 Provisions and Contingent Liabilities

IAS 37 is effective for years beginning on or after July 1, 1999. In the year of adoption, the cumulative-type effect had to be shown as adjustment of the beginning balance of retained earnings. The standard encourages, but does not require, adjustment for the earliest period presented and restatement of prior periods.[247]

FASB Statement No. 5 is effective for fiscal years beginning on or after July 1, 1975. It requires restatement of prior periods presented, unless impracticable, in which case restatement should be made from the date it became practicable. The cumulative-type effect had to be shown in the income statement at the beginning of the earliest period restated or of the period of first adoption of the standard if prior periods could not be restated.[248]

6.4.26 Initial Adjustments Arising from the Application of IFRIC 14

IFRIC 14 provides guidance on when refunds or reductions in future contributions on a defined benefit plan should be regarded as available, how a minimum funding requirement might affect the availability of reductions in future contributions, and when a minimum funding requirement might give rise to a liability. The interpretation is effective for financial periods beginning on or after January 1, 2008. Earlier application is permitted. The initial adjustments arising from the application of IFRIC 14 must affect beginning retained earnings of the first period presented in the first financial statements to which the interpretation applies.[249] The same method of transition applies to the amendments to IFRIC 14 issued in November 2009, effective for annual periods beginning on or after January 1, 2011.[250]

---

[246] *FASB Statement No. 141*, Business Combinations, ¶¶ *59, 61-62; FASB ASC 205-20-50-3 (FASB Statement No. 142, Goodwill and Other Intangible Assets, ¶ 48).*

[247] *IAS 37, ¶¶ 93, 95.*

[248] *FASB Statement No. 5 (as amended by FASB Statement No. 11, Accounting for Contingencies – Transition Method), ¶¶ 20, 104.*

[249] *IFRIC Interpretation No. 14*, IAS 19 – The Limit on a Defined Benefit Asset, Minimum Funding Requirements and their Interaction, ¶¶ *27–28.*

[250] *Amendments to IFRIC 14*, Prepayments of a Minimum Funding Requirement, ¶¶ *27B, 29 (November 2009).*

6.4.27   Income Taxes (Exposure Draft)

The transitional provisions of the IASB's Exposure Draft on income tax (see Chapter 8 later) propose an adjustment to the beginning balance of retained earnings for the tax effects due to the net change in the assets and liabilities existing in the opening statement of financial position of the first annual period beginning on or after the effective date of the new standard. The new standard would apply prospectively thereafter. However, the new intraperiod tax allocation rules introduced by the Exposure Draft and in particular the subsequent tax allocation to profit or loss of certain amounts previously recognized in other comprehensive income or equity must not be applied retrospectively. Therefore, this adjustment to retained earnings would not include any cumulative-effect restatement of amounts previously recognized in other comprehensive income or equity.[251]

The Exposure Draft proposes an amendment to IFRS 1 for the introduction of a new exemption for IFRS first-time adopters with a transition date before that of the new standard. As an accommodation, those entities may elect to maintain IAS 12 for any comparative period presented that starts before the date of issue of the new standard.[252]

The Exposure Draft proposes an amendment to IFRS 1 for the introduction of a new exception for IFRS first-time adopters with a transition date after that of the new standard. Those entities would also apply the new intraperiod tax allocation rules prospectively from its date of transition to IFRSs. The cumulative amounts of tax on items of income and expenses that at the transition date are recognized in accumulated other comprehensive income or that are recognized in equity would not be reclassified to profit and loss on derecognition of the related asset or liability any longer. In fact, those entities must deem those amounts recognized outside profit or loss (either in other comprehensive income or directly in equity) to be zero at the transition date.[253]

On initial application of FASB Statement No. 96, the predecessor of FASB Statement No. 109, in the earliest comparative year presented when the earliest year restated was not presented, an entity had to restate the beginning balance of retained earnings or of the appropriate component of equity affected by the intraperiod tax allocation rules applied, inter alia, to tax benefits of quasi-reorganizations (see Section 5.2.3 previously and Section 6.5.3 later), stock options, and tax on items of other comprehensive income (see Chapter 7 following). A cumulative effect of a change in accounting principle accounted for other situations.[254] FASB Statement No. 109 had similar transitional provisions for all situations where a tax benefit was excluded from comprehensive income and allocated directly to contributed capital or retained earnings. Other circumstances required the recording of a cumulative effect of a change in accounting principle.[255]

6.4.28   Embedded Credit Derivative Features

ASU No. 2010-11 clarifies and limits the breadth of the embedded credit derivative scope exception of Subsections 815-15-15-8 and 15-9 (Paragraph 14B of FASB Statement No. 133),

---

[251] *Exposure Draft*, Income Tax, ¶¶ *50–51, BC115(b) (March 2009)*.

[252] *Exposure Draft*, Income Tax, ¶¶ *C2, BC120 (March 2009)*.

[253] *Exposure Draft*, Income Tax, ¶¶ *C2, BC118 (March 2009)*.

[254] *FASB Statement No. 96*, Accounting for Income Taxes, ¶ *33 (superseded); Implementation Guides – Q&A 96*, A Guide to Implementation of Statement 96 on Accounting for Income Taxes: Questions and Answers, *(superseded)*, ¶ 47.

[255] *FASB Statement No. 109*, ¶ 51.

relating to the transfer of credit risk in the form of subordination of one financial instrument to another. Embedded credit derivative features (other than the concentration of credit risk in the form of subordination of one financial instrument to another), including those in some CDOs (collateralized credit obligations) and synthetic CDOs, are considered embedded derivatives that must be analyzed under Topic 815 (FASB Statement No. 133) for potential bifurcation and separate accounting, provided that the overall contract is not a derivative in its entirety. Bifurcation is not warranted only with respect of the embedded credit derivative feature between the holders of interests in tranches created by subordination. Conversely, analysis for potential bifurcation is required for other embedded credit derivative features, including when the holder of an interest in a tranche of securitized financial instruments has an exposure in potential future payments related to credit risk outside that created by subordination, or in the case of a single-tranche securitization vehicle. These amendments are effective starting from the first fiscal quarter beginning after June 15, 2010. At the date of adoption of the ASU, when bifurcation of a contract containing embedded credit derivative features that no longer qualify for the scope exception is determined to be warranted and the entity does not elect the fair value option, a cumulative-effect adjustment to the beginning balance of retained earnings records the difference between the total carrying amount of the bifurcated components and that of the hybrid instrument before bifurcation. For disclosure purposes, the entity is required to break down the cumulative-effect adjustment into gross gains and gross losses on an instrument-by-instrument basis. In the case where the entity elects to fair value measure an investment in a beneficial interest in a securitized financial asset, beginning retained earnings include the cumulative unrealized gains and losses at the date of adoption. If the entity had reported changes in the fair value of the investment in other comprehensive income, the election as at fair value through earnings implies recycling of accumulated other comprehensive income at the date of adoption.[256]

IFRSs do not have a similar scope exception for embedded credit derivatives.[257]

6.4.29   Initial Application of IFRS 9

IFRS 9 is effective for annual periods beginning on or after January 1, 2013, with earlier application permitted. A recent Exposure Draft proposes to move the effective date of IFRS 9 from January 1, 2013 to January 1, 2015. This is intended to have the same effective date for all steps of the project concerning financial instruments, including the phases still to be completed. Earlier adoption of IFRS 9 would be permitted.[258] When an entity initially applies IFRS 9 at the beginning of a reporting period (which is mandatory if the entity adopts IFRS 9 on or after January 1, 2011), an adjustment to the beginning balance of retained earnings reports any difference between the fair value of an entire hybrid contract under IFRS 9 and the sum of the fair values of the previously-bifurcated nonderivative host and the embedded derivative at the date of initial application of the standard. Conversely, this difference affects profit or loss for an entity that initially applies IFRS 9 during a reporting period. In addition, an adjustment to the beginning balance of retained earnings of the reporting period that includes the date of initial application of IFRS 9 must reflect any difference between the fair value at

---

[256] *FASB ASC 815-15-15-9, 815-15-25-51A, 815-10-65-5 (Accounting Standards Update No. 2010-11, Derivatives and Hedging (Topic 815) – Scope Exception Related to Embedded Credit Derivatives, ¶¶ 4, 8, 13).*

[257] *IFRS 9, ¶¶ 4.3.2, 4.3.3, B4.3.5(f); IAS 39, ¶ AG30(h).*

[258] *Exposure Draft,* Amendments to IFRS 9 Financial Instruments *(November 2009)* and IFRS 9 Financial Instruments *(October 2010):* Mandatory Effective Date *(August 2011).*

the date of initial application of IFRS 9 of an investment in an unquoted equity instrument (or a linked or a related to-be-physically-settled derivative) and its previous carrying amount at cost under IAS 39. Finally, IFRS 9 does not require an entity that adopts the standard for reporting periods beginning before January 1, 2012 to restate prior periods. In such a case, the effect of initial adoption affects the beginning balance of retained earnings or any other component of equity, as applicable.[259]

A similar exemption from restating comparative information under IFRS 9 and related disclosures under IFRS 7 applies to an IFRS first-time adopter that adopts IFRS 9 for reporting periods beginning before January 1, 2012. Any resulting difference with previous GAAP is accounted for as a change in accounting policy (also see Section 6.4.13 previously).[260]

6.4.30   Currency Denomination of Share-Based Payment Awards

ASU No. 2010-13 deals with employee share-based payment transactions where the currency of denomination of the exercise price is that of a market where the entity trades a substantial portion of its equity instruments. It clarifies that such a situation does not trigger liability classification, even when such a currency differs from the functional currency of the entity or from the payroll currency of the employee. The ASU is effective for periods beginning on or after December 15, 2010. Beginning retained earnings must include a separately presented cumulative-effect adjustment concerning all awards outstanding at the beginning of the fiscal year of initial application of the ASU.[261]

6.4.31   Initial Application of FASB Statement No. 167

FASB Statement No. 167 eliminates the quantitative method for determining the primary beneficiary of a variable interest entity (VIE) and replaces it with a primarily qualitative approach to identify which enterprise has the power to direct the activities of a variable interest entity that most significantly impact the entity's economic performance and the obligation to absorb losses of the entity or the right to receive benefits from the entity. The standard requires ongoing reassessments of whether an enterprise is the primary beneficiary of a variable interest entity, as opposed to only when specific events occurred as under previous guidance. It also eliminates the exception based on which a troubled debt restructuring was not an event that required reconsideration of VIE and primary beneficiary status. Enhanced disclosures are required. The standard is effective as of the beginning annual reporting period that begins after November 15, 2009 and related interim periods. Its requirements have been included in ASU 2009-17.

An entity recognizes the equity effects of the initial application of FASB Statement No. 167 as a cumulative adjustment to retained earnings. Separate lines are necessary for the effect of new consolidations and deconsolidations.[262]

---

[259] *IFRS 9, ¶¶ 8.2.2, 8.2.6, 8.2.11, 8.2.12.*
[260] *IFRS 1 (2003 and amended May 2008), ¶¶ 36D, 36E, as amended by IFRS 9; IFRS 1 (Revised November 2009), ¶¶ E1, E2, as amended by IFRS 9.*
[261] *FASB ASC 718-10-25-14A, 718-10-65-2 (FASB Accounting Standards Update No. 2010-13, Compensation – Stock Compensation (Topic 718): Effect of Denominating the Exercise Price of a Share-Based Payment Award in the Currency of the Market in Which the Underlying Equity Security Trades, ¶¶ 2, 4).*
[262] *FASB ASC 810-10-30-8D, 810-10-30-9, 810-10-65-2 (FASB Statement No. 167, Amendments to FASB Interpretation No. 46(R), ¶¶ 5, 6, 7, 9), as amended by Accounting Standards Update*

6.4.32 Embedded Credit Derivative Scope Exception

ASU 2010-11 is effective as of the beginning of the first fiscal quarter beginning after June 15, 2010. It clarifies that only the transfer of credit risk that is created by subordination of one financial instrument to another is an embedded derivative feature that is not subject to potential bifurcation from the host contract and separate accounting as a derivative under Subsection 815-10-15-11 and Section 815-15-25. Conversely, the embedded credit derivative scope exception (Subsections 815-15-15-8 through 15-9) does not apply to other embedded credit derivative features, even if their effects are allocated according to subordination provisions.

By the beginning of the first quarter of adoption of ASU 2010-11, an entity may irrevocably elect fair value measurement for any investment in a beneficial interest in a securitized financial asset. If such an investment was previously carried at fair value with changes in other comprehensive income, the entity must reclassify the accumulated other comprehensive income to beginning retained earnings, as a cumulative effect adjustment. A cumulative effect adjustment to beginning retained earnings also includes the difference between the sum of the individual components of a contract bifurcated under ASU 2010-11 that previously qualified for the scope exception, for which the entity does not elect fair value measurement, and its carrying amount before bifurcation. In the reverse situation (no bifurcation of contracts that were previously bifurcated), no cumulative-effect adjustment arises.[263]

6.4.33 Casino Jackpot Liabilities

ASU No. 20010-16 is effective for financial years, and related interim periods, beginning on or after December 15, 2010. Entities cannot accrue base jackpot liabilities if they are able to avoid payment. The cumulative effect as of the beginning of the period of initial application of this ASU a effects beginning retained earnings.[264] IFRSs have no specific guidance for casinos. However, the concept of a present obligation in IAS 37 is consistent with the conclusions of this ASU.

6.4.34 Insurance Claims and Related Recoveries

Effective for fiscal years, and related interim periods, beginning after December 15, 2010, ASU No. 2010-24 stipulates that health care entities cannot offset anticipated insurance recoveries against medical malpractice claims and similar liabilities. In the period of adoption, beginning retained earnings must reflect any resulting cumulative effect.[265]

6.4.35 Reporting Units with Zero or Negative Carrying Amounts

Under ASU No. 2010-28, a reporting unit with a zero or negative carrying amount must proceed to Step 2 of the goodwill impairment test, even when the fair value of the reporting unit exceeds its carrying amount, if adverse qualitative factors indicate that it is more likely

---

No. 2009-17, Consolidations (Topic 810) – Improvements to Financial Reporting by Enterprises Involved with Variable Interest Entities*).*

[263] *FASB ASC 810-10-65-5 (Accounting Standards Update No. 2010-11,* Derivatives and Hedging (Topic 815) – Scope Exception Related to Embedded Credit Derivatives, *¶¶ 15, BC10).*

[264] *FASB ASC 924-605-65-1 (FASB Accounting Standards Update No. 2010-16,* Entertainment – Casinos (Topic 924) – Accruals for Casino Jackpot Liabilities, *¶ 4).*

[265] *FASB ASC 954-450-65-1 (FASB Accounting Standards Update No. 2010-24,* Health Care Entities (Topic 954) – Presentation of Insurance Claims and Related Insurance Recoveries, *¶ 3).*

than not that an impairment exists. The amendments are effective for fiscal years, and related interim periods, beginning after December 15, 2010 for public companies, and beginning after December 15, 2011 for nonpublic entities. A company must record a cumulative-effect adjustment to beginning retained earnings in the period of adoption of this ASU for any goodwill impairment arising from adopting these amendments.[266]

6.4.36 Joint Arrangements

Effectively for annual periods beginning on or after January 1, 2013, unless earlier applied, the transitional provisions of IFRS 11 require the redetermination of the new classifications starting from the aggregate amounts of assets and liabilities as of the beginning of the earliest period presented as opposed to retrospective application. They require the application of the new classification as equity method under IFRS 11 of an investment that an entity previously carried at proportionate consolidation, or the new configuration as a joint operation of a previously classified equity-method investment, at the beginning of the earliest period presented. The company must adjust beginning retained earnings of the earliest period presented when a reclassification from proportionate consolidation to equity method results in negative net assets for which the investor has no legal or constructive obligation to justify a provision. In the case of the reclassification of an equity-method investment to the accounting for assets and liabilities of a joint operation, any net difference, after an offset with any goodwill of the investment, also results in an adjustment to beginning retained earnings. This also applies in recasting the separate financial statements in which the investor used to account for its investment at cost or at fair value.[267]

IFRS 11 also added an exemption to IFRS 1. When an entity applies IFRS 10 and IFRS 11, it may use this exemption with the same effective date as those standards. This exemption extends the abovementioned transitional provisions of IFRS 11 to IFRS first-time adopters on an elective basis. However, the company must test for impairment the investment under IAS 36 and not IAS 28, irrespective of the existence of impairment indicators, and charge any resulting adjustment to beginning retained earnings of the earliest period presented.[268]

6.4.37 Initial Application of IFRS 10

IFRS 10 replaces IAS 27 and SIC-12. It introduces a single model of consolidation based on control for all types of entities. IFRS 10 is effective for annual periods beginning on or after January 1, 2013, unless earlier applied. The transitional provisions of IFRS 10 require the recording of a cumulative-effect adjustment to the opening balance of equity for any differences arising from the consolidation under IFRS 10 of an investee that was not consolidated under IAS 27 or SIC-12. A similar situation arises for the deconsolidation of a previously consolidated investee. However, the standard mentions equity and not retained earnings, a fact that the IASB proposes to adjust.[269]

---

[266] *FASB ASC 350-20-35-8A, 350-20-35-30, 350-10-65-2 (FASB Accounting Standards Update No. 2010-28,* Intangibles – Goodwill and Other (Topic 350) – When to Perform Step 2 of the Goodwill Impairment Test for Reporting Units with Zero or Negative Carrying Amounts, ¶¶ 2, 3.
[267] *IFRS 11, ¶¶ C1–C13.*
[268] *IFRS 1, as amended by IFRS 11, ¶¶ 39I, D31.*
[269] *IFRS 10, ¶¶ C4, C5.*

6.5 ITEMS THAT MAY AFFECT THE ENDING BALANCE OF RETAINED EARNINGS

The ending balance of retained earnings is ordinarily affected by the net profit or loss of the period and by distributions of dividends. However, there are additional situations when the ending, and not the beginning, balance of retained earnings (as illustrated in Section 6.4 previously), may be affected. These are explained in the following paragraphs.

6.5.1 Cumulative-Type Effect Adjustment under Catch-up Method

As mentioned in Section 6.4.1 previously, before FASB Statement No. 154 and before removal of the allowed alternative treatment from IAS 8, a sort of "catch-up" method (where the cumulative-type adjustment was reported on the face of the income statement in the current period) was the general accounting used for changes in accounting policies. This was named "current-method" under U.S. GAAP. Ultimately, the ending balance, not beginning balance, of retained earnings was affected by such adjustments.

6.5.2 Difference in Redemption Value of Mandatorily Redeemable Shares

Subtopic 480-10 (FASB Statement No. 150) requires liability classification for mandatorily redeemable shares. Those shares that exist at the beginning of the interim period of adoption of the standard must be reclassified from equity to liabilities. On the date of adoption of FASB Statement No. 150, an entity reports any excess of the value of those shares measured under the standard over their book value as a cumulative effect of a change in accounting principle in the income statement (similarly to the "current-method" under APB 20). This creates a deficit in equity in case the redemption price exceeds the entity's equity balance (even if the instruments are reported as liabilities). In the reverse situation of a shortage of redemption price to book value (which is the common stock and retained earnings that are attributable to those shares), the difference between the book value and the liability is reported as an excess of assets over liabilities (equity). Restatement of prior periods is not permitted.

Subsequent adjustments of the reported value of such shares at each reporting date to reflect changes in the redemption amount result in interest cost on mandatorily redeemable shares.[270]

> **Comment:** Subtopic 480-10 (FASB Staff position FAS 150-2) does not state whether this surplus is credited directly in equity or through the income statement as a cumulative-type adjustment. While the illustrative example shows the statement of income with a cumulative transition adjustment in case of loss, it does not illustrate this statement in case of a surplus.

> **Comment:** IAS 32 also classifies mandatorily redeemable shares as financial liabilities. This standard in general requires retrospective application.

---

[270] *FASB ASC 480-10-45-2A (FASB Statement No. 150, ¶¶ 29, A30; FASB Staff Position FAS 150-2*, Accounting for Mandatorily Redeemable Shares Requiring Redemption by Payment of an Amount That Differs from the Book Value of Those Shares, under FASB Statement No. 150).

6.5.3   Quasi-Reorganizations

In the U.S. a quasi-reorganization, also referred to as a "readjustment,"[271] is an informal proceeding, outside of formal bankruptcy codes and without the creation of a new corporate entity, that is intended to avoid legal reorganization or formal bankruptcy in future and cover losses or accumulated deficit in retained earnings under certain conditions. It is a one-off event, under circumstances which would justify an actual reorganization or formation of a new corporation.[272] After formal authorization from stockholders and creditors where required, assets are carried to their fair current values and liabilities to present values, losses are charged to retained earnings, and pre-existing additional paid-in capital is offset by accumulated deficit in retained earnings. In case an accumulated deficit still exists, par value is reduced by transferring capital stock to a new additional paid-in capital account, termed "Paid-in capital for quasi-reorganization" (see Section 5.2.3 previously) that is then totally or partially offset by the remaining accumulated deficit.[273]

A quasi-reorganization that is effected only to eliminate a deficit in retained earnings, without restating assets and liabilities to fair values, is called deficit reorganization. It is not permitted to an SEC registrant, even if this is simply because assets and liabilities are already stated at fair values.[274]

Comment: Consistently with the basic principle of retained earnings, no increase in retained earnings may arise from a deficit reorganization (a paid-in capital for quasi-reorganization account may arise) and no retained earnings may remain.[275] In any case, the procedure cannot result in a write up of net assets.[276] In a broad sense, quasi-organization constitutes another exception to the clean-surplus concept, because asset write downs or other adjustments are not charged to net income.[277]

For an SEC registrant, a deficit reclassification of any nature is considered to be quasi-reorganization and is not permitted unless all prescriptions in Section 210 of the Codification of Financial Reporting Policies are followed. One of these conditions is that no deficit must exist in any surplus account after the quasi-reorganization.[278]

In case of a voluntary change in accounting principle that would be adopted within 12 months following the quasi-reorganization, a registrant should either adopt the new standard early prior to, or as an integral part of, the quasi-reorganization. This is because it is presumed that the accounting change was contemplated at the time of the quasi-reorganization. In case

---

[271]   *FASB ASC 852-20-05-2 (ARB 43, Ch.7A, ¶ 2).*

[272]   *FASB ASC 250-10-S99-1 (Codification of Financial Reporting Releases 210,* Quasi-reorganization*), 250-10-S99-2 (SEC Staff Accounting Bulletin, Topic 5-S,* Quasi-Reorganization*).*

[273]   *FASB ASC 852-20-25-3, 852-20-30-2, 852-20-30-3, 852-20-30-4, 852-20-25-4 (ARB 43, Ch.7A, ¶¶ 3-6).*

[274]   *FASB ASC 250-10-S99-2 (SEC Staff Accounting Bulletin, 5-S).*

[275]   *FASB ASC 852-20-25-4 (ARB 43, Ch.7A, ¶ 6).*

[276]   *FASB ASC 250-10-S99-2 (SEC Staff Accounting Bulletin, 5-S).*

[277]   *FASB ASC 505-10-25-2 (APB 9, ¶ 28).*

[278]   *FASB ASC 250-10-S99-1 (CFRR 210); FASB ASC 250-10-S99-2 (SEC Staff Accounting Bulletin, 5-S).*

of a change in accounting principle that requires retroactive application, the effects of the accounting change on quasi-reorganization adjustments should also be restated.

After a quasi-reorganization, net income is computed starting from the effective date of readjustment and a new retained earnings account is created, similar to that of a new company. At the time of the quasi-reorganization, the accounting principles of the entity should be consistent with those that it plans to use following the reorganization.[279] Retained earnings must mention the effective date of quasi-reorganization for at least 10 years on the face of the balance sheet or longer period if deemed significant (less than 10 years may be justified under exceptional circumstances).[280] Section 210-10-S99 (Regulation S-X) adds that for a period of at least three years retained earnings must indicate the total amount of the deficit eliminated on the face of the balance sheet.[281] After a quasi-reorganization the entity is in a position to distribute dividends again, because the accumulated losses are no longer reflected in retained earnings.

> **Comment:** Broadly speaking, paid-in capital from quasi-reorganization may be assimilated to a reserve with defense of capital and signaling purposes. This is discussed in Section 3.5 previously. Paid-in capital for quasi-reorganization is treated in Section 5.2.3 previously.

> **Comment:** Quasi-reorganization or corporate readjustments are not treated by IFRSs. Quasi-reorganization procedures depend on the specific jurisdiction in which a company is incorporated, as illustrated in Section 3.5.2.2 previously. Such requirements are not considered to be a matter for GAAP, but of national legislation or corporate governance. However, the IASB Framework permits, or better, welcomes their disclosure as it deems it relevant in assisting the informational needs of users of financial statements.[282] In addition to compliance with specific financial reporting that may be mandated by law, disclosure of quasi-reorganization might also be seen as required by IAS 1 as part of capital disclosures, to inform on externally-imposed capital requirements, their nature, and how the entity has complied with them.[283]

> **Comment:** As analyzed in Section 5.4 previously, under U.S. GAAP, additional paid-in capital should not be directly reduced by an entity's operations other than transactions with owners. Quasi-reorganization is an exception to this principle.[284] In fact, bringing overvalued assets to their current value may create a loss or lower income and reduce future depreciation that would be otherwise charged to earnings and retained earnings. Under quasi-reorganization instead the increase in accumulated deficit that arises from adjusting assets and bringing liabilities to their present values is then offset by paid-in capital.

Realized tax benefits of loss carryforwards arising prior to a quasi-reorganization are discussed in Section 8.2.11 later.

---

[279] *FASB ASC 250-10-S99-2 (SEC Staff Accounting Bulletin, 5-S).*
[280] *FASB ASC 852-20-25-5, 852-20-50-2 (ARB 43, Ch.7A, ¶¶ 9-10); ARB 46,* Discontinuance of Dating Earned Surplus, *¶¶ 1-2; Accounting Terminology Bulletin No. 1,* Review and Resume, *¶¶ 68, 69.5.*
[281] *FASB ASC 210-10-S99-1 (Regulation S-X, ¶ 210.5-02.31).*
[282] The Conceptual Framework for Financial Reporting 2010, *¶¶ 4.20, 4.21; IASB Framework, ¶¶ 65-66.*
[283] *IAS 1, ¶ 135.*
[284] *FASB ASC 852-20-25-2 (ARB 43, Ch.7A, ¶ 1).*

6.5.4   Increasing Rate Preferred Stock

Section 4.10 previously explains the accounting for increasing-rate preferred stock. As mentioned, the original discount is amortized at the effective interest method over the period(s) preceding the inception of normal dividend, through a debit to retained earnings.[285]

6.5.5   Redeemable Preferred Stock whose Redemption is Outside Issuer's Control

Section 4.4 previously explains the accounting of an SEC registrant for a preferred stock when its redemption is outside issuer's control and when it does not fall within the scope of Subtopic 480-10 (FASB Statement No. 150). Retained earnings are affected by the adjustment of such instruments to their redemption amount at each reporting period date, when currently redeemable or if redemption is probable. If redeemable at a future determinable date, the security is accreted in each period to the ultimate contractual redemption amount using an appropriate methodology, usually the interest method.[286] Under IAS 32, a mandatorily redeemable preferred share is classified (possibly after split accounting if only a component of the instrument is mandatorily redeemable) as a financial liability. Liability classification also applies under Subtopic 480-10 (FASB Statement No. 150), although with a more limited scope.

6.5.6   Treasury Stock

Section 4.14.2 previously shows how losses on treasury stock transactions and on purchase or retirement of capital stock may reduce retained earnings. Section 4.14.3 previously describes the reclassification of certain treasury stock reserves to retained earnings on first-time adoption of IFRSs.

The *AICPA Accounting Trends & Techniques* show that in 2009 and in 2005, respectively, treasury stock and capital retirement transactions accounted for over 58% and 80% of the charges in retained earnings other than opening balance adjustments, net income or loss and dividends.[287]

6.5.7   Appropriations of Retained Earnings

The topic of appropriations of retained earnings and its relationship with reserve accounting is analyzed in Section 3.5.3 previously.

Comment: Under U.S. GAAP appropriation or de-appropriation of retained earnings technically determines no change in retained earnings, as such designations are part of retained earnings themselves. However, as illustrated in Chapter 3 previously, transfers from/to retained earnings to other components of equity for defense of capital may be ordinarily found in other jurisdictions.

---

[285] *FASB ASC 505-10-S99-7 (SEC Staff Accounting Bulletin, Topic 5-Q,* Increasing Rate Preferred Stock*); International Accounting Standard No. 33,* Earnings per Share, ¶¶ *15, IE 1.*

[286] *FASB ASC 480-10-S99-3A (EITF Topic No. D-98, ¶ 15, as amended by Accounting Standards Update No. 2009-04,* Accounting for Redeemable Equity Instruments*); FASB ASC 480-10-S99-2 (SEC Staff Accounting Bulletin, Topic 3-C,* Redeemable Preferred Stock*); Securities and Exchange Commission, Division of Corporate Finance,* Frequently Requested Accounting and Financial Reporting Interpretations and Guidance, ¶ *I.A (March 31, 2001).*

[287] *AICPA ATT 2010 and AICPA ATT 2006, ¶ Table 5-4.*

> **Example:** In the United Kingdom, when mandatorily redeemable preference shares that are classified as liabilities under IAS 32 are redeemed out of distributable profits, an amount corresponding to the nominal value of the redeemed shares and the amount which would have been recognized in share premium if the instruments were classified as equity must be transferred from retained earnings to a capital redemption reserve in equity.[288]

6.5.8 Capitalization of Retained Earnings

Capitalization of earnings (or of retained earnings) refers to a voluntary or mandatory transfer from retained earnings to a paid-in capital account. Capitalization of retained earnings in case of small stock dividends is discussed in Section 3.5.2.2 previously and Section 5.2.4 previously.

> **Comment:** Depending on jurisdictions, much of the topic of capitalization of retained earnings is a matter of corporate law and defense of capital. This is illustrated in Section 3.5.2.2 previously. Furthermore, as discussed in Section 3.5.3 previously, transfers among "reserves" may be a way of appropriating undistributed earnings that are restricted for distribution or to de-appropriate them in jurisdictions that prescribe such treatment for defense of capital.

6.5.9 Changes in a Parent's Ownership Interest in a Controlled Subsidiary

As Section 5.2.16 previously mentions with reference to mandatorily redeemable noncontrolling interests in temporary equity, the adjustment to noncontrolling interests resulting from a change in a parent's ownership interest with no loss of control may affect retained earnings instead of additional paid-in capital.[289]

6.5.10 Changes in Redemption Value of Basic Ownership Instruments and Components with Redemption Requirements

Under a new approach by the FASB, changes in fair value of basic ownership instruments and components with redemption requirements would be remeasured at each reporting date at their current redemption value, determined as if they had been redeemed at the reporting date. Changes in redemption value would be reported as a separate equity account against an offsetting entry in retained earnings.[290]

> **Comment:** Even though retained earnings would be the counter-account, remeasuring equity is contrary to the IASB Framework and the U.S. Concepts. The transfer from other comprehensive income to retained earnings for revaluation surplus and certain actuarial gains and losses under IFRSs is conceptually different, as it relates to an allocation process (as in the case of depreciation and amortization), the result of derecognition or an initial classification, and not a remeasurement.

---

[288] *The Institute of Chartered Accountants in England and Wales and The Institute of Chartered Accountants of Scotland, TECH 21-05,* Distributable Profits: Implications of IFRS, ¶ 5.28.

[289] *FASB ASC 480-10-S99-3A (EITF Topic No. D-98, ¶ 19A, as amended by Accounting Standards Update No. 2009-04,* Accounting for Redeemable Equity Instruments).

[290] *Financial Accounting Standards Board, Preliminary Views,* Financial Instruments with Characteristics of Equity, *¶ 33 (November 30, 2007).*

6.6 DIRECT TRANSFER TO/FROM RETAINED EARNINGS WITHOUT PASSING THROUGH PROFIT OR LOSS

This Section lists items of income and expense that, under IFRSs, are recognized in other comprehensive income, are not reclassified into profit or loss, but must or may be transferred directly to retained earnings. There is a comprehensive discussion of recycling in Section 7.8 later.

6.6.1 Transfer of Revaluation Surplus to Retained Earnings

Under IAS 16 and IAS 38, tangible and intangible assets, subject to having certain prerequisites, may be measured either at cost or using the so-called "revaluation model." The cost or the revaluation model, once elected, must be applied to each entire class of property, plant, and equipment. Revaluation is credited in other comprehensive income as revaluation surplus.[291] This, and the rationale behind it, are analyzed in Section 7.6.3 later and Section 7.16 later.

> **Comment:** U.S. GAAP does not ordinarily permit write up of property, plant, and equipment to reflect appraisal, market, or current values above cost.[292]

When such net gains are realized (because the revalued asset is either derecognized as disposed of or retired, or through its depreciation or amortization), an entity may optionally transfer the revaluation surplus, net of tax, directly to retained earnings (thus affecting its ending balance) without passing through profit or loss.[293]

> **Comment:** Such transfer to realized profit is computed as the difference between depreciation based on the revalued carrying amount of the asset and depreciation on its original cost. This generally equals, although not always, the net revaluation surplus divided by remaining useful life.

Such transfer also occurs when a parent company loses control of a subsidiary, to the extent that this transfer would have resulted from a transaction at the parent's level, such as the parent directly disposing of an asset to which revaluation surplus relates.[294]

Revaluation surplus, eventually to be transferred to retained earnings, may also arise under other circumstances that result in accounting for revaluation surplus. These are treated in Section 6.6.2 below, Section 6.6.3 following, and Section 6.6.4 later.

6.6.2 Transfer of Owner-Occupied Property to Investment Property

A special case that results in creating revaluation surplus (and thus, a possible subsequent transfer to retained earnings[295]) is when an owner-occupied investment property carried at cost is reclassified to investment property carried at fair value. The difference in bases at the

---

[291] *IAS 16, ¶¶ 31, 36; IAS 38, ¶ 75.*
[292] *APB 6, Status of Accounting Research Bulletins, ¶ 17.*
[293] *IAS 16, ¶ 41; IAS 38, ¶ 87.*
[294] *IAS 27 (2010), ¶¶ 24(e)–35.*
[295] *IAS 40, ¶ 6(2b)(ii).*

date of transfer is brought to revaluation surplus with the rules of IAS 16, not IAS 40. In fact, contrary to IAS 16, under IAS 40, changes in fair value of investment property affect profit and loss, not revaluation surplus. The rationale is that net increases in fair value prior to such transfer must not impact the net income for the current period. Furthermore, the reclassification of revaluation surplus makes that company comparable to one that had applied the revaluation model under IAS 16.[296]

> **Comment:** This treatment seems inconsistent with the transition provision for adopting the fair value model of IAS 40 for the first time, in which case the cumulative-type adjustment is brought to retained earnings (see Section 6.4.10 previously). That case creates comparability among entities that apply IAS 40 (post-change comparability), while the accounting for a transfer from owner-occupied to investment property creates pre-change comparability among entities that applied IAS 16. Worksheet 37 illustrates the changes in use of an asset that justify transfers to or from investment property classification under IAS 40, and the cumulative-type impact of such reclassifications.

6.6.3 Impairment of Fixed Assets Carried at Valuation

Worksheet 38 shows the effects of a decrease in fair value of a tangible asset carried at revaluation model. This affects the amount of revaluation surplus that is possible to transfer to retained earnings. The accounting under International Accounting Standard No. 36, *Impairment of Assets*, arises from the difficulty in distinguishing a downward revaluation versus impairment (reduction in service potential). This accounting affects the amount of revaluation surplus that is subject to the mechanics of transfer to retained earnings explained in Section 6.6.1 previously.

IAS 36 applies prospectively. Therefore neither a cumulative-type adjustment nor a retroactive application applies. As mentioned, there is no comparable provision under U.S. GAAP because neither revaluation of tangible assets nor reversal of an impairment loss is permitted.

6.6.4 Changes in Revaluation Surplus Arising from Changes in Decommissioning and Similar Liabilities

This case, explained in Section 6.4.16 previously, is another situation that originates revaluation surplus that may be subsequently transferred to retained earnings.

6.6.5 Transfer of Accumulated Other Comprehensive Income to Retained Earnings

When an entity initially applies IAS 29 because the economy in which it operates has become hyperinflationary, any pre-existing revaluation surplus is eliminated[297] (see Section 6.4.23 previously).

> **Comment:** This implicitly results in a transfer to retained earnings.

---

[296] *IAS 40, ¶¶ 61, B66.*
[297] *IAS 29, ¶¶ 24–25.*

Under U.S. GAAP there is no revaluation surplus. As explained in Section 7.12 later, at the point its economy becomes highly inflationary that entity is deemed to have a new functional currency corresponding to the reporting currency. In such a situation, the foreign translation adjustment that under the current-rate method had been recognized in other comprehensive income in the previous periods remains so classified. The translated amounts for nonmonetary assets at the end of the prior period become their new accounting bases.[298]

6.6.6   Immediate Transfer of Certain Gains or Losses on Defined Benefit Plans to Retained Earnings

IAS 19, prior to the 2011 amendments, contained an election to recognize all of both actuarial gains and losses on defined benefit plans and any adjustments arising from the asset ceiling limit on defined benefit plans directly in other comprehensive income in the period in which they occur, through the statement of comprehensive income and with immediate and direct transfer to retained earnings without reclassifying to profit or loss. Such election must be applied to all defined benefit plans and all actuarial gains and losses consistently from period to period.[299]

Comment: This is a case where gains or losses are recognized in retained earnings and never in net income, although counterbalanced by increased disclosures.[300] This was intended to be a transitional approach until a final solution in the *Financial Statement Presentation Project.*[301]

Comment: This is a case of transfer from other comprehensive income to retained earnings, but different from the case of transfer of revaluation surplus. Here the transfer is immediate, while for revaluation surplus when the gains or losses become realized. The IASB acknowledges that there would be no rationale in delaying such transfer.[302] The *Financial Statement Presentation Project* Staff viewed this simply as a labeling issue, because such gains or losses are transferred to retained earnings in the period of recognition as in the case of net income.[303] It seems more than a labeling issue because, in contrast to net income, there is no recycling though the income statement (or better, after the 2007 revision of IAS 1, no reclassification to profit or loss). This issue is better analyzed in Section 7.7.4, Section 7.6.3, and Section 7.16 later.

Comment: Note disclosure, not separate presentation within retained earnings, is required.[304] This is consistent with the minimum display requirements under IFRSs, as explained in Section 4.5.1 previously.

---

[298] *FASB ASC 830-10-45-10 (FASB Statement No. 52, ¶ 46); FASB ASC 830-10-45-16 (EITF Topic D-56,* Accounting for a Change in Functional Currency and Deferred Taxes When an Economy Becomes Highly Inflationary*).*

[299] *IAS 19 (2007), ¶¶ 93A–93D, BC48BB–C48EE; IAS 1, ¶ 96.*

[300] *IAS 19 (2007), ¶ BC48S.*

[301] *IAS 19 (2007), ¶¶ BC2, BC48G.*

[302] *IAS 19 (2007), ¶ BC48U.*

[303] *IASB/FASB Meeting, October 24, 2006, Agenda Paper 6C/FASB Memorandum 44C,* Measurement; OCI and Recycling; the Statement of Comprehensive Income, *¶ 64 (October 24, 2006).*

[304] *IAS 19 (2007), ¶ BC48Z.*

> **Comment:** Under both U.S. GAAP and IAS 19 (prior to the 2011 amendments), recognition of pension actuarial gains and losses may be faster than with the corridor approach. Furthermore, before the 2011 revision of IAS 19, an IFRS first-time adopter could use an exemption to recognize in retained earnings all unrecognized cumulative actuarial gains and losses at the date of transition to IFRSs, even though it would use the corridor method for later actuarial gains and losses.[305] However, in U.S. GAAP there is no provision comparable to such transfer to retained earnings. Furthermore, asset ceiling limit adjustments do not exist.
>
> Subtopic 715-20 (FASB Statement No. 158) also requires an adjustment in equity, not in retained earnings but in other comprehensive income, for all unrecognized gains or losses and prior service costs or credits that are not recognized as part of net periodic benefit costs of defined benefit pension and other postretirement plans other than a multiemployer plan (see Section 6.4.17 previously).

The IASB added a project to its agenda in July 2006, for a fundamental review of all aspects of postemployment benefit accounting. Effective for financial years beginning on or after January 1, 2013, with earlier application permitted, IAS 19 has retroactively banned the corridor approach.[306] In addition, under the 2011 revision of IAS 19, faster recognition is no longer an option, because remeasurements of the net defined benefit liability or asset go to other comprehensive income and the immediate recognition is the rule for the other cost components.

6.7 INCOME TAX RELATING TO TRANSACTIONS THAT DIRECTLY AFFECT RETAINED EARNINGS

Chapter 8 analyzes specific issues related to income tax that refer to transactions that directly affect retained earnings.

6.8 PRESENTATION AND DISCLOSURE OF RETAINED EARNINGS

6.8.1 Presentation in the Statement of Financial Position

Under both U.S. GAAP and IFRSs, the presentation of a separate line item for retained earnings on the face of the statement of financial position is a matter of customary practice. ATB 1 supported the display of retained earnings in the balance sheet.[307] Regulation S-X requires the display of retained earnings as part of other stockholders' equity.[308]

Under Subtopic 220-10 (FASB Statement No. 130), accumulated other comprehensive income must be displayed separately from retained earnings and additional paid-in capital on the equity section of the statement of financial position. However, the SEC Staff clarified that a foreign private issuer that under local GAAP reports items of accumulated other comprehensive income in retained earnings is exempted from reclassifying the components of accumulated

---

[305]   *IFRS 1, ¶ D10.*
[306]   *IAS 19 (2011), ¶¶ 172, 173, BC66, BC70.*
[307]   *Accounting Terminology Bulletin No. 1, Review and Resume, ¶¶ 65–66, 68, 69.2.*
[308]   *FASB ASC 210-10-S99-1 (Regulation S-X, ¶ 210.5-02.31(a); FASB ASC 944-210-S99-1 (Regulation S-X, ¶ 210.7-03.24(a)).*

other comprehensive income in case this reconstruction is impracticable and it discloses this fact.[309]

Alternative ways of presenting retained earnings on the face of the statement of financial position may comprise the following formats:

> Beginning balance
> Add: net income
> Less: dividends
> Ending balance

Or, as required by Regulation S-X on the face of the balance sheet[310]:

> Retained earnings
> > Appropriated for . . .
> > Free and unappropriated

Under U.S. GAAP, banks and similar financial institutions must show the portions of retained earnings that are substantially restricted and those that are unrestricted.[311]

Under U.S. GAAP, investment companies must show undistributed net investment income, undistributed net realized gains from investments, and net unrealized appreciation (depreciation) of investments. They may either separately report the foreign currency effect of realized gains or losses from investments into foreign currency transactions or combine it with net realized gains or losses from investments. A company may report unrealized appreciation or depreciation on translation of assets and liabilities in foreign currencies separately or combine it with unrealized gains and losses on investments. However, the company must separately report all other realized or unrealized foreign currency gains and losses. Therefore, it must include realized gains or losses on interest and dividends in the realized gain or loss component of net realized gain or loss. It must include all unrealized foreign currency gains and losses other than those on investments in unrealized appreciation or depreciation on translation of assets and liabilities in foreign currencies. A note must disclose the accounting policy followed.[312]

Comment: IAS 5, then superseded, required a separate display for retained earnings.[313] Now, IAS 1 simply lists "issued capital and reserves" as one of the minimum line items for display on the

---

[309] *FASB ASC 220-10-45-14 (FASB Statement No. 130, ¶ 26); U.S. Securities and Exchange Commission,* International Reporting and Disclosure Issues in the Division of Corporate Finance, *¶ VI.A (November 1, 2004) www.sec.gov (last visited April 26, 2006).*

[310] *FASB ASC 210-10-S99-1 (Regulation S-X, ¶ 210.5-02.31(a)); FASB ASC 944-210-S99-1 (Regulation S-X, ¶ 210.7-03.24(a)).*

[311] *FASB ASC 942-405-55-3, 942-405-55-4 (EITF Issue No. 89-3, ¶¶ Exhibits 89-3A, 89-3B).*

[312] *FASB ASC 946-830-45-4, 946-830-45-36, 946-830-45-37, 946-830-55-12 (AICPA Statement of Position No. 93-4, ¶¶ 34, 35, Appendix B); FASB ASC 946-210-S99-1 (Regulation S-X, ¶ 210.6-04.17) for registered investment companies.*

[313] *International Accounting Standard No. 5,* Information to be Disclosed in Financial Statements, *¶ 17 (superseded).*

face of the statement of financial position.[314] However, subclassifications, such as detail of retained earnings, additional paid-in capital, and other reserves should be disclosed, depending on certain disaggregation criteria, either in the statement of financial position or in the notes.[315] Although not clearly stated in IAS 1, this provision might be read in combination with the one relating the statement of changes in equity (see next Section) to conclude that under the previous version of IAS 1 retained earnings had to be displayed at least on both the statement of changes in equity and the statement of financial position, or in the notes if the entity adopted the statement of recognized income and expenses. Under the latest Revision of IAS 1, retained earnings must be presented on the face of the statement of changes in equity and either on the statement of financial position or in the notes.

Example: In its response to the SEC's review of Form 20-F for the year ended December 31, 2005, a French foreign private issuer adopted such interpretation to justify the disclosure of retained earnings in the notes.[316]

6.8.2 Reconciling Changes in Retained Earnings

Apart from the statement of financial position, alternative statements exist to show retained earnings and their changes.

Under U.S. GAAP, as shown in the following Sections, changes in retained earnings may be shown either as a separate statement of retained earnings, or as a combined statement of income and retained earnings, or as part of the statement of stockholders' equity (corresponding to the statement of changes in equity, under IFRSs), or as note disclosure. The *AICPA Accounting Trends & Techniques* show that the statement of stockholders' equity is the most frequently used.[317] The statement of changes in equity is analyzed in Section 7.9 later.

Common interest realty associations that are cooperatives do not have to disclose components of retained earnings.[318]

Section 505-10-S99 (Regulation S-X) requires analysis of beginning and ending balances and changes of each caption of equity and noncontrolling interests, as note disclosure or as a separate statement of changes in other stockholders' equity.[319]

IAS 1 displays beginning and ending balances and changes in retained earnings in the statement of changes in equity, as for each other component of equity.[320]

---

[314] *IAS 1, ¶ 54.*

[315] *IAS 1, ¶¶ 77, 78(e).*

[316] *Letter by the SEC, File No. 1-10888, ¶ 3 (September 25, 2006). Reply by the company (October 25, 2006) www.sec.gov/divisions/corpfin/ifrs_reviews (last visited January 7, 2008).*

[317] *AICPA ATT 2010 and AICPA ATT 2006, ¶ Table 5-1.*

[318] *FASB ASC 972-205-50-1 (AICPA Accounting and Audit Guide, Common Interest Realty Associations, ¶ 9.12).*

[319] *FASB ASC 505-10-S99-1 (Regulation S-X, ¶ 210.3-04).*

[320] *IAS 1, ¶¶ 106(d), 108.*

Comment: Under the pre-2007 revision of IAS 1, reconciling changes in retained earnings used to be part of either the statement of changes in equity or a note disclosure, if the statement of recognized income and expenses was presented.[321] SEC's Form 20-F uses the same presentation formats as under IFRSs.[322] The 2010 Improvements to IFRSs go back to allow note disclosure for changes in equity.[323]

Example: In its review of Form 20-F for the year ended December 31, 2005 of a Spanish foreign private issuer, the SEC requested separate presentation, not simply within a heading "other reserves," of balances and changes in retained earnings in the statement of changes in equity.[324]

Comment: The U.S. Concepts follow the approach of defining the content that a set of financial statements must represent rather than prescribing specific statements. By contrast, IAS 1 specifically identifies each statement. Within the variety of alternatives used in practice, U.S. Concepts draw no conclusions on the identity, number, or form of those components and, whilst indicating individual statements, do not preclude the possibility to combine statements differently, although aggregation may unduly complicate the information.[325] Among other elements, the U.S. Concepts prescribe net income or earnings to be represented as part of the financial statements.[326] This has given rise to the basic statement of earnings and comprehensive income. This statement may be disaggregated into an income or earning statement, a statement of retained earnings,[327] and a statement of comprehensive income. On the other hand, it may be aggregated into a statement of income and retained earnings, a statement of income and comprehensive income, or a statement of changes in equity. Accordingly, under U.S. GAAP, a full set of financial statements may contain different alternative or additional components with more possible options than IFRSs and substitute terminology. However, ASU 2011-05 recently amended the definition of the full set of financial statements by mentioning the types of statements of income.[328] Worksheet 39 illustrates such relationships and compares them with SEC rules and IFRSs. U.S. Statement of Auditing Standard SAS 29, withdrawn by SAS No. 52,[329] identified the basic set of financial statements under U.S. GAAP. It mentioned a statement of financial position, a statement of income, a statement of retained earnings or a statement of changes in stockholders' equity, a statement of cash flows, a description of accounting policies, notes to financial statements and schedules, and explanatory material that are identified as being part of the basic financial statements. For the purpose of financial statements prepared in conformity with a comprehensive basis of accounting other than GAAP (OCBOA), U.S. auditing standards consider different forms of financial presentations, in addition to the basic financial statements as financial statements for reporting purposes by a U.S. independent auditor. They include a statement

---

[321]   *IAS 1, ¶ 97(b).*

[322]   *Form 20-F, Part I, Item 8.A.1*

[323]   Improvements to IFRSs, Amendments to IAS 1 Presentation of Financial Statements, *¶ 106A (May 2010).*

[324]   *Letter by the SEC, File No. 1-15158, ¶ 14 (September 20, 2006) www.sec.gov/divisions/corpfin/ ifrs_reviews (last visited January 7, 2008).*

[325]   *CON 5, ¶ 14.*

[326]   *CON 5, ¶ 13.*

[327]   *CON 1 (superseded), ¶ 6.*

[328]   *FASB ASC 205-10-45-1A, as amended by ASU 2011-05.*

[329]   *Statement of Auditing Standards No. 29,* Reporting on Information Accompanying the Basic Financial Statements in Auditor-Submitted Documents *(withdrawn by SAS No. 52).*

of operations, or summary of operations, the statement of retained earnings, a statement of assets and liabilities that does not include equity, a statement of operations by product lines, and the statement of cash receipts and disbursements.[330]

Comment: In the United Kingdom, the "movements on reserves" is a tabular form in addition to the "reconciliation of movements in shareholders' funds," required by FRS 3, *Reporting Financial Performance*, a statement that reports the changes in components of equity. The two statements are somewhat equivalent to the statement of changes in equity under IFRSs. Reverses typically include accounts such as share premium, revaluation reserve, and retained earnings.

6.8.3 The Statement of Retained Earnings

The U.S. Concepts acknowledge the use of the statement of retained earnings. Under APB 9, the statement of income and the statement of retained earnings reflect results of operations.[331] Subtopic 230-10 (FASB Statement No. 95) gives results of operations the status of a necessary constituent of a complete set of financial statements.[332] APS 4, which is no longer in force, considered the statement of [changes in] retained earnings as one of the basic financial statements.[333] Worksheet 40 illustrates a sample statement of retained earnings under U.S. GAAP, when presented as a stand-alone statement.

Planning Point: Under U.S. GAAP, the statement of changes in equity is not mandatory for companies that present the statement of financial position, a statement of income, and a statement of retained earnings (or a combined statement of income and retained earnings) and that, prior to ASU 2011-05, have no item of other comprehensive income. On the other hand, whether or not U.S. GAAP requires a statement of retained earnings (or a combined statement of income and retained earnings) is arguable. Strictly, following the definition of a complete set of financial statements in Subtopic 230-10 (FASB Statement No. 95), simple note disclosure of changes in retained earnings would not suffice to represent results of operations, unless the statement of financial position (i.e., one of the basic financial statements) displays changes in retained earnings. Conversely, a statement of changes in equity would be enough, as it includes changes in retained earnings. On the other hand, CON 5[334] does not include the statement of retained earnings in a full set of financial statements. It considers the statement of income and retained earnings as simply a way of differently combining mandatory information. Conversely, Subsection 505-10-S99-1 (Regulation S-X) requires the analysis of beginning and ending balances and changes of each caption of equity and noncontrolling interests, as note disclosure or as a separate statement of changes in other stockholders' equity.[335] In U.S. practice, changes in retained earnings may be shown either as a separate statement of retained earnings, or as a combined statement of income and retained earnings, or as part of the statement of stockholders' equity (corresponding to the statement of changes in equity, under IFRSs), or as

---

[330] *Clarified Statements on Auditing Standards,* Special Considerations – Audits of Financial Statements Prepared in Accordance With Special Purpose Frameworks; AU Section 623, Special Reports.

[331] *APB 9, ¶ 7; CON 5, ¶¶ 24, 30, 33; FASB Current Text, General Standards, F43, ¶ 102.*

[332] *FASB ASC 230-10-15-3 (FASB Statement No. 95, ¶ 3); FASB Statement No. 95, ¶¶ 152, 153.*

[333] *Accounting Principles Board Statement No. 4,* Basic Concepts and Accounting Principles Underlying Financial Statements in Business Enterprises, *¶¶ 13, 191.*

[334] *CON 5, ¶¶ 13, 14.*

[335] *FASB ASC 505-10-S99-1 (Regulation S-X, ¶ 210.3-04).*

note disclosure. According to the *AICPA Accounting Trends & Techniques*, in 2002–2009 about 97–98% of U.S. companies surveyed used the statement of changes in equity to display changes in retained earnings. The remaining companies were equally scattered among the options of the statement of retained earnings, the combined statement of income, and retained earnings and note disclosure.[336]

Comment: The statement of retained earnings shows comparative periods in columns. Therefore, there is an easy and quick cross-reference between the opening and closing balances of retained earnings. Conversely, the use of a statement of changes in equity shows equity components in columns, including retained earnings. Therefore, in order to display comparative information, an entity must compile one format of statement for each comparative period presented.

The statement of retained earnings is not one of the statements within the set of the basic financial statements under IFRSs. IAS 1 separately displays beginning and ending balances and changes in retained earnings in the statement of changes in equity, as for each of the other components of equity.[337]

Example: In its review of Form 20-F for the year ended December 31, 2005 of a Spanish foreign private issuer, the SEC Staff requested separate presentation, not simply within the heading "other reserves," of balances and changes in retained earnings in the statement of changes in equity.[338]

Comment: Under the pre-2007 revision of IAS 1, reconciling changes in retained earnings used to be part of either the statement of changes in equity or a note disclosure, if the entity presented a statement of recognized income and expenses.[339] SEC's Form 20-F adapted the presentation formats to IFRSs.[340]

6.8.4   The Combined Statement of Income and Retained Earnings

Certain U.S. pronouncements mention (or used to mention) a combined statement of income and retained earnings (or earned surplus).[341] Subsection 255-10-55-29 (FASB Statement No. 89) also calls it statement of earnings and retained earnings.[342] Under APB 9, the statement

---

[336] *AICPA ATT 2010 and AICPA ATT 2006, ¶ Table 5-1.*

[337] *IAS 1, ¶¶ 106(d), 108.*

[338] *Letter by the SEC, File No. 1-15158, Note 14 (September 20, 2006).*

[339] *IAS 1, ¶ 97(b).*

[340] *Form 20-F, Part I, Item 8.A.1*

[341] *FASB ASC 255-10-55-53, 255-10-55-54 (FASB Statement No. 89, Financial Reporting and Changing Prices, ¶ 73); APB 9, Reporting the Results of Operations, ¶ 7; APB 15, Earnings per Share, ¶ 92 (superseded); Accounting Principles Board Statement No. 3,* Financial Statements Restated for General Price-Level Changes *(superseded); CON 5,* Recognition and Measurement in Financial Statements of Business Enterprises, *¶ 14.*

[342] *FASB ASC 255-10-55-29 (FASB Statement No. 89, ¶ 53).*

of income and the statement of retained earnings together or their combination in the form of a combined statement of income and retained earnings reflect results of operations.[343] FASB Statement No. 95 gives results of operations with the status of a necessary constituent of a complete set of financial statements.[344] Although still considered acceptable, that was a past practice under ARB 43, Ch. 2B (then superseded). This was considered a manner of evidencing the connecting link of income statements of different periods, thus overcoming the periodic nature of accounting income and possibly computing a long-run income or income-earning capacity of a company. On the other hand, this presentation might become misleading in cases where not all income and expenses passed through the income statement. In addition, as such a statement did not end with net income as a bottom line, there was a risk of creating confusion as to whether net income or other metrics measured an entity's performance.[345] Finally, it mixed items of results of operations (flows) with items of financial position (stock). For these reasons, the then superseded APB 19 required an additional statement of changes in financial position when the combined statement of income and retained earnings was used.[346] One of the options for LLC companies to present changes in members' equity is to combine them with the statement of operations.[347] Common interest realty associations that are cooperatives may use a combined statement of retained earnings and operations if they have no changes in paid-in capital accounts.[348] Worksheet 41 illustrates a sample combined statement of income and retained earnings under U.S. GAAP.

Comment: This statement is typical of UK practice. It is not one of the statements within the set of the basic financial statements under IFRSs. Furthermore, mixing income statement items and balance sheet items would diverge from the cohesiveness working principle of the *Financial Statement Presentation Project* (see Section 1.4.3.1 previously).

The IFRS for small and medium-sized entities permits the use of a statement of income and retained earnings as opposed to a statement of comprehensive income and a statement of changes in equity. Such an entity may elect this simplification when no capital transactions, apart from dividends, have affected equity in the reporting periods presented. Therefore, this statement is limited to the display of dividends, corrections of errors, and changes in accounting policy. In particular, in addition to the items of statement of income, the IFRS for small and medium-sized entities requires the separate display of dividends declared and paid or payable during the period, restatement of retained earnings for corrections of errors, restatement of retained earnings for changes in accounting policy, and beginning and ending retained earnings.[349]

---

[343] *APB 9, ¶ 7; CON 5, ¶¶ 24, 30, 33; FASB Current Text, General Standards, F43, ¶ 102.*

[344] *FASB Statement No. 95, ¶ 152.*

[345] *ARB 43, Ch. 2B,* Combined Statement of Income and Earned Surplus, *¶¶ 1, 3–6 (superseded).*

[346] *APB 19,* Reporting Changes in Financial Position, *¶ 7 (superseded).*

[347] *FASB ASC 272-10-45-1 (Practice Bulletin No. 14,* Accounting and Reporting by Limited Liability Companies and Limited Liability Partnerships, *¶ 8).*

[348] *FASB ASC 972-205-45-16 (AICPA Audit and Accounting Guide,* Common Interest Realty Associations, *¶ 9.14.*

[349] *IFRS for Small and Medium-sized Entities (SMEs), ¶¶ 3.18, 6.1, 6.4, 6.5.*

6.8.5   Development Stage Enterprises

Under U.S. GAAP, a development stage enterprise (as opposed to an established operating enterprise) is an entity that is devoting substantially all of its efforts to establishing a new business with either no principal operations commenced or with a still insignificant amount of revenue. Regulation S-X gives a similar definition. A development stage enterprise (including a development stage subsidiary or other investee) must comply with U.S. GAAP in the same way as other entities. However some additional information must be reported. This includes a "deficit accumulated during the development stage" or equivalent line-item to be displayed in the stockholders' equity section for net losses accumulated since the inception of the entity. Additionally, a statement of stockholders' equity must show each issuance of stock since inception, the number of equity securities and respective total and per-share amounts issued for cash and for other consideration, the nature of any noncash consideration, and the basis used for measurement. Combined disclosure is permitted if those issues are made in the same fiscal year for the same type of consideration and unit amount. The heading of the financial statements must identify the enterprise as development stage and describe the nature of its activities. In the first year in which the entity is no longer in development stage, its financial statements must disclose its previous status. If comparative statements are presented, the abovementioned displays and disclosures are not required. Changes to comparative figures resulting from the adoption of Topic 915 (FASB Statement No. 7) are accounted for as prior period adjustments.[350]

> **Comment:** IFRSs do not provide guidance on the presentational requirements of development stage enterprises.

The SEC Staff clarified that Item 17 filers, but not Item 18 filers, that are development stage enterprises are exempted from these special disclosures.[351]

6.8.6   Additional Disclosures of Retained Earnings

As reported in Section 6.4.2 previously and Section 6.4.3 previously, both U.S. GAAP and IFRSs require specific disclosures for retroactive adjustments of the beginning balance of retained earnings.

In addition, Regulation S-X requires disclosure of any restrictions on retained earnings, including those that may result, upon involuntary liquidation, from the excess of aggregate preferences of preferred shares over par or stated value, and other restrictions of dividends. Such disclosure may be placed either on the face of the financial statements or in the notes. Furthermore, Section 235-10-S99 (Regulation S-X) requires disclosure of the amount of consolidated retained earnings which represents undistributed earnings of 50% or less owned persons accounted for by the equity method.[352]

---

[350]   *FASB ASC 915-10-05-2, 915-205-45-1, 915-210-45-1, 915-235-50-1, 915-235-50-2, 915-205-45-4, 915-205-45-5 (FASB Statement No. 7, ¶¶ 8-15); Regulation S-X, ¶ 210.1-02(h).*

[351]   *AICPA, 2004. AICPA International Practices Task Force Meeting Highlights, September 27, 2004, Washington DC, AICPA, ¶ 3 www.aicpa.org (last visited December 24, 2006).*

[352]   *FASB ASC 235-10-S99-1 (Regulation S-X, ¶¶ 210.4-08(d)(2), 210.4-08(e)).*

Finally, an SEC registrant must disclose whether or not retained earnings available for distribution differ from that presented in SEC financial statements when GAAP or reporting currency differ from that used in its home country.[353]

6.9 DIVIDENDS

IAS 1 requires the presentation of dividends accounted for in equity (in aggregate and per-share amounts) either in the statement of changes in equity or in the notes. It prohibits their presentation in the statement of comprehensive income. In fact, the statement of changes in equity presents owner changes in equity, while the statement of comprehensive income shows non-owner changes in equity.[354] This is in line with the prohibition on detailing comprehensive income in the statement of changes in equity, as Paragraph 1.1.3 previously explains. The *Financial Statement Presentation Project* would confirm this approach.[355] Conversely, the 2005 version of IAS 1 permitted presentation of aggregate and per-share amounts of dividends on the face of the income statement.[356]

> **Comment:** This option was similar to that adopted in UK practice, which resulted in a sort of statement of income and retained earnings, which is still permitted under IFRS for small and medium-sized entities.

IFRS for small and medium-sized entities requires separate presentation of dividends in the statement of changes in equity or separate display of dividends declared and paid or payable during the period in the statement of income and retained earnings if the entity can, and elects to, use this statement.[357]

Subtopic 220-10 (FASB Statement No. 130) does not explain where to present dividends, but its examples show them on the face of the statement of changes in equity.[358] Subtopic 810-10 (ARB 51, as amended) requires separate indication of distributions to owners either in the statement of changes in equity or in the notes,[359] and this comprises dividends. Of course, an entity may also disaggregate changes in retained earnings, including dividends, on the face of the statement of financial position. When presented, the combined statement of income and retained earnings or the statement of retained earnings shows dividends. According to the *AICPA Accounting Trends & Techniques*, in 2009, 2005, and 2002 approximately 54%, 57%, and 62% of survey U.S. GAAP companies, respectively, reported per-share amounts of cash dividends paid to common shareholders in the statement of retained earnings. Those figures change to 32%, 24%, and 37%, respectively, concerning cash dividends paid to preferred shareholders.[360]

---

[353] *AICPA IPTF Summary*, Issues Addressed by the AICPA International Practices Task Force Inception Through March 2003, ¶ E *(March 2003)*.

[354] *IAS 1, ¶¶ 107, 109, BC75.*

[355] *Staff Draft, ¶ 204.*

[356] *IAS 1 (2005), ¶ 95.*

[357] IFRS for SMEs, ¶¶ 6.3(c), 6.5.

[358] *FASB ASC 220-10-55-11, 220-10-55-12 (FASB Statement No. 130, ¶ 131).*

[359] *FASB ASC 810-10-50-1B (ARB 51, ¶ 39(c), as amended by FASB Statement No. 160).*

[360] *AICPA ATT 2010 and AICPA ATT 2006, ¶ Table 5-2.*

Subsection 505-10-S99-1 (Regulation S-X) requires dividends in the separate statement that effects the analysis of changes in equity (i.e., a statement of changes in equity) or in the notes. An entity must include separate indication of the aggregate and per-share amounts of dividends for each class of share.[361] Interim income statements of SEC registrants must display dividends per share.[362] The SEC Staff requires pro forma information when a SEC registrant pays dividends from the proceeds of an offering or when dividends exceed earnings of the current year.[363] Selected financial data of foreign private issuers must include dividends declared per share in the local and the reporting currencies.[364]

Under IFRSs, only the notes must disclose the aggregate and per-share amounts of dividends proposed or declared after the reporting date but before the date of authorization for issue of the IFRS financial statements.[365] This reflects the fact that at the reporting date there is no dividend obligation that meets the criteria for recognition in the statement of financial position. If those declared dividends are in kind, the notes must include the nature, the carrying amount, and the estimated fair value of those assets at the end of the reporting period, including the valuation method used.[366] By contrast, according to the SEC Staff, SEC registrants should retroactively include dividends declared by a subsidiary after the reporting date in the statement of financial position with explanation in the notes or, alternatively, add a statement of financial position on a pro forma basis.[367]

Under IFRSs, the notes must disclose cumulative dividends not recognized. Under U.S. GAAP, either the statement of financial position or the notes inform on cumulative preferred dividends in arrears. Unlike IFRSs, U.S. GAAP adds per-share amounts.[368] SEC registrants must give separate note disclosure of the dividend requirements of material preferred stock of noncontrolling interest.[369] Foreign private issuers must indicate the title and the class of preferred stock of significant subsidiaries with dividends in arrears and the arrearage nature and amount in Form 20-F.[370]

The IFRS statement of changes in equity, the statement of financial position, or the notes must disclose dividend rights, preferences, and restrictions.[371] Under the 2005 version of IAS 1 the statement of changes in equity was not among the options for this.[372] In addition, the notes to consolidated financial statements must indicate the nature and extent of any significant restrictions on cash dividends by subsidiaries and associates.[373] Subsection 505-10-50-3 (FASB Statement No. 129) generically requires the disclosure of dividend preferences of securities

---

[361] *FASB ASC 505-10-S99-1 (Regulation S-X, ¶ 210.3-04).*

[362] *Regulation S-X, ¶ 210.8-03(a)(2); FASB ASC 270-10-S99-1 (Regulation S-X, ¶ 210.10-01(b)(2)).*

[363] *SEC Staff Accounting Bulletin, Topic 1-B.3, Other Matters.*

[364] *Form 20-F, Item 3.A.2.*

[365] *IAS 1, ¶ 137; IAS 10, ¶¶ 13, BC6.*

[366] *IFRIC 17, Distributions of Non-Cash Assets to Owners, ¶ 17.*

[367] *SEC Staff Accounting Bulletin, Topic 1-B.3, Other Matters.*

[368] *FASB ASC 505-10-50-5 (FASB Statement No. 129, Disclosure of Information about Capital Structure, ¶ 7.b); FASB ASC 440-10-50-1 (FASB Statement No. 5, Accounting for Contingencies, ¶ 19).*

[369] *FASB ASC 210-10-S99-1 (Regulation S-X, ¶ 210.5-02.31).*

[370] *Form 20-F, Item 13.B.*

[371] *IAS 1, ¶ 79(a)(v).*

[372] *IAS 1 (2005), ¶ 76(a)(v).*

[373] *IAS 27 (2010), ¶ 41(d); IAS 28 (2010), ¶ 37(f).*

outstanding within the financial statements.[374] Lessees must disclose dividends restrictions pursuant to the lease contract in their financial statements or in the notes.[375] Foreign private issuers must give note disclosure of any dividend currency of publicly held securities that is different from the reporting currency. Their financial statements must prominently indicate, in part, any material exchange restrictions or external controls of the currency of dividend remittances.[376] Furthermore, they must describe dividend rights, respective expiry periods, beneficiary parties, as well as home country exchange controls on remittance of dividends to non-residents, and any other dividend restrictions.[377] Foreign private issuers that register debt securities must also include information on dividend restrictions in Form 20-F.[378] Foreign private issuers must also describe limitations on dividend payments arising from material modifications to the rights of securities.[379] The notes to consolidated financial statements of SEC registrants must explain the terms of any significant restriction on distributions of retained earnings.[380] In condensed consolidating financial information of guarantors and issuers of guaranteed securities, SEC registrants must disclose any restrictions on the ability to obtain funds from subsidiaries through dividends or loans.[381]

In the presence of puttable shares, as is typical for certain investment funds, the classification of dividends as equity deduction versus interest expense depends on whether the entity classifies such instruments as equity or liabilities under IFRSs.[382] For finance companies, U.S. GAAP requires the inclusion of redeemable preferred stock dividends of a parent in the consolidated statement of changes in equity, when the company classifies preferred stock in temporary equity.[383]

6.10   TOWARDS A THEORY OF RETAINED EARNINGS

As demonstrated in this Section, although a well-established concept in practice, retained earnings encompass neither a strong theory background nor consistent application. As shown, the basic theory that retained earnings should be increased by passing through the income statement only is negated in many instances. That, in great part, is a consequence of the result of the debate on the clean-surplus concept.

As mentioned in Section 6.1.2 previously, the meaning of retained earnings is undefined in IFRSs. The topic is complicated by the debate on recycling, that is whether or not certain unrealized income or expenses should be recognized in profit or loss and then in retained earnings as opposed to directly in other comprehensive income and then in profit or loss. This

---

[374]   *FASB ASC 505-10-50-3 (FASB Statement No. 129, ¶ 4).*

[375]   *FASB ASC 840-10-50-2 (FASB Statement No. 13,* Accounting for Leases, *¶ 16.d.iii); IAS 17, ¶¶ 31(e)(iii), 35(d)(iii).*

[376]   *Regulation S-X, ¶ 210.3-20(b).*

[377]   *Form 20-F, Item 10.B.3, Item 10.D.2, Item 10.F.*

[378]   *Form 20-F, Item 14.A.4.*

[379]   *Form 20-F, Instruction to Item 14.B.*

[380]   *FASB ASC 235-10-S99-1 (Regulation S-X, ¶¶ 210.4-08(e)(1), 210.4-08(e)(3)(i)); Regulation S-K, Instruction 6 to ¶ 209.303(a).*

[381]   *FASB ASC 470-10-S99-1 (Regulation S-X, ¶ 210.3-10(i)(9)).*

[382]   *IAS 32, ¶¶ 16A–16F.*

[383]   *FASB ASC 942-405-45-2 (AICPA Statement of Position No. 01-6,* Accounting by Certain Entities (Including Entities With Trade Receivables) That Lend to or Finance the Activities of Others, *¶ 14.l).*

is discussed in Section 7.8 later. Retained earnings, as potentially distributable accumulated income, should, by default, be supposed to be earnings that have been realized unless differently stated. However, depending on GAAP, some gains and losses that are temporary in nature may be occasionally included in earnings. This opens the defense of capital quest for distributable profits, as illustrated in Section 3.5 previously. The IASB responds that defense of capital is not a matter for GAAP and that the association between the nature of profits and retained earnings has yet to be set up.[384]

As all these issues add up, comparisons of available models and suggestions for a comprehensive theory will be discussed in Section 7.21 later, after analysis of recycling and of other comprehensive income.

---

[384] *IAS 19 (2007), ¶ BC48Y.*

7 OTHER COMPREHENSIVE INCOME

7.1 TERMINOLOGY

7.1.1 Comprehensive Income Versus Total Recognized Income and Expense

Comprehensive income is a well-established term in U.S. GAAP pronouncements. *Total recognized income and expense for the period* has long been a substantially equivalent term under IFRSs.

> **Comment:** The different terminology comes from a different approach to elements of financial statements (see Section 7.2.3 later). In fact, contrary to the U.S. Concepts, the IASB Framework does not mention or define *comprehensive income*.[1]

However, the 2007 revision of IAS 1 finally uses both the term *comprehensive income* and *total comprehensive income* and amends IFRSs consistently. Pending the *Joint Conceptual Framework Project*, the IASB Framework does not adopt such terminology yet.

> **Comment:** As part of the *Financial Statement Presentation Project*, initially called *Performance Reporting Project*, the IASB initially adopted the U.S. terminology in its 2003 model.[2] Although during the initial meetings the respective terminologies were used interchangeably until a final decision was taken,[3] later during the project the IASB rejected the term *comprehensive income*, on the basis of the inconsistency with the IASB Framework and with IFRSs.[4] However, the 2007 revision of IAS 1 adopted this term, in order to converge with U.S. GAAP and in view of the suggestions of many respondents to the Exposure Draft and the rejection of the alternative terminology of *recognized income and expense*. In fact, there was no justification as to why "recognized" was mentioned in this expression and not in profit or loss or other items that are also recognized in the financial statements.[5] Therefore, this change appears to be a practical solution with no sound technical or theoretical rationale.

> **Comment:** With reference to IFRSs, this Section explains the reporting of other comprehensive income before and after the amendments to IFRSs made by the 2007 Revision of IAS 1, effective for annual periods beginning on or after January 1, 2009 and the 2011 amendments to IAS 1.

---

[1] *IAS 1, ¶ BC20.*

[2] *Performance Reporting Joint International Group (JIG), Agenda Paper 2*, History of the Performance Reporting Project, *Appendix D:* A Summary of the Differences and Similarities Between the FASB's and IASB's Previously Proposed Models for the Statement of Comprehensive Income, *London (January 2005) www.fasb.org (last visited June 21, 2007).*

[3] *IASB,* Performance Reporting Project Update, *¶ 7 (December 2005) www.iasb.org (last visited April 28, 2006).*

[4] *IASB, Exposure Draft of* Proposed Amendments to IAS 1 Presentation of Financial Statements, *¶ BC18 (March 2006); Agenda Paper 14, Exposure Draft of* Proposed Amendments to IAS 1 Presentation of Financial Statements – Comment Letter Analysis, *¶ 43 (December 14, 2006).*

[5] *IAS 1, ¶¶ BC19–BC20; IASB Update December 2006.*

IAS 1 clarifies that such terminology is not mandatory.[6] CON 5 also calls comprehensive income *total nonowner changes in equity*, and opens the way to the use of alternative names in the future.[7] However, Subtopic 220-10 (FASB Statement No. 130) prefers *comprehensive income* to *total nonowner changes in equity* because it makes reference to a concept of income and is more descriptive of a performance measure, as a preliminary step in case future standards determined that it was ultimately to be reported in a statement of financial performance.[8]

According to the *AICPA Accounting Trends & Techniques*, virtually all of the U.S. GAAP companies surveyed in 2009–2002 that adopted a statement of comprehensive income or a statement of income and comprehensive income used a title containing the word "comprehensive" – therefore either comprehensive income, or comprehensive loss, or comprehensive income (loss). Few companies used the term "comprehensive earnings" or other title.[9]

7.1.2 Other Comprehensive Income Versus Income and Expense Recognized Directly in Equity

The 2007 revision of IAS 1 has now converged to the U.S. terminology of *other comprehensive income*.

Comment: *Income and expense recognized directly in equity* is the expression under IFRSs that has long been the substantial equivalent to *other comprehensive income* under U.S. GAAP, although such a phrase generally applied to single items and not to the whole set of those items of income and expenses. The Exposure Draft to IAS 1 had proposed the expression *other recognized income and expense.*[10]

7.1.3 Comprehensive Income Versus Earnings

Under CON 3, now superseded, *earnings* (see Section 6.1.3 previously) was an undefined term that was reserved for possible subcomponents of comprehensive income,[11] while *comprehensive income* in CON 3 had the same meaning of measure of performance as *earnings* in CON 1.[12] CON 5 expected that the notion of earnings would be subject to future evolution, also as a consequence of the debate on the clean-surplus concept (see Section 6.4.1 previously and Section 7.3 later).

Comment: Contrary to U.S. GAAP, IFRSs do not have *earnings* as an intermediate component of economic performance.

---

[6]   *IAS 1, ¶ 8.*
[7]   *FASB ASC 220-10-45-4 (FASB Statement No. 130, ¶¶ 10); FASB Statement No. 130, ¶ 74; CON 5, ¶¶ 13, 40, 101.*
[8]   *FASB Statement No. 130, ¶¶ 72–74.*
[9]   *AICPA ATT 2010 and AICPA ATT 2006, ¶ Table 4-2.*
[10] *IASB,* Exposure Draft of Proposed Amendments to IAS 1 Presentation of Financial Statements, *¶ 7 (March 2006).*
[11] *CON 3, ¶58.*
[12] *CON 1 (superseded), ¶ 43; CON 5, Footnote 7; CON 6, ¶ 2.*

7.1.4 Comprehensive Income Versus Profits

IFRSs use the term "profit or loss" as U.S. GAAP uses "net income," or "net loss" although IAS 1 clarifies that other terms, such as net income, are acceptable.[13]

Comment: However, the IASB Framework uses the terms "profit" or "profits" as the difference between income (i.e., revenues and gains) and expenses. In particular, profit results from the capital maintenance theory adopted[14] (Section 7.6 later). In that context, profit is used in a sense similar to comprehensive income, therefore including both net income recognized in the income statement and other items of income and expenses recognized outside of the income statement.

7.1.5 Accumulated Other Comprehensive Income

The *AICPA Accounting Trends & Techniques* show that almost all of the approximately 92% survey U.S. GAAP companies that in 2009 presented total accumulated other comprehensive income (in 2005 and 2002, 87% and 88%) used expressions that contained the word "comprehensive" – therefore, either "accumulated other comprehensive income," or "accumulated other comprehensive loss," or "accumulated other comprehensive income (loss)" – on the face of the statement of financial position. Few companies used the term "accumulated other nonowner changes in equity" or other titles. About 5% in 2009 (8% in 2005 and 9% in 2002) displayed accumulated balances by component of accumulated other comprehensive income on the face of the statement of financial position. In 2009, 2005, and 2002, 60%, 55%, and 36%, respectively, disclosed those components in the notes, and 18%, 15%, and 32% in the statement of changes in equity.[15]

Prior to amendments made by the 2007 revision of IAS 1, IFRSs had no term that was equivalent to accumulated other comprehensive income. IAS 1 uses the expression "accumulated balance of each class of other comprehensive income," generally in the context of placing such an item as a separate component of equity.[16]

7.1.6 Financial Performance Measured by Accrual Accounting

The *Joint Conceptual Framework Project* uses the expression "financial performance reflected by accrual accounting," in lieu of "comprehensive income" (under U.S. GAAP), or of "total recognized income and expense for the period" (under IFRSs, prior to the 2007 revision of IAS 1), because it contends that none of the existing terms is believed to communicate the related measuring process.[17]

---

[13] *IAS 1, ¶ 8.*

[14] The Conceptual Framework for Financial Reporting 2010, *¶ 4.58; IASB Framework, ¶ 103.*

[15] *AICPA ATT 2010 and AICPA ATT 2006, ¶¶ Tables 2-39, 2-30.*

[16] *For example: IAS 1, ¶ A4.*

[17] The Conceptual Framework for Financial Reporting 2010, *¶ OB17; IASB Discussion Paper,* Preliminary Views on an Improved Conceptual Framework for Financial Reporting, *¶ BC1.30 (July 2006); FASB Financial Accounting Series, Preliminary Views,* Conceptual Framework for Financial Reporting: Objective of Financial Reporting and Qualitative Characteristics of Decision-Useful Financial Reporting Information, *¶ BC1.30 (July 2006).*

> **Comment:** It is not clear if such a consideration would end up by substituting this new term in accounting standards or in permitting the use of alternative terminology, as currently is the case for IAS 1, CON 5, and Subtopic 220-10 (FASB Statement No. 130), or whether the Boards have deferred such a decision until a revised definition of the elements of financial statements is accomplished as part of the new Joint Conceptual Framework.

7.2   DEFINITIONS OF TERMS

7.2.1   Definition of Comprehensive Income

Currently, both U.S. GAAP and IFRSs identify comprehensive income as an entity's net assets variation during a period other than from transactions and other events (and circumstances, under U.S. GAAP) with owners in their capacity as owners (under U.S. GAAP, also referred to as investment by, and distributions, to owners).[18]

> **Comment:** This designation proceeds from a balance sheet approach (see Section 2.1.4.1 (3) previously).

> **Comment:** The previously used term *total recognized income and expense* was not defined in IFRSs.[19]

> **Comment:** Section 4.3.2 previously explains the linkage between comprehensive income and alternative approaches to consolidated financial statements.

> **Comment:** Section 4.14.2 previously illustrates the application of this linkage to treasury stock accounting.

> **Comment:** Section 6.4.1 previously illustrates the interaction between comprehensive income and a retroactive adjustment to retained earnings.

7.2.2   Definition of Other Comprehensive Income

IAS 1 and Subtopic 220-10 (FASB Statement No. 130) define other comprehensive income similarly, as items of income and expense (revenue, expenses, gains and losses, under U.S. GAAP) that are not recognized in profit or loss (in net income, under U.S. GAAP).[20]

> **Comment:** Therefore, literally, other comprehensive income is comprehensive income other than net income, and is therefore neither paid-in capital or retained earnings.

---

[18] *FASB ASC 220-10-20; CON 3 (superseded), ¶ 59; CON 5, ¶ 39; CON 6, ¶ 70; IAS 1, ¶ 7.*
[19] *IASB, Exposure Draft of Proposed Amendments to IAS 1 Presentation of Financial Statements, ¶ BC17 (March 2006).*
[20] *FASB ASC 220-10-55-6, 220-10-15-4 superseded by ASU 2011-05 (FASB Statement No. 130, ¶ 10); IAS 1, ¶ 7.*

> **Comment:** Although other comprehensive income is defined similarly to U.S. GAAP, the 2007 revision of IAS 1 made a dramatic change. The fact of not being part of profit or loss (as opposed to direct recognition in equity) means that it must no longer be recognized directly in equity. Now, other comprehensive income can only be recognized in the statement of comprehensive income.[21] While under U.S. GAAP, the statement of comprehensive income is one of the alternative presentation formats of comprehensive income (see Section 7.9.1 later), under IAS 1 it becomes a mandatory statement as no item of other comprehensive income can be recognized directly in equity. What previously was directly recognized in equity now is recognized outside profit or loss under the 2007 Revision of IAS 1, but not directly in equity. A similar change had also been proposed as part of the Exposure Draft of FASB Statement No. 130, but the FASB considered it premature before a conceptual reconsideration of comprehensive income and whether or not it should be intended as a measure of performance. It was also rejected as part of the criticism of the statement of income and comprehensive income (see Section 7.9.2 later).[22] Under ASU 2011-05, the statement of changes in equity is no longer an option to display comprehensive income. This is effective for fiscal years ending after December 15, 2012 and subsequent annual and interim periods, with early adoption permitted, and for fiscal years (and related interim periods) beginning after December 15, 2011 for public entities.[23]

> **Comment:** The Basis for Conclusions of IFRS 9 explains that direct recognition in equity of items that do not arise from transactions with owners is not appropriate.[24] Therefore, recognition of other comprehensive income in equity contrasts with the definition of comprehensive income.

IAS 1 lists components of other comprehensive income, such as currency translation adjustment, changes in revaluation surplus, and actuarial gains and losses on defined benefit plans when an entity elects their recognition in the statement of comprehensive income (prior to the 2011 revision of IAS 19), or remeasurements of defined benefit plans under IAS 19 (2011). Other comprehensive income also comprises unrealized gains or losses on available-for-sale financial assets (prior to IFRS 9) and unrealized gains and losses on hedging instruments in a cash flow hedge.[25] Items that have recently been added include gains and losses from investments in equity instruments measured at fair value through other comprehensive income[26] and changes in the fair value of a financial liability designated as at fair value through profit or loss that is attributable to change in the credit risk of the liability, unless this creates or enlarges an accounting mismatch.[27] IAS 12 distinguished items of other comprehensive income from items that are recognized directly in equity, such as retrospective application of a change in accounting policies, correction of an error, and the equity component of a compound financial instrument.[28]

---

[21] *IAS 1, ¶ BC53; IASB, Financial Statement Presentation, Agenda Paper 5,* Performance Reporting – Segment A Sweep Issues, *¶ 25 (January, 2006) www.iasb.org (last visited June 26, 2007).*

[22] *FASB Statement No. 130, ¶¶ 58, 59, 66.*

[23] *FASB ASC 220-10-45-1C, 220-10-65-1 (FASB Accounting Standards Update No. 2011-05,* Comprehensive Income (Topic 220) – Presentation of Comprehensive Income, *¶¶ 8, 10).*

[24] *IFRS 9 (2010), ¶ BC5.44.*

[25] *IAS 1, ¶ 7.*

[26] *IFRS 9, ¶ C12 (November 2009).*

[27] *IFRS 9, ¶ 5.7.7.*

[28] *IAS 12, ¶ 62A.*

> **Planning Point:** As shown in Section 7.8.3 later, this listing is not comprehensive, as other items are part of other comprehensive income under IFRSs (or, better, there are several variants of the topics that the standard mentions). Therefore, this list might be misleading as part of a definition if taken as exclusive. U.S. GAAP provides an inventory of items of other comprehensive income, from existing pronouncements on the subject.[29]

> **Comment:** Hence, IAS 1 gives a self-standing definition of both *other comprehensive income* and *comprehensive income*. The pre-2007 version of IAS 1 did not define *total recognized income and expense* for the period and *items of income and expense recognized directly in equity*.

By analogy, IAS 1 and Subtopic 220-10 (FASB Statement No. 130) use the approach of also defining profit or loss (or net income, under U.S. GAAP) as relatively autonomous terms, that is, the total of income less expenses (revenue, expenses, gains and losses, or comprehensive income, under U.S. GAAP) excluding other comprehensive income.[30]

According to the *AICPA Accounting Trends & Techniques*, cumulative translation adjustment accounted for approximately 31% in 2009 and 33% in 2005 of the components of other comprehensive income that were disclosed by the U.S. GAAP companies surveyed, minimum pension liability for approximately 27% in 2005, and defined benefit postretirement plan adjustments for 30% in 2009, changes in fair value of derivatives for approximately 22%, and unrealized gains or losses on certain investments for approximately 17–18%.[31]

IFRS for SMEs restricts the area of other comprehensive income to three items: foreign currency adjustment, some actuarial gains and losses, and certain types of cash flow hedges and hedge of a net investment in a foreign operation.[32]

7.2.3 Comprehensive Income as an Element of the Financial Statements

Up to the 2007 revision of IAS 1, IFRSs have not even mentioned comprehensive income, as such a concept is not part of the IASB Framework.

> **Comment:** The IASB Framework does not include comprehensive income within the elements of financial statements. On one hand, it does not define profit or loss or net income as opposed to comprehensive income. In fact, the term "income" under the IASB Framework (arguably inappropriately) refers to revenues and gains, not to net income (which in IFRS terminology is referred to as profit or loss). Profit or loss is instead the difference between income and expenses. On the other hand, the term "income" is ambiguous under the IASB Framework, as the Framework relates income as to be recognized in the income statement. For example, IFRIC 17 interprets this as referring to profit and loss in the income statement, as opposed to comprehensive income.[33] A more straightforward interpretation is that income and income statement in the Framework are used as generic concepts

---

[29] *FASB ASC 220-10-55-2 (FASB Statement No. 130, ¶¶ 17, 39), moved to FASB ASC 220-10-45-10A by ASU 2011-05.*

[30] *FASB Statement No. 130, Footnote 4; IAS 1, ¶ 7.*

[31] *AICPA ATT 2010 and AICPA ATT 2006, ¶ Table 4-3.*

[32] IFRS for Small and Medium-Sized Entities, ¶¶ 5.4(b), BC148.

[33] *IFRIC 17, ¶ BC51.*

without distinguishing these two levels. Under the U.S. Concepts revenue, expenses, gains, losses, investments by owners, distributions to owners, and comprehensive income are among the elements of the financial statements. In the context of the elements of financial statements, CON 6 does not even mention net income, although CON 5 debates on the difference between earnings and net income.[34] Interestingly, the U.S. Concepts do not define conceptual characteristics to distinguish comprehensive income from net income. However, in both the conceptual frameworks, profit or loss (or comprehensive income, under the U.S. Concepts) is defined based on a balance sheet approach (see Section 2.1.4.1 (3) previously), in terms of changes in assets and liabilities.

Recently, the IASB and the FASB decided to consider whether to define elements, such as comprehensive income, that are not present in one of the conceptual frameworks.[35]

7.2.4 Computation of Comprehensive Income

CON 5 uses a three-step direct calculation of comprehensive income as earnings, plus or minus cumulative accounting adjustments for a change in accounting principle (the result of computation of those two being net income), plus other nonowner changes in equity (that is, other comprehensive income). IAS 1 computes it directly as the sum of profit or loss for the period and other comprehensive income.[36]

Comprehensive income can also be indirectly derived by following the definition, changes in net assets from nonowner transactions in a period.

> **Planning Point:** The Implementation Guidance of IAS 1 shows a statement of changes in equity that tries to implement the definition of comprehensive income. It shows retained earnings (an equity item) on the face of the statement, and not profit or loss (as resulting from nonowners' transactions). This is in accordance with the categorization working principle of the *Financial Statement Presentation Project* that segregates transactions with owners in their capacity as owners (see Section 1.4.3.2 previously). The caption "total comprehensive income for the year" includes both other comprehensive income and profit or loss for the period. However, the latter component is not evident from the format of the statement as it is included in retained earnings.

7.3 THE ALL-INCLUSIVE OR CLEAN-SURPLUS CONCEPT OF INCOME

7.3.1 Definition of the Clean-Surplus Concept of Income

Both U.S. GAAP and IFRSs acknowledge the "clean-surplus" or "all-inclusive" concept of income, under which all items of income and expenses in a period must be recognized in net income, irrespective of whether or not they consist of results of operations for the period. This is in opposition to the so-called "current operating performance" or "dirty-surplus" concept of income that excludes certain items from net income, such as extraordinary and nonrecurring items. Both U.S. GAAP and IFRSs take an intermediate position between the two approaches,

---

[34] *CON 5, ¶¶ 33–34; CON 6, ¶ 1; IAS 1, ¶ BC51;* The Conceptual Framework for Financial Reporting 2010, *¶ 4.29; IASB Framework, ¶ 74.*

[35] *IASB Update, October 2008; FASB Action Alert, October 20, 2008 Joint Meeting.*

[36] *CON 5, ¶ 44; IAS 1, ¶ 7.*

although with giving prominence to the all-inclusive approach, as discussed in the following Section.[37]

Comment: The 2007 revision of IAS 1 introduces the two-statement approach to reporting income (Section 7.9.2 later). Although this standard maintains the clean-surplus principle, it must rephrase it in the new context. Therefore, all items of income and expense in a period must be recognized in an all-inclusive measure of income (i.e., comprehensive income), although not necessarily in the income statement. Depending on the presentation option that an entity elects and depending on the items, they may be shown in a single statement of comprehensive income or in a separate income statement or in a second statement of comprehensive income.[38]

7.3.2   Pros and Cons of the Clean-Surplus Concept

Worksheet 42 summaries the pros and cons of the "clean-surplus" concept. Most of those elements are illustrated in Section 6.4.1 previously.

Comment: In addition to what is explained in that Section, the all-inclusive concept of income would permit a simpler tracking of the changes in equity and reconciliation of those to the sum of the periodic net incomes. Changes in net assets and changes in net income would be consistent under this approach. Furthermore, the income statement would be a single statement that uses accrual-based information, thus better enabling the prediction of cash flows. The risk of overlooking items that are omitted from the income statement would be eliminated.[39]

Comment: As mentioned in Section 3.5.2.2 previously, Section 5.1 previously, and Section 6.1.1 previously, variations of the term "surplus" exist for both retained earnings and additional paid-in capital. By analogy, "parallel" concepts of clean-surplus also exist for these components of equity that appear in accounting pronouncements. The general rule that increases in retained earnings must be the result of only items that affect the income statement is analogous to a sort of clean-surplus concept applied to retained earnings (Section 6.2 previously). Mirroring general principle postulates that additional paid-in capital should not be directly reduced by an entity's operations other than transactions with owners (Section 5.4 previously). As illustrated in this Book there are several circumstances in which both these general principles are not accomplished. This topic is expanded in the final conclusions for a comprehensive model of the components of equity (Section 7.21 later).

Comment: The clean-surplus concept refers to net income, thus it originates from an income statement view.[40] The symmetrical evidence is that all nonowner changes in net assets during a period must equal a measure of income (a balance sheet view). However, this can be implemented in a continuum, ranging from the all-inclusive to the dirty-surplus concepts. The purest view would consider the clean measure of income to be net income, as presented in the income statement. A broader view

---

[37]   *FASB Statement No. 16, ¶¶ 23, 73; FASB Statement No. 130, ¶ 2; APB 9, ¶¶ 3, 10, 13–15, 17; ARB 43, Ch.8 (superseded), ¶ 6; IAS 1, ¶ 88; IAS 8 (1977) superseded, ¶¶ 4–7.*

[38]   *IAS 1, ¶¶ 81, 88.*

[39]   *APB 9, ¶ 14; Joint International Group on Financial Statement,* Presentation, *presentation by Hiroshi Yamada (June 14, 2005).*

[40]   *APB 9, ¶ 14.*

(resulting in other comprehensive income being a first departure from a pure all-inclusive concept) would deem this measure of income to be comprehensive income, as presented in the statement of comprehensive income, but not directly in equity. An extreme view would consider such metrics to be retained earnings, as presented in a statement of income and retained earnings (see Section 6.8.4 previously).

Comment: The balance sheet view of the clean-surplus concept is traditionally applied to proprietorship equity.[41] That means that net income is considered to be the portion that accrues to the benefit of the controlling stockholders. The clean-surplus concept applied at this level infers that period changes in equity arising from nonowner sources that are attributable to the shareholders of the parent company must equal the cumulative net income. After the final determination that noncontrolling interest is part of equity under Subtopic 810-10 (FASB Statement No. 160) and IAS 27 Revised 2008 (Section 4.3.2 and Section 4.3.3 previously), the clean-surplus concept must be adapted to include entirely net income. Under the proprietary perspective (see Section 2.1 previously), gains and losses accruing to the common shareholders that directly affect equity are dirty-surplus items. This also includes items that affect components of equity different from accumulated other comprehensive income. Examples are certain tax benefits of loss carryforwards (Section 8.2.2 later) and tax benefits of dividends paid to ESOPs (Section 8.2.17.5 later). However, from an entity perspective, equity does not measure only the rights of common shareholders. Different categories of equity, such as common stock, preferred stock, retained earnings, additional paid-in capital, or noncontrolling interests, are supposed to take care of such differences.

Comment: The 2011 Amendments to IAS 1 and ASU 2011-05, by disassociating other comprehensive income from direct recognition in equity, actually enlarge the scope of the clean-surplus: other comprehensive income becomes recognized in income in a statement where income is presented. In other terms, the focus shifts from net income presented in the income statement to comprehensive income presented in the statement of comprehensive income. Here, the clean surplus is implemented either in the same statement (through reclassification of other comprehensive income into profit or loss within that statement), or in two steps through the use of a two-statement approach (that is, the use of both an income statement and a statement of comprehensive income). As mentioned in Section 7.9.2 later, Subtopic 220-10 (FASB Statement No. 130) before ASU 2011-05 also acknowledged this link between the statement of comprehensive income and the all-inclusive concept[42] but considered the move to a single statement of comprehensive income as premature.

Subtopic 250-10 (FASB Statement No. 16) puts the all-inclusive concept of income in relation to other points in accounting literature that reinforce this theory, including the comprehensive allocation method of income taxes, the accounting for changes in estimates, and the accounting for loss contingencies.[43]

7.3.3 Departures from the Clean-Surplus Concept

Both U.S. GAAP and IFRSs depart from a pure clean-surplus model. Firstly, as shown in Section 6.4 previously, items such as corrections of errors or, in certain cases, changes in accounting

---

[41] *APB 9, ¶ 13; ARB 43, Ch.8 (superseded), ¶ 6.*
[42] *FASB ASC 220-10-45-10 (FASB Statement no. 130, ¶¶ 58, 67).*
[43] *FASB ASC 450-20-25-7 (FASB Statement No. 16, ¶¶ 29–37).*

principles as well as other items are reported directly in retained earnings. Secondly, both sets of standards require recognition of other comprehensive income outside of net income.[44]

The term *comprehensive income* itself was criticized for not being comprehensive. Subtopic 220-10 (FASB Statement No. 130) acknowledged this consideration to a certain extent and that the topic would be addressed in a broader-scope project on comprehensive income.[45]

Furthermore, FASB Statement No. 130 maintains outside of its scope certain transactions that have characteristics of both equity transactions with owners and of comprehensive income, such as the direct reduction to stockholders' equity under accounting for Employee Stock Ownership Plans – ESOPs (see Section 4.14.4 previously), or the deduction for unearned or deferred compensation expense under stock options arrangements (see Section 5.2.10 previously), or certain other transactions that directly affect additional paid-in capital or other equity accounts and have characteristics similar to items of other comprehensive income.[46]

Comment: U.S. GAAP does (and IFRSs did) permit other comprehensive income to be recognized directly in equity. That was valid for IFRSs until the 2007 revision of IAS 1, under which other comprehensive income can no longer be recognized directly in equity.

Comment: Under U.S. GAAP, the mechanism of recycling (see Section 7.8 later) should ensure that all items of other comprehensive income pass through profit or loss and thus sooner or later become retained earnings. In this way, cumulative net income over several accounting periods would equal accumulated profit or loss in retained earnings.[47]

More dramatically, as discussed in Section 6.6 previously and Section 7.8.3 later, IFRSs have an additional exception to the all-inclusive concept, i.e., when a category of gains and losses that are recognized in other comprehensive income are then transferred to retained earnings.

7.4 PURPOSE OF REPORTING INCOME AND ITS COMPONENTS

Worksheet 43 summarizes several elements that, mainly within the discussions of the *Financial Statement Presentation Project*, have been used to substantiate the purpose of reporting net income and reasons for considering it as a measure of performance, as compared to earnings, comprehensive income, and other comprehensive income.

7.4.1 Purpose of Reporting Net Income

Net income is traditionally seen as the benchmark measure of performance. It also has a forecasting function, insofar as it is a basis for projecting sustainable profits and cash flows. It is sometimes seen as a measure of the long-term cash flow prospects of the company, a measure of performance that is predictable and sustainable, and a fundamental indicator for valuation purposes to assess enterprise value based on the future expectation of its results.

---

[44] *FASB Statement No. 130, ¶ 3; IAS 1, ¶ 89.*
[45] *FASB Statement No. 130, ¶¶ 70–71.*
[46] *FASB Statement No. 130, ¶¶ 112, 119.*
[47] *Joint International Group on Financial Statement, Minutes of Meeting, September 15, 2006, ¶ 9.*

From an income and expense view, it is the result of the earnings process, metrics of income that is realized and that is measurable with sufficient certainty and reliability[48] or that has at least passed certain tests for recognition,[49] the first input for computing tax, and is a yardstick of distributable profit from the perspective of defense of capital (see Section 3.5.2 previously). For these reasons, it may be conceived as directly related to the results of management's action, a basis for management performance appraisal, a measure of the stewardship of management, and a decision making and control tool.[50]

The Discussion Paper of the *Financial Presentation Project* maintains profit or loss or net income as it acknowledges it as a useful indicator of performance.[51]

7.4.2 Purpose of Reporting Earnings

Under U.S. GAAP, the term earnings has a technical meaning. CON 5 defines "earnings" as net income for the period minus the cumulative effects of a change in accounting principle (see Section 6.4.3 previously) that are recognized in the current period.[52] Under CON 3, now superseded, *earnings* was an undefined term that was reserved for possible subcomponents of comprehensive income,[53] while the term "comprehensive income" (see Section 7.1.3 previously) in CON 3 had the same meaning of measure of performance as *earnings* in CON 1.[54] CON 5 expected that the notion of *earnings* would be subject to future evolution, also as a consequence of the debate on clean-surplus concept (see Section 7.3 previously).

> **Comment:** Contrary to U.S. GAAP, IFRSs do not generally use the term *earnings*, apart from other technical terminology such as earnings per share, and have no such intermediate component of economic performance.

CON 5 defines *earnings* as a measure of period performance that excludes items that do not relate to the current period, as the difference between asset inflows and outflows associated with cash-to-cash cycles that are completed or substantially completed during the period. However, it acknowledges that net income or profit or loss are used in practice as synonyms of earnings.[55]

---

[48] The Conceptual Framework for Financial Reporting 2010, ¶¶ 4.47, 4.48; *IASB Framework*, ¶¶ 92–93; *Minutes of the June 15, 2005 Joint International Group (JIG) on Performance Reporting, ¶ 4 (August 22, 2005) www.fasb.org (last visited June 21, 2007).*

[49] *IAS 40, ¶ B63(f).*

[50] *Performance Reporting Joint International Group (JIG) on Performance Reporting, European CFO Task Force, Presentations by Bo Eriksson, Hiroshi Yamada, Ken Kelly, Takashi Yaekura (June 14–15, 2005) www.fasb.org (last visited June 21, 2007).*

[51] *Discussion Paper,* Preliminary Views on Financial Statement Presentation, *¶ 3.35 (October 2008).*

[52] *CON 5, ¶¶ 34, 42.*

[53] *CON 3, ¶ 58.*

[54] *CON 1 (superseded), ¶ 43; CON 5, Footnote 7; CON 6, ¶ 2; Accounting Terminology Bulletin No. 2, Proceeds, Revenue, Income, Profit, and Earnings (superseded), ¶ 11; U.S. Securities and Exchange Commission Staff, June 13, 2003.* Frequently Asked Questions Regarding the Use of Non-GAAP Financial Measures, *Washington, D.C.: SEC, ¶ Question 14.*

[55] *CON 5, ¶¶ 34–36. Similarly, Accounting Terminology Bulletin No. 2,* Proceeds, Revenue, Income, Profit, and Earnings, *¶ 11.*

> **Comment:** In business language, *earnings* are commonly used to denote "performance," without a specific technical accounting reference.

Earnings are also found in a context of management stewardship and accountability.[56] Furthermore, as shown in Worksheet 43, the term *earnings* has a specific connotation in relation to investor relations, especially to announcements to financial analysts and financial markets, as a preview of yet-to-be-published financial results, hence a basis for the formation of expectations and a starting point for analysis as opposed to a final measure of performance.[57]

Earnings are often mentioned with reference to practices of "earnings management." In the context of this Section, this connotation has to be related to the "quality of earnings" and whether or not the classification of an item into earnings versus other comprehensive income may be informative of a different quality of data, in the sense of greater accuracy, stability, realization, lower volatility, lower risk, etc. This topic is better analyzed in Section 7.4.3 below. Topic 820 (FASB Statement No. 157) requires certain disclosures of recurring fair value measurements subsequent to initial recognition using significant unobservable inputs (Level 3 of the fair value hierarchy) and unrealized gains and losses included in earnings, separate from other comprehensive income, irrespective from whether or not they may be of lesser quality than realized gains or losses. In particular, an entity must illustrate how much of those total gains or losses for the period included in earnings come from changes in unrealized gains or losses relating to assets and liabilities still held at the reporting date. This is intended to give insight into the effects of fair value measurements on earnings for the period.[58] IFRS 13 and the March 2009 amendments to IFRS 7 require similar disclosures, but do not limit the Level 3 disclosures for assets and liabilities still held at the end of the reporting period to unrealized gains or losses.[59]

Finally, earnings have a specialized meaning for calculation of the earnings to fixed charges ratio for registering debt securities.[60]

7.4.3 Purpose of Reporting Other Comprehensive Income

Worksheet 43 illustrates the features that have been identified,[61] mainly as part of the *Financial Statement Presentation Project*, in an attempt to ascertain the characteristics of other

---

[56] *CON 1 (superseded), ¶ 51; IASB, Conceptual Framework Project, Minutes of Meeting, ¶ 46(d) (February 20, 2007) www.iasb.org (last visited June 21, 2007).*

[57] *Performance Reporting Joint International Group (JIG), Agenda Paper 2, History of the Performance Reporting Project, ¶ 29(i), London (January 2005) www.fasb.org (last visited June 21, 2007).*

[58] *FASB ASC 820-10-50-1, 820-10-50-2, 820-10-55-62 moved to 820-10-55-101, 820-10-55-63 moved to 820-10-55-102 (FASB Statement No. 157, ¶¶ 32, A35, C97-C100, as amended by ASU No. 2010-06 and by ASU No. 2011-04).*

[59] *IFRS 13, ¶ 93(f); Amendments to IFRS 7 Financial Instruments, Improving Disclosures about Financial Instruments, ¶ 27B(d) (March 2009), deleted by IFRS 13.*

[60] *Regulation S-K, Instruction 1(C) to ¶ 229.503(d).*

[61] *FASB Statement No. 130, ¶ 60; FASB/IASB, Performance Reporting Joint International Group (JIG), Agenda Paper 2, History of the Performance Reporting Project, ¶¶ 9, 29(a), London (January 2005) www.fasb.org (last visited June 21, 2007); FASB/IASB, Performance Reporting Joint International Group (JIG), Minutes of Meeting, January, 13-14, 2005, ¶ 13, www.fasb.org (last visited June 21,*

comprehensive income. This Section illustrates the application of these characteristics to specific items of other comprehensive income. Section 7.8.2 later further develops the topics in relation to recycling.

Authoritative pronouncements give no sound and solid conceptual theory of other comprehensive income as opposed to net income and the reasons for which a different presentation of such an aggregate would be warranted. No such distinction exists in the IASB Framework. Furthermore, the accounting for other comprehensive income has been developing on a piecemeal basis without a consistent theoretical approach.[62] However, CON 5 highlights the importance of classification and disaggregation in financial statements, based on similarity of characteristics, recurrence, stability, risk, and reliability for the purposes of prediction of future cash flows.[63]

7.4.3.1 The Realization Hypothesis

In certain circumstances, other comprehensive income is found in association with items of profit or loss that are unrealized, as items of other comprehensive income do not generally arise from exchange transaction or results from operations, but rather reflect the remeasurement to fair value of assets or liabilities whose economic effects have not yet completed the earnings process. For example, Subtopic 830-10 (FASB Statement No. 52) and CON 5 justify the recognition of foreign translation adjustment in other comprehensive income based on its unrealized status, although the standard acknowledges possible further developments in relation to the studies on reporting all components of comprehensive income. Sale and complete or substantially complete liquidation of the foreign operation are realization events. Subtopic 830-10 adds that exchange rate changes between the reporting currency and the functional currency of the foreign operation do not affect that subsidiary's cash flows from operations.[64] From a slightly different perspective, IAS 21 justifies the presentation of foreign currency adjustment outside profit or loss because it does not

---

2007); *Performance Reporting Joint International Group (JIG) on Performance Reporting, European CFO Task Force, Presentations by Bo Eriksson, Guido Kerkhoff, Ken Kelly, Walter Schuster, Takashi Yaekura (June 14–15, 2005) www.fasb.org (last visited June 21, 2007); FASB/IASB Financial Statement Presentation Project, Agenda Paper 6C/FASB Memorandum 44C,* Measurement; OCI and Recycling; the Statement of Comprehensive Income, ¶¶ *17, 26, 27, 39, 66 (October 24, 2006) www.iasb.org (last visited June 21, 2007); IASB Meeting, December 14, 2006, Agenda Paper 14:* Exposure Draft of Proposed Amendments to IAS 1 Presentation of Financial Statements – Comment Letter Analysis, ¶ *63 (December 14, 2006); IASB, Financial Statement Presentation Project, Agenda Paper 15A,* Other Comprehensive Income, ¶ *35 (December 14, 2006); FASB, Minutes of Meeting, December 13, 2006,* Financial Statement Presentation – Application of Working Principles (continued), ¶ *8 (December 20, 2006) www.fasb.org (last visited June 21, 2007); IASB, Financial Statement Presentation, Agenda Paper 3B,* Presenting Information about the Cause of Change in Reported Amounts of Assets and Liabilities, ¶ *25 (June 19, 2007) www.iasb.org (last visited June 21, 2007).*

[62] *IAS 41, ¶ B17(f); FASB/IASB Financial Statement Presentation Project, Agenda Paper 6C/FASB Memorandum 44C, Measurement;* OCI and Recycling; the Statement of Comprehensive Income, ¶ *40 (October 24, 2006) www.iasb.org (last visited June 21, 2007); IASB,* Exposure Draft of Proposed Amendments to IAS 1 Presentation of Financial Statements, ¶ *BC13 (March 2006); IASB, Financial Statement Presentation Project, Agenda Paper 9B,* Other Comprehensive Income Presentation, ¶ *60 (March 22, 2007) www.iasb.org (last visited June 21, 2007); IASB, Financial Statement Presentation Project, Agenda Paper 3A,* Basket Transactions and Foreign Currency Translation Adjustments, ¶ *39 (June 19, 2007) www.iasb.org (last visited June 21, 2007).*

[63] *CON 5, ¶ 20.*

[64] *FASB Statement No. 52, ¶¶ 113, 114, 117, 119; CON 5, ¶ 50.*

affect parent's cash flows from operations.[65] The Basis for Conclusions of IFRS 9 reports the realization notion as a common view of other comprehensive income.[66]

> **Comment:** This Book identifies this theory as the "realization hypothesis."

> **Comment:** The IASB Framework mentions that, under a financial capital maintenance concept measured in nominal monetary units, unrealized changes in prices of assets held (holding gains or losses) are not recognized until asset disposal (i.e., realization), although they are conceptually profits. The implementation of this principle through the standards has led to selective recognition of certain holding gains or losses in other comprehensive income, not in profit or loss.[67]

> **Comment:** There are some exceptions to this general rule. Net income may include items that are not fully realized such as a write down of inventory at the lower-of-cost-or-market rule, or an impairment of fixed assets, a change in fair values of trading securities, or of derivative instruments. A point during the *Financial Statement Presentation Project* was whether or not these items should be included in realized profit or loss.[68] Topic 820 (FASB Statement No. 157) requires the disclosure of the effects of fair value measurements on earnings for the period that are attributable to the change in unrealized gains or losses relating to assets and liabilities measured within Level 3 of its fair value hierarchy that are still held at the end of the period.[69] IFRS 13 and the March 2009 amendments to IFRS 7 require similar disclosures, but not limited to unrealized gains or losses.[70]

> **Comment:** The realization hypothesis is not conclusive. For example, the FASB rejected the alternative to report post-acquisition changes in the amounts recognized for assets and liabilities arising from contingencies in other comprehensive income.[71] Furthermore, the IASB Staff labeled the realization rationale as a common misunderstanding.[72]

7.4.3.2   The Timing Difference Hypothesis   Remeasurements of assets or liabilities may arise from changes in prices or from changes in estimates.[73] In that respect, other comprehensive income may also comprise unrealized holding gains or losses, including capital maintenance adjustments (see Section 7.6.3 later).

---

[65]   *IAS 21, ¶ 41.*

[66]   *IFRS 9 (2010), ¶ BC5.54.*

[67]   The Conceptual Framework for Financial Reporting 2010, *¶ 4.63; IASB Framework, ¶ 108.*

[68]   *IASB/FASB, Financial Statement Presentation Project, Agenda Paper 3,* Categorization in a Statement of Earnings and Comprehensive Income, *¶ 45 (June 2005).*

[69]   *FASB ASC 820-10-50-1, 820-10-50-2, 820-10-50-3 (FASB Statement No. 157, ¶¶ 32, C100, as amended by ASU No. 2010-06 and by ASU No. 2011-04).*

[70]   *IFRS 13, ¶ 93(f); Amendments to IFRS 7 Financial Instruments,* Improving Disclosures about Financial Instruments, *¶ 27B(d) (March 2009), deleted by IFRS 13.*

[71]   *FASB Statement No. 141R, ¶ BC241.*

[72]   *Project Summary and Feedback Statement, June 2011.* Presentation of Items of Other Comprehensive Income (Amendments to IAS 1), *page 4.*

[73]   *Discussion Paper,* Preliminary Views on Financial Statement Presentation, *¶ 4.19, Footnote 16 (October 2008).*

In more general terms, other comprehensive income indicates items of income and expenses that have a "timing" difference for recognition in profit or loss. In this sense, it may be seen as a reconciling item between net income and comprehensive income.[74] For example, some respondents to the Exposure Draft concerning own credit risk related to financial liabilities gave this interpretation of unrealized gains and losses in other comprehensive income.[75]

> **Comment:** This Book terms this the "timing difference hypothesis."

7.4.3.3 The Measurement Base Difference Hypothesis

7.4.3.3 The Measurement Base Difference Hypothesis Under another theory, other comprehensive income arises only when a certain basis is adopted in measuring assets or liabilities in the statement of financial position (e.g., fair value) and a different basis (generally, but not always, historical cost) to measure changes in value of those assets or liabilities in the income statement.[76] This is better illustrated in Section 7.7.2 later, on the recycling mechanism. The SEC study on fair value also highlights some interactions between the balance sheet and the income statement that result in other comprehensive income.[77]

> **Comment:** This Book terms this theory the "measurement base difference hypothesis."

7.4.3.4 The Fair Value Measurement and Anticipatory Value Hypotheses Under another view, other comprehensive income would arise from remeasurement to fair value of assets and liabilities whose economic effects have not yet completed the earning process. An elaboration of this concept focuses on the information value of fair value measurements for forecasting purposes.

> **Comment:** This Book refers to these arguments as the "fair value measurement hypothesis" and "anticipatory value hypothesis," respectively.

Fair value adjustments are generally not systematic. Furthermore, the fair value measurement of an asset or a liability must already incorporate the prediction of future cash flows. If this is true, the predictive value of items of other comprehensive income that are remeasurement adjustments would be low or nil. This has been translated in the formula of other comprehensive income as having a "valuation multiple" of one, unless it results from change in value of financial items that are actively managed, generally on a portfolio basis. It is to be noted,

---

[74] *FASB Statement No. 130, ¶ 98; IASB/FASB, Joint International Group (JIG) on Financial Statement Presentation, Agenda Paper 8,* Net Income, Other Comprehensive Income, and Recycling, *¶¶ 7, A4 (September 15, 2006) www.fasb.org (last visited June 21, 2007); IASB Update, October 2006.*

[75] *IFRS 9 (October 2010), ¶ BC5.54.*

[76] *IASB/FASB, Joint International Group (JIG) on Financial Statement Presentation, Agenda Paper 8,* Net Income, Other Comprehensive Income, and Recycling, *¶ 9 (September 15, 2006) www.fasb.org (last visited June 21, 2007); IASB Update, October 2006.*

[77] *United States Securities and Exchange Commission, Office of the Chief Accountant, Division of Corporate Finance,* Report and Recommendations Pursuant to Section 133 of the Emergency Economic Stabilization Act of 2008: Study on Mark-To-Market Accounting *(December 2008), page 18.*

however, that a remeasurement to fair value does not imply per se that such a change in value is recognized as an item of other comprehensive income, as demonstrated by the accounting for trading securities. Remeasurement to fair value is not the only type of value change. Value changes may also include remeasurements of assets and liabilities measured on a cost basis, and these are subject to the same consideration of predictability. Examples of such changes are revision of past estimates, certain impairment losses, and prior period adjustments. Furthermore, non-remeasurement transactions or events may also be distinguished based on their predictive value.

> **Comment:** Fair value changes may have predictive value when they are due to the passage of time. They probably have no such informative meaning if they are due to market factors, revised model estimates, or change in measurement method.

The PAAinE classifies models that distinguish the predictive value of items of the statement of income as the recurring versus nonrecurring model (based on persistence) and as the business model approach (when classification and measurement of items follows the way an entity manages it).[78] Along the lines of the former model, the Discussion Paper of the *Financial Statement Presentation Project* used to distinguish between remeasurements and accruals other than remeasurements (i.e., accrued payable and receivable and systematic allocations such as depreciation, amortization, accretion, and depletion). Remeasurements may be recurring or nonrecurring. Recurring remeasurements may be fair value changes (term used by the FASB) or valuation adjustments (term adopted by the IASB). A valuation adjustment remeasures an asset or a liability to a current value, a concept which may include fair value, fair value less costs to sell, value in use, and net realizable value. The term "recurring" is not used, as opposed to one-off adjustment; instead it refers to the fact that a standard requires such a remeasurement every period.[79]

> **Comment:** Conversely, IFRS 9 follows a business model approach. Therefore, users can adjust their projections of cash flows depending on whether a financial instrument is carried at amortized cost or at fair value through profit or loss, or an equity instrument is considered not for trading but as at fair value through other comprehensive income.

> **Comment:** Currently, several accounting pronouncements require disclosure of inputs and method to determine fair value. Among others, Subtopic 825-10 (FASB Statement No. 107) and IFRS 7 require disclosure of methods and significant assumptions for estimation of fair value of financial instruments. Topic 715 (FASB Statement No. 132(R)) and IAS 19 require information about the assumptions and methods used to estimate defined obligation and other pension items. Topic 820 (FASB Statement No. 157) requires disclosure of inputs used to develop fair value measurements

---

[78] *The Instituto de Contabilidad y Auditoria de Cuentas and EFRAG, 2009.* Pro-Active Accounting Activities in Europe (PAAinE) Performance Reporting, A European Discussion Paper, ¶ 5.4 *www.efrag.org (last visited April 18, 2010).*

[79] *Discussion Paper,* Preliminary Views on Financial Statement Presentation, ¶¶ 4.19, 4.45 *(October 2008).*

on recurring and nonrecurring items. Subtopic 825-10 (FASB Statement No. 159) requires separate presentation of assets and liabilities that are measured pursuant to the fair value option. IAS 1 requires disclosure of assumptions for discounting cash flows and separate presentation of items with different measurement bases.[80]

Comment: Under the 2011 revision of IAS 19, remeasurements of net defined benefit liability or asset go to other comprehensive income. The rationale is that this would isolate information on future cash flow uncertainty and risk and add predictive value.[81]

7.4.3.5 The Volatility Hypothesis Other comprehensive income has also been put in relation to items that are uncertain as to measurability, volatile, unpredictable, nonrecurring, or irrelevant for decision making.[82] The IASB's Chairman also acknowledged the use of other comprehensive income to avoid introducing accounting volatility.[83] The SEC study on fair value also mentions this debate.[84]

Comment: This Book conceptualizes this approach as the "volatility hypothesis."

Firstly, other comprehensive income would remove volatility from reported earnings. For example, Subtopic 320-10 (FASB Statement No. 115) and CON 5 highlight this rationale for reporting unrealized holding gains and losses of available-for-sale securities in equity.[85]

Comment: Volatility of foreign currency adjustment would distort net income. IAS 21 justifies the presentation of foreign currency adjustment outside profit or loss based on the fact that it does not affect cash flows from operations.[86] With regard to postemployment plans, although the IASB rejected the volatility rationale, it accepted it as a practical expedient.[87]

---

[80] *FASB ASC 825-10-50-10, 825-10-50-11, 825-10-50-12 (FASB Statement No. 107, ¶ 10); FASB ASC 715-20-50-1 (FASB Statement No. 132(R), ¶ 5); FASB ASC 820-10-50-1, 820-10-50-2, 820-10-50-3 (FASB Statement No. 157, ¶ 32, as amended by ASU No. 2010-06 and ASU No. 2011-04); FASB ASC 825-10-45-1, 825-10-45-2 (FASB Statement No. 159, ¶ 15); IAS 1, ¶¶ 59, 126; IAS 19 (2007), ¶ 120A; IAS 19 (2011), ¶ 144; IFRS 7, ¶ 27.*

[81] *IAS 19 (2011), ¶¶ BC73, BC88, BC90, BC95, DO15.*

[82] *As an additional example, IAS 41, ¶ B39.*

[83] *Speech by Hans Hoogervorst in Beijing, July 29, 2011.* China and IFRS – an opportunity for leadership in global financial reporting. *[Online] IASB. Available at www.iasb.org (last visited August 15, 2011).*

[84] *United States Securities and Exchange Commission, Office of the Chief Accountant, Division of Corporate Finance,* Report and Recommendations Pursuant to Section 133 of the Emergency Economic Stabilization Act of 2008: Study on Mark-To-Market Accounting *(December 2008), page 18.*

[85] *FASB Statement No. 115, ¶ 94; CON 5, ¶ 50.*

[86] *IAS 21, ¶ 41.*

[87] *IAS 19 (2007), ¶ BC48E.*

> **Comment:** Under the 2011 revision of IAS 19, reporting the remeasurement of net defined benefit liability or asset in other comprehensive income would segregate the volatility inherent in that component.[88]

> **Comment:** The additional removal of volatility is one justification for non-GAAP financial measures, as discussed in Section 7.5.4 later. On the other hand, mitigating volatility in earnings through other comprehensive income would not reduce volatility in reported capital. Whether eliminating volatility is good or bad has been long discussed. A typical counterargument is that volatility that is inherent in a certain business must be reflected in the financial statements and performance indicators, to the extent that fair value reporting is more faithfully representative and appropriate disclosure is provided.[89]

> **Comment:** Under the Exposure Draft on hedge accounting, other comprehensive income would include both gains and losses on a hedged item in a fair value hedge and on the hedging instrument. One of the justifications is that this would remove volatility from other comprehensive income and equity.[90]

Secondly, based on these considerations, other comprehensive income would not have a predictive value of future income or cash flows or in assessing enterprise value for valuation purposes, although it affects the current book value of equity. However, it has been objected that in any case it gives supplementary information on fair value, and that information about measurement uncertainty as a result of changes in risks and opportunities is of value per se.

7.4.3.6   The Core/Noncore Distinction Hypothesis   The concepts of "noncore" activities or "non-operational" performance have also been employed to justify other comprehensive income. However, their main implications relate to the classification of items that make up net income in the income statement. In fact, certain items are often removed from net income to define non-GAAP financial measures of performance (see Section 7.5.4 later).

The meaning of core activities is relative to the individual company, industry, and economic trends and is, to a certain extent, subjective. The AICPA Special Committee of Financial Reporting tried to define core business. This concept tends to mix with that of usual or recurring events or transactions. However, a clear distinction between the characteristics of core business and usual or recurring events is not set: a usual event or transaction that becomes frequent may be classified as core or noncore, depending on circumstances. The Committee suggested a separate presentation of noncore activities on the face of the

---

[88] *IAS 19 (2011), ¶¶ BC65(c), BC72(c); Project Summary and Feedback Statement,* Amendments to IAS 19, Employee Benefits, *page 15.*

[89] *FASB Statement No. 115, ¶ 95.*

[90] *Exposure Draft,* Hedge Accounting, *¶ IN30 (December 2010).*

financial statements, their measurement at fair value, and their charging or crediting directly to equity.[91]

Comment: It is controversial whether net income itself represents the performance of the current operations of an entity (so-called "core earnings"), as extraordinary items are part of net income (U.S. GAAP only), as well as unusual and frequent, or usual but infrequent items. Earnings would be more appropriate to this purpose, as at least cumulative-effect adjustments from a change in accounting principle, if any, are excluded.

Comment: On one hand, other comprehensive income may include items that are related to the core business or current operating cycle, such as revaluation surplus on property, plant and equipment and, on the other hand, items that are not necessarily items related to core business or for which such determination is quite subjective, such as unrealized gains and losses on available-for-sale securities, cash flow hedges, or defined benefit plans.

As an additional point, IAS 19 criticizes the U.S. GAAP additional minimum pension liability (an item of other comprehensive income – see Section 7.18.2 later) as not being on a going concern basis.[92]

7.4.3.7 The Entity's Performance Hypothesis In theory, other comprehensive income items would measure an entity's performance that is not necessarily business performance, or that is beyond management's active control of the normal course of operations.

Comment: This Book labels this scheme as the "entity's performance hypothesis." This theory presents similarities to the core/noncore business distinction, although the two hypotheses do not fully overlap.

Certain pronouncements indicate a leaning towards this assumption. For example, the Basis for Conclusions of IAS 41 justifies the reporting of price changes of biological assets in profit or loss because management might influence them.[93] However, some argued that management is supposed to be responsible for both net income and comprehensive income. The PAAinE notes that over the longer term the difference between management performance and entity performance is blurred.[94]

---

[91] *AICPA Special Committee on Financial Reporting*, Improving Business Reporting – A Customer Focus, *pages 79, 87 (December 1994); FASB Task Force on Financial Performance Reporting by Business Enterprises, Discussion Paper*, Classification of Items of Comprehensive Income, *pages 1–2 (June 2002) www.fasb.org (last visited June 21, 2007)*.

[92] *IAS 19 (2011), ¶ BC105; IAS 19 (2007), ¶ BC65.*

[93] *IAS 41, ¶ B77.*

[94] *The Instituto de Contabilidad y Auditoria de Cuentas and EFRAG, 2009.* Pro-Active Accounting Activities in Europe (PAAinE) Performance Reporting, A European Discussion Paper, *¶ 3.8 www.efrag.org (last visited April 18, 2010)*.

7.4.4   Purpose of Reporting Comprehensive Income

Worksheet 43 compares the features of comprehensive income with those of net income, earnings, and other comprehensive income.

As mentioned in Section 7.2.1 previously, comprehensive income is the overall change in equity from nonowner sources. Such a measure of all changes in equity is the main purpose of reporting comprehensive income according to Subtopic 220-10 (FASB Statement No. 130). Without such an entity, a sum of all changes would be missing, as dispersed between the income statement and the equity section of the statement of financial position.[95] For this reason, it has been sometimes deemed a measure of the entity's performance, i.e., its change in wealth, including events out of management's control, as opposed to current performance and management performance.[96] However, the U.S. Concepts highlight the difficulty to distinguish an entity's performance from management performance.[97]

As a result of the notion of other comprehensive income including remeasurements to fair value, comprehensive income has sometimes been considered as a measure of value or wealth creation as opposed to a measure of performance.

Comment: Depending on which concept of capital maintenance and measurement attributes are used (see Section 7.6 later), both net income and comprehensive income may be considered as a measure of capital maintenance, i.e., what is needed to preserve the equity balance in a period. However, contrary to net income that should include realized price changes (although some gains or losses are unrealized, such as inventory lower-of-cost-or-market adjustments), comprehensive income also comprises unrealized price changes and effects of other interactions with the environment. Therefore, although both permit the computation of return on capital (see Section 7.6.4 later), an accounting system that uses comprehensive income (when a loose clean-surplus concept is adopted) or expands the scope of net income (under a strict clean-surplus concept) leads to a more inclusive measure of total return. However, its utility and scope are affected by the measurement model used (e.g., historical cost versus fair value accounting).

Subtopic 220-10 (FASB Statement No. 130) gives comprehensive income with an informative value on an entity's assets and on the timing and size of future cash flows.[98] On the other hand, as fair value remeasurements are not necessarily predictive of future cash flows, it has been argued that comprehensive income does not give a true picture of financial performance.

Comment: Contrary to comprehensive income, net income is comprehensive only under the strictest clean-surplus concept. All items are supposed to be included in comprehensive income to make earnings manipulation more difficult. However, this does not happen if certain items directly flow to retained earnings. This is the case with IFRSs (see Section 7.16 and Section 7.18.3 later) and with both U.S. GAAP and IFRSs for prior period adjustments (see Section 6.4.1, Section 6.4.2, and Section 6.4.3 previously).

---

[95]   *FASB ASC 220-10-10-1 (FASB Statement No. 130, ¶ 11).*

[96]   *IASB/FASB, Summary of the September 15, 2006 Financial Statement Presentation Joint International Group Meeting, ¶ 26 (October 4, 2006) www.fasb.org (last visited June 21, 2007).*

[97]   *CON 1 (superseded), ¶ 53; CON 5, ¶ 79.*

[98]   *FASB ASC 220-10-10-2 (FASB Statement No. 130, ¶ 12).*

> **Comment:** Net income is affected by the timing of recognition based on accrual accounting. Comprehensive income is less affected because its scope is wider. However, its reach depends on the measurement model that is employed for recognition of related assets and liabilities.

> **Planning Point:** Finally, distinguishing between net income and comprehensive income may be one way, among others, of discriminating income and expenses in order for defense of capital to follow the principles of distributable profits (see Section 3.5.2.2 previously). This Book calls this theory "defense of capital hypothesis."

To the extent other comprehensive income includes capital maintenance adjustments, under capital maintenance theories, comprehensive income has a stable element that differentiates it from net income.

> **Comment:** Section 7.6.3 following demonstrates that both the U.S. Concepts and the IASB Framework chose not to identify another separate element of financial statements to record capital maintenance adjustments. If comprehensive income were eliminated, probably this would be necessary.

Finally, the comprehensive income approach has been often criticized because of its mixed measurement bases. Historical cost is usually the measurement attribute of realized profits. Fair value or other bases that are used for assets and liabilities may give rise to other comprehensive income.

> **Comment:** In summary, net income and comprehensive income have different characteristics, the pros and cons of which have been variously construed as addressing different aspects of financial reporting and informational needs of financial statements users. However, the IASB has not judged those characteristics so univocal as to allow for a clear cut distinction between the two aggregates. Furthermore, the IASB Framework does not identify attributes of items of income and expenses that are part of profit or loss and those that are part of other comprehensive income.[99] Hence, no conclusive statement can be made until a theory of other comprehensive income has been postulated.

7.5 LINKAGE TO THEORIES OF PERFORMANCE

7.5.1 Definition of Performance

Much of the topic on the purpose of reporting comprehensive income versus net income is connected with the debate on the meaning of performance and what indicators of performance should exist.

---

[99] *IAS 1, ¶ BC58; IASB, Exposure Draft of* Proposed Amendments to IAS 1 Presentation of Financial Statements, *¶ BC20 (March 2006).*

> **Comment:** There is no common definition of performance in accounting pronouncements, notwithstanding several attempts to find a common platform.[100] On these grounds, the *Financial Statement Presentation Project* itself started as the *Performance Reporting* Project.

On the other hand, the difficulty in defining performance is rooted in the inherent characteristics and limitations of financial reporting, particularly in that the information it provides is primarily financial in nature and historical, and does not purport to measure the value of a company. The U.S. Concepts distinguish the computation of indicators from their analysis and evaluation, which properly belong to financial analysis and not to financial reporting.[101]

CON 5 gives a definition of earnings as a measure of period performance, as the difference between asset inflows and outflows associated with cash-to-cash cycles that are completed or substantially completed during the period.[102]

> **Comment:** The IASB Framework does not give a straight definition of *performance*. The Joint Conceptual Framework defines financial performance as changes in economic resources and claims.[103]

7.5.2   Economic Versus Financial Performance

Both the former IASB Framework and the U.S. Concepts use the term *performance* in relation to a statement of income under accrual accounting (either income statement or statement of comprehensive income).[104] CON 5 clearly underlines that earnings are the primary measure of performance during a period.[105]

> **Comment:** However, as explained in Section 7.1.3 previously, earnings and comprehensive income overlap in the U.S. Concepts.[106]

Both the IASB Framework and the U.S. Concepts use the term *performance* as measured by income and expenses and hence profit (under CON 6, revenues, expenses, gains and losses) and their combinations, such as gross margin, profit or loss from ordinary activities (under CON 6, income from continuing operations) before or after tax, operating income (CON 6) and profit

---

[100] *Such as the Special Report,* Reporting Financial Performance: A Proposed Approach, *by Kathryn Cearns, published by the members of the former G4+1 standard-setting organizations on September 1999 and the Financial Reporting Exposure Draft (FRED 22),* Reporting Financial Performance, *issued by the UK's Accounting Standards Board (ASB) on December 2000, reported by Ronald J. Bossio,* Reporting Information About Financial Performance of Business Enterprises: Focusing on the Form and Content of Financial Statements *(August 17, 2001).*
[101] *CON 1 (superseded), ¶¶ 18, 21, 41, 48; CON 5, ¶ 28.*
[102] *CON 5, ¶ 36.*
[103] The Conceptual Framework for Financial Reporting 2010, ¶ OB18.
[104] *CON 6, ¶ 77; IASB Framework, ¶ 19 (superseded).*
[105] *CON 5, ¶ 36.*
[106] *CON 5, Footnote 7.*

or loss (IASB Framework), or their derivations, such as return on investment or earnings per share.[107] CON 5 also refers to possible alternative indicators, such as comprehensive income, earnings, or earnings per share.[108] However, the IASB Framework mentions the income statement when it treats the topic of *performance*, while CON 6 refers to comprehensive income.

> **Comment:** Therefore, from an economic perspective, the simplest difference between these two indicators as measure of performance is the different degree of inclusiveness.

However, comprehensive income is not necessarily performance related.

> **Comment:** Comprehensive income measures all value changes in equity during a period, irrespective of whether or not they are business or performance related. As such, it may be deemed an indirect measure of performance. Its meaning related to performance is not fixed. FASB Statement No. 124 argues that changes in net assets are not a measure of performance for not-for-profit organizations, contrary to business enterprises where profits are a major component of such a change.[109] Although Subtopic 220-10 (FASB Statement No. 130) views comprehensive income as the ultimate direction of financial performance, it does not require its presentation as a measure of performance until it has been conceptually addressed by the FASB.[110]

> **Example:** However, the practice of reporting comprehensive income at present shows that net income is judged as incomplete. For example, in the United Kingdom, FRS 3 considers the profit and loss account as not sufficient to show financial performance and therefore complements it with a statement called "statement of total recognized gains and losses" (STRGL).

Financial performance may have meanings that are not exclusively related to a statement of income.

> **Planning Point:** In real-world situations as in financial management theory, performance is not necessarily related to the economic dimension, as is well illustrated by the so-called DuPont decomposition of ROI, where financial efficiency from turnover of assets and capital utilization translates into greater return on investment. As a practical implication, the choice between financial versus economic performance may be both the result of the competitive strategy of the entity and of the relatively sensitive effect that results may have on the specific industry in which an entity operates (e.g., net income in the construction industry will be greatly affected by economic performance, while in a fast moving consumer sector the financial performance, namely turnover of asset, will have a very sensitive impact).

---

[107] *CON 6, ¶ 77;* The Conceptual Framework for Financial Reporting 2010, *¶¶ 4.2, 4.24, 4.28; IASB Framework, ¶¶ 17, 19 (superseded), 47, 69, 73.*

[108] *CON 5, ¶ 22.*

[109] *FASB Statement No. 124,* Accounting for Certain Investments Held by Not-for-Profit Organizations, *¶¶ 46–47.*

[110] *FASB ASC 220-10-45-10 (FASB Statement No. 130, ¶¶ 66, 67).*

> **Comment:** Performance comprises both absolute values and ratios. These indicate how important the interrelationships[111] among individual financial statements (mainly the statement of financial position and the income statement) are in determining performance metrics, as in the case of ROI (Return on Investment), ROE (Return on Equity), IRR (Internal Rate of Return), or EVA (Economic Value Added) indicators.

Certain studies have shown an increase in the relevance of balance sheet, book value information[112] and performance based on nonfinancial information. Also, qualitative considerations are sometimes as important as quantitative financial and nonfinancial information. Companies often employ multiple metrics as opposed to a single indicator of income.[113] This is developed in Section 7.5.4 following.

Now, the *Joint Conceptual Framework Project* breaks down changes in economic resources and claims against the reporting entity into the components of financial performance measured by accrual accounting, financial performance measured by cash flows during a period, and changes in resources and claims that do not result from financial performance.[114]

7.5.3 Specific Relationships with the Financial Statement Presentation Project

As mentioned in the previous Section, performance is often associated with more than one indicator, or with the analysis of the subtotals and components of the income statement, as opposed to simply its bottom line. This also depends on the particular interests of the specific users of financial statements.[115] The U.S. Concepts warn against giving exclusive attention to the bottom line or other condensations.[116] Subtopic 220-10 (FASB Statement No. 130) reiterates this concept with reference to comprehensive income.[117] CON 4 highlights that nonbusiness organizations usually need more that one performance indicator as there is no profit measure.[118] The *Financial Statement Presentation Project* treats this topic in conjunction with the issues of totalization, disaggregation, and categorization.

> **Comment:** IFRSs has somehow gone in the opposite direction so far, by reducing the subcomponents of income and permitting subtotals only when relevant.[119]

---

[111] *CON 5, ¶ 24(b).*

[112] *Ronald J. Bossio,* Reporting Information About Financial Performance of Business Enterprises: Focusing on the Form and Content of Financial Statements, *Footnote 7 (August 17, 2001).*

[113] *FASB Staff,* Summary of User Interviews Reporting Financial Performance by Business Enterprises, *(February 2002); FASB/IASB,* Performance Reporting Joint International Group (JIG), Minutes of Meeting, January, 13–14, 2005, ¶ 13, www.fasb.org *(last visited June 21, 2007).*

[114] The Conceptual Framework for Financial Reporting 2010, ¶¶ OB17, OB20.

[115] *Ronald J. Bossio,* Reporting Information About Financial Performance of Business Enterprises: Focusing on the Form and Content of Financial Statements, *Footnote 76 (August 17, 2001).*

[116] *CON 5, ¶ 22; CON 6, ¶ 77.*

[117] *FASB ASC 220-10-10-3 (FASB Statement No. 130, ¶ 13).*

[118] *CON 4,* Objectives of Financial Reporting by Nonbusiness Organizations, *¶ 9.*

[119] *IAS 1, ¶¶ 55, 85, BC55.*

> **Comment:** One of the reasons for allowing a two-statement approach in IAS 1 (that is, permitting an entity to elect whether to use a statement of comprehensive income or an income statement and a statement of comprehensive income) is to avoid undue focus on the bottom line of comprehensive income (see Section 7.9.2 later).

Defining performance at different subtotals and totals of a statement of income would also evolve from the categorization working principle of the *Financial Statement Presentation Project* (see Section 1.4.3.2 previously). This Project acknowledges that the distinction between business and financial items that is made in corporate finance theory has not yet affected accounting standards.[120]

> **Comment:** The separation between business and financing items (i.e., categorization) can also be read in terms of operating income (return generated by a company that is independent of its capital structure) versus net income, operating leverage versus financing leverage, or ROS and ROI versus ROE, weighted average cost of capital versus cost of debt and cost of equity, or unlevered versus levered cash flows, etc.

Another issue is the question of whom performance should be related to. Performance indicators may refer to the controlling shareholders, i.e., parent company shareholders in consolidated financial statements, or to all the shareholders (see Section 7.3.2 previously for the reflection of this on the clean-surplus concept). Before FASB Statement No. 160 that defines noncontrolling interest as part of equity (see Section 4.3.2 previously), net income and comprehensive income were examples of reporting financial indicators with reference to controlling shareholders. The Joint Conceptual Framework points out that general-purpose external financial reporting is directed to the needs of a wide range of users and adopts an entity perspective (see Section 4.3.2 previously). This fact, however, does not exclude the use of some indicators to address the informational needs of other groups of users, such as earnings per share directed to actual or potential common shareholders, or noncontrolling interest with reference to noncontrolling shareholders.[121]

7.5.4 Non-GAAP Financial Measures

As part of the search for performance indicators, some companies and rating agencies have been reporting certain so-called "non-GAAP measures." Currently, there is no general consensus on the categorization of these measures.[122] They try to take hold of dimensions such as recurring, current operating, predicting value, or core-business earnings, and other characteristics analyzed in Worksheet 43 that, depending on circumstances, might be considered indicative of the concept of performance.

---

[120] *Performance Reporting Joint International Group (JIG), Agenda Paper 2*, History of the Performance Reporting Project, ¶ 26 London (January 2005) www.fasb.org (last visited June 21, 2007).

[121] The Conceptual Framework for Financial Reporting 2010, ¶¶ BC1.15, BC1.16.

[122] *IASB/FASB, Financial Statement Presentation Project, Agenda Paper 3*, Categorization in a Statement of Earnings and Comprehensive Income, ¶ 13 (June 2005).

The U.S. Concepts do not consider certain approaches to be financial reporting, e.g., determining an entity's "earning power," "long-term earning ability," risk assessment, or adjusted, normalized or operating earnings, cash earnings, removing volatility from earnings, or providing other forward-looking information. These are generally thought to be part of financial analysis,[123] although they are justified from a managerial viewpoint and often are the results of new directions in cost accounting, management control, and performance appraisal studies.

Comment: Free cash flow, which is another non-GAAP measure in this context, may be put in relation to the concept of capital maintenance (see Section 7.6 following) because it also highlights normal capital maintenance expenditures.

Comment: Section 7.4.3 previously illustrates that much of the rationale for other comprehensive income is based on the need to distinguish items from net income based on the characteristics mentioned there. When this effort moves to selectively adding items to or deducting items from net income in order to determine a new indicator, the issue becomes that of the so-called "non-GAAP measures."

Under Regulation S-K, if non-GAAP measures are used in filings with the SEC, the registrant must include the most directly comparable GAAP financial measure with equal or greater prominence, a reconciliation with the most directly comparable GAAP financial measure(s), a justification of the usefulness of such information, and a description of the additional purposes for the use of non-GAAP financial measures. In addition, the registrant must not present a non-GAAP measure on the face of a financial statement, the accompanying notes, or the mandatory pro forma financial information, or eliminate or smooth nonrecurring, infrequent or unusual items that are reasonably likely to recur within, or have previously recurred within, two years, or use titles that are equal or similar to GAAP financial measures, or exclude liabilities that may be settled in cash from non-GAAP liquidity measures other than EBIT or EBITDA. Ratios and statistics are not considered as non-GAAP financial measures as defined by Regulation S-K. However, a foreign private issuer may use non-GAAP measures that are required or expressly permitted by a foreign GAAP standard-setter and are related to the foreign GAAP used in the registrant's primary financial statements included in the SEC filing and are included in its annual report for use in the jurisdiction in which it is domiciled, incorporated, or organized or which is intended for distribution to its security holders.[124] Forward-looking information about cash available for distribution, including a reconciliation of expected cash earnings to cash available for distribution, is considered appropriate in registration statements for initial public offerings where the registrant indicates its intention to pay out a significant amount of dividends.[125]

---

[123] *CON 1 (superseded), ¶ 48; CON 5, ¶ 28.*
[124] *Regulation S-K, ¶ 229.10(e); AICPA International Practices Task Force (May 17, 2005).*
[125] *Accounting Staff Members in the Division of Corporation Finance U.S. Securities and Exchange Commission, Washington, D.C.,* Current Accounting and Disclosure Issues in the Division of Corporation Finance, *¶ II.A (December 1, 2005) www.sec.gov (last visited April 26, 2006).*

Comment: IFRSs has no detailed guidance on non-GAAP measures. On one hand, IAS 1 requires additional disclosures when IFRS requirements are insufficient to provide an understanding of the impact of transactions and events on the accounts.[126] On the other hand, IAS 1 does not require but permits the disclosure of results of operating activities or a similar line item, provided that operating items are not excluded even if irregular, infrequent, unusual, or noncash items. The fact the omission conforms to the practice of an industry would not be acceptable grounds for excluding them.[127] The IASB Framework welcomes the separate presentation of unusual, abnormal, and infrequent items in the income statement. It sees subclassifications on the face of the financial statements as relevant, especially when based on source (e.g., ordinary versus incidental activities), to assist users of financial reporting in projecting future cash flows.[128] IAS 1 eliminated the separate presentation of extraordinary items on the face of the statement of comprehensive income. These would in any case require arbitrary allocations.[129] In addition, under IAS 33 and Subtopic 260-10 (FASB Statement No. 128), an entity may disclose non-GAAP per-share amounts, provided it does so in the notes. Under IAS 33, it must disclose basic and diluted amounts with equal prominence, explain the computation of the numerator and whether or not it includes tax, and reconcile these amounts to the statement of comprehensive income or separate income statement items. It must determine the average number of ordinary shares as per IAS 33 rules (under Subtopic 260-10 (FASB Statement No. 128), it must determine the per-share amounts under this pronouncement).[130] Thus, IAS 33 and Subtopic 260-10 (FASB Statement No. 128) do not require the presentation of comprehensive income per share, but do not prohibit it if the above rules are also followed. Subtopic 220-10 (FASB Statement No. 130) does not require it, as it would have been inconsistent with the display of comprehensive income in the statement of changes of equity and the lack of a requirement to consider comprehensive income as a performance indicator.[131] The SEC Staff interprets this flexibility in IFRSs restrictively for foreign private issuers, in the sense that additional captions and subtotals that are not non-GAAP measures are not prohibited, provided they are consistent with IFRSs, are not misleading or inconsistent with IAS 1, and their purpose and usefulness are justified.[132] Subtopic 220-10 (FASB Statement No. 130) delayed the decision on comprehensive income per share pending the conceptual definition of comprehensive income issues.[133] Decisions on per-share measures, including comprehensive income per share or a measure of total changes of an entity's wealth per share, will result from the discussion on totalization, aggregation, and disaggregation guidance in segment B of the *Financial Statement Presentation Project.*[134]

7.5.5 Primary Focus of Financial Reporting

Both the former IASB Framework and the U.S. Concepts underline that financial statements are interrelated as they give different complementary scenarios, including those necessary

---

[126] *IAS 1, ¶ 17(c).*

[127] *IAS 1, ¶¶ BC55–BC56.*

[128] The Conceptual Framework for Financial Reporting 2010, *¶¶ 4.3, 4.27; IASB Framework, ¶¶ 28 (superseded), 48, 72.*

[129] *IAS 1, ¶ BC64.*

[130] *IAS 1, ¶ BC103; FASB Statement No. 128, ¶ 37; IAS 33, ¶ 73; Agenda Paper 14,* Exposure Draft of Proposed Amendments to IAS 1 Presentation of Financial Statements – Comment Letter Analysis, *¶ 94 (December 14, 2006).*

[131] *FASB Statement No. 130, ¶ 77.*

[132] *AICPA International Practices Task Force (November 22, 2005).*

[133] *FASB Statement No. 130, ¶¶ 75–77.*

[134] *IAS 1, ¶¶ BC102-BC103; Agenda Paper 14, Exposure Draft of* Proposed Amendments to IAS 1 Presentation of Financial Statements – Comment Letter Analysis, *¶¶ 97, 99 (December 14, 2006).*

for the evaluation of financial performance.[135] However, CON 6 considers information about performance and status provided by accrual accounting as the primary focus of financial reporting.[136] CON 1 emphasized information about financial performance evidenced by earnings and its components as the primary focus of financial reporting.[137] By contrast, the IASB Framework considered all the statements of equal prominence. The IASB and FASB's Joint Conceptual Framework removes this primary focus connotation from one statement and places it into information about the ability of an entity to generate net cash inflows.

> **Comment:** The emphasis on cash flow prediction is critical in a balance-sheet orientation, as future cash flow generation is functional to asset recognition, and therefore income recognition. The Joint Conceptual Framework states that economic resources and their changes are equally important, although it maintains the importance of accrual accounting to assess an entity's ability to generate net cash inflows. For this purpose, it refers to *financial performance reflected by accrual accounting* instead of comprehensive income (Section 7.1.6 previously).[138] The Discussion Paper of the *Financial Presentation Project* confirms the primacy of accrual accounting over cash-based accounting in estimating future cash flows. The newly-developed (then withdrawn) reconciliation schedule (see Section 7.9.1 later) provided an immediate understanding of the interactions between the two bases of accounting.[139]

7.5.6   Balance Sheet Versus Income-and-Expense View

Net income as a measure of performance is based on an income statement view. On one hand, comprehensive income is still an income concept. CON 6 sees the statement of earnings and comprehensive income as a true statement of performance.[140] On the other hand, the definition of comprehensive income derives from a balance sheet approach. The balance sheet orientation is discussed in Section 2.1.4.1 (3) previously.

> **Comment:** The traditional managerial approach to performance is to appraise a company's operations by means of their effect on the income statement. This is in opposition to a concept based on the balance sheet.

> **Comment:** Comprehensive income is an accounting measure, based on a mixed measurement model. It also includes other comprehensive income that, to a large extent, results from remeasurements to fair value. Thus, comprehensive income, i.e., period changes in net assets from nonowner sources, differs from the traditional managerial approach to performance. It moves towards a determination of book net assets as a proxy for a sort of value of equity adjusted for certain current value measurements. However, this differs from both a market-based and a fair value based determination of the value of the net assets of a company and is not equivalent to changes in net assets in a pure valuation model.

---

[135]   *CON 5, ¶¶ 23, 32; IASB Framework, ¶ 20 (superseded).*
[136]   *CON 6, ¶ 3.*
[137]   *CON 1 (superseded), ¶¶ 43, 55.*
[138]   *CON 8, ¶¶ OB12, OB17, BC1.32.*
[139]   *Discussion Paper*, Preliminary Views on Financial Statement Presentation, *¶¶ 4.26, B18 (October 2008).*
[140]   *CON 5, ¶¶ 24, 30.*

Comment: The financial analyst's approach and the shareholders' value approach are alternative views of performance that also differ from the management approach. Under these theories, the value assigned to a company's decisions equals the present value of the stream of the associated future net cash flows. Again, when determination of fair value is not based on discounted cash flows, it does not necessarily equal present value.

Comment: Although the new Joint Conceptual Framework states that financial performance measured by accrual accounting is not designated as the primary focus of financial reporting, no clear-cut and explicit model seems to emerge at this stage. The framework mixes the "vertical" view of the FASB's existing conceptual framework with the "horizontal" view of the IASB's existing framework. The former is more earnings-based than the IASB's balance sheet approach. The former has multiple objectives from the more general to the more specific, moving from the economic resources and claims in the statement of financial position, to the assessment of their changes with an earnings focus, to ultimately determine liquidity, solvency, funds flows, and the entity's cash generation ability. The latter has the sole objective of usefulness of information, which is served by the three main statements at the same level, through their circular interrelationships to an entity's ability to generate net cash inflows.

7.5.7 Impact of Other Comprehensive Income on Defense of Capital

Recognition of other comprehensive income may be fundamentally in opposition to the legal frameworks in certain jurisdictions.

Comment: In certain countries, typically part of the European Union or where business laws require a minimum level of shareholders' equity or of contributed capital (see Section 3.5.2.2 previously), accounting for items of income or expense in other comprehensive income is not neutral from a defense of capital perspective. If common stock or equity falls below the required thresholds, a recapitalization of the company may be required. In times of financial crisis such an effect may be quite pervasive and may be a very serious corporate issue. These floors are generally assessed on the basis of an entity's financial statements and separate financial statements, not the consolidated financial statements, as under a corporate governance perspective the financial statements of the legal entity are those that are generally relevant, depending of course on the jurisdiction. Recognition of a loss in net income would also affect equity through retained earnings, but at least not immediately, in some cases without triggering an immediate action by shareholders.

7.6 LINKAGE WITH CAPITAL MAINTENANCE CONCEPTS

7.6.1 Definition of Capital Maintenance

Capital maintenance theory seeks to define capital and what an entity must achieve in order to preserve it. Any surplus (or deficit) on the amount needed for such a safeguard is profit (or loss).[141]

There are two basic concepts of capital maintenance. A financial concept of capital sees capital as the net assets or equity of the entity. The focus is on maintaining the capital invested by owners, intended as either its nominal amount or its purchasing power, depending on whether

---

[141] The Conceptual Framework for Financial Reporting 2010, ¶¶ 4.62; IASB Framework, ¶ 107.

nominal monetary units or constant purchasing power accounting is used. A physical concept of capital takes into account the operating output capability that an entity can generate (i.e., its physical, productive capacity or the resources or funds needed to achieve that capacity). Thus, capital is "maintained" if operating capability is preserved. Physical capital maintenance requires the use of current cost accounting, in nominal or constant monetary units.[142]

> **Comment:** As mentioned in Section 2.1.1 previously, the use of "capital" as a substitute for "equity" holds under a financial concept of capital maintenance only.[143]

> **Comment:** Capital maintenance may be put in relationship with the "invested and earned equity model" (see Section 2.1.4.2 (2) previously), because it applies the basic relationship of investment by owners and distributions to them to derive the component that may be defined as maintenance and the excess that may be defined as income.

> **Comment:** Section 3.5.2 previously analyzes the notion of defense of capital. Capital that is defended is also likely to be maintained. Section 4.6 previously explains a different concept, i.e., that of capital management. Capital that is compliant with external statutory requirements is, at least to a certain extent, monitored for maintenance. Capital that is managed from a management internal perspective is supposed to be, but is not necessarily, maintained.

7.6.2 Primary Versus Supplementary Financial Reporting

Both the IASB Framework and CON 5 and CON 6 acknowledge the existence of the two capital maintenance concepts mentioned: the financial capital maintenance concept and the physical capital maintenance model. However, the U.S. Concepts adopt the financial capital maintenance concept only.[144] Initially CON 3 (then superseded) reserved the right to decide which of the two approaches to adopt.[145] The IASB Framework does not sponsor any of them (according to the IASB Framework, an entity may choose the one or the other based on its definition of capital and the needs of the users of its financial statements[146]). The IASB Framework is thought to be applicable in the context of different concepts of capital maintenance, although in practice IFRSs have been developed mainly in line with the financial capital maintenance concept.[147]

> **Comment:** The capital disclosures in IAS 1 (see Section 4.6 previously) take hold of some of this flexibility that is permitted in the IASB Framework.

---

[142] *CON 5, ¶ 47; The Conceptual Framework for Financial Reporting 2010, ¶¶ 4.57, 4.58, 4.61; IASB Framework, ¶¶ 102–103, 106.*

[143] *CON 6, ¶ 213 always equates equity to net assets. Conversely,* The Conceptual Framework for Financial Reporting 2010, *¶ 4.57 (IASB Framework, ¶ 102) relates this equation to a financial concept of capital maintenance.*

[144] *CON 5, ¶ 45; CON 6, ¶¶ 71–72.*

[145] *CON 3 (superseded), ¶ 58.*

[146] The Conceptual Framework for Financial Reporting 2010, *¶ 4.58; IASB Framework, ¶ 103.*

[147] The Conceptual Framework for Financial Reporting 2010, *¶ 4.65; IASB Framework, ¶¶ Preface, 110.*

Comment: The difference in emphasis in the two sets of standards seems to be confirmed by the fact that while current cost accounting under Subtopic 255-10 (FASB Statement No. 89) may be used on a supplementary basis only, IFRSs do not prohibit current cost accounting as a primary basis of reporting. In fact, financial reporting for hyperinflationary economies under IAS 29 applies (and under the superseded IAS 15 might apply) to primary financial statements, irrespective of whether they are on a historical or current cost approach.

Example: The Australian, Canadian, and New Zealand frameworks do not endorse a specific capital maintenance concept, while the UK framework chooses the financial capital approach.[148]

7.6.3 Capital Maintenance Adjustments

Seen at a company overall level, under the regime of the nominal financial capital maintenance concept, income for a period (i.e., profit, as named in the IASB Framework) is earned when, excluding changes from owner sources, the monetary value of ending net assets exceeds the monetary value of net assets at the beginning of the period, which translates into revenues and gains in excess of expenses and losses. Under the constant purchasing power financial capital maintenance concept, the above relation holds but, in addition, such an excess is computed after constant purchasing power has been restated. From the point of view of the physical concept of capital, such excess is valued once the entity's operating capability, excluding changes from owner sources, is preserved.[149]

Comment: As under a balance sheet approach the definition of income is a derivation of the definition of assets and liabilities, the type of capital maintenance adopted affects the recognition and measurement of earned income. Conversely, the type of measurement bases used for assets and liabilities affects capital maintenance and therefore also the recognition of profit or loss.

Capital maintenance adjustments are the changes in capital that are needed to restate the capital balance under the terms of the capital maintenance theory adopted (e.g., purchasing power, or operating capability). Therefore under financial capital maintenance in terms of constant purchasing power and under physical capital maintenance, capital maintenance adjustments are not profit but are deducted (or partially deducted, under the former approach) from the excess of revenues and gains minus expenses and losses in order to compute income.[150] Capital maintenance adjustments mainly refer to unrealized changes in "prices" of assets and liabilities, which are also called "holding gains or losses."[151]

---

[148] *Staff of the Canadian Accounting Standards Boards, Discussion Paper,* Measurement Bases for Financial Accounting – Measurement on Initial Recognition, ¶ B7 *(November 2005).*

[149] The Conceptual Framework for Financial Reporting 2010, ¶¶ 4.24, 4.58–4.60; *IASB Framework,* ¶¶ 69, 103–105.

[150] The Conceptual Framework for Financial Reporting 2010, ¶ 4.60; *IASB Framework,* ¶ 105.

[151] *CON 5,* ¶ 48; The Conceptual Framework for Financial Reporting 2010, ¶ 4.63; *IASB Framework,* ¶ 108.

Comment: There are two ways of picturing this: from the point of view of a balance sheet and from that of an income statement. From a balance sheet perspective, if capital is defined in terms of nominal monetary units, holding gains or losses are profit, not capital maintenance adjustments, to the extent they are recognized and determine changes in equity. However, if accounting standards do not permit their recognition in net income and in equity, they remain unrecognized until eventually realized at disposal of the related asset or extinguishment of the related liability. From an income statement viewpoint, unrealized changes in prices of held assets and owed liabilities are generally not recognized under historical cost accounting. Therefore, if holding price increases are not recognized, they are not included in net income, because no adjustment is made to the asset or liability that affects the income statement, nor do they change equity as capital maintenance adjustments because they are unrecognized. However, holding price decreases are generally recognized as a result of conservatism, as in the case of adjustment of inventories at the lower-of-cost-or-value rule and they are deducted from net income.[152] When a mixed attribute model or fair value accounting are employed under a financial capital maintenance concept, most unrealized changes in prices of assets and liabilities are partially or wholly recognized. Their classification as profit or capital maintenance adjustments depends on whether they are recognized in net income or in other comprehensive income or directly in equity under a capital maintenance concept, as is further explained below in this Section. Under the physical capital maintenance concept, unrealized holding gains and losses are always capital maintenance adjustments because they are deducted from or added to equity.

CON 3 (then superseded) reserved whether or not to select a separate element of financial statements for capital maintenance adjustments, and acknowledged that capital maintenance adjustments might be part of the gains and losses included in other comprehensive income.[153] CON 5 denotes gains and losses corresponding to other comprehensive income as either capital maintenance adjustments or other nonowner changes in equity.[154] CON 6 confirms that capital maintenance adjustments would be a separate element of the financial statements under a physical capital maintenance concept.[155]

Example: Capital maintenance adjustments are a separate element of financial statements under GAAP of New Zealand.

The IASB Framework construes revaluation or restatement of assets and liabilities as capital maintenance adjustments when recognized directly in equity under a capital maintenance concept and also refers to them as "revaluation reserves" (see Section 7.16 later).[156]

Comment: The application of the definition of income and of the criteria for recognition of income in the income statement that are found in the IASB Framework would arguably result in revaluation surplus not being profit recognized in the income statement. In fact, revaluations or fair value remeasurements are neither an increase in assets nor an inflow or an enhancement of assets that determines increase in future economic benefits.[157] However, the IASB Framework states that revaluations or

---

[152] The Conceptual Framework for Financial Reporting 2010, ¶ 4.63; IASB Framework, ¶ 108.

[153] *CON 3 (superseded), ¶ 58.*

[154] *CON 5, ¶ 43.*

[155] *CON 6, ¶ 71.*

[156] The Conceptual Framework for Financial Reporting 2010, ¶ 4.36; IASB Framework, ¶ 81.

[157] The Conceptual Framework for Financial Reporting 2010, ¶¶ 4.25, 4.47; IASB Framework, ¶¶ 70(a), 92.

restatements of assets and liabilities meet the definition of income and expenses.[158] Furthermore, as mentioned, under the definition of financial capital maintenance measured in nominal monetary units revaluation surplus is profit (whether recognized in profit or loss or in other comprehensive income).

Comment: Under the IASB Framework and IFRSs, capital maintenance adjustments are specifically identified as reserves when under a capital maintenance concept they are recognized directly in equity. The IASB Framework does not envisage them as part of other comprehensive income, because it does not acknowledge other comprehensive income. Specific IFRS standards such as IAS 1 and IAS 16,[159] however, include a capital maintenance adjustment such as revaluation surplus in other comprehensive income. Section 3.3 and Section 3.6.6 previously discuss disclosure of capital maintenance adjustments under IFRSs as part of disclosure of equity reserves. Under U.S. GAAP, other comprehensive income is recognized directly in equity and therefore the difference with capital maintenance adjustments is blurred.

Planning Point: However, the inclusion in other comprehensive income appears to be a practical or temporary measure, because being a capital maintenance adjustment would be inconsistent with recycling (at least from a net income viewpoint). This characterization may hold only under the nominal financial capital maintenance concept.

Example: Although this is not a view expressed under IFRSs, revaluation reserve may be conceived as a capital maintenance adjustment. Consequently, it is not recycled under IAS 16 and IAS 38.

Example: One of the conceptual views of cumulative translation adjustment, expressed by Subtopic 830-10 (FASB Statement No. 52), is that it arises from a direct restatement of previously-reported equity as a sort of capital maintenance adjustment (see Section 7.10.4 later).

Comment: Comprehensive income (as opposed to net income) may be seen as a compromise to permit the recording of holding gains or losses in equity through other comprehensive income, even when accounting standards do not allow their recognition in net income. If seen with reference to net income, certain unrealized holding gains or losses would not be recognized in the income statement. If seen from the perspective of comprehensive income, they are part of income (intended as comprehensive income), which in fact corresponds to changes in equity from nonowner sources. For example, a non-impairment reduction in value of available-for-sale financial assets decreases equity as the result of the negative impact on other comprehensive income. Consequently, comprehensive income (not net income) maintains capital for any excess remaining after allowing for this adjustment.

Under the IASB Framework, capital maintenance adjustments are entirely part of equity and not of profit or loss under a physical capital concept. In this case, they are not included in the income statement, even when they meet the definition of income and expenses. The

---

[158] The Conceptual Framework for Financial Reporting 2010, *¶ 4.36; IASB Framework, ¶ 81.*
[159] *IAS 1, ¶¶ 7, 96; IAS 16, ¶¶ 39–40.*

same reasoning applies, but only partially, under financial capital maintenance at constant purchasing power.[160]

> **Comment:** Here, it might be argued that the IASB Framework indirectly acknowledged other comprehensive income, as a mechanism to avoid those items of income or expenses directly hitting the income statement.

> **Comment:** Under the 2007 revision of IAS 1, other comprehensive income, although often consisting of capital maintenance adjustments, is no longer recognized directly in equity, but in the statement of comprehensive income. The IASB Framework mentions that capital maintenance adjustments are part of equity and not of profit and that under certain capital maintenance concepts these adjustments must not be recognized in the income statement. If read literally there is no inconsistency, as it does not state that they must be recognized *directly* in equity and not through the use of another statement (i.e., the statement of comprehensive income). CON 5 instead states that they are recognized *directly* in equity.[161] However, in the IASB Framework profit or loss has to be intended as net income and, as mentioned, the IASB Framework has no such element as comprehensive income. Therefore, it might be argued that, from this angle, recognition in an alternative statement of income is inconsistent with the IASB Framework.

Worksheet 44 illustrates these relationships.

7.6.4 Return on Capital Versus Return of Capital

As a consequence of defining capital and income, the capital maintenance theory distinguishes between return on capital (that is, gain on capital invested by owners) and return of capital or capital recovery (that is, refund to owners of their originally invested capital). Of course, the existence of a profit, that is the surplus based on its definition under the capital maintenance theory, is a prerequisite of positive return on capital.[162]

> **Comment:** When unrealized holding gains and losses are recognized in other comprehensive income, comprehensive income is net of them, and therefore is the return on financial capital under a financial concept of capital maintenance.[163] Under this concept, net income is also a type of return on financial capital, but including only unrealized holding gains and losses that are recognized at that level. Net income under a physical capital maintenance concept is always the return on capital as capital maintenance adjustments are recognized directly in equity. Thus net income reflects only the surplus or defect after such adjustments, consistently with that concept of capital maintenance.[164] Worksheet 44 illustrates these relationships.

---

[160] The Conceptual Framework for Financial Reporting 2010, *¶¶ 4.36, 4.62, 4.63; IASB Framework, ¶¶ 81, 107–108.*

[161] *CON 5, ¶ 48.*

[162] *CON 5, ¶ 46; The Conceptual Framework for Financial Reporting 2010, ¶ 4.60; IASB Framework, ¶ 105.*

[163] *CON 5, Footnote 28; CON 6 ¶ 72.*

[164] *CON 5, ¶ 48.*

CON 3 (superseded) reserved the right to define earnings as return on physical capital or return on financial capital.[165]

7.6.5 Economic Income

Economic income is an economic, not an accounting, concept. It largely corresponds to the accounting concept of capital maintenance, but in terms of wealth, as it makes reference to market values as opposed to accounting income. Economic income is the maximum amount that can be consumed during a period without affecting the enterprise's wealth, apart from withdrawals and other distributions to, and investments from, owners.

> **Comment:** This is also a capital maintenance concept.

Economic income aims at reflecting the creation of the wealth of a company without the cutoffs of accounting periods and therefore accounting conventions of accruals and deferrals, earning process, and realization. Accounting income is a subset of economic income.

> **Comment:** Therefore, economic income also includes holding gains and losses from changes in assets and liabilities that according to GAAP may be segregated as unrealized or not remeasured. Other comprehensive income would have an informative value on such items that are not yet reflected in net income. On the other hand, changes in unrealized gains or losses due to changed economic conditions that are not driven by an entity's transactions (fair value remeasurements) may also affect earnings and similarly provide information about changes in shareholders' wealth. Certain disclosures of unrealized income required by Topic 820 (FASB Statement No. 157), as well as similar disclosures by IFRS 13 and the March 2009 amendments to IFRS 7, have a similar rationale.[166]

> **Comment:** Thus, other comprehensive income may also be seen as a partial connecting link between accounting income and economic income to the extent it recognizes certain unrealized holding gains or losses.

A suggestion made as part of the *Financial Statement Presentation Project* was to create a new "statement of wealth creation and capital allocation" to provide financial statement users with information about how capital is allocated or distributed. Here, differently from comprehensive income, economic income also included financing expenses as part of the whole income potentially distributable to all stakeholders. This statement would have been extended in recording at fair value transactions among owners.[167]

---

[165] *CON 3 (superseded), ¶ 58.*

[166] *FASB ASC 820-10-50-1, 820-10-50-2, 820-10-50-3 (FASB Statement No. 157, ¶¶ 32, as amended by ASU No. 2010-06 and ASU No. 2011-04); FASB Statement No. 157, ¶ C100; IFRS 13, ¶ 93(f); Amendments to IFRS 7 Financial Instruments,* Improving Disclosures about Financial Instruments, *¶ 27B(d) (March 2009), deleted by IFRS 13.*

[167] *IASB, Financial Statement Presentation Project, Agenda Paper 13D,* Statement of Changes in Equity and Other Equity-Related Issues, *¶¶ 30–31 (January 25, 2007).*

> **Comment:** Currently, Subtopic 220-10 (FASB Statement No. 130) clarifies that transactions required by U.S. GAAP to be recognized in additional paid-in capital or other capital accounts must not be displayed in other comprehensive income.[168] By contrast, a concept of "full adoption" of fair value accounting would result in a different concept of equity, from an owner and not from the entity perspective. Additional paid-in capital would record changes at fair value of transactions among owners. The statement of comprehensive income would not only deduct interest expenses to compute comprehensive income but also cost of equity. It would include all types of gains and losses, including capital gains and losses. A new concept of clean-surplus would arise, where a total income would be comprehensive income plus capital gains and loss currently recorded in additional paid-in capital. This would also answer the mixed nature of additional paid-in capital as it is today (see Section 5.4 previously).

7.7   THE OTHER COMPREHENSIVE INCOME DILEMMA

The other comprehensive income dilemma is how to solve certain issues as mentioned below whilst making use of the reporting advantages that other comprehensive income offers. Section 7.4.3 previously illustrates the purpose of other comprehensive income and its pros and cons.

> **Planning Point:** Although some characteristics of other comprehensive income may be debatable, most reasons for such a measure appear to stand in their own right. On the other hand, there are some undesirable implications. Firstly, having two levels of income, i.e., net income and comprehensive income, creates a legitimate doubt concerning what means what and which of the two levels of income should be intended as a measure of performance, as illustrated in Section 7.4.4 previously. Secondly, a double statement of income (an income statement and a statement of comprehensive income) or the use of a subtotal for net income in a single statement of comprehensive income may create uncertainty as to whether or not the one should be combined with the other, or be considered an addendum of the other. Furthermore, the interplay between net income and other comprehensive income determines a mechanism that is called "recycling," which does not yet have a clear conceptual purpose. Recycling is explained in Section 7.8 later.
>
> There are at least five possible solutions to the dilemma, as illustrated in Worksheet 45: 1) adopting alternative recognition model; 2) selecting alternative measurement bases; 3) "quasi-recycling"; 4) directly transferring to retained earnings; and 5) appropriations and/or equity reserves. The first two, however, will eliminate the notion of other comprehensive income itself, so would not solve the issue.

The Discussion Paper of the *Financial Presentation Project* scopes recognition and measurements out of the project, including the definition of items of other comprehensive income and the topic of recycling.[169]

---

[168]   *FASB Statement No. 130, Appendix A, ¶ 119.*
[169]   *Discussion Paper,* Preliminary Views on Financial Statement Presentation, *¶¶ 1.22, 3.33 (October 2008).*

> **Comment:** Is recycling a presentation, recognition, or measurement issue? To the extent recycling an item does impact its measurement it is a measurement issue. To the extent there is a distinction between performance in equity versus performance in income, it is a recognition issue. To the extent it is limited to making a distinction between two categories (such as net income versus comprehensive income) on a "statement of performance" it is a presentation issue.

7.7.1 Rationale for Alternative Recognition Models

Worksheet 46 compares the rationale for recognizing certain gains and losses arising from changes in the value of assets and liabilities in other comprehensive income with alternative recognition models, such as immediate recognition in profit or loss and deferred recognition.

> **Comment:** Adopting a different recognition model may eliminate the need for other comprehensive income. When revising the accounting for pensions and postemployment benefits plans, the IASB found immediate recognition tempting, a fact that in 2011 led to the introduction of immediate recognition for defined benefit plans, even though the basic issues that had prevented the use of this approach are not yet solved.[170]

A long-term goal of the *Financial Statement Presentation Project* is to recognize all current period changes in assets and liabilities in the period in which they occur and present them in a single statement of income with no timing differences of recognition of income and expenses. This would eliminate the recycling mechanism arising from the difference between net income and comprehensive income.[171] However, this would require revisiting both the recognition and measurement attributes of assets and liabilities, topics that fall outside the scope of the project and are better addressed on a specific standard basis (also in consideration of the piecemeal approach under which current accounting for other comprehensive income has arisen). A tentative decision of the project is that the recycling mechanics will be temporarily retained.[172]

> **Example:** Most of the debate on pension accounting is related to alternative recognition methods. Deferred recognition is the accounting model for pensions under pre-2011 IAS 19. The pre-2007 version of IAS 19 adopted an election of immediate recognition in income directly in equity, as opposed to net income. Pre-2011 IAS 19 uses a model that recognizes certain gains and losses in other comprehensive income but with immediate transfer to retained earnings. IAS 19 (2011) goes

---

[170] *IAS 19 (2007), ¶¶ BC41, BC46(a).*

[171] *IASB, Financial Statement Presentation Project, Agenda Paper 3,* Presentation of Income Tax Information, *¶ 14 (March 11, 2008) www.iasb.org (last visited July 28, 2008); IASB Update October 2006.*

[172] *IASB, Financial Statement Presentation Project, Agenda Paper 9B,* Other Comprehensive Income Presentation, *¶¶ 70–71 (March 22, 2007) www.iasb.org (last visited June 21, 2007); IASB, Financial Statement Presentation Project, Agenda Paper 7B,* Totals and Subtotals in the Financial Statements, *¶ 16 (November 15, 2007) www.iasb.org (last visited July 28, 2008); IASB, Financial Statement Presentation Project, Agenda Paper 9A,* Implications of Scope Change, *¶ 16 (June 19, 2008) www.iasb.org (last visited July 28, 2008).*

to immediate recognition in profit or loss but recognition of the remeasurement component in other comprehensive income with no subsequent recycling. Topic 715 (FASB Statement No. 158) continues the past practice of delaying recognition of actuarial gains and losses as a component of net periodic benefit cost but recognizes the entire funded status of a plan in other comprehensive income.

Comment: Alternatively, immediate recognition in income may be seen as a "no-recycling" model, whereby all income and expenses are recognized only once. The IASB considered this approach with reference to cash flow hedges, as the method most consistent with its focus on comprehensive income and with the working principles of the *Financial Statement Presentation Project*. However, it would have serious implications, such as the elimination of cash flow hedge accounting.[173]

Comment: Alternatively, deferred recognition may be seen as the extension of a sort of "basis adjustment" model, whereby income and expenses are deferred in the balance sheet until subsequently recognized in profit or loss (see Section 7.15.2 later for the meaning of basis adjustment in the context of cash flow hedge accounting).[174]

7.7.2   Interaction with Measurement Models

More particularly, the elimination of recycling may have serious consequences on certain standards: it might undermine the conceptual difference between trading securities and available-for-sale securities, change the measurement attributes of available-for-sale financial investments, modify the method for determining foreign currency translation adjustment, eliminate the reason for cash flow hedge accounting to remove the impact of underlying transactions on net income.[175]

Other comprehensive income would not exist if a single measurement basis were used. A mixed measurement model where certain items are measured at fair value, actuarial value, or other bases in the statement of financial position but not in the income statement imposes the necessity of a reconciling item (i.e., other comprehensive income).

Example: The accounting for available-for-sale financial assets at historical cost in the income statement and at fair value in the statement of financial position is an example of a mixed measurement model. Translating a net investment in a foreign operation at foreign exchange rates at transaction dates in the income statement, and at closing foreign exchange rates in the statement of financial position is another example.[176]

---

[173] *IASB Update, July 2002.*

[174] *IASB Update, July 2002.*

[175] *FASB/IASB Financial Statement Presentation Project, Agenda Paper 6C/FASB Memorandum 44C,* Measurement; OCI and Recycling; the Statement of Comprehensive Income, ¶¶ *53–54, 59–62 (October 24, 2006) www.iasb.org (last visited June 21, 2007).*

[176] *IASB/FASB, Joint International Group (JIG) on Financial Statement Presentation, Agenda Paper 8,* Net Income, Other Comprehensive Income, and Recycling, ¶¶ *2–8 (September 15, 2006) www.fasb.org (last visited June 21, 2007); IASB Update, October 2006.*

Comment: Therefore, the full adoption of fair value accounting would eliminate recycling.

One theory asserts that other comprehensive income would remain necessary only when fair value is used in the statement of financial position for nonfinancial investment because showing changes in fair values in the income statement would be inappropriate.[177]

Comment: CON 5 chooses a model of multiple measurement attributes rather than attempting to define exceptions to a single measurement basis. The best measurement attribute depends on its reliability and the nature of the item measured.[178] A mixed measurement model assumes that all individual financial statements have the same or similar prominence and the basis that is most representationally faithful may differ depending on items. Assigning a primary focus on a single statement (see Section 7.5.5 previously) points to the selection of a prevailing measurement basis, as was the case with historical cost for the income statement or may be fair value for the balance sheet.

7.7.3 Quasi-Recycling

"Quasi-recycling" is an expression that the IASB used with reference to cash flow hedging accounting.[179] This Section uses this term extensively. The alternative presentation format of "quasi-recycling" partially solves the dilemma. Section 7.21 later expands on the topic.

Comment: Contrary to the previous two approaches, with alternative presentation models the notion of other comprehensive income remains. To the extent other comprehensive income is supposed to have a positive meaning, this solution saves its information content. If other comprehensive income is recognized directly in equity, it results, by default, in being external to a statement of income and in requiring recycling in order to be computed in that statement. Under this theory, other comprehensive income is recognized directly in a statement of income, renamed as the statement of comprehensive income, and presented as a separate line or otherwise disclosed. This makes it possible to maintain any existing recognition model and measurement bases. Focus shifts from recycling from the equity section of the statement of financial position to the income statement, which would no longer be needed, to "reclassification" from one line to another within the statement of comprehensive income. The dilemma is solved only partially, because two possible indicators of performance still exist, although they may be intended simply to be subtotals with different degrees of inclusiveness.

Comment: IAS 1 follows a similar approach. However, somewhat inconsistently, amounts that standards do not allow to be income or expense of the current period influence the display of comprehensive income for the current period. This method was selected as a practical solution towards a single statement of comprehensive income, which is one of the objectives of the *Financial Statement Presentation Project*.[180]

---

[177] *Performance Reporting Joint International Group (JIG) on Performance Reporting, European CFO Task Force, Presentation by Takashi Yaekura (June 14–15, 2005) www.fasb.org (last visited June 21, 2007).*

[178] *CON 5, ¶¶ 66, 70.*

[179] *IASB Update, July 2002.*

[180] *IASB Update, July 2002.*

> **Comment:** This option has an advantage, to the extent that displaying the change in status of an item of other comprehensive income through recycling or reclassification has informative value (see Section 7.4.3 previously).

7.7.4   Direct Transfer to Retained Earnings

This approach is the one that IFRSs currently follow for revaluation surplus and actuarial gains and losses and for any adjustments arising from the asset ceiling limit on defined benefit plans under the pre-2011 version of IAS 19. Section 6.5 previously analyzes the effect on retained earnings. Section 7.16 and Section 7.18.3 later illustrate the treatment from the point of view of other comprehensive income.

> **Comment:** IAS 19 (2007) explains that this accounting emerged as the result of a pragmatic approach.[181] This Section instead makes autonomous considerations on how a similar model may develop and expands it to meanings that are not expressed under IAS 19 (2007).

> **Comment:** This approach also saves the notion of other comprehensive income, and eliminates recycling. Comprehensive income no longer has any reason to exist (in case of immediate transfer of other comprehensive income to retained earnings, comprehensive income coincides with net income), and is substituted by retained earnings, which would include both the notion of the current comprehensive income and the current retained earnings. However, this model violates the clean-surplus concept, in the sense that income (here net income, and not comprehensive income) does not now include the effect of all transactions and events from nonowner sources. It has also been argued that it may mislead investors by not showing all income and expenses in profit or loss.[182] It also violates the basic principle of retained earnings (see Section 6.2 previously).

> **Planning Point:** There is an easier way to understand this approach. Certain items currently accounted for in other comprehensive income would be renamed as capital maintenance adjustments (see Section 7.6.3 previously). Those adjustments are not income. Therefore, there is no conceptual right to recycle. Other situations of other comprehensive income would be left to one of the other three approaches mentioned above. Retained earnings, currently undefined (see Section 6.1.2 previously), would finally need to find a definition. An additional element of financial statements would need to be defined for capital maintenance adjustments (see Section 7.6.3 previously).

> **Comment:** Section 6.6.6 previously refers to the issue which arose in the *Financial Statement Presentation Project* on whether or not the transfer from other comprehensive income to retained earnings of certain items under IFRSs is simply a labeling issue. This Section shows that it may be a substantial issue to the extent an underlying consistent model is developed.

---

[181]   *IAS 19 (2007), ¶ BC48R.*
[182]   *Joint International Group on Financial Statement, Presentation, presentation by Hiroshi Yamada (June 14, 2005).*

7.7.5   No Recycling

Recognition in other comprehensive income without subsequent recycling seems to be the new model pursued by the IASB. Under IFRS 9, this is the case of equity investments carried at fair value through other comprehensive income, and own credit risk for financial liabilities that are designated as at fair value through profit or loss. The 2011 revision of IAS 19 follows this model for remeasurements of net defined benefit liability or asset.

Comment: However, the no-recycling approach came from a negative rationale, i.e., the lack of criteria for reclassification.[183] The avoidance of distortion of profit or loss and the circumvention of the issues of impairment of equity financial instruments are other reasons.[184] However, even if the effects of impairment on the income statement are bypassed, any inappropriate measurement or failure to measure impairment affects equity. In any event, this approach does not address whether valid reasons exist for reporting items in other comprehensive income. Conversely, IFRS for SMEs gives a practical justification for prohibiting the recycling of exchange differences on monetary items that are in substance part of a net investment in a foreign operation. This avoids tracking for recycling.[185]

7.7.6   Appropriations or Equity Reserves

The fifth approach, further developed in Section 7.21 later, joins the model of immediate recognition in the income statement and the simultaneous appropriation of retained earnings (or of an equity reserve) to disclose and restrict the distributability of an amount corresponding to the unrealized, volatile, or otherwise unqualified earnings. Once the conditions that currently trigger a recycling occur, appropriated retained earnings would be returned to unappropriated retained earnings or the equity reserve reversed.

Comment: This is the model used according to several European local GAAP. Furthermore, it accommodates the legal restrictions that may exist for defense of capital purposes in civil law jurisdictions (see Section 3.5.2 previously and Section 7.5.7 previously).

7.8   RECYCLING

The previous Section placed recycling in the context of different theoretical models. This Section focuses on the mechanics of different types of recycling. It is to be read in conjunction with Section 7.9 later on reporting formats and alternatives.

7.8.1   Definition

The derecognition from other comprehensive income of a portion of gains or losses that have previously been recognized in other comprehensive income and its simultaneous recognition in profit or loss is referred to as "recycling" or "passing through" the income statement (or profit or loss in the statement of comprehensive income). Recycling reverses the amount of

---

[183]   *IAS 19 (2011)*, ¶¶ *BC99, DO4.*
[184]   Chairman of the IASB Addresses ECOFIN Meeting, *March 16, 2010. [Online] Available at www.iasb.org (last visited April 18, 2010).*
[185]   *IFRS for Small and Medium-Sized Entities, ¶ BC123.*

an income and expense item that has been recognized in the same or previous period in other comprehensive income and transfers it to a statement of income for recognition in current income.

Comment: The above definition is stated in general terms that are applicable whether or not other comprehensive income is recognized directly in equity (as may be the case under U.S. GAAP) or in the statement of comprehensive income (as under IFRSs, or as permitted under U.S. GAAP) and whether an income statement only (as may be the case under U.S. GAAP) or a statement of comprehensive income, or both, (as may be the case under both bodies of standards) is adopted.

Recycling is therefore used to avoid double counting the same item of income or expense. Generally speaking, recycling usually arises from a derecognition of assets and liabilities whose gains and losses are recognized in other comprehensive income. Recycling affects both the equity section of the statement of financial position, through a change in the specific other comprehensive income item, and the income statement because such a change passes through profit and loss.

Neither IFRSs nor U.S. GAAP have a general theory of recycling, as the IASB has acknowledged on several occasions.[186] Recycling is not mentioned in the U.S. Concepts and IASB Framework (which, as previously mentioned, does not contain such an element as comprehensive income).[187]

7.8.2 Meaning of Recycling

The mechanism of recycling re-establishes the clean-surplus concept, insofar as the cumulative amount of net income during an entity's lifetime is equal to the cumulative amount of its comprehensive income, because sooner or later other comprehensive income items are recycled.[188]

Comment: Information about reclassification adjustments (i.e., the accounting entries for recycling) is valuable for financial statement users to the extent that other comprehensive income is. Recycling may give information on changes in status of the items of other comprehensive income. Therefore it permits a better understanding of both the equity section of the statement of financial position and the income statement.

For example, changes in status may refer to realization, or resolution of measurement uncertainty and volatility, in order to better assess an entity's timing, amounts, and certainty of future cash flows. Recycling also gives information on different measurement bases used and

---

[186] *IFRS 9 (2010), ¶¶ BC5.44, BC5.55; IAS 19 (2011), ¶ BC99; IAS 19 (2007), ¶ BC48P.*

[187] *FASB/IASB Financial Statement Presentation Project, Agenda Paper 6C/FASB Memorandum 44C, Measurement;* OCI and Recycling; the Statement of Comprehensive Income, ¶ 44 *(October 24, 2006) www.iasb.org (last visited June 21, 2007).*

[188] *IAS 19 (2007), ¶ BC48Q(a); IASB/FASB, Joint International Group (JIG) on Financial Statement Presentation, Agenda Paper 8,* Net Income, Other Comprehensive Income, and Recycling, ¶ 9 *(September 15, 2006) www.fasb.org (last visited June 21, 2007); IASB Update, October 2006.*

the timing differences of recognitions in the statement of financial position and in the income statement.

> **Comment:** As explained in Section 7.8.3 below, this does not happen with minimum additional liability under U.S. GAAP (see Section 7.18.2 later) and does not happen with items that are transferred directly to retained earnings under IFRSs (see Section 7.16 and Section 7.18.3 following).

7.8.3 Classification of Recycling

Worksheet 47 classifies different methods of recycling or reclassifying other comprehensive income that currently exist under U.S. GAAP and IFRSs, as well as under IFRSs prior to the 2007 amendments to IAS 1. Other Sections below explain the accounting for each of those items.

IAS 1 lists the items of other comprehensive income as changes in revaluation surplus, actuarial gains and losses on defined benefit plans when their recognition in the statement of comprehensive income is elected (prior to the 2011 revision of IAS 19), or remeasurements of defined benefit plans under IAS 19 (2011), currency translation adjustment, unrealized gains or losses on available-for-sale financial assets (prior to IFRS 9), and unrealized gains and losses on hedging instruments in a cash flow hedge.[189]

> **Comment:** As mentioned in IFRIC 17, the fact that IAS 1 lists items of other comprehensive income prevents applying them by analogy.[190] However, the Worksheets that follow illustrate that other situations of other comprehensive income exist in IFRSs. These are generally subclassifications of the items mentioned by IAS 1.

Worksheet 48 compares a first set of income and expense items that are recognized as other comprehensive income under U.S. GAAP and IFRSs and subject to recycling. These are subsequently recycled into profit and loss.

> **Comment:** The 2007 Revision of IAS 1 amended other standards. Before such amendments, some items in this worksheet were part of income and expenses that were recognized directly as "a separate component of equity" for which IFRSs did not state explicitly which statements they had to be shown in. It could be inferred from IAS 1 that presentation was possible in one of the two statements permitted (that is, the statement of changes in equity and the statement of recognized income and expenses). Now IFRSs explicitly state that they are recognized as other comprehensive income. IAS 21 now requires the presentation of gains or losses on foreign currency translation in other comprehensive income and of the cumulative amount as a separate component of equity.[191]
>
> For other items IFRSs did not mention that they were recognized as a separate component of equity but rather stated that they were recognized directly in equity through the statement of changes in

---

[189] *IAS 1, ¶ 7.*
[190] *IFRIC 17, ¶ BC48.*
[191] *IAS 21, ¶¶ 41, 45, 48, 52.*

equity, as this term was construed under IAS 1. They are also recycled. Under IAS 1, items of other comprehensive income cannot be presented in the statement of changes in equity, but must be displayed in the statement of comprehensive income.

IFRS 9 replaces the classification of financial assets of IAS 39. The available-for-sale classification for financial assets does not exist anymore.[192] IFRS 9 is effective for annual periods beginning on or after January 1, 2013 (proposed to be moved to 2015). Earlier application is permitted. Unless an entity adopts IFRS 9 for reporting periods beginning before January 1, 2012, the standard requires retrospective application to financial assets existing as of the date of its initial application, irrespective of the business model that an entity used in prior reporting periods.[193]

Worksheet 49 reports the case, under IFRSs, of transfer of accumulated other comprehensive income into the initial carrying amount of the hedged item (so-called "basis adjustment") that is then indirectly reclassified into profit or loss.

Worksheet 50 reports items that are not subject to recycling. The list includes additional pension liability, an item that used to be recognized in other comprehensive income under U.S. GAAP. This item was not recycled. No corresponding concept exists under IFRSs. Under the 2011 Amendments to IAS 1, the statement of profit or loss and other comprehensive income or the statement presenting comprehensive income must total the OCI items that would not be recycled.[194]

Worksheet 51 indicates items that under IAS 19 (2007) may be elected for recognition in other comprehensive income through the statement of comprehensive income only. They are immediately and directly transferred to retained earnings without passing through profit or loss. There is no reclassification adjustment (see Section 7.9.9 later). The 2011 revision of IAS 19 has deleted this option.

> **Comment:** Prior to the amendments made to IFRSs by the 2007 Revision of IAS 1, those items had to be recognized directly in the statement of recognized income and expense. As explained in Section 7.18.3 later, by electing this option, an entity was actually forced to use that statement and could no longer use the statement of changes in equity.

By contrast, the Worksheet includes in other comprehensive income the accounting for period changes in the funded status of defined benefit pension or other postretirement plans and gains or losses and prior service costs or credits that are not recognized as components of net periodic costs, under Topic 715 (FASB Statement No. 158).

Worksheet 52 lists items that, under IFRSs, are directly recognized in other comprehensive income under the special heading "revaluation surplus" through the statement of comprehensive income. These items may be transferred directly to retained earnings either when the asset is consumed or ultimately upon its disposal.

---

[192] *IFRS 9, ¶¶ IN11, 4.1, C9 (amending IFRS 7, ¶ Appendix A), C24 (amending IAS 32, ¶ 12).*
[193] *IFRS 9, ¶¶ 8.1.1, 8.2.1, 8.2.4, 8.2.12.*
[194] *IAS 1, ¶ 82A.*

> **Comment:** Prior to the amendments made to IFRSs by the 2007 Revision of IAS 1, those items were recognized directly in equity through the statement of changes in equity or the statement of recognized income and expense. Because the transfer here is not immediate, this list differs from the one related to transfers to retained earnings.

> **Comment:** This category also introduces a reversal mechanism to account for an impairment of tangible or intangible assets that differs from recycling. In fact, impairment determines an offset between the revaluation surplus and the asset itself (or an impairment valuation account) to the extent a revaluation surplus exists for that asset. Therefore, the reversal of an unrealized gain does not affect the income statement to the extent that gain did not do so.

Worksheet 53 lists the reclassifications of other comprehensive income to the opening balance of retained earnings for the cumulative-effect adjustments that are required or permitted by the transitional provisions of certain standards. Those situations are explained in Section 6.4.10 previously, Section 6.4.11 previously, Section 6.4.12 previously, Section 6.4.15 previously, and Section 6.4.27 previously.

Worksheet 54 shows items, apart from those arising in transactions with owners, that may directly affect more than one component of equity (the list is not necessarily all inclusive).

> **Comment:** These items are classified here as potentially affecting more than one component of equity based on an interpretation under the appropriate standards prior to the amendments made to IFRSs by the 2007 Revision of IAS 1, as explained in Section 6.4.6 and Section 6.4.8 previously. In addition, prior to the amendments made to IFRSs by the 2007 Revision of IAS 1, those items were recognized directly in equity through the statement of changes in equity or the statement of recognized income and expense.

> **Comment:** It is evident that the 2007 Revision of IAS 1 eliminated much of the variety previously existing in IFRSs. Although it is also clear that there are still no consistent and uniform criteria for recycling.[195] The recent developments have introduced other components of other comprehensive income that are not subject to recycling, making the overall picture even more complex.

The Worksheets mentioned above refer to Topic 740 (FASB Statement No. 109) and IAS 12 for the accounting for income tax on items recognized in other comprehensive income. Chapter 8 later illustrates it. As explained in that Chapter, the IASB's Exposure Draft on income tax would change the intraperiod tax rules. Furthermore, the Exposure Draft proposes an amendment to IFRS 1 for the introduction of a new exception for IFRS first-time adopters with a transition date after that of the new standard. Those entities would also apply the new intraperiod tax allocation rules prospectively from its date of transition to IFRSs. The cumulative amounts of tax on items of income and expenses that at the transition date are recognized in accumulated other comprehensive income or that are recognized in equity would not be reclassified to profit and loss on derecognition of the related asset or liability any longer. Those entities must

---

[195] *Agenda Paper 14, Exposure Draft of* Proposed Amendments to IAS 1 Presentation of Financial Statements – Comment Letter Analysis, ¶ 82 *(December 14, 2006).*

deem those amounts recognized outside profit or loss (either in other comprehensive income or directly in equity) to be zero at the transition date.[196]

Section 7.9.11 following reports alternatives for reclassification (i.e., recycling) envisaged as part of the *Financial Statement Presentation Project*.

The Exposure Draft on financial instruments presented an alternative approach to classification and measurement of financial instruments. Under this proposal certain financial instruments would have been measured at fair value, essentially all financial assets that do not have basic loan features and that are not managed on a contractual yield basis and that do not meet the definition of loans and receivables in IAS 39. Any component of fair value changes of such financial assets that is not attributable to the application of an amortized cost basis, impairment loss, or reversal of impairment loss would have been presented in other comprehensive income with no reclassification into profit or loss.[197]

> **Comment:** The rationale of this proposal somehow relates to disaggregating fair value changes based on the information value they provide as discussed in Section 7.4.3 previously. It also looks like a variation of the new category of other comprehensive income recently created by FSP FAS 115-2 and FAS 124-2 in relation to impairment of available-for-sale and held-to-maturity debt securities (see Section 7.14.4 later).

> **Comment:** This approach where no recycling exists and classes of equity might be used to signal different "quality of equity" according to requirements of local jurisdictions can be seen as a particular application of the latest approach envisaged in Section 7.21 later on a comprehensive theory of equity and other comprehensive income.

The Exposure Draft on hedge accounting would require the display of a separate line item in the statement of income for the reclassification of other comprehensive income in a cash flow hedge of a group of items with offsetting hedged risk positions (i.e., a net position hedge). The entity would also have to disclose the related hedging gains or losses.[198]

7.9 REPORTING COMPREHENSIVE INCOME AND OTHER COMPREHENSIVE INCOME

7.9.1 Reporting Alternatives

Worksheet 55 illustrates the logics of alternative structures for presenting comprehensive income and other comprehensive income under U.S. GAAP. A specific statement of comprehensive income, a statement of income and comprehensive income, or the statement of changes in equity are allowed as alternatives. Subtopic 220-10 (FASB Statement No. 130) prefers the first two options.[199]

---

[196] *Exposure Draft*, Income Tax, ¶¶ C2, BC118 (March 2009).
[197] *Exposure Draft*, Financial Instruments: Classification and Measurement, ¶¶ IN14 Question 14, BC38, BC39 (July 2009).
[198] *Exposure Draft*, Hedge Accounting, ¶¶ IN38, IN39, 51, B81, B82, BC176 (December 2010).
[199] *FASB ASC 220-10-45-10 (FASB Statement No. 130, ¶ 67).*

> **Planning Point:** However, effective for fiscal years ending after December 15, 2012 and subsequent annual and interim periods, with early adoption permitted, and for fiscal years (and related interim periods) beginning after December 15, 2011 for public entities, under U.S. GAAP the statement of changes in equity cannot be used to report comprehensive income any longer.[200]

The third option was largely considered to be less transparent and less practical. In fact, under Subtopic 505-10 (APB 12) (when both financial position and results of operations are presented) and Section 505-10-S99 (Regulation S-X) a statement of changes in equity is not mandatory as part of the basic financial statements, as it can be substituted by a separate statement or note disclosure. An entity that chooses the statement of changes in equity to report comprehensive income must include such a statement in basic financial statements and not as a separate statement or note disclosure.[201]

> **Comment:** IAS 1 does not permit a full presentation of comprehensive income in the statement of changes in equity.

> **Comment:** In contrast to the IASB Framework, which has no such distinction, the U.S. Concepts require the display of both net income and comprehensive income as part of the financial statements, not simply disclosure in the notes, although the U.S. Concepts do not prescribe a specific statement and format of comprehensive income.[202]

> **Comment:** Despite the FASB preference for a specific statement of comprehensive income or a statement of income and comprehensive income, most U.S. and Japanese[203] companies use the statement of changes in equity to report comprehensive income. According to the *AICPA Accounting Trends & Techniques*, in 2009–2002 approximately 82–83% of the U.S. GAAP companies surveyed that reported comprehensive income did so in the statement of changes in equity, 13–15% in a separate statement of comprehensive income, and the remainder in the combined statement of income and comprehensive income.[204] After some years, the FASB and the IASB acknowledged that the statement of changes in equity had become a general practice.[205]

Section 505-10-S99 (Regulation S-X) requires the analysis of changes of each caption of stockholders' equity (no longer other stockholders' equity only) and noncontrolling interests either in the form of a separate reconciling statement of the beginning and ending balances, or in the notes. This analysis also includes comprehensive income and other comprehensive

---

[200] *FASB ASC 220-10-45-8 superseded by FASB Accounting Standards Update No. 2011-05,* Compre-hensive Income (Topic 220) – Presentation of Comprehensive Income, ¶¶ 8, BC6.

[201] *FASB ASC 505-10-50-2 (APB Opinion No. 12, ¶ 10); FASB Statement No. 130, ¶¶ 9, 64–65; FASB ASC 505-10-S99-1 (Regulation S-X, ¶ 210.3-04).*

[202] *CON 5, 13; FASB Statement No. 130, ¶ 63.*

[203] *Joint International Group on Financial Statement,* Presentation, *presentation by Hiroshi Yamada (June 14, 2005).*

[204] *AICPA ATT 2010 and AICPA ATT 2006, ¶ Table 4.1.*

[205] *Financial Accounting Standards Advisory Council, June 2005.* Financial Performance Reporting by Business Enterprises, *Attachment E – Appendix 1, ¶ 3(b). www.fasb.org (last visited June 21, 2007).*

income.[206] Foreign private issuers must present a statement of comprehensive income either under U.S. GAAP or home-country GAAP without reconciliation to U.S. GAAP (although it is encouraged). If they present such a statement under U.S. GAAP, they may use any of the formats under Subtopic 220-10 (FASB Statement No. 130).[207] However, ASU 2011-05 prohibits the presentation of comprehensive income and the details of other comprehensive income in the statement of changes in equity.[208] ASU 2011-05 is effective for fiscal years ending after December 15, 2012 and subsequent annual and interim periods, with early adoption permitted, and for fiscal years (and related interim periods) beginning after December 15, 2011 for public entities.

Under IAS 1, items of income and expense must be presented either in the statement of comprehensive income, or in a separate income statement up to profit or loss and in an additional statement of comprehensive income up to comprehensive income, but not in the statement of changes in equity.[209]

Comment: An entity reporting under U.S. GAAP (prior to ASU 2011-05) that elects the statement of changes in equity to present comprehensive income would not be required to prepare a statement of comprehensive income (e.g., it could prepare an income statement). Conversely, an entity reporting under IFRSs must present both the statement of changes in equity and a statement of income.

Comment: The statement of changes in equity contains only a line for total comprehensive income, with separate indication of the portion attributable to controlling and noncontrolling interests, as otherwise totalization of equity would not be possible.[210] The reason presentation of details of comprehensive income is prohibited on the face of the statement of changes in equity is that IAS 1, to implement the categorization working principle established in the *Financial Statement Presentation Project* (see Section 1.4.3.2 previously), does not want to mix changes in equity from nonowner sources with transactions with owners in their capacity as owners, which are displayed in the statement of changes in equity.[211]

Prior to the 2007 amendments to IAS 1, effective for annual periods beginning on or after January 1, 2009, an entity could choose to report comprehensive income either in the statement of changes in equity (SOCIE) or in the so-called statement of recognized income and expense (SORIE). During the *Financial Statement Presentation Project*, the word "recognized" in the title was discarded as recognition is a matter affecting all statements and not just the statement of income and expense. The potential title "total income and expense" was also rejected because it did not sufficiently distinguish components recognized outside profit and loss.[212]

---

[206] *FASB ASC 505-10-S99-1 (Regulation S-X, ¶ 210.3-04).*

[207] *SEC,* Financial Reporting Manual, *¶ 6530.1; AICPA, 1998.* AICPA International Practices Task Force Meeting Highlights, May 28, 1998, *Washington DC, AICPA, ¶ XII. Available at www.aicpa.org (last visited December 24, 2006).*

[208] *FASB ASC 220-10-45-5, 220-10-55-11, 810-10-55-4L, as amended by ASU 2011-05.*

[209] *IAS 1, ¶¶ 81, BC53.*

[210] *IAS 1, ¶ 106(a).*

[211] *IAS 1, ¶ BC49.*

[212] *IASB Meeting, December 14, 2006, Agenda Paper 14: Exposure Draft of* Proposed Amendments to IAS 1 Presentation of Financial Statements – Comment Letter Analysis, *¶ 42 (December 14, 2006).*

> **Comment:** As mentioned in Section 7.2.2 previously, under IFRSs the change from the statement of recognized income and expense to the statement of comprehensive income has a dramatic meaning beyond presentation, because other comprehensive income is no longer recognized directly in equity.

> **Comment:** The statement of recognized income and expense, in most part inherited from UK GAAP, was the IFRS equivalent to the U.S. statement of comprehensive income. The SEC Staff regarded both the statement of total recognized gains and losses under UK GAAP and the statement of changes in equity under IFRSs to be consistent with Subtopic 220-10 (FASB Statement No. 130).[213]

> **Comment:** The EU Accounting Directives refer to the profit and loss account and the balance sheet, not the statement of changes in equity or the statement of comprehensive income. However, the Member States may require or permit additional statements.[214] Some local GAAP in Europe have no such a statement of changes in equity, but similar information is disclosed in the notes, usually in the form of a reconciliation schedule.[215] The EC Commission together with the Member States, through their representatives in the Contact Committee, considered a statement of performance acceptable to the extent that it does not conflict with the layouts of the Fourth Directive.[216] Furthermore, under the EU Modernization Directive, Member States may permit or require a statement of performance instead of a profit and loss account, provided it gives at least equivalent information.[217]

> **Comment:** The format of the statement of changes in equity under IAS 1 has certain features, introduced by the 2007 Revision of the standard: 1) a single line for other comprehensive income versus the previous detailed format; 2) a single line for owners' transactions, then again amended by the 2008 Revision of IAS 27, as discussed in Section 5.3 previously; 3) a new theoretical notion of retrospective adjustments (see Section 6.4.1 previously); and 4) the mandatory attribution of balances to controlling and noncontrolling interests (see Section 7.9.7 later).
>
> For foreign private issuers, Form 20-F accepts one of the options allowed by Subtopic 220-10 (FASB Statement No. 130) for both Item 17 and Item 18, using either U.S. GAAP or home-country GAAP. In any case, a statement is required. Reconciliation to U.S. GAAP is encouraged but not required to a registrant presenting comprehensive income under local GAAP. The disclosure of components of accumulated other comprehensive income (AOCI) is not required under Item 17 if not practical (see Section 7.9.3 later).[218]

---

[213] *U.S. Securities and Exchange Commission,* International Reporting and Disclosure Issues in the Division of Corporate Finance, ¶ *VI.A (November 1, 2004) (last visited April 26, 2006).*

[214] *Fourth Council Directive 78/660/EEC July 25, 1978 Art. 2.1, Art. 2.6.*

[215] *For example, in Italy, Italian OIC – Organismo Italiano di Contabilità, Principio Contabile No. 28, Il Patrimonio Netto, ¶ IV.*

[216] *FEE Study,* Comparison of the EC Accounting Directives and IASs: A Contribution to International Accounting Developments *(April 1999), ¶ 17.*

[217] *Directive 2003/51/EC of the European Parliament and of the Council of June 18, 2003 amending Council Directives 78/660/EEC, 83/349/EEC, 86/635/EEC and 91/674/EEC on the annual and consolidated accounts of certain types of companies, banks and other financial institutions and insurance undertakings (the "Modernization Directive").*

[218] *U.S. Securities and Exchange Commission,* International Reporting and Disclosure Issues in the Division of Corporate Finance, ¶ *VI.A (November 1, 2004) (last visited April 26, 2006).*

The *Financial Statement Presentation Project* proposes to eliminate the existing reporting alternatives of components of comprehensive income. The single statement of comprehensive income would remain the only format. Understandability and comparability among enterprises would be enhanced. Under the 2011 Amendments to IAS 1 and ASU 2011-05, the single statement is divided in two distinct and separate sections for profit or loss and for other comprehensive income. Under the IFRS approach, companies present the components of other comprehensive income that, according to current standards, are subject to reclassification into profit or loss separately from those that are not. An entity that adopts the gross-of-tax method of presenting other comprehensive income is required to display income tax related to those two aggregated categories separately. Due to the difference between the two bodies of standards, the U.S. GAAP approach presents no requirement for distinction of items of other comprehensive income that are subject to recycling from those that that are not, although it maintains the current options of gross- versus net-presentation of items of other comprehensive income. The statement of changes in equity is one of the financial statements, so that reporting in the notes is no longer permitted.[219]

Finally, the Discussion Paper introduced a reconciliation schedule in the notes that reconciles cash flows to comprehensive income and identifies the components of comprehensive income that are cash received or paid other than in transactions with owners, accruals other than remeasurements, recurring fair value change remeasurements or recurring valuation adjustments (see Section 7.4.3 previously), and nonrecurring remeasurements (such as goodwill and inventory impairments, foreign currency translation adjustment, and gains or losses on assets classified as held for sale). The Staff Draft has not reproposed the reconciliation schedule.[220]

7.9.2 Single Versus Two-Statement Approach

As mentioned, both U.S. GAAP and IFRSs permit a single statement of comprehensive income or an income statement plus a statement of comprehensive income. Under U.S. GAAP, the former is also referred to as the (combined) statement of income and comprehensive income or as the (combined) statement of earnings and comprehensive income. ASU 2011-5 introduces the title *Continuous statement of comprehensive income.*[221]

> **Comment:** Initially in the *Financial Statement Presentation Project* this combined statement was called statement of earnings and comprehensive income.[222] The 2011 Amendments to IAS 1 introduce the title *Statement of profit or loss and other comprehensive income.* The purpose is to circumvent the perception of comprehensive income as a superior indicator than profit or loss.[223]

---

[219] *FASB ASC 220-10-45-1A, 220-10-45-8 superseded (Accounting Standards Update No. 2011-05,* Comprehensive Income (Topic 220) – Presentation of Comprehensive Income, ¶ 8); *Amendments to IAS 1,* Presentation of Items of Other Comprehensive Income, ¶¶ 81A, 82A; *Discussion Paper,* Preliminary Views on Financial Statement Presentation, ¶¶ 3.28, 3-29, 3.31, 3.87 (October 2008).

[220] *Discussion Paper,* Preliminary Views on Financial Statement Presentation, ¶¶ 4.19, 4.45 (October 2008).

[221] *FASB ASC 220-10-45-1C (FASB Accounting Standards Update No. 2011-05,* Comprehensive Income (Topic 220) – Presentation of Comprehensive Income, ¶ 8).

[222] *FASB, Minutes of April 21, 2005 Meeting,* Required Financial Statements and Comparative Financial Statements, ¶ 2 (May 13, 2005).

[223] *Amendments to IAS 1,* Presentation of Items of Other Comprehensive Income, ¶¶ 10, 81A; *Exposure Draft,* Presentation of Items of Other Comprehensive Income, ¶¶ 10, BC21 (May 2010).

Comment: Both the IASB and the FASB stated their preference for a single-statement approach (that is, only the statement of comprehensive income) that is more consistent with the IASB Framework and the U.S. Concepts that do not distinguish between profit or loss (or net income) and comprehensive income (the IASB Framework has no comprehensive income element of financial statements – see Section 7.2.3 previously).[224] Furthermore, according to Subtopic 220-10 (FASB Statement No. 130), a single statement approach is more consistent with the clean-surplus concept (see Section 7.3 previously).[225] However, the 2007 Revision of IAS 1 conceived the two-statement approach as a transition measure pending the postulation of a theory on other comprehensive income and conclusive decisions of the *Financial Statement Presentation Project* about the issue of totalization (line items, categories, subtotals, or totals) in financial statements (see Section 1.4.3.5 previously). Similarly, Subtopic 220-10 (FASB Statement No. 130) kept both statements, because it considered a single statement of financial performance premature prior to the solution of the conceptual issues on reporting comprehensive income.[226] Furthermore, many prefer this approach to maintain a primary focus on the income statement (see Section 7.5.5 previously), and to leave net income as an established measure of performance while comprehensive income would be a measure of change of net assets and not necessarily performance related. This would remove the focus from the bottom line only (see Section 7.5.3 previously). However, a single statement would adhere to the cohesiveness working principle (see Section 1.4.3.1 previously).[227] According to other opinions, having two statements of performance, or statements that claim to be so, may be confusing and may undermine comparability.[228] The SEC study on fair value accounting recommends the display of other comprehensive income in the income statement.[229]

Example: A two-statement approach is also followed in the United Kingdom by FRS 3, *Reporting Financial Performance*, which considers it necessary to complement the profit and loss account with a "statement of total recognized gains and losses" (STRGL).

The *Financial Statement Presentation Project* has been long debating these two approaches. The Discussion Paper proposes a single statement of comprehensive income with a subtotal of profit or loss or net income and a separate section that displays other comprehensive income with the same prominence as the other sections.[230] This approach is considered superior because it permits the disclosure of net income and comprehensive income in one and the same place.[231] In July 2009 the IASB and the FASB decided to address the single statement in

---

[224] *FASB ASC 220-10-45-10 (FASB Statement No. 130, ¶ 67); IAS 1, ¶¶ 81, BC51.*

[225] *FASB ASC 220-10-45-10 (FASB Statement No. 130, ¶¶ 58, 67).*

[226] *FASB Statement No. 130, ¶ 59.*

[227] *IAS 1, ¶¶ BC50–BC54; FASB/IASB Financial Statement Presentation Project, Agenda Paper 6C/FASB Memorandum 44C,* Measurement; OCI and Recycling; the Statement of Comprehensive Income, *¶ 76 (October 24, 2006) www.iasb.org (last visited June 21, 2007); IASB Meeting, December 14, 2006, Agenda Paper 14:* Exposure Draft of Proposed Amendments to IAS 1 Presentation of Financial Statements – Comment Letter Analysis, *¶¶ 62–63 (December 14, 2006).*

[228] *FASB Statement No. 130, ¶ 60; IASB Meeting, December 14, 2006, Agenda Paper 14:* Exposure Draft of Proposed Amendments to IAS 1 Presentation of Financial Statements – Comment Letter Analysis, *¶ 58 (December 14, 2006).*

[229] *United States Securities and Exchange Commission, Office of the Chief Accountant, Division of Corporate Finance,* Report and Recommendations Pursuant to Section 133 of the Emergency Economic Stabilization Act of 2008: Study on Mark-To-Market Accounting *(December 2008), pages 9–10, 204.*

[230] *Discussion Paper, Preliminary Views on Financial Statement Presentation, ¶ 3.24 (October 2008).*

[231] *IASB Update, April 2005; Financial Accounting Standards Advisory Council,* Financial Performance Reporting by Business Enterprises, *Attachment E – Appendix 1, ¶ 5 (June 2005) (last visited June 21,*

a separate project. In October 2009, they decided to develop a convergent, although separate, guidance. As part of the latest tentative decisions, the two-statement approach in IAS 1 (i.e., an income statement and a combined statement of income and comprehensive income) would be eliminated. However, the 2011 Amendments to IAS 1 and ASU 2011-05 have not yet incorporated this step. ASU 2011-05 deleted the current option available under U.S. GAAP to present comprehensive income in the statement of changes in equity.[232]

7.9.3   Display Requirements

Worksheet 56 shows the minimum display requirements under U.S. GAAP for each presentation alternative mentioned in the previous Section.

Worksheet 57 lists the minimum presentation requirements under current IFRSs. Worksheet 58 shows the requirements prior to the amendments by the 2007 Revision of IAS 1. Both diagrams illustrate those requirements as contrasted with U.S. GAAP minimum requirements and terminology. Of course, those exhibits show items related to the topic of comprehensive income only (not to prior period adjustments, dividends, or other capital accounts).

> **Comment:** These are minimum display requirements. In addition, as usual for each statement, under both bodies of standards, materiality governs the aggregation in classes of similar items or the disaggregation of items of a dissimilar nature or function.[233]

IFRSs, as a result of the *Business Combination Project*, require determination of the portions of profit or loss and total comprehensive income that are attributable to noncontrolling interests and to present total comprehensive income for the period separately in the newly-established single statement of comprehensive income or in the income statement and in the statement of comprehensive income (when the two-statement approach is elected).[234] U.S. GAAP also requires the display of amounts of net income and comprehensive income that are attributable to noncontrolling interests on the face of the income statement or the statement of comprehensive income.[235] FASB Statement No. 160 also amends FASB Statement No. 130 to require the display of comprehensive income attributed to controlling and noncontrolling interests on the face of the statement where comprehensive income is presented.[236]

Under both U.S. GAAP and IFRSs, the part of income from continuing operations, discontinued operations, and extraordinary items (U.S. GAAP only) that is attributed to the parent

---

2007) www.fasb.org; FASB/IASB Financial Statement Presentation Project, Agenda Paper 6C/FASB Memorandum 44C, Measurement; OCI and Recycling; the Statement of Comprehensive Income, ¶ 75 (October 24, 2006) (last visited June 21, 2007) www.iasb.org.

[232]   *FASB ASC 220-10-45-8 superseded by FASB Accounting Standards Update No. 2011-05, Comprehensive Income (Topic 220) – Presentation of Comprehensive Income, ¶ 8.*

[233]   *IAS 1, ¶ 86.*

[234]   *IAS 1, ¶¶ 54, 82, 83; IAS 27 (2010), ¶¶ 27–28.*

[235]   *FASB ASC 810-10-50-1A, 810-10-55-4J, 810-10-55-AK (ARB 51, ¶¶ 38(a), A4, A5, as amended by FASB Statement No. 160).*

[236]   *FASB Statement No. 130, ¶ 14, as amended by FASB Statement No. 160, ¶ C9.*

must be disclosed either on the face of the income statement (U.S. GAAP) or the statement of comprehensive income (IFRSs) or in the notes.[237]

The Implementation Guidance of Subtopic 220-10 (FASB Statement No. 130) illustrates the closing of accounts and the transfer of other comprehensive income (a nominal account) to accumulated other comprehensive income (a real, balance sheet account).[238] As shown, under Subtopic 220-10 (FASB Statement No. 130), accumulated other comprehensive income must be displayed separately from both retained earnings and additional paid-in capital on the equity section of the statement of financial position. Furthermore, each component of the accumulated balances must be shown on the face of the statement of financial position, statement of changes in equity, or in the notes. This is not required under Item 17 of Form 20-F. However, effective for fiscal years ending on or after December 15, 2011, all issuers will have to comply with Item 18 rather than Item 17. Furthermore, the SEC Staff clarified that a foreign private issuer that under local GAAP reports items of accumulated other comprehensive income in retained earnings is exempted from reclassifying the components of accumulated other comprehensive income in case this reconstruction is impracticable and it discloses this fact.[239] For insurance companies, Regulation S-X requires the display of unrealized appreciation or depreciation of equity securities less applicable deferred taxes on the face of the statement of financial position.[240]

Planning Point: Effective for fiscal years ending after December 15, 2012 and subsequent annual and interim periods, with early adoption permitted, and for fiscal years (and related interim periods) beginning after December 15, 2011 for public entities, ASU 2011-05 mentions changes in balances of AOCI and not the balances by themselves. Furthermore, it simply refers to financial statements or the notes as opposed to the statement of financial position, the statement of changes in equity, or the notes. However, the examples in ASU 2011-05 consider only the statement of changes in equity and the notes, not the statement of financial position. The statement of changes in equity may also display total AOCI.[241] Conversely, the example of statement of changes in equity in IAS 1 has columns for the components of accumulated other comprehensive income and not a column for the total. The May 2010 *Improvements to IFRSs* permit note disclosure of the effects on equity of each component of other comprehensive income. This would make the statement simpler, similarly to what ASU 2011-05 does.[242]

The *AICPA Accounting Trends & Techniques* shows that 60% of the U.S. GAAP companies surveyed in 2009 (55% in 2005 and 36% in 2002) displayed balances of component of accumulated other comprehensive income in the notes, and 18%, 15%, and 32%, respectively, in the statement of changes in equity. About 5%, 9%, and 8%, respectively, used the statement

---

[237] *FASB ASC 810-10-50-1A (ARB 51, as amended, ¶ 38(b)); IFRS 5, as amended by IAS 27 (2008), ¶ 33(d).*

[238] *FASB ASC 220-10-55-27 (FASB Statement No. 130, ¶ 139).*

[239] *FASB ASC 220-10-45-14 (FASB Statement No. 130, ¶ 26); U.S. Securities and Exchange Commission,* International Reporting and Disclosure Issues in the Division of Corporate Finance, *¶ VI.A (November 1, 2004) (last visited April 26, 2006) www.sec.gov; U.S. Securities and Exchange Commission, Release No. 33-8959,* Foreign Issuer Reporting Enhancements, *¶ II.E (December 2008) (last visited October 11, 2009) www.sec.gov.*

[240] *FASB ASC 944-210-S99-1 (Regulation S-X 210.7-03.23).*

[241] *FASB ASC 220-10-45-14A, 220-10-55-11, 220-10-55-15, 220-10-55-16 (ASU 2011-05).*

[242] *IAS 1, ¶ 106(d)(iii), 106A, as amended by* Improvements to IFRSs, *May 2010.*

of financial position, no more than 2% in the statement of comprehensive income, and 15% in 2009 (16% in 2005 and 19% in 2002) did not present any component. 2–4% had no accumulated other comprehensive income at all.[243]

Although IFRSs require the separate recognition of each class of other comprehensive income, IAS 1 does not require separate presentation of accumulated other comprehensive income on the face of the statement of financial position. However, the statement of changes in equity must separately show the opening and closing balances, and changes thereof, of each component of equity, including the accumulated balance of each class of other comprehensive income.[244] As part of the *Annual Improvements*, in May 2010 the IASB amended IAS 1 to clarify that an entity could either present in the reconciliation the analysis of each item of other comprehensive income in the statement of changes in equity or disclose it in the notes.[245] IFRS for SMEs requires the presentation of items of accumulated other comprehensive income in the statement of financial position or disclosure in the notes.[246]

Under IFRS 5, a subsidiary that is acquired and held exclusively with a view to resale meets the criteria to be classified as held for sale. IFRS 5 requires that cumulative income or expenses that relate to a noncurrent asset (or disposal group) classified as held for sale and that is recognized in other comprehensive income must be separately presented in the equity section of the consolidated statement of financial position.[247] On the contrary, in such a case Subtopic 360-10 (FASB Statement No. 144) does not mandate specific presentation in equity.

Recently, the IASB and the FASB tentatively decided that the fact that an item of other comprehensive income relates to discontinued operations warrants separate presentation, likely into discontinued operations.[248]

Worksheet 59 shows sample formats of the statement of changes in equity.

In addition, for recurring fair value measurements subsequent to initial recognition using significant unobservable inputs (Level 3 of the fair value hierarchy), Subtopic 820-10 (FASB Statement No. 157) requires disclosure of the segregation of the total gains or losses for the period recognized into the amount that is included in earnings and the amount that is recognized in other comprehensive income and the respective line items.[249] Similar disclosures are contained in IFRS 13 and the March 2009 Amendment to IFRS 7.[250]

The Exposure Draft on hedge accounting proposes to enrich the IAS 1 reconciliation of accumulated other comprehensive income in the statement of changes in equity or in the

---

[243] *AICPA ATT 2010 and AICPA ATT 2006, ¶ Table 2-40.*

[244] *IAS 1, ¶¶ 106(d), 108.*

[245] Improvements to IFRSs, Amendments to IAS 1 Presentation of Financial Statements, *¶ 106A (May 2010); IASB Update, page 4 (February 2009).*

[246] IFRS for Small and Medium-Sized Entities, *¶ 4.11.*

[247] *IFRS 5, ¶ 38.*

[248] *IASB Update, July 2009; IASB Update, March 11, 2010.*

[249] *FASB ASC 820-10-50-1, 820-10-50-2, 820-10-50-3, 820-10-55-62, 820-10-55-63 (FASB Statement No. 157, ¶¶ 32, A35, as amended by ASU No. 2010-06 and ASU No. 2011-04).*

[250] IFRS 13, *¶ 93(f); Amendments to IFRS 7 Financial Instruments*, Improving Disclosures about Financial Instruments, *¶ 27B(d) (March 2009), deleted by IFRS 13.*

notes, in order to highlight the effects of hedge accounting on equity and the statement of comprehensive income. Such disclosure would comprise information on amounts arising from changes in the value of hedging instruments, reclassification of hedging gains or losses in net position hedges, reclassification adjustments in cash flow hedges, and the amounts related to time value of options that hedge transaction related hedged items and time period related hedged items. The Exposure Draft would also require additional information in tabular format of the effects of hedge accounting segregated by hedge type.[251]

FSP FAS 115-2 and FAS 124-2 (see Section 7.14.4 later) introduced a new category of other comprehensive income for the portion of other-than-temporary impairment that is not related to a credit loss for a held-to-maturity security. The carrying amount of the debt security increases (with no effect in earnings) over its remaining life through a prospective accretion from other comprehensive income to its amortized cost, until the security is sold, matures, or another other-than-temporary impairment is recognized in earnings. In addition, when a portion of other-than-temporary impairment of held-to-maturity and available-for-sale securities has been recognized in earnings as required by the FSP, the statement that reports the components of accumulated other comprehensive income (see Section 7.9.1 previously) must separately display the amounts related to held-to-maturity and available-for-sale securities. This new format of presentation applies to both debt held-to-maturity and available-for-sale securities and equity available-for-sale securities.[252]

Finally, Section 6.4.5 previously mentions the disclosure requirements under U.S. GAAP relating to the effects of a change in reporting entity on other comprehensive income and other appropriate equity caption for all periods presented.

In a context of interim reporting, Subtopic 220-10 (FASB Statement No. 130) requires a total for comprehensive income, not its components, although it explains that it expects an entity to explain significant other comprehensive income amounts in interim periods.[253]

Comment: Although the standard does not qualify the type of enterprise to which such requirement applies, its Basis for Conclusions explains that this is required in condensed interim financial statements of publicly traded enterprises.

From its effective date, ASU 2011-05 extends the presentation of the components of net income and other comprehensive income in condensed interim financial statements.[254]

Unlike annual financial statements, Form 20-F does not provide guidance about comprehensive income in interim reporting. In any case, a statement is required.[255]

---

[251] *Exposure Draft,* Hedge Accounting, ¶¶ *IN41, 51, 52, BC201, BC203 (December 2010).*
[252] *FSP FAS 115-2 and FAS 124-2, ¶¶ 11, 18, 34, 37.*
[253] *FASB ASC 220-10-45-18 (FASB Statement No. 130, ¶ 27); FASB Statement No. 130, ¶¶ 124, 125; FASB ASC 270-10-50-1 (APB 28, ¶ 30.a).*
[254] *FASB ASC 220-10-45-18, as amended by ASU 2011-05.*
[255] *SEC, International, November 1, 2004, ¶ VI.A.*

Under the *Financial Statement Presentation Project*, the statement of comprehensive income should indicate the type of activity (i.e., operating, investing, financing, or discontinued operations) to which each item of other comprehensive income does or will relate, except for foreign currency translation adjustment on a consolidated subsidiary or, under IFRSs prior to IFRS 11, on a proportionately consolidated joint venture. Under the 2011 Amendments to IAS 1 and ASU 2011-05, the statement shows a total for other comprehensive income and each of its components. Under the IFRS approach, the statement segregates items of other comprehensive income that are subject to reclassification to profit or loss from those that are not. An entity that adopts the gross-of-tax method of presenting other comprehensive income is required to separately display income tax related to those two aggregated categories. Due to the difference between the two bodies of standards, the FASB version has no requirement for distinction of items of other comprehensive income that are recycled from those that that are not.[256]

7.9.4 Designing for Dual-Reporting Equivalent Statement of Changes in Equity

Worksheet 60 proposes reconciliation between some items required to be displayed in the statement of changes in equity or disclosed under IFRSs and the same statement under Subtopic 220-10 (FASB Statement No. 130). Worksheet 61 gives the same illustration with reference to IFRSs prior to the amendments by the 2007 Revision of IAS 1.

Planning Point: This provides a view of reconciliation that is needed under a dual-reporting environment and layout interventions that an accounting information system must make to allow both formats of presentation.

Comment: The Implementation Guidance of IAS 1 shows a row for total comprehensive income that crosses a column for retained earnings. This illustration is somehow misleading. Its meaning is illustrated in the footnotes to the statement of changes in equity. For example, a change of retained earnings attributable to total comprehensive income may be due to profit or loss for the period attributable to owners of the parent, plus actuarial gains or losses on defined benefit plans net of tax attributable to owners of the parent (under the pre-2011 version of IAS 19).

Comment: An important change is that IAS 1 introduces a separate row for the transfer of revaluation surplus to retained earnings in the display of the statement of changes in equity, as shown in the Implementation Guidance of the standard. The lack of a total for comprehensive income is clearly observable. This has probably been done on purpose, as this statement must not report detail of comprehensive income, apart from what is strictly necessary to compute totals of rows and columns. On the other hand, the fact of having a line for comprehensive income, but not a full total may be confusing to some users of financial statements.

---

[256] *FASB ASV 220-10-45-1A; FASB ASC 220-10-45-8 superseded by FASB Accounting Standards Update No. 2011-05*, Comprehensive Income (Topic 220) – Presentation of Comprehensive Income, ¶ 8; *Amendments to IAS 1*, Presentation of Items of Other Comprehensive Income, ¶¶ 81A, 82A; *Discussion Paper*, Preliminary Views on Financial Statement Presentation, ¶ 3.25 (October 2008); *FASB and IASB*, Staff Draft of an Exposure Draft on Financial Statement Presentation, ¶¶ 104, 139, 151, 162 (July 2010).

> **Comment:** Section 6.4.3 previously explains subtle differences between the examples provided by IAS 8 and Subtopic 250-10 (FASB Statement No. 154) and some inconsistencies between IAS 1 and IAS 8 in reporting the effects of retrospective application or retrospective restatement in the statement of changes in equity.

The 2008 Revision of IAS 27, effective for annual periods beginning on or after July 1, 2009, amended the statement of changes in equity to detail the beginning and ending balances and to indicate, separately, period changes of each component of equity that results from profit or loss and from each item of other comprehensive income.

> **Comment:** There is a perceived inconsistency between the requirement to detail all changes in each class of other comprehensive income and the general principle that the statement of changes in equity must not present nonowner changes in equity. This results in a compromise, that is, a single row for total comprehensive income but explanations of changes in the footnotes to the statement.

Subtopic 810-10 (FASB Statement No. 160) contains a similar requirement, with certain differences, as explained in Section 7.9.7 following.

> **Planning Point:** Effective for fiscal years ending after December 15, 2012 and subsequent annual and interim periods, with early adoption permitted, and for fiscal years (and related interim periods) beginning after December 15, 2011 for public entities, under ASU 2011-05 the statement of changes in equity is no longer an option to report comprehensive income. Under U.S. GAAP, like IAS 1, the statement of changes in equity no longer shows details of other comprehensive income. However, unlike IAS 1, it must show a total for other comprehensive income and net income, a fact that IAS 1 prohibits. Unlike IAS 1, the examples shown in the ASU do not display a total or a column for comprehensive income, while IAS 1 requires a total for comprehensive income.[257]

7.9.5 Designing for Dual-Reporting Equivalent Statement of Comprehensive Income

Worksheet 62 compares the statement of comprehensive income under IFRSs and U.S. GAAP. Worksheet 63 compares the statement of recognized income and expense under IFRSs, prior to the 2007 amendments made by IAS 1, with the statement of comprehensive income under U.S. GAAP.

> **Comment:** Under IAS 1 and IAS 28 an investor in an associate or a venturer in a joint venture accounted for at equity method adjusts its carrying amount of the investment for its share (after tax and minority interest) of the changes in the investee's other comprehensive income. It displays its share of the changes in the investee's other comprehensive income in its consolidated statement of comprehensive income. Prior to the 2007 amendments of IAS 1, it adjusted its equity for its share in income and expense that the investor had recognized directly in equity.[258] Subtopic 323-10

---

[257] *FASB ASC 220-10-55-11, 220-10-55-12, 810-10-55-4L (ASU 2011-05).*

[258] *IAS 1, ¶ 82(h); IAS 28 (2010), ¶¶ 11, 39.*

(FASB Statement No. 130) also requires display for the investor's share of an investee's equity adjustments for other comprehensive income, but it does not clarify how it should be displayed. It also permits the combining with the investor's other comprehensive income items.[259]

7.9.6   Retrospective Accounting Adjustments

The previously existing statement of recognized income and expense used to display the effect of changes in accounting policy and correction of errors accounted for under IAS 8.[260] Now, under IAS 1, the statement of changes in equity must show the effect of changes in accounting policy and correction of errors accounted for by a retroactive approach under IAS 8.[261] IAS 1 asserts the abovementioned point mainly with reference to retained earnings but confirms that in the context of adjustments to each component of equity.[262]

> **Planning Point:** The previous treatment is no longer permitted in the newly-developed statement of comprehensive income or statement of income and comprehensive income, because these adjustments are considered simply a reconciling item and not part of comprehensive income as they do not arise from changes in net assets during the period. The standard clarifies that in reply to some comment letters to the Exposure Draft of the amendments to IAS 1.[263] However, the IASB did not consider it necessary to remove the inconsistency in the definition of "total comprehensive income" that does not explicitly exclude such adjustments[264] (also see Section 6.4.1 previously).

Under FASB Statement No. 130, prior period adjustments should not be displayed in comprehensive income for the period as, in effect, they recast the comprehensive income of prior periods.[265] Instead, CON 5 and FASB Statement No. 130 consider cumulative accounting adjustments (which U.S. GAAP used to report under the current-method prior to FASB Statement No. 154) as part of comprehensive income as they are recognized in the current period as changes in equity and therefore meet the definition of comprehensive income under the U.S. Concepts.[266] Arguably, here a different way of accounting (by a retroactive approach or by the catch-up method) for like transactions or events determines a different scope for an element of the financial statements by the simple fact that focus shifts from the period of occurrence of the original transaction to the period of reporting of the adjustment.

> **Example:** A French foreign private issuer replied to the SEC Staff, in the context of the review of Form 20-F for the fiscal year ended December 31, 2005 containing financial statements prepared for the first time on the basis of IFRSs. The company applied the treatment under FASB Statement

[259] *FASB ASC 323-10-35-18, 323-10-45-3 (FASB Statement No. 130. ¶¶ 121–122).*

[260] *IAS 1, ¶ 96(d).*

[261] *IAS 1, ¶ 106(b); IAS 1, ¶ 96(d).*

[262] *IAS 1, ¶ 110.*

[263] *IASB Meeting, December 14, 2006, Agenda Paper 14: Exposure Draft of Proposed Amendments to IAS 1 Presentation of Financial Statements – Comment Letter Analysis, ¶ 53 (December 14, 2006).*

[264] *IAS 1, ¶ 7, IASB Meeting, December 14, 2006, Agenda Paper 14: Exposure Draft of Proposed Amendments to IAS 1 Presentation of Financial Statements – Comment Letter Analysis, ¶ 55 (December 14, 2006).*

[265] *FASB Statement No. 130, ¶¶ 106.*

[266] *FASB Statement No. 130, ¶ 79; CON 5, ¶ 39.*

No. 130 (based on which prior period adjustments that would affect other comprehensive income must not be displayed in comprehensive income for the period as they recast the comprehensive income of prior periods) to the IFRS financial report.[267] At the time of these letters, the 2007 Revision of IAS 1 was not yet issued.

Comment: In stating that cumulative accounting adjustments are part of comprehensive income, FASB Statement No. 130 does not take a position on whether they should be part of net income or other comprehensive income. It leaves them in net income simply because that determination is outside of the scope of the standard.[268]

7.9.7 Attribution to Controlling and Noncontrolling Interests

IFRSs and Subtopic 810-10 (FASB Statement No. 160) require that the portion of profit or loss and comprehensive income that is attributable to owners of the parent company and to noncontrolling interest be displayed as allocation of those total amounts and not as an expense item. Such allocations hold even if noncontrolling interest ends up with a deficit balance. The same holds for reconciliation of equity balances and each item of other comprehensive income in the statement of changes in equity or in the notes.[269] Under IAS 1, the statement of changes in equity must also present both allocations of comprehensive income.[270] IFRS 10 adds that the entities must also allocate each item of other comprehensive income.[271]

In the year of adoption of FASB Statement No. 160 an entity must disclose pro forma consolidated net income attributable to the parent and pro forma earnings per share as computed previously under ARB 51, if significantly different.[272]

Comment: All the above is consistent with the entity theory of consolidation and in line with the recent evolution of accounting for noncontrolling interest (see Section 4.3.2 previously and Section 4.3.3 previously).

The new format of the statement of changes in equity, if seen from a consolidated perspective, also conveys information on the effects of transactions with noncontrolling interests that do not result in a loss of control on the equity of the owners of the parent, although regarding this, IAS 27 added a specific schedule to be disclosed in the notes,[273] to converge with Subtopic

---

[267] *Letters by the SEC, File No. 1-15234, Note 37 (September 7, 2006), Note 36. Reply by the company (November 24, 2006) www.sec.gov/divisions/corpfin/ifrs_reviews (last visited January 7, 2008).*

[268] *FASB Statement No. 130, ¶¶ 81–85.*

[269] *FASB ASC 810-10-45-21, 810-10-50-1A, 810-10-55-4J, 810-10-55K, 810-10-55-AL (ARB 51, ¶¶ 31, 38(a), 38(c), A4–A6, as amended by FASB Statement No. 160); IAS 1, ¶¶ 83, 106(a), BC59; IAS 27 (2010), ¶ 28.*

[270] *IAS 1, ¶ 106(a).*

[271] *IFRS 10, ¶ B94.*

[272] *FASB ASC 810-10-65-1 (FASB Statement No. 160, ¶¶ 6); FASB Statement No. 160, ¶ B74.*

[273] *IAS 27 (2010), ¶¶ 41(e), A4, BC68–BC70.*

810-10 (FASB Statement No. 160) that requires this schedule.[274] IFRS 12 confirms such a schedule.[275]

FASB Statement No. 160 also amends FASB Statement No. 130 to require the display of comprehensive income attributed to controlling and noncontrolling interests on the face of the statement where comprehensive income is presented.[276]

Furthermore, under Subtopic 810-10 (FASB Statement No. 160), a parent with one or more less-than-wholly-owned subsidiaries must disclose a reconciliation of beginning and ending balances of total equity and its allocation to controlling and noncontrolling interests either in the consolidated statement of changes in equity or in the notes, with separate presentation of net income, other comprehensive income, and contributions from and distributions to owners and other capital transactions.[277] One reason for permitting note disclosure is that a company not registered with the SEC is not obligated to present the statement of changes in equity[278] (also see Section 7.9.1 previously). Apart from total comprehensive income, IAS 1 as part of balances reconciliation in the statement of changes in equity does not state the attribution to controlling and noncontrolling interests. However, this is shown in the Implementation Guidance.[279]

Comment: There are subtle differences for the latter requirement. Firstly, unlike IAS 1, Subtopic 810-10 (FASB Statement No. 160) allows note disclosure as an option. This is because nonregistered companies are not obliged to present the statement of changes in equity.[280] Secondly, the wording of IAS 1 literally calls for showing the change in equity balances arising from profit or loss, each item of other comprehensive income, and transactions with owners. The illustration of changes in balances with an explanation in footnotes is enough to reach the disclosure objective without violating the prohibition on those details of comprehensive income. Instead, the wording of Subtopic 810-10 (FASB Statement No. 160) requires showing net income, each component of other comprehensive income, and transactions with owners. Implementation Guidance shows these differences. However, effective for fiscal years ending after December 15, 2012 and subsequent annual and interim periods, with early adoption permitted, and for fiscal years (and related interim periods) beginning after December 15, 2011 for public entities, ASU 2011-05 shows the attribution of only net income and the total of other comprehensive income to noncontrolling interests on the face of the statement of changes in equity.[281]

Comment: The *Financial Statement Presentation Project* had noted that the current statement of changes in equity does not provide information about changes between ownership interests.[282]

---

[274] *FASB ASC 810-10-50-1A (ARB 51, ¶ 38(d), as amended by FASB Statement No. 160).*

[275] *IFRS 12, ¶ 18.*

[276] *FASB Statement No. 130, ¶ 14, as amended by FASB Statement No. 160, ¶ C9.*

[277] *FASB ASC 810-10-50-1A (ARB 51, ¶ 38(c), as amended by FASB Statement No. 160).*

[278] *FASB Statement No. 160, ¶¶ B66, A6.*

[279] *FASB ASC 810-10-50-1A, 810-10-55-AL (ARB 51, ¶¶ 38(c), A6, as amended by FASB Statement No. 160); IAS 1, ¶ 106(d) as amended by IAS 27 (2008); IAS 27 (2010), ¶ 28.*

[280] *FASB Statement No. 160, ¶ B66.*

[281] *FASB ASC 220-10-45-8 superseded, 220-10-55-11, 220-10-55-12, 810-10-55-4L as amended by ASU 2011-05.*

[282] *IASB, Financial Statement Presentation Project, Agenda Paper 13D, Statement of Changes in Equity and Other Equity-Related Issues, ¶ 33 (January 25, 2007).*

Planning Point: Some local GAAP require reconciliation between the net income and shareholders' equity in a parent's separate financial statements and those in the consolidated financial statements. For example, Italian accounting standards require this statement in the notes to the consolidated financial statements.[283] The Italian Consob requires listed parent companies to include such a statement in the management commentary to the consolidated financial statements.[284] IFRSs and U.S. GAAP do not require such a statement. This is unfortunate as it is quite informative and a valid consolidation control tool.

Example: In response to the review of Form 20-F of an Italian foreign private issuer for the year ended December 31, 2005, the company explained to the SEC that this form is required by Italian Standards.[285]

When consolidated financial statements include a less-than-wholly-owned subsidiary that holds available-for-sale investments, other comprehensive income must be adjusted against noncontrolling interest at the same time the subsidiary recognizes changes in value of its available-for-sale investments in other comprehensive income. This entry records the noncontrolling interest's share of the subsidiary's other comprehensive income and related changes.[286] Similarly, under IAS 27, noncontrolling interests include their proportionate share of each component of other comprehensive income.[287]

Subsection 210-10-S99-1 (Rule 3-04) now requires an analysis of changes of each caption of stockholders' equity, no longer other stockholders' equity only. Under Subsection 210-10-S99-1 (Regulation S-X), other stockholders' equity includes additional paid-in capital, other paid-in capital accounts, and retained earnings.[288] Regulation S-X does not require a reconciliation of total equity balances, because Subsection 480-10-S99-1 (CFRR 211) prohibits SEC registrants that have redeemable preferred stock to use a stockholders' equity heading inclusive of redeemable preferred stock.[289] The SEC Staff identified two methods for SEC registrants to comply with this rule and at the same time effect the equity reconciliation required by Subtopic 810-10 (ARB 51) and Subsection 210-10-S99-1 (Rule 3-04). A separate column for redeemable preferred stock in the equity reconciliation should not add up to total equity. A row or supplemental table can show the allocation of net income to controlling interests, nonredeemable noncontrolling interests, and redeemable noncontrolling interests. Alternatively, if the equity reconciliation excludes redeemable preferred stock, a supplemental

---

[283] *OIC – Organismo Italiano di Contabilità, Principio Contabile No. 17*, Il Bilancio Consolidato, ¶ 8.4; *OIC 4*, Fusione e Scissione, *page 4*.

[284] *Consob, DEM/6064293 (July 2006).*

[285] *Letter by the SEC, File No. 001-14090, Note 23 (September 28, 2006). Reply by the company (October 28, 2006) www.sec.gov/divisions/corpfin/ifrs_reviews (last visited January 7, 2008).*

[286] *FASB ASC 320-10-S99-2 (EITF Topic D-41, Adjustments in Assets and Liabilities for Holding Gains and Losses as Related to the Implementation of FASB Statement No. 115, as amended by Accounting Standards Update No. 2010-04, Accounting for Various Topics, Technical Corrections to SEC Paragraphs, ¶ 9).*

[287] *IAS 27 (2010), ¶ 28.*

[288] *FASB ASC 210-10-S99-1 (Regulation S-X, ¶ 210.5-02.30).*

[289] *FASB ASC 480-10-S99-1 (Codification of Financial Reporting Release, CFRR 211, Redeemable Preferred Stock, ¶¶ 1, 3).*

table would reconcile beginning and ending balances of redeemable noncontrolling interests. Net income would parenthetically explain the portion allocated to redeemable noncontrolling interests.[290]

Nonregistered investment partnerships that report capital by investor class must include cumulative unrealized gains and losses into the ending balances of each class of shareholders' or partners' interest in that entity at the balance sheet date, as if net assets were realized and distributed based on the partnership's governing documents.[291]

7.9.8 Prominence of Presentation

IAS 1 states that all financial statements of a complete set of financial statements must be presented with equal prominence.[292] Under Subsection 220-10-45-8 (FASB Statement No. 130) comprehensive income must be reported in a statement with equal prominence as other statements that are part of the full set of financial statements.

Comment: The topic of the level of prominence of comprehensive income is linked to both whether or not financial performance must be the primary focus of financial reporting and whether performance must be defined in terms of a single indicator or multiple measures. Section 7.5.5 previously and Section 7.5.3 previously explain the mixed views on these subjects. The fact that Subtopic 220-10 (FASB Statement No. 130) does not characterize comprehensive income as a measure of performance reinforces the need for equal prominence.[293] IAS 1 embraces the view of multiple measures of performance to support the equal prominence of financial statements.[294]

Planning Point: The U.S. Concepts directly require information on comprehensive income, as it is an element of the financial statements (the U.S. Concepts approach to defining the components of a full set of financial statements is described in Section 6.8.2 previously). Subtopic 220-10 (FASB Statement No. 130) implements this prescriptively. IFRSs, prior to the 2007 amendments made by IAS 1 have done it indirectly as a part of a statement of changes in equity, by requiring disclosure of items of income and expense that are recognized directly in equity. Currently, comprehensive income derives indirectly from two concepts that are not defined as elements in the IASB Framework, i.e., net income and other comprehensive income (see Section 7.2.3 previously).

The goal of equal prominence may be achieved in at least three different ways. A first way is through a statement of comprehensive income that shows both net income and comprehensive income. A second way is, under both IFRSs and U.S. GAAP (no longer under ASU 2011-05), by means of the requirement that a combined statement of income and comprehensive

---

[290] AICPA, *SEC Regulations Committee, 2009.* Joint Meeting with SEC Staff, June 23, 2009. *Washington DC, AICPA, ¶ V.B. [Online] AICPA. Available at www.aicpa.org (last visited July 9, 2010) (hereinafter SEC Regulations Committee, June 23, 2009).*

[291] AICPA, *TIS Section 6910*, Investment Companies, *¶ 29*.

[292] *IAS 1, ¶ 11.*

[293] *FASB Statement No. 130, ¶ 66.*

[294] *IAS 1, ¶ BC22.*

income starts with net income. ASU 2011-05 and the 2011 Amendments to IAS 1 add that that statement must also present a total of other comprehensive income.[295] IAS 1 adds that the separate income statement must be placed immediately before the statement of comprehensive income if a two-statement approach is followed.[296] ASU 2011-05 inserts this requirement, effective for fiscal years ending after December 15, 2012 and subsequent annual and interim periods, with early adoption permitted, and for fiscal years (and related interim periods) beginning after December 15, 2011 for public entities.[297]

Comment: Although both net income and comprehensive income are evidenced in the same statement, under the former approach one (net income) is a component of the other (comprehensive income). This aspect of the issue of prominence is, in general, being analyzed as part of the working principle of disaggregation of the *Financial Statement Presentation Project* (see Section 1.4.3.5 previously).

Subtopic 220-10 (FASB Statement No. 130) calls these two layouts "reconciled formats," because comprehensive income is reconciled to net income through other comprehensive income. In order to have a reconciled format, the statement of changes in equity must permit the totalization of net income and other comprehensive income to arrive at comprehensive income.[298]

Comment: The statement of changes in equity in IAS 1 is not a "reconciled statement": net income must not be displayed in such a statement. The 2008 amendments by IAS 27 do not result in a "reconciled statement," because they introduced the display of the impact of net income and other comprehensive income on each component of equity in the footnotes to the statement. From its effective date, ASU 2011-05 no longer permits the presentation of comprehensive income on the face of the statement of changes in equity, which therefore loses its characteristic of reconciled format under U.S. GAAP.

Comment: In the *Financial Statement Presentation Project*, the IASB Staff was of the view that the statement of comprehensive income should start with comprehensive operating income inclusive of other comprehensive income, not profit or loss. This was intended to facilitate the transition to the IASB long-term goal of having comprehensive income only.[299]

The statement of changes in equity has been criticized for not presenting other comprehensive income with the same prominence as net income in a statement of performance.[300]

---

[295] *FASB ASC 220-10-45-1B, 220-10-45-8 then superseded by ASU 2011-05 (FASB Statement No. 130, ¶¶ 22); FASB Statement No. 130, ¶ 99; IAS 1 (2011), ¶¶ 81A, BC57.*

[296] *IAS 1, ¶ 12.*

[297] *FASB ASC 220-10-45-1, as amended by ASU 2011-05.*

[298] *FASB Statement No. 130, ¶¶ 98–99.*

[299] *IASB, Financial Statement Presentation, Agenda Paper No. 15B, The Statement of Cash Flows, ¶ 45 (December 14, 2006) www.iasb.org (last visited June 21, 2007).*

[300] *FASB Statement No. 130, Dissenting Opinions.*

> **Comment:** In fact, it might be inferred that under IAS 1 such a statement is not intended as a statement of performance.

7.9.9 Reclassification Adjustments

Recently IAS 1 converged to FASB Statement No. 130 in using the expression *reclassification adjustment*, i.e., reclassification of other comprehensive income items, which were recognized in the current or previous periods, into current profit or loss.[301]

> **Comment:** The Exposure Draft of the 2007 Amendment to IAS 1 was modified to clarify that the recognition in other comprehensive income could happen both in the current and in previous periods. This clarification was intended to extend the accounting for reclassification adjustments to interim reporting, when other comprehensive income has been recorded in previous interim periods that are part of the current annual period.[302]

> **Comment:** In a strict sense, the term *reclassification adjustment* refers to the accounting entry of recycling. However, it is sometimes used as a substitute for recycling (Section 7.8 previously).[303] A reclassification adjustment entry requires a separate adjustment and is not automatic.

A reclassification adjustment avoids double hitting comprehensive income, once as other comprehensive income in the current or prior periods, then as net income when other comprehensive income is recycled to the income statement, for example in case of disposal of available-for-sale securities (prior to IFRS 9) or of a foreign operation or when in a cash flow hedge a hedged forecast cash flows affect profit or loss.[304]

> **Comment:** Therefore the accounting entry will debit a loss (or credit a gain) in net income and credit (or debit) a "reclassification adjustment" in other comprehensive income.
>
> Subtopic 830-30 (FASB Statement No. 52) requires the reporting of reclassification adjustment of cumulative translation adjustment as part of the gain or loss on sale or liquidation.[305] U.S. GAAP, prior to ASU 2011-05, presents reclassification adjustments for each item of other comprehensive income either as a separate line in a financial statement in which comprehensive income is shown or combined with each period change in the specific other comprehensive income item with disclosure in the notes. ASU 2011-05 eliminates the note disclosure option.

---

[301] *FASB Statement No. 130, ¶ 18; IAS 1, ¶ 7.*
[302] *IAS 1, ¶¶ BC72–BC73; IASB Update, December 2006; IASB Meeting, December 14, 2006, Agenda Paper 14: IASB, Exposure Draft of Proposed Amendments to IAS 1 Presentation of Financial Statements – Comment Letter Analysis, ¶¶ 79–81 (December 14, 2006).*
[303] *IAS 1, ¶ BC70.*
[304] *FASB ASC 220-10-45-15 (FASB Statement No. 130, ¶ 18); IAS 1, ¶¶ 93 (amended by IFRS 9), 95 (amended by IFRS 9).*
[305] *FASB ASC 830-30-40-1 (FASB Statement No. 52, ¶ 14).*

> **Comment:** The former is referred to as "gross display" under U.S. GAAP, and "gross presentation," under IFRSs. The latter is called "net display" under U.S. GAAP, and "net presentation" or "aggregated presentation," under IFRSs.[306]

Gross display may be either next to each item of other comprehensive income or in a single section where all reclassification adjustments are shown. Each one must be labeled as appropriate.

> **Comment:** IAS 1 does not indicate these two formats of gross display. The Implementation Guidance shows a gross presentation with reclassification adjustments next to each item of other comprehensive income. In any case, IAS 1 requires disclosure of reclassification adjustments per item of other comprehensive income.[307]

Under U.S. GAAP, a reclassification adjustment used not to apply to minimum pension liability adjustments under FASB Statement No. 87 (see Section 7.18.2 later), as its determination was considered to be impractical.[308] Minimum pension liability required net display only.[309] FASB Statement No. 158 has eliminated this item.

The purpose of disclosing those adjustments is to reconcile the amounts that are included as income and expenses in different periods through net income and other comprehensive income and permit a computation of total gain or loss associated with the specific asset or liability. Furthermore, depending on jurisdictions, tax rates applicable to items of other comprehensive income may differ from those of components of net income, and this may be significant information.[310]

> **Comment:** Although they are different concepts, the gross and net presentation formats interact with the gross-of-tax and net-of tax formats that are explained in the Section 7.9.10 following.

In fact, the gross display has the advantage of directly tracing the reclassification adjustment from other comprehensive income to the income statement items which are presented on a before-tax basis, without the need for additional disclosure. On the other hand, the net display is consistent with the equity section of the statement of financial position and with equity in the statement of changes in equity, as on an after-tax basis.[311] Finally, net display avoids cluttering the face of the financial statements.[312]

---

[306] *IAS 1, ¶¶ BC65, IG6(b).*

[307] *IAS 1, ¶¶ IN8, IN14.*

[308] *FASB ASC 220-10-45-17 (FASB Statement No. 130, ¶ 20); FASB Statement No. 130, ¶¶ 92, 94.*

[309] *FASB Statement No. 130, ¶ 21 (eliminated by FASB Statement No. 158, ¶ F4(d)).*

[310] *IAS 1, ¶¶ IN14, BC66, BC68, BC69.*

[311] *FASB Statement No. 130, ¶¶ 100, 103; IAS 1, ¶ BC65.*

[312] *IASB Meeting, December 14, 2006, Agenda Paper 14: Exposure Draft of* Proposed Amendments to IAS 1 Presentation of Financial Statements – Comment Letter Analysis, *¶ 76 (December 14, 2006).*

> **Comment:** Gross display follows an income view. Net display has a balance sheet orientation (Section 2.1.4.1 (3) previously). The disclosure refers to each item of other comprehensive income, not to net income. Thus, the income statement does not distinguish the portion of realized gains or losses that are due to reclassification adjustments.[313] Note that IAS 1 defines reclassification adjustments as an integral part of other comprehensive income.[314]

> **Planning Point:** Under the FASB new approach for reporting comprehensive income, the statement of changes in equity cannot any longer display other comprehensive income (as previously under U.S. GAAP). In this respect, it converges with IAS 1. However, unlike IAS 1, ASU 2011-05 requires the presentation of the effects of reclassification adjustments by component of net income and of other comprehensive income. In effect, this prohibits net presentation of reclassification adjustments. A proposed ASU would defer the requirement that the statement where net income is presented must also show the effects of reclassification adjustments by component of net income.[315] ASU 2011-05 is effective for fiscal years ending after December 15, 2012 and subsequent annual and interim periods, with early adoption permitted, and for fiscal years (and related interim periods) beginning after December 15, 2011 for public entities.[316] IAS 1 after IFRS 9 adds gains and losses from reclassifying financial assets to fair value to minimum line items, but this is not about recycling.[317]

Contrary to U.S. GAAP, the previous Revision of IAS 1 did not require general disclosure of recycling. However, IAS 32[318] used to, and IFRS 7 (prior to amendments by IFRS 9) does prescribe separate disclosure on the face of the financial statements (now on the face of the statement of comprehensive income) or in the notes of the current period reclassification adjustments of available-for-sale financial assets and of cash flow hedges (the latter only in the notes).[319] IAS 1 requires either gross or net presentation of reclassification adjustments in the statement of comprehensive income.[320]

FSP FAS 115-2 and FAS 124-2 amends FASB Statement No. 130 to clarify that a reclassification adjustment of the new separate category of accumulated other comprehensive income relating to held-to-maturity securities that under the FSP originates from other-than-temporary impairment not related to a credit loss only applies to the case of a sale of the security, maturity, or of an additional credit loss (see Section 7.14.4 later). Conversely, in all other instances that separate category of other comprehensive income is amortized over the remaining life of the security through a prospective accretion from other comprehensive income to its amortized cost with no effect on earnings.[321]

---

[313] *IAS 1, ¶ 93.*

[314] *IAS 1, ¶ 7.*

[315] *Proposed Accounting Standards Update,* Comprehensive Income (Topic 220) – Deferral of the Effective Date for Amendments of Items Out of Accumulated Other Comprehensive Income in Accounting Standards Update No. 2011-05 *(October 2011).*

[316] *FASB ASC 220-10-45-8 superseded, 220-10-45-17 (FASB Accounting Standards Update No. 2011-05,* Comprehensive Income (Topic 220) – Presentation of Comprehensive Income, *¶ 8, BC6).*

[317] *IAS 1, ¶ 82(ca).*

[318] *IAS 32 (Revised 2003), ¶ 94(h).*

[319] *IFRS 7, ¶¶ 20(a)(ii) (deleted by IFRS 9), 23(d).*

[320] *IAS 1, ¶¶ 92, 94.*

[321] *FSP FAS 115-2 and FAS 124-2, ¶¶ 11, 34, 37, A3(c).*

Under IFRSs, reclassification adjustments do not apply to other comprehensive income items that are transferred directly to retained earnings (see Section 7.16 and Section 7.18.3 later).[322] For a discussion of the meaning of capital maintenance adjustments see Section 7.6.3 previously.

The *Financial Statement Presentation Project* proposes the reclassification of items of other comprehensive income to the same categories, if necessary with several lines, as the asset or liability in the statement of financial position that originated that item.[323] Under the FASB and IASB new approach for reporting comprehensive income, the statement of changes in equity no longer displays other comprehensive income (as currently under IAS 1).[324] Reclassification adjustments remain in the statement of comprehensive income. Under the 2011 Amendments to IAS 1, companies present the components of other comprehensive income that, according to current standards, are subject to reclassification into profit or loss separately from those that are not.[325] Due to the difference between the two bodies of standards, ASU 2001-05 presents no requirement for distinction of items of other comprehensive income into these two categories. The Feedback Statement explains that this gives an indication of the future impact of recycling on profit or loss.[326]

7.9.10 Gross- Versus Net-of-Tax Display

An entity must separately disclose income tax relating to each component of other comprehensive income, including those attributable to reclassification adjustments, either in the statement of comprehensive income (under IFRSs) or in the statement that reports those components (under U.S. GAAP) or in the notes (see Section 7.9.1 previously and Section 8.2.12 later).[327] Under both U.S. GAAP and IFRSs, a net-of-tax (also called "post-tax" display or "net presentation," under IFRSs) or "gross-of tax" presentation (also known as "pre-tax" display or "gross presentation," under IFRSs) is possible. The former combines the items of other comprehensive income and the related tax. The latter reports the gross amount of the components of other comprehensive income and the aggregated income tax effects in one line. Detail of tax for each component is disclosed in the notes, both in gross presentation and in net presentation when it does not give such a level of detail.[328] These two formats interlink with similar concepts used for reclassification adjustments, and Section 7.9.9 above explains the pros and cons of these two layouts.

The Implementation Guidance of IAS 1 and the Illustrative Examples of FASB Statement No. 130 illustrate a gross presentation of the statement of comprehensive income where income tax

---

[322] *IAS 1, ¶ 96.*

[323] *FASB and IASB,* Staff Draft of an Exposure Draft on Financial Statement Presentation, *¶ 163 (July 2010); Discussion Paper,* Preliminary Views on Financial Statement Presentation, *¶¶ 3.26, 3.41 (October 2008).*

[324] *FASB ASC 220-10-45-8 superseded by FASB Accounting Standards Update No. 2011-05,* Comprehensive Income (Topic 220) – Presentation of Comprehensive Income, *¶ 8.*

[325] *Amendments to IAS 1,* Presentation of Items of Other Comprehensive Income, *¶ 82A; IASB Update, October 2009.*

[326] *Project Summary and Feedback Statement, Amendments to IAS 1,* Presentation of Items of Other Comprehensive Income, *page 9.*

[327] *FASB ASC 220-10-45-12 (FASB Statement No. 130, ¶ 25); IAS 1, ¶¶ IN8, IN14, 90, 91; IAS 12, ¶ 81(ab).*

[328] *FASB ASC 220-10-45-11 (FASB Statement No. 130, ¶ 24); IAS 1, ¶¶ 91, BC65.*

related to components of other comprehensive income is displayed in a single line, and details related to each single item are disclosed in the notes. A variation of the net-presentation format might be parenthetical explanation of tax amounts on the face of the statement that reports other comprehensive income. ASU 2011-05 removes the characterization of parenthetical explanation.[329] Worksheet 64 compares these different formats.

The identification of the tax impact must refer to each individual item of other comprehensive income. The pros include clarity and transparency of information, especially for financial analysis, and inference of different tax rates that may be applicable depending on jurisdiction. The cons comprise the fact that tax allocation, depending on sector, may be relatively arbitrary and not immediately available (see Section 8.1 later), and the lack of consistency in applying such a treatment to other comprehensive income only and not to all other items of the statement of comprehensive income. However, the Exposure Draft on income tax would allocate income tax to the components of comprehensive income (such as income from continuing operations, discontinued operations, and other comprehensive income) and equity.[330] The note disclosure of the tax effects distinguishes the before-tax, tax, and after-tax amounts of each component of other comprehensive income for the current and comparative periods. In the presence of reclassification adjustments, both under gross and net presentation, details of income tax must refer to both the gain and loss recorded in other comprehensive income that arises in the period as well as the related reclassification adjustment.[331] In addition, an SEC registrant must reconcile the tax amount to the applicable statutory Federal income tax rate or rates.[332]

According to the *AICPA Accounting Trends & Techniques*, in 2009 and 2005, respectively, approximately 52% and 63% of the companies surveyed that disclosed tax effects on other comprehensive income did it on the face of a statement (net presentation).[333]

Gross- versus net-of-tax presentation is a topic of the *Financial Statement Presentation Project*. Net presentation violates the cohesiveness principle (see Section 1.4.3.1 previously). A tentative decision is that gross presentation should be the general rule, unless additional information in a gross presentation provides no incremental value.[334] Other issues related to income tax accounting are discussed in Section 8.2 later.[335]

Under the 2011 Amendments to IAS 1, an entity that adopts the gross-of-tax method of presenting other comprehensive income is required to give a separate display of income tax related to the two aggregated categories of the components of other comprehensive income that, according to current standards, are subject to reclassification into profit or loss separately from those that are not.[336] The 2011 Amendments to IAS 1 and ASU 2011-05 maintain the current options of gross versus net presentation of items of other comprehensive income.

---

[329] *FASB ASC 220-10-55-13, 220-10-55-14, 220-10-55-26 (FASB Statement No. 130, ¶¶ 131, 138); IAS 1, Guidance on Implementing, Part I; FASB ASC 220-10-55-8B, as amended by ASU 2011-05.*

[330] *Exposure Draft, Income Tax, ¶ 29 (March 2009).*

[331] *IAS 1, ¶¶ BC66–BC68.*

[332] *FASB ASC 210-10-S99-2 (SEC Staff Accounting Bulletin, Topic 6-H, ¶ 4.I.3,* Net of Tax Presentation*).*

[333] *AICPA ATT 2010 and AICPA ATT 2006, ¶ Table 4-1.*

[334] *IASB Update, December 2006.*

[335] *IASB, Financial Statement Presentation Project, Agenda Paper 15A,* Other Comprehensive Income, *¶ 34 (December 14, 2006).*

[336] *Amendments to IAS 1,* Presentation of Items of Other Comprehensive Income, *¶ 82A; IASB Update, October 2009.*

As explained in Chapter 8 later, the IASB's Exposure Draft on income tax would change the intraperiod tax rules. Furthermore, the Exposure Draft proposes an amendment to IFRS 1 for the introduction of a new exception for IFRS first-time adopters with a transition date after that of the new standard. Those entities would also apply the new intraperiod tax allocation rules prospectively from their dates of transition to IFRSs. The cumulative amounts of tax on items of income and expenses that at the transition date are recognized in accumulated other comprehensive income or that are recognized in equity would not be reclassified to profit and loss on derecognition of the related asset or liability any longer. Those entities must deem those amounts recognized outside profit or loss (either in other comprehensive income or directly in equity) to be zero at the transition date.[337]

7.9.11   Other Inputs from the Financial Statement Presentation Project

Worksheet 65 illustrates certain financial statements layout dimensions that can be found in current accounting pronouncements and their interactions from the perspective of financial statement users.

Comment: In trying to define new or revised formats for financial statements, the *Financial Statement Presentation Project* moves from the working principles illustrated in Section 1.4.3 previously. The Project develops various considerations, some of which are analyzed in the Sections above, with the objective of determining cohesive layouts across the financial statements. A detailed analysis of the proposals of the Project falls outside the scope of this Book.

Cohesiveness among financial statements (see Section 1.4.3.1 previously) was initially thought to be the governing working principle which seeks to address the question of complementary characteristics in displaying the same categories (such as operating, financing, investment, discontinued operations, income tax, others) on the face of each financial statement. An issue is whether cohesiveness should be applied at category or line-item level. The line-item level cohesiveness interpretation would result in modifying certain current approaches (e.g., mandating the use of the direct method of the statement of cash flows or eliminating the need for reconciliation between such a statement and the statement of comprehensive income).[338]

Comment: In effect, as the cohesiveness model would cut across the financial statements, the issue becomes which statement should lead, if any. Each individual statement has a different focus, and the considerations that apply to one are not necessarily valid for another. Depending on the main focus of financial reporting (see Section 7.5.5 previously), one statement may be seen as the starting point or simply as a reconciliation of the perspectives of other statements. For example, the statement of cash flows may be conceived as reconciliation between the statement of financial position and the statement of comprehensive income or as a self-standing perspective. Also a statement of changes in net assets may be seen as reconciliation between a beginning and an ending statement of financial position or an expansion of the statement of comprehensive income or a variant of the statement of changes in equity. Section 2.1.4.1 (3) previously recaps the debate on the balance sheet as opposed to the income-and-expense approaches.

---

[337] *Exposure Draft*, Income Tax, ¶¶ C2, BC118 (March 2009).
[338] *Financial Accounting Standards Advisory Council Meeting, Attachment F (March 20, 2007).*

The Project has been studying alternative statements, such as a reconciliation of the statements of cash flows and comprehensive income, a statement of financial position reconciliation, or a statement of comprehensive income matrix to show the cause of changes in assets or liabilities.[339] The Discussion Paper of the *Financial Statement Presentation Project* introduced a reconciliation schedule between cash flows and comprehensive income in the notes, along certain dimensions explained in Section 7.4.3 previously, then withdrawn by the Staff Draft.

> **Comment:** Again, part of the debate on these statements is about what financial statement should lead, e.g., the statement of financial position, the statement of comprehensive income, or the statement of cash flow. Again, this topic is in turn linked to the concept of focus of financial reporting.

The Project also discussed whether or not a statement of changes in net assets should be presented, as an expansion of the statement of comprehensive income. In some ways, this is linked to the discussion on whether or not comprehensive income is an indicator of performance and on the cohesiveness among financial statements. However, to put it briefly, such a statement would provide similar information to the statement of changes in equity.

> **Comment:** In effect, there is no specific statement other than the statement of changes in equity that provides information about investment by and distributions to owners. The U.S. Concepts consider them an element of the financial statements and require such a statement.[340]

In particular, the Project distinguishes operating activities from financial activities on the face of the financial statements and tries to determine whether or not and which of these sections should prevail over the other. This would parallel the finance theory whereby operating decisions are generally disconnected from financing decisions and would assist users in a better understanding of the capital structure and the associated cost of the capital of a company. A principle initially emerging as part of the Project is that a performance statement should make it possible to distinguish the return on total capital employed from the return on equity.[341]

> **Comment:** The definition of operating activities is much influenced by the issue of the distinguishing features of items of net income as opposed to items of other comprehensive income, such as relation to core business, recurrence, etc. (see Section 7.4 previously).

[339] For example, IASB/FASB, *Financial Statement Presentation Project, Agenda Paper 3,* Categorization in a Statement of Earnings and Comprehensive Income, *(June 2005); IASB, Financial Statement Presentation, Agenda Paper 9A,* Presentation of Changes in Assets and Liabilities, ¶ 14 (March 22, 2007); IASB, *Financial Statement Presentation, Agenda Paper 3B,* Presenting Information about the Cause of Change in Reported Amounts of Assets and Liabilities, ¶¶ 12, 29 (June 19, 2007) www.iasb.org (last visited June 21, 2007); IASB Update, July 2007.
[340] CON 5, ¶¶ 55, 56.
[341] FASB Task Force on Financial Performance Reporting by Business Enterprises, Discussion Paper, Classification of Items of Comprehensive Income, *page 10 (June 2002) www.fasb.org (last visited June 21, 2007).*

The project has provided different definitions of financial activities. The definition and classification of "treasury assets," the concept of "gross" versus "net-debt," the concept of "operating working capital" as opposed to "working capital," whether or not some assets should be part of the notion of financing, and whether or not an investment category should exist are different angles that are part of the picture.

Comment: The classification of an item as financial or operating works around different interpretations (sometimes, misinterpretations) of these terms. This distinction may refer to the nature of the relationships underlying an item (e.g., trade versus other financial receivables – a view that is typical of IAS 1), or to the underlying contractual rights and obligations (e.g., financial assets and financial liabilities under IAS 32), or to its task (e.g., held for investment, for trading, for sale, kept available for sale, or for productive operations – a view that is typical of accounting for financial instruments under IAS 39 or tangible assets under IAS 16 and IAS 40), or to the organizational unit or the business segment within a company that holds or manages an item (e.g., an operating business unit as opposed to a treasury center – a view that is typical of segment reporting under IAS 14 and IFRS 8), and under the functional approach of the Discussion Paper how financial assets and liabilities are used within the entity.[342]

As mentioned, the separation between changes in equity from nonowner sources from transactions with owners in their capacity as owners is a fundamental point in implementing the categorization working principle. This is consistent with the definition of comprehensive income in the conceptual frameworks. In addition, risk and return characteristics of these two areas differ. These considerations resulted in one decision in favor of the exclusion of details of other comprehensive income from the layout of the statement of changes in equity in the 2007 Revision of IAS 1. Additionally, the statement of changes in equity is now less congested with changes in other comprehensive income of the period.[343]

A particular implementation issue of the cohesiveness principle is whether or not equity financing should be part of the financing section. To a certain extent, equity is interchangeable with debt financing and a financing section would give an idea of an entity's total capitalization. On the other hand, by separating the two types of transactions, accounting would catch up with finance theory, whereby operating decisions are analyzed separately from their financing. Furthermore, having an overall finance section would not be cohesive with a statement of changes in equity only. The solution to this point is to some extent linked to the results of the *Financial Instruments with Characteristics of Equity Project* – former *Financial Instruments: Liabilities and Equity Project*. The Staff Draft suggests separate debt and equity categories within the

---

[342] *Discussion Paper*, Preliminary Views on Financial Statement Presentation, ¶ 2.62 *(October 2008)*.

[343] *IASB*, Exposure Draft of Proposed Amendments to IAS 1 Presentation of Financial Statements, ¶ *BC18 (March 2006); IASB, Financial Statement Presentation, Agenda Paper 17*, Application of Working Principles, ¶ *50 (July 21, 2006) www.iasb.org (last visited June 21, 2007); Agenda Paper 14*, Exposure Draft of Proposed Amendments to IAS 1 Presentation of Financial Statements – Comment Letter Analysis, ¶ *44 (December 14, 2006); IASB, Financial Statement Presentation Project, Agenda Paper 13D*, Statement of Changes in Equity and Other Equity-Related Issues, ¶¶ *5, 14, 22 (January 25, 2007)*.

financing section. However, this distinction would be operational only in the statement of financial position.[344]

One of the main points of the Project is whether or not reclassification (i.e., recycling) should exist. Different presentation alternatives of the statement of comprehensive income arise if recycling is maintained. These include a separate section for other comprehensive income with equal prominence as the business, financing, income tax, and discontinued operations sections (this is the current proposal), or the display within each functional section or category to which the related event or transaction relates, or a subcategory of each functional section or category. Reclassification might occur within or among the sections and categories. Reclassification from the other comprehensive income section to the other sections or categories in the statement of comprehensive income is the solution so far selected. In addition, new standards are adding components of other comprehensive income that are not subject to recycling (for example, see Section 7.19 and 7.20 later).

A parallel issue is whether or not there should be a net income subtotal. The long-term goal of the IASB is to present all current period changes in assets and liabilities in one of the functional categories on the statement of comprehensive income so as to eliminate recycling and substitute the concept of comprehensive income for that of net income.[345] The 2011 Amendments to IAS 1 and ASU 2011-05 confirm a subtotal for profit or loss or net income.[346]

Another suggestion of the Project is whether or not the statement of comprehensive income should include a short- versus long-term classification, based on the classification of the related asset or liability in the statement of financial position. Long-term classification would distinguish unrealized price changes (generally items of other comprehensive income) from short-term consumption of assets.[347]

Disaggregation on the financial statements might follow several dimensions, such as segregating remeasurements from transactions unrelated to remeasurement, further drilled down based on persistence, measurement subjectivity, measurement bases, transactions with third parties, predictive value of fair value changes, cash and noncash items, or the other dimensions that Section 7.4 previously discusses as determinants of other comprehensive versus net income. The *Financial Statement Presentation Project* has selected persistence (i.e., the fact of an

---

[344] *FASB and IASB*, Staff Draft of an Exposure Draft on Financial Statement Presentation, ¶¶ *62, 84, 95 (July 2010); IASB, Financial Statement Presentation Project, Agenda Paper 9*, Application of Working Principles, ¶ *11 (September 19, 2006) www.iasb.org (last visited June 21, 2007); FASB Memoranda No. 46A-C, IASB Agenda Papers No. 13A, C, and D*, Financial Statement Presentation – Discontinued Operations, Hybrid Entities, and Equity-Related Issues, ¶ *46 (January 31, 2007) www.fasb.org (last visited June 21, 2007); IASB, Financial Statement Presentation Project, Agenda Paper 13D*, Statement of Changes in Equity and Other Equity-Related Issues, ¶ *23 (January 25, 2007).*

[345] *IASB, Financial Statement Presentation Project, Agenda Paper 15A*, Other Comprehensive Income, *(December 14, 2006); FASB Memoranda No. 44A-F, IASB Agenda Paper No. 6A-F*, Financial Statement Presentation, ¶ *63 www.fasb.org (last visited June 21, 2007); FASB/IASB*, Project Updates, Financial Statement Presentation - Joint Project of the IASB and FASB, *Updated: January 12, 2007*, ¶ *9 www.fasb.org (last visited January 16, 2007).*

[346] *FASB ASC 220-10-45-1A; IAS 1*, ¶ *10A, as amended by Amendments to IAS 1*, Presentation of Items of Other Comprehensive Income.

[347] *IASB, Financial Statement Presentation Project, Agenda Paper 9B*, Other Comprehensive Income Presentation, ¶¶ *7–19 (March 22, 2007) www.iasb.org (last visited June 21, 2007).*

item being indicative of its future amounts) and subjectivity as the primary disaggregation characteristics of comprehensive income to predict future cash flows.[348]

Comment: The emphasis of disaggregation along value-enhancing dimensions, such as the ability to predict value, reflects, to a certain extent, a management view of financial data for internal decisions, forecasting, capital budgeting, planning, and controlling. This perspective, if taken to the limit, would likely call for a revision of the hierarchy of financial statement users, whereby today management is not included in the first layer. The hierarchy of quality characteristics may also need to be revised. The distinction between general accounting and management accounting would partially blur. The limitation, mentioned in the conceptual frameworks, that the assessment of the value of an enterprise is not an objective of financial reporting would likely be rephrased. All this was somehow inherent in the initial idea of the *Performance Reporting Project*.

Other aspects of the layout of the statement of comprehensive income discussed in the Project, such as presentation by nature of expense as opposed to function, fall outside the scope of this Book.

7.10 FOREIGN CURRENCY TRANSLATION ADJUSTMENT

7.10.1 The Reporting Currency Issue in an International Context

Under FASB Statement No. 52, the reporting currency is the currency of preparation of the financial statements.[349] IAS 21 calls the currency in which financial statements are presented the presentation currency.[350] The functional currency is that of the primary economic environment in which an entity operates, that is the primary currency in which an entity conducts its business.[351] IAS 21 (Revised 1993) used to call it the measurement currency. The determination of the functional currency is made based on certain tests.

U.S. GAAP and IFRSs start from different historical and geographical premises with reference to the topic of the presentation currency. Worksheet 66 illustrates the options available in an international context.

Comment: Multinationals reporting under IFRSs may need to adapt to legal requirements of different jurisdictions. Multinational groups traditionally face the issue that the financial statements of single members of the group may be presented in a currency that is different from the one used in the consolidated financial statements. Depending on specific cases in an international context, however, multinational companies may face the situation of being included in consolidated financial statements where the reporting currency is different from that of the parent company. Also, they may comprise operations with a number of functional currencies. They may use several currencies both for external reporting as well as for management control. Finally, because of the existence of some country requirements for a domestic or foreign group to report in the local currency, they may be in the

---

[348] *FASB and IASB,* Staff Draft of an Exposure Draft on Financial Statement Presentation, ¶¶ *BC204, BC226 (July 2010); Discussion Paper,* Preliminary Views on Financial Statement Presentation, *¶¶ 4.23–4.24 (October 2008).*

[349] *FASB Statement No. 52, ¶ 162.*

[350] *IAS 1, ¶ BC4.*

[351] *FASB ASC 830-10-45-2 (FASB Statement No. 52, ¶ 5); IAS 21, ¶ 8.*

situation to produce dual currency statements. All these are circumstances where they may need to report in a currency other than their functional currency. For this reason, IFRSs permit the use of any presentation currency or currencies for consolidated, or an entity's financial statements, as well as for parent's, investor's, or joint venturer's separate financial statements.[352] Thus, for the purpose of IFRS financial reporting, entities reporting under IFRSs need not prepare dual currency statements if a particular jurisdiction mandates the use of a specific currency. The difference in importance that U.S. GAAP gives to this subject is shown by the fact that FASB Statement No. 52 scopes out the translation of financial statements to a currency different from an entity's reporting currency or a translation for purposes other than consolidation, combination, or the equity method, e.g., the choice of a reporting currency by a stand-alone entity. Under this standard, the reporting currency is the currency in which the reporting enterprise prepares its financial statements. The reporting enterprise includes either the group (i.e., through consolidated or combined financial statement) or the parent or investor through equity method accounting.[353] However, under U.S. GAAP an entity may not have more than one reporting currency. By equating these two points, the reporting currency of the parent will be the reporting currency of the consolidated financial statements.

Furthermore, IFRSs, due to their international nature, refer to the generic term "units of currency." Conversely, U.S. GAAP generally reasons in U.S. dollar amounts. Most U.S. entities report in U.S. dollars. Although Subtopic 830-10 (FASB Statement No. 52) permits the use of a reporting currency other than the U.S. dollar, as in the case of a foreign enterprise that uses the local currency as the reporting currency in its financial statements prepared in conformity with U.S. GAAP, it generally refers to consolidated financial statements as those prepared in the reporting currency of the consolidated enterprise (the U.S. dollar for U.S. companies), rather than any other currency.[354] Under Section 205-10-S99 (Regulation S-X), a U.S.-incorporated registrant must present its financial statements in U.S. dollars. The use of a functional currency other than the USD as the reporting currency is allowed to such registrants in rare instances where little or no assets are held and few operations are made in the U.S. and transactions are substantially in that single foreign functional currency.[355] Conversely, all foreign private issuers are permitted to present primary financial statements in U.S. dollars or in any other currency. However, in case of change of the reporting currency, the issuer must recast its financial statements as if the new currency had been used since at least the earliest period presented in the filing.[356] Although the reporting currency of financial statements can be freely selected, the functional currency should be, for operations not located in a hyperinflationary environment, the currency that is used for measurement.[357] Under Regulation S-X, financial statements of acquirees or equity investees can be prepared either in their currency or in the issuer's currency (USD for a domestic issuer).[358]

---

[352] *IAS 21, ¶¶ 18–19, 38, BC12–BC13.*

[353] *FASB Statement No. 52, Appendix E, ¶ 2.*

[354] *FASB ASC 830-10-15-4 (FASB Statement No. 52, Footnote 2, ¶ 4).*

[355] *FASB ASC 205-10-S99-1 (Regulation S-X, ¶ 210.4-01(b); U.S. Securities and Exchange Commission,* International Reporting and Disclosure Issues in the Division of Corporate Finance, *VIII.E (November 1, 2004) www.sec.gov (last visited April 26, 2006).*

[356] *Regulation S-X, ¶ 210.3-20(d), (e).*

[357] *Regulation S-X, ¶ 210.3-20(a); U.S. Securities and Exchange Commission,* International Reporting and Disclosure Issues in the Division of Corporate Finance, *VIII.B (November 1, 2004) www.sec.gov (last visited April 26, 2006).*

[358] *U.S. Securities and Exchange Commission,* International Reporting and Disclosure Issues in the Division of Corporate Finance, *VIII.A (November 1, 2004) www.sec.gov (last visited April 26, 2006).*

> **Comment:** This issue may have a strong impact on financial statements, as accumulated foreign currency translation may end up being the main item of accumulated other comprehensive income of some multinationals.

7.10.2 Foreign Currency Translation Methods

Under U.S. GAAP, translation adjustment results from the so-called "current rate method," which, with certain exceptions, basically translates balance sheet items at the closing rate as of the reporting date and income statement items at actual or average rates. This applies in reporting a foreign subsidiary or an equity-method investee in a currency (the reporting currency, thus generally the U.S. dollar) when such an entity has a functional currency that is different from that of the U.S. reporting parent or investor.[359] Conversely, the "remeasurement method," as opposed to translation, applies when the subsidiary's or associate's books are kept in a local currency other than the functional currency. If the functional currency is different from the parent's reporting currency, remeasurement into the functional currency of the foreign entity first and translation to the reporting currency afterwards would apply.[360]

IAS 21 uses a translation method similar to the one used in U.S. GAAP but, as mentioned, extends it to the general topic of adopting a presentation currency that is different from the functional currency of any entity, even if not for consolidation, combination or equity-method accounting.[361]

> **Comment:** U.S GAAP generally has no such equivalent situation, as U.S. companies generally report in USD, and consolidated financial statements are the only general-purpose financial statements.[362] The use of a currency other than the reporting currency for purposes other than consolidation, combination, or the equity method is scoped out of Subtopic 830-10 (FASB Statement No. 52) and arguably might be accounted for as a convenience translation.[363]

With reference to this topic, reporting under IFRSs versus U.S. GAAP (when, under U.S. GAAP the convenience translation interpretation is used) has a triple impact on accumulated other comprehensive income. Firstly, under IFRSs accumulated other comprehensive income also includes a portion of translation adjustment arising from translating a parent's functional currency to the presentation currency of the group. However, the foreign currency exposure arising from the relationships between the functional currency of a parent entity and the reporting currency of the group cannot be designated as a hedged risk in a hedge of a net investment in a foreign operation, and therefore cannot be offset.[364] Finally, this presentation currency component of the translation adjustment will be reclassified to profit or loss at disposal of the net operation.

---

[359] *FASB ASC 830-30-45-12 (FASB Statement No. 52, ¶ 13); FASB Statement No. 52, ¶¶ 69, 138.*

[360] *FASB ASC 830-10-45-17, 830-10-45-17 (FASB Statement No. 52, ¶¶ 10, 47; IAS 21, ¶ 34.*

[361] *IAS 21, ¶¶ IN14; 38, BC7.*

[362] *FASB Statement No. 94, Consolidation of All Majority-Owned Subsidiaries, ¶ 15; APB 18, ¶ 14; FASB ASC 810-10-45-11 (ARB 51, ¶ 24, as amended by FASB Statement No. 160); AICPA TPA 1400.32, Parent-Only Financial Statements and Relationship to GAAP.*

[363] *FASB ASC 830-10-15-7 (FASB Statement No. 52, ¶ 2).*

[364] *IFRIC Interpretation No. 16, Hedges of a Net Investment in a Foreign Operation, ¶¶ 12, BC14.*

A convenience translation is a translation of financial statements or portions thereof in a currency other than the presentation currency (and, also, the functional currency, under IFRSs) that is not necessarily prepared by using GAAP translation methods.[365]

> **Comment:** For the reasons given in the introduction to this Paragraph, under IAS 21 a convenience translation may also exist in an entity's financial statements or in its separate financial statements, in which case the currency is different from both the reporting and the functional currency.

Both IAS 21 and Regulation S-X do not require or encourage convenience translation, but they do not prohibit it. IAS 21 mandates that it is clearly identified as supplementary information, disclosing the currency, the functional currency, and the method used for such a convenience translation. Regulation S-X requires that it is limited to only the most recent fiscal year and any subsequent interim period presented, and that all amounts presented in a given period are computed at the same most recent closing exchange rate of the filing, unless a more recent rate is materially different. If financial statements are incorporated by reference to a previously filed Form 20-F, an amendment to reflect a more recent exchange rate is not required.[366]

> **Comment:** Worksheet 67 compares the presentation of foreign currency translation adjustment, and related concepts, under U.S. GAAP, Regulation S-X and IFRSs. A detailed explanation of foreign currency translation and related issues falls outside the scope of this Book.

Under IAS 21, when the group presentation currency is different from the parent's functional currency, the use of the direct method or the step-by-step method of consolidation does not, in aggregate, affect the financial statements in the presentation currency nor does it affect the overall translation adjustment.[367] Under the direct consolidation method, the ultimate parent company directly consolidates an indirectly-owned foreign operation and translates the foreign operation financial statements from their functional currency into the group presentation currency. Under the step-by-step method of consolidation, an intermediate parent consolidates and translates the foreign operation financial statements from their functional currency into its own functional currency, and then the ultimate parent consolidates the intermediate parent and translates the intermediate parent's financial statements from the functional currency into the group presentation currency. However, the amount of other comprehensive income attributable to an individual foreign operation (in case more than one exists) varies depending on which of the two methods is used. In fact, with the step-by-step method the ultimate parent translates the cumulative foreign currency translation as determined by the intermediate parent. Therefore, the choice of the method would not be neutral, as the impact on net income and other comprehensive income changes depends on the methods, on which individual foreign operation is disposed of and when, and which net investment in a foreign operation is being hedged. In order to implement this equivalence (which, however, IAS 21 does not mandate at individual net investment level, as both methods are legitimate), an entity that uses the

---

[365] *IAS 21, ¶¶ 57, BC14.*
[366] *Regulation S-X, ¶ 210.3-20(b); SEC, Financial Reporting Manual, ¶¶ 6620.5, 6620.6; U.S. Securities and Exchange Commission, International Reporting and Disclosure Issues in the Division of Corporate Finance, VIII.D (November 1, 2004) (last visited April 26, 2006); IAS 21, ¶¶ 54, BC14.*
[367] *IAS 21, ¶ BC18.*

step-by-step method may eliminate the difference between the two methods, provided it does so as an accounting policy that is applied to all net investments, by reclassifying on disposal of the foreign operations the amounts relating to each foreign operation that would have arisen if the direct method of consolidation had been used.[368]

7.10.3 Impact on Other Comprehensive Income

Under both sets of standards, translation adjustment is displayed in accumulated other comprehensive income (or, under IAS 21, in a separate component of equity) and, for the portion of the period, in other comprehensive income in the statement where this is shown. For the latter, IAS 21 generically mentions disclosure for the statement of comprehensive income, and separate presentation of cumulative translation adjustment in a separate component of equity in the statement of financial position.[369] Under U.S. GAAP, the amount on the statement of financial position is called "translation adjustment," but it is a cumulative figure, i.e., cumulative translation adjustment.

Comment: IFRSs call translation adjustment "gains or losses arising from translating the financial statements of a foreign operation," or "net exchange difference recognized in other comprehensive income and accumulated in a separate component of equity," or "(cumulative) translation differences."[370]

Finally, an IFRS first-time adopter may elect to zero out any cumulative translation differences that existed at the date of transition to IFRSs, instead of retroactively restating them, without giving an undue cost or effort justification. Subsequent disposal will generate gains or losses only with reference to translation differences arising after the transition date.[371] The SEC Staff rejected a similar accommodation under U.S. GAAP for foreign private issuers.[372]

7.10.4 The Concept of Net Investment

Translation adjustment may be seen as the result of one application of the "net investment" concept. This also represents the rationale for displaying translation adjustment in other comprehensive income. The notion of net investment sees a foreign entity that is a subsidiary or an equity-method investee as a whole set of financial relationships that are stand-alone and established independently of, and separately from, its parent company. Cash flows from operations of the reporting entity (the parent company) are not impacted by the foreign operation's individual assets and liabilities, as these are supposed to hedge each other (the concept of economic hedge). Only the parent's investment in such an entity (that is, its share in the foreign entity's unhedged net assets) is what is exposed to currency risk. Prior to divestment, the foreign exchange impact of translating such unhedged net assets is so uncertain as to require recognition as an unrealized item in other comprehensive income and not net

---

[368] *IFRIC Interpretation No. 16, ¶¶ 17, AG8, BC8, BC36–BC39.*

[369] *FASB Statement No. 52, ¶ 13; IAS 21, ¶¶ 39(c), 41, 52(b).*

[370] *IAS 1, ¶ 7; IAS 21, ¶ 52(b), IFRS 1, ¶ D13.*

[371] *IFRS 1, ¶¶ D13, BC55.*

[372] *AICPA International Practices Task Force, ¶ 9(a) (November 22, 2005) www.aicpa.org (last visited December 24, 2006).*

income.[373] Conversely, the remeasurement method assumes that the functional currency of the transactions of the foreign subsidiary is the same as that of the parent and thus remeasurement gain or loss impacts net income and the cash flow statement.

> **Comment:** Although IAS 21 does not speculate much on the net investment theory, it also defines the net investment in a foreign operation as the reporting entity's interest in its net assets and underlines that the reason why exchange differences are not recognized in profit and loss is that they do not significantly affect cash flows from operation.[374]

A difference in functional currencies between the foreign operation and the parent determines an economic exchange rate risk exposure to changes in cash flows or fair values of the overall net investment. By contrast, the use of a presentation currency different from the parent's functional currency does not per se expose the group to a greater currency risk, but simply to translation exchange differences that will not materialize in any economic impact. Also, an entity may elect a presentation currency and change it over time.[375]

Based on an alternative view, translation adjustment would result simply from a mechanical restating of previously reported equity and, as such, is reported as a reconciling item in equity, not in net income. This direct restating of equity is a sort of capital maintenance adjustment (see Section 7.6.3 previously), contrary to the "net investment" approach where translation adjustment is part of comprehensive income.[376]

> **Comment:** However, under this view, contrary to what happens under Subtopic 830-10 (FASB Statement No. 52), translation adjustment would not be recycled (see Section 7.6.3 previously).

Consequently, translation adjustment is a matter for the reporting entity only (the consolidated entity and, under U.S. GAAP only, the parent or investor financial statements when an investee is accounted for at equity method). Therefore it is presented in consolidated, combined, parent-only (U.S. GAAP only), or investor-only statements (U.S. GAAP only) and has no effect on the subsidiary or investee's financial statements. Under IFRSs, translation adjustment also affects the individual financial statements of an investor that has no subsidiaries and jointly controlled entities.[377] Instead, remeasurement gain or loss that arises with the remeasurement method affects the subsidiary's income statement in the year of occurrence. It is then also reported in the parent's income statement and in the consolidated income statement.

7.10.5   Recycling

Under U.S. GAAP, accumulated translation adjustment remains in other comprehensive income until sale or complete or substantially complete liquidation of the related net investment, in which period it is recycled to the income statement as part of the realized gain or loss on sale

---

[373] *FASB Statement No. 52, ¶¶ 69(d), 94, 95, 111, 113.*
[374] *IAS 21, ¶¶ 8, 41.*
[375] *IAS 21, ¶ BC 25C(b); IFRIC Interpretation No. 16, ¶¶ BC13, BC30.*
[376] *FASB Statement No. 52, ¶¶ 114, 116.*
[377] *IAS 27, ¶ 6; IAS 28 (2011), ¶ IN8; IAS 28 (2010), ¶¶ IN8, 4.*

or liquidation.[378] FASB Statement No. 52 requires the reporting of reclassification adjustment of cumulative translation adjustment as part of the gain or loss on sale or liquidation.[379] Additional events or transactions, such as a subsidiary's issuance of additional stock, a subsidiary's full or partial liquidation of its assets and liabilities, distribution of dividends, payment of long-term intercompany accounts, and any other form of reduction in the parent's or investor's net investment do not trigger recycling. This is because a sale or disposal determines realized gains or losses, while the other situations mentioned are either not fully realized or relate to specific flows and not to the net investment in itself, which remains outstanding with the associated uncertain currency exposure.[380] Under FASB Interpretation No. 37, recycling applies only to the pro rata portion of the accumulated translation adjustment in case of the disposal of part of an equity-method investment in a foreign entity, but not in case of partial liquidation.[381] Conversely, under IFRSs, whole or partial sale, liquidation, repayment of share capital, and whole or partial abandonment of the foreign operation, are all whole or partial disposal events that determine recycling.[382]

Comment: As stated, liquidation is a disposal event. Instead, liquidation is not an event that determines the classification of a subsidiary or an investment as held for sale under IFRS 5, because their carrying amounts would not be recovered principally through a sale transaction.

Under the 2008 Revision of IAS 27, effectively for annual periods beginning on or after July 1, 2009, a loss of control of a subsidiary, a loss of significant influence over an associate, and a loss of joint control over a jointly controlled entity (before IFRS 11) that includes a foreign operation are considered as disposal events that determine the reclassification of the exchange differences accumulated in other comprehensive income into profit or loss (entirely, in the case that subsidiary is wholly-owned), even if the entity retains an interest in the former subsidiary, associate, or jointly controlled entity or the former subsidiary becomes an associate or a jointly controlled entity. This change in nature of the investment is considered a significant economic event to trigger reclassification. However, if the subsidiary that included a foreign operation is less-than-wholly-owned, the share attributable to the noncontrolling interest is derecognized but not reclassified to profit or loss. In case of a partial disposal of a subsidiary that includes a foreign operation (therefore a change in the parent's interest in a subsidiary that does not result in a loss of control), the proportionate share of accumulated exchange differences recognized in other comprehensive income that is disposed of must be reallocated to the noncontrolling interest in the foreign operation (therefore, it is accounted for as an equity transaction between owners in their capacity as owners). All other forms of partial disposals (excluding the payment of a dividend paid out of postacquisition earnings) of a foreign operation other than through a subsidiary (for example, a reduction in ownership interest in an associate or jointly controlled entity that includes a foreign operation) trigger

---

[378] *FASB ASC 830-30-40-1 (FASB Statement No. 52, ¶ 14; FASB Statement No. 52, ¶ 119; FASB ASC 220-10-45-16 (FASB Statement No. 130, ¶ 19).*

[379] *FASB Statement No. 52, ¶ 14.*

[380] *FASB ASC 830-30-40-3 (FASB Statement No. 52, ¶¶ 111, 119; FASB Interpretation No. 37,* Accounting for Translation Adjustments upon Sale of Part of an Investment in a Foreign Entity, *¶¶ 7–8).*

[381] *FASB ASC 830-30-40-2, 830-30-40-3 (FASB Interpretation No. 37,* Accounting for Translation Adjustments upon Sale of Part of an Investment in a Foreign Entity, *¶¶ 2, 8.*

[382] *IAS 21, ¶¶ 48–49.*

the reclassification of the parent's proportionate share of exchange differences accumulated in other comprehensive income in profit or loss.[383] IFRS 11 amends IAS 21 to redefine a loss of joint control, when significant influence is maintained, as a partial disposal and not as a disposal, hence with reallocation and not reclassification of other comprehensive income.[384] Subtopic 810-10 (FASB Statement No. 160) also requires full recycling in case of a loss of control of a consolidated subsidiary and reattribution to noncontrolling interests in case of change in an interest in a subsidiary with no loss of control.[385] Section 7.17 later expands this topic.

Finally, effective for annual periods beginning on or after January 1, 2009, the amendments to IFRS 1 and IAS 27 eliminate the return of capital in the form of dividends paid out of preacquisition profits as a case of partial disposal that determines recycling.[386]

Comment: The distribution of a business (e.g., in a spin off) to an entity's owners acting in their capacity of owners may be in the scope of IFRIC 17, provided certain other situations exist. This interpretation requires that any difference between the (net) assets carrying amount and the carrying amount of the dividend payable (i.e., adjusted to the fair value of the net assets to be distributed) be recognized in profit or loss upon settlement of the dividend payable.[387] On one hand, this seems consistent with the income recognition of the disposal of a subsidiary with loss of control under IAS 27. On the other hand, as explained above, the 2008 revision of IAS 27 excluded the payment of dividends as an event of disposal or partial disposal of an interest in a foreign operation. Furthermore, IAS 27 refers to payment of dividends, while IFRC 17 distinguished between declaration (i.e., when, according to jurisdictions, the entity has no longer discretion) and settlement. Upon declaration, the dividend payable is measured at the fair value of the net assets to be distributed and any subsequent adjustment of the carrying amount of the dividend payable before settlement affects equity.[388] Only upon settlement profit or loss is affected.

Under both sets of standards, there is no recycling upon impairment of a net investment (be it due to losses of the foreign operation or because of an impairment recognized by the investor[389]), because a write down must be recorded before translation and consolidation.[390]

Under both U.S. GAAP and IFRSs, in case of a change of functional currency from a foreign currency to the reporting currency, accumulated translation adjustment remains in equity until disposal.[391] In the reverse case, under U.S. GAAP, except for the case of an economy that ceases to be highly inflationary (see Section 7.12 later), the adjustment that arises on

---

[383]   *IAS 27 (2010), ¶¶ A6, BCA1.*

[384]   *IFRS 11, ¶¶ D34, BC40; IASB Update, March 3, 2010.*

[385]   *FASB ASC 810-10-45-24 (ARB 51, ¶ 34, as amended by FASB Statement No. 160); FASB Statement No. 160, ¶ B53; FASB ASC 830-30-40-2 (FASB Interpretation No. 37, as amended by FASB Statement No. 160, Footnote 2).*

[386]   *Amendments to IFRS 1,* First-time Adoption of International Financial Reporting Standards *and IAS 27,* Consolidated and Separate Financial Statements, Cost of an Investment in a Subsidiary, Jointly Controlled Entity or Associate, *¶¶ 45B, BCA1 (May 2008).*

[387]   *IFRIC 17, ¶¶ 13, 14, BC14, BC27, BC57.*

[388]   *IFRIC 17, ¶¶ 10, 11, 13.*

[389]   *IAS 27 (2010), ¶ A6.*

[390]   *FASB Statement No. 52, ¶ 118; IAS 21, ¶ 49.*

[391]   *FASB ASC 830-10-45-10 (FASB Statement No. 52, ¶ 46); IAS 21, ¶ 37.*

translation of nonmonetary assets at current rate, as of the date of change, is recognized in other comprehensive income.[392] Under IFRSs, balances for nonmonetary items translated at exchange rates at the date of change become their new historical bases. The translation procedure pertinent to the new functional currency applies prospectively from the date of change.[393] Worksheet 69 illustrates the accounting for a change in functional currency. Under Regulation S-X, the same reporting currency used by a registrant or its predecessor must be maintained for all periods in a filing. However, if an issuer elects to change its reporting currency, all periods presented must be retroactively restated, and this fact and reasons for it must be disclosed in a note.[394]

Subtopic 830-30 (EITF Issue No. 01-5), contrary to IFRSs, for the purpose of impairment testing includes the accumulated foreign currency translation adjustment (including the gain or loss from an effective hedge of the net investment) in the carrying amount of a consolidated or an equity-method investment in a foreign entity that is held for disposal, if a committed plan to dispose of the investment will cause a whole or partial recycling.[395]

Comment: Under IFRSs, the classification of an asset or a disposal group as held for sale does not trigger a reclassification adjustment. In effect, a commitment to a sale plan involving loss of control of a subsidiary is different from a sale. Under IFRSs, the former now determines held for sale classification and, therefore, separate presentation of accumulated other comprehensive income. The latter, instead, calls for a reclassification adjustment.

7.10.6   Separate and Entity's Financial Statements

Under U.S. GAAP, (cumulative) translation adjustment is also recognized in the parent-only or investor-only financial statements, where a parent or an investor accounts for the subsidiary or the investee at equity method in its financial statements.

Comment: Under IAS 27 and IAS 28 a parent or an investor cannot account for a subsidiary or associate at equity method in their separate financial statements. Therefore, from the perspective of separate financial statements, those subsidiaries and associates would be scoped out of IAS 21, as the reporting entity's separate financial statements do not include them. If the parent uses the cost method to account for its investee in its separate financial statements, the investment account will remain stated at cost. If instead the parent accounts for the subsidiary or the investee at fair value under IAS 39 as an available-for-sale financial asset that is a nonmonetary item under IAS 21, a foreign exchange difference will arise, as IAS 21 requires that nonmonetary items that are measured at fair value in a foreign currency be translated using the exchange rates at the date when the fair value is determined.[396] Under IAS 39, this fair value remeasurement would go directly to other

---

[392] *FASB ASC 830-10-45-9 (FASB Statement No. 52, ¶ 46).*

[393] *IAS 21, ¶¶ 35, 37.*

[394] *Regulation S-X, ¶ 210.3-20(e); U.S. Securities and Exchange Commission,* International Reporting and Disclosure Issues in the Division of Corporate Finance, *VIII.C (November 1, 2004) (last visited April 26, 2006).*

[395] *FASB ASC 830-30-45-13 (EITF Issue No. 01-5,* Application of FASB Statement No. 52 to an Investment Being Evaluated for Impairment That Will Be Disposed of, *¶ 5); IFRS 5, ¶¶ BC37–BC38.*

[396] *IAS 21, ¶ 23(c).*

> comprehensive income, including any related exchange difference (see Section 7.14.2 later). Similar conclusions could be drawn for the separate financial statements of a venturer in a jointly controlled entity, which under IFRSs would use either the cost or fair value method, as opposed to the equity method under U.S. GAAP.

However, an investor uses the equity method in its entity's (not separate) financial statements only when it has no subsidiaries and no joint ventures. In such a case, IAS 21 provisions for direct recognition in other comprehensive income of the translation adjustment would apply. This situation would be treated similarly to U.S. GAAP where the investor accounts for the investee at equity method.

7.10.7   Computation of the Currency Translation Adjustment

Translation adjustment is essentially a mechanism to balance the statement of financial position. It may also be computed directly or indirectly. Thus, based on the so-called "indirect" calculation, translation adjustment equals total assets minus total liabilities minus equity, before and after translation of all items has been made according to the rules of the current-rate method. Based on the "direct" (or "cross-check") calculation, subject to certain variations, translation adjustment amounts to the beginning balance of net assets times the difference between current rate and prior period's current rate, plus net income times the difference between current rate and weighted-average rate.[397]

Under U.S. GAAP, translation of goodwill and fair value adjustments in a business combination concerning a foreign entity for which the foreign currency is its functional currency also follows the functional currency approach and its translation rules. Therefore, in consolidation worksheets they are translated into the parent's reporting currency at current rates. Subsequently, these are translated at current rates. Therefore, changes in current rates affect foreign currency adjustment. Additionally, subsequent amortization of fair value adjustments and any impairment of goodwill are translated at average rates. Hence, the difference between closing rates and average rates also affects foreign translation adjustment. In conclusion, accumulated foreign currency adjustment reported in the consolidated statement of financial position is the translation adjustment at the date of business combination, subsequent translation adjustment, and current and past adjustments resulting from the translation of amortization of fair value adjustments and any impairment of goodwill. Under the remeasurement method (when the subsidiary's foreign currency is not its functional currency), goodwill is remeasured at historical rate.[398]

In a business combination involving a foreign acquiree, IAS 21 requires the quantification of goodwill and fair value adjustments in the functional currency of the foreign entity and then their translation at closing rates. It does not permit treating them as nonmonetary items of the acquirer that must be translated at the historical rate.[399] However, on this topic, an IFRS first-time adopter may elect not to apply IAS 21 retrospectively to any past business

---

[397]   *FASB ASC 830-30-45-3, 830-20-30-3, 830-30-45-6 (FASB Statement No. 52, ¶¶ 12, 27; IAS 21, ¶ 41).*

[398]   *FASB ASC 830-10-15-5 (FASB Statement No. 52, ¶¶ 48, 101).*

[399]   *IAS 21, ¶ 47.*

combinations, to apply it to all, or to apply it only to those past business combinations that it retrospectively restates under IFRS 3.[400]

Under U.S. GAAP and IFRSs, accumulated translation adjustment attributable to noncontrolling interest is reported as part of noncontrolling interest.[401] Noncontrolling interests are determined at their fair value at business combination date or, under IFRS 3 only, at noncontrolling interest's proportionate share of the acquiree's net identifiable assets. In both cases, translation is at the exchange rate at the date of business combination. In consolidation in subsequent years, noncontrolling interests in the statement of financial position include their share of accumulated foreign currency adjustment. Accumulated foreign currency adjustment is the sum of the original balance, foreign currency adjustment of subsequent years, and current and past adjustments to foreign currency adjustment arising from amortization of the fair value adjustments of the business combination. As the exchange rates used to determine all these components are different, the noncontrolling interest's portion of accumulated foreign currency adjustment is more easily computed after translation in reporting currency.

7.10.8 Disclosures

Under U.S. GAAP, a separate statement titled "equity adjustment from foreign currency translation" or similar headline, the statement of changes in equity, or the notes must disclose at least the beginning and ending balances of the accumulated translation adjustment, the adjustment arising in the period, the related income taxes, and the reclassification adjustment. It must also report gains and losses on economic hedges of a net investment in a foreign entity and on long-term items that are in substance part of a net investment in a foreign entity. Those disclosures are in addition to the ordinary analysis of changes in all equity accounts.[402] ASU 2011-05 eliminates the statement of changes in equity as a manner of reporting details of other comprehensive income. IAS 21 requires a note disclosure of amounts and balances reconciliation of net exchange differences recognized in accumulated other comprehensive income and other comprehensive income. In addition, an entity must disclose the fact and reason for adopting a presentation currency that is different from its functional currency, and reason for a change in functional currency.[403] The notes, under both IAS 27(R) and Subtopic 810-10 (FASB Statement No. 160), must include a schedule of the effects of any change in the parent's interest in a subsidiary that do not result in a loss of control on the equity attributable to the parent. In case of loss of control of a subsidiary, the entity must disclose in which lines of the statement of comprehensive income the gain or loss is recognized, if disclosure is not separate.[404] Finally, IAS 34, as amended by the 2008 Revision of IFRS 3, requires the disclosure of the effects of changes in the interim period due to obtaining or losing control or subsidiaries and long-term investments.[405]

Section 7.11 and Section 7.13 following explain additional specific situations of translation adjustment.

---

[400] *IFRS 1, ¶¶ C2, C3, IG21A.*

[401] *FASB ASC 830-10-15-5 (FASB Statement No. 52, ¶ 101); IAS 21, ¶ 41.*

[402] *FASB ASC 830-30-50-1, 830-30-45-20, 830-30-45-19 (FASB Statement No. 52, ¶¶ 31, 142.*

[403] *IAS 21, ¶¶ 52(b), 53–54.*

[404] *IAS 27 (2010), ¶¶ 41(e), 41(f)(ii).*

[405] *IAS 34, as amended by IFRS 3, ¶ 16(i).*

7.10.9 Specific Relationships with the Financial Statement Presentation Project

The *Financial Statement Presentation Project* has been discussing accumulated foreign currency translation adjustment. It has been evidenced as having both some of the characteristics that have been associated with other comprehensive income (see Section 7.4.3 previously) as well as other attributes that would not be typical of such a category, such as being nonexceptional, indeed a recurring and operating item. In particular, translation adjustment would comprise large and volatile unrealized holding gains or losses, which are related to market value change and relatively beyond control of management (although geographical areas of presence and hedging strategies may be selected).[406]

As to the categorization working principle (see Section 1.4.3.2 previously), foreign currency translation adjustment poses the particular issue that while on parent- or investor-only financial statements it may be classified in the same category as that of the equity-method investee to which it relates, on consolidated financial statements there is no single asset or liability to which it may be associated. This would open to the alternatives of either allocating it to several categories in case of consolidated subsidiaries or proportionately consolidated joint ventures prior to IFRS 11 (nonetheless, likely a costly, cumbersome, and relatively arbitrary process), or presenting it in the category which represents the predominant characteristic of the underlying investment. Alternatively, it would be presented in the operating category, or in an "other business profit income" or equivalent category, as a separate section, or in the category where the investment was prior to consolidation or in that in which it is displayed in the parent's separate financial statements. Consistency with the net investment concept would dictate no allocation, because only net assets are exposed to foreign currency risk. Finally, the issue of allocating foreign currency translation has an impact in defining whether or not there should be a separate section for other comprehensive income in the financial statements.[407] Based on the Discussion Paper and Staff Draft of the *Financial Statement Presentation Project*, identification of the sections of categories would not be required for foreign currency translation adjustment on a consolidated subsidiary (or a proportionately consolidated joint venture under IFRSs prior to IFRS 11). Conversely, gain or loss on remeasurement of the financial statements of an entity into its functional currency would be allocated to the same sections or categories as the underlying assets and liabilities.[408]

---

[406] *IASB/FASB, Financial Statement Presentation Project, Agenda Paper 3,* Categorization in a Statement of Earnings and Comprehensive Income, *¶ 51 (June 2005); Performance Reporting Joint International Group (JIG) on Performance Reporting, European CFO Task Force, Presentation by Guido Kerkhoff (June 14–15, 2005) www.fasb.org (last visited June 21, 2007).*

[407] *IASB, Financial Statement Presentation Project, Agenda Paper 15A,* Other Comprehensive Income, *¶¶ 21, 23, 24 (December 14, 2006) www.iasb.org (last visited June 21, 2007); IASB, Financial Statement Presentation Project, Agenda Paper 9B,* Other Comprehensive Income Presentation, *¶¶ 28, 31, 36, 37, 41 (March 22, 2007) www.iasb.org (last visited June 21, 2007); FASB Memorandum No. 50A-D,* Financial Statement Presentation – Disaggregating Changes in Assets and Liabilities, Presentation of Other Comprehensive Income Items, and Cash Equivalents, *¶¶ 71, 72, 74, 77 (March 27, 2007) www.fasb.org (last visited June 21, 2007); IASB, Financial Statement Presentation, Agenda Paper 3B,* Presenting Information about the Cause of Change in Reported Amounts of Assets and Liabilities, *¶¶ 41, 43 (June 19, 2007) www.iasb.org (last visited June 21, 2007).*

[408] *Discussion Paper,* Preliminary Views on Financial Statement Presentation, *¶¶ 3.25, 3.40, 3.63, 3.68, 3.69 (October 2008); FASB and IASB,* Staff Draft of an Exposure Draft on Financial Statement Presentation, *¶¶ 138, 139, BC162, BC165–BC167 (July 2010).*

An additional issue has been whether or not to allocate the impact of recycling into various categories. An approach is to display the foreign currency translation in an "acquisitions and disposals" section because it is recycled on disposal of the net investment. This is related to the concept of "integrated basket transactions," of which the sale or liquidation of an investment in a consolidated subsidiary, proportionately consolidated jointly controlled entity prior to IFRS 11 (not of equity-method investments) would be an example. The concept of basket transactions includes both the acquisition and the disposal of multiple assets or a combination of assets and liabilities. If the disposal meets the definition of a component of an entity, the note would also give disclosures on discontinued operations.[409]

Another way of seeing the issue of allocation is from the angle of the cohesiveness working principle (see Section 1.4.3.1 previously), especially depending on whether or not a statement of financial position reconciliation would be part of the basic financial statements. If this statement were to be used, the allocation of foreign currency translation would facilitate this reconciliation, otherwise a residual caption would be needed.[410]

Comment: The interlink of the cohesiveness and the categorization principles first poses the issue of whether or not cumulative foreign currency translation should be recognized as a single line item in the equity section of the statement of financial position or whether it should be broken down into the separate categories of financial statements. Depending on the answer, both the statement of comprehensive income and statement of financial position reconciliation would or would not allocate the unrecycled or the recycled (or reclassified) amounts.

7.11 CERTAIN LONG-TERM ITEMS

7.11.1 Long-Term Items that are in Substance Part of a Net Investment in Foreign Operations

Both Topic 830 (FASB Statement No. 52) and IAS 21 expand the treatment as foreign currency translation adjustment (i.e., recognition in other comprehensive income) to exchange differences arising on certain intercompany foreign currency transactions (monetary items, under IFRSs). These must be transactions for which settlement is not planned, or anticipated (under U.S. GAAP), or likely to occur (under IAS 21) in the foreseeable future.

Comment: U.S. GAAP adds combined financial statements. Full IFRSs (contrary to IFRSs for small and medium-sized entities) currently do not treat combined financial statements. IFRSs prior to IFRS 11, in contrast to U.S. GAAP, add proportionately consolidated financial statements.

---

[409] *Financial Statement Presentation Project, Agenda Paper 9B*, Other Comprehensive Income Presentation, ¶ 34 *(March 22, 2007) www.iasb.org (last visited June 21, 2007)*; IASB, *Financial Statement Presentation Project, Agenda Paper 3A*, Basket Transactions and Foreign Currency Translation Adjustments, ¶¶ 3, 44–45 *(June 19, 2007) www.iasb.org (last visited June 21, 2007)*.

[410] IASB, *Financial Statement Presentation, Agenda Paper 3B*, Presenting Information about the Cause of Change in Reported Amounts of Assets and Liabilities, ¶¶ 44, 46 *(June 19, 2007) www.iasb.org (last visited June 21, 2007)*.

Comment: This accounting applies for the purpose of the financial statements where a foreign operation is consolidated, proportionately consolidated (under IFRSs prior to IFRS 11), or combined (under U.S. GAAP). U.S. GAAP recognized these exchange differences in foreign currency translation adjustment when parent-only or investor-only financial statements incorporate an equity-method investee, or a branch. Conversely, IFRSs also add that the parent recognizes such exchange differences in profit or loss in its separate financial statements if the monetary item is denominated in a currency that is different from its functional currency. The foreign operation does the same in its financial statements if the monetary item is denominated in a currency that is different from its functional currency.[411]

Under IAS 21, the accounting in other comprehensive income in the consolidated financial statements is irrespective of the currency in which the monetary item is denominated (this provision is different from that contained in the 2003 version of IAS 21).[412] Therefore, as the result of the December 2005 Amendment to IAS 21,[413] when the monetary item is denominated in a currency other than the functional currency of either the reporting entity or the foreign operation, the consolidated financial statements (or the financial statements that include the reporting entity and the foreign operation) will initially recognize the exchange differences in foreign translation adjustment in other comprehensive income and no longer in profit or loss.

Example: The Corporate Reporting Standing Committee (EECS), a forum of the EU National Enforcers of Financial Information, assessed that a change in currency of an intercompany loan that was part of a net investment in a subsidiary did not trigger any recycling because the redenomination did not have any effect on the functional currency of the subsidiary and hence was not a disposal.[414]

Comment: Topic 830 (FASB Statement No. 52) refers to intercompany transactions and balances, but does not state which entities may be part of those transactions. IAS 21 specifies that they may be among any subsidiary of the consolidated group, not necessarily with the reporting entity,[415] or between the parent and an associate, but not between an associate and its net investment in a foreign operation, because the reporting entity does not control the associate's investment.[416] IFRIC 16 explains that the group, as opposed to a parent or an individual entity, is the relevant reporting entity, and the fact that the net investment is held through an intermediary does not affect its economic risk. The currency denomination of the monetary item or which company within the group is part of the transaction is irrelevant to the accounting treatment in the consolidated financial statements of a parent that directly or indirectly has a net investment in that foreign operation.[417] This is in contrast with U.S. GAAP and practice that generally view the accounting for a net investment in a foreign

[411] *IAS 21, ¶¶ 32, 33.*
[412] *IAS 21, ¶¶ BC25C, BC25D.*
[413] *Amendment to IAS 21* The Effect of Changes In Foreign Exchange Rate, Net Investment in a Foreign Operation *(December 2005).*
[414] *Committee of European Securities Regulators (CESR), 2007. CESR/07-120,* Extract from EECS's Database of Enforcement Decisions, *Paris: CESR, ¶ Decision ref. EECS/0407-15. [Online] CESR. Available at www.cesr.eu (last visited July 20, 2010).*
[415] *IAS 21, ¶¶ 15A, BC25E.*
[416] *IAS 21, ¶¶ 8, BC25F ; IASB Update, June 2005.*
[417] *IAS 21, ¶ BC25D; IFRIC 16, ¶ BC29.*

operation from the perspective of the U.S. parent company (the reporting enterprise), although FASB Statement No. 52 widely defines a reporting enterprise as an entity or group to which financial statements are referred.[418]

Provided that such items are in the nature of long-term investment, examples comprise long-term receivables from, or loans or payables to, a foreign operation, but not trade receivables or payables or other short-term intercompany transactions and balances. Subtopic 830-20 (FASB Statement No. 52) also includes an advance or a demand note payable.[419]

Comment: The rationale for the accounting in other comprehensive income is that those items are considered to be part of the concept of a net investment (see Section 7.10.4 previously), or in IFRSs terms, an in-substance net investment in a foreign operation.[420] IAS 21 states that they are similar in nature to an equity investment in a foreign operation.[421] Arguably, if they do not have a planned or likely settlement, they are somehow akin to not having a contractual obligation (which would meet one of the criteria for definition of an equity instrument under IAS 32[422]). On the other hand, the fact of being a monetary item (a category that also includes a variable number of the entity's own equity instruments[423]) would meet one of the criteria for the definition of a financial liability under IAS 32.[424] Furthermore, as the items must be monetary, they cannot be equity securities (which are not monetary in the meaning given to this term by IAS 21, i.e., corresponding to a fixed or determinable amount).

Comment: Subtopic 830-10 (FASB Statement No. 52) does not require that the item be monetary. IAS 21 does not explain why it must be monetary. Under IAS 21, an item is monetary if it embodies a right to receive (or an obligation to deliver) a fixed or determinable number of units of currency.[425] Firstly, insofar as it is monetary, it represents a commitment to convert one currency into another with an associated currency risk exposure.[426] Secondly, closing exchange rates apply to remeasurement of monetary items from a local currency to the functional currency,[427] in the same way as closing rates pertain to the translation of assets and liabilities from an entity's functional currency to a different presentation currency. Thirdly, an equity security (a nonmonetary item, in the IAS 21 meaning) would itself be a net investment in a foreign operation, if incorporated in consolidated or combined financial statements or accounted for at equity methods. Finally, gains and losses, including exchange differences computed at closing rates, arising from fair valuation of an available-for-sale equity instrument under IAS 39 or an equity investment carried through other comprehensive income under IFRS 9 (i.e., when not incorporated in consolidated or combined financial statements or accounted for at equity method) would also be accounted for in other comprehensive income, as explained in Section 7.14.2 later.

[418] *FASB Statement No. 52, Appendix E.*
[419] *FASB ASC 830-20-35-3, 830-20-35-4 (FASB Statement No. 52, ¶¶ 20(b), 131; IAS 21, ¶¶ 15, 32.*
[420] *FASB ASC 830-20-35-4 (FASB Statement No. 52, ¶ 131); IAS 21, ¶ 15.*
[421] *IAS 21, ¶ BC25D.*
[422] *IAS 32, ¶ 16.*
[423] *IAS 21, ¶ 16.*
[424] *IAS 32, ¶ 11.*
[425] *IAS 21, ¶¶ 8, 16.*
[426] *IAS 21, ¶ 45.*
[427] *IAS 21, ¶ 34.*

IAS 21, IFRS 9, and IAS 39 interact with each other. IFRS 9 and IAS 39 apply for the purpose of measuring and recognizing a financial asset or liability in the financial statement of the foreign operation. If the foreign operation classifies the item as at fair value through profit or loss it would be measured at fair value with changes recognized in profit or loss. IAS 21 applies in translating the foreign operation financial statements into the currency of the parent company that consolidates the foreign operation. The income statement of the foreign operation (hence including the impact of the item classified as at fair value through profit or loss) is translated at the exchange rates at the dates of each transaction or at average rate as a practical approximation. The monetary item (a balance sheet item) is translated at closing rate. The difference is recognized in translation adjustment in other comprehensive income.[428]

> **Comment:** Prior to IFRS 9, if the foreign operation classified the item as an available-for-sale debt financial asset, the impact on the income statement, as computed in the foreign currency, in the financial statements of the foreign operation was limited to the interest income and impairment loss, while the changes in the fair value, as computed in the foreign currency, was recognized in the equity of the foreign operation (see Section 7.14.2 later).

Subtopic 830-30 (FASB Statement No. 52) requires disclosure of such intercompany items as part of the reconciling note on accumulated foreign currency translation adjustments[429] (see Section 7.10.8 previously).

Unlike full IFRSs, IFRS for SMEs prohibits a reclassification adjustment related to exchange differences on monetary items that are in substance part of a net investment in a foreign operation.[430]

7.11.2   Long-Term Interests that are in Substance Part of a Net Investment in an Associate

The previous section illustrates the accounting for a net investment in a foreign operation. An analogy may be drawn between this concept of in-substance net investment in a foreign operation and the notion of non-equity long-term interests that are in substance part of the net investment in an associate under IAS 28 or in-substance common stock under APB 18, EITF Issue No. 98-13, Section 323-10-35 (EITF Issue No. 02-14), and Section 323-10-35 (EITF Topic D-68)[431] (see Section 2.2.3, Section 2.2.4, and Section 2.2.5 previously) for the purpose of loss recognition on such investments.[432]

---

[428]   *IAS 39, ¶ E.3.3 (as amended by IFRS 9).*

[429]   *FASB ASC 830-30-50-1, 830-30-45-20 (FASB Statement No. 52, ¶ 31).*

[430]   IFRS for Small and Medium-Sized Entities, ¶¶ 30.13, BC68(c), BC123.

[431]   *FASB ASC 323-10-35-23 (EITF Issue No. 02-14,* Whether an Investor Should Apply the Equity Method of Accounting to Investments Other Than Common Stock; *EITF Issue No. 98-13,* Accounting by an Equity Method Investor for Investee Losses When the Investor Has Loans to and Investments in Other Securities of an Investee); *FASB ASC 323-10-35-19 (EITF Topic D-68,* Accounting by an Equity Method Investor for Investee Losses When the Investor Has Loans to and Investments in Other Securities of an Investee).

[432]   *IASB Update, February 2002 also highlights that those other non-equity instruments should be consistent with the net investment concept in IAS 21.*

Comment: Under IAS 28, for the purpose of recognizing an investor's share of losses in an associate, such investments also include items for which settlement is neither planned nor likely to occur in the foreseeable future, such as long-term receivables or loans (excluding trade receivables and payables, and secured loans or similar long-term receivables with adequate collateral), advances, and debt securities including mandatorily redeemable preferred stock. Although not part of their definition, such items are mentioned to be non-equity interests or non-equity investments.[433] EITF Issue No. 02-14 also calls them investments in an entity without distinguishing whether or not they must be non-equity interests. Its examples cover several types of preferred stock and warrants. However, for the purpose of IAS 21, as the item must be a monetary item, it cannot be an equity security. To the extent that a monetary item is a non-equity instrument that falls under both the scope of in-substance common stock under EITF Issue No. 02-14 and long-term interest that in substance forms part of the investor's net investment in an associate, it is likely to be within the scope of IAS 21. The investor will record its share in the foreign currency adjustment in other comprehensive income as explained in the previous Section, as well as its share in the associate's changes in components of other comprehensive income (such as cash flow hedges reserve, etc.) in the investor's other comprehensive income. However, IAS 28 does not go this far apart from equity method loss pickup.

7.12 HIGHLY INFLATIONARY ECONOMIES

Reporting for highly inflationary economies, and the related effects on deferred taxes, can be looked at from the perspective of the foreign entity that operates in a hyperinflationary economy or from the viewpoint of its consolidated or parent's financial statements. Furthermore, different treatments exist for primary and supplemental financial reporting. Section 6.4.23 previously explains the impact of accounting for hyperinflation on retained earnings. This Section analyzes the accounting for hyperinflation and its impact on other comprehensive income. Section 8.2.16 later explains its implications on income taxes. Worksheet 68 summaries the topic by comparing the methods under U.S. GAAP and IFRSs and their impact on other comprehensive income and deferred taxes.

From the perspective of the foreign entity, U.S. GAAP considers its general price-level financial statements where required or permitted by home-country GAAP, restated retroactively to the purchasing power unit at the date of the most recent balance sheet, expressed in its local currency of operation and presented under U.S. GAAP as primary financial statements preferable only when intended for readers in the U.S.[434] A foreign private issuer presenting its financial statements in a foreign currency that is hyperinflationary must either present additional restated statements or accompany those primary statements by historical cost/constant currency or current cost supplemental reporting (see following).[435] Conversely, IAS 29 uses the so-called "restatement approach" to a foreign entity that operates in a highly inflationary economy. When the functional currency is the currency of a highly inflationary economy, the IAS 29 restatement approach is similar to a retrospective application as if the entity had always applied the restatement approach.[436] IAS 29 requires the restatement of its primary financial

[433] *IAS 28 (2010), ¶ 29.*
[434] *Accounting Principle Board Statement No. 3,* Financial Statements Restated for General Price-Level Changes, *(superseded) ¶ 26; U.S. Securities and Exchange Commission,* International Reporting and Disclosure Issues in the Division of Corporate Finance, *¶ XI.A.3,* Reporting in Highly Inflationary Economies, *(November 1, 2004).*
[435] *Regulation S-X, ¶ 210.3-20(c).*
[436] *IFRIC 7, ¶ B17.*

statements, including comparative information, into measuring units current as of the latest reporting date. As clarified by IFRIC 7, in its first hyperinflationary period, the entity must restate the opening balances in the earliest comparative period presented for nonmonetary assets or liabilities under IAS 29, starting from their acquisition or assumption dates if they have been measured at historical cost, or from their latest valuation if carried under other bases (as for the case of investment property).[437] However, if an IFRS first-time adopter uses the election to consider the fair values at transition date of certain nonmonetary assets as their deemed costs (see Section 7.16.1 later), it applies IAS 29 from that date without restating those assets from their acquisition dates.[438] Section 6.6.5 previously explains how a pre-existing revaluation surplus will be implicitly transferred to retained earnings as a result of the first application of IAS 29.

For the purpose of reporting an investment in foreign entities (i.e., associates or subsidiaries) operating in highly inflationary economies in primary consolidated or parent's financial statements, or for the purpose of the foreign entity reporting in U.S. dollars, U.S. GAAP applies the remeasurement method (see Section 7.10.2 previously) to a highly inflationary economy, as if the functional currency of the foreign entity were the reporting currency of the reporting entity (i.e., of its parent).[439] Of course, this assumes that the reporting currency is a more stable one (typically, the USD).

> **Comment:** This aims at avoiding the so-called "disappearing plant phenomenon" by using historical rates that are higher than current rates. This method which is internationally known as the "stable foreign currency" or "hard currency" approach approximates the effect of hyperinflation to the extent to which changes in exchange rates are representative of the change in inflation.

The remeasurement of investment in foreign entities is a prospective approach. Instead, contrary to U.S. GAAP, under IFRSs a foreign entity cannot avoid restatement under IAS 29 by selecting the presentation currency of its parent as its functional currency.[440]

For the purpose of reporting investments in foreign entities in consolidated or parent's separate financial statements when a foreign entity reports its restated financial statements in a foreign currency, those amounts that are restated under IAS 29 are then translated into presentation currency at the exchange rates current as of the most recent reporting date. The same applies when such a foreign entity elects a different presentation currency. IAS 21 stipulates that the current rate is also used for income, expenses, and equity items. If both the parent and the subsidiary operate and report in different highly inflationary economies, the restatement under IAS 29 is first applied to that subsidiary, and is then translated into the presentation currency of the parent at current rate and included in the consolidated financial statements to which IAS 29 is then applied. Comparatives are also adjusted for changes in the price level.[441]

---

[437] *IFRIC 7,* Applying the Restatement Approach under IAS 29 Financial Reporting in Hyperinflationary Economies, ¶ 3.

[438] *IFRS 1, ¶ IG34; IFRIC 7, ¶ BC12.*

[439] *FASB ASC 830-10-45-11 (FASB Statement No. 52, ¶ 11).*

[440] *IAS 21, ¶ 14; IAS 29,* Financial Reporting in Hyperinflationary Economies, ¶ 8.

[441] *IAS 29, ¶¶ 34, 35.*

> **Comment:** The situation depicted in IAS 21 of a translation of a hyperinflationary currency into another hyperinflationary presentation currency would not arise under U.S. GAAP for consolidated financial statements of domestic enterprises where the reporting currency must be the U.S. dollar and would unlikely exist for foreign enterprises. The topic is better analyzed in Section 7.10.1 previously.

However, if the presentation currency is that of a non-hyperinflationary economy, comparative information remains that which had been prepared in that presentation currency in prior year(s) statements, without any additional adjustment for changes in price level or in foreign exchange rates.[442] Hence, the parent of a foreign subsidiary that operates in an economy that becomes hyperinflationary in the current period would not adjust the comparative periods of its subsidiary.

U.S. GAAP does not allow this restate-translation method which holds under IAS 29 and IAS 21 in primary financial statements. However, SEC Form 20-F contains an accommodation that permits foreign private issuers reporting under IFRSs that use such a method to omit the disclosure of the effects of the different method of accounting for inflation in hyperinflationary economies (see Section 6.4.23 previously).[443] Nevertheless a registrant may voluntarily elect financial statements under Subtopic 255-10 (FASB Statement No. 89) as supplementary information (see below).[444] Form 20-F also permits foreign private issuers to file price-level adjusted primary financial statements under the historical cost/constant currency or current cost approach with the SEC and not present the same reconciliations, but the basis for accounting must be stated and the fact that such reconciliation is not presented must be disclosed.[445]

> **Comment:** Therefore, contrary to the basic IAS 29 restatement approach for the purpose of the foreign entity, and similarly to U.S. GAAP, in this case only the translation is accounted for prospectively.

Specific procedures apply when an economy begins or ceases to be hyperinflationary. IFRSs do not see the moving into a state of hyperinflation as necessarily corresponding to a change in functional currency, and therefore account for these two events differently.[446] Worksheet 69 illustrates the accounting for a change in functional currency, both in non-hyperinflationary and hyperinflationary contexts. Under U.S. GAAP, if the foreign currency of a foreign entity used to be its functional currency (thus the current-rate method of translation was used – see Section 7.10.2 previously), at the point its economy becomes highly inflationary that entity is deemed to have a new functional currency corresponding to the reporting currency. In such a situation, the foreign translation adjustment that under the current-rate method had been recognized in other comprehensive income in the previous periods remains so classified. The translated amounts for nonmonetary assets at the end of the prior period become

---

[442]   *IAS 21, ¶¶ IN14(b)–(c), 42-43; IAS 29, ¶ 20.*
[443]   *SEC Form 20-F, ¶ Item 17. (c).(2)(iv)(B).*
[444]   *Regulation S-K, ¶¶ 229.303, Instructions to Paragraph 303(a), 8*
[445]   *SEC Form 20-F, ¶ Item 17.(c).(2)(iv)(A).*
[446]   *IFRIC 7, ¶ BC15.*

their new accounting bases.[447] Under IFRSs, as explained previously, when an economy becomes hyperinflationary the restatement also applies retrospectively from the beginning of that period.[448]

Conversely, when an economy is no longer considered highly inflationary for accounting purposes, under U.S. GAAP a foreign entity is no longer deemed to have its functional currency equal to the reporting currency for the purpose of the accounting in the consolidated or in the parent's financial statements. On the contrary, redetermination of the functional currency is required.[449] In this situation, at the date of change, the reporting currency amounts of non-monetary assets (net of accumulated depreciation or amortization) and nonmonetary liabilities of the foreign entity whose functional currency is the foreign currency must be translated into the local currency at current rate. From that moment onwards the current-rate method of translation applies. This creates new local currency balances, different from those that would result from translating historical-rate nonmonetary items at a much lower current rate.[450]

Under IAS 21, when an economy ceases to be hyperinflationary, the latest restated amounts under IAS 29 become the new historical cost bases. The current-rate method of translation into the presentation currency applies to those amounts.[451] Both U.S. GAAP and IAS 21 accounts for a change in functional currency prospectively from the date of change.[452]

Subtopic 255-10 (FASB Statement No. 89) encourages, but does not require, a business enterprise that reports in U.S. dollars under U.S. GAAP to disclose supplementary information on current cost/constant purchasing power accounting.[453] Conversely, IAS 29 does not permit restated information as supplemental financial statements. The IASB withdrew IAS 15, *Information Reflecting the Effect of Changing Prices*, about purchasing power/current cost accounting. Furthermore, in its primary financial statements, an entity that operates in a hyperinflationary economy must use the same IAS 29 procedures irrespective of whether it uses historical cost or current cost accounting.[454] Under Subtopic 255-10 (FASB Statement No. 89), an entity that has significant foreign operations and uses the U.S. dollar as its functional currency must use the U.S. dollar CPI-U (Consumer Price Index for All Urban Consumers) to restate current costs into units of constant purchasing power or current cost. When significant foreign operations use a foreign currency as their functional currency, the reporting entity may use either the restate-translate method or the translate-restate method. Based on the former, financial statements expressed in current cost/nominal functional currency of the foreign operation are first restated into units of constant purchasing power based on a broad-based

---

[447] *FASB ASC 830-10-45-10 (FASB Statement No. 52, ¶ 46); FASB ASC 830-10-45-16 (EITF Topic D-56,* Accounting for a Change in Functional Currency and Deferred Taxes When an Economy Becomes Highly Inflationary*).*

[448] *IAS 29, ¶ 4; IFRIC 7, ¶ BC7.*

[449] *Securities and Exchange Commission, Division of Corporate Finance,* Frequently Requested Accounting and Financial Reporting Interpretations and Guidance, *¶ I.D (March 31, 2001).*

[450] *FASB ASC 830-10-45-15) (EITF Issue No. 92-4,* Accounting for a Change in Functional Currency When an Economy Ceases to Be Considered Highly Inflationary*).*

[451] *IAS 21, ¶ 43.*

[452] *FASB ASC 830-10-45-7 (FASB Statement No. 52, ¶ 9); IAS 21, ¶ 35.*

[453] *FASB ASC 255-10-50-1 (FASB Statement No. 89,* Financial Reporting and Changing Prices, *¶¶ 1, 3).*

[454] *IAS 29, ¶¶ 6–8.*

measure of the change in general purchasing power and then translated into the reporting currency. Under this method, a parity adjustment measures the difference between local and U.S. inflation on net assets. Based on the latter method, current cost/nominal functional currency information is first translated into the reporting currency and then restated into units of constant purchasing power based on the U.S. dollar CPI-U. In both cases, the cumulative foreign translation adjustment on a current cost basis is reported net of any related income tax that was allocated to it on the primary financial statements. However, under the restate-translate method, the cumulative foreign translation adjustment may be stated net of the aggregate parity adjustment. The sum of the parity adjustment and the translation adjustment measures any differential impact of foreign exchange rate changes over inflation.[455]

Comment: When the functional currency is the currency of a highly inflationary economy, IFRSs require a sort of restate-translation method in primary financial statements, similar to the first of the two methods that a company may elect for supplemental reporting under Subtopic 255-10 (FASB Statement No. 89). However, contrary to Subtopic 255-10 (FASB Statement No. 89) for supplemental financial statements, in this case IAS 21 requires this method for the current period only together with a translation method that also applies the current rate to income and expenses items. If changes in exchange rates perfectly offset the differential between inflation rates, the two standards would likely get the same results for comparative information. If changes in exchange rates do not fully compensate for differential inflation, under Subtopic 255-10 (FASB Statement No. 89) other comprehensive income will include this discrepancy, resulting from the difference between foreign translation adjustment and the parity adjustment.

7.13 HEDGES OF A NET INVESTMENT IN FOREIGN OPERATIONS

This Section analyzes a hedge of a net investment in a foreign operation with reference to the impact on other comprehensive income. Other aspects of the topic fall outside the scope of this Book.

A hedge of a net investment in a foreign operation applies only to financial statements that include the foreign operation (see Section 7.10.1 previously).[456]

Comment: Therefore, in the case of a branch it is possible that net investment hedge accounting be applied at entity's financial statements level. IFRS 11 adds the case of financial statements that include a joint operation.[457]

Under both U.S. GAAP and IFRSs, a hedge of a net investment in a foreign operation is a hedge of a foreign currency exposure of an entity's interest in the net assets of a foreign operation, not a fair value hedge of the change in the value of an equity-method investment or a consolidated subsidiary, which, by the way, cannot be designed as hedged items as they are already part of the reporting entity's financial statements that incorporate such investments.[458]

---

[455] *FASB ASC 255-10-50-9, FASB ASC 255-10-50-44 to FASB ASC 255-10-50-49 (FASB Statement No. 89,* Financial Reporting and Changing Prices, *¶¶ 9, 36–39); FASB Statement No. 89, ¶ 44.*

[456] *IFRIC 16, ¶ 2.*

[457] *IFRIC 16, Footnote to ¶ 2, as amended by IFRS 11.*

[458] *FASB Statement No. 133, ¶ 455; IAS 39, ¶ AG99.*

IAS 39 specifies that a hedge of a net investment in a foreign operation may also include a hedge of a monetary item that is accounted for as part of the net investment (see Section 7.11.1 previously).[459]

Under both U.S. GAAP and IFRSs, the portion of gain and loss on the hedging instrument (the gain or loss on a hedging derivative instrument or the foreign currency transaction gain or loss on a nonderivative hedging instrument) that is determined to be effective under the hedging criteria, is recognized in other comprehensive income as for a cash flow hedge, while the ineffective portion is placed in profit or loss. Subsequently, on disposal or partial disposal of the foreign operation (therefore, also including a loss of control, a loss of significant influence or a loss of joint control, and partial disposals as explained in Section 7.17 later), the amount corresponding to the effective portion of the hedge is reclassified in profit or loss (under U.S. GAAP, recycled into earnings).[460]

Comment: FASB Statement No. 133 used to include the component of other comprehensive income referred to the effective portion of a gain and loss on net investment hedges into cumulative translation adjustment.[461] IAS 39 does not state whether or not it is to be displayed separately from translation differences. IFRIC 16 confirms that the gain or loss on the hedging instrument that is determined to be an effective hedge of the net investment is included with the foreign exchange differences arising on translation and that the reclassification adjustment comes from the foreign currency translation reserve. However, the amount that is reclassified in respect of cumulative gain or loss on the hedging instrument that was determined to be an effective hedge under IAS 39 is logically different from the amount that is reclassified in respect of exchange differences on the net investment in that foreign operation in accordance with IAS 21. This standard requires presentation of the latter cumulative amount in a separate component of equity. IAS 39 requires the identification of the effective hedge for recognition purpose.[462]

The step-by-step method of consolidation may end up with a reclassification adjustment that differs from the amount used to determine hedge effectiveness, although the choice of the consolidation method does not affect the assessment of the effectiveness of the hedge. Under IFRSs, this difference may be eliminated by an adjustment as explained in Section 7.10.2 previously.[463]

In addition, Subtopic 830-20 (FASB Statement No. 52) accounts for transaction gains and losses attributable to a foreign currency transaction that is designated an economic hedge of a net investment in a foreign entity as a translation adjustment in other comprehensive income, to the extent to which the hedge is affective and from its designation date.[464]

---

[459]   *IAS 39, ¶ 102.*

[460]   *FASB ASC 815-20-35-1, 815-35-35-1 (FASB Statement No. 133, ¶¶ 18(d)(4), 42); IAS 39 (as amended by IAS 27 (2008)), ¶ 102.*

[461]   *FASB Statement No. 133, ¶ 45(c) (superseded).*

[462]   *IAS 39, ¶ 102(a); IFRIC 16, ¶¶ 3, 16–17, BC33–BC34.*

[463]   *IFRIC 16, ¶¶ 48, AG7.*

[464]   *FASB ASC 830-20-35-3 (FASB Statement No. 52, ¶ 20(a)); FASB Statement No. 52, ¶¶ 128-129; FASB Statement No. 133, ¶ 477.*

> **Comment:** The term *economic hedge* has several meanings. It generally indicates two symmetric positions that hedge each other's risk exposure, but the hedging relationship does not meet all of the conditions for hedge accounting. In other circumstances, *economic hedge* refers to a natural hedge, that is where both the hedging transaction and the hedged item are already accounted in the same manner (e.g., both in profit or loss) and therefore no need for hedge accounting arises. Conversely, hedge accounting is thought to eliminate volatility between two opposite positions that would not otherwise be accounted for symmetrically. IFRSs do not use the expression *economic hedge*. Under IFRSs, a derivative in an economic hedge that does not qualify for hedge accounting would generally be accounted for as a derivative held for trading.

Under Subtopic 815-20 (FASB Statement No. 133), a premium or discount on a foreign currency forward contract that is designated and is effective as a hedge of the foreign exchange exposure of an entity's net investment in a foreign operation must be accounted together with the translation adjustment. That is different from previous guidance under FASB Statement No. 52 that permitted separate amortization in earnings.[465]

Under U.S. GAAP, both a derivative or a nonderivative financial instrument that may give rise to a foreign currency transaction gain or loss under Topic 830 (FASB Statement No. 52) (therefore excluding a nonderivative financial instrument that is reported at fair value with changes in fair value recognized in earnings) may be designated as a hedging instrument of the foreign currency exposure of a net investment in a foreign entity in consolidated financial statements. As a prerequisite, the net investment must be denominated in a currency other than the functional currency of the entity that has the risk exposure, and either that entity or another member of the consolidated group with the same functional currency as that entity must be a party to the hedging instrument. No intermediate or ultimate parent with a different functional currency may be party to that hedging instrument.[466]

> **Comment:** An available-for-sale security would be a nonderivative financial instrument that may give rise to a foreign currency transaction gain or loss under Topic 830 (FASB Statement No. 52).

By contrast, under IFRSs, both derivative and nonderivative financial assets or liabilities or combinations thereof may be designated as hedging instruments of foreign currency risk, irrespective of which entity within the group holds the hedging instrument. A similar treatment applies to a cash flow hedge and to a monetary item that is in substance part of a net investment in a foreign operation.[467] This is because the identity of the entity that holds the hedging instrument, or its functional currency, does not affect the nature of the economic risk arising from the foreign currency exposure to the ultimate parent entity. Furthermore, the functional

---

[465] *FASB ASC 815-20-25-132 (Statement 133 Implementation Issue No. H6, Foreign Currency Hedges: Accounting for Premium or Discount on a Forward Contract Used as the Hedging Instrument in a Net Investment Hedge).*

[466] *FASB ASC 815-20-25-30, 815-20-25-66 (FASB Statement No. 133, ¶¶ 40(a), 40(b), 42); FASB ASC 815-20-25-23, 815-20-25-27, 815-20-25-30 (FASB Statement No. 133 Implementation Issue No. H1, Foreign Currency Hedges: Hedging at the Operating Unit Level).*

[467] *IAS 39, ¶¶ 9, 72, F.2.14; IAS 21, ¶¶ 15A, BC25D; IFRIC 16, ¶¶ BC26–BC29.*

currency of the entity holding the instrument is irrelevant in determining the effectiveness of the hedge, which instead depends on the functional currency of the parent entity (ultimate, intermediate, or direct) that is indicated in the hedge documentation.[468] The hedged risk may be designated as the exposure between the functional currency of the foreign operation and that of any of its immediate, intermediate, or ultimate parent entities. As an exception, IFRIC 16 did not permit hedge accounting if the hedging instrument was held by the foreign operation that was being hedged. Here, hedging was considered unnecessary because the foreign exchange differences between the parent's functional currency and the functional currency of the net investment would also affect other comprehensive income, because the hedging instrument was denominated in the same functional currency of the net investment and was part of it.[469] However, a subsequent review of this point showed that without hedge accounting part of the foreign exchange difference arising from the hedging instrument might be included in consolidated profit or loss as opposed to translation reserve in other comprehensive income, as this depends on which is the parent that is designated in the hedge and its functional currency. Therefore, the IASB issued an amendment to IFRIC 16 to eliminate this exception. The amendment is effective for annual periods beginning on or after July 1, 2009 with prospective application.[470]

Comment: Under IFRSs, hedge accounting applies only to foreign exchange differences involving functional currencies, not to a different presentation currency.[471] As explained in Section 7.10.1 previously, the fact that IFRSs permit translation in a presentation currency different from the parent's functional currency, but not its hedge creates a comparability difference between companies reporting under IFRSs and U.S. GAAP, which does not permit either.

Under Section 830-30-45 (EITF Issue No. 01-5),[472] differently from IFRSs, the gain or loss from an effective hedge of a net investment in a foreign operation must also be computed in the carrying amount of the investment for purposes of impairment evaluation, when the reporting entity has committed to a plan for its disposal and if that planned disposal will cause recycling to income (see Section 7.10.5 previously).

In addition to the information required by IAS 21 (see Section 7.10.8 previously), IFRS 7 requires the disclosure of each type of hedge, the hedge risk, the financial instruments designated as hedging instruments, their fair values at the reporting date. For net investment hedges, an entity must disclose the ineffectiveness recognized in profit or loss.[473] Except for the last one, IAS 32 contained similar disclosures. In addition to the information required by Topic 830 (FASB Statement No. 52) and Subtopic 220-10 (FASB Statement 130) (see Section 7.10.8 previously), FASB Statement No. 133 used to require information on gains or losses included in the cumulative translation adjustment during the period.[474] FASB Statement No. 161 amends

---

[468]   *IFRIC 16, ¶¶ 14, 15, AG4, BC23, BC25–BC30.*

[469]   *IFRIC 16, ¶¶ 14, BC24.*

[470]   Improvements to IFRSs, *Amendment to IFRIC Interpretation 16 Hedges of a Net Investment in a Foreign Operation (April 2009);* Post-implementation Revisions to IFRIC Interpretations, *Proposed Amendments to IFRIC 9 and IFRIC 16 (January 2009).*

[471]   *IFRIC 16, ¶¶ 10, 12.*

[472]   *FASB ASC 830-30-45-13 (EITF Issue No. 01-5, ¶ 5).*

[473]   *IFRS 7, ¶¶ 22, 24.*

[474]   *FASB Statement No. 133, ¶ 45(c) (superseded).*

Topic 815 (FASB Statement No. 133) to require, among other disclosures, tabular-format information about fair value amounts and the line item(s) in the statement of financial position of all derivative instruments and of nonderivative instruments that are designated and qualify as hedging instruments including foreign currency exposure of a net investment in a foreign operation. Asset and liabilities instruments must be separately presented, segregated by hedging and no-hedging designations, and by type of derivative contract. An entity must also disclose the location and amount of gains and losses reported in the statement of financial performance or, where applicable, in other comprehensive income on derivative instruments and related hedged items. Gains and losses must also be separately presented by type of hedge (fair value, cash flow, and net investment hedges) and nonhedging derivatives, and by type of derivative contract. With reference to cash flow hedges and net investment hedges, such information must be segregated by the effective portion of gains and losses on derivative instruments that was recognized in other comprehensive income in the current period, the amount reclassified into earnings during the current period, the ineffective portion, and the portion excluded from the assessment of hedge effectiveness.[475] Under both sets of standards, the abovementioned disclosures are in addition to those relating to hedging strategy and policy.

7.14 AVAILABLE-FOR-SALE INVESTMENTS

7.14.1 Unrealized Holding Gains or Losses on Available-for-Sale Investments

IFRS 9 replaces the classification of financial assets of IAS 39. Under IFRS 9, the available-for-sale classification for financial assets does not exist anymore.[476] IFRS 9 is effective for annual periods beginning on or after January 1, 2013 (proposed to be moved to 2015). Earlier application is permitted. Unless an entity adopts IFRS 9 for reporting periods beginning before January 1, 2012, the standard requires retrospective application to financial assets existing as of the date of its initial application, irrespective of the business model that an entity used in prior reporting periods.[477] This Section illustrates the accounting under U.S. GAAP and IFRS prior to IFRS 9.

Under both U.S. GAAP and IFRSs (prior to IFRS 9), available-for-sale financial assets are a residual category of financial assets. Contrary to U.S. GAAP, IAS 39 also permitted a company to designate a nonderivative financial asset as available for sale.[478] IAS 39 allowed designation as available for sale only on initial recognition of a financial asset. In addition, an entity that applied IFRSs before January 1, 2005 might designate a previously recognized financial asset as available for sale on initial application of the 2004 Revision of IAS 39. All cumulative changes in fair value would be recognized in a separate component in equity, until reclassification in profit or loss on subsequent impairment or derecognition. Comparative information on the financial asset would be reclassified. The entity would disclose the fair value at the date of designation, and the carrying amount and classification in the prior financial statements.[479]

---

[475] *FASB Statement No. 161*, Disclosures about Derivative Instruments and Hedging Activities, ¶ 3.
[476] *IFRS 9, ¶¶ IN11, 4.1, C9 (amending IFRS 7, ¶ Appendix A), C24 (amending IAS 32, ¶ 12).*
[477] *IFRS 9, ¶¶ 8.1.1, 8.2.1, 8.2.4, 8.2.12.*
[478] *FASB ASC 320-10-35-1 (FASB Statement No. 115, ¶ 12(b)); IAS 39, ¶ 9 (deleted by IFRS 9).*
[479] *IAS 39, ¶¶ 105, BC63A.*

> **Comment:** As part of the more general approach discussed in Section 2.1.3 previously, IAS 39 used to refer to available-for-sale financial assets while Topic 320 (FASB Statement No. 115) refers to available-for-sale securities.

As a general rule under both U.S. GAAP and IFRSs (prior to IFRS 9), gains or losses arising from changes in fair value of available-for-sale financial assets that are not part of a hedging relationship (see Section 7.14.3 following) are recognized in other comprehensive income. Under both U.S. GAAP and IFRSs, the above recognition rule excludes dividend income on available-for-sale equity instruments (equity securities, under U.S. GAAP) and interest income (including premium/discount amortization calculated at effective interest rate) on available-for-sale financial assets (debt securities, under U.S. GAAP).[480] For insurance companies, Regulation S-X requires the display of unrealized appreciation or depreciation of equity securities less applicable deferred taxes on the face of the statement of financial position.[481]

> **Comment:** Section 7.14.2 and Section 7.14.4 following explain certain additional exclusions from this rule under IFRSs for foreign exchange differences and impairment losses, respectively.

> **Comment:** Therefore, this is a mixed model where interest income is recorded in profit or loss as part of accounting for an instrument at amortized cost, while fair value remeasurement applies at each reporting date and affects other comprehensive income.

> **Comment:** FASB Statement No. 115 terms these gains or losses unrealized holding gains or losses, consistently with certain theories on other comprehensive income (see Section 7.4.3 previously). An unrealized holding gain or loss is the change in fair value of the instrument, exclusive of impairment loss and recognized and unpaid dividend and interest income.[482] FASB Statement No. 115 also considers additional reasons for reporting them in other comprehensive income: mitigating volatility in earnings arising from changes in fair value of long-term investments, reducing mismatching in earnings resulting from the fact that related liabilities are not measured at fair value, and maintaining unrealized gains and losses in accumulated other comprehensive income to mitigate "gains trading" upon transfer among categories.[483] As a response to the financial market crisis, under FSP FAS 115-2 and FAS 124-2 (see Section 7.14.4 following) the portion of the total other-than-temporary impairment of a held-to-maturity or an available-for-sale security that is related to all factors other than a credit loss is also recognized in other comprehensive income. Furthermore, the statement that reports the components of accumulated other comprehensive income (see Section 7.9.1 previously) must separately display the amounts related to held-to-maturity and available-for-sale securities for which a portion of the other-than-temporary impairment has been recognized in earnings.[484]

---

[480]   *FASB ASC 320-10-35-1, 320-10-35-4 (FASB Statement No. 115, ¶¶ 13–14); IAS 39, ¶ 55 (amended by IFRS 9).*

[481]   *FASB ASC 944-210-S99-1 (Regulation S-X 210.7-03.23).*

[482]   *FASB Statement No. 115, ¶ 137.*

[483]   *FASB Statement No. 115, ¶¶ 79, 85, 94.*

[484]   *FSP FAS 115-2 and FAS 124-2, ¶¶ 30, 37.*

> **Comment:** The previous revision of IAS 1 stated that unrealized gains and losses were recognized directly as a separate component of equity through the statement of changes in equity. The Implementation Guidance used to term the reserve for changes in value of available-for-sale instruments in the statement of changes in equity "valuation gains (losses) taken to equity."

However, if an available-for-sale financial asset is designated as a hedged item in a fair value hedge, the gain or loss that is attributable to the hedged risk is recognized in profit or loss (see Section 7.14.3 following).[485]

Under U.S. GAAP, a transfer of a security classified as held-to-maturity into the available-for-sale category determines the recognition in other comprehensive income of the unrealized gain or loss at the date of transfer.[486] Similarly, under IFRSs prior to IFRS 9, this accounting used to apply to the difference between the fair value of the financial asset at the time of transfer and its carrying amount.[487]

> **Comment:** "Reclassification" is the IFRS term for a transfer between categories of financial assets.

Accumulated other comprehensive income is recycled (reclassified, under IFRSs) into profit or loss when the asset is impaired, or derecognized (sold, collected, or otherwise disposed of).[488]

Under IAS 39, derecognition also included the purchase by another company of a company, whose shares the entity kept as available-for-sale financial assets, in exchange for the shares of the acquirer.[489]

Under IAS 39 prior to IFRS 9, in a transfer of a financial asset in general (and of an available-for-sale financial asset in particular) where only a part of a financial asset qualified for derecognition, a reclassification adjustment was limited to the portion of the related cumulative other comprehensive income that was allocated, based on the relative fair values of those parts, to the derecognized part.[490]

The scope of IFRIC 17 also includes the distribution of available-for-sale securities to owners acting in their capacity as owners, provided all other criteria under this interpretation are met.[491]

> **Comment:** Therefore, when an entity settles the dividend payable, gains or losses accumulated in other comprehensive income will be reclassified to profit or loss.

---

[485] *FASB ASC 320-10-35-1 (FASB Statement No. 115, ¶ 13); IAS 39, ¶ 89(b).*
[486] *FASB ASC 320-10-35-10 (FASB Statement No. 115, ¶ 15(c)).*
[487] *IAS 39, ¶ 51.*
[488] *IAS 1, ¶ 93 (as amended by IFRS 9); IAS 39, ¶ 55.*
[489] *IAS 39, ¶ E.3.1 (deleted by IFRS 9).*
[490] *IAS 39, ¶¶ 27, 34.*
[491] *IFRIC Interpretation 17,* Distributions of Non-cash Assets to Owners, *¶ IE1.*

Section 7.17.1 and Section 7.17.3 later explain recycling (reclassification, under IFRSs) in connection with a loss of control of a subsidiary, the loss of significant influence of an associate, or the loss of joint control of a jointly controlled entity.

Under U.S. GAAP, a transfer into the trading category would also trigger recycling, as the gain or loss accumulated in other comprehensive income is deemed to be realized. If there is a net loss at transfer, a previous unrecognized gain is netted to recognize the net loss.[492] Furthermore, FASB Statement No. 133 permits an entity, at the date of initial application of the standard, to transfer any available-for-sale securities into the trading category with the aforementioned accounting.[493] By contrast, IFRSs prohibited subsequent reclassifications from or to the category of at fair value through profit or loss (of which the held-for-trading classification is part).[494] However, the 2008 amendments to IAS 39 and to IFRS 7 (effective on or after July 1, 2008) permitted an entity to reclassify a nonderivative financial asset classified as at fair value through profit or loss that was not designated as such upon initial recognition out of this category only under rare circumstances. This was allowed if the instrument was no longer held for the purpose of selling or repurchasing it in the near term. An entity might reclassify an instrument that would have met the definition of loans and receivables if it had not been required to be classified as held for trading at initial recognition, provided the entity intended to hold it for the foreseeable future or until maturity, any gains and losses already recognized in profit or loss were not reversed, and appropriate disclosures were provided under IFRS 7. As subsequently clarified in November 2008,[495] the amendments permitted some backdating to July 1, 2008 as part of the transitional arrangements, as long as the reclassification was made before November 1, 2008 and the reclassification was not backdated to a date before July 1, 2008. These amendments, thought of as a short-term relief for some entities in the 2008 financial crisis following an urgent request from Europe, were intended to converge to FASB Statement No. 115 and FASB Statement No. 65 concerning reclassifications out of the trading category.[496] IFRS 9 does not have available-for-sale and loans and receivables categories for financial assets. The standard now requires reclassification of financial assets to the extent an entity changes its business model for managing financial assets.[497] IFRS 9 does not repropose the abovementioned temporary provisions concerning reclassifications.

Under U.S. GAAP, if an available-for-sale debt security is transferred to the held-to-maturity category, the unrealized holding gain or loss at the date of transfer remains in accumulated other comprehensive income and is subsequently amortized to income over the period until maturity as an adjustment of yield using the effective interest method. This amortization has an opposite sign to the amortization of the premium or discount at effective interest method that is determined for the newly-classified held-to-maturity debt security for the difference between

---

[492] *FASB ASC 320-10-35-10 (FASB Statement No. 115, ¶ 15(b)); FASB ASC 320-10-40-2 (Implementation Guides, Q&A 115, ¶ 39).*

[493] *FASB Statement No. 133, ¶ 55.*

[494] *IAS 39, ¶ 50 before October 2008 amendments.*

[495] *Amendments to IAS 39 and IFRS 7,* Reclassification of Financial Assets – Effective Date and Transition *(November 2008).*

[496] *IASB,* Reclassification of Financial Assets – Amendments to IAS 39 Financial Instruments: Recognition and Measurement and IFRS 7 Financial Instruments: Disclosures, ¶¶ 50, 50B, 50C, 50D *(paragraphs deleted by IFRS 9), BC104A (October 2008).*

[497] *IFRS 9 (October 2010), ¶ 4.4.1; IFRS 9 (November 2009), ¶ 4.9.*

its fair value at the date of transfer and its par value (maturity amount, under IFRSs prior to IFRS 9). The two will cancel or mitigate each other.[498] IAS 39 added that if the resulting financial asset has no fixed maturity, the gain or loss remains in equity until impairment or derecognition.[499]

Similarly to this treatment, but with no effect on earnings, the portion of other-than-temporary impairment not related to a credit loss for a held-to-maturity security that under FSP FAS 115-2 and FAS 124-2 must be accounted for in a separate category of other comprehensive income is amortized over the remaining life of the security through a prospective accretion from other comprehensive income to its amortized cost, until the security is sold, matures, or another other-than-temporary impairment is recognized in earnings. The FSP amends FASB Statement No. 130 to clarify that a reclassification adjustment of the new separate category of accumulated other comprehensive income relating to held-to-maturity securities that under the FSP originates from other-than-temporary impairment not related to a credit loss only applies to the case of a sale of the security, maturity, or of an additional credit loss (see Section 7.14.4 later).[500]

The 2008 amendments to IAS 39 and to IFRS 7 mentioned above (effective on or after July 1, 2008) permitted an entity to reclassify an available-for-sale financial asset to the loans and receivables category if that instrument would have met the definition of loans and receivables if it had not been required to be classified as available for sale and the entity intended to hold it for the foreseeable future or until maturity. This reclassification had to be made at the fair value of the instrument at the reclassification date (subject to a limited backdating as explained above) and it had to be accounted for as in the case of a transfer to a held-to-maturity financial asset.[501]

The previous version of IAS 39 permitted, as an accounting policy, an option to recognize unrealized gains and losses on all available-for-sale financial assets either in equity or in profit or loss. This was eliminated when the standard introduced the option to measure a financial asset or financial liability at fair value with gains and losses recognized in profit or loss (see also Section 6.4.12 previously and see Section 6.4.14 previously). Under FASB Statement No. 159 (effective for the fiscal year that begins after November 15, 2007), an entity may also elect to use the fair value option for eligible items, including available-for-sale securities. Cumulative unrealized gains or losses on those securities at the effective date must be reclassified from other comprehensive income to the beginning balance of retained earnings as a cumulative-effect adjustment to be separately disclosed.[502] This treatment is different from the ordinary one prescribed by Topic 320 (FASB Statement No. 115), based on which a reclassification from available-for-sale securities to trading securities determines the recognition of a gain or

---

[498] *FASB ASC 320-10-35-10 (FASB Statement No. 115, ¶¶ 15(d), Footnote 3, 15(b)); FASB ASC 320-10-35-16, 320-10-55-24, 320-10-55-25 (Implementation Guides, Q&A 115, ¶¶ 43, 45); IAS 39, ¶ 54 (deleted by IFRS 9).*

[499] *IAS 39, ¶ 54(b) (deleted by IFRS 9).*

[500] *FSP FAS 115-2 and FAS 124-2, ¶¶ 11, 34, 37, A3(c).*

[501] *IASB, Reclassification of Financial Assets – Amendments to IAS 39 Financial Instruments: Recognition and Measurement and IFRS 7 Financial Instruments: Disclosures, ¶¶ 50E-50F (October 2008) (deleted by IFRS 9).*

[502] *FASB Statement No. 159, ¶ 28.*

loss in current earnings, including the amount that had been recognized in other comprehensive income.[503]

Incremental direct costs of available-for-sale debt securities are amortized at effective interest method under Subtopic 310-20 (FASB Statement No. 91).[504] Under IAS 39 prior to IFRS 9, transaction costs on an available-for-sale financial asset (such as fees, commissions, and other incremental costs) were included as part of its initial measurement, but not those upon its transfer or disposal. Once recognized, transaction costs on available-for-sale financial assets were included in equity as part of a change in fair value at its remeasurement at the end of the next reporting date. In addition, if a debt available-for-sale financial asset had a finite life with fixed or determinable payments, transaction costs were amortized in profit or loss at the effective interest method. Otherwise they were expensed on asset derecognition or impairment.[505] At initial measurement, IFRS 9 instead adds directly attributable transaction costs to the initial measurement of only financial assets that are not at fair value through profit or loss, therefore those that are measured at fair value though other comprehensive income.[506]

Subtopic 320-10 (FASB Statement No. 115) requires the disclosure of the aggregate fair value of available-for-sale securities, and total gains (or total losses), by major security type, for securities with net gain (or net loss) in accumulated other comprehensive income for each period for which a statement of financial position is presented.[507] It also requires information on the proceeds from sale, the resulting realized gross gains and losses recycled to earnings, the gross gains and gross losses from transfer into the trading category, whether specific identification, average cost or other basis is used to determine the sale and transfer amount of a security, the amount in net unrealized holding gain or loss arising in the period, and the amount recycled in the period.[508] An entity must also disclose contractual maturities of available-for-sale debt securities, and the net carrying amount of securities transferred from the held-to-maturity category and the circumstances for the transfer, as these are supposed to be rare[509]. Under IFRS 7 prior to amendments by IFRS 9, an entity had to disclose net gains or net losses on available-for-sale financial assets either on the face of the statement of comprehensive income or in the notes, separately showing current-period amounts and reclassification adjustments. It also had to describe the criteria used for designating financial assets as available for sale. As part of the market risk disclosures, the sensitivity analysis of equity to each type of market risk to which the entity was exposed at the reporting date also had to include the impact of available-for-sale financial assets[510]. Of course, under both sets

---

[503] *FASB ASC 320-10-35-10 (FASB Statement No. 115, ¶ 15); FASB Statement No. 159, ¶ 29.*

[504] *FASB ASC 310-20-35-2 (FASB Statement No. 91, Accounting for Nonrefundable Fees and Costs Associated with Originating or Acquiring Loans and Initial Direct Costs of Leases, ¶ 5); FASB Statement No. 91, ¶ 6.*

[505] *IAS 39, ¶¶ 43 (deleted by IFRS 9), 46 (deleted by IFRS 9), AG6, AG13, AG67 (deleted by IFRS 9), E.1.1 (amended by IFRS 9).*

[506] *IFRS 9, ¶¶ 5.1.1, B5.4.*

[507] *FASB ASC 320-10-50-2 (FASB Statement No. 115, ¶ 19).*

[508] *FASB ASC 320-10-50-9 (FASB Statement No. 115, ¶¶ 21(a)–(d)).*

[509] *FASB ASC 320-10-50-2, 320-10-50-3, 320-10-50-10 (FASB Statement No. 115, ¶¶ 20, 22); FASB Statement No. 115, ¶ 85.*

[510] *IFRS 7, ¶¶ 20(a)(ii) (deleted by IFRS 9), 40(a), B5(b) (deleted by IFRS 9), B27 (amended by IFRS 9).*

of standards, the abovementioned disclosures are (or were, under IFRSs) in addition to those generally required for other comprehensive income.

If an IFRS first-time adopter that under its previous GAAP used to measure certain investments at fair value and classify the change in fair value outside profit or loss reclassifies those financial assets as available for sale on initial application of IAS 39 (prior to IFRS 9), it has to recognize the pre-IAS 39 revaluation gain in a separate component of equity (also see Section 6.4.14 previously).[511]

Comment: The 2007 Revision of IAS 1 did not amend this "separate component of equity" to other comprehensive income. The December 2009 version of IFRSs maintains this terminology. Hence, it arguably has to be displayed separately from other comprehensive income that is accumulated after the initial adoption of IAS 39. According to a different opinion, the pre-IAS 39 component would be accounted in the same equity reserve.[512] In any case, in the pre-IFRS 9 accounting, subsequent reclassifications to profit on loss on derecognition or impairment apply to both the components of equity. IFRS 9 amends IFRS 1 to consider a reclassification to instruments at fair value through other comprehensive income, in which case a subsequent derecognition does not determine a reclassification adjustment but simply an elective transfer to a different caption in equity.[513]

Prior to IFRS 9, an IFRS first-time adopter might, at the date of transition to IFRSs, redesignate previously recognized financial instruments as available-for-sale financial assets. It had to disclose their fair values at the date of designation, and their carrying amounts and classifications in the prior financial statements.[514]

Comment: The Implementation Guidance of IFRS 1 includes the gains relating to the difference between fair value at transition date and carrying amount under prior GAAP in a "revaluation reserve" ("revaluation surplus" in IFRS 1 restructured in 2008) in the reconciliation of total comprehensive income.[515] Arguably, this term is inappropriate, as under IFRSs revaluation is used for tangible and intangible assets carried at revaluation model (not fair value model).

Finally, when consolidated financial statements include a less-than-wholly-owned subsidiary that holds available-for-sale investments, other comprehensive income must be adjusted against noncontrolling interest at the same time the subsidiary recognizes changes in value of its available-for-sale investments in other comprehensive income. This entry records the noncontrolling interest's share of the subsidiary's other comprehensive income and related changes.[516]

---

[511] *IFRS 1, ¶ IG59.*

[512] *ABI – Associazione Bancaria Italiana, Soluzioni IAS No. 16 (March 10, 2006).*

[513] *IFRS 1, ¶ IG59 (amended by IFRS 9).*

[514] *IFRS 1, ¶¶ D19 (amended by IFRS 9), 29 (amended by IFRS 9), BC63A, BC81.*

[515] *IFRS 1 (both June 2005 and Restructured November 2008), ¶ IG 63 Example 11.*

[516] *FASB ASC 320-10-S99-2 (EITF Topic D-41,* Adjustments in Assets and Liabilities for Holding Gains and Losses as Related to the Implementation of FASB Statement No. 115, *as amended by Accounting Standards Update No. 2010-04,* Accounting for Various Topics, Technical Corrections to SEC Paragraphs, *¶ 9).*

Similarly, under IAS 27, noncontrolling interests include their proportionate share of each component of other comprehensive income.[517]

The *Financial Statement Presentation Project* has discussed the way of displaying gains and losses on available-for-sale financial assets. Separate line items for realized and unrealized gains and losses in the investment income category have been considered an option. Alternatively, the cohesiveness principle would lead to classifying gains and losses in the same category as that of the related security on the face of the statement of financial position (for nonfinancial institutions, generally, financing or investing categories). Finally, fair value changes in financial instruments have been considered candidates for inclusion in the "remeasurement" classification in the financial statements.[518] After IFRS 9, the topic remains under U.S. GAAP only. The Staff Draft maintains unrealized gains or losses on available-for-sale securities in the other comprehensive income section of the statement of comprehensive income, labeled as operating activities[519].

7.14.2   Foreign Exchange Differences on Available-for-Sale Investments

The previous Section illustrates the general rule for recognition and presentation of available-for-sale investments. Worksheet 70 contrasts the treatment of foreign exchange differences that arise when available-for-sale instruments are denominated in a foreign currency under U.S. GAAP and IFRSs.

Under IAS 21, the exchange differences arising from subsequent measurement of foreign-currency-denominated monetary items that do not form part of a net investment in a foreign operation (see Section 7.11.1 previously) are recognized in profit or loss in the period in which such differences arise. However, if the item is nonmonetary, the recognition of the exchange differences is diverted to the accounting for the gains or losses of the nonmonetary item itself (see Section 7.16.2 later).[520] Prior to IFRS 9, IAS 39 used to override this rule for available-for-sale debt financial assets.[521] As an available-for-sale debt financial asset (hence a monetary item) was accounted for at a mixed model where interest income and impairment loss are brought to profit or loss, while valuation changes were recorded in other comprehensive income, the exchange differences followed the treatments of the respective items to which they referred. The cumulative adjustment in other comprehensive income, including the component of exchange differences, was computed as the balance between the fair value of the available-for-sale monetary financial asset in the functional currency of the reporting entity and the amortized cost adjusted for any impairment translated at the appropriate closing rate.[522] The

---

[517]   *IAS 27 (2010), ¶ 28.*

[518]   *Performance Reporting Joint International Group (JIG), Agenda Paper 2,* History of the Performance Reporting Project, *¶ 22 London (January 2005) www.fasb.org (last visited June 21, 2007); IASB, Financial Statement Presentation Project, Agenda Paper 15A,* Other Comprehensive Income, *¶¶ 11, 25 (December 14, 2006); FASB/IASB Financial Statement Presentation Project, Agenda Paper 6C/FASB Memorandum 44C,* Measurement; OCI and Recycling; the Statement of Comprehensive Income, *¶ 41 (October 24, 2006) www.iasb.org (last visited June 21, 2007).*

[519]   *FASB and IASB,* Staff Draft of an Exposure Draft on Financial Statement Presentation, *¶ IG32 (July 2010).*

[520]   *IAS 21, ¶¶ 28, 30.*

[521]   *IAS 39, ¶ AG83 (amended by IFRS 9).*

[522]   *IAS 39, ¶ E.3.2.*

gains or losses in other comprehensive income and those in profit and loss could not be offset by each other.[523] Conversely, exchange differences on an available-for-sale equity instrument (that is, a nonmonetary item) were all recognized in other comprehensive income, even when they referred to dividend income or an impairment loss. As an available-for-sale asset was remeasured at fair value, the exchange rate applied for translating from the foreign currency of denomination to the functional currency of the holding entity was the closing rate at the remeasurement date (usually, the reporting date). If the instrument was carried at cost because it was an equity financial asset whose fair value could not be reliably measured, it was translated at historical rate.[524] Under IFRS 9, the foreign exchange gain or loss of an equity instrument that is carried at fair value through other comprehensive income keeps on affecting other comprehensive income.[525] Under U.S. GAAP, the entire portion of the change in fair value of an available-for-sale debt security attributable to changes in exchange rates must be reported in other comprehensive income.[526]

Example: In relation to the SEC's review of Form 20-F of a foreign private issuer from Belgium for the fiscal year ended December 21, 2005 containing financial statements prepared for the first time on the basis of IFRSs, the company explained a difference in reporting unrealized loss on securities in other comprehensive income under IFRSs and under U.S. GAAP. Under U.S. GAAP, exchange rate fluctuations recognized in the changes in unrealized foreign exchange gains and losses were recorded at historical exchange rates, and under IFRSs at the closing exchange rates.[527]

In summary, whether foreign exchange differences on available-for-sale financial assets impacted profit or loss or other comprehensive income depended on whether the asset was monetary or nonmonetary (IFRSs only), whether the exchange differences related to change in amortized cost or in fair value (IFRSs only), whether or not the asset is designated as a hedging instrument in a cash flow hedge (see Section 7.15.1 later) or in a hedge of a net investment of a foreign operation (see Section 7.13 previously), or whether or not it is a monetary item that forms part of a net investment of a foreign operation and therefore the exchange differences result from translating its financial statements (see Section 7.11.1 previously).[528]

7.14.3 Available-for-Sale Investments under Hedge Accounting

Section 7.13 previously explains that an available-for-sale financial asset may be designated as a hedging instrument of a net investment in a foreign operation. This Section treats other hedging situations, where hedge accounting overrides, as an exception, the treatment illustrated for available-for-sale financial assets.

---

[523] *IAS 39, ¶ E.3.3 (amended by IFRS 9).*

[524] *IAS 21, ¶¶ 23(b)-(c), IAS 39, ¶ 46(c) (deleted by IFRS 9).*

[525] *IFRS 9, ¶ B.5.14.*

[526] *FASB ASC 830-20-35-6 (EITF Issue No. 96-15, Accounting for the Effects of Changes in Foreign Exchange Rates on Foreign-Currency-Denominated Available-for-Sale Debt Securities).*

[527] *Letters by the SEC, File No. 1-15180, Note 18 (September 21, 2006). Reply by the company (October 31, 2006) www.sec.gov/divisions/corpfin/ifrs_reviews (last visited January 7, 2008).*

[528] *IAS 39, ¶ E.3.3 (amended by IFRS 9).*

Under both U.S. GAAP and IFRSs, as an exception to the general measurement rule for available-for-sale financial assets, if a foreign-currency-denominated nonmonetary available-for-sale financial asset (as stated, under IFRS 9 available-for-sale financial assets do not exist any longer) is designated as a hedged item in a fair value hedge of the exposure to changes in foreign currency rates, it is remeasured at fair value (and thus, under IAS 21, translated at closing rate[529]), and the gain or loss attributable to the hedged risk is recognized in profit or loss (instead of in other comprehensive income, prior to IFRS 9), including the related foreign exchange differences.[530] Under IFRSs prior to IFRS 9, the portion excluded from the assessment of the hedge effectiveness was recognized according to the fair value remeasurement general rule, i.e., in other comprehensive income if it was related to an available-for-sale investment.[531]

Subtopic 815-25 (FASB Statement No. 133) requires disclosure of net gain or loss of the hedged item reported in earnings in the period due to hedge's ineffectiveness and the derivative hedging instrument's gain or loss of the excluded portion.[532] As explained in Section 7.13 previously, FASB Statement No. 161 reinforced the requirements for disclosing the line items where gains or losses are reported.[533] IFRS 7 requires, together with other information, disclosure of the gains and losses of the hedging instrument and those of the hedged item attributable to the hedged risk.[534]

If a foreign-currency-denominated monetary available-for-sale financial asset is designated as a hedging instrument against the exposure to changes in foreign currency rates in a cash flow hedge, the exchange differences of the portion of the gain or loss on a designated hedging instrument that is determined to be an effective hedge are recognized in other comprehensive income, while IAS 21 would ordinarily require recognition in other comprehensive income only for the exchange differences on the remeasurement portion (see Section 7.14.2 previously).[535] Under U.S. GAAP, a nonderivative instrument cannot be designated as a hedging instrument of a foreign-currency-denominated forecasted transaction.

7.14.4 Impairment of an Available-for-Sale Financial Asset

Under both FASB Statement No. 115 (prior to FSP FAS 115-2 and FAS 124-2) and IAS 39 prior to IFRS 9 an impairment of an available-for-sale financial asset leads to recycling (reclassification to profit or loss, under IFRSs) of the cumulative loss that has been recognized in other comprehensive income, even though the asset has not been derecognized.[536] Under IFRSs, the amount that was recycled also included any portion that was attributable to foreign currency that, depending on whether or not the asset was monetary or nonmonetary, had previously been recognized in other comprehensive income (see Section 7.14.2 previously).[537]

---

[529] *IAS 21, ¶¶ 23(b)-(c); IAS 39, ¶ E.3.4 (amended by IFRS 9).*

[530] *FASB ASC 320-10-35-1 (FASB Statement No. 115, ¶ 13); FASB ASC 815-20-35-6, 815-20-25-37 (FASB Statement No. 133, ¶¶ 23, 38); IAS 39, ¶ 89(b) (amended by IFRS 9).*

[531] *IAS 39, ¶¶ 55 (amended by IFRS 9), 90 (amended by IFRS 9).*

[532] *FASB ASC 815-25-50-1 (FASB Statement No. 133, ¶ 45(a)).*

[533] *FASB Statement No. 161, ¶ 3.*

[534] *IFRS 7, ¶ 24.*

[535] *IAS 39, ¶¶ 95(a), E.3.3 (amended by IFRS 9); IAS 21, ¶ 27.*

[536] *IAS 39, ¶¶ 67, IG E.4.9 (deleted by IFRS 9).*

[537] *IAS 39, ¶ E.4.9 (deleted by IFRS 9).*

> **Comment:** Under both U.S. GAAP and IFRSs prior to IFRS 9, a decrease in fair value that is not impairment (or other-than-temporary impairment, under U.S. GAAP) does not determine a reclassification adjustment,[538] but would be accounted for in other comprehensive income as would any other remeasurement to fair value of an available-for-sale financial asset. The determination of when a decrease in fair value is impairment falls outside the scope of this Book.

While U.S. GAAP does not permit a reversal of impairment until the available-for-sale investment is liquidated,[539] IAS 39 followed an approach that is similar to the reversal only for an available-for-sale debt instrument, but not for an available-for-sale equity instrument. In the latter case, any subsequent increase in fair value had to be recognized directly in other comprehensive income and not through profit or loss, because it was not deemed to be a reversal. The reason given was that distinguishing between impairment, reversal, and other increases in value was difficult, impractical, and somewhat arbitrary.[540] Reversal of an impairment of an available-for-sale equity instrument was also prohibited in interim reporting, even if a smaller loss or none would have been recognized had an impairment assessment been made only at a subsequent reporting period date. The IFRIC acknowledged that this prohibition created a conflict with IAS 34 that requires year-to-date measures in interim financial statements.[541] Instead, reversal of an impairment loss of an investment in an associate follows the rules of IAS 36, which permits the reversal of impairment losses for assets other than goodwill, to the extent that the recoverable amount of the investment subsequently increases.[542]

A reversal of an impairment of an available-for-sale debt instrument in profit or loss (in line with other situations under IFRSs, such as inventories, loans and receivables, held-to-maturity assets, or debt instruments) was permitted only to the extent that the increase in fair value was objectively due to an event that was subsequent to the impairment recognition.[543]

> **Comment:** The mechanism of reversal of impairment for tangible and intangible assets carried at revaluation model under IAS 16 and IAS 38 differs (see Section 7.16.3 later).

On April 2009, the FASB issued FSP FAS 115-2 and FAS 124-2.[544] In the context of the financial markets crisis, it follows the Emergency Economic Stabilization Act and the SEC study on mark-to-market accounting in late 2008.[545] Under the FSP, when an entity has concluded that other-than-temporary impairment has occurred for an available-for-sale or

---

[538] *FASB ASC 320-10-35-18 (FASB Statement No. 115, ¶ 16); IAS 39, ¶ E.4.10.*
[539] *FASB Statement No. 115, ¶ 16.*
[540] *IAS 39, ¶¶ IN22 (deleted by IFRS 9), 69 (deleted by IFRS 9), BC125 (deleted by IFRS 9), BC130 (deleted by IFRS 9), BC221.*
[541] *IFRIC Interpretation No. 10,* Interim Financial Reporting and Impairment, *¶¶ 8 (amended by IFRS 9), BC3, BC9 (amended by IFRS 9).*
[542] Improvements to IFRSs, *Part I, Amendments to IAS 28 (May 2008).*
[543] *IAS 39, ¶¶ 70 (deleted by IFRS 9), BC128 (deleted by IFRS 9).*
[544] *FSP FAS 115-2 and FAS 124-2, ¶¶ 18, 20–22, 28–33, 35–37.*
[545] *United States Securities and Exchange Commission, Office of the Chief Accountant, Division of Corporate Finance,* Report and Recommendations Pursuant to Section 133 of the Emergency Economic Stabilization Act of 2008: Study on Mark-To-Market Accounting *(December 2008).*

held-to-maturity debt security because the entity has the intent to sell the debt security or there is available evidence to assess that more likely than not it will be required to sell the debt security before the recovery of its amortized cost basis, it must recognize the other-than-temporary impairment (i.e., the entire difference between the investment's amortized cost basis and its fair value at the balance sheet date) in earnings. When neither of these two conditions is met, if a credit loss (i.e., the difference between the present value of the cash flows expected to be collected and the amortized cost basis) exists, other-than-temporary impairment has also occurred. In such a case the entity must recognize the amount of the total other-than-temporary impairment related to the credit loss in earnings, while the amount of the total other-than-temporary impairment related to all other factors in other comprehensive income, net of applicable taxes. The previous amortized cost basis of the investment less the other-than-temporary impairment recognized in earnings becomes its new basis. That new basis is adjusted for accretion and amortization but cannot be written up for subsequent recoveries in fair value. Subsequent changes (different from additional other-than-temporary impairments) in fair value of an available-for-sale security will affect other comprehensive income. The statement that reports the components of accumulated other comprehensive income (i.e., the statement of financial position, the statement of changes in equity – see Section 7.9.1 previously) must separately disclose the amounts related to held-to-maturity and available-for-sale securities for which a portion of the other-than-temporary impairment has been recognized in earnings. The statement of earnings (i.e., the income statement or the statement of income and comprehensive income) must show the current period net impairment loss recognized in earnings as the difference between total other-than-temporary impairment loss and the portion recognized in other comprehensive income. These formats of presentation also apply to equity available-for-sale securities. The FSP integrates some of the disclosures required by Topic 320 (FASB Statement No. 115) and introduces new ones, including a tabular rollforward of the credit losses recognized in earnings. The FSP is effective for interim and annual periods ending after June 15, 2009. It applies to existing and new investments held as of the beginning of the interim period in which it is adopted. Restatement of comparative information is not mandated.

On March 20, 2009 the IASB published a request for views on FASB Proposed FSP No. FAS 157-e, Determining Whether a Market is Not Active and a Transaction is Not Distressed (then FSP FAS 157-4, Determining Fair Value When the Volume and Level of Activity for the Asset or Liability Have Significantly Decreased and Identifying Transactions That Are Not Orderly), and Proposed FSP No. FAS 115-a, FAS 124-a, and EITF 99-20-b, Recognition and Presentation of Other-Than-Temporary Impairments (then FSP FAS 115-2 and FAS 124-2 and FSP EITF 99-20-1).[546] On April 24, 2009 the IASB announced a detailed six-month timetable for publishing a proposed replacement of IAS 39. In particular, the IASB did not give an immediate response to the new requirements about impairment, in order to avoid piecemeal changes in a field where U.S. GAAP and IFRS approaches and models differ. The IASB decided to reconsider impairment requirements as part of the comprehensive revision of IAS 39.[547] As a further step, in November 2009 the IASB issued IFRS 9.

---

[546] *IASB*, Request for Views on Proposed FASB Amendments on Fair Value Measurement and Proposed FASB Amendments to Impairment Requirements for Certain Investments in Debt and Equity Securities *(March 2009)*.

[547] *IASB*, IASB sets out timetable for IAS 39 replacement and its conclusions on FASB FSPs*, (April 24, 2009) (last visited April 29, 2009) www.iasb.org*.

7.14.5 Acquisition of Control

If a company that holds an available-for-sale equity investment subsequently obtains control of this investee (i.e., a business combination achieved in stages), the accumulated other comprehensive income is reclassified into profit or loss as if it were a disposal of the previously held equity interest. This is because, although the investment is not sold, on consolidation the investment account is derecognized from the consolidated financial statements, as happens when an available-for-sale security is derecognized.[548] Of course, IFRS 9 does not contemplate this situation for available-for-sale financial assets any longer.

The acquirer must disclose the amounts reclassified, and in which line item of the statement of comprehensive income the gain or loss is recognized.[549]

7.15 CASH FLOW HEDGES

7.15.1 Impact on Other Comprehensive Income

This Section treats cash flow hedges to the extent of the topic of other comprehensive income.

Both Topic 815 (FASB Statement No. 133) and IAS 39 recognize the effective portion of the gain or loss on the hedging instrument in a cash flow hedge in other comprehensive income, while the ineffective portion is recognized in profit or loss (under U.S. GAAP, earnings). The amount recognized in accumulated other comprehensive income is limited to the lesser, from inception of the hedge, of the cumulative gain or loss on the hedging instrument (minus the excluded portion and the already recycled amounts, under U.S. GAAP) or the cumulative change in expected future cash flows on the hedged transaction (under U.S. GAAP, the portion of the cumulative gain or loss on the hedging instrument necessary to offset the cumulative change in expected future cash flows on the hedged transaction, less the already recycled amounts). In this calculation U.S. GAAP excludes previous effectiveness assessment periods in which hedge accounting has not been applied because it is not permitted based on retrospective evaluation. Under IAS 39, any portion of gains or losses on the hedging instrument that is excluded from the assessment of hedge effectiveness is recognized following the general rule for recognition of financial instruments (therefore depending on the type of hedged item), while this recognition is in earnings under U.S. GAAP.[550]

Accumulated other comprehensive income with respect to the cash flow hedge is reclassified into profit or loss (recycled into earnings, under U.S. GAAP) in the period(s) when the hedged forecast transaction occurs (under U.S. GAAP) or when the transaction cash flows affect profit or loss (under U.S. GAAP, the transaction affects earnings), or when the asset acquired or the liability assumed affects profit or loss (under U.S. GAAP, earnings) if the transaction results in the acquisition of an asset or the incurring of a liability, or when the forecast transaction is no longer expected (under U.S. GAAP, probable) to occur (with certain exceptions, under U.S. GAAP). Expiration or sale of the hedging instrument, revocation of the designation, the fact

---

[548] *FASB ASC 805-10-25-10 (FASB Statement No. 141(R), ¶ 48); FASB Statement No. 141(R), ¶ B388; IFRS 3, ¶¶ 42 (amended by IFRS 9), BC389, DO11.*

[549] *IFRS 3, ¶ B64(p).*

[550] *FASB ASC 815-20-35-1, 815-30-35-3 (FASB Statement No. 133, ¶ 30, as amended by Accounting Standards Update No. 2010-08, Technical Corrections to Various Topics, ¶ 45); IAS 39, ¶¶ 95, 96.*

that a hedge may no longer meet the hedge accounting criteria or, under IFRSs, the fact that the forecasted transaction may no longer be highly probable do not trigger a reclassification adjustment. In addition a loss must be immediately recycled to the extent of the cumulative gain in other comprehensive income that is not expected to be recovered.[551] Under U.S. GAAP, an impairment or recovery for the related asset determines the recycling of a net loss or net gain.[552]

Under IFRSs, the same recognition exceptions to foreign exchange gains and losses as for a monetary item that is designated as a hedging instrument in a hedge of a net investment in a foreign operation (see Section 7.13 previously) also apply when a monetary item is designated as a hedging instrument in cash flow hedge.[553]

Contrary to IAS 39, Subtopic 815-30 (FASB Statement No. 133) requires a separate presentation of the net gain or loss on derivative instruments designated and qualifying as cash flow hedging instruments within other comprehensive income. The statement of financial position or the statement of changes in equity or the notes where the components of accumulated other comprehensive income are disclosed under Topic 220 (FASB Statement No. 130) must also include the beginning and ending accumulated derivative gain or loss, the net gain or loss that arises in the period, and respective net reclassification adjustments.[554]

Topic 815 (FASB Statement No. 133) requires the disclosure, among others things, of the ineffective portion recognized in earnings, the excluded portion of the net gain or loss of a derivative hedging instrument that is recognized in earnings and the line items where it is reported, a list of which transactions or events would trigger recycling, the estimated net amount that is expected to be recycled in the next 12 months, and the amount that has been recycled because of the probability that the forecasted transaction would not occur.[555] Section 7.13 previously explains additional disclosure requirements introduced by FASB Statement No. 161. Among other disclosures, IFRS 7 requires information on the amount recognized in other comprehensive income during the period, reclassification adjustments of the period, with statement of comprehensive income line-item detail, the ineffective portion, in what period the cash flows are expected to occur, and when they are expected to affect profit or loss.[556]

An IFRS first-time adopter that under previous GAAP had deferred gains and losses in a cash flow hedge of a forecast transaction must recognize them in other comprehensive income, if at the date of transition to IFRSs the hedged forecast transaction is still expected to occur, even though not highly probable. Any net cumulative gain or loss that had been reclassified to equity on initial application of IAS 39 remains in equity until reclassified under cash flow hedge accounting.[557]

---

[551] *FASB ASC 815-30-35-38 to FASB ASC 815-30-35-41, 815-30-40-1, 815-30-40-2, 815-30-40-4, 815-30-40-5 (FASB Statement No. 133, ¶¶ 31, 32, 33); IAS 39, ¶¶ 97-101; Improvements to IFRSs, Amendments to IAS 39, ¶¶ 97, 100 (April 2009).*

[552] *FASB ASC 815-30-35-43 (FASB Statement No. 133, ¶ 35).*

[553] *IAS 39, ¶ AG83 (amended by IFRS 9).*

[554] *FASB ASC 815-30-45-1, 815-30-50-2 (FASB Statement No. 133, ¶¶ 46, 47).*

[555] *FASB Statement No. 133, ¶¶ 44C(b), 45(b).*

[556] *IFRS 7, ¶¶ 23, 24(b).*

[557] *IFRS 1, ¶ IG60B.*

Different views for presentation of cash flow hedging were proposed in the *Financial Statement Presentation Project*. One approach is to relate gains and losses on cash flow hedges to the section, category, or subcategory of the statement of comprehensive income that corresponds to the asset or liability that originates the cash flows to hedge or to the section, category, or subcategory that will be affected by the forecast transaction when it occurs.[558] The Discussion Paper and the Staff Draft of the *Financial Statement Presentation Project* have selected this approach.[559] Based on an opposite approach, the hedging instrument would be in the section of the statement of financial position that corresponds to the classification of gains or losses in the statement of comprehensive income.[560] Another option discussed was to present separate categories relating to both the operating and financing sections in the statement of comprehensive income.[561] The IASB and the FASB *Financial Instruments Project* will pursue a review of hedge accounting.

7.15.2 Basis Adjustment

Basis adjustment is an accounting policy that a company reporting under IFRSs may elect, provided it applies it consistently to all eligible cash flow hedges. In a cash flow hedge of a forecast transaction (such as an anticipated transaction arising from the purchase of an asset or the issuing of a liability), "basis adjustment" refers to the inclusion of the cumulative gain or loss, that is recognized in other comprehensive income to the extent the hedge is effective, into the initial cost or other carrying amount of a nonfinancial asset or nonfinancial liability once the hedged transaction takes place. Basis adjustment may also occur when a forecasted transaction becomes a firm commitment for which fair value hedge accounting is applied. The adjustment in the basis of the asset or liability will subsequently hit profit or loss, for example in the form of interest income or expense, depreciation, cost of sale (if the asset is inventory), or gain or loss on disposal.[562] U.S. GAAP does not permit basis adjustment.

Worksheet 71 compares this situation under IFRSs with the ordinary recycling with U.S. GAAP, and illustrates the pros and cons of basis adjustment.

Comment: Technically, basis adjustment relates to cash flow hedge accounting. However, under both U.S. GAAP and IFRSs, a fair value hedge results in a similar effect as basis adjustment from the perspective of a hedged asset, in the sense that the gain or loss on the hedged item attributable to the hedged risk is included in the carrying amount of the hedged item (adjustment of the basis). Contrary to a cash flow hedge, however, the gain or loss is currently recognized in profit or loss. A fair value hedge of a firm commitment also results in the recognition of an asset or liability that includes the adjustment for the cumulative gain or loss attributable to the hedged risk.[563]

---

[558] IASB, *Financial Statement Presentation Project, Agenda Paper 9A*, Implications of Scope Change, ¶ 14 (June 19, 2008) www.iasb.org (last visited July 28, 2008).

[559] *Discussion Paper*, Preliminary Views on Financial Statement Presentation, ¶ 3.39 (October 2008); *FASB and IASB*, Staff Draft of an Exposure Draft on Financial Statement Presentation, ¶¶ 103, 104 (July 2010).

[560] IASB, *Financial Statement Presentation Project, Agenda Paper 15A*, Other Comprehensive Income, ¶ 26 (December 14, 2006).

[561] *IASB Update, July 2002*.

[562] *IAS 39, ¶¶ 98-99*

[563] *FASB ASC 815-10-05-4 (FASB Statement No. 133, ¶ 4); IAS 39, ¶¶ 93, BC158.*

Conversely, when the asset or liability that arises from a forecast transaction is financial, both U.S. GAAP and IFRSs require that cumulative other comprehensive income remain in equity and a reclassification adjustment be made in the same period or periods in which the hedged forecast cash flows hit profit or loss (IFRSs) or the hedged forecast transaction affects earnings (U.S. GAAP).[564]

7.16   REVALUATION MODEL

7.16.1   Revaluation Surplus

Under APB 6[565] property, plant and equipment, except as a result of a quasi-reorganization (Section 6.5.3 previously), cannot be written up by an entity to reflect appraisal, market, or current values above cost, although this pronouncement leaves room for a possible exemption for foreign operations in serious inflation or currency devaluation economies. ATB 1 reserved a specific caption in stockholders' equity to revaluation of fixed assets, i.e., "excess of appraised or fair value of fixed assets over cost" or "appreciation of fixed assets."[566] Conversely, as an accounting policy under IAS 16, property, plant, and equipment may be measured, subsequently to their initial recognition, using the revaluation model. In order to apply the revaluation model, the fair value of an item of property, plant, and equipment must be reliably measurable. The revalued amount of a property, plant, and equipment is the fair value at date of measurement less any subsequent accumulated depreciation and impairment. A company that chooses the revaluation model must apply it simultaneously, not selectively, to the entire class of property, plant, or equipment to which that asset belongs. However, the revaluation of each class may be completed on a rolling basis, provided all the class is revalued within a short period of time and the amounts are kept updated. Revaluation must occur regularly enough so that carrying amounts are not materially different from the fair value at the reporting date. The frequency depends on the changes in fair value of the asset. The accumulated depreciation at the date of revaluation is either restated proportionately with the change in the gross carrying amount of the asset (the so-called "proportional method") or eliminated against the gross carrying amount of the asset so that the net amount is brought up to the revalued amount (the so-called "gross method").[567] The IFRS Interpretations Committee clarifies that under the proportionate restatement the adjustment to the gross amount may differ from the adjustment to accumulated depreciation to take a revision of residual value, useful life, or depreciation method into consideration.[568]

> **Comment:** Under both methods, revaluation surplus changes by the difference between revalued amount (i.e., the new carrying amount) and the previous net carrying amount, net of any applicable deferred tax. With the second method, however, accumulated depreciation is written back. This method follows a sort of "fresh-start" concept, whereby accumulated depreciation is reset as it were a new asset. Both methods affect the gross book value and accumulated depreciation. Conversely, IAS 16 does not contemplate "asymmetrical" methods found in certain local GAAP sometimes in connection with revaluation mandated or permitted pursuant to special laws, such as revaluing the gross book value only or reducing the accumulated depreciation only. In particular, the latter

[564] *FASB ASC 815-30-35-38, 815-30-35-39 (FASB Statement No. 133, ¶ 31); IAS 39, ¶ 97;* Improvements to IFRSs, Amendments to IAS 39, ¶¶ 97, 100 (April 2009).
[565] *APB 6, ¶ 17.*
[566] *Accounting Terminology Bulletin No. 1, ¶ 69.6.*
[567] *IAS 16, ¶¶ 29, 31, 34–36, 38.*
[568] *IFRIC Update, May 2011.*

> method would conceptually refer to a changed residual life as opposed to a revalued amount and it would be like retroactively restating equity, through other comprehensive income, for the cumulated depreciation that has reduced equity through a charge to net income (unlike U.S. GAAP, under IFRSs, this treatment would not even be permitted as a method of accounting for a change in remaining life). Worksheet 72 compares all these accounting methods.

Under IAS 38, with the same rules explained above, an entity may also apply the revaluation model to the subsequent measurement of recognized intangible assets, provided fair value can be determined by reference to an active market. However, if other intangible assets of a same class do not possess the characteristics for the application of the revaluation model, an asset belonging to that class must be carried at the cost model.[569] The revaluation model is also applicable to intangible assets with indefinite useful lives, in which case the revalued amount would not be diminished by the subsequent accumulated amortization.[570]

> **Comment:** IAS 38 acknowledges that such a market may be highly unlikely in practice. Frequency of transactions and availability of information must be such that prices provide sufficient evidence of fair value.[571] This, in addition to the other constraints mentioned, limits in effect the applicability of the revaluation model to intangible assets.

A revaluation surplus is recognized in other comprehensive income, unless it reverses a revaluation decrease of the same asset that has previously been recognized in profit or loss, in which case it affects profit or loss to that extent. In case of a revaluation decrease, any existing revaluation surplus credit balance referred to that asset is first reversed in other comprehensive income and any excess is expensed.[572]

> **Comment:** In other terms, all changes in fair value below depreciated or amortized historical cost are expensed as impairments and recognized in income as reversals of impairments, and all changes in fair value above depreciated or amortized historical cost are recognized in other comprehensive income as revaluation increases or decreases. This is different from the pattern used for reversal of impairment of available-for-sale financial assets (see Section 7.14.4 previously).

> **Comment:** Depreciation that is made before the end of the reporting period is computed on the latest revalued carrying amount over the remaining useful life and taking into consideration the latest updated residual value.

As explained in Section 6.4.10 previously, the revaluation model under IAS 16 and IAS 38 differs from the fair value model of investment property under IAS 40. Although both methods are based on fair value, the latter recognizes changes in fair value in profit or loss and not in other comprehensive income.

---

[569] *IAS 38, ¶ 75.*
[570] *IAS 38, ¶¶ BC73, BC76–BC77.*
[571] *IAS 38, ¶¶ 8, 78, 81, BCZ36(b).*
[572] *IAS 16, ¶¶ 39–40.*

> **Comment:** IFRSs present several models of recognition of changes in fair value: 1) full recognition in profit or loss, as in the case of investment property under IAS 40, biological assets under IAS 41, or the fair value option for financial instruments under IAS 39; 2) a quasi-full recognition in other comprehensive income, as in the case of available-for-sale debt instruments (apart from certain items, such as interest income or impairment, as explained in Section 7.14.1 previously); 3) increases in other comprehensive income, except for impairment, and decreases in profit or loss, as in the case of available-for-sale equity instruments (see Section 7.14.4 previously); and 4) net increases over depreciated or amortized cost recognized in other comprehensive income and net decreases in profit or loss, as for the revaluation model under IAS 16 and IAS 38.

The Basis for Conclusions of IAS 40 contrasts different views on recognition of fair value changes. On one hand, recognition in profit or loss would make it unnecessary to determine when changes in fair values are required to be recycled. It would overcome the accounting mismatch between items related to investment property that are recognized in the income statement, such as net rental income, maintenance expenses, and items that would be recognized in other comprehensive income, such as changes in fair values and depreciation. On the other hand, uncertainty, variability, and illiquidity of market value, although certain investment properties may be held for trading purposes, would support recognizing market value changes in other comprehensive income (see Section 7.4.3 previously). Also, market prices are outside of management control.[573] In addition, as net income does not reflect changes in the fair value of the debt arising from changes in interest rates, net income should not be affected by the impact of changes in interest rates in the fair value of the financed properties.[574]

IFRS 5 requires the inclusion of an adjustment to a noncurrent asset that loses its status as held for sale into continuing operations, although it does not mention separate presentation or disclosure. However, if the asset was carried at revaluation model before being classified as held for sale, the adjustment follows the rules of changes in revaluation surplus.[575]

Section 6.6.2 previously illustrates the accounting for a transfer from owner-occupied investment property carried at cost to investment property carried at the fair value model.

Section 6.6.1 previously explains the mechanism of transfer of revaluation surplus to retained earnings.

Section 7.17.1 and Section 7.17.3 later explain that on a whole disposal or a loss of control of a subsidiary, a whole disposal or a loss of significant influence over an associate, and a whole disposal or a loss of joint control over a jointly controlled entity accumulated other comprehensive income is reclassified to profit or loss. In these situations, accumulated revaluation surplus is transferred to retained earnings.

---

[573] *Performance Reporting Joint International Group (JIG) on Performance Reporting, European CFO Task Force, Presentations by Malcolm Cheetham (June 14–15, 2005) www.fasb.org (last visited June 21, 2007).*

[574] *IAS 40, ¶¶ BC63, BC65.*

[575] *IFRS 5, ¶ 28.*

> **Comment:** Section 7.6.3 previously explains the linkage between revaluation surplus and the concept of capital maintenance. This relationship is realized in part under IFRSs, but the standard does not make any explicit reference to capital maintenance.

For each class of assets, IFRSs require the disclosure of the beginning and ending revaluation surplus, its increases and decreases, and any restrictions on the distribution of the balance to shareholders. IFRSs require separate presentation in equity of cumulative revaluation surplus. In addition, an entity must inform about the effective date of the revaluation, the involvement of an independent valuer (IAS 16 only), the estimation methods and significant fair value assumptions, the use of observable prices in an active market, recent market transactions on arm's length terms or other valuation techniques (IAS 16 only, prior to IFRS 13), and the pro forma amount as if the cost model had been used. Entities must conform to the disclosures required by IFRS 13, as applicable.[576]

> **Comment:** With reference to the disclosure of the effects of the cost model, in the United Kingdom, FRS 3, *Reporting Financial Performance* requires, in case of material differences between the reported profit and the historical cost profit, a "note of historical cost profits and losses" to be placed immediately following the profit and loss account or the statement of total recognized gains and losses. This note must show how the reported profit on ordinary activities before taxation would change (usually increased) by adding back the impact of depreciation on asset revaluation and any excess gain (or shortage loss) on disposal that would have been realized in the absence of revaluation.

> **Comment:** With reference to the disclosure on restrictions on the distribution under IAS 16, Section 3.5.2 previously explains the concept of defense of capital in connection with revaluation or other equity reserves.

As an additional disclosure for intangible assets, a company must explain whether the revaluation model or the cost model is used for an intangible asset that is acquired by way of a government grant and initially recognized at fair value.[577]

For an item of property, plant, and equipment, or for an intangible asset that is eligible under the revaluation model or an investment property carried at cost model, an IFRS first-time adopter may elect to use the fair value at the date of transition to IFRSs as the deemed cost at that date. The first IFRS financial statements must disclose the aggregate fair values and the aggregate adjustments to the carrying amounts reported under previous GAAP for each applicable line item of the statement of financial position. A revaluation that is already available because it was made under previous GAAP qualifies, provided that at the date of valuation it was broadly comparable to fair value or reflected a measure of changing prices, such as changes in a general or specific price index, applied to cost or depreciated cost. An event-driven fair value measurement under previous GAAP, e.g., for an IPO or a privatization, also qualifies. These two situations would not give rise to a restatement at the date of transition, because this already applied under previous GAAP. Those accommodations are intended as a

---

[576] *IFRS 13, ¶ D57; IFRS 1, ¶ IG10; IAS 16, ¶¶ 39, 40, 73, 77; IAS 38, ¶¶ 85, 86.*
[577] *IAS 38, ¶ 122(c)(iii).*

cost-effective solution when the retrospective application of IFRSs would involve undue cost or effort in collecting, reconstructing, or estimating historical cost. A company, however, does not need to demonstrate such an undue cost or effort. The requirement to revalue the entire class to which the asset belongs does not apply, so as to avoid revaluing asset that would immediately be reduced as impaired. If an IFRS first-time adopter chooses the cost model as its subsequent accounting policy, the resulting adjustments affect the opening balance of retained earnings. If the entity chooses the revaluation model in IAS 16 for some or all eligible assets as its subsequent accounting policy, their cost or deemed cost at the transition date will be compared to their revalued carrying amount at the same date in order to determine the cumulative revaluation surplus. The resulting cumulative revaluation surplus at the transition date must be separately presented in equity.[578] The IASB recently extended the exemption to event-driven revaluations that occurred after the date of transition to IFRSs but no later than the period covered by an entity's first IFRS financial statements.[579]

Example: Government-owned enterprises in the People's Republic of China revalue property, plant, and equipment as part of a process of "corporatization" in contemplation of a public offering of securities. In this case, the SEC Staff did not consider this accommodation applicable, unless reliable historical cost records have never been maintained. In fact, those revalued amounts are established by government policy rather than being fair value based.[580]

Comment: An issue is how to treat revaluation of tangible assets that, depending on jurisdictions, might be permitted under previous GAAP. Questions concerning jurisdictional approaches have arisen as mentioned in Section 3.6.2 previously. Those equity reserves must be reversed if revaluation was not compliant with the criteria mentioned under IFRS 1.[581] Section 3.6.8 previously mentions the fact that under certain jurisdictions an equity reserve for deemed cost valuation has been imposed.

Example: In banking financial statements, Italy's Banca d'Italia requires the disclosure of revaluation reserves, which existed prior to the first-time adoption of IFRSs, in a note and in the statement of changes in equity.[582]

The SEC Staff clarified that, for a foreign private issuer, a revaluation surplus in accordance with IFRSs or other home country GAAP had to be maintained in the statement of other comprehensive income that is presented in Item 17 and Item 18 of Form 20-F.[583]

---

[578] *IFRS 1, ¶¶ 30, D5–D8, BC41–BC42, BC45, BC95, IG8–IG11, IG50, IG51.*

[579] *IFRS 1, ¶¶ 39E, D8, BC46A, BC46B, as amended by* Improvements to IFRSs *(May 2010).*

[580] *U.S. Securities and Exchange Commission,* International Reporting and Disclosure Issues in the Division of Corporate Finance, *Appendix A,* Country Specific Issues, *¶ 6 (November 1, 2004) (last visited April 26, 2006).*

[581] *For example, instructions by Italian OIC – Organismo Italiano di Contabilità,* Guida Operativa per la Transizione ai Principi Contabili Internazionali (IAS/IFRS) *(October 2005), ¶ 3.3.*

[582] *Banca d'Italia, Circolare No. 262,* I bilanci delle banche: schemi e regole di compilazione *(December 30, 2005), published in Supplemento ordinario n. 12 alla Gazzetta Ufficiale n. 11, Serie generale (January 14, 2006).*

[583] *U.S. Securities and Exchange Commission,* International Reporting and Disclosure Issues in the Division of Corporate Finance, *¶ VI.A (November 1, 2004) (last visited April 26, 2006).*

In the *Financial Statement Presentation Project*, revaluation surplus would be classified in the operating income category on the statement of comprehensive income or, less likely, in the investing category, although the other gains and losses section was proposed.[584] The Discussion Paper illustrates it as part of the other comprehensive income category with reference to the operating category.[585] The Staff Draft does not give examples of its classification.

7.16.2 Exchange Differences on Nonmonetary Items

Under IAS 21, exchange differences on a gain or loss on nonmonetary items follow the recognition rule of that gain or loss. They are recognized in other comprehensive income or in profit or loss depending on where that gain or loss has been recognized.

Example: A nonmonetary item that is denominated in a foreign currency and is measured at fair value, such as a tangible asset carried at revaluation model, is reported at subsequent reporting period dates by using the exchange rates at the date of valuation. In such a case, the resulting exchange difference that arises is recognized in other comprehensive income.[586]

Comment: There is no equivalent rule under U.S. GAAP.

7.16.3 Impairments of Fixed Assets Carried at Valuation

IFRSs define an impairment of an item of property, plant, and equipment or an intangible asset as the excess of its carrying amount over its recoverable amount, which is the higher of the asset's net selling price and its value in use.[587] IAS 36 establishes the accounting for an impairment loss.

Worksheet 38 shows the effects of a decrease in fair value of an item of property, plant, and equipment carried at the revaluation model.

Comment: Different concepts may interact in setting the accounting for a decrease in value. Firstly, a distinction may be attempted between a revaluation decrease (or a reversal of revaluation) versus a devaluation (or a downward revaluation) versus an impairment. A revaluation may also differ from a reversal of impairment or reversal of devaluation. Secondly, a decrease in value may be temporary or other-than-temporary. Thirdly, it may be due to changes in fair value or other determinants. Finally, it may relate to events that are prior to or subsequent to a previous increase in value. These points, as well as the evaluation of impairment and procedures for impairment testing, fall outside the scope of this Book.

---

[584] *Performance Reporting Joint International Group (JIG), Agenda Paper 2,* History of the Performance Reporting Project, ¶ 25, London (January 2005) www.fasb.org (last visited June 21, 2007); IASB, *Financial Statement Presentation Project, Agenda Paper 15A,* Other Comprehensive Income, ¶ 29 (December 14, 2006).

[585] *Discussion Paper,* Preliminary Views on Financial Statement Presentation, ¶ A8 (October 2008).

[586] *IAS 21, ¶¶ 23(c), 30–31.*

[587] *IAS 16, ¶ 6; IAS 38, ¶ 8; IAS 36, ¶ 59.*

A company accounts for an impairment loss of an asset carried at the revaluation model as a revaluation decrease (i.e., a decrease of the revaluation surplus for that asset to the extent that the impairment loss does not exceed the revaluation surplus for the same asset and as an expense for any excess). When an impairment loss is greater that the asset's carrying amount, a liability must be recognized if and only if required by another standard.[588]

> **Comment:** IAS 16 and IAS 38 deduct any cumulative impairment from the carrying amount of a tangible or intangible asset. To trace this, an impairment loss would be accounted for though an impairment account (an asset valuation account) which measures the accumulated impairment loss of that asset.

> **Comment:** In contrast to an impairment of an available-for-sale financial asset (see Section 7.14.4 previously) that determines a reclassification adjustment (the cumulative other comprehensive loss is removed and recognized in profit or loss even though the asset has not been derecognized), an impairment of a tangible or an intangible asset determines an offset between the revaluation surplus and the asset itself to the extent a revaluation surplus exists for that asset. Therefore, the reversal of an unrealized gain does not hit the income statement to the extent that the gain did not do so.

An impairment loss is recognized as a separate economic event from any compensation from third parties for items of property, plant, and equipment that were impaired, lost, or given up, or any subsequent purchase or construction of replacement assets. Either the income statement or a note must report the related amount that is included in profit or loss.[589] Similarly under U.S. GAAP, a gain or loss is recognized as a separate event in case of an involuntary conversion from nonmonetary to monetary assets, that is, a forced disposition of nonmonetary assets, due to casualty, theft, condemnation, or threat of condemnation.[590]

A reversal of an impairment loss of an asset carried at the revaluation model is recognized as income to the extent that an impairment loss on the same asset was previously expensed, and in other comprehensive income as an increase to revaluation surplus for that asset for any excess. A reversal is recognized to the extent that it does not increase the net carrying amount as if no impairment loss had been recognized.[591]

Therefore, under IFRSs, an impairment loss is treated in the same way as a reversal of revaluation increase (or revaluation decrease), as also is a reversal of impairment accounted for as a reversal of revaluation decrease (or a revaluation increase). This accounting treatment arises from the difficulty in distinguishing a downward revaluation versus impairment (reduction in service potential).[592] However, the fact of considering a material change in value taken individually or applied to the enterprise as a whole, impairment, or reversal of impairment as

[588] *IAS 36, ¶¶ 60, 62.*
[589] *IAS 16, ¶¶ 66, 74(d).*
[590] *FASB ASC 605-40-25-3 (FASB Interpretation No. 30,* Accounting for Involuntary Conversions of Nonmonetary Assets to Monetary Assets, *¶ 11).*
[591] *IAS 36, ¶¶ 117, 119–120.*
[592] *IAS 36, ¶ BCZ111.*

opposed to a revaluation or a reversal of a revaluation triggers the need for complying with IAS 36 disclosures which are more extensive than those required by IAS 16 and IAS 38.[593]

Comment: Worksheet 73 compares some pros and cons for recognition of a reversal of an impairment loss in other comprehensive income versus profit or loss.

Comment: Under U.S. GAAP, there is no comparable provision for reversal of an impairment loss, as neither revaluation of tangible assets nor reversal of an impairment loss is permitted.

For each class of tangible and intangible assets, disclosures required by IFRSs include, among other things, separate information on the amount recognized and reversed during the period in profit or loss and directly in equity, respectively. The beginning and ending balances of accumulated impairment may be aggregated with accumulated depreciation.[594] Such disclosures may be given within the reconciliation of the carrying amount of the asset classes. In addition, a company that applies segment reporting must give reconciliation of impairment losses to each reportable segment under IFRS 8. An entity must also disclose the detail of impairment and reversal of impairment in profit or loss and in other comprehensive income during the period for each reportable segment under IFRS 8 (if that entity reports segment information). For each impairment or reversal that is individually material, an entity must explain the respective events and circumstances, the items or cash-generating unit involved, the respective amounts (by class of assets, if referred to a cash-generating unit) and the reportable primary segments under IFRS 8, any change of and reason for changing the way of aggregating assets of the cash-generating unit, and certain information on the determination of the recoverable amount. If impairment losses or reversal are material only in aggregate, an entity must describe the main classes of assets affected and the respective events and circumstances.[595]

An IFRS first-time adopter accounts for reversal of an impairment loss under IAS 36 whether it was recognized under previous GAAP or on transition to IFRSs. It must provide IAS 36 disclosures for an impairment loss or a reversal recognized in its opening IFRS statement of financial position.[596]

7.16.4 Changes in an Existing Decommissioning Liability

Section 6.6.4 previously explains the accounting for a change in estimate of a decommissioning, restoration, or similar liability.

Any change in revaluation surplus arising from a change in the related decommissioning liability must be separately identified and disclosed on the face of the statement of comprehensive income (under the previous Revision of IAS 1, in the statement of changes in equity).[597]

---

[593] *IAS 36, ¶ BCZ112.*
[594] *IAS 16, ¶ 73; IAS 38, ¶ 118; IAS 36, ¶¶ 126, 128.*
[595] *IAS 36, ¶¶ 129–131.*
[596] *IFRS 1, ¶¶ 24(c), IG43.*
[597] *IFRIC 1, ¶¶ 6(d), BC29.*

7.16.5 Noncurrent Assets Ceased to be Classified as Held for Sale

Under IFRS 5, an entity discontinues the held for sale classification for a noncurrent asset that no longer meets the requirements for such a categorization. In such a case, it remeasures it at the lower of its recoverable amount or its carrying amount as if it had not been classified as held for sale. Such a redetermination affects revaluation surplus of assets that the company previously carried, and still carries at revaluation model.[598]

7.17 CONSOLIDATION, DECONSOLIDATION, AND CHANGE IN INTEREST IN AN INVESTMENT

Worksheet 74 summarizes the accounting for other comprehensive income as the result of a disposal of a subsidiary, an associate, or a joint venture, as well as for a loss of control (a loss of a controlling interest, under U.S. GAAP) of a subsidiary, a loss of significant influence of an associate, or a loss of joint control of a joint venture, or a partial disposal of those entities, both before and after the 2008 Revision of IAS 27, under IFRS 11 and the issuance of FASB Statement No. 160. Those topics are treated in this and the following Sections.

7.17.1 Disposal or Loss of Control of a Subsidiary

With the 2008 amendments of IAS 27 and FASB Statement No. 160, effective, respectively, for fiscal years beginning on or after July 1, 2009 and for fiscal years and interim periods within those fiscal years beginning on or after December 15, 2008, a disposal or a loss of control of a subsidiary (whether the result of a change in ownership or other circumstances) is considered a significant economic event that triggers the reclassification into profit or loss of any amounts accumulated in other comprehensive income with respect to that subsidiary, even if the entity retains an interest in the former subsidiary or the former subsidiary becomes an associate or a jointly controlled entity. The consolidated financial statements take account of the reclassification adjustment of any accumulated other comprehensive income related to the subsidiary's assets or liabilities as if the parent had made a direct disposal of those assets or liabilities. This is because the parent no longer controls the subsidiary's individual assets and liabilities and the parent–subsidiary relationship ceases to exist. As a loss of control causes deconsolidation, at that date, any noncontrolling interests in a partially-owned former subsidiary are derecognized, including their share of accumulated other comprehensive income, which is, however, not reclassified to profit or loss. As those amendments apply prospectively both for an entity that already reports under IFRSs and an IFRS first-time adopter, a loss of control that occurred before the effective date of the amendments or the date of transition to IFRSs does not give rise to a restatement. However, an IFRS first-time adopter that elects to apply IFRS 3 retrospectively to past business combinations must apply those amendments to IAS 27 from the same date.[599] A recent Accounting Standards Update clarifies that under U.S. GAAP, unlike IFRSs, deconsolidation due to a loss of control is limited to a subsidiary or a group of assets that are a business or nonprofit activity, excluding

---

[598] *IFRS 5, ¶¶ 26–28.*

[599] *FASB ASC 810-10-40-4, 810-10-40-5 (ARB 51, ¶¶ 35, 36, as amended by FASB Statement No. 160); FASB Statement No. 160, ¶¶ B53, B55; 36(a); IFRS 10, ¶¶ B98, B99; IAS 27 (2010), ¶¶ 34(b), 34(e), 35 (as amended by IFRS 9), 45(c), BC54, BC55, BC56; IFRS 1, ¶ B7.*

a transaction that is in substance a sale of real estate or conveyance of oil and gas mineral rights, or subsidiaries that are not businesses or nonprofit activities if the substance of the transaction is not addressed by other standards.[600] Deconsolidation may also result from a transfer of an interest in a subsidiary (under the Accounting Standard Update, if that is a business or nonprofit activity) to an equity-method investee or to a joint venture investee or in exchange for a joint venture interest or to an entity in exchange for a noncontrolling interest in that purchasing entity. The Accounting Standard Update expands this treatment to a transfer of a group of assets that constitute a business or nonprofit activity, excluding a transaction that is in substance a sale of real estate or conveyance of oil and gas mineral rights.[601] Conversely, the IFRS Interpretations Committee acknowledged the existence of a conflict between full gain or loss recognition under IAS 27 and partial recognition under SIC-13 in the case of a contribution of an interest in a subsidiary to a jointly controlled entity or an associate against a noncontrolling interest, when this transaction results in a loss of control of the subsidiary. Although IFRS 11 reproposes the provisions of SIC-13 with reference to a transaction with a joint operation, the 2011 Revision of IAS 28 limits the exception to the recognition of gains and losses to the case of a lack of commercial substance.[602]

Section 7.10.5 previously explains the treatment of exchange differences on a loss of control of a subsidiary that includes a net investment in a foreign operation. Section 7.13 previously mentions the recycling of the effective portion of a hedge of a net investment in a foreign operation in conjunction with the "disposal" event.

Section 8.2.17.4 later mentions the indefinite reversal exemption from recognizing deferred tax on undistributed earnings of subsidiaries, associates, branches, and joint ventures. Under the Exposure Draft on income tax, a loss of control of an exempted foreign subsidiary would trigger the loss of its exempt status.[603]

Prior to the 2008 Revision of IAS 27 and to FASB Statement No. 160, disposal or a loss of control of a subsidiary, a loss of significant influence of an associate, or a loss of joint control of a jointly controlled entity under IAS 31 caused deconsolidation or discontinuation of the equity method, or of the equity method or proportionate consolidation under IAS 31, respectively. From that moment the investment was accounted for based on its new status. However, both IFRSs and U.S. GAAP provided no explicit guidance on recycling in such situations.[604]

---

[600] *FASB ASC 810-10-40-3A (Accounting Standards Update No. 2010-02,* Accounting and Reporting for Decreases in Ownership of a Subsidiary – a Scope Clarification, *¶ 3); EITF Issue No. 08-10,* Selected Statement 160 Implementation Questions, *¶ 5.*

[601] *FASB ASC 845-10-30-25 (EITF Issue No. 08-10,* Selected Statement 160 Implementation Questions, *¶ 6; Accounting Standards Update No. 2010-02,* Accounting and Reporting for Decreases in Ownership of a Subsidiary – a Scope Clarification, *¶ 13).*

[602] *IFRS 10, ¶ B98; IFRS 11, ¶ B34; IAS 28 (2010), ¶¶ 30, BC32–BC37; IAS 27 (2010), ¶ 34; SIC-13,* Jointly Controlled Entities – Non-Monetary Contributions by Venturers, *¶ 5; IFRIC Update, May 2011.*

[603] *Exposure Draft,* Income Tax, *¶ B8 (March 2009).*

[604] *FASB ASC 323-10-35-35, 323-10-35-36 (APB 18, ¶¶ 19(f), 19(l)); IAS 27 (2010), ¶¶ IN9, 21; IAS 28 (2010), ¶¶ IN10, 10; IAS 31, ¶ IN8.*

IAS 34, as amended by the 2008 Revision of IFRS 3, requires the disclosure of the effects of changes in the interim period due to obtaining or losing control of subsidiaries and long-term investments.[605]

Effectively for annual periods beginning on or after July 1, 2009, a commitment to a sale plan involving loss of control of a subsidiary triggers the classification of all the assets and liabilities of that subsidiary as held for sale (not simply the portion expected to be disposed of), if the IFRS 5 criteria for such classification are met. The parent company must disclose the information required for discontinued operations.[606]

> **Comment:** Therefore, consolidated financial statements must separately present accumulated other comprehensive income of the subsidiary (see Section 7.17.5 later).

The accounting for loss of control does not apply to nonreciprocal transfers to owners, including a spin off, to which APB 29 applies. The IASB also excluded these topics from the scope of the *Business Combinations Project*.[607]

> **Comment:** However, the distribution of a business (e.g., in a spin off) to an entity's owners acting in their capacity of owners may be within the scope of IFRIC 17, provided certain other situations exist. Upon declaration, the dividend payable is measured at the fair value of the net assets to be distributed and any subsequent adjustment of the carrying amount of the dividend payable before settlement affects equity. Any difference between the (net) assets carrying amount and the carrying amount of the dividend payable (i.e., adjusted to the fair value of the net assets to be distributed) upon settlement of the dividend payable must be recognized in profit or loss.[608]

The *Financial Statement Presentation Project* posed the issue of the financial statements classification of a loss of control or changes in the interests of a subsidiary or in a jointly controlled entity to which proportionate consolidation applies (prior to IFRS 11) and whether they meet the definition of a basket transaction (see Section 7.10.9 previously) or not because they are considered an equity transaction.[609]

7.17.2   Changes in a Parent's Interest in a Subsidiary

Under the 2008 amendments to IAS 27 and Subtopic 810-10 (FASB Statement No. 160), a change in a parent's ownership interest in a subsidiary that does not result in a loss of control (also called "partial disposal" in case of a decrease in the controlling interest, especially with

---

[605]   *IAS 34, as amended by IFRS 3, ¶ 16(i).*

[606]   *IFRS 5, as amended by* IFRS Improvements, *¶¶ 8A, 36A (May 2008).*

[607]   *FASB ASC 810-10-40-5 (ARB 51, ¶ 36, as amended by FASB Statement No. 160); IAS 27 (2010), ¶ BC57.*

[608]   *IFRIC 17, ¶¶ 10, 11-14, BC14, BC27, BC57.*

[609]   *IASB, Financial Statement Presentation Project, Agenda Paper 3A,* Basket Transactions and Foreign Currency Translation Adjustments, *¶ 25 (June 19, 2007) www.iasb.org (last visited June 21, 2007).*

reference to a net investment in a foreign operation[610]) is accounted for as an equity transaction with owners in their capacity as owners. This is in line with considering noncontrolling interests a separate component of equity (see Section 4.3.2 previously). This is also because a change in ownership interest simply changes the controlling share of net income but does not determine a change in control, which would require revising the business combination accounting. Such an event triggers an adjustment between the carrying amounts of the controlling and noncontrolling interests. Any difference between the fair value of the consideration paid or received for such a transaction and the above adjustment of noncontrolling interests, directly affects controlling interest in equity. The proportionate share of accumulated other comprehensive income that is disposed of must be reallocated from the controlling to the noncontrolling interest.[611] Section 4.14.10 previously treats certain aspects related to this topic. Section 7.9.7 previously explains that in consolidated financial statements noncontrolling interest must reflect the noncontrolling interest's share of (changes in) other comprehensive income arising from available-for-sale investments of a less-than-wholly-owned subsidiary. Unlike IFRSs, under a recent Accounting Standard Update this accounting for a decrease in the parent's ownership interest as an equity transaction would apply only to subsidiaries that are businesses or nonprofit activities, excluding a transaction that is in substance a sale of real estate or a conveyance of oil and gas mineral rights, or subsidiaries that are not businesses or nonprofit activities if the substance of the transaction is not addressed by other standards.[612]

Comment: Therefore, a purchase of an additional interest in a controlled subsidiary at a consideration paid in excess of book value determines a loss recognized in equity attributable to the controlling interest. Subtopic 810 (FASB Statement No. 160) explains that additional paid-in capital is reduced by the excess amount paid. In addition, the reallocation of other comprehensive income is accounted for as an increase in the controlling interest's proportionate share of other comprehensive income counterbalanced by a decrease in additional paid-in capital.[613]

IFRIC 17 confirms that an entity's distribution of some of its ownership interests in a subsidiary to the entity's owners acting in their quality as owners, where there is no loss of control of that subsidiary, is out of the scope of this interpretation and must be accounted for under IAS 27.[614]

Section 7.10.5 previously explains the treatment of exchange differences on a partial disposal of a subsidiary that includes a net investment in a foreign operation. Section 7.13 previously explains the accounting for the effective portion of a hedge of a net investment in a foreign operation in conjunction with a partial disposal of such a subsidiary.

IFRSs and U.S. GAAP, and recently Regulation S-X, converged to require a specific schedule in a note to the consolidated financial statements about the effects on the equity of the

---

[610]   *IAS 21, ¶ 48D.*

[611]   *FASB ASC 810-10-45-23 (ARB 51, ¶ 33, as amended by FASB Statement No. 160); FASB Statement No. 160, ¶ B44; IAS 27 (2010), ¶¶ 30, 31, BC42, BC46, BC47.*

[612]   *FASB ASC 810-10-45-21A (Accounting Standards Update No. 2010-02,* Accounting and Reporting for Decreases in Ownership of a Subsidiary – a Scope Clarification, *¶ 5).*

[613]   *FASB ASC 810-10-45-24 (ARB 51, ¶ 34, as amended by FASB Statement No. 160).*

[614]   *IFRIC 17, ¶ 7.*

owners of the parent of transactions with noncontrolling interests that do not result in a loss of control.[615]

A change in ownership interests in a subsidiary after control is obtained, that occurred before the effective date of the amendments or the date of transition to IFRSs, does not give rise to a restatement. However, an IFRS first-time adopter that elects to apply IFRS 3 retrospectively to past business combinations must apply the amendments to IAS 27 from the same date.[616]

Prior to the 2008 Revision of IAS 27, under IAS 21 and IAS 39, a partial disposal determined a proportionate recycling of the cumulative exchange difference from translation adjustment for the parent's portion. In that context, Section 4.14.10 previously and Section 7.10.5 previously explain how such a partial disposal was treated under U.S. GAAP prior to FASB Statement No. 160.

7.17.3 Loss of Significant Influence of an Associate and Loss of Joint Control of a Joint Venture

By analogy with the loss of control of a subsidiary, under IAS 28 and IAS 31 as amended by the 2008 Revision of IAS 27, effectively for annual periods beginning on or after July 1, 2009 a loss of significant influence over an associate or a loss of joint control over a jointly controlled entity also determines a reclassification adjustment, even if the investor or venturer retains an interest in the former associate or jointly controlled entity.[617]

> **Comment:** This applies in consolidated financial statements and in the financial statements of an investor that has no subsidiaries or joint ventures (otherwise the equity method cannot be used).

The 2011 Revision of IAS 28 confirms these effects resulting from an investment ceasing to be an associate or joint venture. No remeasurement of the retained interest occurs when an investment in an associate becomes an investment in a joint venture and vice versa. The new standard in any event requires the equity method.[618] IFRS 11 amends IAS 21 to redefine a loss of joint control, when significant influence is maintained, as a partial disposal and not as a disposal, hence requiring the recycling of only the parent's proportionate share of exchange differences accumulated in other comprehensive income.[619]

The FASB considered this topic to be outside of the scope of the *Business Combinations Project*.[620] EITF Issue No. 08-6 clarifies that a share issuance by an equity-method investee is equivalent to a partial disposal of the investment by the investor.[621] Under U.S. GAAP,

---

[615] *IAS 27 (2010), ¶¶ 41(e), BC70; Regulation S-X, ¶ 210.3-04, as amended by* FASB Accounting Standadrds Update No. 2010-21, Accounting for Technical Amendments to Various SEC Rules and Schedules, Amendments to SEC Paragraphs Pursuant to Release No. 33-9026: Technical Amendments to Rules, Forms, Schedules and Codification of Financial Reporting Policies.

[616] *IAS 27 (2010), ¶ 45(b); IFRS 1, ¶ B7.*

[617] *IAS 28 (2010), ¶ 19A; IAS 31, ¶ 45B; IAS 27 (2010), ¶ BC64.*

[618] *IAS 28 (2010), ¶ 9, 22–24.*

[619] *IFRS 11, ¶¶ D34, BCA5; IASB Update, March 3, 2010.*

[620] *IAS 27 (2010), ¶ BC64.*

[621] *EITF Issue No. 08-6,* Equity Method Investment Accounting Considerations, *¶ 9.*

a change in an investor's interest in an equity-method investee with no loss of significant influence, even when due to a capital transaction by the investee, determines a change in the investor's investment account on the statement of financial position, counterbalanced by a change in the investor's proportionate share in accumulated other comprehensive income of the investee within equity. The investor displays its proportionate share in accumulated other comprehensive income of the investee separately or combined with its own other comprehensive income items in the statement where it presents other comprehensive income (see Section 7.9.1 previously). This treatment applies at the date the significant influence is lost. Net income is not impacted, except for any excess of other comprehensive income over the investment account.[622]

Section 7.10.5 previously explains the treatment of exchange differences on a disposal of an associate or joint arrangement that includes a net investment in a foreign operation. Section 7.13 previously explains the accounting for the effective portion of a hedge of a net investment in a foreign operation in conjunction with the disposal of an associate or jointly controlled entity.

An Exposure Draft proposed to extend the classification as held for sale to all the assets and liabilities of an interest in an associate or jointly controlled entity when the entity is committed to a sale plan involving loss of significant influence or loss of joint control, respectively. Later, the IASB removed this proposal from the Annual Improvements process. IAS 28 Revised 2011 permits the classification of a portion of an investment in an associate or joint venture as held for sale if its disposal meets the requirements in IFRS 5. However, even if a company classifies a portion of an interest in an associate or joint venture as held for sale based on IFRS 5, the equity method applies to the retained interest that does not meet the IFRS 5 criteria, to the extent that the entity maintains significant influence or joint control.[623]

7.17.4 Changes in an Interest in an Associate or a Joint Venture

The 2008 amendments of IAS 28 and IAS 31 provide specific guidance for the accounting for a reduction in an investor's interest in an associate or in a venturer's interest in a jointly controlled entity with no loss in significant influence or no loss in joint control, respectively. This determines a reclassification adjustment for the investor's share of the accumulated other comprehensive income that the investee would have reclassified to profit or loss in case of disposal of its assets or liabilities related to that other comprehensive income. The 2011 Revision of IAS 28 confirms these provisions.[624] The 2008 Revision of IAS 27 amends the provisions of IAS 21 relating to when such entities include a net investment in a foreign operation.[625] In this case, a reclassification adjustment of the cumulative translation adjustment to profit or loss exists only for the investor's or venturer's proportionate interest.

---

[622] *FASB ASC 323-10-35-18 (FASB Statement No. 130, ¶ 121); FASB ASC 323-10-35-39 (FASB Staff Position APB 18-1,* Accounting by an Investor for Its Proportionate Share of Accumulated Other Comprehensive Income of an Investee Accounted for under the Equity Method in Accordance with APB Opinion No. 18 upon a Loss of Significant Influence, *¶ 4).*

[623] *IAS 28 (2011), ¶¶ 20, BC23–BC27, BC56(c); Exposure Draft,* Improvements to IFRSs, Proposed Amendments to IFRS 5 Non-current Assets Held for Sale and Discontinued Operations, *¶ 8A (August 2009); IASB Update, March 2010.*

[624] *IAS 28 (2011), ¶ 25 ; IAS 28 (2010), ¶ 19A; IAS 31, ¶ 45B.*

[625] *IAS 21, ¶ 48D.*

This topic is outside of the scope of the FASB's *Business Combinations Project*. Section 7.10.5 previously explains the treatment under U.S. GAAP with reference to a net investment in a foreign operation.

7.17.5   Classification as Noncurrent Assets Held for Sale

Under IFRS 5, a subsidiary that is acquired and held exclusively with a view to resale would ordinarily meet the criteria to be classified as held for sale. IFRS 5 requires that cumulative income or expenses that relate to a noncurrent asset (or disposal group) classified as held for sale and that is recognized in other comprehensive income must be separately presented in the equity section of the consolidated statement of financial position.[626] On the contrary, in such a case Subtopic 360-10 (FASB Statement No. 144) does not mandate specific presentation in equity.

Under both IFRSs and U.S. GAAP, as illustrated in Section 7.10.5 previously, the accumulated foreign currency translation adjustment related to the translation of a foreign operation with a functional currency that is different from the foreign currency of the consolidating entity or from the presentation currency of the group (functional currency of the reporting entity only, under U.S. GAAP) is reclassified to profit or loss when the held for sale subsidiary that included the net investment is sold.[627] The same treatment applies, in general, in case of disposal or loss of control of a subsidiary, even though it is classified as held for sale (see Section 7.17.1 previously).

Effectively for annual periods beginning on or after July 1, 2009 a commitment to a sale plan involving loss of control of a subsidiary triggers the classification of all the assets and liabilities of that subsidiary as held for sale (not just the portion expected to be disposed of), provided the IFRS 5 criteria for such classification are met. The parent company must disclose the information required for discontinued operations.[628]

7.17.6   Associate's Other Comprehensive Income

As explained in Section 6.4.6 previously, under IAS 28 an investor accounts for an associate's income or expense that is recognized in other comprehensive income by adjusting the investment account with a counterbalancing entry in other comprehensive income, after any adjustments to conform to the investor's accounting policies.[629]

> **Comment:** In this way, the investment in an associate also reflects the investor's proportionate interest in the changes in fair value of the associate's items of property, plant, and equipment or other items for which fair value changes are recognized in other comprehensive income.

A similar treatment applies under U.S. GAAP, both for changes in an equity-method investee's other comprehensive income arising from unrealized holding gains or losses on its investments

---

[626]   *IFRS 5, ¶ 38.*

[627]   *IFRS 5, ¶¶ BC37–BC38.*

[628]   *IFRS 5, as amended by* IFRS Improvements *(May 2008), ¶¶ 8A, 36A.*

[629]   *IAS 28 (2010), ¶¶ 11, 27, 39.*

in debt and equity securities (e.g., available-for-sale securities),[630] and in general for an equity-method investee's adjustments in other comprehensive income.[631]

Under IAS 1, the investor separately presents in the statement of comprehensive income its proportionate share of an equity-method investee's other comprehensive income.[632] Similar treatment applies to a venturer's proportionate share of the other comprehensive income of a joint-controlled entity accounted for at equity method.[633] An enterprise has an election under Subtopic 232-10 (FASB Statement No. 130) either to separately display the adjustments in its other comprehensive income relating to its proportionate share of an equity-method investee's adjustments in other comprehensive income or to aggregate it with its own items, as per the available display alternatives under the standard. However, from the effective date of ASU 2011-05, the statement of changes in equity is no longer an option to present the details of other comprehensive income.[634]

Section 7.11.2 previously explains the accounting in the investor's other comprehensive income for long-term interests that are in substance part of the net investment in an equity-method investment.

IFRS 12, effective for annual periods beginning on or after January 1, 2013, if not earlier applied, requires the disclosure, among other points as part of summarized financial information, of other comprehensive income and comprehensive income of material associates and joint ventures, and the aggregate amount for individually immaterial associates and individually immaterial joint ventures.[635]

7.17.7 Companies that have All Shares Subject to Mandatory Redemption

An entity that has no equity instruments outstanding and, under FASB Statement No. 150, presents all shares as subject to mandatory redemption in the liability section of the statement of financial position must disclose separately, contrary to IAS 32, the components of such instruments that would be par value, additional paid-in capital, retained earnings, accumulated other comprehensive income, had the instrument not been classified as a liability.[636]

7.18 PENSION ACCOUNTING

7.18.1 Impact of Pension Accounting on Other Comprehensive Income

FASB Statement No. 158 resulted from a project that the FASB added to its agenda in November 2005 to comprehensively reconsider the accounting for postretirement benefits. Under Topic 715 (FASB Statement No. 158), a business entity that sponsors a single-employer defined benefit plan must recognize the funded status of the benefit plan (i.e., the difference between

---

[630] *FASB Technical Bulletin No. 79-19,* Investor's Accounting for Unrealized Losses on Marketable Securities Owned by an Equity Method Investee, ¶ 6.

[631] *FASB ASC 323-10-35-18 (FASB Statement No. 130, ¶ 121).*

[632] *IAS 1, ¶ 82(g) and (h).*

[633] *IASB Update, page 7 (June 2007).*

[634] *FASB ASC 323-10-45-3 (FASB Statement No. 130, ¶¶ 121–122).*

[635] *IFRS 12,* Disclosure of Interests in Other Entities, ¶¶ B12, B16.

[636] *FASB Statement No. 150, ¶¶ 28, B60.*

the fair value of plan assets and the benefit obligation) on the statement of financial position. The provisions of the standard for measuring plan assets and defined benefit obligations at year-end of the fiscal year of adoption are effective for fiscal years ending after December 15, 2008. The provisions of the standard for recognition of the funded status of a benefit plan are effective as of the end of the fiscal years ending after December 15, 2006 for an employer with publicly traded equity securities, and after June 15, 2007 for others. Section 6.4.17 previously explains the transitional provisions of the standard that impact on retained earnings and current earnings. In addition, on the first application of the standard, an employer must adjust the net-of-tax balance of accumulated other comprehensive income, as of the date of adoption of the recognition and disclosure provisions of the standard, by the unrecognized components mentioned above that are not included in net periodic benefit cost at that date.[637]

The employer must then recognize in other comprehensive income the gains or losses and prior service costs or credits that arise during the period, which are unrecognized under FASB Statement No. 87 and FASB Statement No. 106. A reclassification adjustment arises with the subsequent recognition of those items as components of net periodic benefit cost over the average remaining service period, as well as of the transition assets or obligations that are still outstanding from the initial application of FASB Statement No. 87 and FASB Statement No. 106.[638]

Comment: IAS 19 (2007) recognizes an expense for past service costs over the vesting period, unlike U.S. GAAP, or immediately to the extent that the related benefits are already vested. Under IAS 19 (2011), past service costs follow immediate recognition.[639]

Separately for pension plans and other postretirement benefit plans, the notes must disclose (including comparative information) other comprehensive income arising in the period and reclassification adjustments, detailed into net gain or loss and net prior service cost or credit, broken down into current-period amounts, reclassification adjustment, and reclassification adjustment of the net transition asset or obligation. The disclosure must include the breakdown of accumulated other comprehensive income by net gain or loss, net prior service cost or credit, and net transition asset or obligation. With the same detail, the note must give information on the amount of accumulated other comprehensive income expected to be recycled over the next fiscal year.[640] However, FASB Statement No. 130 as amended by FASB Statement No. 158 shows those current period items of other comprehensive income and reclassification adjustments on the face of the statement of comprehensive income and those items of accumulated other comprehensive income on the face of the statement of changes in equity.[641] For not-for-profit organizations, FASB Statement No. 158 permits separate line(s) or note disclosure of other comprehensive income and reclassification adjustments for pension plans and

---

[637] *FASB ASC 715-20-65-1, 715-20-55-5 (FASB Statement No. 158, ¶¶ 12, 13, 15, A2); FASB Statement No. 158, ¶ 16(a).*

[638] *FASB Statement No. 158, ¶ 4.*

[639] *IAS 19 (2011), ¶ 102; IAS 19 (2007), ¶ 96.*

[640] *FASB ASC 715-20-50-1 (FASB Statement No. 132R, ¶¶ 5.i, 5.ii, 5.s., 8.h, 8.hh, 8.n, 10A, 10B, 10C, 10D, C3; FASB Statement No. 158, ¶¶ 7.a, 7.b, 7.d), as amended by ASU 2010-06,* Fair Value Measurements and Disclosures (Topic 820) – Improving Disclosures about Fair Value Measurements, *¶ 10.*

[641] *FASB Statement No. 130, ¶ 131, as amended by FASB Statement No. 158.*

other postretirement benefit plans. In the former case, they must show items within changes in unrestricted net assets, and health care organizations outside a performance indicator of operations.[642] An SEC registrant must consider whether disclosure of the expected periods of recycling of items recognized in other comprehensive income is necessary in Management Discussion and Analysis.[643]

Entities must separately disclose the effects of the initial application of the measurement provisions of FASB Statement No. 158 on accumulated other comprehensive income either in the statement of changes in equity or in the notes.[644]

7.18.2 Minimum Pension Liability

FASB Statement No. 158 eliminates the need for a minimum pension liability, and therefore the previous requirement under FASB Statement No. 87 to recognize it. It also removes the related disclosures under FASB Statement No. 132(R) and amended other pronouncements on the topic.[645]

FASB Statement No. 87 for pension plans, but not FASB Statement No. 106 for postretirement plans other than pensions, required recognition of a minimum pension liability. As noted in Section 7.8.3 previously there was no recycling for minimum additional liability, as its determination was considered not to be practical.[646]

Minimum pension liability is equal to the unfunded accumulated pension benefit obligation, which results from the deferred recognition of items such as actuarial losses, prior service cost, and transition amounts. It is computed as the accumulated benefit obligation (ABO), which is the value of accrued benefits if the entity discontinued the plan without considering an allowance for future salary increases, minus the fair value of plan assets, minus any recognized accrued (or plus prepaid) pension costs.[647] The additional pension liability account is an adjustment of the accrued/prepaid pension costs to arrive at the unfunded accumulated pension benefit obligation. For presentation purposes, it is combined with accrued/prepaid pension costs in order to reflect the minimum pension liability.[648] Its counterbalance is an intangible asset equal to the amount of unrecognized prior service cost and a loss (net of tax benefits) in other comprehensive income for any excess.[649]

Minimum pension liability limits the unrecognized net liability in the statement of financial position. However, IAS 19 rejects such a liability, as it does not consider the ABO to reflect the going concern assumption. It does not meet the definition of a liability under the IASB

---

[642] *FASB Statement No. 158, ¶¶ 8.c, 8.d, 10.a, 10.b; AICPA Audit and Accounting Guide,* Health Care Organizations.

[643] *Accounting Staff Members in the Division of Corporation Finance U.S. Securities and Exchange Commission, Washington, D.C.,* Current Accounting and Disclosure Issues in the Division of Corporation Finance, *¶ II.J (November 30, 2006) www.sec.gov (last visited February 5, 2007).*

[644] *FASB ASC 715-20-65-1 (FASB Statement No. 158, ¶ 21); FASB Statement No. 158, ¶ B60.*

[645] *FASB Statement No. 158, ¶¶ B36, B61, C2(k), (l), (p), E1(e), (n).*

[646] *FASB ASC 220-10-45-17 (FASB Statement No. 130, ¶ 20); FASB Statement No. 130, ¶¶ 92, 94.*

[647] *FASB ASC 715-30-25-2 (FASB Statement No. 87, ¶ 36).*

[648] *FASB Statement No. 87, ¶ Appendix B, Illustration 5 (superseded).*

[649] *FASB ASC 715-30-25-3 (FASB Statement No. 87, ¶ 37).*

Framework, because some of the underlying circumstances would not be past events but possibly contingent liabilities to be disclosed as nonadjusting events under IAS 10.[650] In fact, it is intended to recognize any additional obligation in excess of the recognized liability that would arise from a discontinuation of the plan as of the reporting period date, or if employees with vested benefits left the company as of the reporting period date and therefore their fully vested benefits, or even larger amount because of the shorter discounting period, exceeded the unrecognized deferred amounts.[651]

During the *Financial Statement Presentation Project*, some commenters considered the minimum pension liability adjustment and the funded status of a defined benefit plan to be outside the control of management.[652]

7.18.3   The IAS 19 Model for Remeasurements of Net Defined Benefit Liability or Asset

The IASB added a project to its agenda in July 2006 for a review of postemployment benefit accounting. The project initially proposed possible alternatives for recognition and presentation of gains and losses into profit or loss; or the cost of service into profit or loss and other items into other comprehensive income; or the cost of service, interest costs, and imputed income on assets into profit or loss and all remeasurements into other comprehensive income.[653] Under the 2011 revision of IAS 19, effective for financial years beginning on or after January 1, 2013, other comprehensive income includes the remeasurements of the net defined benefit liability or assets (this does not apply to other long-term employee benefits). Such remeasurements include actuarial gains and losses. It also comprises any difference between actual return on plan assets and changes in the effect of the asset ceiling and the net interest cost on the net defined benefit liability or asset that is instead accounted for in the income statement. Conversely, unlike prior service costs under U.S. GAAP, remeasurements accounted for in other comprehensive income exclude past service costs. Therefore, under Revised IAS 19, the previous option to recognize actuarial gains and losses in other comprehensive income with immediate direct transfer to retained earnings is no longer valid. Furthermore, the previous option of faster recognition in profit or loss is no longer an option. Unlike U.S. GAAP, these remeasurements are not subject to reclassification adjustments. However, an entity may want to transfer this part of other comprehensive income to other components of equity, while, under the previous version of IAS 19, transfer to retained earnings was mandatory. An entity must explain the composition of the remeasurements component of other comprehensive income. A transition provision of the 2011 revision of IAS 19 exempts entities from retrospectively recasting the capitalization of employee benefit costs in tangible assets, inventories, or other assets before the beginning of the earliest period presented when adopting the amendments to IAS 19.[654] The 2011 revision of IAS 19 also eliminated the IFRS 1 accommodation for

---

[650]   *FASB Statement No. 87, ¶¶ 152, 153; IAS 19 (2011), ¶ BC105; IAS 19 (2007), ¶ BC65.*

[651]   *IAS 19 (2007), ¶ BC63.*

[652]   *Performance Reporting Joint International Group (JIG) on Performance Reporting, European CFO Task Force, Presentations by Malcolm Cheetham (June 14–15, 2005) www.fasb.org (last visited June 21, 2007).*

[653]   *IASB Insight, Q1/Q2, 2008.*

[654]   *IAS 19 (2011), ¶¶ IN6(i)(ii), 120(c), 122, 127, 141, 154, 172, BC65(c), B66(c), BC88, BC93, BC100, BCC276.*

defined benefit plans starting from when an IFRS first-time adopter applies the revised IAS 19, with retrospective application.[655]

During the *Financial Statement Presentation Project*, actuarial gains and losses have been considered candidates for inclusion in the "remeasurement" classification in the financial statements and pension service cost in the non-remeasurement classification. Actuarial gains and losses and prior service costs and credits would be classified in the operating income category or other gains and losses category. Pension obligations have also been proposed for the financing section. It has been noted that accounting for pensions and other postretirement benefits do not lend themselves to line-item cohesiveness.[656]

7.18.4 The Pre-2011 IAS 19 Model for Actuarial Gains and Losses and Adjustment for Asset Ceiling

Under both FASB Statement No. 87 and pre-2011 IAS 19, recognition of pension actuarial gains and losses may be faster than with the corridor approach, provided it is systematic, consistently applied over time, similarly to both gains and losses, and disclosed.[657] The recognition of actuarial gains and losses in full in profit or loss when they occur may be considered a special case of this faster recognition.

> **Comment:** This may have had a pervasive impact, for example for covenants or agreements that are linked to net income.

Effective for financial years beginning on or after January 1, 2013, with earlier application permitted, IAS 19 has retroactively banned the corridor approach.[658] Therefore, faster recognition is not an option any longer, because remeasurements of the net defined benefit liability or asset go to other comprehensive income and the immediate recognition is the rule for the other cost components.

IAS 19, for annual periods ending on or after December 16, 2004 and with retroactive application, adds an option for a company to entirely recognize in the period of occurrence actuarial gains and losses and any adjustments arising from the asset ceiling (which does not exist under U.S. GAAP) outside profit or loss (rephrased by the 2007 Revision of IAS 1 as in other comprehensive income). To make this election, an entity must apply this pattern to all

---

[655] *IAS 19 (2011), ¶¶ A1–A3, BC270.*

[656] *FASB/IASB Financial Statement Presentation Project, Agenda Paper 6C/FASB Memorandum 44C,* Measurement; OCI and Recycling; the Statement of Comprehensive Income, *¶ 29 (October 24, 2006) www.iasb.org (last visited June 21, 2007); FASB/IASB,* Summary of the September 15, 2006 Financial Statement Presentation Joint International Group Meeting, *¶¶ 7–8 (October 4, 2006); IASB, Financial Statement Presentation Project, Agenda Paper 15A,* Other Comprehensive Income, *¶¶ 10, 27 (December 14, 2006); FASB Memoranda No. 50A-D,* Financial Statement Presentation – Disaggregating Changes in Assets and Liabilities, Presentation of Other Comprehensive Income Items, and Cash Equivalents, *¶ 3 (March 21, 2007); Discussion Paper,* Preliminary Views on Financial Statement Presentation, *¶ 4.34 (October 2008); FASB and IASB,* Staff Draft of an Exposure Draft on Financial Statement Presentation, *¶ IG13 (July 2010).*

[657] *FASB ASC 715-30-35-25 (FASB Statement No. 87, ¶ 33); IAS 19 (2007), ¶ 93.*

[658] *IAS 19 (2011), ¶¶ 172, 173, BC67(a), BC70.*

of its defined benefit plans, and all of its actuarial gains and losses and any asset ceiling limit adjustments. Before the amendments made by the 2007 Revision of IAS 1, this election was done directly in the statement of recognized income and expense only, with the consequence that showing all items of income and expense that directly affected equity on the statement of changes in equity was no longer an option.[659]

> **Comment:** After the amendments made by the 2007 Revision of IAS 1, the statement of comprehensive income has a different meaning and is no longer a format that is alternative to the statement of changes in equity. Therefore, in this new meaning, the election translates into direct recognition in other comprehensive income in the statement of comprehensive income.[660]

> **Comment:** Under the unamended version of IAS 19, the election had the consequence of forcing a company to choose the statement of recognized income and expense and not the statement of changes in equity and eliminated the latter as a primary statement for all other income and expense items that were recognized directly to equity. That also might have impacted covenants or agreements that had been linked with financial statements. The new change may have a reverse impact. Under IAS 1, by definition, the statement of changes in equity must not show the items of other comprehensive income. Therefore, that prohibition is no longer necessary.

> **Example:** The SEC Staff, in its review of Form 20-F of a French foreign private issuer for the fiscal year ended December 31, 2005 containing financial statements prepared for the first time on the basis of IFRSs, challenged the presentation in the statement of changes in equity and not in the statement of recognized income and expense. The company had elected to recognize actuarial gains and losses outside profit and loss as permitted by IAS 19.[661]

An entity that makes this election must immediately transfer those gains or losses to retained earnings. Therefore there is no recycling.[662] Section 6.6.5 previously expands on the impact on retained earnings.

> **Comment:** Even if recognized in other comprehensive income, gains and losses are not subsequently reclassified in the statement of comprehensive income because they are immediately transferred to retained earnings.

> **Comment:** There is no comparable provision under U.S. GAAP. Under Topic 715 (FASB Statement No. 158), actuarial gains and losses that are initially recognized in other comprehensive income ultimately are recycled to earnings. This is a fundamental difference with the direct transfer to retained earnings under IAS 19 (2007).

---

[659] *IAS 19 (2007), ¶¶ 93A–93C.*

[660] *IAS 1, ¶ A16.*

[661] *Letter by the SEC, File No. 1-15248, Note 13 (September 25, 2006). Reply by the company (December 19, 2006) www.sec.gov/divisions/corpfin/ifrs_reviews (last visited January 7, 2008).*

[662] *IAS 19 (2007), ¶ 93D.*

The use of a statement of recognized income and expense and the prohibition of recycling were not necessarily an indication of the IASB considerations on reporting comprehensive income in general. The treatment used in IAS 19 (2007) was largely influenced by the UK standard FRS 17, *Retirement Benefits.*[663] The IASB considered that this method gave more transparent information than deferred recognition and emphasized those items as being items of income or expense. It was considered a temporary solution, given that immediate recognition in profit and loss was still judged premature.[664]

Comment: Most of the debate on pension accounting is related to alternative recognition methods. Deferred recognition has been the accounting model for pensions up to the 2011 revision of IAS 19. The election under the pre-2007 version of IAS 19 adopted a form of immediate recognition in "quasi-income," not net income but directly in equity. Pre-2011 IAS 19 uses a model that recognizes certain gains and losses in other comprehensive income but with immediate transfer to retained earnings. Topic 715 (FASB Statement No. 158) continues the past practice of delaying recognition of actuarial gains and losses as a component of net periodic benefit cost but it recognizes the entire funded status of a plan in other comprehensive income. Section 7.7.1 previously compares rationales for different recognition models.

According to a 2007 survey of European publicly listed and unlisted companies, 37% of preparers adopted immediate recognition of actuarial gains and losses. 74% of them recognized these in equity and the remainder in profit or loss. 44% of preparers used the corridor approach. The other companies (19%) did not have defined benefit plans.[665] A pan-European survey on IFRS 2006 financial statements found that 49% of the survey companies reported actuarial gains and losses in equity, 8% fully recognized them in profit or loss, 39% through the corridor method, and 4% did not disclose the method used.[666]

An IFRS first-time adopter may use an exemption to recognize in retained earnings all unrecognized cumulative actuarial gains and losses at the date of transition to IFRSs, even though, under the pre-2011 version of IAS 19, it will use the corridor method for later actuarial gains and losses.[667] The 2011 revision of IAS 19 deletes this accommodation.

An entity must disclose, in addition to the other information required for defined benefit plans, its accounting policy for recognizing actuarial gains and losses, the amount recognized in other comprehensive income for actuarial gains and losses and for the effect of the asset ceiling limit (prior to the 2011 revision of IAS 19), and the aggregate amount recognized in cumulative other comprehensive income.[668]

---

[663] *IAS 19 (2007), ¶ BC48F; IASB Update, September 2004.*

[664] *IAS 19 (2007), ¶¶ BC48G, BC48I, BC48K.*

[665] *The Institute of Chartered Accountants in England and Wales (ICAEW), 2007.* EU Implementation of IFRS and the Fair Value Directive, a Report for the European Commission, *¶¶ 15.1, 15.2. [On line] London: ICAEW. Available at www.icaew.com/ecifrsstudy (last visited July 31, 2010).*

[666] *Ineum Consulting, 2008.* Evaluation of the Application of IFRS in the 2006 Financial Statements of EU Companies, Report to the European Commission, *¶ 13.6. France: Ineum Consulting.*

[667] *IFRS 1, ¶ D10.*

[668] *IAS 19 (2007), ¶¶ 120A(a), 120A(h), 120A(i).*

> **Example:** The SEC Staff, in its review of Form 20-F of a French foreign private issuer for the fiscal year ended December 31, 2005 requested disclosures on accumulated other comprehensive income, as information on other comprehensive income of the period was not sufficient to comply with IAS 19. The company had elected to recognize actuarial gains and losses outside profit and loss as permitted by IAS 19.[669]

7.19   RECENT DEVELOPMENTS FOR FINANCIAL INSTRUMENTS

7.19.1   Investments in Equity Instruments Designated as at Fair Value Through Other Comprehensive Income

IFRS 9 on financial instruments amends the definition of other comprehensive income in IAS 1[670] to add a new category of other comprehensive income relating to investments in equity instruments that are not held for trading and that are not part of a hedging relationship. The Exposure Draft initially referred to these instruments as purchased for strategic purposes (as opposed to trading purposes or investments held for realizing dividends and capital gains), as generally purchased to create or preserve a long-term operating relationship with another entity, or to create other noncontractual benefits. However, the Exposure Draft proposed, and IFRS 9 confirms, that developing a notion of a strategic investment would not be operative. At initial recognition, entities would have an irrevocable election to present subsequent changes in the fair value of those equity instruments and any related foreign exchange gain or loss in other comprehensive income. This election is on an instrument-by-instrument basis. Unlike IFRS 9, the Exposure Draft included related dividends in other comprehensive income. This new class creates a category of instruments measured at fair value through (or in) other comprehensive income.[671]

> **Comment:** The rationale states some arguments similar to those discussed in Section 7.5 previously on the theory of performance and in Section 7.4.3 previously on differentiating the information value of fair value remeasurements. In fact, this classification is intended to separately report changes in fair value gains that may not be indicative of the performance of the entity and to highlight the implications of fair value changes for such equity instruments.[672]

> **Comment:** As part of its new framework, IFRS 9 eliminates the previous category of available-for-sale financial assets and introduces the new category of financial assets at fair value through other comprehensive income.

---

[669] *Letter by the SEC, File No. 1-15248, Note 35 (February 14, 2007) www.sec.gov/divisions/corpfin/ifrs_reviews (last visited January 7, 2008).*

[670] *IFRS 9 (November 2009), ¶ C12.*

[671] *IFRS 9 (October 2010), ¶¶ 5.7.5, 5.7.6, B5.7.1, B5.7.3; IFRS 9 (November 2009), ¶¶ 5.4.4, 5.4.5, B5.12, B5.14, BC86(a), BC86(c), BC118(f); Exposure Draft,* Financial Instruments: Classification and Measurement, *¶¶ IN14 Question 10, 5, 19, 21, 22, B26, B27, BC68, BC70, BC72 (July 2009).*

[672] *IFRS 9 (November 2009), ¶¶ BC83, BC84; Exposure Draft,* Financial Instruments: Classification and Measurement, *¶¶ BC68, BC69, BC71 (July 2009).*

This component of other comprehensive income would not be subject to reclassification to profit or loss and impairment requirements would not apply to those investments. However, reclassification from other comprehensive income to other components of equity would be permitted.[673] In consideration of the long-term duration of this type of investments, recycling would distort profit or loss. In addition, avoiding recycling was an expedient to bypass the issue of impairment for equity instruments,[674] an issue that had already proved to be critical for available-for-sale equity instruments.

> **Comment:** This approach where no recycling exists and classes of equity might be used to signal different "quality of equity" according to requirements of local jurisdictions can be seen as a particular application of the latest approach envisaged in Section 7.21 later on a comprehensive theory of equity and other comprehensive income.

IFRS 7, as amended, requires the disclosure of the carrying amount of such a category of equity instruments either in the statement of financial position or in the notes. In addition, an entity must disclose the type of investments, the reason for such a format of display, their ending fair values, recognized dividends on investments that are have been derecognized in the period and, separately, on those that are still held at the reporting date, any reclassification of other comprehensive income to other components of equity and related rationale, cumulative gain or loss on disposal, including the reasons for disposing of the investments and their fair value at that date. Either the statement of comprehensive income or the notes must disclose net gains or net losses on financial assets measured at fair value through other comprehensive income.[675]

At the date of its initial application, IFRS 9 permits the designation of an investment in an equity instrument as at fair value through other comprehensive income, to be assessed on the basis of the facts and circumstances that exist at that date. Retrospective application is required.[676]

On IFRS first-time adoption, any previously-existing cumulative gains or losses that under prior GAAP had been recognized outside profit or loss with respect to an equity instrument that on initial application of IFRS 9 is classified at fair value through other comprehensive income remain in a separate component of equity. Subsequent changes in other comprehensive income sum up in that component.[677]

An IFRS first-time adopter that uses such a designation under IFRS 9 must consider the facts and circumstances that exist at the transition date.[678]

---

[673] *IFRS 9 (October 2010), ¶ B5.7.1; IFRS 9 (November 2009), ¶¶ B5.12, BC86(b); Exposure Draft, Financial Instruments: Classification and Measurement, ¶ BC73 (July 2009).*

[674] *IASB News, March 16, 2010.* Chairman of the IASB Addresses ECOFIN Meeting. *IASB [Online] [Available at www.ifrs.org].*

[675] *IFRS 7, ¶¶ 8, 11A, 11B, 20(a)(viii) as amended by IFRS 9 (November 2009), ¶ C8.*

[676] *IFRS 9, ¶¶ 8.2.7, B8.1.*

[677] *IFRS 1, ¶ IG59 (as amended by IFRS 9).*

[678] *IFRS 1 (2003 and amended May 2008), ¶ 34F, as amended by IFRS 9; IFRS 1 (Revised November 2009), ¶ D19B, as amended by IFRS 9.*

7.19.2   Changes in Credit Risk of Certain Financial Liabilities

IFRS 9 (October 2010) introduces a new component of other comprehensive income for the portion of change in the fair value related to a change in the credit risk of a financial liability that is designated at fair value through profit or loss. There is no recycling for this component. The standard waives this treatment in the case where it would determine or increase an accounting mismatch in profit or loss.[679] IFRS 7 requires specific disclosures, including the accumulated change in fair value that is attributable to changes in the credit risk of those liabilities, any period transfer of accumulated other comprehensive income to other equity captions, and the realization of accumulated other comprehensive income through the derecognition of liabilities in the current period.[680]

> **Comment:** Accounting tells us that an increase in the credit risk of such a financial liability produces a counter-intuitive increase in equity, conservatively accounted for as other comprehensive income. Finance theory (Modigliani-Miller) tells us what the other part of the story might be. An increase of cost of debt reduces the value of debt. However, over a certain limit, this would also increase the required cost of equity, which would reduce the value of equity, therefore not affecting the value of the firm in efficient markets. However, financial reporting does not purport to measure the value of a firm.

7.19.3   The FASB's Proposed Model for Financial Instruments

The FASB has proposed a new approach for financial instruments. This is different from IFRS 9 in many aspects. As part of this model, an entity that holds a financial instrument for collection or payment of contractual cash flows would be required to present both amortized cost and a sort of reconciliation to fair value in the statement of financial position. Related interest income or expense, credit impairment, and realized gains and losses would be part of net income, while other qualifying changes in fair value would affect other comprehensive income.[681]

7.19.4   Proposed Fair Value Hedge Accounting

On December 9, 2010, the IASB published an Exposure Draft on hedge accounting. In particular, the statement of financial position would present the hedging gain or loss on the hedged item in a fair value hedge as a separate line, next to the related hedged asset or liability or the unrecognized firm commitment. Other comprehensive income would include both the hedging gain or loss on the hedged item and the change in the fair value of the hedging instrument, with a zero net effect. A transfer from other comprehensive income to profit or loss would highlight the ineffective portion. The hedging gain or loss on a hedged item that is a financial instrument carried at amortized cost would be amortized to profit or loss, while it would adjust the initial carrying amount of a nonfinancial asset or liability arising from a firm commitment. The company would have to disclose the change in the value of the hedged item, the amount of other comprehensive income relating to the hedging instrument, the hedge

---

[679] *IFRS 9 (October 2010), ¶¶ 5.7.1(c), 5.7.7, 5.7.8, B5.7.9.*

[680] *IFRS 7, ¶¶ 10, 11.*

[681] *FASB, Proposed Accounting Standards Update,* Accounting for Financial Instruments and Revisions to the Accounting for Derivative Instruments and Hedging Activities – Financial Instruments (Topic 825) and Derivatives and Hedging (Topic 815) *(May 2010).*

ineffectiveness, and its location in the statement of income. The statement of changes in equity or the notes would illustrate the changes in accumulated other comprehensive income.[682]

7.19.5   Proposed Accounting for Undesignated Time Value of an Option Contract

Under the Exposure Draft on hedge accounting, an entity that designates as a hedging instrument only the changes in the intrinsic value of an option contract would recognize the changes in the fair value of the undesignated time value of the option in other comprehensive income for the amount that relates to the hedged item. This treatment is different from the current classification of the time value portion as at fair value through profit or loss. The subsequent accounting varies depending on whether the option hedges a transaction related or a time period related hedged item. In the case of an option that hedges a transaction related hedged item, reclassification adjustments occur as the hedged expected future cash flows hit profit or loss. However, the entity would transfer accumulated other comprehensive income increases to the basis of a nonfinancial asset or liability or a fair value hedged firm commitment that arises from the hedged item. In the case of an option that hedges a time period related hedged item, recycling would apply over the term of the hedging relationship based on a rational method. The accumulated other comprehensive income and its recycling is computed by reference to the relationship between the actual time value and the part replicated by an option that would perfectly match the hedged item (the aligned time value). Discontinuation of hedge accounting would trigger immediate reclassification of the remaining amount of accumulated other comprehensive income.[683]

7.20   SHADOW ACCOUNTING

IFRS 4 permits insurers a change of accounting policies to use shadow accounting. This practice is permitted only when the measurement of an insurance liability (or related deferred acquisition costs and related intangible assets) is driven directly by asset values or realized gains and losses on assets held. In such a case, if the unrealized gains or losses of the asset are recognized in other comprehensive income, for example in revaluation surplus, the insurer may recognize the corresponding adjustments to the measurement of the insurer liability in other comprehensive income.[684]

According to a 2007 survey of European publicly listed and unlisted companies, 54% of sample insurance companies used shadow accounting as permitted by IFRS 4.[685]

7.21   TOWARDS A COMPREHENSIVE MODEL OF EQUITY AND OTHER COMPREHENSIVE INCOME

The previous Sections have illustrated different models of accounting for items of other comprehensive income and related issues. As shown, a conclusive theoretical and consistent implementation solution is still some time away. This Section presents a summary and a re-interpretation of alternative models that may result from the suggestions discussed in the

---

[682]   *Exposure Draft,* Hedge Accounting, ¶¶ *IN29, 26–28, 51, 52 (December 2010).*

[683]   *Exposure Draft,* Hedge Accounting, ¶¶ *IN33–IN35, 33, B68, B69 (December 2010).*

[684]   *IFRS 4, ¶¶ 30, BC152, IG6–IG10, BC181–BC184.*

[685]   *The Institute of Chartered Accountants in England and Wales (ICAEW), 2007.* EU Implementation of IFRS and the Fair Value Directive, a Report for the European Commission, ¶ *18.1. [Online] London: ICAEW. Available at www.icaew.com/ecifrsstudy (last visited July 31, 2010).*

Book, particularly with reference to the theories of other comprehensive income, retained earnings, and additional paid-in capital.

Comment: In effect, the issue of what should be intended as financial performance and what should be the level of quality of earnings that must be guaranteed by GAAP is part of the dispute on other comprehensive income. However, it is to be noted that the fact of being unrealized does not necessarily infer that a gain or a loss is of lower quality.[686] By looking at quality of earnings only, the debate focuses on the income statement or the statement of comprehensive income. Eventually, however, quality of earnings is translated into quality of equity. Different dimensions enter into the equation: achieving a high quality of information, maintaining the clean-surplus concept, having a clear definition of performance, getting to a definition of retained earnings, maintaining defense of capital legal frameworks in effect, and preserving independence from measurement and recognition models. The difficult is to find a conceptually rigorous and cost-effective way of balancing these different aspects.

Planning Point: A first approach (number 1) distinguishes between net income and comprehensive income. This is the traditional approach of recognizing other comprehensive income directly in equity but not in the income statement. U.S. GAAP currently adopts this approach. Items of other comprehensive income are somehow placed in a "waiting line" until they meet certain thresholds sufficiently for recognition as net income, in which case they are recycled through to the income statement. Such a "waiting line" consists in being part of equity, but not yet part of retained earnings. Eventually, net income accrues to retained earnings. Thus, equity comprises items that flow through and items that pass over the income statement. In a sense, accumulated other comprehensive income may be considered, although it is not necessarily, a "second-tier" equity, or a lesser "quality" component of equity.

A second approach (number 2) distinguishes net income from comprehensive income, by placing other comprehensive income in an "expanded" statement of performance. Possibly, a single statement of income exists. However, income has two (or three) levels or bottom lines, such as earnings, net income, and comprehensive income. Their meaning may be minimized by considering them simply as subtotals. Here there is no recycling, but a "quasi-recycling,"[687] which is simply a reclassification from one level to another. The model may be further complicated by reclassifying within or across subcategories of the statement, such as an operating section, a financing one, and other sections. There is still a "waiting line," but no recognition in equity without passing through such a statement of performance. In other terms, to the extent this categorization may represent a different "quality of earnings" it is directly highlighted in this statement. The display of different "qualities of equity" occurs only to the extent accumulated other comprehensive income is also reflected in equity. However, clean-surplus concept of income exists to the extent accumulated other comprehensive income is not presented as a component of equity.

A third model (number 3) is a compromise between the previous two. There are two statements of performance (i.e., an income statement and a statement of comprehensive income) so that providing information on the different qualities of earnings is achieved through double statements. IFRSs currently follow this approach. This model may be conceived as a variant of either the first or the second approach, depending on whether or not other comprehensive income is recognized directly in equity.

---

[686] *FASB Statement No. 157, ¶ C97.*
[687] *IASB Update, July 2002 uses the expression "quasi-recycling."*

A "disclosure-based" approach (number 4) consists in providing such information simply in the notes. Of course, note disclosures may also be an integral part of any of the other approaches. For example, Subtopic 820-10 (FASB Statement No. 157) requires a reconciliation of beginning and ending balances of recurring fair value measurements within Level 3 of the fair value hierarchy, that is, when unobservable inputs to valuation are used, in order to show the effect of those measurements on period earnings or changes in net assets, how much is due to changes in unrealized gains or losses of assets and liabilities outstanding at the reporting date, and in which items of the statement of income gains or losses are reported.[688]

As a further alternative (number 5), instead of recognizing items of comprehensive income and warranting them particular presentation formats, non-recognition (that is, setting more stringent recognition criteria) is another option that is currently followed by some local GAAP. This approach enforces a strict clean-surplus concept and a robust quality of earnings. It is the natural solution for countries where accounting standards have a strong legal derivation. However, this method follows a conservative income-and-expense view that on most occasions is not consistent with asset and liability recognition under a balance sheet orientation.

As a variant (number 6) to some of the approaches mentioned, a new element of the financial statements that is different from other comprehensive income may be used for capital maintenance adjustments only. Therefore there would be no recycling for these items. This approach appears to be rigorous in distinguishing items that currently are classified as other comprehensive income as such and as capital maintenance adjustments. The issue of recycling would conceptually be eliminated for those items that would result as capital maintenance adjustments, with no need for a transfer to retained earnings, as currently employed by the IFRS revaluation model and IAS 19 (2007). However, the extension of this no-recycling mechanism to other items of other comprehensive income that are not capital adjustments, as currently pursued by the IASB, is not based on any clear rationale.

Another approach (number 7) is the temporary equity versus permanent equity model under SEC rules. After all, this is also a way of disclosing two different "qualities" of equity, although most items that are recognized in temporary equity arise from capital transactions.

Another approach (number 8) is to report fair value adjustments and other items that are currently reported in other comprehensive income in a separate column in the statement of income. They would cross-cut all line items of the income statement, a fact that would immediately explain the composition of each item. Then, the total of this column is reported after net income to compute comprehensive income. This approach would eliminate the recycling of most of the other comprehensive items. UBS has proposed an example of this approach.[689]

Finally, certain jurisdictions, especially in continental Europe, have long been employing another method (number 9), which consists in appropriating retained earnings or creating special reserves within equity (as described in Chapter 3 previously) to the extent that certain items that are unrealized or are of a lesser "earnings quality" are recognized. This approach has several advantages. Firstly, the clean-surplus concept is maintained, as all items of income and expense enter into the computation of net income. Secondly, reserve accounting ensures disclosure of quality of equity and supports its preservation. In a sense, this is not new to IFRSs because, as illustrated in Section 3.2.2 previously, other comprehensive income is a component of equity reserves. Thirdly, a single concept of income exists, although possibly with subtotals. The peculiarity of this approach is that the income

---

[688] *FASB ASC 820-10-50-2 (FASB Statement No. 157, ¶ 32, as amended by ASU No. 2010-06 and ASU No. 2011-04).*

[689] *Cooper, S., April 16, 2007.* UBS Investment Research, Financial Reporting for Investors *www.ubs.com (last visited July 26, 2011).*

statement no longer needs an indicator other than net income (i.e., comprehensive income) nor is a statement of comprehensive income required. Furthermore, there is no recycling. If deemed necessary, reclassification on the face of the statement of income may be maintained. Instead of having other comprehensive income that recycles into net income which transfers to retained earnings, under this approach net income transfers to retained earnings, with a parallel process of appropriation and de-appropriation of retained earnings or reserves. Furthermore, as there is no other comprehensive income and no recycling, presentation becomes independent of measurement and recognition. Finally, in a certain sense, this approach would find a solution to the clean-surplus issue applied to additional paid-in capital (see Section 5.4 previously) and to retained earnings (see Section 6.10 previously). In fact, equity reserves would be created, increased, or reduced as a result of items of income and expenses that arise from nonowner transactions and that are recognized in the income statement. Such a mechanism would affect retained earnings, where effected through appropriations and reversals of appropriations of retained earnings, or special paid-in capital accounts. A consistent definition of retained earnings, still an undefined term as demonstrated in Section 6.1.2 previously, would determine whether these reserves should be intended as appropriations of retained earnings or paid-in capital accounts. Finally, and of utmost importance, defense of capital notions under the specific jurisdictions would be unaffected and most of the current conflicts with IFRSs that often lead to jurisdictional versions of IFRSs would be avoided.

Finally, the most complete model would probably arise from the combination of model numbers 2, 8, and model number 9. A statement of comprehensive income presents the advantages mentioned of having both a single concept of income and providing information on different qualities of earnings. On the other hand, appropriations and equity reserves convey information on different qualities of equity. This presentation format would be independent on the measurement bases and recognition criteria adopted. Presentation on the face of the statement of income and in the equity section of the statement of financial position represents the quality of earnings and equity irrespective of whether or not a single or multiple-base measurement model exists. A particular application similar to this approach is explained in Section 7.19 previously.

Worksheet 75 compares these approaches.

8 PRESENTATION OF TAXES ON EQUITY ITEMS

8.1 INTRAPERIOD TAX ALLOCATION TO EQUITY

8.1.1 Definition of Intraperiod Tax Allocation

Under Subtopic 740-20 (FASB Statement No. 109), as a general rule, the difference between total income tax expense or benefit and income tax calculated on income from continuing operations is allocated to all items other than continuing operations, such as discontinued operations, extraordinary items, cumulative effect of a change in accounting principle, other comprehensive income, prior period adjustments, and other items recognized directly in stockholders' equity. Intraperiod tax allocation is the U.S. GAAP term for this process of allocation.[1]

Comment: IFRSs do not use the expression "intraperiod tax allocation." However, as a matter of fact, IFRSs also apportion income tax to the different items of income and expenses.

Intraperiod tax allocation is one of the topics of the *Financial Statement Presentation Project*[2] as well as of the short-term convergence project on income tax. Opponents of intraperiod tax allocation claim that, by definition, any related procedure is arbitrary, even when the allocation rules are unambiguous, as may be the case under U.S. GAAP. Furthermore, on certain occasions it may be simpler not to trace backwards. The typical example is a change in valuation allowance related to a loss carryforward that arose in a previous period from losses recognized in different components of comprehensive income or equity.[3] This perspective views income taxes essentially as transactions with tax authorities that are separate from the underlying transactions. Income tax would be a sort of appropriation of income to tax authorities (see Section 3.5.3.3 previously). This view would be consistent with the arguments which the FASB is proposing as part of *Financial Instruments with Characteristics of Equity Project* – former *Financial Instruments: Liabilities and Equity Project* that equity issuance costs should be expensed because they are not transactions with owners (see Section 4.11 previously). Furthermore, as financing decisions and their related tax impact influence each other, disaggregation of pre-tax income would be consistent with finance theory, whereby

---

[1] *FASB ASC 740-20-45-2, 740-20-45-8, 740-20-45-12, 740-20-45-14 (FASB Statement No. 109, ¶¶ 35, 38).*

[2] *FASB, User Advisory Council, Minutes of Meeting, October 3, 2006, ¶¶ 37, 40, 41 (October 31, 2006); IASB Meeting, September 19, 2006, Agenda Paper 9,* Application of Working Principles, *¶¶ 44, 47, 53, 61 (September 2006) www.iasb.org (last visited June 21, 2007); FASB, FASB Memorandum No. 43,* Financial Statement Presentation – Application of Working Principles (continued), *¶ 14 (September 26, 2006) www.fasb.org (last visited June 21, 2007); IASB, Financial Statement Presentation Project, Agenda Paper 15A,* Other Comprehensive Income, *¶¶ 53, 55 (December 14, 2006); Agenda Paper 14,* Exposure Draft of Proposed Amendments to IAS 1 Presentation of Financial Statements – Comment Letter Analysis *(December 14, 2006), ¶ 87.*

[3] *Exposure Draft,* Income Tax, *¶ BC92–BC93 (March 2009).*

operating decisions are analyzed before their financing. A single picture of income tax would assist users in assessing the effectiveness of an entity's tax planning strategies. Furthermore, intraperiod tax allocation would be eliminated and income taxes would be included in income only. Finally, if income taxes are transactions with tax authorities (i.e., non-owners), they must not be recognized directly in equity but in comprehensive income. Taxes related to items of other comprehensive income would be considered to be a transaction separate from the original transaction that gives rise to other comprehensive income. Net-of-tax display of items of other comprehensive income would be eliminated.

> **Comment:** The *Financial Statement Presentation Project* raised the issue that the theory that income tax must be separate from the related transaction and deferred tax accounting may be inconsistent. Both IAS 12 and Topic 740 (FASB Statement No. 109) follow the balance sheet liability method. Based on deferred tax accounting, deferred tax liabilities and assets arise from temporary differences between tax and financial reporting bases of assets and liabilities. In contrast to income statement liability method and the deferred method that were used in the past, the balance sheet liability method of intraperiod tax allocation does not correlate deferred taxes to pretax accounting income or to the difference between net income for financial reporting and for tax reporting. As a consequence, presenting income tax in relation to the income statement sections or its line items would be inconsistent with that basic assumption of accounting for deferred tax. However, under the balance sheet liability method, not all deferred taxes may be associated to income statement items. In fact, unlike IAS 12, the Exposure Draft on income tax proposed a revised definition of temporary differences that included items originating other than from assets and liabilities, such as the carryforward of unused tax losses and of unused tax credits.[4] On the other hand, allocating deferred taxes to balance sheet categories or items would result in grossing up assets and liabilities, a method which was also eliminated by FASB Statement No. 109. There are other examples where accounting literature is contrary to the principle of "integral transactions," as was the case under IAS 23 prior to the March 2007 amendments for capitalization of interest expenses to a specific asset, a method that was not the benchmark treatment and whose justification required that strict rules be followed.

> **Comment:** This Chapter mentions the IASB's Exposure Draft on income taxes published in March 2009. However, in October 2009, the IASB decided not to go forward with the Exposure Draft and to re-introduce some of its proposals. It also resolved to address specific issues concerning income taxes in the short term and conduct a fundamental review with the FASB in a longer period.[5]
>
> In contrast, management's perspective generally tends to consider the effects of tax together with the transactions to which they relate. Even if arbitrary to some extent, the allocation process may be useful. This perspective views income tax as integral to the related transaction. Disclosure of the tax impact of each equity item provides more information, transparency on tax rates, and valuation allowances. The Discussion Paper concludes that intraperiod tax allocation assists users of financial statements in assessing future cash flow prospects and dynamics. However, the Boards did not support allocation to segments and categories within those sections, as this would make it more complex and arbitrary.[6] An intermediate view would allocate income tax only to significant items or to items where this apportionment is clearly more objective.

---

[4] *IAS 12, ¶ 5; Exposure Draft*, Income Tax, *¶¶ 1, Appendix A (March 2009).*
[5] *Amendments to IAS 12*, Deferred Tax: Recovery of Underlying Assets, *¶ BC3; IASB Update, November 2009; IASB Update, March 2010.*
[6] *Discussion Paper*, Preliminary Views on Financial Statement Presentation, *¶¶ 2.75, 3.55, 3.58, 3.60 (October 2008).*

There are several differences between the two bodies of standards on the topic of intraperiod tax allocation to equity. The following Sections explain these dissimilarities. As explained in Section 8.2.18 later, the Discussion Paper proposes to maintain the existing requirements for allocating and presenting income taxes in the statement of comprehensive income. However, as part of the *Income Tax Short-Term Convergence Project*, the IASB agreed to amend IAS 12 to adopt the intraperiod tax allocation requirements of Topic 740 (FASB Statement No. 109),[7] an approach that the Exposure Draft on income tax has subsequently proposed.

8.1.2 Initial Recognition Versus Backwards Tracing

Under Topic 740 (FASB Statement No. 109), income tax on income from continuing operations is computed on the pretax income or loss from continuing operations. However, income tax on income from continuing operations also includes the tax effect that arises from certain remeasurements due to current-year changes in deferred tax even if related to prior-year equity items. For example, under most circumstances this would be the case of the initial recognition of a deferred tax asset (i.e., reduction or elimination of the opening balance of the related valuation allowance) due to changes in circumstances that cause new judgment concerning its future realization. However, in certain cases, the tax effects of a change in the valuation allowance on deferred tax assets (including the initial recognition of an operating loss carryforward) are always allocated to other comprehensive income or other components of equity as the items to which they refer to, as explained in Section 8.2.1 and Section 8.2.2 later. Therefore, for those special cases, U.S. GAAP applies a concept of backwards tracing. Other changes in the balance of the valuation allowance follow the intraperiod tax allocation general rules. A change in tax laws or rates, a change in tax status (see Section 8.2.4 later), or the payment of certain tax-deductible dividends (see Section 8.2.17.3 later)[8] are other occurrences where the tax effect is part of income tax on income from continuing operations.

By contrast, under IAS 12 current and deferred income taxes follow a single rule, that is, the recognition of tax effects in or outside profit or loss (i.e., in other comprehensive income or directly in equity) mirrors the location of the related underlying transaction or event, irrespective of whether recognized in the current or in a previous period.[9]

Comment: This is called "backwards tracing." In general, Topic 740 (FASB Statement No. 109) does not adopt backwards tracing. By mandating income recognition as a general rule for those changes, U.S. GAAP avoids the implementation issues of backwards tracing and the need for tracking the history of previous transactions from the start. This eliminates the practical issues of computing the tax effects on prior year's transactions when there are many different types of temporary differences, incremental tax rates, and operating loss and credit carryforwards and carrybacks.[10]

An option discussed in the *Financial Statement Presentation Project* is to present income taxes in a single section in the statement of comprehensive income. This would eliminate backwards

---

[7]   IASB, *Project Update*, Short-Term Convergence: Income Taxes *(June 2007)*.
[8]   FASB ASC 740-10-45-20, 740-20-45-8, 740-20-45-11, 740-20-45-3 *(FASB Statement No. 109, ¶¶ 26, 35–37)*.
[9]   IAS 12, *¶¶ Objective, 58, 61A*.
[10]   FASB ASC 740-10-30-23 *(FASB Statement No. 109, ¶ 103)*.

tracing and the need for truing up the items recognized in equity. The Staff Draft has an income tax section, but it does not waive any income tax accounting requirements.[11] However, according to the Exposure Draft on income tax (now frozen), an entity would have initially allocated current and deferred income tax expense and the tax benefit from a deferred tax asset (including the effect of a valuation allowance) across the components of comprehensive income and equity where it records the related transaction or other event. The entity would have recognized any subsequent change in the tax expense previously recognized, other than a change in valuation allowance, in profit or loss for the year from continuing operations.[12] On one hand, this approach would eliminate the need for tracing back the source of the related transaction or other event. On the other hand, it would be necessary to keep a record of taxes that are originally classified in other comprehensive income in order to recognize subsequent changes in those tax effects in profit or loss.[13]

Comment: Therefore the proposed standard would have eliminated backwards tracing for those changes. The Basis for Conclusions seemed to give more weight to the goal of convergence and to the character of more detailed prescriptive guidance in U.S. GAAP (although simplified in the proposal made in the Exposure Draft) than to sound conceptual considerations. Conversely, the Exposure Draft (now frozen) presented an alternative solution for discussion, based on which, the allocation of subsequent changes in the deferred tax expense or benefit and of changes in valuation allowances would have followed the components of comprehensive income and equity of the related transaction or other event. However, this method would have improved the IAS 12 approach by spelling out the allocation rules. The Exposure Draft also considered the residual case of when original tax effects of a transaction or event do not affect comprehensive income or equity. The subsequent changes in tax effects would have been allocated to continuing operations or discontinued operations as appropriate.[14]

Comment: In the convergence effort, the Exposure Draft used the term "continuing operations," which is undefined and not used under IFRSs except for IAS 33 and the 2007 Revision of IAS 1.

8.1.3   Allocation Rules

Under U.S. GAAP intraperiod tax allocation reflects the individual effects of each item along a certain formula.[15] By contrast, IAS 12 simply requires an appropriate reasonable pro rata allocation to equity of taxable items or any other appropriate method, in case the tax rate applicable to a specific taxable equity item cannot be determined or such determination is too difficult (e.g., in certain situations of graduated tax rates, or of a change in assessment of tax recovery, or of a change in tax rates or tax rules).[16] The Exposure Draft on income tax (now frozen) proposed allocation rules in line with those U.S. GAAP requirements.[17]

---

[11]   *FASB and IASB*, Staff Draft of an Exposure Draft on Financial Statement Presentation, ¶¶ 62, 66, 98 *(July 2010); IASB Meeting, September 19, 2006, Agenda Paper 9,* Application of Working Principles, ¶ 62 *(September 2006) www.iasb.org (last visited June 21, 2007).*

[12]   *Exposure Draft,* Income Tax, ¶¶ 29, 33, B34 *(March 2009).*

[13]   *Exposure Draft,* Income Tax, ¶ BC126 *(March 2009).*

[14]   *Exposure Draft,* Income Tax, ¶¶ 29A–34A, B34A–B36A, BC96–BC97 *(March 2009).*

[15]   *FASB ASC 740-20-45-14 (FASB Statement No. 109, ¶ 38).*

[16]   *IAS 12, ¶ 63.*

[17]   *Exposure Draft,* Income Tax, ¶ 34 *(March 2009).*

> **Comment:** Contrary to what would be expected, backwards tracing would require more complex rules of accounting. Conversely, the provisions of IAS 12 on this subject are quite vague. The Exposure Draft admitted that IAS 12 does not provide detailed guidance, e.g., on allocation methods or where to present any difference between total tax and tax allocated to the individual components.[18]

> **Comment:** IAS 12 has neither general nor such specific rules as U.S. GAAP, nor does it explain how to make such an allocation. The fact that under IFRSs, intraperiod tax allocation is not as sophisticated as under U.S. GAAP derives, in part, from the relatively simpler profit and loss structure under IFRSs in comparison to U.S. GAAP. Under IFRSs, the statement of comprehensive income does not include extraordinary items or the cumulative effect of a change in accounting principle, except in the rare case of the prospective application of a change in accounting principle under the IAS 8 impracticability exception (see Section 6.4.3 previously). Recently, FASB Statement No. 154 also removed the cumulative effect of a change in accounting principle caption from the income statement.

8.2 INCOME TAX RECOGNIZED IN EQUITY

8.2.1 General Rules

Under U.S. GAAP, the tax benefits of deductible temporary differences or of an operating loss carryforward occurring during the year are recognized in equity in the following circumstances: 1) retrospective changes in the beginning balance of retained earnings; 2) other comprehensive income items; 3) a change in contributed capital, such as deductible expenditures reported as a reduction of the proceeds of issued capital stock (see Section 8.2.5 later); 4) expenses for employee stock options recognized differently for financial reporting and tax purposes (see Section 8.2.8 later); 5) dividends that are paid on unallocated shares held by an ESOP and charged to retained earnings (see Section 8.2.17.5 later); and 6) a deductible difference or an operating loss carryforward that existed at the date of a quasi-reorganization (see Section 8.2.11 later).[19]

Conversely, IAS 12 follows the general backwards tracing rule. Therefore equity will report the current or deferred income tax related to the items that are directly recognized directly in equity.

On initial application of FASB Statement No. 96, the predecessor of FASB Statement No. 109, in the earliest comparative year presented when the earliest year restated was not presented, an entity had to restate the beginning balance of retained earnings or of the appropriate component of equity affected by the intraperiod tax allocation rules applied, inter alia, to tax benefits of quasi-reorganizations (see Section 5.2.3 and Section 6.5.3 previously), stock options, tax on items of other comprehensive income (see Chapter 7 previously). A cumulative effect of a change in accounting principle accounted for other situations.[20] FASB Statement No. 109 had the same transitional provisions for all situations where a tax benefit is excluded from comprehensive income and allocated directly to contributed capital or retained earnings.

---

[18]　*Exposure Draft*, Income Tax, ¶ BC94 (March 2009).

[19]　*FASB ASC 740-20-45-11, 740-20-45-3 (FASB Statement No. 109, ¶¶ 36–37).*

[20]　*FASB Statement No. 96, Accounting for Income Taxes, ¶ 33 (superseded); Implementation Guides – Q&A 96, (superseded), ¶ 47.*

Other circumstances required the recording of a cumulative effect of a change in accounting principle.[21]

8.2.2 Tax Benefits of an Operating Loss Carryforward and Carryback

The topic of intraperiod allocation of tax benefit arising from a net operating loss carryforward or carryback may be analyzed from the perspective of the accounting in the period it arises or of the treatment or its first recognition of a carryforward (i.e., elimination of the related valuation allowance) in subsequent periods or of a subsequent change in estimates.

In the period in which a net operating loss arises, the general intraperiod allocation rules apply (see Section 8.1.2 previously). In particular, a current and deferred tax benefit arising from a loss from continuing operations in the current period is allocated to continuing operations even if the loss offsets a current, past, or future period capital gain in extraordinary items.[22]

A simple adjustment to the valuation allowance because of a change in estimate about whether the income tax benefits of deductible temporary differences or net operating loss or tax credit carryforwards are more likely than not to be realizable affects income from continuing operations.[23]

Under all other circumstances, except the special cases mentioned below, Topic 740 (FASB Statement No. 109) requires the allocation of the current and deferred tax benefits of an operating loss carryforward that resulted in a prior year or the tax benefit of an operating loss carryback to the same classification as the component of the source of the income or loss in the current year. The events that produced the loss in a previous year or the source of the expected future taxable income that will realize a current period deferred tax asset or carryforward are irrelevant. The standard's arguments are based on the grounds that this treatment is more understandable and avoids tracing back tax benefits to the transactions that originated the operating loss in previous years.[24] For example, the tax benefit of a loss carryback refund in the current year is recognized in continuing operations in the same manner as the source of the operating loss in the current year (i.e., that of the refund), not as the taxes paid on another component (e.g., on extraordinary items) in a previous period that it offsets.[25] As another example, the tax benefit of an operating loss carryforward that arose in a previous year but is first recognized (i.e., the valuation allowance is eliminated) in the current year is allocated to extraordinary items if it offsets the current or deferred tax consequences of that extraordinary gain. Conversely, the tax benefit of a previous year extraordinary loss first recognized in the current year is allocated to continuing operations if it offsets the current or deferred tax consequences of income from continuing operations of the current year.[26] Therefore, the tax benefits will be allocated to equity to the extent that the source of the tax benefit in the current year arises from equity.

---

[21] *FASB Statement No. 109, ¶ 51.*

[22] *FASB ASC 740-10-30-18, 740-10-25-3 (FASB Statement No. 109, ¶¶ 245(b), 274.*

[23] *FASB ASC 740-10-45-20, 740-20-45-11, 740-20-45-3 (FASB Statement No. 109, ¶¶ 26, 36–37).*

[24] *FASB ASC 740-10-45-20, 740-20-45-3, 740-10-55-38 (FASB Statement No. 109, ¶¶ 26, 37, 141, 245).*

[25] *FASB Statement No. 109, ¶ 245(b); IASB, Educational Section,* Allocation to Shareholders Equity ('Backwards Tracing'), *¶ 28 (September 21, 2004).*

[26] *FASB Statement No. 109, ¶ 245(a).*

However, the tax benefits of a deductible temporary difference or of an operating loss carryforward occurring during the year, as well as their first recognition by the subsequent elimination of the related valuation allowances, are recognized directly in other comprehensive income or in other components of equity in certain cases. This happens in the case of 1) a change in contributed capital, such as deductible expenditures reported as a reduction of the proceeds of issued capital stock (see Section 8.2.5 later); 2) expenses for employee stock options recognized differently for financial reporting and tax purposes (see Section 8.2.8 later); 3) dividends that are paid on unallocated shares held by an ESOP and that are charged to retained earnings (see Section 8.2.17.5 later); and 4) a deductible difference or an operating loss carryforward that existed at the date of a quasi-reorganization (see Section 8.2.11 later).

A special rule (outside the scope of this Book) applies to the first recognition (i.e., the elimination of the valuation allowance) of tax benefits relating to deferred tax assets that were recognized at the acquisition date in a business combination and for which a tax benefit is first recognized in subsequent years. However, under EITF Issue No. 99-15, the reduction or elimination of the valuation allowance had to be included in income from continuing operations to the extent it resulted from a change in tax law or regulation, irrespective of whether that reduction had occurred in the period of the tax law change or in a subsequent period.[27] Subtopic 805-10 (FASB Statement No. 141(R)) amended FASB Statement No. 109 to require a different accounting (reduction of goodwill and a bargain purchase gain for any excess) limited to changes in valuation allowances that are adjusted within the measurement period as defined in that standard and that result from new information about facts and circumstances that existed at the acquisition date. All other changes follow the rules applicable to changes in valuation allowances. It also nullified EITF Issue No. 99-15. These new rules apply prospectively to business combinations in which the acquisition date is on or after the beginning of the first annual period beginning on or after December 15, 2008.[28]

IAS 12 has no specific rules for allocation of the tax benefits arising from an operating loss carryforward or carryback,[29] as under the standard the allocation criteria (unlike U.S. GAAP) as well as the recognition criteria (like U.S. GAAP) of deferred tax assets are irrespective of the type of the related benefits, whether they arise from deductible temporary differences, unused tax losses, or unused tax credits. Unlike IAS 12, the Exposure Draft on income tax (now frozen) would have introduced the accounting for valuation allowances. Furthermore, it would have better clarified that in the year of origination the allocation of the effect of a deferred tax asset, as well as of a simultaneously recognized valuation allowance, should follow the same component of comprehensive income or equity as the event or transaction giving rise to the temporary difference, tax loss, or tax credit, irrespective of which is the source of the taxable income that recovers or is expected to recover that tax benefit.[30]

The *Financial Statement Presentation Project* has discussed several options regarding this topic. As an operating loss carryforward is not ordinarily allocable to a specific transaction,

---

[27] *EITF Issue No. 99-15*, Accounting for Decreases in Deferred Tax Asset Valuation Allowances Established in a Purchase Business Combination As a Result of a Change in Tax Regulation *(nullified by FASB Statement No. 141(R), ¶ F4)*.

[28] *FASB ASC 805-10-65-1 (FASB Statement No. 141(R), ¶ 77); FASB Statement No. 141(R), ¶¶ E22(d), E22(e), F4(u).*

[29] *IAS 12, ¶ 35.*

[30] *Exposure Draft, Income Tax, ¶¶ 23, B34-B35 (March 2009).*

this would lead to choosing a single line item to present income tax. On the other hand, realizing the tax benefits arising from an operating loss carryforward may be the very reason for entering into a specific transaction, hence they would be considered an integral part of that transaction.[31]

With reference to intraperiod allocation of subsequent changes of a valuation allowance, including on operating loss carryforwards, the Exposure Draft on income tax (now frozen) proposed to move towards the U.S. GAAP approach. IFRS 3 accounts for the subsequent realization of a deferred tax acquired in a business combination that was unrecognized at the acquisition date similarly to the requirement under Topic 805 (FASB Statement 141(R)) as mentioned above. The Exposure Draft would have extended the same treatment to a subsequent change in the related valuation allowance.[32] Like U.S. GAAP, the tax effects of changes in valuation allowances due to changes in circumstances that cause a change in judgment about the recoverability of deferred taxes in future years would be allocated to continuing operations.[33] Backwards tracing to equity would be maintained only when a change in valuation allowance refers to deferred taxes arising from transactions with equity holders in their capacity as equity holders, except distributions to them.[34] Here the Exposure Draft was generic while Topic 740 (FASB Statement No. 109) is specific to situations well known under U.S. GAAP. Finally, in all other cases the tax effects of a change in valuation allowance would be allocated, similarly to U.S. GAAP, to the component in which the income is recognized.[35]

IAS 12 requires the disclosure of both a current and a deferred tax benefit arising from the use in the current year of a previously unrecognized tax loss, tax credit, or temporary difference of a prior period.[36] The Exposure Draft would have replaced this point with the disclosure of any change in a valuation allowance, including a change relating to a tax benefit that reduces current tax expense. Furthermore, detail of any valuation allowance, respective changes, and events and circumstances for those changes would have been required.[37] Under IAS 12, an entity must also separately disclose the amount and the expiry dates of deductible temporary differences, unused tax losses, and unused tax credits for which it recognized no deferred tax assets. An entity must inform on deferred tax assets and deferred tax liabilities (segmented in relation with each type of temporary differences, unused tax losses, and unused tax credits) recognized for each period presented and deferred tax income or expense if not implicit in that disclosure.[38] The Exposure Draft would have replaced these requirements with a reconciliation of beginning and ending balances of deferred tax liabilities and assets, period changes (including separate indication of the effect of reversal of temporary differences, tax rates changes, change in tax status, tax uncertainties) as well as expiry dates for each type of temporary differences, unused tax losses, and unused tax credits.[39]

---

[31] *IASB Meeting, September 19, 2006, Agenda Paper 9,* Application of Working Principles, ¶¶ 49–50 (*September 2006*) *www.iasb.org (last visited June 21, 2007).*

[32] *IFRS 3, ¶ C4; IAS 12, ¶ 68; Exposure Draft,* Income Tax, ¶¶ B36(a), B40 (March 2009).

[33] *Exposure Draft,* Income Tax, ¶ B36(c)(ii) (March 2009).

[34] *Exposure Draft,* Income Tax, ¶ B36(b) (March 2009).

[35] *Exposure Draft,* Income Tax, ¶ B36(c)(i) (March 2009).

[36] *IAS 12, ¶¶ 80(e), 80(f).*

[37] *Exposure Draft,* Income Tax, ¶¶ 41(g), 47 (March 2009).

[38] *IAS 12, ¶¶ 81(e), 81(g).*

[39] *Exposure Draft,* Income Tax, ¶ 46 (March 2009).

8.2.3 Certain Transactions with or Among Shareholders

Under EITF Issue No. 94-10, the tax effects of a change in the tax bases of assets and liabilities that, depending on jurisdiction, may arise from transactions among or with shareholders and any valuation allowance that arises for deferred tax assets as a result of these changes in tax bases must be included initially in equity. Subsequent changes in valuation allowance must be reported in the income statement. As an example, in the U.S. a whole purchase of stock that is treated as purchase of assets for tax purposes and not for financial reporting changes the tax bases of that company's assets and liabilities and thus the related deferred tax assets and liabilities.

Conversely, if transactions with or among shareholders change the expectations of realization of a deferred tax asset (thus a change in the valuation allowance or a write off of the deferred tax asset), their income tax effects must be included in the income statement. In the U.S., a change in ownership in excess of 50% that may limit the future utilization of operating loss carryforward is an example.[40] IFRSs have no guidance on this topic apart from the issue of a change in status of an entity or its shareholders, which is treated in Section 8.2.4 below.

> **Comment:** The latter situation is analogous to a change due to other external events such as in enacted income tax rates.

In the *Financial Statement Presentation Project*, the IASB Staff proposal of presenting income tax in a separate section of the statement of comprehensive income might be extended to income taxes related to transactions with owners.[41]

8.2.4 Changes in Tax Laws and Tax Status

Under Topic 740 (FASB Statement No. 109), a change in deferred taxes that arises from a change in the tax laws (including tax rates) must affect income from continuing operations. Therefore, tax on income from continuing operations includes both the impact due to deferred taxes on the current period tax provision and the effect of the tax law change on the temporary differences that at the date of change are not yet reversed, even where the previously recorded deferred taxes were originally not recorded in income from continuing operations.

Under Topic 740 (FASB Statement No. 109), a change in deferred taxes that arises from a change in the tax status of an entity from taxable to nontaxable or vice versa must affect income from continuing operations. Such a change in tax status is recognized from the date of enactment of the tax law. The effects of an election for a voluntary change in tax status are recognized on the date of approval, or of the filing if approval is not required. For example, a C-corporation that before the end of the fiscal year files for S-corporation status will reverse deferred taxes in the fiscal year of filing. An S-corporation that files for C-corporation status

---

[40] *FASB ASC 740-20-45-11, 740-10-45-21 (EITF Issue No. 94-10,* Accounting by a Company for the Income Tax Effects of Transactions among or with Its Shareholders under FASB Statement No. 109*)*.

[41] *IASB Meeting, September 19, 2006, Agenda Paper 9,* Application of Working Principles, *¶ 63 (September 2006) www.iasb.org (last visited June 21, 2007).*

will record deferred taxes for any net tax benefit or obligation for unreversed temporary differences existing at the date the change becomes effective. The adjustments to deferred taxes arising from both types of changes must be disclosed.[42]

Section 8.2.2 previously mentions the special case of changes in valuation allowances relating to deferred tax assets that were recognized at the acquisition date in a business combination, including when resulting from a change in tax law or regulation.

Under IAS 12, any change in deferred taxes resulting from a change in tax rates or tax laws is recognized by the normal backwards tracing rules, i.e., in profit or loss unless it relates to items that are recognized in a prior period(s) in other comprehensive income or directly in equity.[43]

SIC-25 does not specifically deal with incorporated businesses switching to pass-through entities or vice versa, but in general with a change in the tax status of an entity or its shareholders. Under SIC-25, the tax consequences of a change in the tax status of an entity or its shareholders (such as a change in current or deferred tax assets or liabilities resulting from a change in tax impact of recovering or settling the carrying amount of the related asset or liability, also as a result of different applicable tax rates or tax incentives) must not be accounted for outside profit or loss, unless this is required by backwards tracing, i.e., the related transaction or event was recorded in other comprehensive income or directly in equity in the same or different period (See Section 8.1.2 previously), as may be the case of property, plant, and equipment carried at revaluation model. Therefore, the cumulative tax impact in equity is the amount that would have resulted as if the new tax status had been previously applied. Examples may be an initial public offering, the restructuring of an entity's equity, or the fact that the controlling shareholders are moving abroad.[44]

Hence, on this topic SIC-25 has a wider scope than Topic 740 (FASB Statement No. 109), as it is not limited to change in tax status from taxable to nontaxable and vice versa or to the consequences on deferred taxes only.

As part of the *Income Tax Short-Term Convergence Project*, the IASB decided to supersede SIC-25 and to converge to Topic 740 (FASB Statement No. 109) concerning the effective date of both an election for a voluntary change in tax status and a change in tax status that results from a change in tax law. However, IAS 12 and the Exposure Draft also include a law that is substantially enacted within the scope of this topic, although the concept of substantively enactment would be reformulated to accommodate the legal practice in different jurisdictions, including the U.S. Furthermore, as the Exposure Draft would have aligned intraperiod tax allocation with the U.S. GAAP requirements (see Section 8.1.2 previously), changes in tax rates, laws, or the taxable status of the entity would have had an effect on profit or loss even for deferred taxes related to an item recognized in other comprehensive income or directly in equity in a prior period.[45]

---

[42] *FASB ASC 740-10-45-15, 740-10-45-19, 740-10-40-6, 740-10-25-32, 740-10-25-33 (FASB Statement No. 109, ¶¶ 27–28); FASB Statement No. 109, ¶¶ 45(g), 112–113.*
[43] *IAS 12, ¶¶ 60, 80(d).*
[44] *SIC-25, Income Taxes – Changes in the Tax Status of an Entity or its Shareholders, ¶¶ 1–2, 4, 8.*
[45] *Exposure Draft, Income Tax, ¶¶ 54, B26, B27, BC90 (March 2009).*

> **Comment:** Arguably in contrast with such a conclusion, the Exposure Draft stated a change in tax rate as a typical example of a situation where backwards tracing would be the natural and intuitive solution, because there is no related non-tax amount that is recognized in the current period.[46]

IAS 12 and Topic 740 (FASB Statement No. 109) require the disclosure of the effect of changes in tax rates (or, under IAS 12, new taxes) on deferred tax expense or income. Under IAS 12, this may be shown as an adjustment to opening deferred tax liabilities or assets in a schedule that justifies deferred taxes and their period changes and in the reconciliation schedule that explains the relationship between tax expense and the accounting profit.[47] IAS 12 also requires an explanation of changes in tax rates compared to the previous accounting period.[48] Contrary to Topic 740 (FASB Statement No. 109), IFRSs require the disclosure of any significant effect in current or deferred taxes from changes in tax rates or laws substantively enacted after the reporting date. The Exposure Draft would have removed this requirement because it was already part of IAS 10.[49] In line with U.S. GAAP, the Exposure Draft would have required the disclosure of adjustments to deferred taxes arising from a change in tax status of the entity or its shareholders.[50]

8.2.5   Income Tax on Equity Issuing Costs

Section 4.11 previously explains the accounting for equity issuing costs and transaction costs in general. Income tax on equity issuing costs (under U.S. GAAP) or transaction costs (under IAS 32) that are presented in equity as a reduction of the proceeds and that are immediately deductible or amortizable for tax purposes are part of current or deferred tax credited or charged directly to equity.[51] The accounting entries may be as in the following example:

    Cash (proceeds)
    Income taxes payable (reduction due to the tax benefits)
        Common stock
        Additional paid-in capital – common stock (net-of-tax-benefit issuing costs) (*)
        Accounts payable (issuing costs)
        (*) Share premium under IFRSs.

As mentioned, under IFRSs, such an amount must be disclosed separately.[52] Under U.S. GAAP, however, this happens only in the period in which the transaction occurs. In subsequent periods any change in income tax affects current earnings.[53]

However, the 2011 Exposure Draft *Improvements to IFRSs* proposes to eliminate the references to income tax on transaction costs in IAS 32 to make clear that the general criteria in IAS 12

---

[46]   *Exposure Draft*, Income Tax, ¶ *BC91 (March 2009).*

[47]   *FASB ASC 740-10-50-9 (FASB Statement No. 109, ¶ 45(g)); IAS 12, ¶¶ 80(d), Appendix B Example 2.*

[48]   *IAS 12, ¶ 81(d).*

[49]   *IAS 10, ¶ 22(h); IAS 12, ¶ 88; Exposure Draft, Income Tax, ¶ BC105(a) (March 2009).*

[50]   *FASB ASC 740-10-50-9 (FASB Statement No. 109, ¶ 45(g)); Exposure Draft, Income Tax, ¶ 41(f) (March 2009).*

[51]   *FASB Statement No. 109, ¶ 36(c); IAS 32, ¶¶ IN15, 35, 37, 39, BC33.*

[52]   *IAS 32, ¶ 39.*

[53]   *FASB ASC 740-20-45-11 (FASB Statement No. 109, ¶ 36).*

apply, i.e., income tax affects profit or loss, except when the underlying transaction or event originates from other comprehensive income or is recognized directly in equity.[54]

The Exposure Draft on income tax, on proposing the elimination of backwards tracing, would have amended IAS 32 to remove the presentation of transaction costs of an equity transaction net of any related income tax benefit,[55] unless they arise in the same period of the transaction.

8.2.6   Income Tax on Compound Instruments

Under IFRSs, the deferred tax liability on a compound instrument (such as a convertible bond), to the extent a temporary difference exists on its initial recognition, is charged directly to the equity components of the compound instrument which is thus reported net of tax. Subsequent changes in the deferred tax liability affect profit or loss because these changes result from the recognition of the imputed discount as interest expense in the income statement.[56]

> **Comment:** This subject currently pertains to IFRSs, not to U.S. GAAP, which has no split accounting.

> **Example:** For example, on initial recognition a temporary difference may exist if the tax basis of the convertible debt includes the entire amount of the instrument, while split accounting requires the recognition of both a liability and an equity component. An entity must recognize a deferred tax liability at the time of the transaction because the initial recognition of the instrument affects taxable profit or loss and therefore the transaction does not fall within the IAS 12 exception[57] for recognition of deferred taxation on initial recognition of an asset or liability. From the perspective of the income statement, the deferred tax liability at the end of each period corresponds to the aggregate income tax deduction on the difference between the nominal interest expense and the imputed interest expense for the remaining life of the instrument.

8.2.7   Income Tax on a Beneficial Conversion Feature

Section 5.2.8 previously explains the accounting for a convertible debt security with a beneficial conversion feature. Under U.S. GAAP, when such a convertible instrument is considered as a single debt instrument for tax purposes, deferred tax on the temporary difference due to the difference between tax and financial reporting bases must be recognized as an adjustment to additional paid-in capital.[58]

8.2.8   Income Tax on Share-Based Payment Transactions

Both IFRS 2 and Topic 718 (FASB Statement No. 123(R)) require recognition of compensation cost relating to share-based payment transactions in net income. When an item is recognized as an expense and not as a liability in the period it is incurred (i.e., the remuneration expense

---

[54]   *IAS 12, ¶¶ 52B, 58; Exposure Draft,* Improvements to IFRSs *(June 2011); IASB Update, March 2010.*

[55]   *Exposure Draft,* Income Tax, *¶ C5 (March 2009).*

[56]   *IAS 12, ¶¶ 23, Appendix B, Example 4.*

[57]   *IAS 12, ¶ 15(b).*

[58]   *FASB ASC 740-10-55-51 (EITF Issue No. 05-8,* Income Tax Consequences of Issuing Convertible Debt with a Beneficial Conversion Feature*).*

recognized for accounting purposes), the difference between its tax basis and its carrying amount of nil (as no liability is recorded) is also a deductible temporary difference. If no component is deductible for tax purposes, no temporary difference arises, as there will be no difference between the tax base (nil) and the financial reporting base (nil, because the remuneration is expensed).[59]

Generally speaking, a difference between the cumulative compensation expense recorded for financial reporting purposes and the amount that the tax rules permit an entity to deduct on the remuneration paid in shares, stock options, or similar arrangements may be the result of many factors. It may originate from a timing lag due to the use of a measurement date for accounting purposes (e.g., grant date under both U.S. GAAP and IFRS 2) that is different from that admitted for taxation (typically, for example, share option exercise date). Also, the measurement methods used may differ (e.g., intrinsic value for tax purposes versus fair value for financial reporting, thus the time value component of the instrument may not be deductible for tax purposes), the rules for treatment of forfeitures may be at variance, or other specific tax deduction rules may exist under a specific tax jurisdiction.[60]

Worksheet 76 summarizes the IFRSs and U.S. GAAP logics, computation procedures, and entries to account for income taxes on equity-settled share-based payment arrangements.

> **Comment:** There are certain differences between U.S. GAAP and IFRSs, as explained below. The two sets of standards assume different rationales and procedures to arrive at a conclusion and accounting that are similar, but only to a certain extent. The SEC Staff reminded foreign private issuers that, although measurement provisions of IFRS 2 and Topic 718 (FASB Statement No. 123(R)) would ordinarily not produce Form 20-F reconciling items, these may result from certain differences between the two standards.[61]

Firstly, IFRSs and U.S. GAAP differ in accounting for an excess income tax benefit in share-based payment arrangements, in the sense that both apply equity recognition to an excess income tax benefit, but with different recognition limits. An excess income tax benefit refers to the excess of the realized tax deduction reported on a tax return (under IFRSs, the estimated, or subsequently realized, future tax deduction) over the tax effects on the cumulative compensation expense recognized for financial reporting purposes. As per the general intraperiod tax allocation rule under IAS 12, backwards tracing applies. Therefore, IFRSs require the recognition in profit or loss of income tax benefits to the extent the estimated or actual tax deduction corresponds to the cumulative compensation expense recognized in profit or loss for financial reporting purposes. Any tax deduction in excess of the cumulative expense recognized for financial reporting purposes must then refer to an equity component, and must therefore be recognized directly in equity as it occurs.[62] Under IFRSs, the rationale for recognizing tax effects both within profit or loss and outside profit or loss is that, in addition to an employee remuneration expense that is compensation cost in nature, a portion of the tax deduction also refers to an equity item to the extent the arrangement is also a

---

[59] *IFRS 2, ¶ BC312; IAS 12, ¶ 26(a).*

[60] *FASB ASC 718-740-05-4 (FASB Statement No. 123(R), ¶ 58); IAS 12, ¶ 68A; IFRS 2, ¶ BC315.*

[61] *FASB ASC 718-10-S99-1 (SEC Staff Accounting Bulletin, Topic 14-L, Application of the Measurement Provisions of Statement 123R to Foreign Private Issuers).*

[62] *IAS 12, ¶ 68C.*

share-based transaction, in which case taxes must be traced back to equity. The portion recognized directly in equity is not limited to the excess relating to changes in value of an equity interest, because other reasons may exist, depending on the jurisdiction, such as differences in valuation methodology. As IFRSs, on account of their international nature, must be applicable to any tax jurisdiction, such an accounting must be irrespective of the specific determinants to which the tax rules may attribute this excess tax benefit in a specific tax jurisdiction.

> **Comment:** Consistent with IAS 12, backwards tracing would require income recognition for income tax related to the portion of an excess tax benefit arising from an increase of share price, because a change in fair value of an equity instrument is not recognized in equity.

U.S. GAAP recognizes the income tax effects in the income statement, based on deferred tax assets computed on the cumulative expense recorded for financial reporting purposes for instruments classified as equity that will ordinarily result in a future tax deduction.[63] Any excess tax benefit (i.e., the realized tax deduction that exceeds the total expense recognized in the financial statements) is credited in equity, i.e., in additional paid-in capital. The rationale for recognition both in net income and directly in equity is that U.S. GAAP also views an equity-settled share-based payment arrangement as two embedded transactions, i.e., service rendered in exchange for shares (therefore, a transaction that must affect the income statement), and the share option exercise or the vesting of shares (i.e., an equity transaction between the entity and employees acting in their quality of shareholders). This is because under grant date measurement, any change in the value of the equity instruments after grant date is seen a matter of equity holders acting as such and not as employees.[64] However, Topic 718 (FASB Statement No. 123(R)) limits the equity recognition of an excess tax benefit to the extent that such an excess results from changes in the fair value of the entity's shares between the measurement date for financial reporting and the later measurement date for tax purposes.[65] This is because U.S. GAAP is tied to the U.S. tax system, where excess tax deductions are due to the increase in the intrinsic value of the equity instrument after the grant date (generally at the exercise date for share options and at the vesting date for shares). Hence, only the tax effect related to the increase of share price is considered an equity component.[66] An entity does not credit additional paid-in capital to the extent a realized tax deduction from an existing net operating loss carryforward reduces taxes payable.[67] Under EITF Issue No. 06-11, when dividends or dividend equivalents that are paid to employees on nonvested equity shares or share units during the vesting period or on outstanding share options before their exercise are tax deductible even if charged to retained earnings, the realized income tax benefits is recognized as an increase in additional paid-in capital and is included in the so-called "APIC pool" (see below).[68]

---

[63] *FASB ASC 718-740-25-2, 718-740-30-1 (FASB Statement No. 123(R), ¶ 59).*

[64] *FASB Statement No. 109, ¶ 143; FASB Statement No. 123(R), ¶¶ B209, B224; IFRS 2, ¶¶ BC317–BC320.*

[65] *FASB ASC 718-740-45-2, 718-740-35-3 (FASB Statement No. 123(R), ¶ 62).*

[66] *FASB Statement No. 123(R), ¶¶ B208–B209; IFRS 2, ¶ BC328.*

[67] *FASB ASC 718-740-25-10 (FASB Statement No. 123(R), Footnote 82).*

[68] *FASB ASC 718-740-45-8 to 718-740-45-12 (EITF Issue No. 06-11,* Accounting for Income Tax Benefits of Dividend on Share-Based Payment Awards*).*

Secondly, under IFRSs, deferred taxes are kept posted every period based on the entity's updated estimate of the tax base of the employee services received to date, which corresponds to the expected tax deduction that the specific tax jurisdiction would permit in future periods. When such a tax base is not known at the end of the period, it must be estimated based on information available at the end of the period. If a determination of share prices at a future date is needed under that tax jurisdiction, the entity must then estimate the share prices at the end of the reporting period.[69] This fine tuning estimation process ensures that the cumulative tax benefit that is recognized over time does not exceed actual deductible tax benefits.[70] Thanks to this mechanism, no unrecovered deferred tax should arise, nor should it be recognized as it does not meet the definition of an asset under the IASB Framework.[71] As a consequence, no permanent tax difference should exist. Contrary to IFRSs, U.S. GAAP does not update deferred taxes on the cumulative expense, which was recorded at the award grant-date fair value, based on a new estimate of what future tax deductions would be at subsequent reporting dates due to changes in the current fair value of share prices.[72] The rationale of Topic 718 (FASB Statement No. 123(R)) for not considering changes in share prices during the requisite service period is that contractually the employees, not the employer, bear that risk of those changes and the employees render the service in the requisite period to earn their right to benefit from the option irrespective of any share price change. To confirm this view, even if the option were cancelled, the remaining unrecognized compensation cost at the date of cancellation would be recognized.[73] The two transactions (employees rendering services and equity issuing) are accounted for separately and must not interfere with each other as the benefit the employer receives from service rendered does not depend on changes in share price and therefore compensation cost must not be affected by those changes. Therefore, differences between cumulative expense and tax deduction are likely to arise in each vesting period. Unrecovered deferred taxes (i.e., on a permanent difference) may arise to the extent a cumulative expense that exceeds the actual tax benefit is recorded. Insofar as they are unrecoverable and as during the vesting period they are not reversed as they arise, at vesting or exercise they are written off to equity as a final adjustment against any remaining additional paid-in capital resulting from excess tax benefits from previous awards (the so-called "APIC pool").[74]

Thirdly, under U.S. GAAP, this write off follows a portfolio approach, as any remaining additional paid-in capital that arose from excess tax benefits as a result of previous awards is first written off, prior to recognizing the remainder in the income statement.[75] The same treatment applies in the reverse situation of tax deficiencies (i.e., where the recognized tax deduction is less than the total expense recognized for accounting purposes). As mentioned, the need for a final adjustment to write off an excess income tax benefit cannot arise under IFRS 2. By definition tax deficiencies do not arise under IFRS 2 during the vesting period because estimated tax deduction is updated each period. A tax deficiency that arises in the

---

[69] *IAS 12, ¶ 68B; IFRS 2, ¶ BC324.*

[70] *IFRS 2, ¶ BC327.*

[71] *IFRS 2, ¶ BC325.*

[72] *FASB ASC 718-740-30-2 (FASB Statement No. 123(R), ¶ 61); FASB Statement No. 123(R), ¶ B207.*

[73] *FASB Statement No. 123(R), ¶¶ B159–B160, B163–B164, B221–B222.*

[74] *FASB ASC 718-20-55-23 (FASB Statement No. 123(R), ¶ A95).*

[75] *FASB ASC 718-740-35-5, 718-740-45-4 (FASB Statement No. 123(R), ¶ 63); FASB Statement No. 123(R), ¶¶ B210, B269.*

vesting or exercise period is recognized in profit or loss.[76] This determination is made on an individual instrument basis.

Finally, contrary to IFRS 2, Topic 718 (FASB Statement No. 123(R)) does include the time value component of the instrument, due to the use of fair value for financial reporting versus intrinsic value for tax purposes, in computing deferred taxes for an award of share options, as the standard computes deferred tax based on the grant-date fair value of the award, or calculated value for certain nonpublic entities. IFRS 2 computes deferred tax based on the intrinsic value of the award that can be deductible for tax purposes when the tax benefit is recognized. Therefore, for example, Topic 718 (FASB Statement No. 123(R)) recognizes deferred taxes for an at-the-money share option, while IFRS 2 does not do so until that award is in-the-money. IFRS 2 considers the recognition of a deferred tax asset that is not likely to be recovered, as under Topic 718 (FASB Statement No. 123(R)) may be the case of share options that are significantly out-of-the-money, to be against the recognition criteria of IAS 12, the definition of asset in the IASB Framework, and the impairment rules.[77]

Presentation of deferred tax related to equity-settled share-based payment transactions in the equity section of the statement of financial position would ordinarily follow the display of the underlying item, on a net basis, as a separate item or parenthetically disclosed. IFRSs do not explain the display of an equity-settled share-based payment transaction itself (see Section 5.2.10 previously).

A broad-based employee stock plan or "all-employee" plan is an employee share purchase plan that applies to all or substantially all employees.[78] Topic 718 (FASB Statement No. 123(R)) establishes specific criteria for a broad-based plan to be considered a noncompensatory plan.[79] No deferred taxes are recorded for noncompensatory plans under U.S. GAAP and any excess tax is recognized at exercise in additional paid-in capital. This circumstance does not arise under IFRS 2 as it does not exempt broad-based employee share purchase plans from expense recognition as it considers them to represent employee remuneration anyway.[80]

Under Section 718-10-25 (EITF Issue No. 00-16), payroll taxes and social security on stock-based compensation must be expensed and a liability must be recognized at the date of the event that determines the measurement and payment of the tax for tax purposes, which is generally the exercise date for stock options and the vesting date for restricted stock.[81] Payroll taxes and social security must be presented as operating expenses in the income statement.[82] Although IFRS 2 has no specific guidance in this respect, under IFRSs, they should be accrued over the same period or periods in which share-based compensation cost is expensed.

---

[76] *IFRS 2, ¶ BC326.*

[77] *FASB Statement No. 123(R), ¶¶ B219-B220, B268; IFRS 2, ¶ BC325.*

[78] *FASB Statement No. 123, Accounting for Stock-Based Compensation, (superseded), ¶ 234; IFRS 2, ¶ BC8.*

[79] *FASB ASC 718-50-25-1 (FASB Statement No. 123(R), ¶ 12).*

[80] *IFRS 2, ¶¶ BC11, BC17.*

[81] *FASB ASC 718-10-25-22 (EITF Issue No. 00-16, Recognition and Measurement of Employer Payroll Taxes on Employee Stock-Based Compensation).*

[82] *FASB ASC 718-10-25-23 (EITF Topic No. D-83, Accounting for Payroll Taxes Associated with Stock Option Exercises).*

8.2.9 Tax on Corrections of Errors and Changes in Accounting Principles

Under both U.S. GAAP and IFRSs, income tax effect, if any, on the restatement for a correction of prior period errors or income tax on the retroactive application of changes in accounting principles or policies is part of the net adjustment to the opening balance of retained earnings. Topic 250 (FASB Statement No. 154) considers tax impact as part of the direct effect of a change in accounting principle. IAS 12 requires separate disclosure of those tax effects. The Implementation Guidance of IAS 8 shows their parenthetical disclosure.[83]

> **Comment:** As explained in Section 6.4.1 previously, the cumulative effect of a retrospective application of an accounting policy is recognized directly in equity, i.e., in retained earnings. Under U.S. GAAP, should a deferred tax arise from a retrospective application of an accounting principle, a subsequent remeasurement of such deferred tax liability or asset that had been recognized as the result of a retrospective application of an accounting principle affects net income. Under IFRSs, it is controversial whether this subsequent remeasurement must be recognized in equity or in profit or loss when the item would be ordinarily accounted for in profit or loss under the new accounting policy. The issue is similar to that discussed in Section 8.2.4 previously with reference to a subsequent-period change in tax rate.[84]

8.2.10 Income Tax Impact from IFRS First-Time Adoption

8.2.10.1 General Effects of the Tax System In general, most tax accounting systems in the world produce tax returns through adjustments to the financial statements. As the first-time adoption of IFRSs has changed the financial statements results as compared with previous local GAAP, each specific jurisdiction which has adopted IFRSs has faced the issue of whether or not and how to change the tax system to avoid tax impacts that companies would face under that jurisdiction as a result of the migration to IFRSs. This topic falls outside the scope of this Book.

8.2.10.2 The First-Time Adoption Reserve As explained in Section 6.4.4 previously, under IFRS 1 most of the adjustments related to the transition to IFRSs affect retained earnings or other components of equity, as appropriate. Depending on jurisdiction, as explained in Section 3.6.7 and Section 3.6.8 previously, a specific FTA (First-Time-Adoption) reserve may have arisen and certain equity reserves may have been required for defense of capital or taxation purposes. This topic interrelates with the discussion of Section 8.2.13 later about tax on revaluation surplus and Section 8.2.17.4 later about undistributed versus distributed earnings tax rates. In fact, depending on the solution given by a specific tax system, the FTA reserve, the revaluation reserve for deemed cost under IFRS 1, and other newly-created equity reserves may be subject to different tax rates depending on whether or not they are distributed, used for deficit reorganization, or capitalized to contributed capital.

---

[83] *FASB ASC 740-20-45-11 (FASB Statement No. 109, ¶ 36(a); FASB Statement No. 109, ¶ 142; FASB ASC 250-10-45-8 (FASB Statement No. 154, ¶¶ 2(g), 10); IAS 8, ¶¶ 4, Implementation Guidance, Example 2; IAS 12, ¶¶ 62A(a), 80(h), 81(a).*

[84] *For an interpretation in line with the jurisdictional interpretation explained in Section 8.2.10.3, see Ernst & Young, International GAAP (2005), Chapter 24, ¶ 6.1.2.*

8.2.10.3   Subsequent Changes in Tax Rates and Tax Laws   A change in tax rates or tax laws that are enacted or substantively enacted subsequent to the end of the first IFRS reporting period affects deferred income taxes that resulted from IFRS 1 transition adjustments.[85] An issue arises as to whether such an effect should be accounted for inside or outside profit or loss in the period of change.

Comment: IAS 12, not IFRS 1, applies to subsequent financial statements. IFRS 1 does not operate any override of IAS 12 or IAS 1. Under IAS 12, a change in deferred taxes arising from changes in tax rates or tax laws affects profit or loss unless the entity recognized the underlying item outside profit or loss (i.e., the so-called backwards tracing). Outside profit or loss means other comprehensive income or a direct adjustment to equity items, including opening retained earnings.[86] When upon transition date an IFRS 1 adjustment affected accumulated other comprehensive income, a change in deferred taxes arising from a subsequent change in tax rates or tax laws affects other comprehensive income, on the grounds of the ordinary IAS 12 rule.[87] IAS 12 does not say whether it adjusts accumulated other comprehensive income or other comprehensive income. However, after the 2007 Revision of IAS 1, other comprehensive income is outside profit or loss but no longer a direct component of equity.

The treatment of transition adjustments that affected opening retained earnings is more complex. On one hand, adjustments to opening retained earnings measure a retrospective application of accounting policy or a correction of errors that under IFRSs would have affected profit or loss in periods prior to the transition date. By analogy, in consolidation procedures, adjustments to opening retained earnings concern items that affected profit or loss of prior periods. On the other hand, from a balance sheet perspective, retained earnings are a component of equity.[88] Furthermore, IAS 12 classifies a retrospective adjustment to the opening balance of retained earnings as outside profit or loss and as a direct debit or credit in equity. IAS 1 classifies retrospective adjustments and retrospective restatements as reconciling items and not as changes in equity in the period, either from transactions with owners, or from profit or loss or other comprehensive income (see Section 7.9.6 previously).[89] All this would exclude such deferred taxes referring to items that are classified within profit or loss. A basic principle in IFRSs, rigidly applied in IAS 10, is that recognition and classification (for example, the current versus noncurrent distinction) reflect the situation and status at the date of reporting, with no forward looking to situations that do not exist at the reporting date or that may arise or be reversed depending on future decisions of management. Backwards tracing looks to the past, not to the future. Therefore, the subsequent measurement model of an item under IFRSs should not affect the counter-account of changes in deferred taxes. On the contrary, according to certain jurisdictional interpretations, the income tax effects of a subsequent change in tax rate would be recorded within profit or loss or outside profit or loss depending on where the item would ordinarily be accounted for under IFRSs in a context of non-first-time adoption of IFRSs. A change in deferred taxes on a deemed cost of fixed assets due to a subsequent change in tax rates would affect profit or loss, because this is a one-off effect that does not correspond to an existing subsequent measurement model under IFRSs. According to a second jurisdictional view concerning the banking sector, it would be accounted for in retained earnings.[90]

---

[85]   *IFRS 1, ¶ IG6.*

[86]   *IAS 12, ¶ 60.*

[87]   *IAS 12, ¶¶ 61A, 62A.*

[88]   *IAS 1, ¶ 108.*

[89]   *IAS 1, ¶¶ 110, BC74.*

[90]   *Assirevi, February 21, 2008. OPI 10,* Valutazione successiva delle imposte differite sulle differenze temporanee sorte in sede di transizione agli IFRS; *Tavolo di coordinamento tra Banca d'Italia, Consob ed Isvap in materia di applicazione degli IAS/IFRS, February 21, 2008. Documento No. 1,* Trattamento contabile delle variazioni della fiscalità differita derivanti dalla Legge Finanziaria 2008; *ABI, February 28, 2008. Soluzioni IAS No. 48.*

8.2.11   Income Tax on Temporary Differences at the Date of a Quasi-Reorganization

Under U.S. GAAP, income tax benefits of deductible differences and carryforwards that existed as of the date of a quasi-reorganization (see Section 5.2.3 and Section 6.5.3 previously) must be credited to contributed capital if those benefits are recognized in subsequent periods (including through the offset of a valuation allowance), irrespective of whether losses that created the operating loss carryforward have been charged to income or contributed capital before the quasi-reorganization. The rationale is that the net income after quasi-reorganization should not be affected by those benefits that relate to prior periods because a quasi-reorganization creates a new basis of accounting. An operating loss carryforward is likely to arise for a company that goes through quasi-reorganization. In such a situation, at the date of the quasi-reorganization a deferred tax asset for the potential future tax benefits would not likely meet the requirements for recognition. A subsequent recognition or decrease of a valuation allowance due to changes in circumstances is expensed in an item called "taxes not payable in cash" with a corresponding credit to paid-in capital. Topic 740 (FASB Statement No. 109) grandfathers a quasi-reorganization that has been made in the form of a deficit reclassification (see Section 6.5.3 previously) and whose income tax was accounted for under the previous FASB Statement No. 96. In this case, as an exception, the subsequent realization of the tax benefits is recognized in net income (or, in case of a net operating loss carryforward, it is reported as the source of taxable income in the current period) and then reclassified from retained earnings to contributed capital. An entity must disclose the date of the quasi-reorganization, how tax has been reported, the separate tax impact of the quasi-reorganization on the aggregate and per-share income from continuing operations, income before extraordinary items and net income, and if the aforementioned exception was used.[91] Taxes not payable in cash are not items of other comprehensive income.[92]

IFRSs have no specific guidance on this subject. The general backwards tracing rules would apply.[93]

8.2.12   Tax on Items of Other Comprehensive Income

Section 7.9.9 and Section 7.9.10 previously explain gross-of-tax and net-of-tax presentations of other comprehensive income and their respective pros and cons, including their effects on traceability, clarity and transparency, tax rates information, cluttering of financial statements, and consistency with the accounting for other items in the statement of comprehensive income.

---

[91] *FASB Statement No. 16, ¶¶ 32, 34; FASB ASC 740-20-45-11, 852-740-45-3 (FASB Statement No. 109, ¶¶ 36(g), 39; FASB Statement No. 109, ¶¶ 146-147; FASB Statement No. 130, ¶ 113; FASB ASC 852-20-S99-2 (SEC Staff Accounting Bulletin, Topic 5-S); FASB ASC 852-740-55-2 to FASB ASC 852-740-55-6 (Implementation Guides – Q&A 109, ¶¶ 9-10; Implementation Guides – Q&A 96, (superseded), ¶¶ 26, 27, 38; AICPA Accounting Interpretations AIN-APB 11*, Accounting for Income Taxes: Accounting Interpretations of APB Opinion No. 11 *(superseded), ¶ 16; FASB ASC 852-10-15-1 (AICPA Statement of Position No. 90-7*, Financial Reporting by Entities in Reorganization Under the Bankruptcy Code*).*

[92] *FASB ASC 220-10-55-3 moved to 220-10-45-10B by ASU 2011-05; FASB Statement No. 130, ¶ 115.*

[93] *IASB*, Allocations to Shareholders' Equity ('Backwards Tracing') *(September 21, 2004), Footnote 12 www.iasb.org (last visited September 29, 2008).*

> **Comment:** Net-of-tax presentation of certain items (e.g., discontinued operations, extraordinary items, cumulative effect of a change in accounting principle, and other comprehensive income) or the need for disclosing applicable tax in case of a choice between gross- or net-of-tax displays would require intraperiod tax allocation.

> **Comment:** Arguably, the recycling (under IFRSs, reclassification) of other comprehensive income (see Section 7.8 previously) would also determine an implicit corresponding reversal of the related deferred taxes that had been recognized in other comprehensive income. As mentioned in Section 8.1.2 previously, the Exposure Draft on income tax would have changed the intraperiod tax allocation rules. On one hand, this approach would eliminate the need for tracing back the source of the related transaction or other event. On the other hand, until recycling it would have been necessary to keep a record of taxes that are originally classified in other comprehensive income in order to recognize subsequent changes in those tax effects in profit or loss.[94] The Exposure Draft proposed an amendment to IFRS 1 for the introduction of a new exception for IFRS first-time adopters with a transition date after that of the new standard. Those entities would have also applied the new intraperiod tax allocation rules prospectively from their date of transition to IFRSs. The cumulative amounts of tax on items of income and expense that at the transition date are recognized in accumulated other comprehensive income or that are recognized in equity would not have been reclassified to profit and loss on derecognition of the related asset or liability any longer. Those entities would have deemed those amounts recognized outside profit or loss (either in other comprehensive income or directly in equity) to be zero at the transition date.[95]

8.2.13   Tax on Revaluation Surplus

Worksheet 77 shows the IFRSs accounting for the revaluation of property, plant, and equipment in a situation where this accounting revaluation does not affect the tax base of the asset (i.e., it is made for financial reporting purposes only). A temporary difference may arise. If it also affects the tax base for the same amount, no deferred tax will arise. As a side aspect, the Exposure Draft on income tax specified that a fair value measurement incorporates the market participants' assumptions about the tax consequences of recovering or settling the asset or liability.[96]

> **Comment:** A situation may exist where at the date of revaluation there is no temporary difference (i.e., both the accounting and tax bases of the asset are revalued for the same amount), but temporary differences occur in subsequent periods. This may arise for example from a difference in the inception of depreciation or amortization of the revalued asset between tax and financial reporting.

The deferred tax that arises on revaluation surplus is recognized in other comprehensive income as a charge to revaluation surplus.[97]

Subsequently, any optional transfer of the revaluation surplus related to that asset directly to retained earnings in view of its realization in the period (see Section 6.6.1 previously) is also

---

[94] *Exposure Draft,* Income Tax, ¶ BC126 (March 2009).
[95] *Exposure Draft,* Income Tax, ¶¶ C2, BC118 (March 2009).
[96] *Exposure Draft,* Income Tax, ¶ B14 (March 2009).
[97] *IAS 12,* ¶¶ 20, 61A, 62(a).

made net of any related deferred tax.[98] The ending balance of revaluation surplus will be the revaluation surplus net of tax, less any transfer net of tax.

Comment: Additional disclosure may be required, because deferred tax income or expense recognized for each period presented may not be apparent from the changes in the amounts recognized in the statement of financial position. In fact, revaluation surplus is shown net of both any deferred tax and of any transfer related to the depreciation of the asset. The ending balance is the beginning net-of-tax balance of revaluation minus the net-of-tax difference between depreciation based on revalued and historical cost amounts.

Conversely, under IAS 12 the tax effects of an asset revaluation that is effected for tax purposes only and is not related to an accounting revaluation in the current, a previous, or a future period affects profit or loss.[99]

Comment: In certain tax jurisdictions an entity may have the option to have the tax base of the revalued asset adjusted to the revalued carrying amount by paying a "substitute" or similar income tax. By analogy with IAS 12, this substitute tax expense would be recognized against revaluation surplus. On the other hand, a previously recognized deferred tax asset would be reversed because, by the effect of the "substitute" tax, the temporary difference between the accounting and tax bases would be zeroed.

Revaluing a nonmonetary asset is different from its restatement for financial reporting purposes in a hyperinflationary economy, which instead generates a charge of deferred tax in profit or loss if no corresponding restatement is allowed for tax purposes. Section 8.2.16 following treats this subject further.[100]

Section 8.2.17.4 following analyzes the tax effects of the interaction of a revaluation reserve with its distribution to shareholders.

8.2.14 Income Tax on Foreign Currency Translation Adjustment

Under both IFRSs and U.S. GAAP (under the latter only for the tax effects occurring during the current year – the Exposure Draft, *Income Tax* (March 2009) proposed to adopt the same solution for IFRSs), the deferred income taxes on foreign currency translation adjustment (see Section 7.10 previously) are debited or credited directly to other comprehensive income, to the extent recognition of deferred taxes is not exempted as in the case of indefinite reversal assumption of unremitted earnings of foreign operations. They must be separately disclosed in the notes.[101]

---

[98] *IAS 12, ¶ 64.*
[99] *IAS 12, ¶ 65.*
[100] *IAS 12, ¶ 18.*
[101] *FASB ASC 830-30-45-21, 830-30-45-20 (FASB Statement No. 52, ¶¶ 23, 24, 31(c)); FASB ASC 740-20-45-11, 740-20-55-24 (FASB Statement No. 109, ¶¶ 36(b), 276); IAS 12, ¶¶ 38(b), 62(c), Appendix B, Example 3; IAS 21, ¶ 50.*

8.2.15   Deferred Tax on Foreign Nonmonetary Assets and Liabilities

On this issue Topic 740 (FASB Statement No. 109) has an exception to the general principle of comprehensive recognition of deferred taxes on temporary differences. Contrary to IAS 12,[102] the standard prohibits the recognition of deferred taxes for temporary differences on foreign nonmonetary assets and liabilities that are remeasured under Topic 830 (FASB Statement No. 52) from the local to the functional currency using historical rates that result from a change in foreign exchange rates or the indexing for tax purposes. These tax benefits are recognized only when realized on the tax return. The rationale is that FASB Topic 830 (Statement No. 52) does not recognize gains and losses due to changes in exchange rates on foreign nonmonetary assets when the U.S. dollar is the functional currency.[103] This would include the case of highly inflationary economies or of foreign operations where the books are kept in a local currency and the tax basis of nonmonetary assets or liabilities is determined in the local currency, while the reporting currency, not the foreign currency, is the functional currency of the foreign operation. In these situations, under both U.S. GAAP and IFRSs the basis of those assets and liabilities in terms of functional currency for financial reporting purposes does not change over time, as historical rates are maintained. However, while a change in foreign exchange rates does not change the foreign tax basis of those assets and liabilities in the jurisdiction of the foreign operation, it would likely change their tax basis in the reporting currency for the reporting entity, as well as the amount needed in the future to recover their costs expressed in the reporting currency. From a different perspective, if those foreign assets and liabilities were accounted for by the foreign operation directly on a U.S. set of books, a change in exchange rates or an indexing for tax purposes would change their foreign tax basis and again create a temporary difference because their accounting basis would not change. Thus, a temporary difference arises under any of those circumstances.[104]

The Exposure Draft, *Income Tax* (March 2009) retained the guidance in IAS 12.[105]

> **Comment:** However, the Exposure Draft did not explain a solution to the dilemma mentioned in Topic 740 (FASB Statement No. 109).

As part of the *Income Tax Short-Term Convergence Project*, the FASB considered the option to converge with IAS 12 on this subject.[106]

As part of the *Financial Statement Presentation Project* and *Income Tax Short-Term Convergence Project*, the decision on whether or not to allocate and how to present any allocation of income tax to the foreign currency translation adjustment is consequential on the decision on

---

[102]   *IAS 12, ¶¶ IN2, 41.*

[103]   *FASB ASC 740-10-25-3 (FASB Statement No. 109, ¶ 9(f)); FASB Statement No. 109, ¶ 119.*

[104]   *FASB Statement No. 109, ¶ 118; FASB, Minutes of December 15, 2004 Meeting, Board Memorandum 8, Intercompany Transfers and Foreign Currency (December 30, 2004), ¶ 24 www.fasb.org (last visited September 29, 2008).*

[105]   *Exposure Draft, Income Tax, ¶ BC51 (March 2009).*

[106]   IASB, *Minutes of July 2005 Meeting, Agenda Paper 8*, Short-Term Convergence: Income Taxes – Cover Note, *¶ 16-33 www.iasb.org (last visited September 29, 2008).*

whether or not the foreign currency translation adjustment itself should be allocated, and how, in the statement of comprehensive income (see Section 7.10.9 previously).[107]

8.2.16 Income Tax in Highly Inflationary Economies

Section 6.4.23 previously illustrates the accounting for highly inflationary economies and its impact on retained earnings. Section 7.12 previously explains the impact on other comprehensive income. Worksheet 68 summarizes the topic by comparing the methods under U.S. GAAP and IFRSs and their impact on other comprehensive income and deferred taxes.

From the perspective of the foreign entity, U.S. GAAP considers the general price-level financial statements of a the foreign entity, restated retroactively to the purchasing power unit at the date of the most recent balance sheet, as the preferable primary financial statements, but only when intended for readers in the U.S., where required or permitted by home-country GAAP, expressed in its local currency of operation and presented under U.S. GAAP.[108] Highly inflationary jurisdictions often require the indexing for tax purposes of certain assets and liabilities. In general price-level financial statements at end-of-current-year purchasing power units under APS 3, end-of-period deferred taxes are computed on the temporary difference between indexed tax basis and price-level restated amount. The change in deferred taxes resulting from remeasuring deferred taxes at the end of the prior period to units of current general purchasing power at the end of the current period impacts the income statement.[109]

For the purpose of reporting an investment in foreign entities (i.e., associates or subsidiaries) operating in highly inflationary economies in primary consolidated or parent's financial statements, or for the purpose of a foreign entity reporting in U.S. dollars, U.S. GAAP applies the remeasurement method to a highly inflationary economy (see Section 7.10.2 previously and Section 7.12 previously), as if the functional currency of the foreign entity were the reporting currency of the reporting entity (i.e., of its parent).[110] Section 7.12 previously explains that under U.S. GAAP, contrary to IFRSs, when the reporting currency is the functional currency, the indexing on nonmonetary assets and liabilities that are remeasured at historical cost for financial reporting purposes does not give rise to the recognition of deferred tax assets. This prohibition tends to avoid a deferred tax asset in highly inflationary economies that would arise when the tax jurisdiction requires an indexing for tax purpose and U.S. GAAP maintains historical exchange rates because the USD is the functional currency.[111] Topic 255 (FASB Statement No. 89) also does not adjust deferred taxes for any temporary difference that may result from the use of current cost/constant purchasing power in supplemental

---

[107]   IASB, *Financial Statement Presentation, Agenda Paper 3*, Presentation of Income Tax Information, *(March 11, 2008) ¶ 18.*

[108]   *Accounting Principle Board Statement No. 3*, Financial Statements Restated for General Price-Level Changes, *¶ 26; U.S. Securities and Exchange Commission*, International Reporting and Disclosure Issues *in the Division of Corporate Finance, ¶ XI.A.3*, Reporting in Highly Inflationary Economies, *(November 1, 2004).*

[109]   *FASB ASC 830-740-25-5, 830-740-30-1 (EITF Issue No. 93-9, Application of FASB Statement No. 109 in Foreign Financial Statements Restated for General Price-Level Changes).*

[110]   *FASB ASC 830-10-45-11 (FASB Statement No. 52, ¶ 11).*

[111]   *FASB ASC 740-10-25-3, 740-10-25-20 (FASB Statement No. 109, ¶¶ 9(f), 11(g)); FASB Statement No. 109, ¶¶ 114(b), 120.*

financial statements.[112] However, when the remeasurement method is applied (i.e., the reporting currency is the functional currency), Topic 740 (FASB Statement No. 109) requires the remeasurement of pre-existing deferred taxes at current rates after a change in exchange rates and this is reported in net income.[113] In fact, deferred taxes are considered monetary items both for the purpose of applying the remeasurement method and for supplemental information under Topic 255 (FASB Statement No. 89).[114]

Worksheet 69 illustrates the accounting for a change in functional currency, both in non-hyperinflationary and hyperinflationary contexts. Under U.S. GAAP, on the date of a change in functional currency from the reporting currency to a foreign currency because the foreign economy ceases to be highly inflationary, a taxable temporary difference ordinarily arises because the foreign currency tax bases of the nonmonetary assets would be lower than their functional currency (i.e., foreign currency) accounting bases. The related deferred tax liability is charged to the cumulative transaction adjustment in other comprehensive income and not to the income tax expense.[115]

Conversely, both IAS 29 and IAS 21 refer to the standard determination of deferred taxes under IAS 12.[116] A temporary difference may also arise on nonmonetary items when IAS 29 is applied and no indexing (or no equivalent adjustment) is done for tax purposes. In this case, deferred taxes are recognized and allocated based on the ordinary backwards tracing rules. Hence, they are allocated to profit or loss, except for the portion that refers to any revaluation surplus of those nonmonetary assets.[117] As a result of a restatement under IAS 29, the financial reporting bases of nonmonetary assets and liabilities change. As IAS 29 applies retrospectively, related deferred taxes must also change. Although it may be argued that deferred taxes might be considered monetary items (see above), restating them with the method applicable to monetary items would not result in the remeasurement of deferred assets as if the economy had always been hyperinflationary. Therefore, when an entity restates financial statements under IAS 29 for the first time, it must first re-determine these deferred taxes as of the beginning of the current period and of any comparative period presented, but after having restated their accounting bases as of the beginning of that period by applying the measurement unit at that date. In fact, the determination of deferred taxes follows IAS 12, i.e., it is based on the temporary differences between the restated accounting bases of nonmonetary items and their tax bases, and not by applying a general price index to unrestated deferred taxes as they were nonmonetary items. Once the entity has determined the deferred taxes in this way as of the beginning of each period, it must restate them at measuring current units as of the end of that period by multiplying them by the conversion factor corresponding to the general price index from the opening date of the respective period to the end date of the same period. Then, in order to show comparative information in subsequent periods, the entity applies the change in the measuring units for that subsequent period directly to the restated balances of deferred taxes at the end of the previous period. The restatement change in deferred taxes on

---

[112] *FASB ASC 255-10-50-41 (FASB Statement No. 89, ¶ 33).*

[113] *FASB ASC 830-740-45-1 (FASB Statement No. 109, ¶ 230).*

[114] *FASB Statement No. 52, ¶ 54; FASB ASC 255-10-55-1 (FASB Statement No. 89, ¶ 96).*

[115] *FASB ASC 830-740-45-2 (EITF Issue No. 92-8, Accounting for the Income Tax Effects under FASB Statement No. 109 of a Change in Functional Currency When an Economy Ceases to Be Considered Highly Inflationary).*

[116] *IAS 21, ¶ 50; IAS 29, ¶ 32.*

[117] *IAS 12, ¶ A18.*

nonmonetary items affects profit or loss. In case of a nonmonetary asset, for example, the impact is the net effect of two components. On one hand, a decrease in tax expense (i.e., from a decrease in deferred tax liability) results from a lower taxable temporary difference related to the nonmonetary asset. On the other hand, if the indexing for tax purposes of a nonmonetary asset is nil or lower than its restatement for financial reporting purposes, the current period profit or loss is hit by the increase of deferred tax liability corresponding to the loss of purchasing power that is not compensated by a corresponding indexing of the tax base of a nonmonetary asset. In this way, the loss on tax base because of inflation is charged to the current period profit or loss, as part of the so-called "gain or loss on the net monetary position" under IAS 29. This effect would otherwise be included in the opening equity if the nonmonetary assets in comparative periods were restated by using the general price index from the opening date of the comparative period to the end of the current period instead of that of the same comparative period.[118]

Comment: IFRIC 7 starts from determining deferred taxes on restated opening balances of current and prior period, while EITF Issue No. 93-9 remeasures deferred taxes from the end of the previous period. Under EITF Issue No. 93-9 such a restatement affects beginning equity, while under IAS 29 it affects profit or loss.

8.2.17 Income Tax on Dividends

8.2.17.1 Classification of Income Tax on Dividends Under Topic 480 (FASB Statement No. 150), dividends on mandatorily redeemable shares or other instruments classified as liabilities under the standard are reported as interest cost.[119] Similarly, under IAS 32, the classification of a financial instrument in the form of shares as equity or financial liability determines whether the related dividends are reflected in equity or in the income statement (i.e., as a distribution of retained earnings or as interest expenses). Furthermore, under IFRSs, if based on the contractual arrangements dividend distribution is mandatory or accrues to the redemption amount of an instrument, dividends are classified as interest expenses.[120]

The related income tax classification in the income statement or in equity follows the classification of the underlying financial instrument. However, the IASB notes an inconsistency between such a treatment under IAS 32 and the requirement in IAS 12 to report tax on dividends in profit or loss, except when dividends originate from other comprehensive income or transactions recognized directly in equity. The IASB interprets that IAS 32 does not intend to waive IAS 12. The 2011 Exposure Draft *Improvements to IFRSs* proposes to make this clear.[121]

IAS 1 requests presentation of dividends accounted for in equity either in the statement of changes in equity or in the notes and prohibits their presentation in the statement of comprehensive income, as owner changes in equity must be presented in the statement of changes in equity separately from non-owner changes in equity (presented in the statement of

---

[118] *IAS 29, ¶ 9; IFRIC 7, ¶¶ 4–5, IE5–IE6, BC22–BC25.*

[119] *FASB ASC 480-10-45-3, 480-10-55-8 (FASB Statement No. 150, ¶¶ 22, A5); FASB Statement No. 150, ¶ B69.*

[120] *IAS 32, ¶¶ 35, 36, AG37.*

[121] *IAS 12, ¶¶ 52B, 58; Exposure Draft,* Improvements to IFRSs *(June 2011); IASB Update, March 2010.*

comprehensive income).[122] The pre-2007 version of IAS 1 also permitted presentation on the face of the income statement.[123]

> **Comment:** This option was similar to that adopted in the UK practice, used to compute beginning and ending retained earnings on the face of the income statement.

IAS 32 encourages, but does not require, separate display of dividends classified as an expense because, depending on tax jurisdiction, tax implications may differ from those of interest.[124] However, IFRS 7 requires the disclosure of the dividend and interest breakdown of net gains and losses for each category of financial instruments, also including financial liabilities classified as at fair value through profit or loss.[125]

8.2.17.2 Withholding Tax on Dividends   Certain jurisdictions assess withholding taxes on dividends. Those withholding taxes may be fully or partially refundable to the dividend recipient. In addition, depending on the jurisdiction, a foreign resident may claim a foreign tax credit which may interact with withholding tax provisions of a bilateral treaty for the avoidance of double taxation with the country of residence of the dividend recipient. Under IAS 12, withholding tax on dividends paid or payable to tax authorities on behalf of the entity's shareholders (including when distributed by a subsidiary, associate, or jointly controlled entity to its parent, investor, or venturer, respectively) directly reduces retained earnings as part of the net dividend, in the entity or separate financial statements of the dividend-distributing company, irrespective of whether the distributing entity pays net dividends to shareholders and withholds tax at the source or the corporation itself bears the tax charge.[126]

> **Comment:** U.S. GAAP is not so explicit on the recognition of withholding tax for a dividend-distributing company. However, Subtopic 740-10 (EITF Issue No. 95-9) indirectly confirms the recognition of withholding tax in equity. In fact, the Issue states that withholding tax assessed on a corporation on distributed dividends for the benefit of the recipients of the dividend must be recorded in equity as withholding tax as part of the dividend distribution in the corporation's individual financial statements, provided such a tax is payable only in connection with an actual dividend distribution, it does not reduce other future taxes of the corporation, and shareholders receive a tax credit (in the form of a refund or reduction of taxes) for an amount that is no lower irrespective of their tax status.[127] Furthermore, Topic 740 (FASB Statement No. 109) does not clearly list withholding tax on dividend as an item allocated to income from continuing operations. Under this analysis, the general intraperiod allocation rule of equity display of tax on items that are recognized in equity would apply, provided those underlying items refer to the current period.

Under IFRSs, if under a specific jurisdiction intercompany dividend income is taxable, the dividend-receiving parent recognizes related taxes in its separate financial statements,

---

[122] *IAS 1, ¶¶ 107, BC75.*
[123] *IAS 1 (2005), ¶ 95.*
[124] *IAS 32, ¶ 40.*
[125] *IFRS 7, ¶¶ B5(e), BC34.*
[126] *IAS 12, ¶¶ 2, 65A.*
[127] *FASB ASC 740-10-15-4 (EITF Issue No. 95-9, Accounting for Tax Effects of Dividends in France in Accordance With FASB Statement No. 109).*

including those withheld by the subsidiary. For financial reporting purposes, the entity recognizes a deferred tax liability when dividends are declared by the reporting date, even if not paid (assuming that in that jurisdiction dividends are taxable at payment date), while it recognizes a current tax payable in the period dividends are paid. The entity recognizes a tax liability inclusive of any tax, including withholding tax, on the accrued dividend receivable.[128]

Under U.S. GAAP, the company that receives dividends must take into account any applicable taxes, including withholding taxes. Withholding taxes related to future distribution of dividends must also be considered when deferred taxes are recognized on undistributed earnings of subsidiaries and dividends distribution is planned. Under Topic 740 (FASB Statement No. 109), an entity must measure deferred tax liability for undistributed earnings based on dividends so as to include the net effect of dividend-received deductions, withholding taxes, or any applicable foreign tax credits. In assessing whether or not a deferred tax asset for an investment in a subsidiary meets the future reversal threshold for recognition, the future distribution of dividends of the subsidiary must not be considered, unless to the extent of a deferred tax liability that has been recognized for undistributed earnings. Therefore the future realization of tax benefits must not depend on reversal of deferred tax liability for undistributed earnings that has not or will not be recognized.[129] Depending on the percentage ownership interest, certain jurisdictions make a corporate dividends-received deduction on dividends received from certain subsidiaries available to certain parent corporations that do not, or cannot, file consolidated income tax returns. Such an amount is deducted for taxable income but not for accounting purposes. Therefore, the amount of dividends corresponding to the dividends-received deduction creates a permanent difference for which no deferred taxes are recorded.

Under the general rules of IAS 12, withholding tax on intragroup dividends affects profit or loss in the consolidated statement of comprehensive income (as opposed to retained earnings in the distributing entity's financial statements). In fact, withholding tax is not eliminated in the consolidated financial statements, in contrast to the dividends (dividend income for the parent company and retained earnings for the subsidiary, assuming the subsidiary is accounted at cost method under IFRSs). Thus, withholding tax cannot be referred to any equity item any longer.[130] Worksheet 78 illustrates the accounting for income taxes on intercompany dividends.

Comment: U.S. GAAP is silent on whether or not income tax on intercompany dividends is eliminated in consolidation, and whether or not the treatment of income tax on intercompany unrealized profits (i.e., on assets remaining within the group) should be applied by analogy (e.g., in the case where a dividend receivable exists at the reporting date). In fact, Topic 740 (FASB Statement No. 109), differently from the previous FASB Statement No. 96, prohibits the recognition of deferred tax assets on intercompany unrealized profits, because they are eliminated in consolidation. This is an exception under U.S. GAAP to the comprehensive recognition of deferred taxes. This tax basis difference is given by the difference between the tax basis of the assets in the jurisdiction of the "buyer" and their cost in the consolidated statement of financial position.[131] A deferred tax asset is instead recognized

---

[128] *IAS 12, ¶¶ 7, Appendix B, Example 3; IAS 18*, Revenue, *¶ 30.*

[129] *FASB ASC 942-740-25-4, 740-30-25-13, 740-10-55-24 (FASB Statement No. 109, ¶¶ 34, 237); FASB Statement No. 109, ¶ 174.*

[130] *IAS 12, ¶ B11; IAS 27 (2010), ¶ 25.*

[131] *FASB ASC 740-10-25-3 (FASB Statement No. 109, ¶ 9(e)); FASB Statement No. 109, ¶¶ 114(c), 124.*

to offset the current taxes that the "seller" has paid on intercompany profits that remain unrealized and suspended in the asset in the consolidated statement of financial position. Alternatively, those intercompany profits must be appropriately reduced.[132] IAS 12 however applies the general principle of tax accounting that recognizes deferred taxes on temporary differences between tax and financial reporting bases. This results in a deferred tax asset on intercompany unrecognized profit at buyers' tax rate. This difference between the two sets of standards may be briefly summarized in that under IFRSs deferred tax effect of intercompany unrealized profit is recognized at the buyer's tax rate, while under U.S. GAAP reference is made to the seller's tax rate. The Exposure Draft on income tax confirmed that recognizing a deferred tax is not in conflict with consolidation accounting because the payment of income tax and the change in tax jurisdiction are events with external parties and, as such, they must be faithfully represented.[133]

Disclosure on accounting policy will also include a description of taxes applicable to taxes and withholding tax on dividends, other comprehensive income, and other equity items. Topic 740 (FASB Statement No. 109), in contrast to the superseded FASB Statement No. 96, has no requirement of specific disclosure of withholding tax on dividend that would be payable upon remittance of foreign earnings.[134] For foreign private issuers, SEC Regulation K requires disclosure on taxes and withholding taxes to U.S. common shareholders under a registrant's foreign country rules and provisions of reciprocal tax treaties, if any.[135] Form 20-F requires disclosure on taxes and withholding taxes to shareholders of the host countries, provisions of anti-double tax treaties, if any, and whether or not the reporting entity assumes responsibility for the withholding of tax at source.[136]

8.2.17.3 Tax-Deductible Dividends

Depending on the specific circumstances and jurisdiction certain dividends may be tax-deductible. If dividends are tax-deductible, Topic 740 (FASB Statement No. 109) in general requires the allocation of the related income tax benefit to income from continuing operations. The standard justifies this on the grounds that those dividends substantially provide a tax exemption of a corresponding amount of earnings.[137]

Comment: The accounting under IFRSs is controversial. On one hand, if under a specific jurisdiction dividends are tax-deductible, IAS 32 specifies that dividends must be debited directly to equity net of the associated income tax benefit.[138] On the other hand, IAS 12 requires recognizing the income tax consequences of dividends in net profit or loss.[139] The IFRIC reaffirmed that the classification in net profit or loss of income tax on tax-deductible dividends under IAS 12 applies to any tax-deductible payments that are made on own equity instruments.[140]

---

[132] *FASB ASC 810-10-45-8 (ARB 51, ¶ 17).*

[133] *Exposure Draft,* Income Tax, *¶¶ BC46-BC47 (March 2009).*

[134] *FASB Statement No. 109, ¶ 175; FASB Statement No. 96,* Accounting for Income Taxes, *(superseded) ¶ 25.*

[135] *SEC Regulation K, ¶ 229.201, Instructions to Item 201, 4.B; 229.202, Instructions to Item 202, 2.C-D.*

[136] *SEC Form 20-F, Part I, Item 10.E.*

[137] *FASB ASC 740-20-45-8 (FASB Statement No. 109, ¶ 35); FASB Statement No. 109, ¶ 145.*

[138] *IAS 32, ¶ 35.*

[139] *IAS 12, ¶ 52B.*

[140] *IFRIC Update, February 2003.*

8.2.17.4 Undistributed Versus Distributed Earnings Tax Rates In certain jurisdictions different tax rates may apply to distributed versus undistributed earnings. Alternatively, a distribution of the net profit or retained earnings may trigger the payment or refund of income taxes. This payment or refund generally corresponds to the difference between the tax computed at the undistributed earnings rates applicable to the taxable income for the period to which the tax return refers and the tax computed at the distributed earnings rates in effect in the period in which dividend is distributed (i.e., the period in which the tax credit is included in the tax return).

Example: This would be the case for Germany and Italy.

The topic may be analyzed from the standpoint of a subsidiary in whose jurisdiction these tax rules are effective, or from the perspective of the consolidated financial statements, or from the point of view of a parent company where these tax rules exist in its jurisdiction but not in the jurisdiction of its subsidiary.

Under IAS 12, from the perspective of the entity (subsidiary or parent) under whose tax jurisdiction the above rules apply, the income tax effects of dividends (e.g., benefit or expense due at the lower or higher tax rates) are recognized in the current period only when dividends have been declared by the reporting period date (i.e., when a liability arises). Therefore, if the dividends are declared after the reporting date, current tax expense in the statement of comprehensive income must reflect the tax rates applicable to undistributed earnings and no deferred tax assets or liabilities on the effects of potential tax impacts from the future distribution of dividends are recognized. Deferred tax assets or liabilities on other items are also computed at the tax rates applicable to undistributed earnings. The income tax refund or payment that is triggered by the payment of dividends in a subsequent period will be recognized in current tax in the statement of comprehensive income, not in retained earnings, in the period of recognition for tax purposes (even if dividends are recognized in equity). The rationale is that those benefits relate more to past income-producing transactions than to the distribution decision itself.

Comment: The above rationale stated in IAS 12 is consistent with the abovementioned position of Topic 740 (FASB Statement No. 109) for recognizing income tax on tax-deductible dividends in income from continuing operations. However, the fact that the income tax effects hit the income statement is somehow inconsistent with one of the two interpretations of the recognition of tax-deductible dividends mentioned in the previous Section.

Under IFRSs, of course, backwards tracing rules may require recognition in equity of some portion of those income tax consequences of dividends.

Comment: For example, this may refer to a portion of that dividend that is paid out of profit arising from transactions or events that have been recognized directly in equity, or to withholding tax on dividends.

Conversely, the Exposure Draft on income tax proposed to compute current and deferred taxes at the distributed rate. The topic of the income tax effects of dividends has been debated for a long time as part of the short-term convergence project on income tax.[141]

Comment: It justifies this on the grounds of more alleged useful information to users of financial statements, especially in the case of tax-exempt entities, such as real estate investment trusts and cooperative societies in some jurisdictions and of the general approach of using the rate expected to apply in measuring deferred tax assets and liabilities. On the other hand, this seems contrary to the hitherto rigorous use of the reporting date as the cut-off point to assess whether or not a distribution declaration creates an obligation to pay cash as dividends or distribute other assets, as IFRIC 17 recently confirmed.[142]

Subtopic 740-10 (EITF Issue No. 95-10) uses a similar accounting to IAS 12 for the purpose of the financial statements of a foreign corporation reporting under U.S. GAAP that pays dividends and that obtains a tax credit or tax refund in connection with such a payment in the foreign jurisdiction.[143] However, this consensus applies only to the situation where the undistributed tax rate is higher than the distributed tax rate.

Comment: As drafted, there is another subtle difference between the Subtopic 740-10 (EITF Issue No. 95-10) and the IAS 12 position on this subject. Subtopic 740-10 (EITF Issue No. 95-10) makes reference to the tax perspective (i.e., taxable income and tax credit in two different tax returns). IAS 12, in analyzing whether or not the income tax effects of dividends should be recognized in the period of earning of net income makes reference to dividend declaration from a financial reporting perspective, not dividend payment for tax purposes. To explain, in case the undistributed tax rate is higher than the distributed tax rate, neither U.S. GAAP nor IFRSs recognize the deferred tax asset (arising from the difference in rates) in the period in which taxable income is taxed if dividends are declared and distributed in a subsequent period. However, IAS 12 would recognize a deferred tax asset, while Subtopic 740-10 (EITF Issue No. 95-10) would not, if dividends are declared from profits earned in the same period but paid in a subsequent period. Furthermore, under EITF Issue No. 95-10 the corporation recognizes a reduction on current income tax expense in the period the tax credits are included in its tax returns (which generally corresponds to the date of payment), but under IAS 12 a change in deferred tax (i.e., its remeasurement at distributed earnings rate) is triggered by the dividend declaration in the subsequent year while a reduction in current income tax expense (and a reversal of deferred taxes) occurs at dividend payment. IFRIC 17 clarifies the meaning of declaration of dividends for IFRS financial reporting purposes. This is when it is no longer at the discretion of the entity, a moment that may vary with corporate governance framework depending on jurisdiction (e.g., approval by shareholders as opposed to declaration by management or board of directors).[144]

Subtopic 740-10 (EITF Issue No. 95-10) indirectly confirms that those tax effects of dividend payments are recognized in the income statement.

---

[141] *FASB*, Short-Term Convergence – Income Taxes, *Minutes of the March 30, 2005 Board Meeting (March 30, 2005)*.

[142] *Exposure Draft*, Income Tax, *¶¶ B31, BC79–BC81 (March 2009); IFRIC 17, ¶ 10*.

[143] *FASB ASC 740-10-25-40 (EITF Issue No. 95-10*, Accounting for Tax Credits Related to Dividend Payments in Accordance with FASB Statement No. 109).

[144] *IFRIC 17, ¶ 10*.

Comment: A similar conclusion may be reached by reading EITF Issue No. 95-9 (see Section 8.2.17.2 previously). If tax assessed on a corporation on dividend distribution affects other future taxes of the corporation, it is not considered withholding tax for the purpose of the Issue and it is not subject to its requirement of direct recognition in equity. Arguably, in this case to the extent the distribution of dividends determines income tax effects on earnings and they would be considered tax-deductible dividends, those effects would be recognized in income from continuing operations (see Section 8.2.17.3 previously).

Comment: The topic discussed in this Section interacts with that analyzed in Section 8.2.13 previously. Depending on jurisdiction, similar situations often arise with revaluation reserves. The issue is whether or not the rules of the potential effects of dividends apply to distribution of equity reserves, such as revaluation reserves. As explained, if a temporary difference arises from a revaluation, IAS 12 requires the recognition of deferred taxes, which is made in other comprehensive income if revaluation is made for financial reporting purposes in a past, in the current, or in a future period, or in profit or loss if the adjustment is done for tax purposes only. On the other hand, when different tax rates apply to this revaluation reserve depending on whether or not it is distributed to shareholders, the measurement of deferred taxes will be computed based on tax rates applicable to undistributed earnings and no deferred taxes are recognized in the current period on the effects of a distribution that may be effected in the future. Therefore, IAS 12 appears to be clear in requiring the recognition of deferred taxes on such reserves based on undistributed earnings rate, but it distinguishes between recognition and measurement criteria. Arguably, if the undistributed earnings rate is nil and no earnings are distributed, no deferred taxes are recognized. However, jurisdictional interpretations have arisen on whether or not deferred tax must be recognized at all on these special equity reserves. Certain authoritative interpretations in Italy have claimed that either no deferred tax must be recognized or that a judgment of probability of payment dividends must be made to determine whether deferred tax must be recognized, mainly based on the analogy of the application of the treatment required for undistributed profits of subsidiaries, associates, branches, and joint ventures.[145]

Example: In certain jurisdictions, some equity reserves (see Section 3.5.4 previously) may be taxable only to the extent they are distributed to shareholders. In Italy, certain revaluation reserves that are required or allowed by act of specific laws are taxable only if distributed (not if capitalized or used for deficit reorganization) unless a substitutive tax has been paid, in which case those equity reserves become free and unappropriated.

Example: A French foreign private issuer replied to the SEC Staff in its review of the company Form 20-F for the fiscal year ending December 31, 2005 containing financial statements prepared for the first time on the basis of IFRSs, that it recognized no deferred tax liability on certain tax-free reserves of its Greek subsidiary as they were subject to no tax unless distributed.[146]

---

[145] *OIC – Organismo Italiano di Contabilità,* Guida Operativa per la Transizione ai Principi Contabili Internazionali (IAS/IFRS) *(October 2005), ¶ Chapter 17.3.3; ABI – Associazione Bancaria Italiana, Soluzioni IAS ABI No. 2 (November 21, 2005).*

[146] *Letter by the SEC, File No. 1-15218, Note 3 (September 12, 2006). Reply by the company (October 23, 2006) www.sec.gov/divisions/corpfin/ifrs_reviews (last visited January 7, 2008).*

Comment: Contrary to these interpretations, under U.S. GAAP the indefinite reversal exemption cannot be applied by analogy. In fact, a related issue is whether or not the indefinite reversal exemption applies to the portion of the undistributed earnings of a subsidiary that is subject to different tax rates in case of distribution. U.S. GAAP clarifies that a U.S. parent must not apply the indefinite reversal criterion (see below) on the so-called "inside basis differences," such as the portion of undistributed earnings of an Italian (or other foreign) subsidiary corresponding to the temporary difference of a revaluation reserve taxable in case of distribution. An inside basis difference is a temporary difference within the foreign entity, i.e., between the carrying amount of an item of the foreign entity in the consolidated financial statements and its tax basis in the tax jurisdiction of that individual group entity. An outside basis difference is a temporary difference between the carrying amount of the investment in a subsidiary, associate, or jointly controlled entity and its tax basis in the tax jurisdiction of the parent, investor, or joint venturer. The entity must recognize deferred taxes on temporary inside basis differences.[147] Although it does not clearly state it, the Exposure Draft on Income Taxes suggested similar scope exclusion for inside basis differences.[148]

From the perspective of the consolidated financial statements of the entity that receives dividends, an issue arises on how to account for the tax effects of undistributed earnings of subsidiaries, associates, joint ventures, or branches in which jurisdiction tax rates on undistributed and distributed earnings differ and how this interacts with the indefinite reversal exemptions under respective GAAP. U.S. GAAP has an indefinite reversal exemption, which however is currently limited to undistributed earnings of foreign subsidiaries or corporate joint ventures when the reporting entity is able to overcome the presumption of repatriation of the foreign earnings based on certain evidence.[149] There is no exemption for undistributed earnings of domestic subsidiaries or domestic corporate joint ventures that are essentially permanent in duration and for which it is not apparent that the temporary difference will reverse in the foreseeable future if they arose in fiscal years beginning after December 15, 1992, or for undistributed earnings of any other investees (such as an equity-method investee). This exemption must not be applied by analogy with temporary differences other than those specified in the pronouncement.[150] A deferred tax asset on the excess of the tax basis over the carrying amount of an investment in a subsidiary or corporate joint venture (even if domestic) that is essentially permanent in duration and for which it is apparent that the temporary difference will reverse in the foreseeable future must be recognized.[151] U.S. GAAP prohibits recognition of a tax benefit possibly arising from lower tax rates or tax deductions in connection with future distribution of dividends of subsidiaries when the parent has recognized no deferred tax in consolidated financial statements due to indefinite reversal exemption. Therefore, in these situations the undistributed earnings rates must be used to compute income tax.[152] If on

---

[147]   *FASB ASC 740-30-25-17, 830-740-25-7 (EITF Issue No. 93-16,* Application of FASB Statement No. 109 to Basis Differences within Foreign Subsidiaries That Meet the Indefinite Reversal Criterion of APB Opinion No. 23*); Exposure Draft of a Proposed IFRS for Small and Medium-sized Entities (February 2007), ¶ 28.11.*

[148]   *Exposure Draft,* Income Tax, *¶ BC39, BC44 (March 2009).*

[149]   *FASB ASC 740-30-25-6, 740-30-25-17, 740-30-25-19 (APB 23, ¶¶ 10, 12).*

[150]   *FASB ASC 740-10-25-3, 740-30-15-4, 740-30-25-5 (FASB Statement No. 109, ¶¶ 31, 32).*

[151]   *FASB ASC 740-30-25-9 (FASB Statement No. 109, ¶ 34).*

[152]   *FASB ASC 740-30-25-14 (FASB Statement No. 109, ¶ 145); FASB ASC 840-40-25-14 (EITF Issue No. 95-20,* Measurement in the Consolidated Financial Statements of a Parent of the Tax Effects Related to the Operations of a Foreign Subsidiary That Receives Tax Credits Related to Dividend Payments*).*

the other hand the parent has not elected for the exemption for foreign unremitted earnings, both deferred taxes on undistributed earnings of the subsidiary and the income tax effects of future dividend payment (e.g., a tax credit) must be recognized in the current period based on tax rates applicable to distributed earnings.[153] In practice, the higher of the distributed or undistributed rate is often used.[154]

Comment: Generally speaking, the accounting required by IAS 12 on undistributed earnings rate applies to any reporting entity, whether a subsidiary, parent, or consolidated entity. The situation gets more complex when considering the interaction with the indefinite reversal exemption. IAS 12 also has a sort of indefinite reversal exemption, based on which deferred tax liabilities are not recognized under certain circumstances. Unlike U.S. GAAP, this exemption is not limited to foreign subsidiaries only and is also permitted to associates and branches.[155] The Exposure Draft proposed to restrict this exemption to investments in foreign subsidiaries and joint ventures (like U.S. GAAP) or branches that are essentially permanent in duration and to prohibit it for associates. Unlike U.S. GAAP, the recognition of deferred tax assets on domestic subsidiaries and joint ventures would not be exempted.[156] IAS 12 explains the accounting for income tax on undistributed earnings of subsidiaries, associates, joint ventures, or branches. It also clarifies that the impracticability of determining the amount of unrecognized deferred tax liabilities on those undistributed earnings may translate into impracticability in computing the potential income tax consequences of dividends.[157] However, it does not provide guidance as to the specific situation where, under a parent's jurisdiction, equity reserves that may be subject to different tax rates depending on whether or not they are distributed take their origin, in whole or in part, from undistributed profits of those entities included in the consolidated financial statements. Certain jurisdictional interpretations have directed that in such situations, an entity that is exempted from recognizing deferred tax liabilities on taxable differences associated with investment subsidiaries, associates, joint ventures, or branches would be in the position, if respective criteria are met, of not recognizing these deferred taxes at all, not only to the extent of the effects of a future distribution of dividends.[158] However, as explained above, the exemption from recognizing a deferred tax liability is not permitted to the extent such temporary difference is an inside basis difference.

Under IFRSs, an entity must disclose the potential income tax impact of payment of dividend, the fact that some consequences are not practicably determinable, the main determinants of these consequences, and the main characteristics of the income tax system. In a parent's separate financial statements, these disclosures apply to the parent's undistributed earnings and not to those of its subsidiaries or investees. In addition, the disclosure of the potential income tax impacts of payment of dividend must include the situation when dividends are declared or proposed before authorization for issue of the financial statements but have not been recognized as a liability.[159] As Topic 740 (FASB Statement No. 109) does not require these disclosures, the FASB tentatively agreed as part of the short-term project on income taxes to converge with the IASB.[160] Finally, as the IASB's Exposure Draft proposed to move to the distributed

---

[153] *FASB ASC 840-40-25-14 (EITF Issue No. 95-20).*
[154] *Exposure Draft, Income Tax, ¶ BC77 (March 2009).*
[155] *IAS 12, ¶ 39.*
[156] *Exposure Draft, Income Tax, ¶¶ IN8(f), B5, BC133(a) (March 2009).*
[157] *IAS 12, ¶ 87C.*
[158] *OIC – Organismo Italiano di Contabilità,* Guida Operativa per la Transizione ai Principi Contabili Internazionali (IAS/IFRS) *(October 2005), ¶ Chapter 17.3.3.*
[159] *IAS 12, ¶¶ 52A–52B, 81(g)(i), 82A, 87A–87B.*
[160] *FASB, Short-Term Convergence – Income Taxes, Revised Minutes of the June 15, 2005 Board Meeting (June 23, 2005), ¶ 32.*

earnings rate, most of those disclosures would be eliminated. An entity would be required to explain its estimates relating to future distributions and their impact on the tax rate used.[161]

8.2.17.5   Income Tax on Dividends on ESOP Shares   Section 4.14.4 previously discusses certain relationships between accounting for share-based payment transactions, ESOPs, and similar employee benefit trusts and treasury shares.

An ESOP (employee stock ownership plan) is an employee benefit plan under the Employee Retirement Income Security Act of 1974 (ERISA) and the Internal Revenue Code (IRC) of 1986 consisting in a stock bonus plan, or combination stock bonus and money purchase pension plan, designed to invest primarily in employer stock. Under SOP 93-6, dividends on unallocated shares held by a leveraged ESOP are reported in the sponsor's income statement as compensation expenses if paid to plan participants, or as reductions of debt or accrued interest. Dividends on allocated ESOP shares are debited to retained earnings, because once allocated the shares belong to participants' accounts and the employer no longer has control over the dividends. Dividends on shares held by a nonleveraged ESOP are generally charged to retained earnings.[162] Under Topic 740 (FASB Statement No. 109) however, by analogy with the general treatment of income tax on tax-deductible dividends in the income statement (see Section 8.2.17.3 previously), any income tax benefits of tax-deductible dividends on ESOP shares are credited in income from continuing operations, except in the case where shares are unallocated and dividends charged to retained earnings.[163]

IFRSs have no explicit guidance on ESOPs. In theory, the accounting for income tax on ESOP dividends is interlinked to several issues that underline certain inconsistencies.

Comment: Firstly, as U.S. GAAP seeks to treat ESOPs consistently with stock option plans, ESOPs are within the scope of IFRS 2, as a form of equity-compensation plan, provided equity instruments are granted to employees in exchange for their employee service. An ESOP in substance implements share-based awards to an entity's employees through an employee benefit trust.

From a different angle, an ESOP is also a broad-based employee share plan. IFRSs use expressions such as "employee share trusts" and "employee share purchase plans," which also might include ESOP arrangements. As mentioned above, IFRS 2 does not contain exemptions for those plans.[164]

However, the characterization of shares held by an ESOP under the specific circumstances has to be determined. In consolidated financial statements, share-based payment transactions effected through a benefit trust would be accounted for under IFRS 2 as equity-settled or cash-settled depending on their classification. For the purpose of individual or separate financial statements, a transfer of an entity's equity instruments in exchange for goods or services is an equity-settled share-based payment irrespective of whether the entity itself, its parent, or its subsidiary grants the rights to the shares or whether the entity itself or a third party settles the transaction.[165] Under IFRIC 11, the fact that an

---

[161]   *Exposure Draft, Income Tax), ¶ 48(a) (March 2009).*
[162]   *FASB ASC 718-40-15-3 (AICPA Statement of Position No. 93-6, Employer's Accounting for Employee Stock Ownership Plans, ¶¶ 21, 22, 42).*
[163]   *FASB ASC 740-20-45-8, 740-20-45-11 (FASB Statement No. 109, ¶¶ 35, 144); FASB Statement No. 109, ¶ 36(f); AICPA Statement of Position No. 93-6, ¶ 51.*
[164]   *IFRIC Amendment to SIC-12, Scope of SIC-12, Consolidation – Special Purpose Entities, ¶ 15B; IASB Update, September 2003.*
[165]   *FASB ASC 718-10-15-4 (FASB Statement No. 123(R), ¶ 11); IFRS 2, ¶ 3; IFRIC, ¶ 7.*

entity may choose or be required to purchase its own shares on the market or from a shareholder to be used in exchange for employee services does not negate the nature of the transaction as an equity-settled share-based payment transaction.[166]

This topic is also related to whether or not an ESOP should be consolidated by the sponsor or employer. IFRSs acknowledge the existence of employee benefit trusts and treat them especially for the purpose of determining whether or not they should be consolidated by the employer.[167] The Amendment of SIC-12 removed the previous scope exclusion of equity compensation plans from that interpretation, for the purposes of consolidating those plans.[168] The consolidation model of IFRS 10 applies to all types of entities.[169]

IFRS 2 and IAS 32 extend treasury shares accounting (i.e., equity treatment, as Section 4.14 previously explains) to an entity's own shares issued or cancelled in connection with share-based payment.[170] On the other hand, if the ESOP were determined to hold shares on behalf of others (i.e., the employer), those shares would not be treated as property of the ESOP but as employer's treasury shares under IAS 32.[171] However, the IFRIC analyzed whether treasury stock accounting should also apply to the separate financial statements of an entity sponsoring an employee benefit trust, that is, whether the employee benefit trust should be considered an extension of the sponsoring entity or whether the investment in the employee benefit trust should be recorded as an asset (a separate legal entity view). The IFRIC decided not to take the issue onto its agenda. The topic was related to the notion of "entity" being analyzed in the *Conceptual Framework Project* and to whether or not to account for the net investment in the trust, an issue that was related to the revision of IAS 27.[172]

Of course, the legal treatment of dividends on own shares falls under defense of capital regulations (see Section 3.5.2 previously). For example, in certain jurisdictions, dividends declared in respect of own shares proportionally accrue to the other shares outstanding.

Furthermore, the nature of dividends on ESOP shares as distribution of profit or as interest expenses must be determined. By contrast, U.S. GAAP seeks to treat income tax on dividends consistently with the substance and classification of ESOP shares. However, FSP FAS 150-4 explicitly excludes ESOPs from the scope of Topic 480 (FASB Statement No. 150).[173] A similar provision is missing under IFRSs. As explained above, IAS 32 classifies dividends either as interest expenses or as reduction of retained earnings (i.e., a distribution of profits) depending on whether the substance, not the legal form, of the underlying shares is that of a financial liability or of an equity instrument, respectively. If, based on contractual arrangements, distribution of dividends is mandatory or accrues to the redemption amount of an instrument, dividends are classified as interest expenses. Similarly, an obligation (such as under a forward contract) to purchase its own shares for cash where the entity cannot avoid settlement in cash or another financial asset or where the settlement is decided by the counterparty or depends on specified future events or circumstances beyond the control of the entity establish a financial liability for that amount of cash.[174] Based on that, the accounting of tax-deductible dividends as compensation costs or interest expense would be consistent with the classification of

---

[166] *IFRIC 11, ¶ 7 (then incorporated into IFRS 2).*
[167] *IFRS 2, ¶ BC70.*
[168] *IFRIC Amendment to SIC-12*, Scope of SIC-12, Consolidation – Special Purpose Entities.
[169] *IAS 19 (2011), ¶ Footnote to BC181.*
[170] *IAS 32, ¶ 4f(ii); IFRS 2, ¶ BC333.*
[171] *IAS 32, ¶ AG36.*
[172] *IFRIC Update, May 2006; IFRIC Update, November 2006.*
[173] *FASB ASC 480-10-15-8 (FASB Staff Position FAS 150-4*, Issuers' Accounting for Employee Stock Ownership Plans under FASB Statement No. 150, *¶ 3).*
[174] *IAS 32, ¶¶ BC10–BC12.*

related income tax benefits in the statement of comprehensive income (see Section 8.2.17.3 previously). On the other hand, based on IAS 32 treasury shares accounting (see Section 4.14.2 previously), IFRS 2 specifies that dividends on own shares, even when permitted under a specific jurisdiction, cannot be recognized as revenue or expense.[175]

8.2.18   Presentation of Income Tax

In current standards, presentation of income taxes follows both a gross-display on the face of the statement of comprehensive income, for income from continuing operations (U.S. GAAP only) and profit before tax (IFRSs only), and a net-display pattern for discontinued operations, extraordinary items (U.S. GAAP only), and either a net-of-tax or gross-of tax presentation for other comprehensive income.

> **Comment:** The 2007 amendments to IAS 1 amended IAS 12 to require the display of income tax related to profit or loss from ordinary activities (although undefined under IFRSs) in the statement of comprehensive income or in the income statement if the entity elects to use both statements.[176] The Exposure Draft on income tax would have deleted this requirement once intraperiod tax allocation was adopted.

An issue discussed in the *Financial Statement Presentation Project* is whether or not income tax should be a single line, and whether it should be allocated to the primary section or to all the sections of the statement of comprehensive income. The former case would translate in a gross display consisting in presenting all items on a pretax basis, including discontinued operations, extraordinary items (U.S. GAAP only), and so on. Having income tax in multiple sections would also eliminate a subtotal for income before tax. Presenting income tax as a separate section or within sections (and not simply as a line item as currently) would, in effect, eliminate the dichotomy between income before tax and net income. On the other hand, it would violate the cohesiveness principle (see Section 1.4.3.1 previously) and be open to the critics of intraperiod tax allocation. If income tax were allocated to a primary section of the statement of comprehensive income, an option would remain for either gross or net presentation in this section. However, income taxes do not arise solely from business or financing transactions. A tentative conclusion was that gross display should be the general rule for all items, unless net presentation is required or permitted by a standard or additional information provided in a gross presentation does not provide incremental values. As an example, this might be the case of a gain or loss on disposal of an ancillary piece of equipment.[177]

> **Comment:** Whether or not a net presentation provides incremental value is quite subjective. For example, tax impact is critical in project finance deals. However, the same project must be first analyzed from the operating side. As another example, a variant of the free cash flow approach

---

[175]   *IFRS 2, ¶ BC73.*

[176]   *IAS 1, ¶¶ 77, 77A.*

[177]   *FASB, User Advisory Council, Minutes of Meeting, October 3, 2006, ¶ 34 (October 31, 2006); IASB, Financial Statement Presentation Project, Agenda Paper 15A, Other Comprehensive Income, ¶ 34 (December 14, 2006); IASB Meeting, September 19, 2006, Agenda Paper 9, Application of Working Principles, ¶¶ 56, 116 (September 2006) www.iasb.org (last visited June 21, 2007); FASB, FASB Memorandum No. 43, Financial Statement Presentation – Application of Working Principles (continued), ¶¶ 14, 42 (September 26, 2006) www.fasb.org (last visited June 21, 2007).*

> separates the cash tax impact on free cash flow components from the cash tax impact on interests arising from financing after determining the free cash flow. Therefore, in practice, both views are used in business.

Finally, the Discussion Paper and the Staff Draft end up with maintaining the existing requirements for allocating and presenting income taxes in the statement of comprehensive income, because this contributes to the assessment of the amount, timing, and uncertainty of future cash flows, as required by the disaggregation objective. Furthermore, after-tax income from continuing operations has been considered an important indicator to retain.[178] While the Exposure Draft on income tax dealt with both intraperiod tax allocation and presentation of deferred taxes on the face of the statement of financial position (the latter topic is outside the scope of this Book), it did not take a position on the issue of the gross versus net presentation of income taxes on the face of the statement of comprehensive income.

8.2.19   Other Disclosures of Income Tax Allocated To Equity

Both IAS 12 and Topic 740 (FASB Statement No. 109) require disclosure of the total current and deferred tax allocated directly to equity and of tax expense or income related to changes in accounting policies and corrections of errors.[179] IAS 12 requires the detail of income tax for each component of other comprehensive income.[180] Topic 740 (FASB Statement No. 109) prescribes the disclosure of income tax expense or benefit allocated to items other than continuing operations and specifically the components of income tax attributable to income from continuing operations.[181] Section 235-10-S99 (Regulation S-X) gives guidance for specific disclosure of the various components of income tax expense.[182] The SEC Staff interpreted that an overall disclosure of income tax by intraperiod allocation nature (such as to continuing operations, discontinued operations, extraordinary items, cumulative effects of an accounting change, and direct charges and credits to shareholders' equity) is sufficient without the need for detailing the amount related to Federal, State, Foreign taxes, etc. for each nature of allocation.[183]

> **Example:** The SEC Staff, in its review of Form 20-F of an Italian foreign private issuer for the fiscal year ended December 31, 2005 containing financial statements prepared for the first time on the basis of IFRSs, requested the disclosure of current and deferred taxes charged or credited to equity.[184]

Section 8.2.12 previously explains the disclosure requirements of tax on items of other comprehensive income. Section 8.2.17.3 previously elucidates disclosure requirements of tax-deductible dividends.

---

[178]   *FASB and IASB*, Staff Draft of an Exposure Draft on Financial Statement Presentation, ¶¶ *98, BC111 (July 2010); Discussion Paper,* Preliminary Views on Financial Statement Presentation, ¶¶ *2.21, 2.75, 3.55, 3.62 (October 2008).*

[179]   *IAS 12, ¶¶ 80(h), 81(a).*

[180]   *IAS 12, ¶ 81(ab).*

[181]   *FASB ASC 740-10-50-9, 740-10-50-10 (FASB Statement No. 109, ¶¶ 45, 46).*

[182]   *FASB ASC 235-10-S99-1 (Regulation S-X, ¶ 210.4-08(h)).*

[183]   *FASB ASC 740-10-S99-1 (SEC Staff Accounting Bulletin, Topic 6-I.7,* Tax Expense Components vs. "Overall" Presentation*).*

[184]   *Letter by the SEC, File No. 1-14970, Note 3 (December 19, 2006). Reply by the company (January 30, 2007) www.sec.gov/divisions/corpfin/ifrs_reviews (last visited January 7, 2008).*

BIBLIOGRAPHY

OFFICIAL

Please see Worksheet 1.

UNOFFICIAL

Allegrini, M., Quagli, A., and Zattarin, S. (eds), *Principi contabili internazionali – Casi risolti* (IPSOA, 2006).

Barton, P. C. and Sager, C. R., "Sixth Circuit Court of Appeals Reverses Debt-Versus-Equity Issue," *The CPA Journal* (April 2007).

Bellandi, F., *I principi contabili internazionali: una sfida per dirigenti e manager* (IASItalia, 2005).

Bellandi, F., "Dual Reporting Under U.S. GAAP and IFRS – Layout of the Statement of Financial Position for Commercial and Industrial Entities," *The CPA Journal* (December 2007).

Bellandi, F., *The Handbook to IFRS Transition and to IFRS U.S. GAAP Dual Reporting, Interpretation, Implementation and Application to Grey Areas* (John Wiley & Sons, Ltd., 2012).

Bloomer, C. (ed.), Financial Accounting Standard Board, *The IASC – U.S. Comparison Project: A Report on the Similarities and Differences between IASC Standards and U.S. GAAP* (1999).

Bonham, M., Curtis, M., Davies, M., Dekker, P., Denton, T., Moore, R., Richards, H., Wilkinson-Riddle, G., and Wilson, A. (Ernst & Young), *International GAAP*, (LexisNexis).

Calderisi, M. C., Bowman, D., and Cohen, D. (eds), *Accounting Trends & Techniques*. 64th edn (New York: AICPA, 2010).

Cantino, V. and Devalle, A. (eds), *Impatto degli IAS/IFRS sui processi gestionali* (IPSOA, 2005).

Cearns, K., September 1999 Special Report, Reporting Financial Performance: A Proposed Approach, published by the members of the former G4+1 standard-setting organizations (September 1999).

Cook, D., Connor, L., Crisp, R., Dekker, P., Pankhurst, M., and Wilson, A. (Ernst & Young), *IFRS/US GAAP Comparison* (LexisNexis).

Danjou, P. and Baranger, S., Autorité Des Marchés Financiers, "IFRS et information financière – Recommandations et réflexions de l'Autorité des Marchés Financiers" (January 17, 2006).

Epstein, B. J. and Ali Mirza, A., *Interpretation and Application of International Accounting and Financial Reporting Standards*.

Epstein, B. J., Black, E. L., Nach, R., and Delaney, P. R., *GAAP* (John Wiley & Sons, Ltd., 2004).

Giussani, A., Nava, P., Portalupi, A., *Principi contabili internazionali*, Memento Pratico IPSOA – Francis Lefebvre.

Griffiths, M., *Purchase by Companies of Their Own Shares* (ACCA Global, 2000).

Huefner, R. J., Largay, III J. A., and Hamlen, S. S., *Advanced Financial Accounting* (DAME Thomson Learning, 2002).

Johnson, L. T. and Lennard, A., January 1998 Special Report, Reporting Financial Performance: Current Developments and Future Directions, published by the members of the former G4+1 (1998).

Lever, K., *Comprehensive Income: Would Luca Pacioli Turn in His Grave?* (ACCA Global, 2007).

Lofe, Y. and Calderisi, M. C. (eds), *Accounting Trends & Techniques*. 60th edn (New York: AICPA, 2006).

Mulford, C. W. and Comiskey, E. E., *The Financial Number Game* (John Wiley & Sons, Ltd., 2002).

Pretorious, J.T., *Capital Maintenance Doctrine in South Africa Corporate Law* (ACCA Global, 2000).

Stein, N., *Reporting Performance* (ACCA Global, 2003).

Walters, P. D. and Bowman, D., *IFRS Accounting Trends & Techniques – 2009* (New York: AICPA, 2010).

Walton, P., *The Comprehensive Income Statement* (ACCA Global, 2007).

Walton, P., Haller, A., and Raffournier, B. (eds), *International Accounting* (Thomson, 2002).

White, G. I., Sondhi, A. C., and Fried, D., *The Analysis and Use of Financial Statements* (John Wiley & Sons, Ltd., 2003).

ACCA, "DP2 – The Performance Reporting Debate. What (if Anything) Is Wrong with the Good Old Income Statement?" (April 2007).

Accounting Standards Committee of Germany on behalf of the European Financial Reporting Advisory Group and the German Accounting Standards Board under the Pro-active Accounting Activities in Europe Initiative of the European Financial Reporting Advisory Group and the European National Standard Setters, *Distinguishing Between Liabilities and Equity – Preliminary Views on the Classification of Liabilities and Equity and Under International Financial Reporting Standards*, (Brussels/Berlin, 2007).

AICPA Special Committee on Financial Reporting, Improving Business Reporting – A Customer Focus (December 1994).

Association for Investment Management and Research (AIMR), Financial Reporting in the 1990s and Beyond (November 1993).

Autorité Des Marchés Financiers, "Points relevés par l'AMF à l'occasion des premières communications sur la transition aux normes IFRS" (2005).

Autorité Des Marchés Financiers, "Les recommandations de l'AMF en matière d'information comptable dans la perspective de l'arrêté des comptes 2006" (December 2006).

BDO Stoy Hayward, "2006 IFRS Survey, International Financial Reporting Standards and the Mid-Market" (2006).

Citigate Dewe Rogerson Fallonstewart, "The Adoption of International Financial Reporting Standards, Who should lead the way?" (March 2005).

Commission of The European Communities, "Comments concerning certain Articles of the Regulation (EC) No 1606/2002 of the European Parliament and of the Council of 19 July 2002 on the application of international accounting standards and the Fourth Council Directive 78/660/EEC of 25 July 1978 and the Seventh Council Directive 83/349/EEC of 13 June 1983 on accounting" (2003).

The Committee of European Securities Regulators, CESR/03-323e, "European Regulation on the Application of IFRS in 2005 – Recommendation for Additional Guidance Regarding the Transition to IFRS" (2003).

The Committee of European Securities Regulators, CESR/05-230b, "Technical Advice on Equivalence of Certain Third Country GAAP and on Description of Certain Third Countries Mechanisms of Enforcement of Financial Information" (2005).

The Committee of European Securities Regulators, CESR/05-758, "CESR Reminds Issuers and Investors about the Importance of Clear and Transparent Disclosure on the Use of Any Options Made Available by Applicable Financial Reporting Standards" (January 12, 2006).

The Committee of European Securities Regulators, CESR/07-163, "CESR publishes key information from its database of enforcement decisions taken by EU National Enforcers of financial information (IFRS)" (2007).

Cooper, S., April 16, 2007. *UBS Investment Research, Financial Reporting for Investors.* (2007).

Deloitte, "IFRS Financial Statements – Key Considerations for Preparers" (2005).

Deloitte, IFRSs, and US GAAP, "A Pocket Comparison."

Ernst & Young, "Converting to IFRS – An Analysis of Implementation Issues" (2005).

Ernst & Young, "IFRS in Individual Company Accounts" (2005).

Ernst & Young, "IFRS, The Implications for the Building Materials Sector" (2005).

Ernst & Young, "Observations on the Implementation of IFRS" (2006).

Ernst & Young, "The Impact or IFRS on European Banks – 2005 Reporting" (2006).

Ernst & Young, "International GAAP Illustrative Financial Statements" (2007).

Fédération des Experts Comptables Européens, FEE Study, "Comparison of the EC Accounting Directives and IASs: A Contribution to International Accounting Developments" (April 1999).

Fédération des Experts Comptables Européens, "Accounting Standard Setting in Europe" (2000).

Fédération des Experts Comptables Européens, FEE Study, "To What Extent Can Options in International Accounting Standards Be Used For Consolidated Accounts Under the EC Accounting Directives?" (2000).

Fédération des Experts Comptables Européens, "Financial Reporting: Convergence, Equivalence And Mutual Recognition," FEE Position Paper (March 2006).

Finharmony, "IAS/IFRS L'impact du passage sur les sociétés du CAC 40" (May 2005).

IASB Press Release, "No new major standards to be effective before 2009" (December 2006).

IASPlus, "Use of IFRSs for Reporting by Domestic Listed and Unlisted Companies by Country and Region" (January 4, 2007).

Il Sole 24 Ore, *Guida ai principi contabili internazionali.*

Ineum Consulting, 2008. *Evaluation of the Application of IFRS in the 2006 Financial Statements of EU Companies, Report to the European Commission.*

The Institute of Chartered Accountants in England and Wales and The Institute of Chartered Accountants of Scotland, TECH 21/05, *Distributable Profits: Implication of IFRS* (2005).

The Institute of Chartered Accountants in England and Wales (ICAEW), 2007. *EU Implementation of IFRS and the Fair Value Directive, a Report for the European Commission.*

The Institute of Chartered Accountants in England and Wales and by The Institute of Chartered Accountants of Scotland, TECH 3/07, *Guidance on The Determination of Realised Profits and Losses in the Context of Distributions Under The Companies Act 1985* (2007).

The Institute of Chartered Accountants in England and Wales, "EU Implementation of IFRS and the Fair Value Directive, A Report for the European Commission," (October 2007).

The Instituto de Contabilidad y Auditoria de Cuentas and EFRAG. "Pro-Active Accounting Activities in Europe (PAAinE), Discussion Paper 2, The Performance reporting Debate, What (if anything) is wrong with the good old income statement? (2006).

The Instituto de Contabilidad y Auditoria de Cuentas and EFRAG. "Pro-Active Accounting Activities in Europe (PAAinE), Performance Reporting, A European Discussion Paper" (2009).

International Federation of Accountants, "Perspectives on the Global Application of IFRS" (2007).

IOSCO Press Release, "Regulators to Share Information on International Financial Reporting Standards" (2007).

KPMG, "International Financial Reporting Standards (IFRS) Survey of First-time Adoption" (2005).

KPMG, "On the Threshold of IFRS," Analyst Research Survey (November 2005).

Mazars, "IFRS 2005 European Survey" (2005).

MEDEF Survey – "Chief Financial Officers and the IFRS" (October 2006).

OIC – Organismo Italiano di Contabilità, *Guida Operativa per la Transizione ai Principi Contabili Internazionali (IAS/IFRS)* (October 2005).

OIC – Organismo Italiano di Contabilità, *Guida Operativa sulla informativa di bilancio prevista per i soggetti che adottano i principi contabili internazionali* (2007).

OIC – Organismo Italiano di Contabilità, *Guida Operativa – Aspetti applicativi dei principi IAS/IFRS* (2008).

Ordre des Experts-Comptables, "Retours d'expérience sur les nouveautés comptables 2005" (2006).

Osservatorio Bilanci Sezione di Ragioneria – Dipartimento di Economia Aziendale Università degli Studi di Torino, "Summit 2005, Rapporto sui bilanci 2005 delle società quotate," Summa (2006).

PriceWaterhouseCoopers, International Financial Reporting Standards, "Ready to Take the Plunge?" (May 2004).

PriceWaterhouseCoopers, "International Financial Reporting Standard – Ready to Take-off?" (December 2004).

PriceWaterhouseCoopers, "Illustrative Corporate Consolidated Financial Statements."

PriceWaterhouseCoopers, "Similarities and Differences – A Comparison of IFRS and US GAAP."

Protiviti, Insight No. 6 2005, "Transizione agli IAS/IFRS – 2 Il Debutto delle Società italiane (aggiornamento alle semestrali 2005)" (December 2005).

Securities and Exchange Commission, Press Release No. 2006-17, "Accounting Standards: SEC Chairman Cox and EU Commissioner McCreevy Affirm Commitment to Elimination of the Need for Reconciliation Requirements" (February 8, 2006).

Securities and Exchange Commission, Press Release No. 2006-130, "SEC and CESR Launch Work Plan Focused on Financial Reporting" (2006).

Securities and Exchange Commission, "Observations in the Review of IFRS Financial Statements" (July 2007).

Securities and Exchange Commission, Release No. 33-8831, "Concept Release on Allowing U.S. Issuers to Prepare Financial Statements in Accordance With International Financial Reporting Standards" (August 2007).

Securities and Exchange Commission, "Acceptance from Foreign Private Issuers of Financial Statements Prepared in Accordance with International Financial Reporting Standards Without Reconciliation to U.S. GAAP" (March 4, 2008).

Special Committee Report of the Business Reporting Research Project, "Improving Business Reporting: Insights into Enhancing Voluntary Disclosures" (January 2001).

UK's Accounting Standards Board (ASB) Financial Reporting Exposure Draft (FRED 22), Reporting Financial Performance (December 2000).

United Nations Conference on Trade and Development, "Review of Practical Implementation Issues of International Financial Reporting Standards" (2005).

INDEX